T0375636

The Scientific MBA

5th edition

G. A. Mohr
BE, MEngSci (Melb.), PhD (Camb.)
CEO, Transworld Research & Innovation (TRI)
World Hons Mult.; Member, World Innovation Foundation (London)
Former CEO International Arts & Sciences College (IASC)

Balboa Press books may be ordered through booksellers or by contacting:

Balboa Press
A Division of Hay House
1663 Liberty Drive
Bloomington, IN 47403
www.balboapress.com.au
1 (877) 407-4847

ISBN: 978-1-5043-0989-9 (sc)
ISBN: 978-1-5043-0990-5 (e)

Print information available on the last page.

Balboa Press rev. date: 08/23/2017

Introduction

The 'scientific MBA' is a course that was developed at IASC from 1995 onwards. It was disseminated usually as the Diploma and Bachelor of Business Science.

In April 1996, a lady with a PhD working for a leading publisher wrote to me:

I'm not exactly sure I understand what the intended market is - most existing MBA programs (as you have correctly identified as being found on every street corner) are not (with some exceptions) M&S oriented precisely because the market demand is not for business degrees addressing these skills in detail, much as a more scientifically angled course of study may be needed.

This course serves that need (with a generous 12 point font size for easy reading).

This is the fifth and final edition of the summary course notes for this course, not counting many addenda and corrigenda to the prior editions over the years.

The Dip.Bus.Sci. or DBS was awarded for passing BP, BL, BF, MP, MR, IE and ME and a few sections only of the other 7 subjects. The B.Bus.Sci. was awarded for also passing subjects MS, IT, NM, OT, OR, PP and FM. On completion of all 14 subjects and completion of a thesis based on a minimum of six months intensive research, or its equivalent, the Master of Business Science (MBS) degree was awarded.

Like any MBA course, the DBS/MBS covers a range of specialist areas such as Management, Finance, HRM, Marketing and Operations but it concentrates on the more mathematical/scientific areas such as OR (Operations Research) and the lead-up Maths for this (MS), then adding much new material such as application of the Finite Element Method (FEM) to the Operations Research and Project Planning (PP).

Those more interested in Marketing, however, need only concentrate their career efforts in that area. As with any course, they will over time forget much of the material, if not most, but they should make an effort to deepen their knowledge of their chosen specialization by self-education via books and other sources.

As for the importance of a more mathematical business course, the Westpac Numeracy study found a positive correlation between an Australian adult's income and their level of maths education, those who had completed years 11-12 maths earning an average of $7,000 more/year in their careers than those who had completed to only years 7-10.

Thanks to Edwin Fear and Richard Sinclair for 'testing' the 1st edition of the course, and for their collaboration on a number of recent books noted in the reference lists.

I wish them and present readers the best of luck with their careers.

Geoff Mohr, 2017
CEO, Transworld Research & Innovation
Formerly CEO, International Arts & Sciences College (IASC)

Transworld
Research &
Innovation

The Scientific MBA

TABLE OF CONTENTS

BUSINESS POLICY (BP)

For these two, rightly taken, are the gravest of sciences, being the arts of arts; the one for judgment, the other for ornament, Francis Bacon on logic and rhetoric.

BP: BUSINESS POLICY

Each subject of this course is presented as a chapter of this book, each section corresponding to a lecture. The following section of this chapter outlines the structure of the course, the general motivation for it, and notes a few examples of key references for the course, this text being the backbone of the course. To typical sections/lectures of the course students/readers should commit at least an hour of extra study, adding further study in readily accessible and relevant media such as textbooks, newspapers, television etc. Towards the end of some chapters/subjects exercises are suggested. Keep your exercise work and notes for each subject in a separate folder, to which newly acquired material may be added in following years. Some areas, ideas, programs etc. may prove of special interest, however, and these should be worked upon a good deal.

BP1. The DBS/MBS course

This course was developed to meet a need for a more logical approach to business/commerce than is given in the traditional MBA courses that are now so ubiquitous. Bearing in mind that these take their name from the Harvard MBA which began in the 1960s, and that it was Wassily Leontief who introduced a little mathematics such as *input-output analysis* to the Harvard Business School in 1931, it would seem long overdue that some attempt to bring the MBA up to scratch in modern mathematics in as painless as possible a way is overdue. This course was written with that aim.

This book is based on a course of lectures written and given in 1995+ by the author at the *International Arts & Sciences College* (IASC) in Melbourne, Australia. The 'A & S' of the name was inspired by Francis Bacon's second book on the Advancement of Learning, where, speaking of logic and rhetoric, subjects which he studied at Cambridge for two years, commencing at the age of twelve, he wrote: *For these two, rightly taken, are the gravest of sciences, being the arts of arts; the one for judgment, the other for ornament.*

Indeed, it is interesting to note that the Harvard Business School was originally founded as a graduate department of *arts and sciences.* It is also interesting to reflect, what are arts and sciences? Though few realize it, science, strictly speaking, is study with a view to acquiring new knowledge, whereas art is the business of applying that knowledge. Very often the two overlap, of course, but it would surprise most of us to realize that a carpenter, for example, is an *artisan* and, therefore, practices an art.

So too, for another example, is an engineer or applied scientist, unless he or she deliberately engage in theoretical research.

The course is a well balanced combination of 'A & S'. It has fourteen subjects and was originally divided into two halves, the first of which was the Diploma of Business Science (DBS) and the second the Bachelor of Business Science (MBS). On completion of both of these and completion of a thesis based on a minimum of six months intensive research, or its equivalent, the Master of Business Science (MBS) degree was to be awarded.

Soon, however, it was decided to simply run the course as a concise, efficient 'business science' course, and the MBS was never, in fact, awarded.

It is hoped that students and readers of this book will get a job in a relevant business or start their own and, using a little *science,* succeed, over time furthering their studies of 'BizSci' so that, if not at the outset, they will ere long have second to none knowledge of *modern* business. This unique course in outline is:

The DBS/MBS program

Part I:	**BP**	Business Policy {+ Mohr's Laws, new idea development}
	BL	Business Law (and company law)
	MS	Maths and Stats - for beginners {including queueing theory}
	BF	Business Finance {+ forecasting techniques}
	MP	Management Psychology - including HRM sociology
	MR	Market Research (& marketing) {+ psychology of attitudes}
	IT	Information Technology (& computing) {including programming}
Part II:	**NM**	Numerical Methods {+ penalty etc. transformation methods}
	IE	International Economics (Macroeconomics) {+ time stepping models}
	ME	Managerial Economics (Microeconomic) {+ input-output analysis}
	OT	Optimization Techniques {+ nonlinear problems made simple}
	OR	Operations Research {+ direct LP for distribution}
	PP	Project Planning {+ optimization of planning networks}
	FM	Finite Methods {+ network models via Mohr's Law & infinity conditions}
Part III:		Follow up study/thesis etc.: 6 months min., 18 months max (EFT)

Examples of material unique to the course are shown in { }. Most of this was developed at IASC and was not available from anywhere else in the world.

Some of the motivations for this course are well stated by F.W. Taylor in his *Principles of Scientific Management* (Harper, New York NY 1911) where he argues that:

1. The whole country loses daily by inefficiency in everything we do.
2. The remedy? Systematic management based on scientific principles, not some 'super manager(s).'
3. Business science rests on clear laws, rules and principles applicable to individual acts and to large corporations and will yield big results.

Desirable prerequisites for students/readers of this course are

a. Interested and motivated and at least of moderate intelligence.

b. At least a little knowledge of high school mathematics, a willingness to suffer a smallish dose of statistics and a little knowledge of computing with a PC.

For the purposes of the DBS the following assumptions are made:

☑ In BL (Business Law) lectures are based on Australian Law but this has much in common with British Law and, in turn US and international law.
☑ There is no management accounting (MA) subject. An introduction to accounting is given in BL and BF and for most users simple spreadsheet packages should serve their needs. For the nuances of taxation law, however, specialist advice is recommended.
☑ For the purpose of the word science I take mathematics to be a subset of science. The word *art* I then take to mean *application.* Then, for example, *applied science* I take to mean technology. Then *engineering* and its allied disciplines are a subset of applied science.

Some of the sources of material upon which the DBS is based are given in the reference lists at the end of each subject's chapter, but the author's work underpins the course, as might be hoped, just a couple of examples of the many possible being:

Mohr GA, Milner HR, *A Microcomputer Introduction to the Finite Element Method,* Pitman (1986), Heinemann (1987).
Mohr GA, *Finite Elements for Solids, Fluids, and Optimization.* OUP, Oxford (1992).
Mohr GA, *The Pretentious Persuaders,* Horizon, Sydney (2012, 2014).
Mohr GA, *Elementary Thinking for the 21st Century,* Xlibris, Sydney (2014).
Mohr GA, *The History and Psychology of Human Conflict,* Horizon, Sydney (2014).
Mohr GA, Richard Sinclair & Edwin Fear, *The Evolving Universe,* Xlibris, Sydney (2015).
Mohr GA & Edwin Fear, *The Brainwashed,* Inspiring Publishers, Canberra (2016).
Mohr GA, Richard Sinclair & Edwin Fear, *Human Intelligence, Learning & Behaviour,* Inspiring Publishers, Canberra (2017).

BP2 Elements of Business Policy

Perhaps the three basic considerations of business policy formulation are *objectives, means* and *constraints.* With each of these there are both *qualitative* and *quantitative* matters to consider. Briefly considering each of these in turn:

Objectives.

Qualitative objectives might include good corporate image, customer loyalty (see MR), product quality and personnel loyalty (see MP).

Quantitative objectives might include maximum sales (see MR) and maximum profit (see ME).

In this context the term *management by objectives (MBO)* is worth note and decision theory (see BP4) is an example of this.

Means.

Qualitative means towards one's aims might include corporate strategy and tactics, a company structure and/or role model (see BP5).

Quantitative means might include available finance (see BF), material and human resources.

Constraints.

Qualitative constraints will include legal restrictions (see BL) as well, of course, as human limitations.

Quantitative constraints will include finance limits, worker limitations and resistance (see MP), material and human resource limits and market size (see MR).

Note that there are *internal constraints* (work force size) and *external constraints* (laws etc.) and one should have both *short term* and *long term plans.* In following chapters these and many other pertinent subjects are considered in detail.

Finally, in speaking of objectives here, we are at the outset of any business enterprise originally involved in the question of ideas that might be said to be the 'top line' in our endeavours.

Business ideas

Not to be taken too seriously, here are a few ideas that I have collected over a fairly short time. Some are not all that good but perhaps one or two might be of interest?

❖ **AV equipment**: as a lecturer I have never had access to an 'opaque projector' whereas 'overhead projectors' always abound. Opaque projectors are simple mirror affairs and are much too expensive (and RGB projectors more so).

❖ **Beverages:** tea, coffee etc. are big business for some. So are Milo etc. Here I find half to a third as much very cheap 'home brand' cocoa + sugar OK instead!

❖ **Booze**: your own pub, let alone brewery or distillery, can be a license to print money. Technically speaking brewing is pretty simple. There are very few home brew shops around, I notice, and this could be a growth business.

❖ **Calendars:** Calendars can be reused every few years (e.g. 1993 & 1999 were the same) so why not sell a calendars on that basis?

❖ **Cars:** Clive Sinclair's electric car cost a small fraction of the cost of an ICE monster but I fear GM etc. will make the electric car dear(er).

❖ **Clothes:** Did you realize that the simple tie comes from the Romans who had it ready as an emergency binding for wounds. Do we really need it or the other ridiculous junk we are expected to wear? By the way - the Romans did wear undies!

❖ **Computers:** I see a market now for simple and cheaper PCs reminiscent of the early ones with free software etc. and believe the Indians are producing such a thing for education purposes.

❖ **Confectionery:** Things like Russian (vanilla) fudge, peppermint nougat bars and chocolates to order from a home made shop I distantly remember in my childhood. I also wonder why well known local sweets have never been exported (desirably including ideas from such home made shops). After all, Mars bars began that way.

❖ **Cosmetics:** A business where you multiply the cost of common ingredients by a large number. Some slightly necessary products like Clearasil are pretty dear as a result of monopoly. Likewise with Listerine.

❖ **Cures:** The snake oil salesman is surely not dead at all. Surely I could promise to prevent baldness using brushes, shampoos, hormones, prayer, etc.

❖ **Diet:** Various big selling books and high profile organizations make this big business. Myself a pocket book of calorie/cholesterol/fat/salt etc. tables I bought second hand for 10 cents finally did the trick for me! (But to be honest you do need to study at least a couple of other books to see what ideas etc. are extant.). A small pocket counter to check your calorie intake through the day would be a good idea too.

❖ **Disposable:** Baron Biche gave us the disposable biro, shaver and lighter. Now we have disposable watches etc. What next I wonder?

❖ **Exercise:** Home exercise gear is now a big business. A package with a booklet of exercises and a couple of small hand and leg weights might be worthwhile product.

❖ **Export:** Something most of us neglect somewhat. Local confectionery, booze, fast food etc. products should be exportable at least within one's world region to begin with. You can take on Coke/McDonald's etc. later on.

❖ **Fast food:** I would not mind a fast food chain that sold a *variety* of things such as pies, fish fillets, chicken nuggets or fillets, 'bread burgers,' sandwiches (various breads or fillings), small fruit pies and even just plain fruit juice and milk at more like cost price. I also see a market for health FF shops with vegetarian etc. stuff.

❖ **Food:** I can see a market for more high fibre, low calorie foods for diet conscious people trying to loose weight or keep it down.

❖ **Furniture:** A few old fashioned items like the bulky traditional couch could surely be improved on with a little thought and IKEA etc. try this.

❖ **Import:** From booze and restaurants to cars is it always more posh/clever to buy foreign? Surely advertisers could overcome this! On the other hand, becoming an importer yourself, as long as a bank backs you, can be very lucrative.

❖ **Packaging:** I used to buy cardboard milk cartons which had to be opened by making a spout with scissors. I gave up and pay a little more for a better package.

❖ **Shops:** Thinking just what kind of shop I would start just down the road is just about the toughest question I know (if my money is at risk!). I mention home brew shops under booze above but the trouble is that the most hard up people probably cannott afford the small set up cost and might not even have a roof over their head. I also see a greater market for 'game shops' that might sell cheap computer games, board games and other paraphernalia associated with games.

❖ **Soft drinks:** Why the Coke vs Pepsi war consumes the world I do not know. I am happy with, indeed, prefer, 'home brand' floavoured mineral water from the super market when it's boiling hot weather. Generally my drinks of preference are decaf., tea and cocoa in that order as the day progresses, plus a little booze in the evening.

❖ **Toothpaste:** Why not add a little antiseptic (as in Listerine) to this? Not a bad idea to use 'tooth string' as my mother used to call it daily. Find the right cotton and cut to suit and this will save you a lot on 'dental floss' and the same applies to countless other things. It will also save a lot at the dentist.

❖ **Vegetables:** With mad cow disease etc. why eat 'mystery bags' (sausages), chicken nuggets complete with ground up beaks etc. You can buy fresh potatoes, carrots and beans cheaply by the kilo and keep them in the fridge and microwave them to get a quick, healthy and cheap dinner (+ fish fillets or just gravy on the spuds to simulate meat!).

I get better ideas daily but don't record them. Sometimes it might be helpful to start by considering categories of basic need such as food, cooking, heating, clothing, shelter, health and so on.

But that's all folks! Just which one of the above would I start up down the road? It depends what road etc. and, anyway, I should want a partner and would want to talk it all over with he or she first. If we could not agree then it might be best not to start at all.

BP3 Business meetings

In business, as in politics, meetings are an important part of the process. As in parliament, standard procedures should be followed in calling, running and reporting meetings.

To publicize an impending meeting an agenda paper is distributed, for example:

BULLDUST ASSOCIATION OF VICTORIA

Annual General Meeting to be held at 1, Spring St at 8:00 p.m. on Thursday 10/8/99.

BUSINESS

1. President's opening remarks.
2. Apologies.
3. Minutes of the AGM held on 12/8/98.
4. Business arising out of the minutes.
5. Correspondence.
6. Business arising out of the correspondence.
7. President's report (AGM only).
8. Treasurer's report.
9. Election of new members.
10. Subcommittee reports/Reports from delegates.
11. Election of office bearers:
    - President
    - Vice-presidents (2)
    - Secretary
    - Treasurer
    - Committee (5)
12. Election of auditor.
13. Guest speaker: Mr J.C. Smith, former Prime Minister, on "Politics Today."
14. Motions on notice:

a. Mr Jones to move, "That the secretary be granted an honorarium of ten dollars ($10)."

b. Mrs Brown to move, "That the Government be requested to reduce the sales tax on bulldust."

15. General business.
16. Notice of motions.
17. Date of next meeting.
18. Close.

During such a meeting the secretary will keep notes and these are used to prepare the *minutes* of the meeting, copies of which are sent to members and other interested parties prior to the next meeting.

These should cover such items as: Present; Apologies; 1. Minutes of previous meeting; 2. Financial report; 3. Issue A: report on discussion, suggestions, resolutions etc.; 4. Issue B: report on; 5. General business, discussion etc.; 6. Next meeting - date/time. "The meeting then closed." Signed . . . . Chairman.

In the matter of meetings of businesses and associations the following additional subjects are worth consideration:

Chairperson. The chairperson's duties are simply to ensure that the agenda is followed and to deal with motions.

Motions. A motion is a proposed *resolution*. It may be:

a. Procedural, for example "That the meeting adjourn."

b. Substantive, for example "That ABC's account be paid."

A motion is dealt with as follows:

Mover: states (preferably in writing) the motion and explains it.
Seconder: (called by the CP) speaks for the motion.
Speaker(s): (") alternatively speak against/for the motion.
Mover: (") summarizes the case for the motion.
Chairperson: "The motion is that - - -."
"The question is that the motion be agreed to."
"Those in favour?"
"Those against?"
"I declare the motion carried/lost."

Note that motions can be: 1. In parts (a), (b) etc.

2. Amended.
3. Rescinded.
4. Foreshadowed.

Procedural motions. These generally have two functions:

a. To dispose of business, for example "That the meeting adjourn" or "That the speaker be no longer heard."

b. To deal with business, for example to vary the order of business or to call for a vote ("That the motion be put").

"Point of order". This exclamation to the Chairperson is a complaint, for example, that the speaker has taken too long, it out of order (poor language) or is not speaking on the subject.

Voting methods: These include

1. Voices/show of hands.
2. Division.
3. Poll or ballot (which may be secret).

Constitutions: Associations, companies etc. should have a constitution that contains usually standard clauses governing behaviour of the company and its members, the running of meetings and other matters requiring rules. Some of the most common clauses are: Name, objectives, membership and subscription clauses.

Meetings, committee, elections and quorum clauses.
Finance, dissolution, voting and amendments clauses.
Interpretations, delegations, open/closed meetings and expulsion clauses.

Standing orders: These are the rules for the procedure of meetings, for example setting time limits for meetings and stating the procedure for putting motions.

Election systems: Prior to an election such matters as the following should be considered:

1. A call for nominations.
2. Provision for postal or proxy votes.
3. Appointment of a returning officer.
4. Method of election, for example:

a. First past the post, or b. Preferential/proportional/points systems.

On matters such as 4(b) above the reader may require a little further reading to learn more detail but, generally, so far as meetings are concerned, it is also not a bad idea to attend one or two properly run ones.

There are also a few rare books on procedure for meetings. I remember buying one over 20 years ago and taking great delight in moving "That the speaker be no longer heard until he can speak to the meeting properly prepared" (the chap kept fumbling through pages of his proposal and changing his mind when asked any question). I am sure they had never heard of such a motion. Anyway it was carried and the offender gave me dirty looks around the institution for weeks afterwards.

BP5 Decision Theory

Decision theory is a somewhat imprecise term that refers to techniques for making business decisions. A few simple examples are given in this section but many more appear throughout the text.

Decision matrices.

An example is the 'prisoner dilemma matrix' where two prisoners are questioned separately. What happens if neither, one or both confess?

Prisoner B	Prisoner A		
		Confess	Don't
	Confess	Both - 20 years	A Life B 10 years
	Don't	A 10 years B Life	Both - free

Decision tables:

A good example is the following table of the performance of three categories of stocks and shares under boom, steady and slump market conditions.

	Boom (a)	Steady (b)	Slump (c)
Gilt edged (x)	5 %	5	5
Speculative (y)	20	0	-10
Unit trusts (z)	10	5	0

What then is the best mix of shares to buy?

The *deterministic solution* is as follows. For a 10 year cycle time in business conditions assume $a = 1$, $b = 6$ and $c = 3$. Then the profit (%) from each of the three share types is:

x: 5 + 30 + 15 = 50
y: 20 - 30 = -10
z: 10 + 30 = 40

so that one should buy *x* or *z* but not *y* (unless boom conditions are assured for a known period).

Probability trees.

The simplest example is that of tossing a coin three times. What are the possible outcomes?

This is a special case of the *binomial distribution* (see MS9) and, for example, the probability of three successive heads is

$$P(HHH) = (1/2)^3 = 1/8$$

as it is for all other possible sequences when P(H) = P(T). Probability trees are of little use but the idea can be incorporated with that of a decision tree to assist in important business decisions.

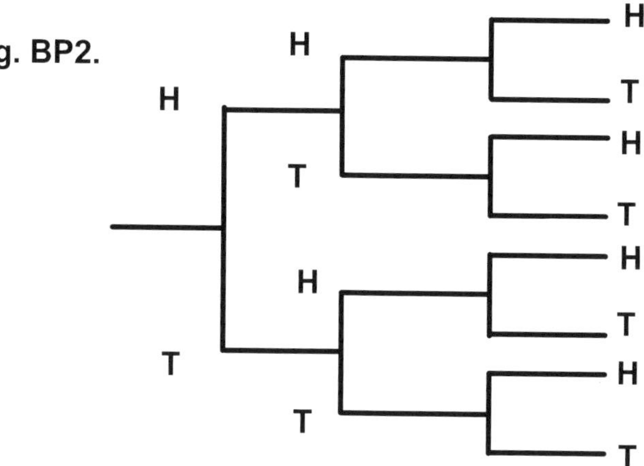

Fig. BP2.

Decision trees

These help show what alternatives are open to use when we have to make a business decision. A simple example is that of a manufacturer asked by a supermarket chain to make a 'home brand' version of its product. The resulting decision tree looks like this:

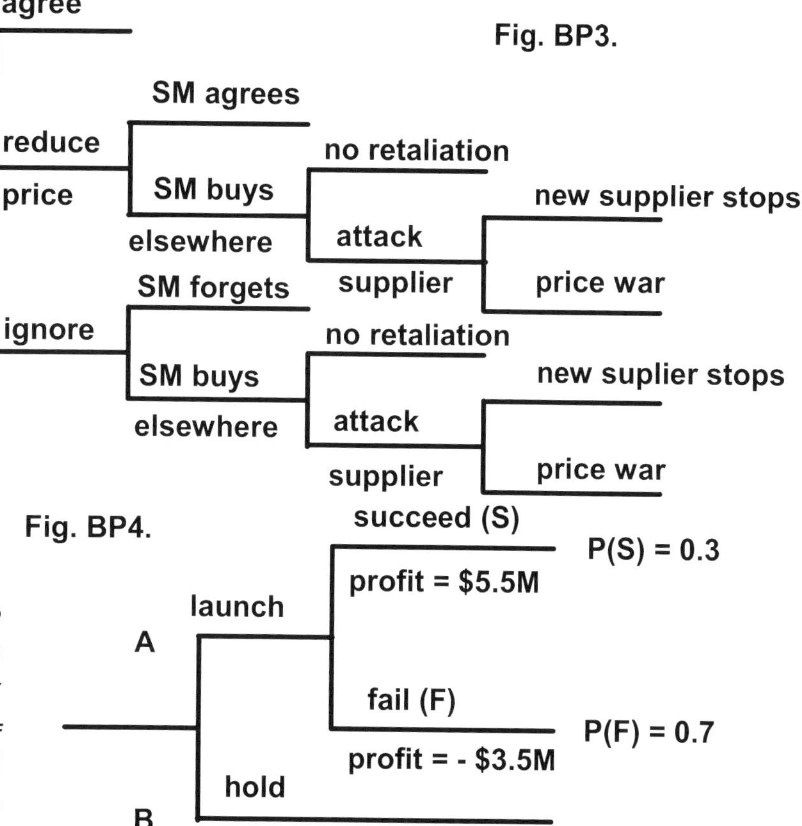

Fig. BP3.

Fig. BP4.

Now probabilities can be attached to the branches of the tree, though it may be of some help in decision making as it stands.

As a simple example of this, consider the problem of deciding whether to launch a rocket at a certain time or not. With probabilities and profit figures attached the decision tree is:

Then the *expected monetary value (EMV)* of a launch is *0.3(5.5) - 0.7(3.5) = - $0.8M* so we should decide to hold. With more optimistic figures, for example *P(S) = 0.7* and *P(F) = 0.3,* the EMV of A is $2.85M and the launch decision is much more favourable, though perhaps still not certain.

There are also a great many ratios and indices used in business to gauge the performance and profitability and these, in turn, are much used in decision making. An example only is the *ROCE* or *return on capital expenditure*, that is the ratio of the percentage net profit to rate of capital turnover. Another is the *PE ratio* (i.e. price/earnings ratio per share) and this is often given in the daily share listings of newspapers. Details of some of the many other such ratios are given in Sec. BF9.

BP5 Corporate Structure

Corporate structure is the hierarchical structure and communication channels giving rise to the chain of command and response in a company or organization. Some of the basic types of corporate structure are as follows:

[1] Functional structure. This is the usual structure for small companies and corresponds to one division of type (2) below.

[2] Divisional structure. For a corporation with just two divisions this of the form of Fig. BP5.

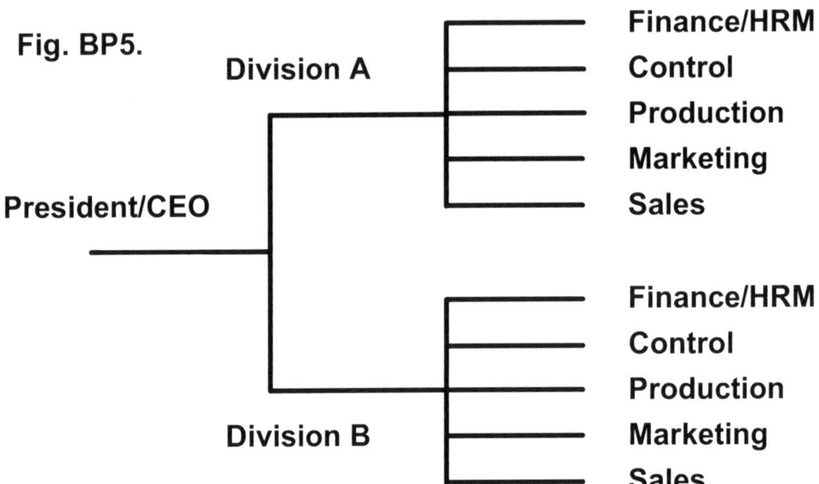

Fig. BP5.

[3] Matrix Structure

Note that in Fig. BP5 Finance and HRM are combined into one group, but not in Fig. BP6. Similarly, marketing and sales might often by one group, for example. In a very small business, of course, the boss or owner is HRM/control/marketing, finance is the bank a few doors away and the few employees may be production and sales, including the boss!

CEO
HRM
Finance
Control
Production
Marketing
Sales
Proj. Mngr A
Proj. Mngr B
Proj. Mngr C
Proj. Mngr D

Fig. BP6 Matrix organizational structure

[4] Ring structure.

This is typical of political parties, voluntary organizations etc. Such structures can be described approximately as follows:

Centre = president/CEO
Inner ring = secretary/treasurer/vice presidents etc.
+ presidents of committees for finance/membership/PR etc.
+ chairmen of branches
Outer ring 1 = clusters of members of each committee
Outer ring 2 = clusters of members of each branch

In the outer rings the 'clusters' are like satellites (at the same radius) and each is another group of members which in turn holds meetings etc., the committee presidents and branch chairpersons reporting back to the inner ring or *board* or *central committee.*

Thus committee chairpersons and branch presidents have to attend two lots of meetings, as will many members when these are delegates from the branches, as is often the case.

In the case of political parties the central committee is the elected members of the party in parliament. These 'politicians' often have to attend committee and branch meetings, as well as those of parliament, and are therefore often busier than we sometimes imagine.

Some additional aspects of such corporate structures are:

Fig. BP7

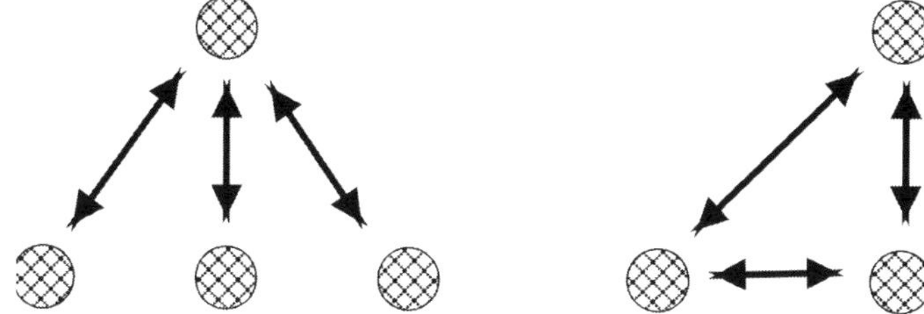

a. hierarchical or 'one to one' structure is as shown on the left in Fig. BP7.

b. A mixture of hierarchical and group structure is shown on the right in Fig. BP7.

c. Responsibilities of members may overlap, for example project manager A in Fig. BP6 is involved in two groups, that is CEO/PMA/PMB/PMC/PMD and PMA/MHR/MF/MC - -, where MHR = manager of human resources etc.

d. It is usually in the interests of middle level members that lower levels do not know the chain of command.

e. It is usually in the interests of both higher and lower levels that the chain of command is known.

Generally, for example, case (b) is a more efficient structure than (a).

In case (d) middle level members are more empowered by ignorance of the chain of command by their subordinates. Whether this situation is in the interests of the company, however, is very doubtful and, indeed, it usually is not.

Such comments are merely a beginning in looking at the nuances of command structures. Further aspects of communication are considered elsewhere in the course, for example in MP (Management Psychology) and have important applications in production control and efficiency (see PP) and industrial relations (see BL).

Finally, it should be noted that managers should be seeking to ensure that *effective communication* occurs throughout the corporate structure and it is not difficult to personally check that information has been properly passed on from time to time. That the information is understandable and is being given to people capable of understanding it are matters considered later in the course, for example in MR (Market Research) and MP (Management Psychology).

MP6 Functions of a Manager

Except for the general manager or CEO each member of the board of a corporation usually manages a particular function of the corporation such as engineering, sales, accounting etc. Every manager, however, is likely to have various responsibilities, including:

1. Planning. Selection of objectives and policies, programs and procedures to achieve them.
2. Organizing. Forming a corporate structure and assigning tasks to the members of this.
3. Staffing. Selection of staff (see MP where HRM is discussed).
4. Direction. Using the chain of command (see also MP where leadership and related matters are discussed).
5. Control. Act appropriately on accounting, marketing, sales, production and control information.
6. Coordination. Facilitate horizontal reciprocal communication (for example between accounting and purchasing) at planning stage and ensure that it continues.

The nature of management. The following are useful examples of this:
1. A manager may type his own letters sometimes but the secretary never manages (in theory at least!).
2. Technical v. management skills: middle managers may use both, in contrast to higher and lower level management which usually use only one of these two skills (guess which!).
3. Material v. human resources: managers usually deal with human resources who in turn deal with material resources directly or indirectly.

Authority. Two important aspects of authority are:
1. We can assume that authority has been delegated via the hierarchy to a manager but effective authority depends upon its *acceptance* by subordinates.
2. Acceptance of authority depends upon such factors as
a. Orders are understood, fit for the purpose of the company, fit the interests of those given them and they are mentally and physically able to carry them out.
b. Group pressure.
c. Competence or personal authority of the manager.
d. Automatic acceptance (for example of routine orders).

Limits of authority. The amount of authority possessed by members of a company can often by represented by the 'inverted pyramid' shown in Fig. BP8.

Other constraints on management authority include:
a. Limitations on human capacity.
b. Climate, geography, physical laws etc.
c. Economic constraints.
d. Relevant laws.

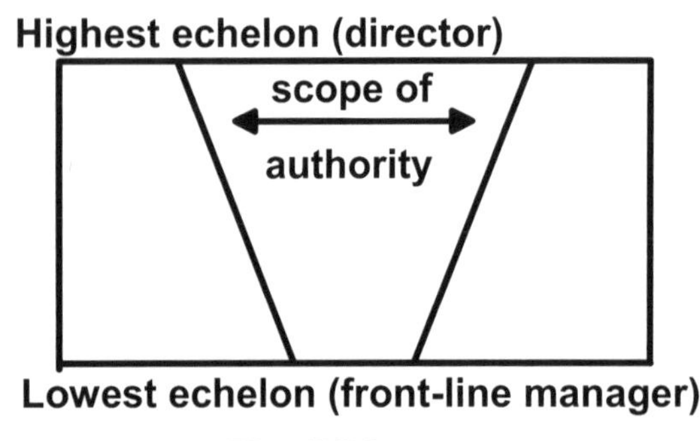

Fig. BP8.

Responsibility

It should be realized that authority and responsibility are not synonymous as sometimes assumed. Responsibility is equivalent to obligation, however. For example, if you are assigned *responsibility* for a task you have an obligation to see that it is done. You may have authority to delegate the responsibility but somewhere down the line the buck stops and somebody is actually responsible for doing it themselves. That is, *that* somebody has no further to look but a shovel or whatever to do the job.

Delegation of authority

When delegating authority consider the following points:

1. The person delegating must have appropriate seniority and the delegate must be trustworthy.
2. Delegating involves assignment of a task, at least indirectly via the chain of command.
3. Such delegation may be written or verbal.
4. Delegation must be clearly understood and involve tasks that are feasible etc.
5. There should be *feedback, e.g.* task now complete or why not do it this way?
6. Recovery of authority: delegated authority can be withdrawn and reassigned when necessary.
7. Decentralization of authority (via delegation) is, in theory at least, better for company growth and may be the means of achieving that growth.
8. Reward success. When authority is successfully delegated the delegates may be entitled to higher pay or privileges.

Principles of delegation

The following 'principles of delegation' are sometimes worth bearing in mind as aids to effective management:

1. The principle of functional definition. The duties of members of an organization should be defined, for example by *job descriptions.*
2. The scalar principle. When seeking a decision (but not necessarily for information) follow the line of command.
3. The 'level principle' of authority. Pass decisions that you cannot make or do not have authority to *up.*
4. Principle of unity of command: each subordinate reporting to only one superior.
5. Principle of delegation to obtain results (not to share out power).
6. Principle of absolute responsibility. Responsibility cannot be delegated: a manager is responsible for tasks assigned and for those they are assigned to.

SUMMARY: Amongst many other things, managers must

- ❖ have responsibility for given functions
- ❖ have authority over given people
- ❖ plan, control etc.
- ❖ make decisions
- ❖ manage people, that is, delegate

It is, of course, not quite as simple as that, but if some notice is given to words such as *responsibility* and *delegation* that is a good start.

Finally you should know clearly what your duties are, how to perform them and, of course, be capable of doing do. It is also desirable that you can do it all well !

BP7 Business Policy Formulation

In this and the following section business policy formulation is discussed, giving attention to product selection, development and marketing, production of a product, financial policy and HRM policy.

First, however, it should be noted that policy may come from the following sources:

a. Original policy, that is, based on objectives decided by the directors of the company.

b. Developed policy, that is, derived from decisions made as a result of problems encountered and other feedback.

c. Imposed (externally) policy, for example by Government, union demands or conditions etc.

More important, however, is an awareness of the various matters for which policy may be required and many of these are discussed in the remainder of BP7 and in BP8.

Pricing policy formulation

This involves such considerations as:

1. Product selection. Choose your product for a market, that is, to meet a need.
2. Product development. R & D etc. should be directed at the chosen product and not at peripheral or irrelevant problems.
3. Product production. This is discussed below.
4. Product pricing. The following factors should be considered:

a. Set the price for a particular market subdivision. In turn R & D should be based on this.
b. The price must not exceed cost + a margin that the market will bear.
c. Prices should be reviewed regularly.
d. Prices may be allowed to vary regionally or an average price used.
e. For a cheap image use prices like $99.95 whereas for a prestige image use $200 etc.

5. Sales promotion. Policy for this may be based on:

a. Pricing, advertising, packaging, distribution, grading or quality, market research and other feedback.
b. Reputation for good product, good service and fair dealing.
c. Availability of supplies.
d. Good resale value (for example cars).

1. Distribution channels. For many products wholesale and retail distribution networks are already established. Many businesses such as chain stores and supermarkets establish their own distribution systems but some small businesses may choose direct marketing.

Product policy formulation

This involves decisions on such matters as:

1. Whether or not to make the product or part or component of it. As we all know a lot of 'branding' goes on (using the term in the same way as with cattle). Reasons for farming out whole or part production of a product can include lack of facilities, expertise, capital or time and also a desire to avoid 'booming' at a level of production that will only be temporary.
2. How many to make? The decision can be based on advance orders and sales forecasts. Some degree or risk is often unavoidable, however, for example when forecasts depend on assumptions about future macroeconomic conditions.
3. Production stabilization. Variations in demand owing to seasonal factors can be dealt with by staff layoffs, producing 'fill in' products or by giving price concessions at off peak times (for example in the travel and accommodation industries or in long distance phone call charges).

4. Inventory policy. This depends on the tolerable delays in supply (for example cars compared to planes), the variability in demand and production costs and capital supply. Like most aspects of policy, that for inventory needs regular checks and reviews.

Financial policy formulation

This involves such considerations as:

[1] Capital procurement. Capital may be acquired from such sources as:

a. Private funds, for example from partners or family members in the case of a small business.

b. Public share issues (by proprietary limited companies). Companies with large assets and/or earnings can borrow accordingly and in some cases are effectively immortal and thus considered safe. Going public, however, does entail some loss of control.

c. Company profits. Part of these is sometimes returned to investors as dividends but usually most is reinvested.

d. Mortgaging company assets such as offices etc. to cover losses.

e. Sale of assets such as property holdings or subsidiary companies.

f. Loans from banks, finance or insurance companies or government agencies and instrumentalities.

In securing loans the term of the loan, the rate of interest and any restrictions on company operation that may be a condition of the loan must be considered.

For example, public utilities usually use long term loans because of high project costs and a stable long term market, then reinvesting part in the stock market. Small businesses, on the other hand, usually use short term loans from family, partners or friends or the local bank, sometimes via an overdraft.

[2] Cash and depreciation allowances. 'Depreciation reserve accounting' in which depreciation is overestimated allows cash to accumulate and this should be reinvested.

[3] Is it better to own or lease? When taxes are high it is often better to lease, the cost being tax deductible, than to fund from equity.

[4] Working capital (WC). Provision of this is vital or things would grind to a halt. In relation to WC note that:

a. WC = current (assets - liabilities), where 'current' means to be 'converted' during the current year of operation, that is, current assets will be sold and current liabilities will be liquidated.

b. It is the cash part of the WC (not the 'surplus account' which involves non liquid assets such as inventory) that ensures the day to day operation of the company, that is, pays the bills.

c. Companies with credit sales, expensive or specialized products or long production cycles need more WC.

d. It is the current assets (that is cash and marketable securities) which are maintained by a line of credit from a bank but such loans should only be used to fund the cyclical deficits in WC.

[5] Profit disposition. Using a high depreciation allowance reduces profit, in turn reducing taxes and dividends (it also helps to understate inventory and put tooling and R & D costs as current expenses). Whether issuing dividends or reinvesting pushes shares higher is a difficult question, but most shareholders prefer the latter course hoping for share price gains.

BP8 Business Policy Formulation (cont.)

Personnel and PR policy formation

This involves policy to be used in dealing with members of the company, unions, the media and the public. Examples of particular importance include:

[1] Selection and training.

In the selection and training of staff the following factors should be considered:

a. For selection of staff at lower levels is a more casual procedure sufficient?

b. At all levels minimum education and experience requirements should be specified clearly.

c. Should in house training be used? Should this be done in the classroom, at conferences or seminars, by committees, by one on one coaching or by job rotation, or by some mix of these approaches?

d. For selection of staff at higher levels should there be a strict internal promotion procedure or should the process be open to both external and internal candidates?

e. Should relatives or friends of present staff be excluded?

f. Should geographical, personal factors etc. be considered?

[2] Compensation.

This can be via wages, profit sharing, bonuses and perks. In setting different levels of remuneration through the hierarchy of the company it is often preferable to use an openly disclosed basis.

[3] Employee benefits and morale.

Such factors as leave provisions, pensions, company cafeterias, working conditions, social and recreational activities, clubs, staff lounges etc. contribute to morale. Proper provision of insurance and medical aid is also important.

[4] Union relations.

Examples of three approaches to union matters are:

a. Managerial staff communicate with the union which in turn communicates with its members.

b. Management communicates with an arbitrator who in turn communicates with the union and thence its members.

c. Front line management listens to and ignores or settles worker issues.

In practice any of such approaches may be used depending upon circumstances.

[5] PR.

The modern CEO gives news releases, speeches etc. on the financial affairs of the company, if not country. The modern company director also supports charities, education, community affairs, sport and politics. These are merely examples, however, of how modern PR involves a great deal more than just product advertisement.

Guidelines for effective policy

1. It should be in writing and be understood. It should greatly assist delegation. At the very least it should be based on a known company structure and constitution.
2. It should be based on objectives.

3. It should be *consistent*, for example don't advertise a product as new or unique and cut the cost as well.
4. Policies, rules and procedures are needed in that order, policies being the *aims,* rules being *who does what* and procedures being *how to do it.*
5. Policies should be regularly reviewed and adjusted by senior management or by an independent consultant.

Strategy

Strategy is used to expedite policy and tactics are the steps used in a particular strategy. An example of a tactic might be not too discrete inquiries to another bank, supplier etc., when wanting better treatment from the present one.

Finally, there will be feedback resulting from the actions based on policy. This may result in changes to BP at board level and this, of course, is essentially the stuff of management.

BP9 Change Management

Change management refers to the organization of new business locations, new product manufacture, use of new techniques and equipment etc. Many companies, consultants and executives now specialize in CM, some basic areas of interest being:

Resistance to change

This stems from fear of extra work or hassle, loss of entitlements, that the change is not in worker interests, mistrust of management, fear of being unable to cope with or learn new techniques etc. Most of all, however, if the change is aimed at 'productivity improvement' there will be fear of job losses (not without reason).

Overcoming resistance to change

Some ways in which resistance to change can be reduced include:
1. Explain the problem and the solution being implemented.
2. Allow participation in decision making and change.
3. Personal encouragement and assistance through time off to reorganize personal matters, counseling, retraining and cash allowances.
4. Negotiation with individuals and/or unions.
5. Manipulation, for example foreign cooperation by causing a need for it.
6. Coercion using implicit or explicit threats.

Needless to say, the 'softer' approaches are to be preferred and coercion etc. should only be used as a last resort.

Internal and external climate

Internal climate is the 'culture' of the company and embodies how things are done and how people are treated.

The external climate is that of the industry in which the company operates, the economy of the country of operation, the international economy, the state of technology in the industry, the available resources, changes in the industry and the company goals (which are external to most company members).

In change management change is generally motivated by the state of the external climate and one usually aims to disturb the internal climate as little as possible.

Six key questions about a change plan

- Is there *one* clear overall objective for which there are sufficient resources?
- *Who* are the stakeholders in this change and what are their motives and incentives?
- *What* are the gains and the losses? (Is the problem worth solving?)
- *When* are the changes needed? (Will the problem go away?)
- *Why* hasn't the problem been solved already?
- *How* likely is success?

An example of the effects of changes was the banking system in the early 1980s. With the introduction of new technology and deregulation of bank products and areas of operation came greater competition. This led to smaller margins on deposits and loans. Hence new loans were needed to make up for poor loans which were failing. This led to high loan losses and closure of some banks.

The lesson? The banks diversified, including financial services and other new products in their operations. Loan officers were asked to limit expansion of their loan portfolios and concentrate instead on providing greater services to existing customers.

Useful 'levers' for change management

There are many points in the operating system of a company at which change managers can use a little *leverage* to bring about change. These include:

1. Job design. For example the choice between single production line and parallel production lines will be a major decision.
2. Performance evaluation systems. Feedback from these should be used to improve productivity.
3. Incentive/reward systems. Cash or benefit lures, of course, can be used to motivate change etc.
4. Recruiting systems. Will changes in the criteria for these be helpful, if not a necessary aspect of change management.
5. Control systems. Changes in performance indicators and permitted variances can be used to facilitate change.
6. Information systems. The feedback from these will monitor changes.
7. Planning systems. Feedback from various sources should be acted upon in preparing future plans.

Clearly dealing with all the possible 'levers' is not an easy task, but the patient manager will look at each of his levers periodically to see if some useful adjustment is warranted.

'People levers' in change management

In addition to the 'system' levers within the operating system of a company 'people levers,' that is the personal techniques a manager uses in dealing with people, are an important part of change management. These include:

1. Management style. This involves self management, personal image etc. and skills in dealing with information, meetings and people.
2. Communication style. This involves choice of content in communication, the medium used, one's personal tone and demeanor etc., the timing of communication and the sequence in which information is dealt with.

3. Conflict resolution style. Various possible approaches to conflict resolution include:
(a) negotiation and bargaining openly and freely.
(b) Restrict two way interchange between parties, aiming more for one way information flow from the top.
(c) Restrict information exchange to a 'menu'.
(d) Concentrate on determining the causes of the conflict and deal with these impersonally.
(e) Individual counseling.

Dealing with people is, of course, by no means easy. It requires patience and understanding, a good rapport with people and a heavy duty 'fuse.' That, however, is what management is all about and why, sometimes, managers fall by the wayside.

Action plan for change management

We have discussed various aspects of change management. Most important, however, is formation of a plan of action to bring about required changes. Very briefly, this should include:

Problem summary and desired outcome (both short and long term).
Key objectives and how to communicate these.
Management strategy and who is responsible for implementing it.
Action step: detail the steps, their timing and location and the people to carry them out.
Contingency plans: where possible it is useful to anticipate possible problems and make contingency plans.

In conclusion, it will be apparent that whilst such problems as resistance to change make change management sound difficult, there are a few saving graces. These include the fact that 'levers' for change already exist in the company operating system so that, given a good change plan which gives due attention to people affected by the change, things will usually go fairly smoothly.

BP10 Management Communication

The purpose of management communication is to facilitate planning and coordination of company activities. As it is a day to day task that takes up a good deal of time well thought out lines of communication are worthwhile, as are appropriate means of and procedures for communication. In the following section such matters are dealt with briefly.

Communication structure.
Some simple examples are shown in Fig. BP9.

The circle structure gives slower communication. It has no leader and is better liked by the group and encourages better group loyalty and better productivity. This structure tends to deal with ambiguous information better than others.

The chain structure gives the slowest communication and the centre of the chain (C) tends to be the leader.

Fig. BP9

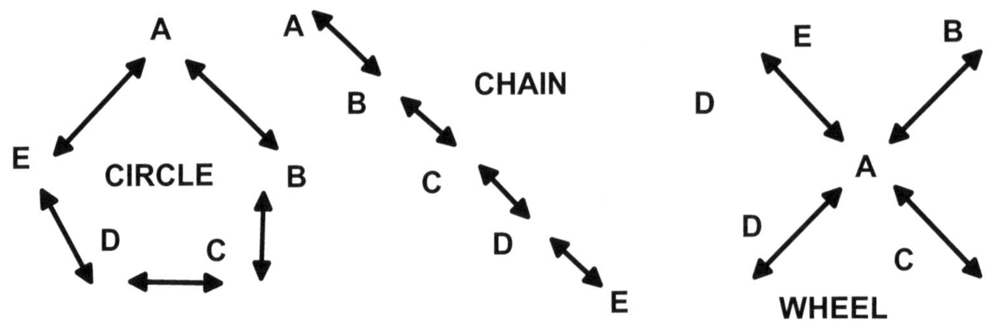

The wheel structure gives the quickest communication and the centre of the wheel (A) tends to be the leader. This structure, however, is slower in adapting to change.

Sometimes one way, rather than two way, communication is desirable from the management point of view but generally management should encourage *upward communication.*

Means of communication

1. Internal memos and letters, for example for hiring and firing.
2. Full written reports, for example for expansion plans.
3. Group reports, for example on the environment.
4. Press releases, for example announcing product recalls.
5. Annual reports, particularly to release accounting information.
6. Prepared speeches, for example for AGMs.
7. Spontaneous media contact, for example in the case of takeovers or company crises.
8. Meetings, particularly for routine business.
9. Interviews, for example to deal with conflict resolution.

Procedure for communication

Amongst many other things, the following steps should be considered in dealing with communication of important matters:

[1] Decide

a. What you want to say and what you should say.

b. The means of communication and the background and detail information to be included in it.

c. What you recommend and how strongly.

d. When: now, later or never?

e. Who are your audience and tailor your message style, scope etc. for that audience.

[2] Check your material and modify as needed.

[3] Estimate

a. Likely questions and make sure they are covered.

b. Likely response from both primary and secondary audiences.

c. Likely short and long term results.

[4] Adopt an appropriate style of communication, for example in line with your 'brand personality.'

Communication quality

Effective management communication will have some of the following qualities:

1. Good, interesting ideas.
2. The message is presented with conviction and a knowledge air.
3. Style of presentation is relaxed, perhaps with a little humour.
4. The message has an ambience of honesty.
5. Sensitivity to audience interests and concerns is evident.

An example of a lack of such sensitivity was a company that gave firing notices to 5% of its workers but no information to the rest who were left wondering when they too would receive notices.

An example of a better approach was Johnson & Johnson faced with the scare of discovery of several poisoned bottles of a product, there being rumours of several deaths as a result. J & J immediately formed a task force of advertising and PR people, management, brokers, pollsters and politicians and ordered a full product recall. The product was then reissued with a new 'tamper resistant' packaging. This prompt action saved the day, though there was a new scare five years later.

Management communication checklist

The following checklist is useful for both personal and company use:

1. Is good management communication a high priority?
2. Do you think before communicating?
3. Are communications clear and concise?
4. Do communications answer important questions?
5. Are communications tailored for their intended or target audience(s)?
6. Are both the content and style of communications satisfactory?
7. Do communications incorporate any of the qualities discussed above?
8. Are there any important business policies that have not been disseminated or which staff might need reminding of?

Conclusion

Ranging from corridor talk to memos to written reports and public media presentations many managers have to spend a great deal of time and effort on communication. Throw in meetings, both scheduled and impromptu, and there may well be little time left.

All the more important, therefore, that communication be given a little thought from time to time as a great deal of time can be saved in the long run if unnecessary or repetitive communication can be eliminated and other essential communication is made more effective.

BP11. Case study: beginning as a one man business

In his mid 20s Jim joined a US manufacturer of specialist medical equipment as, he thought, a sales manager selling a single item with no competition.

The job description led him to believe that he would be in charge of a few sales staff but he found himself the sole representative in the UK. He stuck it out for five years, however, by which time he was competing with equipment from 20 other companies and needed to be selling a product range rather than a single piece of specialist equipment to make a living.

Following a suggestion from a friend, Jim decided to become an independent agent for the single item of the US company, adding a small range of other manufacturer's products to his stock, taking out a smallish loan for this purpose.

Things soon went much better and his bank offered him a larger loan that would allow him to add more lines and employ a salesperson. Should he accept?

Deciding to expand

Jim was advised to base his decision on:

a. His main business objectives.
b. Predicted sales of new lines based on his experience.
c. A cash flow forecast for his predicted sales volume.

He listed his main objectives as:

1. Maximum *sales* (not profit), at least in the short term.
2. *Growth* into a larger company with comfortable offices.
3. Enough *profit* to provide a satisfactory living.
4. The *welfare* of the sick on whom his medical equipment was used.

He also decided that appropriate marketing policies for these objectives would be low margins and product diversity, to which end he had several new lines in mind.

Based on these considerations the decision was obviously to accept the loan offer, stock a wider range and employ and extra man. His business has continued to grow ever since.

He now has a typical *small business* with a manager (himself), a secretary, a sales manager and several sales representatives.

With a large business or corporation there is a board of directors and a divisional structure involving large numbers of people. Decisions to expand, however, are based on much the same principles used in the foregoing example.

For examples of the affairs of bigger business one need only consult the business pages of the appropriate newspapers to learn a little about what goes on.

With small and large business, however, one will find that is usually unwarranted expansion, for example from one shop to two, which leads to disaster. This is often because increased borrowing, ostensibly to finance expansion, is often used to cover losses. That is, there is probably a stronger case for contraction of the business, but then the outstanding losses will be difficult and certainly slower to cover. This is a classic dilemma in which it does, however, seem clear that the sensible objective is survival, not expansion.

BP12. Some principles and laws of business

We are all much indebted to Cyril Parkinson and Laurence Peter who proposed, a little tongue in cheek, some of the most celebrated principles and laws of business. It was not long, however, before it was realized how true to life they really were. Indeed, they apply to anything ranging from domestic life to large corporations and are well worth a little study.

Parkinson's Law (of administration) **(1958)**: *work expands to fill the time available (for its completion).*

This was conceived with the peacetime navy in mind but may well apply even better elsewhere. As a result of this law the growth in the administration separates from the work to be done. Administration officers multiply subordinates, not rivals, thereby making work for each other.

That Francis Bacon went up to Cambridge at twelve was mentioned in BP1 and it seems that Parkinson's Law applies well to education for I cannot believe that 12 years at school, which is what I endured, is necessary for all but the slowest of minds, for example the teachers! With the proliferation of Universities and tertiary courses in recent decades it seems that the problem is growing ever worse!

Parkinson's Law of Triviality: *Committees will pass major decisions without demur but prognosticate interminably over trivia.*

Parkinson's Law of Expenditure: *Expenditure rises to meet income.*
I am left breathless! These three gems put Newton's laws of motion (three) in the shade and, years later, Parkinson concluded with one overall law:

Parkinson's 'The Law' (of the vacuum, or Hoover's Law): *Action expands to fill the void created by human failure.*

The Peter Principle (1969): *In a hierarchy every employee tends to rise to his own level of incompetence (and then stays there).*
A corollary is: *In time every post tends to be occupied by an employee who is incompetent to carry out his duties.*
More brilliant stuff and I cannot recommend Peter's book too strongly. Promotion to your level of incompetence Peter calls the *final placement* and devises many brilliant strategies to achieve or avoid it.

Pareto's Law (1967): *In most situations a relatively small percentage of certain objects contributes a relatively high percentage of output.*
This is the basis of *contribution-by-value analysis* (also called ABC analysis). For instance 15-30 percent of the population contributes 70-90 percent of the tax revenue, 20 percent of the employees in an office may do 80 percent of the work, or 20 percent of the items in inventory may account for 80 percent of the sales.
As an example of ABC analysis, the percentage of total dollar annual sales for each product are calculated and tabulated in descending order. Then the cumulative percentage contribution is added as a final column to show how much, say, the first 20% of products contributes.
This law points out that there are exceptions to Parkinson's Law and the Peter Principle and there are a few workers who do not 'pad out' their day and contribute more than Peter's incompetent managers.

Mohr's Laws
These are ten laws about human behaviour proposed by Geoff Mohr (1993). The first (ML1) is called *Playground Principle* and asserts that there are three basic personality types, namely assertive (A), neutral (B) and placid (C). These neatly correspond to the Greek classifications of *ectomorph, mesomorph* and *endomorph* and thus are nothing new.
What is new, however, is that Mohr claims that you will encounter and have difficulty with opposing types around age nine in the playground and, in every new group of people you have to deal with throughout life, you find that the same types remain. Indeed, the problems

may get worse as some people enter second childhood prematurely with such diseases as SDAT (senile dementia of the Alzheimer's type). So at least it is some help to be warned.

The other laws concern themselves with sex (ML7), achievement etc., and thus can be compared to the Ten Commandments given to Moses. The fifth that great philosopher Zorba himself agreed with: "A man must have a little madness - - ." The ninth (ML9), however, is that *Murphy is God (MIG)*, and all history seems to prove it, clearly in agreement with Parkinson's law of the vacuum and the Peter Principle. The ten laws are summarized briefly in Table BP1 where, despite the great brevity, the general ideas should be fairly clear after a while, so clear that you might feel like taking a powder!

Table BP1.

Law number	Law name	Subject	Principle
1	Mohr's morphology	human personality	Playground principle
2	Mohr's malady	hierarchy & power	law of the jungle etc.
3	Mohr's mentation	education	brainwashing etc.
4	Mohr's metamorphosis	life in three 'boxes'	i.e. home/pub/coffin
5	Mohr's mechanism	achievement	madness required
6	Mohr's misanthropy	nuclear family	explodes
7	Mohr's mirage	sex	myth of love etc.
8	Mohr's motto	power	power corrupts
9	Mohr's mantra	man's history	Murphy is God (MIG)
10	Mohr's metrology	the final judgment	?/10

Mohr's Metrology

This is the tenth of Mohr's Laws (ML10) shown in Table BP1 and requires a little elaboration. It asserts that all human traits can be measured out of ten. Madness, for example, is not a black and white thing, and we should be given a score, though this may vary a little according to such factors as the weather and countless others that hardly need mention.

This law can be used to calculate the *meaning of life.* To this end we sum all the possible scores, that is 0, 1, 2 - - - 10, to obtain 55.

Dividing this result by the number of scores (11) we obtain the answer 5.5. This is not correct, however, as a score of 10 (perfection) is not possible (for example perfect sanity would surely constitute insanity).

Hence the corrected calculation of the 'MOL' is 45/11 = 4.090909 - - . This pleasing result indicates that we are all doomed to failure in the end, if not sooner. *Note too that I had the number recurrence above stated incorrectly with only one digit recurring and a switch girl at Cambridge corrected me, whereas I have never got much sense from academics the world over!* Thanks Martine! Indeed, I have given up and the frustrations of trying did my sanity no good at all and did much to ruin it.

Note too that the playground principle (ML1) can be generalized to fit onto the Mohr scale (1 to10) by subdividing the personality types A, B and C into three degrees. Then type A3 rates 9, that is maximum aggression, once again a score of 10 being disallowed (meltdown). Then type C1 rates 1 on the Mohr scale of aggression. This is maximum placidity, practically speaking, as zero corresponds to petrifaction.

The Mohr scale is also useful in the study of *ethics* where the questions of what is 'right' and what is 'good' are put, quickly followed by the question: "how good?" For this purpose the Mohr scale provides a set or ordinal numbers where, for example, 9 is the maximum goodness (10 would be too good to be true).

Whilst some of this discussion is in humour, it is, however, often well worthwhile to avoid jumping to the conclusion that 'so and so is a ratbag' and instead give him a score out of 10. This might help you see things a little more objectively.

There are countless other Mohr's laws and principles, for example Mohr's Law of War *(DON'T PANIC !!)* and ten rules for making decisions (e.g. don't take first offer), so that the laws of Table BP1 are sometimes called Mohr's Laws of Life. Thus some seriously useful Mohr's laws appear in the text, for example Mohr's laws of money and distribution (3), along with a number of new methods developed by he.

Exercise.

At the close of most subjects' chapters of this course some sort of exercise is given. Here I would simply suggest pondering some sort of business ideas of one's own; implicitly perhaps what kind of shop would you start just down the road? I am not at all sure what I would do. I would really need to know the exact location, the available finance, be able to estimate the market for my chosen product and I would want a helper or two!

BP References

I. Adamson, R. Kennedy, *Sinclair and the 'Sunrise' Technology,* Penguin, UK, 1986.

K.M. Bartel, D.C. Martin, *Management,* 2nd edn, McGraw-Hill, New York, 1994.

J. Carey (ed.), *The Faber Book of Science,* Faber, London, 1995.

R. Carter, *Business Administration,* 2nd edn, Heinemann, London, 1986.

Lord Chesterfield, Against revenues from drunkenness and vice, in *International University Reading Course,* section 8, International University Society, Nottingham.

D. Clark, *Economic Update,* 9th edn, Financial Review Library, Melbourne, 1995.

J.C. Collins, J.I. Porras, Building your company's vision, *Harvard Business Review,* Sept-Oct 1996.

Davis, JW, *An Introduction to Public Administration,* The Free Press, NY 1974.

E. de Bono, *Lateral Thinking for Management,* Pelican, UK, 1982.

J. Dwyer, *The Business Communication Handbook,* 3rd edn, Prentice-Hall, Sydney 1993.

M. Dwyer, K. Marshall, *Guide to MBA programs in Australia,* The Financial Review Library, Melbourne, 1993.

J. Elkington, *Cannibals with Forks: The Triple Bottom Line of 21st Century Business*, Capstone, Oxford, 1999.

G. Hamel, Strategy as revolution, *Harvard Business Review,* July-Aug. 1996.

J.M. Hanna, E.L. Popham, R.S. Tilton, *Secretarial Procedures and Administration,* South-Western, Cincinnati OH, 1978.

E.F. Huse, *Management, 2nd edn,* West, St Paul MN, 1982.

A. Johnston (ed.), *Francis Bacon,* Batesford, London, 1965.

F.J. Kelly, H.M. Kelly, *What They Really Teach You at Harvard Business School,* Grafton, London, 1988.

T. Kempner, *The Penguin Management Handbook,* 4th edn, Penguin, UK, 1987.

C.H. Kepner, B.B. Tregoe, *The New Rational Manager,* Princeton Research Press, Princeton NJ. 1981.

H. Koontz, C. O'Donnell, *Principles of Management,* 3rd edn, McGraw-Hill, New York, 1964.

H. Lorayne, *How to Develop a Super Power Memory,* Fell, Hollywood FA, 1990.

J.L. Massie, *Essentials of Management,* 3rd edn, Prentice-Hall, Englewood Cliffs NJ, 1979.

McCormack, M.H., *What They Don't Teach You at Harvard Business School,* Collins, Glasgow. 1984.

T. Morden, *Business Strategy and Planning: Text and Cases,* McGraw-Hill, London. 1973.

W.R. Niblett (ed.), *Higher Education, Demand and Response,* Tavistock, London, 1969.

Mohr GA, Power AS, The Tertiary Study Objectives of Victorian Secondary Students, *Australian Journal of Advanced Education,* pp 18-19, August 1977.

Mohr GA, Chemical inhibition of corrosion in reinforced concrete, *Int. J. of Arts & Sciences,* Vol. 1, No. 2, pp 50-59, 2001.

Mohr GA, *The Pretentious Persuaders, A Brief History & Science of Mass Persuasion,* Horizon Publishing Group, Sydney, 2012 (edn 1), 2014 (edn 2).

Mohr GA, *The Doomsday Calculation, The End of the Human Race,* Xlibris (2012).

Mohr GA, *The War of the Sexes: Women Are Getting On Top,* Xlibris (2012).

Mohr GA, Richard Sinclair & Edwin Fear, *Human Intelligence, Learning & Behaviour,* Inspiring Publishers, Canberra (2017).

M. Nicholas, *The World's Greatest Cranks and Crackpots,* Exeter, New York NY, 1984.

J.N. Nisberg, *The Random House Book of Business Terms,* Random House, NY, 1988.

F. Odle, *The Picture Story of British Inventions,* World Distributors, London, 1966.

C.N. Parkinson, *The Law,* Schwartz, Melbourne, 1980.

L.J. Peter and R. Hull, *The Peter Principle, Why Things Go Wrong,* Souvenir Press, London, 1969.

N.E. Renton, *Guide for Meetings and Organizations,* 6th edn, Law Book Co, Melbourne, 1992.

S.P. Robbins, *Management,* 3rd edn, Prentice-Hall, Englewood Cliffs NJ, 1991.

Sir David Ross, *Foundations of Ethics,* Oxford University Press, Oxford, 1939.

C.J. Slaybough, Pareto's Law and Modern Management, *Management Services,* March-April 1967.

F. Addington Symonds, *Teach Yourself Commercial Correspondence,* 2nd edn, The English Universities Ltd, London, 1957.

F.W. Taylor, The principles of scientific management, in *Management and Motivation,* eds V.H. Vroom and E.L. Deci, Penguin, Harmondsworth, 1970.

H.J. Vander Zwaag, *Sport Management,* MacMillan, New York, 1984.

J.K. Van Fleet, *Van Fleet's Master Guide for Managers,* Parker, West Nyack NY 1978.

J.O. Whitney, Strategy as revolution, *Harvard Business Review,* July-Aug. 1996.

M. Wrice, *First Steps in Retail Management,* MacMillan, Melbourne, 1998.

_____, *Three Steps to More Skillful Management,* Rydge Publ. Ltd, Sydney, 1975.

BUSINESS LAW (BL)

All virtue is summed up in dealing justly. Aristotle.

In the following chapter we briefly discuss business law, including commercial law, company law and industrial law. Most attention is given to company law as it is this which will be of more immediate concern to those wishing to start their own business or expand an existing one. The discussion of company law applies to Australian conditions but, as the relevant law terms stem from British law, most of this material will be relevant, at least approximately, in most other countries.

BL1 Introduction to Business Law

In the following chapter we take business law to include three areas:

[1] Commercial/Mercantile Law.

Commercial law includes such matters as

a. The general principles of contracts.

b. Laws relating to the sale of goods, the use of agents, insurance of goods, the issue of guarantees and the use of negotiable instruments.

c. Laws relating to consumer protection (this area is sometimes referred to as 'business law') and monopoly control laws (this area is sometimes referred to as 'economic law').

d. International treaties on such matters as air transport and protection of industrial property.

[2] Company Law.

Company law is generally laid down in a *Companies Act* or *Code* involving a great deal of legislation which is a fertile ground for legal debate. This legislation covers such matters as:

a. Registration of companies, company constitutions.

b. Partnerships or mergers (by acquisition or combination).

c. Bankruptcy, liquidation and company deregistration.

d. Share trading (in Australia this is controlled by the *Australian Securities and Investments Commission (ASIC)*).

e. Auditing and taxation

f. Types of company, for example proprietary limited (liability) companies.

[3] Industrial Law.

This lays down the general principles of 'boss v. worker" conduct and involves:

a. Employment contracts and health and safety legislation ('labour law").

b. Laws controlling the operation of trade unions.

c. Laws governing collective bargaining (unions usually prefer negotiation rather than resort to the law).

d. Laws governing industrial tribunals.

e. New legislation, for example EO laws.

f. Workplace bullying.

Finally, it is worth noting a few important properties of companies:

1. They act as a *body corporate* (legally equivalent to a person which in turn is equivalent to the combined membership of the company).
2. They can sue, be sued and acquire, hold or sell property.
3. They have perpetual succession ('don't die') and are a separate entity to the members (called the *veil of corporation*), whereas partnerships or trusts are represented by individual members.

BL2. Commercial Law

Some of the matters involved in commercial law include:

❖ *Agency,* for example brokers, real estate and mercantile agents or *factors.* Such people act for the *principal* for a fee and may be bound by contract to do so.

❖ *Bankers' commercial credits.* A bank guarantees to 'cover' (and in turn an overseas bank does also) your export shipment up to a certain limit when given a *draft* (see negotiable instruments) and the shipping documents.

❖ *Bills of exchange/Negotiable instruments.* Negotiable document embodying a debt, for example promissory notes.

❖ *Bills of lading.* Issued by a ship owner for sea freight. The exporter sends these to the importer, who may in turn give them to a third party to collect the goods after shipment.

❖ *Charter party.* A contract of ship hire specifying the period of hire and the purpose.

❖ *CIF contracts,* that is, cost, insurance and freight contracts. These include negotiable instruments, insurance policies and invoices. The buyer pays for goods on receipt of the CIF contracts and uses them to claim the goods. An FOB (free on board) contract is the special case when the buyer pays for the insurance and freight.

❖ *Consumer credit act (UK).* This requires credit and hire purchase companies to hold a licence and has provisions regarding advertising, information (for example true interest rates must be stated), cooling off periods, recovery of goods and freedom of information (FOI) on credit ratings held by the company.

❖ *Copyright* or right or production or reproduction of work (not ideas). No registration of copyright is required (as is the case for patents and trade marks).

❖ *Data protection act (UK).* This involves FOI for information stored by computer (not manually filed information) and stipulates legal and fairness conventions for the collection and use of personal data.

❖ *Exclusions clauses.* These are inserted into contracts to limit liability in the event of death, injury or other mishap.

❖ *Goodwill* (in law). This refers to any 'benefit arising from connection or reputation' of a business. Thus when purchasing a business the price may include the goodwill associated with it.

❖ *Guarantees.* A guarantee stipulates liability for a debt incurred by some wrongful act (but is not equivalent to an indemnity). Guarantees are sometimes given by a third party (a *guarantor*) and should be in writing.

❖ *Insurance contracts.* The term *assurance* is used where the contingency in question is inevitable. The insured party is obliged to divulge information regarding the level of risk, to ensure that he has an 'insurable interest' in the subject of the policy (that is, he stands to lose in the event of the contingency) and must not claim more than is lost or stipulated in the policy.

❖ *Insurance Law.* This stipulates that insurance contracts must be in good faith and based on true information (see insurance contracts).

❖ *Mareva injunction (UK).* Named after a landmark case such an injunction is sought to prevent asset removal from a company, for example during liquidation.

❖ *Patents.* New devices which have actual practical application may be able to be patented. The use of a chemical for any purpose is not patentable, the chemical already existing, but if it is applied in some novel way, perhaps using some special apparatus, a patent may be obtainable. For a small fee notice can be given of a patent application and this gives some temporary protection.

❖ *Product liability.* In most countries the producer is liable for faults and resulting losses.

❖ *Resale price maintenance law.* This was introduced to discourage the practice of manufacturers dictating the price at which retailers could sell their products. This is now legal only if the retailer buys directly from the manufacturer and agrees to any pricing policies of the manufacturer.

❖ *Restraint of trade.* This involves unreasonable restrictions in employment or trade, for example where a company by some means unfairly restricts the prospects of another, perhaps in collusion with other parties. Where such restraint is deemed by the law to be fair to all parties and the public, however, it is held to be legal. An example is when the seller of a business sells a business and its 'goodwill' and agrees not to compete with the business thereafter. The seller is restricted here by his own consent. In Australia such matters are covered by the *Trade Practices Act.*

❖ *Sale of goods.* Goods are sold under conditions and warrantees. Warrantees are usually in writing but conditions implied by the sale of the goods, for example, the goods must fit the description given of them and be for the purpose claimed for them. If the conditions are breached the buyer may treat the contract as discharged and claim damages. The same applies when a warranty is breached except that the amount the buyer may claim is usually stipulated in the warranty. In Australia such matters are governed by the *Consumer Affairs Act.*

❖ *Supply of goods and services.* The laws relating to the supply of services are much the same as those for the sale of goods but, in addition, it is required that services be provided in a reasonable time, with reasonable care and skill and at a fair price.

❖ *Trade marks.* These must be registered in much the same way as business names (see BL3) and can be sold with a company.

❖ *Vicarious liability.* This involves the liability a company may have for its employee's actions. For example, if A lends a car to B, partly for A's purposes, then A is liable for B's civil wrongs *(torts)* and persons injured by B in an accident can sue both A and B.

The foregoing points, of course, are meant merely as an introduction to some of the key areas of commercial law. From these, however, it will be clear that businesses engaged in export or import have many special concerns unique to these activities.

It will also be clear that any kind of business involves legal obligations and restrictions and it is important to have at least some rudimentary knowledge of these.

BL3. Company Law

Incorporation

In forming a company several steps are involved:

[1] Reservation of name.

Application must be made to the companies office, along with payment of a modest fee. A name search is then conducted to ensure that the chosen name is not too similar to an existing one. If so an alternative name must be used.

This could be the name for a small business, such as a shop. For P/L companies standard company constitutions can be sued to minimize set up cost but there are still annual reporting obligations and charges.

[2] Establishment of company records.

In the matter of company records and the like the following are required:

a. Company seal, for example share certificates must bear this.
b. Registers of: (i) Directors, principal executive officers and secretaries.
(ii) Company members and debenture holders.
(iii) Directors' interests (shares, debentures etc.).
(iv) Substantial shareholders.
(v) Assets, for example property holdings.
These should be kept at the registered office of the company.
c. Minutes of general meetings and board of directors meetings must be filed.
d. Records of allotment of shares.
e. Company accounts.
f. Company registered office. The company name should be displayed here and also on company letters and other documents of transaction.
g. A 'public officer' responsible for all tax matters must be appointed.
h. Companies should have a bank account in the company name.

All manner of other records may be kept relating the day to day affairs of the company, but most of the above are legally necessary for companies which issue public shares.

Types of companies.

[1] Companies with liability (of members). These include:

a. Companies limited by shares. Liability is limited to any amounts unpaid on shares held by members.
b. Companies limited by guarantee. Liability is limited to amounts agreed to by members at the time of incorporation.
c. Companies limited by shares and guarantee. These are very rare.
d. Unlimited companies. Some (mutual) investment companies are unlimited. They hold assets as investments and do not involve as great risk or accountability requirements as limited companies.
e. No liability (N.L.) companies. Only mining companies can be N.L. (and they cannot be proprietary companies). Shareholders of N.L. companies forfeit their shares if they don't pay a call.

[2] Proprietary or public companies.

Proprietary companies are by far the most common kind. They are often family companies and fund themselves privately. Sometimes, however, these expand to become public companies.

Public companies are usually large and raise capital through the stock exchange. They must therefore be accountable for their use of these public funds and disclose their financial affairs at AGMs etc.

Exempt proprietary companies are often family companies. These are exempt from disclosure of their finances but a public company cannot hold shares in an exempt company. Exempt companies need not have an auditor, simply including financial statements with their taxation return, along with a signed statement by two directors that they believe the company's accounts are fair and proper.

[3] Holding and subsidiary companies.

A holding company is a company which has subsidiary companies. It controls the boards of these as well as the majority of the shares and votes at general meetings. Too complex to discuss here, there are legal restrictions on the transfer of funds between *related companies* (such as holding and subsidiary companies) and their directors. For example, directors of the holding company cannot lend to directors of a subsidiary.

[4] Recognized and foreign companies.

In Australia a company incorporated in a particular state can be 'recognized' in others simply by notifying the companies office of its address in any other state in which it wishes to operate. This eliminates the need for separate incorporation in the other states.

Foreign companies can take advantage of this procedure, only needing to incorporate in one state.

[5] Investment companies.

Investment companies must be recognized as such by the securities commission. Such companies engage primarily in the business of investment in 'marketable securities', that is shares, debentures and government securities.

Such companies are subject to restrictions on how much, in relation to their tangible assets, they can borrow, invest in any single company or underwrite share issues. They must also state in their prospectuses and articles whether their objective is overseas or local investment, or both.

[6] Trustee companies.

These are now popular as a means of holding family or company funds. They often have only a minimum possible issued capital and are thus referred to as '$2 companies'. They therefore have no real liability to creditors but can distribute funds to their members with tax only being paid once by these members.

On the detailed workings of, for example, trustee companies, the brief notes given here are only an introduction and, for practical purposes, expert advice may be required. Some idea of what the term 'limited' means in association with a company, however, is important, as is some idea of what is required to set up (incorporate) a company.

Finally, note that public and statutory authorities run by the government, Crown agencies, the public trustee (of deceased estate etc.) and most professional societies, unions and charities are not companies in the sense of the companies code. For example, some Universities are public authorities funded directly by government whilst others are incorporated and partly or wholly privately funded.

BL4. Company Constitutions

Memorandum of association.

A company must have a memorandum of association before it can be registered and this must contain the following clauses:

a. The name of the company.
b. Its share capital and the nominal value of the shares.
c. Statement whether limited, guarantee, unlimited or N.L.
d. Statement of association saying that the subscribers to the company agree to its incorporation.
e. The names, addresses and share holdings of its subscribers.

Additional clauses that are sometimes required include:

f. Further powers of the company, for example to distribute property to its members.
g. Objectives of the company, for example to mine for gold (such clauses are less binding than they once were).

Alterations to the memorandum must, for example, be by a resolution passed by 75% of the members.

Articles of association.

Limited or N.L. companies do not require their own articles, in which case they are covered by 'model articles' which are part of company laws. Guarantee and unlimited companies must provide their own articles.

The effect of the articles is to establish a contract between the company and its members and between the members themselves, who are then bound by changes in the memorandum or articles whether they voted for them or not.

The articles should contain the following clauses:

a. Type of company and the corresponding requirements as to the number of members as well as the issuing of shares.
b. Method of issuing shares and rights of shareholders.
c. *Lien* (possession of property until a debt on it is paid) on shares.
d. Method of issuing a call on shares.
e. Method of share transfer.
f. Method of share transmission.
g. Condition under which shares are forfeited.
h. Provision allowing conversion of shares into stock (and vice versa).
i. Provision allowing alteration of share capital.
j. Make up of share capital of the company (for example numbers of ordinary and 'class' shares) and voting rights associated with each share type.
k. Provision for notice in calling general meetings.
l. Required proceedings at general meetings.

m. Procedure for appointment, removal and remuneration of directors.
n. Provision for appointment of a permanent governing director.
o. Provision for appointment of a managing director.
p. Provision for appointment of associate directors.
q. Provisions for terms of office of the secretary.
r. Restrictions on use of the company seal.
s. Restrictions on access to company records.
t. Provision that company reserves may be reinvested or distributed.
u. Provision for capitalization of profits (for example by paying up unissued shares and distributing these to members according to their share rights).
v. Provision for notices (of general meetings, for example).
w. Conditions for winding up of the company.
x. Provision for indemnification of officers of the company for any liability incurred by company duties (given Court judgment is in their favour).

Alterations of the articles can be made by special resolution at a general meeting (though these may be invalid if they discriminate against certain shareholders, for example).

Many of the items listed above will, in practice, require several clauses so that company articles can become quite lengthy documents, particularly when new clauses have been added over the years.

Liability of a company

The last clause above is a useful reminder that the question of company liability is an important one worth further discussion. In particular the following points are of note:

[1] Acts of employees.

A company can be held liable for the torts of employees engaged in company duties as legally they are judges to be the 'mind and will' of the company. Hence the courts may charge the manager(s) responsible for the duties of the errant employees, holding that they are vicariously liable (see BL2).

Whether the acts in question were intentional or deliberate is, or course, a key consideration in judgment, as is whether the erring party knew they were committing a wrong. An example might be when a sales person sells an article at full price, unaware of a new advertisement of a reduced price. If this is believed he will be found innocent of any wrong doing.

[2] Acts of agents.

Persons acting under contract with a company who commit torts may in some cases be deemed to be acting as employees of the company, which may then be vicariously liable.

The authority of such agents may be actual (in writing) or apparent, that is whether the principal leads the third person or outsider to believe that the agent has authority.

A special case is that of pre-incorporation contracts made by a 'promoter' in the process of setting up a company. If illegal acts are committed in the process the promoter and/or the company may be held responsible.

[3] Sale of goods.

Violation of the laws of sale of goods (see BL2) once again may involve an offending officer of the company and/or the company in litigation. Where an officer misrepresents a product and misled a customer he alone is generally liable. When the product is faulty, on the other hand, the company, of course, is liable. A company, however, cannot be imprisoned, for example, and the manager deemed responsible for the problem will be sought by the court.

In conclusion, there are a great many legal matters to be considered at the very outset in forming a company and, once it is formed, it has many legal obligations.

BL5. Prospectuses and Shares

A major reason for the existence of companies is so that they can pool funds contributed by many individuals to finance activities which could not be afforded by a single person. This is achieved by issuing shares. When the issue is a public one a prospectus is required and various legal requirements are involved in these matters.

Prospectuses

These must accompany share application forms given out in response to 'an offer to the public' (by a public company) and a copy must be registered with the Securities Commission.

They are required to contain the following information:

a. A minimum number of shares required. No shares can be issued until subscriptions for this number of shares have been obtained.
b. A statement that no shares will be issued on the basis of this prospectus after six months.
c. A statement whether application has been made for stock exchange listing (if listing is obtained the issue becomes void).
d. Details of interests and remuneration of directors and promoters of the company.
e. Details of any property to be acquired from the process of the issue.
f. Voting rights of the issue.
g. Report by a registered auditor setting out the profit and loss and dividends paid for the last five years.
h. If the prospectus is for a debenture issue state that the company may retain part of oversubscriptions.

If the prospectus includes a statement by an expert (on the virtues of the issue) it must be also stated that written consent has been given to include his statement.

Advertising

Advertising of a share issue should be limited to the nature of the company and details of the shares (that is type etc.). Verbal or written 'hawking' is not allowed and the company is liable for misstatements and nondisclosures.

Shares

A share in a company is an interest in it equal to \$x,, where x is the nominal, market or par value. 'Stock' in a company is a collection of shares expressed as a monetary value. 'Options' are contracts to issue shares to option holders at a later date. Shares can also be issued 'at a premium', that is, at a price higher than the par value.

Authorized share capital

The authorized or nominal share capital of a company is that prescribed in its memorandum. More shares than this cannot be issued but commonly only part of the authorized shares are issued. This is the *issued capital* and the amount unpaid on this is the *reserve capital* or *uncalled capital.* At any time the company can make a call on this owed money.

The authorized capital can be changed by resolution but cannot, of course, be less than the issued capital.

Allotment of shares

For shares to be allotted the minimum subscription must be received and if the issue is oversubscribed applicants are obliged to accept fewer shares than applied for. In the case of a new company, for example, shares can be issued for other than cash to acquire assets. Shares can also be issued at a premium but not at a discount (except in the case of N.L. companies). The latter restriction can be circumvented by issuing partly paid shares with no intention of a call on them before winding up.

Classes of shares

Different classes of shares have different rights to dividends, voting and liquidation payments and this should be detailed in the articles. Preference shares, for example, have priority in payment on liquidation and when redeemable are equivalent to a means of borrowing by the company. Rights of a class of shares can be varied by resolution of 75% of votes.

Maintenance of issued capital

Limited liability companies are required to maintain their share capital. This is so that they cannot escape creditors by, for example, buying their own shares or funding others to do so. For the same reason a subsidiary company cannot hold shares in a holding company. Also for this reason, dividends can only be taken from profits.

Members of a company

Subscribers to the original memorandum and shareholders are members of a company and can vote, receive dividends, share assets (or debts) on wind up and can hold shares on behalf of others (that is, act as trustee).

There must be a register of company members and substantial shareholders (holding more than 10% of any class of shares) must notify the company of their holding and the reason for it. On forfeiture or sale of their shares, on the other hand, shareholders are no longer members of the company.

Share certificates

These should state the company name, the class of shares, their nominal value and the extent to which they are paid up.

Transfer of shares

A transfer of shares must be affected in writing and the document of transfer is usually signed by the transferor and transferee. The transfer document and share certificates should then be lodged with the company so that its register can be amended accordingly.

Transmission of shares occurs when the holder dies, is incapacitated or bankrupted. Then the shares vest in the executor(s) of the holder's will, his personal representative or the trustee in bankruptcy.

Conclusion

To those new to them, even the basics of prospectuses and shares, like most of business law, will seem a little daunting. Like the requirements for incorporation, however, most of the matters discussed are really fairly obvious practical considerations.

Moreover, as in the case of accounting, where use of an example set of accounts is very helpful, it is very helpful to obtain a sample company memorandum and articles, prospectus etc. and compare these with the requirements listed in this and other books.

BL6. Dividends and Debentures

Dividends

Dividends should only be paid out of profits, and then after sufficient cash has been held in reserve for company operations.

That dividends will be paid is declared by the directors at a general meeting, when the amount to be paid is also announced and this amount is then owed immediately and preferential shareholders have priority of payment,

If the articles permit *interim dividends* can be declared and, should the circumstances of the company change for the worse, the declaration can be rescinded.

Debentures

Debentures are a means by which a company can raise *loan capital* and the ratio of this to *share capital* is called the *gearing* of the company. The following points are important in debenture transactions:

a. Debenture holders are creditors and have priority of payment on wind up.
b. *Convertible* debentures or notes can be converted to shares.
c. *Mortgage debentures* can only be issued on the basis of a first mortgage over land held by the company described in the prospectus.
d. Debentures may also be *secured* by a charge over tangible property of the company.
e. Debentures which are not secured are called *unsecured notes.*
f. When debentures are issued a *trustee* must be appointed and he holds the *trust deed* and may inspect the company records at liberty.
g. The trust deed states the limit of borrowing entailed and states the obligation of the business to conduct its affairs properly and accountably and may place limits on future borrowing.
h. Debenture holders are entitled to a copy of the auditor's report and if holders of 10% or more of the debenture stock apply to hold a meeting to consider the company accounts the company must hold such a meeting of all debenture holders.
i. Debentures are transferred in much the same way as shares.

Company charges

Debentures are usually secured by a *charge* or mortgage over company property. Such charges may be fixed or floating and related to assets (property, patents held, crops etc.), reserve share capital or mortgages, liens or pledges held by the company,

Floating charges relate to a *category* of assets, such as property or shares, and the company is free to trade such assets for others of the same kind. Such charges are *crystallized* when the company is wound up or defaults on conditions of the trust deed.

Company charges must be registered with the securities commission and a register of *chargees* (lenders) must be kept by the *chargor* (company).

Conclusion

Dividends are a relatively simple matter, the primary consideration being that a company is obliged to maintain its share capital. Debentures, however, are a little more complicated but here we encounter the interesting issue of *gearing*, that is the ratio of *debt to equity*, and this is an important factor in business finance matters.

BL7. Management of Companies

The board of directors

The board is responsible for running the company and even a general meeting of members cannot direct the board, generally having only the right to elect directors, though as in politics, members can exert 'public pressure.' The board can delegate to the MD and committees and has the power to issue shares, calls, cheques, receipts, and dividends, and to call GMs (there must be at least one meeting annually, that is, the AGM).

The *proceedings* of the board are by way of meeting, which require notice and a quorum (two unless articled otherwise) and minutes, resolutions signed by all directors (which take effect on the date of the last signature) and through delegations, for example of accounting matters to one director.

The board may include non-executive directors, often persons of considerable reputation and experience, to contribute to broader policy discussion rather than the day to day affairs of the company.

The powers and duties of directors

1. Some proprietary companies, for example family companies, appoint a governing director who has full control of the company.
2. BODs usually appoint a managing director (MD) who has all the powers of the board and is sometimes appointed under contract.
3. The chairman of directors, often a 'prestigious' person, has no real powers and simply chairs meetings and signs the minutes.
4. Committees of directors may be appointed to deal with some particular aspect of business, for example overseas operations.
5. Alternative directors may be appointed to replace directors unavailable for health or other reasons for a limited period.
6. Associate directors with limited attendance and voting rights can be appointed if required.
7. Nominee directors are those appointed by a holding company.
8. Directors are appointed by subscribing to the original memorandum or thereafter by a general meeting.
9. Casual vacancies resulting from death or resignation are filled by the board.
10. Directors may be required to have a *share qualification*, that is, some minimum share holding.
11. Directors must be at least 18 and must not have been convicted of a criminal offence in the last five years (for example bankruptcy). They cannot be a registered auditor, receiver or liquidator.
12. Directors are only appointed annually if older than 72.
13. Directors are usually retired in rotation, when they become eligible for re-election.
14. Directors can be removed by resolution at a general meeting.
15. The annual accounts must show the *emoluments* (money and other benefits) received by directors and shareholders can demand an audited statement of payments to each director.

The company secretary

A company must have at least one secretary. The secretary is appointed by the board (and can be a member of this) and the secretary or agent thereof is required to be present at the company's registered office during the hours when the office is required to be open and accessible to the public.

The secretary is responsible for the minutes of meetings and the general administration of the company, for example lodging the annual return.

Large companies, or course, often have many secretaries, as well as assistant or deputy secretaries.

Duties of officers of a company

Officers of a company have a *fiduciary* (in trust) obligation to exercise proper care, diligence, skill and discretion in carrying out their duties.

Breach of duty, which may involve misuse of funds or information, bribes etc., may be remedied by dismissal, fines in compensation, return of property or restriction of benefits.

Meetings

Companies are required to hold their first AGM within 18 months of incorporation and subsequent AGMs within six months of the end of each financial year (roughly the same timing applies to submission of their returns).

Limited public and N.L. companies must hold a statutory meeting within three months of allotment of shares pursuant to issue of a prospectus. At this meeting full details of the share allotment must be provided.

The directors have the power to call an extraordinary general meeting at any time and can also be requisitioned to do so by a sufficient number of members or members with a sufficient voting entitlement (including a single member).

Class meetings of holders of certain classes of shares can be called. These, like general meetings, require at least 14 days notice, though a meeting convened for the passing of a special resolution requires at least 21 days notice.

Notice of meetings must be in writing and a quorum and chairman are required. Voting is usually by a show of hands, although a poll can be called for and proxy votes are permitted, though usually only in a poll.

Ordinary resolutions require only a majority but special resolutions may require some higher proportion of the votes. Such results must, of course, be recorded in the minutes of the meeting.

Powers of majority shareholders

Sometimes a majority or controlling shareholder or member may have greater power than a director by virtue of his 'perceived authority' and directors may accept his direction.

Minority shareholders, on the other hand, generally have little or no power. An exception is where some act of the company is illegal or denies the personal rights of a shareholder. In such cases the member may take legal action and/or apply to the securities commission for a ruling. If the company is found guilty of a serious offence (for example fraud) then orders may be given for it to be wound up.

Conclusion

In the foregoing discussion we have concentrated on the management role of the board and its obligations to shareholders. This is because it is here that legal obligations are most heavily concentrated.

It should be realised that companies are managed through a corporate structure which also involves various legal obligations at its various levels, for example occupational health and safety at the 'coal face' of company operations.

BL8. Company Accounts

The proper keeping of company accounts is, of course, vitally important. Some of the relevant obligations of a company include:

[1] Annual returns must be lodged with the securities commission. The company address, the accounts from the AGM, details of 'charges', a summary of share capital, a lists of shareholders, a list of company executive officers and the name of the auditor should be included. Exempt proprietary companies, however, need not include accounts with their return can include a statement by an auditor instead.

[2] Accounting records must be kept. These must be a record of transactions and finances, including invoices and receipts etc. Directors are able to inspect these at any time and the records must be amenable to this.

[3] Directors are obliged to ensure accuracy of the accounts, for example by writing off bad debts and dealing with doubtful ones, also writing down over valued assets.

[4] Before the auditor reports on them (preparatory to the AGM) a directors' statement must be attached to the accounts and this should state:

a. That the profit and loss account and balance sheet give a true and fair view.
b. That the company can pay its debts as they fall due.
c. That the accounts are made out in accordance with accepted standards.

[5] A director's report must be prepared and presented at the AGM. This must include the following information:

a. A list of directors.
b. The principal activities of the company and any changes in these.
c. The net profit or loss after tax.
d. Dividends declared or paid during the financial year and any dividends recommended by the directors now.
e. Review of company operations and significant changes in its affairs.
f. Likely developments and results thereof in the coming year.
g. Details of any share options granted and shares issued as a result.
h. Details of any benefits accorded directors other than those shown in the accounts.

[6] Group accounts are those for a holding company and its subsidiaries. These must satisfy the same requirements as company accounts.

[7] *Disclosure* requirements. At the AGM directors must provide all members of the company with copies of:

a. The profit and loss account for the last financial year (f.y.).
b. The balance sheet as at the end of the last f.y.
c. The directors' report.
d. The auditor's report (unless exempted from this requirement).
e. The director's statement.

[8] Auditors are not required by exempt proprietary companies, when a signed statement by at least two directors that the accounts are fair and proper must be attached to them.
[9] When an auditor is required to be appointed this must be done within one month of incorporation. The auditor must be registered as such (and therefore experienced and qualified in accounting and company law).

Conclusion

Trite though it may sound, 'accountability in accounting' is crucially important in good business. To many accounting is a daunting and tedious subject and the more so when legal matters are also included. This combination, however, is the crux of our financial system.

BL9. The Securities Industry

In Australia the securities industry is controlled by the Australian Securities and Investments Commission (ASIC). Companies which issue shares must be registered with this and must register prospectuses for share issues with ASIC. Shares are then traded on the Australian Stock Exchange, an amalgamation of the exchanges in the capital cities of each state.

Functions of ASIC

[1] The *objectives* of ASIC are to promote business certainty and reduce business costs, to promote efficient markets and to preserve investor confidence.
[2] The *powers* of ASIC include
a. It can prohibit trading in stock(s).
b. It can require information disclosure of a company.
c. It licenses dealers, investment advisers and their representatives.
d. It regulates the stock exchanges.

Functions of the stock exchange

The principal function of the exchanges, of course, is to facilitate trade in securities. Companies, as well as individuals, can be members of the exchange and it has the power to list and delist shares.

Prohibited practices

Prohibited practices include *short selling* (shares not owned by the seller), *insider trading* (for example directors of a company trading in their own shares), issuing *false information* (which may affect share prices) and *market manipulation* (for example a group of investors pooling their funds and then selling a stock successively from one to the other to raise its price, thereby inducing others to buy, and then selling at a profit).

Takeovers

The conduct of company takeovers is governed by the 'Takeover Code' {The Companies (Acquisition of Shares) Act}, This is not aimed at preventing takeovers (in contrast to the Trade Practices Act which aims to prevent restrictive trade practices such as monopolies) but at ensuring that they are fairly conducted. This imposes the following conditions:
[1] Any person is prohibited from holding more than 20% of the voting shares in a target company (or cannot increase their holding if it is already greater than 20%).

[2] Generally a person can only acquire more than 20% of the shares in a target company in three ways:
a. By acquiring not more than 3% of the shares every three months (a *creeping* takeover).
b. By making a written takeover bid which must remain open for at least one month and not more than six months.
c. By making a takeover announcement on the stock exchange which takes effect two weeks after the announcement and must remain effective for one month.
[3] A person is deemed to have acquired a 'relevant interest' in shares if he has control over their voting rights. This is aimed at, for example, the situation where two or more people buy, say, 18% of the shares with a view to these 'associated' people gaining control. Then a person with a relevant interest in the shares is deemed to have acquired for the purposes of [1].
[4] Exemptions to [1] are allowed if:
a. The shares are acquired under a will.
b. The shares are allotted pursuant to a prospectus.
c. The acquisition is approved by a GM of the target company of ASIC.
d. The company does not have more than 15 members.
[5] A takeover bidder cannot forecast profits etc. without ASIC approval.
[6] A target company cannot make statements on asset values etc. without ASIC approval.
[7] A bidder cannot withdraw the bid without good reason before it becomes effective or before the minimum period has elapsed.
[8] A target company cannot issue shares to 'friends' or give bonuses to its directors as a 'bail out' strategy.

Powers of ASIC

Powers which the securities commission has at its disposal in the matter of takeovers include:
[1] It can exempt a bidder from part or all of the Code restrictions.
[2] It can declare conduct in relation to a (proposed) takeover unacceptable and apply to the court to:
a. Require the purchaser/bidder to dispose of shares.
b. Restrain the purchaser/bidder from using the voting rights of the shares.
c. Direct the target company not to give dividends to the purchaser.
d. Order that the shares in question be vested in ASIC.

ASIC can also exercise similar restraints on its own initiative but disposal of the shares must be ordered by the court.

The role of stockbrokers

Traditionally broking houses have played a leading role in the new issues market. A company may maintain a continuing relationship with a broking house, which advises it on fund raising and the terms of a new issue of securities.

It is also common for the same broker or an associated company to underwrite the issue, that is take up any portion of the issue which is not taken up by other investors within a given period. Sometimes a broker will undertake to sell the issue to clients and institutional investors.

Larger broking houses also frequently assist companies contemplating a takeover or merger and act as intermediaries for such moves.

Many broking houses now provide a service in the short term money market, acting as an agent in the intercompany market, accepting short term deposits and re-lending them, and operating in the commercial bills market. Most brokers, however, provide such services through associated merchant banks.

The role of merchant banks

Many of the early merchant banks were partially owned by a broking house and most large broking houses still have a close association with a merchant bank. Through these associations merchant banks provide much the same services as the larger broking houses and vice versa.

Conclusion

The securities industry is the heart of our economic system, enabling companies to be 'launched' and to grow. Many important legal controls for this system have evolved over time and are vital to its well being.

BL10. Temporary Insolvency

Temporary or technical insolvency can be dealt with in several ways. These include:

[1] Schemes of arrangement.

These are agreements between members of a company and its creditors designed to avoid winding up the company. There are several types of schemes of arrangement, the most common of these being:

a. *Moratorium schemes* where debt payments are deferred and creditors appoint a manager and an advisory committee to run the company

b. *Compromise schemes* where creditors accept part payment or shares in lieu of payment.

c. Combinations of (a) and (b).

Such schemes are implemented by a member or director applying to the court for an order for a meeting of members and/or creditors to be convened to initiate a proposed scheme. If the proposal is approved by a sufficient majority then it is binding.

Under such schemes share capital can be reorganized, assets can be transferred, companies can be amalgamated etc.

The scheme manager must be a registered liquidator unless court approval is sought otherwise.

[2] Investigations and inspections.

The relevant minister of the government (state or federal) can order the securities commission to conduct a special investigation if an application for such is received from

a. Members holding not less than 5% of the shares.

b. A prescribed number of members of the company.

c. The trustee for the debenture holders of the holders themselves.

d. The trustee or representative for holders of prescribed interests or the interest holders.

e. The company.

The commission, or an inspector appointed by it, then conducts an investigation and provides a report to the company, the requesters of the investigation and other interested parties.

As a result of this report corrective action may be taken by the company, civil or criminal proceedings may be instigated or a receiver may be appointed by the court.

[3] Receivership.

The term 'receiver' means receiver and manager. A receiver may be appointed by

a. Debenture holders when the company defaults on a due payment, is operating at a loss or reduces its capital.

b. The court as a result of an application by a mortgagee if the company defaults in payment of a secured debt.

A receiver must be a registered liquidator or an authorized and independent trustee company and the appointment must be notified to the company, the securities commission, the taxation department and notice that a receiver has been appointed should appear on company documents.

The duties and powers of a receiver include:

a. The receiver supersedes the board of directors and carries on any business of the company.

b. To sell the charged property relating to the 'defaulted' debentures and discharge the secured debt, first paying tax, and outstanding wages.

c. To report any offences by members of the company.

Generally, however, a receiver is authorized to carry out any legal and proper act necessary in discharging his duties.

Periods of receivership are generally as short as possible. In some cases the company is able to resume normal business and in others, when the insolvency cannot be remedied, the company is placed in liquidation and the receiver's agency ceases.

[4] Official management.

Official management is a statutory moratorium scheme of arrangement initiated by the company or its creditors by resolution at a meeting for that purpose As a result an official manager is appointed by the creditors. The official manager need not be registered or hold any particular qualifications (but is usually an experienced receiver and liquidator). Notice that an official manager has been appointed must appear on all company documents.

The official manager meets with the creditors every six months to report on the financial position of the company. When conducting the company's business he must comply with any directions of creditors passed by special resolution at meetings of which special notice has been given.

A creditors' meeting may appoint a committee of management made up of three persons appointed by the creditors and two appointed by the members. This committee is allowed to advise and assist the official manager in the management of the company.

The powers of the official manager to dispose of property other than during the normal course of business are limited to small sums of money unless approval is given by the committee of management, but then only limited sums of money are allowed. Larger 'disposals' must be approved by resolution at a meeting of creditors of which special notice is given.

Official management, though seemingly a sound procedure, is rare and schemes of arrangement, though they involve more complex and time consuming procedures, are more flexible and more commonly used.

Official management and schemes of arrangement are terminated when and if the company has traded out of difficulty. If, on the other hand, the 'interim' manager is of the view that the company will not be able to pay its debts by continued operation he must call a meeting of creditors for the purpose of voluntary winding up.

Conclusion

When a company is unable to pay its creditors it is usually in their interests, as well as in the interests of the members and shareholders, to at least delay receivership or liquidation from which they often stand to be paid only a small fraction of what they are owed. Hence the alternative courses discussed here are at least worth consideration.

BL11. Liquidations

Liquidation or winding up is the process by which a company's assets are collected, its debts paid in part or full and, in the latter instance, the surplus, if any, is distributed amongst its members. There are three modes of winding up:

<u>[1] Members' voluntary winding up</u>. A members' voluntary winding up is initiated by special resolution of the company and can only proceed if the company is solvent and the directors make a declaration to this effect and lodge it with the securities commission. The members then appoint a liquidator and have supervisory powers over his or her conduct of the liquidation.

<u>[2] Creditor's voluntary winding up</u>. This occurs when, during the course of a members' voluntary winding up, it is found that the company is insolvent. A creditors meeting must then be called at which they must nominate a liquidator or, when a liquidator has already been appointed, they have the option of appointing a new one.

<u>[3] Compulsory winding up</u>. Compulsory winding up occurs as a result of a court application by the company, its creditors, a shareholder or 'contributory', a liquidator in a voluntary winding up, the securities commission or an official manager.

Applicants must advertise that they have applied and notify the commission. This makes the application pubic knowledge and permits time to apply for an injunction against the application by the company.

Grounds for granting of the application include:

a. The company is insolvent (the usual grounds) in the judgment of the court or because it fails to meet a demand for payment.
b. Default by the company in lodging reports or holding meetings.
c. The company does not commence business within a year of incorporation or suspends business for a year or more.
d. The company has too few members (compared to that required).
e. Self interested or unjust actions by directors.
f. Company conduct prejudicial to the interests of members.
g. Where the commission reports an opinion for winding up.

If the court grants the application it appoints a liquidator.

Liquidation. The liquidator must be a registered liquidator or an 'official' liquidator appointed by the court (except in a members' voluntary winding up of an exempt proprietary company). His powers are those of the board and he opens his own accounts to conduct the liquidation.

The liquidator then makes compromises with creditors and shareholders and sells the company assets and distributes the proceeds according to 'priority' (for example preference shares have priority over ordinary).

When this process is complete the liquidator so advises the commission and the company is dissolved (and de-registered).

Conclusion

A company effectively ceases business when a liquidator is appointed, if not before, and its documents must carry the notice 'in liquidation'. The liquidator may retain a skeleton staff, however, to facilitate the accumulation and sale of assets.

BL12. Industrial Law

Industrial law and industrial relations are large subjects of considerable importance in many industries. Some of the key matters involved include:

❖ *Apprenticeship.* A contract of apprenticeship does not differ significantly from other employment contracts. Key features are that they usually involve *minors* (under 18) whose parents or guardians may be party to the contract.

❖ *Arbitration.* Commercial arbitration involves settlement of commercial disputes, for example concerning violation of patent rights. Industrial arbitration involves disputes over wages and conditions or employment and may be dealt with by the courts, an ombudsman, solicitors, government agencies or an arbitration commission.

❖ *Collective agreements in law.* Such agreements between unions and companies may include such clauses as 'no strike' promises in return for commitments on job security etc. Such agreements have limited application to individuals.

❖ *Collective bargaining.* Group bargaining about wages and/or conditions of work. This is based on established principles and seeks to keep third party intervention to a minimum.

❖ *Conciliation.* Conciliation involves bringing the parties together with a view to persuading them to settle their differences themselves. The Australian Conciliation and Arbitration Commission and the Court of 'C &A' are example of organizations with this responsibility.

❖ *Disabled persons.* Under EO and other legislation employers of more than a certain number of people may be obliged to employ disabled persons.

❖ *Discrimination.* Much legislation concerning equal pay, EO, maternity rights, gender and racial discrimination and the like now exists.

❖ *Dismissal.* Persons dismissed without due notice and/or cause may sue for compensation and, in exceptional cases, for reinstatement.

❖ *Employment contracts.* These may include a specified period of employment, remuneration and other conditions. In relation to the period of employment these are not binding under certain circumstances, for example misconduct or incompetence of an employee.

❖ *Equal opportunity.* EO in employment (of different gender, race etc.) is now widely practised and appeals concerning denial of EO are now common.

❖ *Equal pay.* Equal pay legislation whereby women must be paid equally with men for 'like work' has been in force in most countries for over 20 years and has done much towards equalizing the earnings of men and women.

❖ *Factories act.* This governs employers' liability for working conditions, safety etc. The government provides factory inspectors to ensure safe and proper working conditions. Building inspectors have the same responsibility in relation to the building industry.

❖ *Freedom of association.* Legislation establishing this as a right prevents dismissal on the grounds of membership of a professional society or trade union.

❖ *Guarantee pay.* This is a guarantee of payment of an employee when no suitable work is available for a limited period.

❖ *Heath and safety legislation.* There is now a great deal of such legislation requiring, for example, companies to provide written safety policies and unions to provide safety representatives. This legislation is policed by inspectors who have the right to test materials and conduct investigations.

❖ *Industrial training act.* This governs the obligation of employers in certain industries to provide or contribute to the cost of training of employees. Such legislation is particularly important in relation to the safe use of manufacturing and construction equipment, for example.

❖ *Maternity rights.* These include leave with pay for a limited period and retention of employment. Some limited paternity rights also exist now.

❖ *Office employment.* Safety legislation for this is similar to that in the factories act.

❖ *Picketing.* Legislation exists to protect the rights of picketers but if they threaten or endanger property or people they can be charged.

❖ *Redundancy.* When an employee is made redundant by adjustment of manpower requirements he is entitled to redundancy pay unless it can be proved that dismissal was not due to redundancy.

❖ *Right to work.* See Discrimination.

❖ *Sick pay.* This is governed by employment contracts but there are minimum statutory requirements except in the case of casual or short term workers.

❖ *Strike.* Strike, 'go-slow' and 'work to rule' are the main weapons of 'industrial action' by unions. Such matters are resolved be negotiation, conciliation and arbitration or by legal action.

❖ *Trade dispute.* A trade dispute is sometimes a long term dispute (for example by school teachers) in which such actions as strikes may play little or no part. Such matters are resolved by the same means as strikes.

❖ *Trade union.* Organization of workers whose principal purposes include the regulation of relations with employers etc. Registration of unions is voluntary, as is membership thereof usually. Election of office beaters and votes for strike action may be required to be by secret ballot.

❖ *Transfer of undertakings.* By law contracts of those employed by a company taken over by another are automatically transferred to the new owner.

❖ *Unfair dismissal.* Dismissal includes 'constructive dismissal' where the employee leaves in response to a substantial breach of contract on the part of the employer. When a complaint is filed the employer must show reasonable grounds for dismissal.

❖ *Wage systems.* Two main systems are time-rates and piece-rates and often these are combined. Another is 'payment by results' (PBR). Many other variations which may include bonuses and other incentives may be used.

Conclusion

Industrial and industrial relations is, of course, a much larger field than this, though it is , perhaps, more important for an employee to be aware of his individual rights.

In Australia there are many organizations concerned with such matters, for example the Australian Council of Trade Unions (ACTU), the Australian Council of Salaried and Professional Associations (ACSPA) and the Australian Workers Union (AWU). The ACTU, for example, has a very high profile and can exert some pressure on governments. For those related to any union, however, a little legal advice is sometimes well worthwhile.

BL References

Dabsckeck, B and Niland, J. *Industrial Relations in Australia.* Allen & Unwin, Sydney. 1981.

Epstein, D.G., Landers, J.M. and Nickles, S.H. *Debtors and Creditors.* West, St Paul MN. 1988.

Ford, G.W., Hearn, J.M. and Lansbury, R.D> (eds). *Australian Labour Relations,* 3rd edn. MacMillan, Melbourne. 1980.

Gibson, A. and Kelsen, I. *Essentials of Australian Business Law,* 3rd end. Pitman, Melbourne. 1989.

Gillies, P. *Business Law,* 7th edn. Federation Press, Sydney. 1995.

Hall,T. *White Collar Crime in Australia.* Harper & Row, Sydney. 1979.

Kaye, B. Compliance and corporate culture: making the most out of codes of ethics. *Aust. J. Management*, vol. 21, no. 1. 1996.

Lipton, P, and Herzberg, A. *Understanding Company Law,* 4th edn. Law Book Co., Sydney. 1992.

Mohr GA, The History and Psychology of Human Conflict, Horizon Publishing Group, Sydney, 2014.

Mohr GA, Elementary Thinking for the 21st Century, Xlibris, Sydney, 2014.

Plowman, D., Deery S. and Fisher, C. *Australian Industrial Relations.* McGraw-Hill, Sydney. 1980.

Townsend, P. (ed). *The Concept of Poverty.* Heinemann, London. 1971.

______. *'A True and Fair View' and the Reporting Obligations of Directors and Auditors.* Australian Securities Commission, Melbourne. 1984.

______. *Memorandum of Articles of Association of ---- Investments P/L.*, Australia, 1998.

MATHEMATICS & STATISTICS (MS)

Instructing a savage in advanced techniques does not change him into a civilized person; it changes him into an efficient savage. Carlo Cipolla.

This chapter briefly reviews some basics of classical mathematics as a prelude to the introduction of *numerical methods* in the next chapter. Some knowledge of *polynomials, differentiation* and *integration*, for example, is needed in the Finite Element Method and the optimization techniques that are the core of the this book.

MS1. Mathematical functions

Explicit functions. Explicit functions are expressed symbolically in the form $y = f(x)$ where x is the *independent variable* and y is the *dependent variable.* An example is

(MS1) $$y = x^2 \qquad -3 < x < 3$$

where the function is defined in the range or interval -3 to 3 and is a parabola passing through the origin (as an exercise plot this on graph paper and on your computer if you have never done so).

Implicit functions. Implicit functions are expressed symbolically in the form $f(x,y) = 0$. An example is

(MS2) $$x^2 + y^2 = 9$$

which is a circle of radius 3 centered at the origin (convert the equation to explicit form and plot it as an exercise).

Single valued functions. For these solutions of $f(x,y) = 0$ give one and only one value of y corresponding to each value of x. Examples are $f(x,y) = x - y + 2$ (straight line) and $f(x,y) = x^2 - y + 1$ (parabola). On the other hand relations such as $y^2 = | x |$ and $sin(y) = x$ define *two-valued* and *many-valued* functions of x respectively.

Polynomials. A polynomial of *degree n* is a function of the form

(MS3) $$a_n x^2 + a_{n-1} x^{n-1} + - - - + a_1 x + a_0$$

in which the coefficients (the *a's l)* are constants and n is an integer. The quotient $p(x)/q(x)$ of one polynomial by another is called a *rational* function of x (a rational number can be expressed in the form r/s where r and s are integers whereas an irrational number cannot be expressed in this way, for example π and $\sqrt{2}$).

Transcendental functions. These are infinite polynomials. Examples include the trigonometric functions and the exponential, hyperbolic and logarithm functions. Examples of these infinite polynomials are given in the next section.

Periodic functions. These repeat themselves at regular intervals. For example sin *(x)* and cos *(x)* are periodic with period 2π, tan *(x)* has period p and sin *(px/a)* has period *a*.

The *trigonometric* functions are so called because they are defined by the ratios of the sides of a right angled triangle:

sin(A) = BC/AC
cos(A) = AB/AC
tan(A) = BC/AB = *slope* of AC

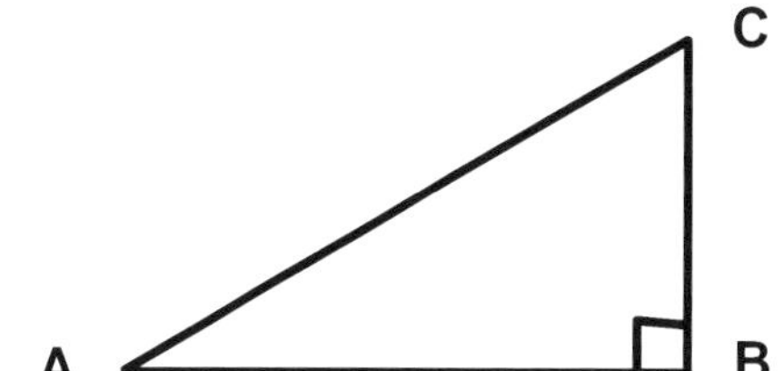

Fig. MS1 Trigonometric functions

and their periodicity arises as the hypotenuse AC revolves through successive circles of rotation (anticlockwise so that angle A increases). Here recall that 360 degrees (a full revolution) equals 2π in *radians.*

Then it can easily be shown that, for example, sin (180 - A) = sin (A) and sin (180 + A) = - sin (A). The signs of these relationships are remembered by the CAST rule which is represented by the diagram

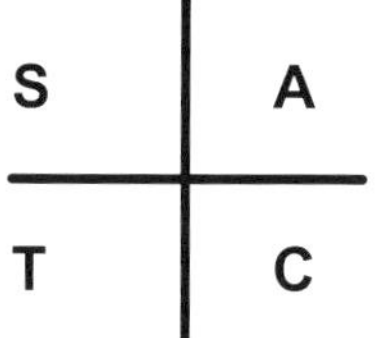

Fig. MS2. The CAST rule.

It indicates that sin( ) is positive in the second quadrant, tan( ) in the third, cos( ) in the fourth and all are positive in the first. This is a good example of a *mnemonic* (here taking the form of an *acronym*). As an exercise verify the CAST rule for 90 ±, 180 ± and 270 ± using such simple cases as A = 30° (given by BC = 1, AC = 2 and AB = √3, so that sin(30°) = ½ = cos(60°)) or A = 45° (given by AB = BC = 1 and AC = √2, so that tan(45°) = 1).

Even functions. *f(x)* is an even function if *f(-x) = f(x)* and is an *odd function* if *f(-x) = -f(x)*. For example x^2, cos(x) and $x$sin(x) are even functions and x^3, sin(x) and $x\cos^2(x)$ are odd functions. Generally functions are neither even nor odd but any function can be expressed as a sum of even and odd functions using the identity:

$$f(x) = (1/2)\{f(x) + f(-x)\} + \{f(x) - f(-x)\}$$

Logarithms. If $y = b^x$ we say that x is the logarithm of y to the *base b* and write $x = \log_b(y)$. Historically logarithms were used to calculate the products of numbers using the rule:

$$\text{(MS4)} \qquad \log_b(yz) = \log_b(y) + \log_b(z)$$

and tables of logarithms, a task eliminated by the electronic calculator.

Generally the base 10 is used so that, for example, $\log_{10}(10) = 1$ and $\log_{10}(100) = 2$ etc. *Natural logarithms,* however, where the base is the *exponential number e* are perhaps more important theoretically.

The exponential function $y = e^x$ or exp (x) is the solution of the *differential equation* $dy/dx = y$ when $y = 1$ at $x = 0$. This solution is discussed in Sec. MS4 and the infinite series expression for exp (x) is given in Sec. MS3.

Finally the following rules for logarithms are worth note:

(i) $y = e^{ln(y)}$

(ii) $x = \ln(e^x)$

(iii) $a^x = e^{x ln(a)}$, where $\ln(\ ) = \log_e(\ )$.

MS2. Standard Mathematical Curves and Functions

Some standard functions which should be familiar in graphical form include:

Straight line: $y = ax + b$ is a straight line with *intercepts* $x = -b/a$ and $y = b$ on the x and y axes respectively and *slope* a.

Circle: $(x - a)^2 + (y - b)^2 = R^2$ is a circle of area $A = \pi R^2$ centred at $x = a$ and $y = b$, that is at the point (a,b).

Ellipse: $(x/a)^2 + (y/b)^2 = 1$ is an ellipse of area $A = \pi ab$ centred at the *origin* $(x = y = 0)$.

Hyperbola: $(x/a)^2 - (y/b)^2 = 1$ is a pair of rectangular hyperbolae with *asymptotes* $y = \pm bx/a$.

$y = ax/(b + x)$ is a pair of hyperbolae with asymptotes $y = a$ and $x = -b$. The particular case is discussed further in Sec. BF12.

Polynomial: $y = a + bx + cx^2 + dx^3 + ex^4 + fx^5 - - - (const.)^n$ and the special cases $n = 2$ (parabola or *quadratic*), $n = 3$ *(cubic)*, $n = 4$ *(quartic)* and $n = 5$ *(quintic)* are much used in practice (for example in the Finite Element Method, see FM).

Note that a parabola has one *turning point,* a cubic curve two (because the equation for the *slope* dy/dx is quadratic and therefore has two *roots,* that is, solutions to $dy/dx = 0$), a quartic curve has three 'TPs' and so on.

Exponential: $y = ak^x$ or $y = e^{kx}$ in the special case of the exponential function and the infinite series expression for this is given below.

Periodic: $y = \sin(kx)$, $\cos(kx)$ and $\tan(kx)$. The sin( ) and cos( ) functions are much used in the study of alternating electrical currents and the vibration of machinery etc.

Curve sketching. In drawing such functions attention should be given to:
i. Symmetry (?), intercepts (with the axes) and asymptotes.
ii. Turning points, curvature at TPs (> 0 for a minimum, < 0 for a maximum, and = 0 for a point of inflexion).
iii. Range restrictions and discontinuities (e.g. $y = \tan(x)$).

Translation of axes. To shift the origin of a function to $x = a$, $y = b$ simply replace x by $(x - a)$ and y by $(y - b)$ throughout the function.

Rotation of axes. If the axes are rotated anticlockwise by an angle ϕ then the coordinates x', y' relative to these new axes are given by

(MS5) $$\begin{Bmatrix} x' \\ y' \end{Bmatrix} = \begin{bmatrix} c & s \\ -s & c \end{bmatrix} \begin{Bmatrix} x \\ y \end{Bmatrix}$$

where the result is written in matrix form and $c = \cos(\phi)$, $s = \sin(\phi)$. [As a useful exercise see if you can prove this with a simple diagram].

It can easily be shown that the inverse of the 2 x 2 matrix is the *transpose* of the original matrix (see Sec. MS5), so that $x = cx' - sy'$ and $y = sx' + cy'$.

As an exercise substitute these results into the equation $x^2 - y^2 = 1$ to obtain the equation for hyperbolae with the axes as asymptotes (note: use $\phi = 45^0$ so that $c = -1/\sqrt{2}$, $s = 1/\sqrt{2}$).

The transcendental functions. These are represented by infinite series or polynomials. These are obtained using *McLaurin's formula.* To develop this from first principles we write an infinite polynomial for some function $g(x)$:

$$g(x) = c_1 + c_2 x + c_3 x^2 + c_4 x^3 + - - -$$

Differentiating $g(x)$ several times [differentiation is discussed in the next section]

$$g'(x) = c_2 + 2c_3 x + 3c_4 x^2 + - - -, \text{ that is, } c_2 = g'(0)$$
$$g''(x) = 2c_3 + 6c_4 + - - -, \text{ that is, } c_3 = g''(0)/2$$
$$g'''(x) = 6c_4 + - - -, \text{ that is, } c_4 = g'''(0)/6$$

and so on . Thus, the coefficients of the polynomial can be expressed in terms of the various derivatives at the origin. Then substituting these results into the original polynomial for $g(x)$ we obtain by induction

(MS6) $$g(x) = g(0) + xg'(0) + x^2 g''(0)/2 + x^3 g'''(0)/6 + - - - + x^2 g^n(0)/n!$$

which is McClaurin's formula.

From this the infinite series for the transcendental functions can be obtained, for example

$$e^x = 1 + x + x^2/2 + x^3/!3 + x^4/4! + - - \qquad |\, x \,| < \infty$$

$$\ln(1+x) = x - x^2/2 + x^3/3 - x^4/4 + - - - \qquad -1 < x \leq 1$$

$$\sin(x) = x - x^3/3! + x^5/5! - x^6/6! + - - - \qquad |\, x \,| < \infty$$

$$\cos(x) = 1 - x^2/2! + x^4/4! - x^6/6! + - - - \qquad |\, x \,| < \infty$$

In each of these cases the ratio of successive coefficients is less than unity and approaches zero so that the series converges.

Note also that e^x repeats itself upon differentiation and this is the unique property of the exponential function for which it was created.

Taylor's theorem. This is for the value of a function at a distance (usually small) h from the point $x = a$. This is obtained simply by replacing zero by *'a'* and x by h in Eqn MS6.

Conclusion. In following chapters some familiarity with the equations for such simple functions as straight lines, parabolas and hyperbolae will be needed, for example in attempting to fit curves to graphs of share or currency variations.

To have some understanding of the mathematical forms involved in the oscillations in functions, therefore, it is also important to have familiarity with the exponential function and its series expression.

MS3. Basic calculus

Differentiation. The *first derivative* $f'(x)$ of a function $f(x)$ with respect to x is defined as

$$\text{(MS7)} \qquad f'(x) = d(\, f(x)\,)/\, d(x) = Lim_{\delta x \to 0}\, [f(x + \delta x) - f(x)] \,/\, \delta x$$

where δx is an infinitesimal increment in x. Then to take second and higher order derivatives the process is repeated successively.

Using this definition the first derivative of x^2, for example, is

$$f'(x) = d(f(x))/d(x) = Lim_{\delta x \to 0}\, [(x + \delta x)^2 - x^2] \,/\, \delta x = Lim_{\delta x \to 0}[2x + \delta x] = 2x$$

from which it can be inferred that $d(x^n)/dx = nx^{n-1}$.

Three rules which are especially useful for calculating derivatives are:

(MS8) *Product rule (PR):* $d(uv)/dx = u(dv/dx) + v(du/dx)$

(MS9) *Quotient rule (QR):* $d(u/v) = [v(du/dx) - u(dv/dx)]/v^2$

(MS10) *Chain rule (CR):* $dy/dx = (dy/du)/(du/dx), \;\; y = f(u)$

where u and v are functions of x.

As simple exercises the reader may verify the following examples:
(i) PR: $y = e^x \tan(x)$ gives $y' = e^x \sec^2(x) + \tan(x)(xe^x)$
(ii) QR: $y = \ln(x)/x$ gives $y' = (1 - \ln(x))/x^2$
(iii) CR: $y = (2x^2 + 3)^3 + 2$ gives $y' = 12x(2x^2 + 3)^2$

Applications of differentiation. Elementary examples include:
(a) Calculation of velocities (dx/dt) and accelerations (d^2x/dt^2).
(b) Properties of curves:

Fig. MS3
Arc length and slope for a curve.

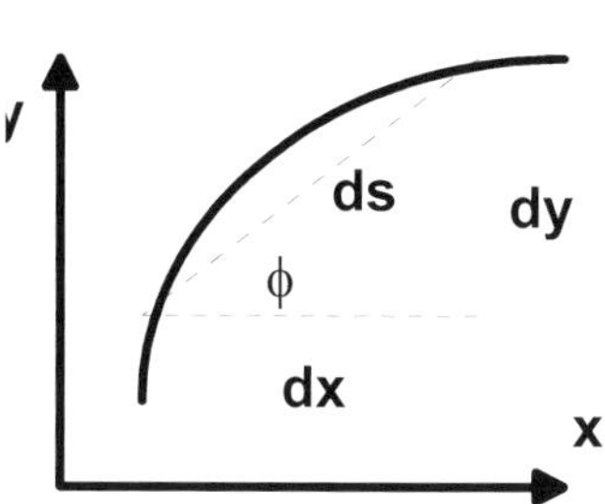

Slope = $\phi = \tan^{-1}(dy/dx)$

Arc length $ds^2 = dx^2 + dy^2$

giving $s = \int \sqrt{(1 + (dy/dx)^2)}\, dx$

Curvature:

$$\begin{aligned}\kappa &= 1/R = d(slope)/d(arc) \\ &= d\phi/ds = (d\phi/d\tan\phi)(d\tan\phi/dx)(dx/ds) \\ &= (1/\sec^2\phi)(dy'/dx)(1 + (y')^2)^{-1/2} = y''/[1 + (y')^2]^{3/2}\end{aligned}$$

Centre of curvature: $x_c = x - R\sin(\phi)$, $y = y + R\cos(\phi)$

Turning points: $y'' > 0$ for a minimum
$y'' < 0$ for a maximum [before the TP $y' > 0$, after it $y' < 0$ so that y' is Decreasing, hence y'' (the rate of change in y') is < 0.
$y'' = 0$ indicates a point of inflexion.

Finally, a list of some standard derivatives is given in the following table. As shown this also can be used to obtain indefinite integrals (i.e. without *numerical* limits) by reverse differentiation (that is, reading the table backwards)

Integral ←←←		Derivative deduced using
→→→	Derivative	
x^n	nx^{n-1}	PR
e^x	e^x	Take as definition
e^{ax}	ae^{ax}	PR
log (x)	1/x	log definition and CR
log (f(x))	f′(x)/f(x)	CR
a^x	log (a) a^x	from $a^x = e^{x\log a}$
sin (x)	cos (x)	from sin x = $(e^{ix} - e^{-ix})/2$

cos (x)	- sin (x)	from cos x = $(e^{ix} + e^{ix})/2$
tan (x)	$\sec^2$ (x)	QR
cosec (x)	- cosec (x) cot (x)	CR
sec (x)	sec (x) tan (x)	CR
cot (x)	- cosec^2 (x)	CR
sinh (x)	cosh (x)	from sinh x = $(e^x - e^{-x})/2$
cosh (x)	sinh (x)	from cosh x = $(e^x + e^{-x})/2$
tanh (x)	sech^2 (x)	QR
$\sin^{-1}$ (x)	$1/\sqrt{(1 - x^2)}$	These usually appear as integration exercises by substitution but may also be deduced directly by substitutions (e.g. $y = \sin^{-1}(x)$ and invert and differentiate etc.) or the 'e' definitions.
$\cos^{-1}$ (x)	$-1/\sqrt{(1 - x^2)}$	
$\tan^{-1}$ (x)	$1/(1 + x^2)$	
$\sinh^{-1}$ (x)	$1/\sqrt{(x^2 + 1)}$	
$\cosh^{-1}$ (x)	$1/\sqrt{(x^2 + 1)}$	

Integration. The two basic types of integral are:

Definite integral: $\int_a^b f(x)\,dx,\ \int_c^d y(t)\,dt$
where *a, b* are boundary conditions and *c* is an initial condition.

Indefinite integral: $\int f(x)\,dx = F(x) + C$
where *F(x)* is the anti derivative and *C* is a constant.

Analytical integration. Useful examples include:
(a) *Back* or *reverse differentiation:*
$de^{kx}/dx = ke^{kx}$ gives $\int e^{kx}\,dx = e^{kx}/k + C$

(b) *Substitution:* for the integral $\int (1 + x^2)^{-3/2}\,dx$ put $x = \tan(u)$, giving

$$I = \int(\sec^2(u)\,du)/(\sec^2(u))^{3/2} = \int \cos(u)\,du = \sin(u) + C = x/\sqrt{\{1 + x^2)} + C$$

(c) *Integration by parts:* for this we use the following formula based on the product rule:

$$\int u\,(dv/dx)\,dx = uv\,| - \int (du/dx)\,v\,dx$$

where | denotes term evaluated at the boundary.
A useful example of the latter 'IBP' process is:

$$\int x^2 e^x\,dx = x^2 e^x - 2\int x\,e^x\,dx = x^2 e^x - 2[xe^x - \int e^x dx]$$
$$= x^2 e^x - 2xe^x + 2e^x + C$$

from which the *reduction formula* for integration of $x^n e^{ax}$ is obtained by inference.

Applications of integration.

Fig. MS4.
Infinitesimal strip
of the area under a curve.

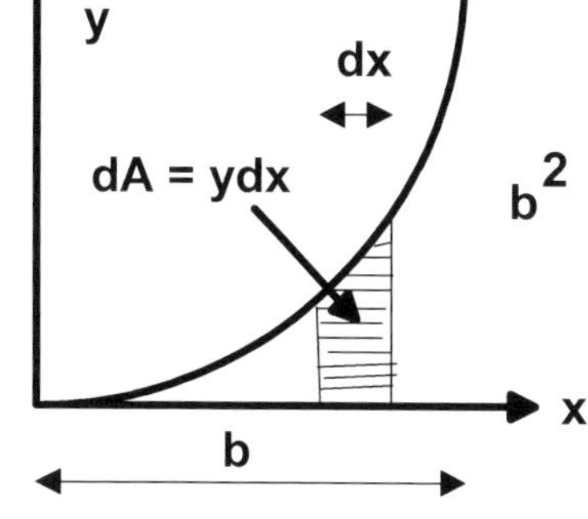

(a) Areas under curves are calculated as

$\int_a^b y\,dx$

(b) Centroids of areas are given by

$x_c = \int x\,dA / \int dA, \quad y_c = \int y\,dA / \int dA$

(c) Volumes, for example for a solid of revolution (about the *x* axis) $V = \int \pi y^2\,dx$

(d) First and second moments of area are calculated as $\int y\,dA$ and $\int y^2\,dA$, first moments of area being used in (b).

As a very simple example we calculate the area under the parabola $y = x^2$ between $x = 0$ & $x = b$.

$$A = \int dA = \int y\,dx = \int_0^b x^2\,dx = [x^3/3]_0^b = b^3/3$$

or one third of the rectangle bounded by $x = b$, $y = b^2$ and the axes.

As an exercise the reader should verify that $x_c = 3b/4$ and $y_c = 3b^2/5$

Conclusion

At least a little calculus is useful, for example to find turning points in cost functions in economics and in the theory of optimization. Indeed optimization is of crucial importance in business science and one of the major objectives of this text.

MS4. Differential equations

Ordinary differential equations. ODEs are those involving only one independent variable and of these useful examples are:

(i) $dy/dx - x = 0$

is a *first order* ODE (involving only first derivatives) the solution of which is given by integration as

$$y \mid = x^2/2 \mid$$

where | denotes that boundary values must be given for the interval over which the DE applies.

(ii) (MS11) $dx/dt = kx$

is the growth law for populations and is *separable* so it can be written in the form

$$\int dx / x = \int k\,dt$$

giving, with the inclusion of the initial values, the exponential growth law

(MS12) $\ln x - \ln x_0 = k(t - t_0)$, or $x - x_0 = \exp[k(t - t_0)]$

where k is the *growth factor.*

As an example, suppose that every 25 years 0.5(children - deaths) result per person, giving $k = 0.02$. This will give a 22% increase in population in 10 years, 2.7 times in 50 years (not very different from what happened from 1935 to 1985) and 2.7 times in the next 50 years (i.e. 7.3 times for 100 years). Now the growth factor is closer to 0.014, doubling us in 50 years, but the disturbing message should be clear.

(iii)

$$x = A\cos(\omega t + a)$$

describes vibration and writing $x' = -A\sin(\omega t + a)$ and $x'' = -\omega^2 A\cos(\omega t + a)$

it is clear that (MS13) $x'' + \omega^2 x = 0$

which is the form of differential equation that governs vibrations.

Analytical solution of ODEs

(1) ODEs take the general form *F(y″, y′, x etc.) = f(x)* and analytical solutions seek a *complementary function* for the case when *f(x) = 0* and a *particular solution* to augments this for the right side function.

(2) Such solutions can be obtained by techniques such as:

a. *Integration factors* $\lambda = \exp(\int P(x)dx)$ for the equation $y' + Py = Q$.
b. *Auxiliary equations* formed by substituting $y = \exp(mt)$.
c. Tthe *Laplace transform,* multiplying *F( )* by an exponential term.
d. *Power series,* giving a polynomial solution.

Compared to numerical methods, such techniques have limited application, though the Laplace transform is worth note when discontinuities are involved.

For the purposes of this very limited introduction, therefore, simple cases that can be directly integrated or are separable must suffice and a useful vibration example is solved numerically in Sec. NM10.

Partial differential equations. PDEs are those involving two or more independent variables. For example, in *potential flow* problems the distribution of the *potential function* $\phi = \phi(x,y)$ in two dimensions possesses *partial derivatives* $\partial\phi/\partial x$ and $\partial\phi/\partial y$ which are calculated by respectively holding y and x constant and then obtaining an expression for the partial derivatives in the normal way.

For example if

$$\phi = ax^2 + 2hxy + by^2 + 2gx + 2fy + c$$

$$\text{then } \phi_x = \partial\phi/\partial x = 2ax + 2hy + 2g$$

$$\phi_y = \partial\phi/\partial y = 2hx + 2by + 2f$$

The PDE governing potential flow problems is *LaPlace's equation* which is

(MS14) $\nabla^2\phi = \partial^2\phi/\partial x^2 + \partial^2\phi/\partial y^2 = 0$

where $\nabla^2\phi$ is the *Laplacian* operator. Then the particular case $\nabla^2\phi = const.$ is *Poisson's equation* and this governs *plane torsion* problems.

Including the time dimension two other well known PDEs are the *wave equation*

(MS15) $\partial^2 u/\partial t^2 = c^2\nabla^2 u$

(MS16) and $\partial^2 T/\partial t = c\,\nabla^2 T$

which is the *diffusion equation*, respectively having application to vibration and transient heat flow problems.

Analytical solution of PDEs

PDEs for steady state two dimensional problems can be solved analytically using *Fourier series.* This involves 'fitting' solutions which are the sum of sin( ) or cos( ) terms to each direction to satisfy the boundary conditions and then the product of these solves the 2D problem.

When the problem is time dependent also then the LaPlace transform and fast Fourier transform techniques prove useful. Such techniques have limited application, however, and numerical techniques are now more popular.

Numerical solution of PDEs

When numerical methods are used four basic types of physical problem can be written in matrix form:

(i) *Equilibrium problems.* These are steady state distributions of stress, temperature, electrical or magnetic potential, fluid pressure or potential etc. For these only the *K* and *Q* terms of Eqn MS17 are needed.

(ii) *Diffusion problems.* These involve transient fluxes of matter or energy governed by a *velocity law.* These require the *C, K, Q* and *Q(t)* terms of Eqn MS17.

(iii) *Inertial problems.* These involve vibrations governed by an *acceleration law.* These are expressed as a matrix equation of the form

(MS17) $M\{D''\} + C\{D'\} + K\{D\} = \{Q\} + \{Q(t)\}$

where *M, C* and *K* are *mass, damping* and *stiffness* matrices, *D'* and *D"* are the derivatives of the field variables and *Q* and *Q(t)* are constant and time dependent forcing loads.
(iv) *Eigenvalue problems.* Omitting the load and *C* terms in Eqn MS17 and writing each element of the vector *{D}* as $e_i \sin(\omega t + a_i)$ so that each element of the acceleration vector *{D"}* is $-\omega^2 e_i \sin(\omega t + a_i)$ we obtain the eigenvalue problem

$$(MS18) \qquad (K - \lambda M)\{e\} = \{0\}$$

in which various *eigenvalues* of $\omega^2 = \lambda$ correspond to *eigenvectors {e}* which are in vibration problems, for example, the modes of *free vibration.*

Conclusion
PDEs are largely beyond the scope of the present text at present but the potential flow problem of Eqn MS14 is solved in chapter FM, providing a useful example of application of the *Finite Element Method (FEM)* to a two dimensional equilibrium problem. Such solutions can be used to approximately analyze traffic flow and other problems of relevance in business science.

MS5. Matrices

We have already encountered matrices in passing and here some of the basic manipulations with matrices are discussed. First, however, we observe that matrices are used as a way of writing simultaneous equations such as

$$2x + 2y + 2z = 12$$
$$2x + 3y + 4z = 20$$
$$2x + 4y + 3z = 19$$

which can be written

$$(MS19) \qquad A\{x\} = \begin{bmatrix} 2 & 2 & 2 \\ 2 & 3 & 4 \\ 2 & 4 & 3 \end{bmatrix} \begin{Bmatrix} x \\ y \\ x \end{Bmatrix} = \begin{Bmatrix} 12 \\ 20 \\ 19 \end{Bmatrix} = \{b\}$$

using a 3 (rows) x 3 (columns) coefficient matrix *A.*

Special matrices. Special types of matrix include:
(i) *Diagonal matrix:* the entries are elsewhere zero.
(ii) *Unit matrix:* a diagonal matrix with all non-zero entries = 1.
Denoted *I* and the *leading diagonal* (starting top left) entries all = 1.
(iii) *Null matrix:* all entries zero. Denoted *O.*
(iv) *Symmetric matrix:* entry ij = entry ji (row j & column i), that is symmetric across the *leading diagonal* which runs from top left to bottom right.
(v) *Triangular matrix:* entries above or below leading diagonal zero.

Addition and subtraction of matrices. Add or subtract corresponding entries (the matrices must be the same size).

Scalar multiplication of matrices. Multiply all entries by the number.

Differentiation and integration of matrices. Operate in the same way on each entry.
Transpose of a matrix. Interchange rows and columns. For example:

$$A = \begin{bmatrix} 1 & 2 & 3 \\ 0 & -1 & 4 \end{bmatrix} \qquad A^t = \begin{bmatrix} 1 & 0 \\ 2 & -1 \\ 3 & 4 \end{bmatrix} \quad (\textit{tranpose})$$

Matrix multiplication. As an example we multiply a 3 x 3 matrix A with a 3 x 2 matrix B, yielding a 3 x 2 matrix $C = AB$ which is given by the *algorithm*

$$\text{(MS20)} \quad c_{ij} = \Sigma_{k=1}^{3} a_{ij}\, b_{kj} = \{\textit{row i of A}\}\ \textit{mutlipied into}\{\textit{column j of B}\}$$

and we say that row i of A is multiplied with column j of B, but only multiplying corresponding entries together and summing the result (this corresponds to a vector dot product, see Sec. MS6). Note that to permit such multiplication A and B must be *compatible*, that is the number of columns in A must equal the number of rows in B, as in the following

$$AB = \begin{bmatrix} 1 & -1 & 2 \\ 0 & 3 & 4 \\ -2 & 5 & -1 \end{bmatrix} \begin{bmatrix} 2 & 0 \\ -1 & 3 \\ 1 & 1 \end{bmatrix} = \begin{bmatrix} 5 & -1 \\ 1 & 13 \\ -10 & 14 \end{bmatrix} = C$$

The following rules pertaining to matrix multiplication are also noteworthy:

a. $AI = A$ (I = unit or identity matrix)
b. $A(B + C) = AB + AC$
c. $(AB)^t = B^t A^t$
d. AA^t yields a symmetric matrix.

Determinant of a matrix. The determinant of a (square) matrix

$$A = \begin{bmatrix} x & y & z \\ a & b & c \\ d & e & f \end{bmatrix}$$

is

$$\det(A) = |A| = \Sigma(\textit{entries of any row or column} \times \textit{their 'cofactors'})$$

where the cofactor of an entry is the *signed minor*, that is the determinant of the matrix given by omitting the row and column of that entry and given the sign corresponding to the pattern of alternating signs through rows and columns begun with a + sign at the top left.

Hence we obtain the *LaPlace expansion*

$$\text{(MS21)} \quad |A| = x\begin{vmatrix} b & c \\ e & f \end{vmatrix} - y\begin{vmatrix} a & c \\ d & f \end{vmatrix} + z\begin{vmatrix} a & b \\ d & e \end{vmatrix}$$

where the first 2 x 2 determinant = bf - ce *(cross product)*, likewise the others.

Determinants have important application in some techniques of solving eigenvalue problems. They also provide a formal (but not practical) means of inverting matrices and solving matrix equations. Another application is obtained by writing

$$\text{(MS22)} \quad \begin{vmatrix} 1 & 1 & 1 \\ x_1 & x_2 & x_3 \\ y_1 & y_2 & y_3 \end{vmatrix} = 0$$

which gives the equation for the line joining the points (x_1, y_1) and (x_2, y_2).

Replacing x and y by x_3 and y_3 above one also obtains three times the area of a triangle with vertices at (x_1, y_1) etc.

Matrix inverse

The inverse of a matrix A is defined as

$$\text{(MS23)} \quad A^{-1} = adj(A)/\mid A \mid = [cof(A)]^t/\mid A \mid$$

where adj(A) denotes the *adjoint* of A which is the transpose of the matrix of cofactors.

Note that an inverse does not exist if $\mid A \mid = 0$ when A is said to be *singular.* This occurs if any two or more rows of columns of A are not independent (and $\mid A \mid = 0$ can be used as a test for this).

Using Eqn MS23 the inverse of the matrix of Eqn MS19 is obtained and used as shown below to obtain the solution for $\{x\}$ in this equation.

$$\text{(MS24)} \quad \begin{Bmatrix} x \\ y \\ x \end{Bmatrix} = (-1/6)\begin{bmatrix} -7 & 2 & 2 \\ 2 & 2 & -4 \\ 2 & -4 & 2 \end{bmatrix}\begin{Bmatrix} 12 \\ 20 \\ 19 \end{Bmatrix} = \begin{Bmatrix} 1 \\ 2 \\ 3 \end{Bmatrix}$$

and the reader should check the cofactor calculations etc. leading to this result as an exercise.

Finally, the following identities involving matrix inverses are worth note:

(a) $A^{-1}A = I$, (b) $(A^{-1})^t = (A^t)^{-1}$, (c) $(AB)^{-1} = B^{-1} A^{-1}$

Conclusion

Matrices are much used in the remainder of the text, for example in linear programming and in input-output analysis. For these and other applications efficient methods of inverting matrices and thus solving matrix equations will be discussed.

MS6. Vectors

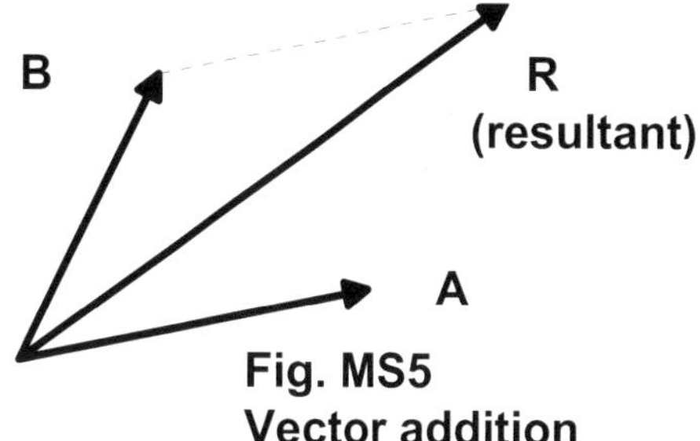

Fig. MS5
Vector addition

Vectors have *magnitude, direction* and *sense* and a point of application whereas scalars have only magnitude. Most readers will also recall the triangle and parallelogram rules for vector addition illustrated in Fig. MS5.

Unit vectors. For most vector operations it is convenient to define *unit vectors,* that is vectors parallel to the axes *x, y* and *z* of unit magnitude. Denoting these *i, j* and *k* for simplicity (a 'hat' ^ or bold type is often used) the *position vector* of the point P (x,y,z) is

$$\vec{OP} = xi + yj + zk = \mid OP \mid (li + mj + nk) \ with \ \mid OP \mid = \sqrt{(x^2 + y^2 + z^2}$$

where *l, m, n* are the *direction cosines* of this vector.

Scalar dot products. The dot product of vectors $\vec{A}$ *and* $\vec{B}$ is given by

$$\text{(MS25)} \qquad \vec{A} \cdot \vec{B} = \mid A \mid \mid B \mid \cos(\phi) = \mid A \mid \times \{component\ of\ \vec{B}\ parallel\ to\ \vec{A}\}$$

where ϕ is the angle between the two vectors. Useful results of this include:

(a) i · i = j ·j = k ·k = 1 (parallel vectors)
 i ·j = j ·k = k ·i = 0 (perpendicular vectors)
(b) (2i - 3j + k) ·(4i + 2j - 2k) = 8 - 6 - 2 =0 (i.e. perpendicular)
(c) if the equation of the normal to a plane is $\vec{n} = n_1 i + n_2 j + n_3 k$ and $B(b_1,b_2,b_3)$ is a point in the plane then for any point $P(x,y,z)$ in the plane

$$(\vec{OP} - \vec{OB}) \cdot \vec{n} = 0$$

$$or\ (x - b_1)n_1 + (y - b_2)n_2 + (z - b_3)n_3 = 0$$

$$or\ n_1 x + n_2 y + n_3 z = b_1 n_1 + b_2 n_2 + b_3 n_3 = const.$$

gives the equation of the plane.

Vector (cross) products. The cross product of vectors $\vec{A}$ *and* $\vec{B}$ is given by

$$\text{(MS27)} \qquad \vec{A} \times \vec{B} = \mid A \mid \mid B \mid \sin(\phi)\,(\vec{n})$$

where $\vec{n}$ is a unit vector normal to the plane containing the vectors being multiplied.
The magnitude of the cross product is equal the area of the parallelogram formed by them in their plan and the direction of the unit normal vector is given by the right hand screw rule, that is the direction of a right hand screw rotating from $\vec{A}$ *to* $\vec{B}$.

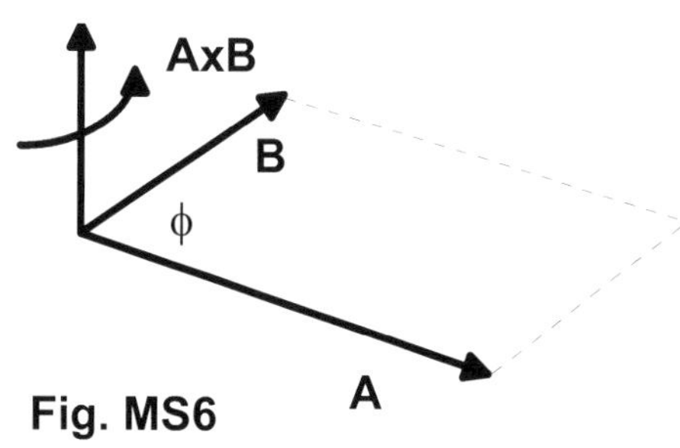

Fig. MS6

Useful results of the vector cross product include:

(a) i × i = j × j = k × k = 0 (parallel vectors)
i × j = k, j × k = I, k × i = j
j × i = - k, k × j = -1, i × k = -j

(b) The vector cross product can be written as

$$\vec{A} \times \vec{B} = \begin{vmatrix} i & j & k \\ A_1 & A_2 & A_3 \\ B_1 & B_2 & B_3 \end{vmatrix}$$

where A_1 etc. are the components of the vectors.

(c) The vector cross product is the usual means of determining the direction of a normal to a plane. In turn result (c) for scalar products can then be used to find the equation of the plane.

Complex numbers

These have *real* and *imaginary* parts and

can be written

$z = x + iy$ where $i = \sqrt{(-1)}$ ('jot')

$= r(\cos(\phi) + i \sin(\phi)) = r \text{ cis } (\phi) = r \angle\phi$

where $r = \sqrt{(x^2 + y^2)}$ and $\phi = \tan^{-1}(y/x)$.

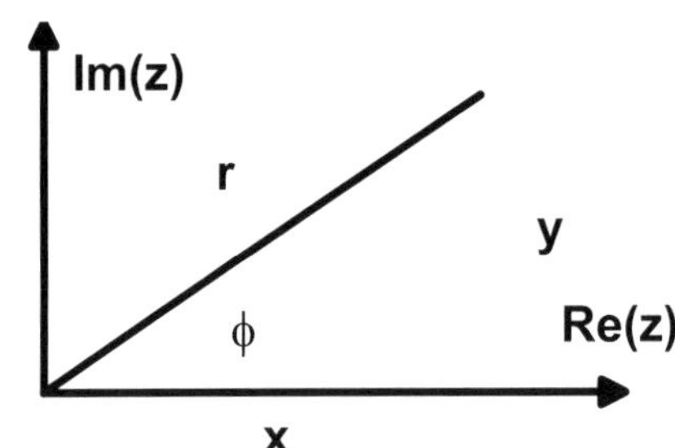

Fig. MS7 An Argand diagram

Basic operations with complex numbers are accomplished as follows:

i. Addition (and subtraction): real and imaginary parts are added (or subtracted).
ii. Multiplication: $z_1 z_2 = r_1 r_2 \text{ cis } (\phi_1 + \phi_2)$, i.e. the angles add.
iii. Division: $z_1 / z_2 = (r_1 / r_2) \text{ cis } (\phi_1 + \phi_2)$, i.e. the angles subtract.

Exponential form

$z = r e^{i\phi}$ where $e^{i\phi} = \text{cis } (\phi)$ follows from the series expressions for cos( ) and sin( ). Then AC electric currents can be written in the form $I_0 \exp(i (\omega t + \phi))$ where ω is the angular frequency.

Conclusion

Vectors and complex numbers (equivalent to two dimensional vectors) are discussed briefly as general (mathematical) knowledge and an interesting example of complex numbers is given in Sec. MS12 as an exercise.

MS7. The Algebra of Sets

The algebra of sets or *Boolean algebra* forms the basis for a sound grasp of statistics whilst the notion of sets themselves has immediate application in business science, for example, where a set might be a market. At the outset the following notation and terms are defined:

a. $a \in A$ denotes that *a* is a *member* of set *A*.

b. $a \notin A$ denotes that *a* is not a member of *A*.

c. $B \subset A$ denotes that set *B* is a *subset* of set *A*.

d. $B \subseteq A$ denotes that set *B* is a subset of *A* and may be identical to *A*.

e. $A \cap B$ is the *intersection* of *A* and *B*, that is, it contains those members common to both *A* and *B*.

f. $A \cup B$ is the *union* of *A* and *B*, that is, it contains all members of both *A* and *B*.

g. $A \cap B = \phi$ where ϕ is the *null set,* indicates that *A* and *B* have no common members and are *disjoint* sets.

h. I is the *universal set*, that is it contains the entire population.

i. A' is the *complements* of *A* and contains all members of *I*, except those in *A*. Then it follows that $A' \cup A = I$ *and* $A' \cap A = \phi$ identities.

Venn diagrams

These are a useful means of illustrating the relationships between sets, for example:

$A \cap (B \cap C)$ is the cross hatched area.

$A \cap (B \cup C)$ is the all the hatched areas.

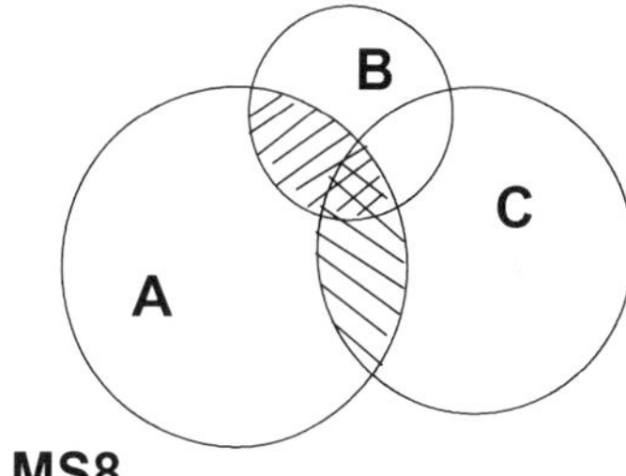

Fig. MS8

Switching circuits.

Boolean logic is very useful in the analysis of switching circuits. Consider, for example, the two circuits (a) and in Fig. MS9.

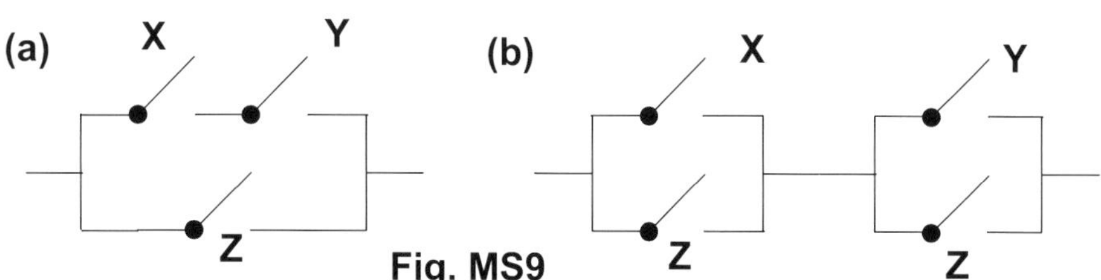

Fig. MS9

Noting that $\cap$ corresponds to switches in *series* and $\cup$ corresponds to *parallel* switches circuit (a) can be represented by the expression

$$\text{(MS28)} \qquad T = (X \cap Y) \cup Z = Z \cup (X \cap Y) = (Z \cup X) \cap (Z \cup Y)$$

which represents circuit (b) so that the two circuits are equivalent.

This can be verified by constructing a *truth table* of all possible outcomes:

X	Y	Z	(X ∩Y)∪Z	(Z ∪X)∩(Z ∪Y)
0	0	0	0	0
1	0	0	0	0
1	1	0	1	1
1	0	1	1	1
0	1	1	1	1
1	1	1	1	1
0	1	0	0	0
0	0	1	1	1

The truth table confirms the equivalence of the two circuits. In practice, however, the truth table is often formed first (because we know the desired outcomes) and the corresponding circuit deduced from the table.

Conclusion

Sets are a particularly relevant concept in both statistics and business science where, for example, a subset might be a segment of a market which a product is aimed at. Then the concepts of union and intersection etc. of Boolean algebra are particularly useful, particularly in conjunction with a basic knowledge of statistics.

MS8. Discrete Probability Models

Discrete probability models are those where outcomes are 'yes or no', that is they either happen or they don't and there is no measurement of the 'degree' of an outcome. A common example is that of tossing coins, perhaps in pairs. As another example consider tossing two dice and form a table for the outcome or *sample space (S):*

		dice 1					
dice 2		1	2	3	4	5	6
	1	1,1	1,2	1,3	1,4	1,5	1,6
	2	2,1	2,2	2,3	2,4	2,5	2,6
	3	3,1	3,2	3,3	3,4	3,5	3,6
	4	4,1	4,2	4,3	4,4	4,5	4,6
	5	5,1	5,2	5,3	5,4	5,5	5,6
	6	6,1	6,2	6,3	6,4	6,5	6,6

Then the probability of a total of four (for the two dice) is given by

p(A) = (number of outcomes in A)/(number of outcomes in S) = 3/36 = ½

Also, the following identities are important:

i. p(S) = 1 (i.e. 'total probability' = 1)

ii. p(ϕ) = 0 (where ϕ is a null set)

iii. p(A') = 1 - p(a) (where A' is the complement of A)

Addition rule. The general rule for addition of probabilities is

(MS29) $p(A = (B \cup C)) = p(B) + p(C) - p(B \cap C)$

where the last term is zero if the sets B and C are *mutually exclusive.*

As examples of the application of this rule consider the following:

(a) One card is taken form a pack of 52 cards. What is the probability that the card is red and an ace? The result is simply
$p(A) = 26/52 + 4/52 - 2/52 = 28/52 = 7/13$

(b) The probability that a man watches TV in the evening is 0.6, the probability that he listens to the radio is 0.3 and the probability that he does both is 0.15. What is the probability that he does neither? The result is given by

$p(V \cup R) = p(V) + p(R) - p(V \cap R) = 0.6 + 0.3 - 0.15 = 0.75$

so that $p(\text{neither}) = 1 - p(V \cup R) = 0.25$

and illustrating this result using a Venn diagram is suggested as a useful exercise for the interested reader.

Multiplication rule. The *conditional probability* of event A occurring *subject* to event B having occurred is given by

(MS30) $p(A/B) = p(A \cap B)/p(B)$

As an example consider rolling two dice. What is the probability that their total is greater than 8 (event A) given that the first die gives 4 (event B). The sample space for $A \cap B$ is { (4,5), (4,6) } and p(B) = 1/6, so that the result is given by

$p(A/B) = (2/36)/(1/6) = 1/3$

Independent events. When events A and B are *statistically independent* then $p(A \cap B) = p(A).p(B)$ so that p(A/B) in Eqn MS30 reduces to p(A) so that here conditional probability does not exist..

For example, when a single die is rolled twice, what is the probability of two sixes? The result is simply

$p(\text{two sixes}) = p(6 \cap 6) = (1/6)(1/6) = 1/36$

Tree diagrams

These provide a useful way of enumerating probabilities when there are several outcomes arising from compounding events. As an example, suppose a die is thrown three times and success occurs with each throw if the score exceeds two. Then p(success) = 2/3 and p(failure) = 1 - p = 1/3. Then all possible outcomes are given by the tree diagram of Fig. MS10.

2/3 S 8/27
2/3 S 1/3 F 4/27
2/3 S 1/3 F 2/3 S 4/27
1/3 F 2/27
2/3 S 2/3 S 4/27
1/3 F 1/3 F 2/27
1/3 F 2/3 S 2/27
1/3 F 1/27
$\Sigma = 1$

Fig. MS10

To evaluate the probability of a particular outcome, such as SFS, the probabilities along the relevant branches of the tree are multiplied to obtain

P(SFS) = (2/3)(1/3)2/3) = 4/27

and the results for all such outcomes are shown in the diagram.

Then to calculate the probability of at least two successes we note that the relevant mutually exclusive outcomes are SSS, SSf, SFS, and FSS and sum their probabilities:

$p(\geq 2\ S) = (8 + 4 + 4 + 4)/27 = 20/27$

Graphical solutions

These require a good deal of ingenuity to construct but are particularly useful for certain types of problem. An example is that of a commuter who has to travel from A to D, changing buses at B and C. The maximum waiting time at both B and C is 8 minutes and any lesser wait is equally likely.

The commuter can afford a total wait of 13 minutes without being late. What is the probability of being late? The problem can be solved graphically as shown below.

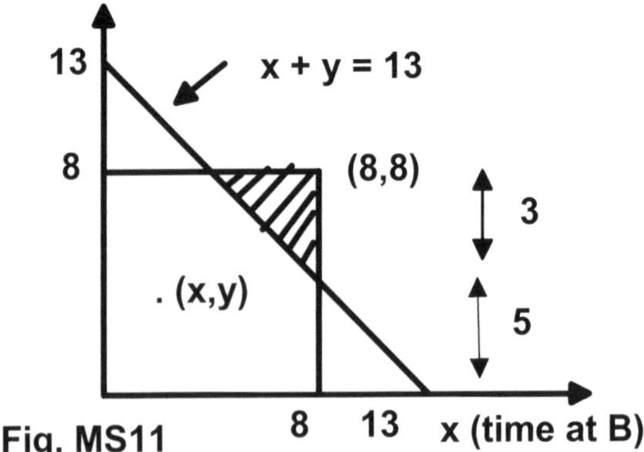

Fig. MS11

The waiting times here vary continuously and the problem is not strictly a discrete probability one. By way of analogy with the table of outcomes for two dice given at the start of the section, however, we draw an 8 x 8 'box' and the coordinates of any point in this are the two waiting times.

Then the line $x + y = 13$ is crossed when the commuter is late and hence the shaded area, taken as a proportion of the total feasible area (in the box) gives the probability of being late as

p(late at D) = (9/2)/64 = 9/128

providing a good example of how the simplest problems in statistics may yield the most interesting solutions.

MS9. Probability distributions

First we consider two *discrete probability distributions,* the binomial distribution and the Poisson distribution. In the interests of brevity much of the terminology will be introduced along the way, rather than at the outset. The concepts of *expected value, mean* and *variance* will, it is hoped become clearer after several different types of probability distribution have been considered.

Binomial distribution

When a 'trial' has two outcomes which we label success (with probability p) and failure (with probability q = 1 - p) then the results of 'experiments' which consist of several trials are given by

(MS31) $$p(r) = {}^nC_r\, p^r\, q^{n-r} \text{ where } {}^nC_r = n!/[(n-r)!\,r!]$$

where *p(r)* is the probability of *r* successes in *n* trials and ${}^nC_r$ is the number of *combinations* or ways in which *r* items can be chosen from *n* items.

The *mean* and *variance* for the binomial distribution are given by

(MS32) $$M = E(x) = np,\ var(X) = E([X - M]^2) = npq$$

where *E( )* denotes *expected value,* that is the *population mean* (as distinct) from the *sample mean* which, as a matter of 'chance' may differ).

As an example suppose we are sampling manufactured items for which there are 0.5% defective items on average. If the items are packed in cartons of 100 then the probability of no defects in a carton is

$p(0) = (99.5/100)^{100} = 0.606$

and the probability of at least two defects in a carton is given by

$p(1) = 100(99.5/100)^{99}(0.5/100) = 0.304$

so that $p(\geq 2) = 1 - p(0) - p(1) = 0.090$

and clearly such problems are of interest in business science.

Poisson distribution

The Poisson distribution is useful in studying accident rates, numbers of defects in manufactured articles, variations in traffic flow etc. It gives the probability of *r* events occurring in an interval

(MS33) $$p(r) = \lambda^r e^{-\lambda}/r!$$

where λ is the average number of events for that interval, that is λ is the mean of distribution and it is also the variance.

As an example consider a telephone exchange with 8 lines which averages 6 calls per minute. What is the probability that a caller can't connect within one minute? This is the probability of 9 or more calls in the one minute. Using Eqn MS33 with $\lambda = 6$ this is

$$\sum_{r=9}^{\infty} 6^r e^{-6}/r! = 1 - \sum_{r=0}^{8} 6^r e^{-6}/r!$$

and we calculate the probabilities to be summed using

$$p(0) = e^{-6} = 0.0025, \quad p(r+1) = \lambda p(r)/(r+1)$$

giving the table

r	λ/(r + 1)	p(r)
0	6	0.0025
1	3	0.015
2	2	0.045
3	1.5	0.09
4	1.2	0.135
5	1	0.162
6	6/7	0.162
7	0.75	0.1389
8		0.1042
		Σ = 0.8546

giving the answer
$p(\geq 9) = 1 - 0.8546 = 0.1454$ (4 d.p.)

Approximation of the binomial distribution

The binomial distribution becomes tedious to use when n is large and p (or q) is very small. Then substituting $p = l/n$ (from mean = np for the binomial distribution) into the formula for the binomial distribution (Eqn MS31) it is easily shown that as $n \to \infty$ (and thus $p \to 0$) that it reduces to the formula for the Poisson distribution.

Then for the example of items with 0.5% defects packed in cartons of 100 used for the binomial distribution earlier we now obtain

$$p(0) = e^{-0.5} = 0.606(5)$$

and $p(1) = 0.5p(0) = 0.303$
so that $p(\geq 2) = 1 - p(0) - p(1) = 0.090$

exactly the same result as obtained originally.

MS10. Continuous Probability Distributions

With continuous probability distributions occurrence of some variable with precisely a particular value will have an infinitesimal probability. We concern ourselves, therefore, with the probability of variables lying within a particular *range.* This requires that we define a *probability density function (pdf),* a simple example of which is shown in Fig. MS12.

This pdf is written as

$$f(x) = \lambda(1 - x)$$

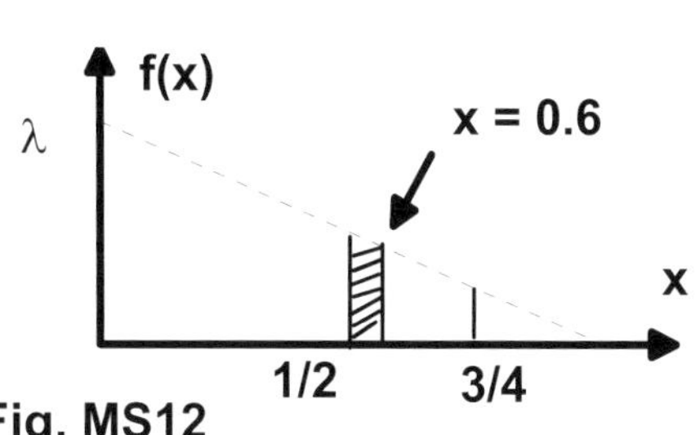

Fig. MS12

and this must obey the conditions
$f(x) \geq 0$ for all x in the sample space and

(MS34) $$\int_{-\infty}^{\infty} f(x)\,dx = 1$$

here replacing the limits by the limits ½ and ¾, giving

$$\int_{1/2}^{3/4} \lambda(1 - x)dx = \lambda[x - x^2/2]_{1/2}^{3/4} = \lambda\{(24-9)-(16 - 4)\}/32 = 3\lambda/32 = 1$$

so that $\lambda = 32/3$. Then the shaded area shown in Fig. MS12 is given by

$$p(0.5 \leq x \leq 0.6) = 0.48$$

and the reader should verify this result as an exercise.

Measures of central tendency and spread

These are obtained as follows:

(i) *Mean:*

(MS35) $$M = E(x) = \int_{-\infty}^{\infty} x\,f(x)\,dx$$

(ii) *Median:* the value m for which the integral of Eqn MS35 = ½ when either the upper or lower limit is replaces by *m.*

(iii) *Variance:*

(MS36) $$var(x) = \int_{-\infty}^{\infty} (x - M)^2 f(x)\,dx = \int_{-\infty}^{\infty} x^2 f(x)dx - M^2 = E(X^2) - (E(x))^2$$

Cumulative distribution function

The *cdf* gives the probability of all events up to and including a particular value, that is

(MS37) $F(x_0) = p(X \leq x_0) = {}_{-\infty}\int^{x_0} f(x)\,dx$

For example, for the pdf of Fig. MS12 the cdf is

$$F(x) = {}_{1/2}\int^{x} \{32(1 - x)/3\}\,dx = 32x(1 - x/2)/3 - 4$$

giving a parabola between (1/2, 0) and (3/4, 1) in Fig. MS12, that is the cdf begins at zero and rises to a value of unity (as do all cdf's).

Negative exponential distribution

This distribution is given by $p(\dot{X} > x) = \exp(-\lambda x)$ so that its cdf is

(MS38) $F(x) = p(X \leq x) = 1 - \exp(-\lambda x)$

Differentiating Eqn MS38 with respect to x gives the pdf

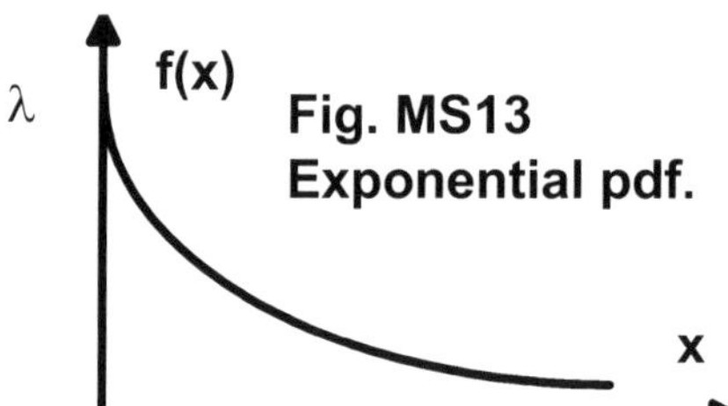

Fig. MS13 Exponential pdf.

(MS39) $f(x) = \lambda \exp(-\lambda x)$

and the mean and variance are given by

(MS40) $M = E(X) = 1/\lambda\,,\ var(X) = \sigma^2(X) = 1/\lambda^2$

so that the *standard deviation* σ for an exponential distribution is equal to the mean.

Shifted exponential distribution

This is obtained by shifting the negative exponential distribution, giving

$$p(X > x) = \exp[-(x - c)/x^*],\ \textit{where}\ x^* = 1/\lambda$$

from which the cdf and pdf follow in the same fashion as for the exponential distribution.

Normal distribution

This normal distribution (sometimes called the Gaussian distribution) is so called because we *normalize* the horizontal scale, scaling in terms of the *standard deviation* σ (also shifting the origin to $x = M$) as shown in Fig. MS14.

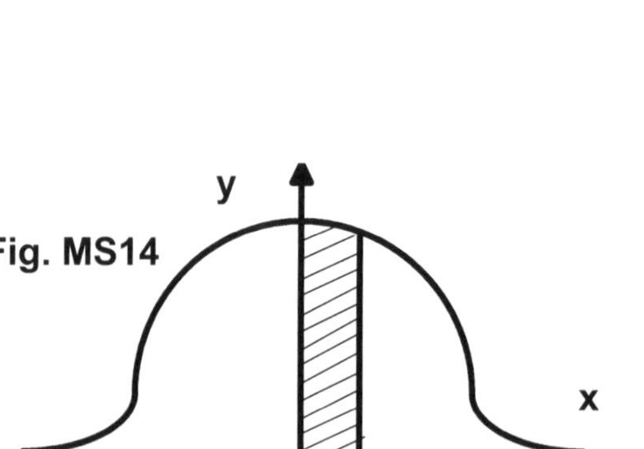

Fig. MS14

The pdf is

(MS42) $y = f(x) = (1/(\sigma\sqrt{2\pi})\exp[-\{(x - M)/\sigma\}^2/2]$

which might be described as a shifted 'exponential parabola' (for which a parabola is sometimes used as an approximation, indeed a parabola might be more appropriate in some cases if infinite 'tails' are not practically possible).

Tables for the normal distribution usually give the area hatched in Fig. MS14, that is

(MS43) $p(0 \le x - M \le k\sigma) \simeq 34\%$ *for* $k = 1$ *or* $\simeq 48\%$ *for* $k = 2$

and the reader should verify the values cited in Eqn MS43 using the program NUMINT given in \MBS1 of the course Basics disc. Such tables usually denote $z = (x - M)/\sigma$. Now let us write

$$\int_{-\infty}^{\infty} \exp(-z^2)\, dz = I$$

Then the square of this integral can be written as

$$I^2 = \int\int \exp(-x^2 - y^2)\, dxdy$$

Expressing this result in terms of *polar coordinates* we obtain

$$I^2 = \int_0^{\infty} \exp(-r^2)\, r dr \int_0^{2\pi} d\theta = 2\pi\,[-\exp(-r^2)/2]_0^{\infty} = \pi$$

and hence we obtain $I = \sqrt{\pi}$. If we had commenced with a divisor of 2 for the exponent (i.e. as in Eqn MS42) then the result would have been $I = \sqrt{2\pi}$, explaining the appearance of such a term in the pdf for the normal distribution.

Examples

(a) Machine parts are made with a mean diameter of 1.535 cm and a standard deviation of 0.005. The probability that a part has a diameter between 1.535 and 1.543 cm is given by calculating

$$z = (x - M)/\sigma = (1.543 - 1.535)/0.005 = 1.6$$

for which the normal distribution probability is 44.5%.

(b) A product is made with a mean weight of 18.2 and 10% of these items have a weight greater than 18.7. Then we have

$$p(18.2 \le x \le 18.7) = 0.40$$

and interpolating in a Normal Distribution table gives $z = 1.28$. Therefore

$$z = (18.7 - 18.2)/\sigma = 0.5/\sigma = 1.28, \text{ giving } \sigma = 0.39.$$

Confidence intervals

The limits within which there is a 95% probability that a variable will lie if normally distributed are determined by finding that value of z in the normal tables that corresponds to $F(z) = 0.475$ (or 0.975 if the range for $F(z)$ extends to $-\infty$), namely $z = 1.96$. Then the 95% *confidence interval* for a normally distributed variable is

(MS44) $$M - 1.96\sigma \leq x \leq M + 1.96\sigma$$

Note that $F(z) = 0.475$ (not 0.45) was used because we are considering the *two tails* of the distribution.

Then if we seek the 95% confidence interval for the mean x_{av} of a sample of n items this is given by

(MS45) $$x_{av} \pm 1.96\sigma(x_{av})$$

where $\sigma(x_{av}) = \sigma/\sqrt{n}$ is the *standard error* of the mean.

Finally, where the standard deviation is not known it can be estimated by calculating the *sample standard deviation* as

(MS46) $$SD = \sqrt{\{[\,\Sigma(x - M)^2]/(n-1)\}} = \sqrt{\{(SS - S^2/n)/(n-1)\}}$$

where $SS = \Sigma x^2$ *and* $S = \Sigma x$ in the second form, the *raw score formula*. Here *n-1* is used to give the SD of the 'population' (use *n* for the variability of the sample itself).

Conclusion

To some of us statistics is a painful subject. The brief treatment given here should, however, be a useful revision exercise to those with some familiarity with the subject. Others may need additional reading from any introductory text on the subject.

Applications of the normal distribution are to be found in the chapter on business finance (BF). In addition, linear regression is introduced in Sec. IE11 and the Pearson correlation coefficient and the Chi-square or O-E test are introduced in Sec. MR7. Finally, the following section gives a brief introduction to queueing theory and this is a subset of statistics of obvious interest in business.

MS11. Queueing Theory

Queueing Theory is a branch of statistics which, as the name suggests studies in detail the behaviour of queues of various types, for example *deterministic models* in which a fixed pattern of (customer) arrivals is assumed. We begin discussion with this case and then discuss queues in which arrivals are Poisson distributed, as are the service times.

Deterministic models: D/D/1/K case.

Here the first D denotes that the arrival or *gap time* is deterministic and the second that the *service time* is also. The 'one' indicates that there is one *channel* or server and K is the *system capacity* (most queueing models assume an infinite capacity but finite capacity models are much more useful).

We now assume a fixed arrival rate = a per minute, so that the gap time = $1/a$ mins, and a fixed service rate = s per minute, so that the service time = $1/s$ mins [these are, of course, average times]. Then the number of customers in the queue at any time is

$$n(t) = int(at) - int(st - a/s)$$

where int( ) denotes truncation to the lowest integer value.

As an example let $1/s = 4$ (service time), $1/a = 2$ (gap time) and $K = 2$ (system capacity) and assume that arrivals who cannot find a place in the queue *baulk* the system. Then the problem can be represented as shown in Fig. MS15.

The diagram completely describes the problem and shows, for example, that the first baulk occurs at time $t = 8$.

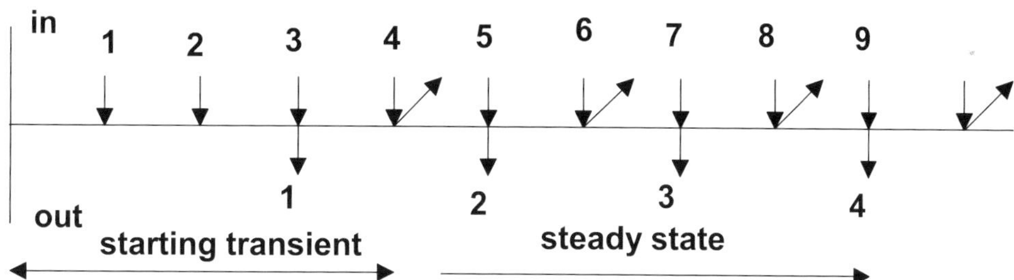

Fig. MS15. Deterministic queueing model.

Markov models: M/M/c/K case

Here M indicates a Markov or random model using a Poisson distribution for both the arrival gap times and the service times. There are c channels and the system capacity is once again finite and equal to K.

Then using the same process as in the telephone exchange example of Sec. MS9 the probability of n customers being in the system is given by

$$\text{(MS47a)} \quad p_n \; r^n p_0/n! \qquad 0 \leq n < c$$

$$\text{(MS47b)} \quad = r^n p_0/c^{n-c}c! \qquad c \leq n \leq K \;\; \text{where } r = a/s$$

and substituting these results in the 'boundary condition' ${}_{n=0}\Sigma^K \; p_n = 1$ we obtain

$$p_0 = [(r^c/c!)\{1 - z^{K-c+1})/(1 - z)\} + {}_{n=0}\Sigma^{c-1} \; r^n/n!]^{-1}$$

where $z = a/cs$ and the { } term is replaced by $\{K - c + 1\}$ if $z = 1$, is the probability of zero customers in the system

Similarly it can also be shown that the expected length of the queue is

$$\text{(MS49)} \quad L_q = \{p_0(cz)^c z\}/\{c!(1-z)^2\}[1 - z^{K-c+1} - (1-z)(K-c+1)\,z^{K-c}]$$

and the expected number of customers in the system (in service in the queue) is

$$\text{(MS50)} \quad L = L_q + c - p_0 \, {}_{n=0}\Sigma^{c=1}(c-n)(zc)^n/n!$$

The expected waiting time in the system is given by

$$\text{(MS51)} \quad W = L/a', \text{ where } a' = a(1-p_K)$$

where a' is the 'effective' arrival rate, and the expected waiting time in the queue is simply

$$\text{(MS52)} \quad W_q = W - 1/s \quad (or\ L_q/a')$$

Example: consider a car inspection centre with three bays $(c = 3)$ for one car and space for only four further cars to queue, so that $K = 7$. Assume Poisson distributed arrivals at an average of one per minute (a = 1) and that the service time is also Poisson distributed with an average of 6 minutes (s = 1/6) so that we have $r = a/s = 6$ and $z = a/cs = 2$.

Than applying Eqns MS47 - MS52 we obtain

$$p_0 = [(6^3/3!)\{1-2^5)/(1-2)\} + {}_0\sum^{2} 6^n/n!]^{-1} = 1/1141 = 0.00088$$

$$L_q = (p_o 6^3 \times 2)/3!(-1)^2[1 - 2^5 + 5 \times 2^4] = 3528p_0 = 3.09$$

$$L = 3.09 + 3 - p_0 \, {}_0\sum^{2}(3-n)6^n/n! = 6.06$$

$$W = L/a(1 - p_7) = L/(1 - p_0 6^7 3^4 3!) = 12.3 \text{ mins}$$

$$W_q = W - 1/s = 12.3 - 6 = 6.3 \text{ mins}$$

and from these details it can be decided whether to alter the system.

Erlang's loss formula: M/M/c/c case

This is much used in such application as telecommunications system design. It gives the probability of the system being busy as

$$\text{(MS53)} \quad p_c = (r^c/c!)/({}_0\Sigma^c\ r^n/n!) \quad (r = a/s)$$

and this result is, in fact, independent of the service time distribution.

As an example consider an exchange which has an average of 84.3 calls per hour (a) with an average duration of 0.103 hours $(1/s)$. If we can allow only one busy signal every two hours, how many lines are needed? The solution is obtained by writing

$$p_c = \text{(calls busy in 2 hours)/(calls in 2 hours)} = 1/2a = (8.7^c/c!)({}_0\Sigma^c\ 8.7^n/n!)$$

Then a series of curves for different values of r plotted with values of p_c as the vertical axis and numbers of channels (c) as the horizontal axis (such curves are given in many texts on queueing theory) may be consulted, yielding the result $c = 16$, which is the required number of telephone lines in our example. Alternatively, a short computer program can easily be written to provide this result.

Conclusion

Queueing theory may seem an esoteric subject but simple deterministic models are easily applied and prove very useful in many applications.

Markovian models result in complicated formulas, but these are not difficult to use in practice, as the car inspection centre example given for the *M/M/c/K* case demonstrates. Special cases of this worth note are *M/M/1/∞* in which the distribution of waiting times is called the Erlang distribution and *M/M/∞* models where there is unlimited service so that the problem reduces to that of applying a Poisson distribution to the service times.

MS12. A Simple Exercise in Relativity

At first sight it might seem out of place, but the relativity exercise considered here brings into play many of the concepts introduced in earlier sections, for example calculus, complex numbers and vector dot products.

4-D space

In 4-D space we allow a point (x_1,x_2,x_3,x_4) to move to $(x_1+dx_1,x_2+dx_2,x_3+dx_3,x_4+dx_4)$ and write the square of the distance moved in the quadratic form:

$$\text{(MS54)} \quad ds^2 = g_{11}dx_1^2 + g_{22}dx_2^2 + g_{33}dx_3^2 + g_{44}dx_4^2 + 2g_{12}dx_1dx_2 - - -$$

where the coefficients g_{11} etc. are functions of x_1,x_2,x_3,x_4 and there are six 'cross' or g_{ij} terms.

3-D space + time

Using rectangular coordinates the 'cross' terms in Eqn MS54 vanish (equivalent to taking a vector dot product) and the coefficients g_{11} etc. reduce to unity so that we have

$$ds^2 = dx^2 + dy^2 + dz^2 + dy_4^2$$

Now we let $dy_4 = i\,c\,dt$, assuming now that c is real (recall that 'i' $=\sqrt{-1}$), giving

$$\text{(MS55)} \quad ds^2 = dx^2 + dy^2 + dz^2 - c^2dt$$

A moving clock

Consider a clock moving (slowly) from $(x_1,0,0)$ to $(x_2,0,0)$. The reading of the clock will be proportional to $\int ds$ where

$$\text{(MS56)} \quad -ds^2 = c^2dt^2 - dx^2 = c^2dt^2(1 - (dx/dt)^2/c^2)$$

so that , denoting the speed $dx/dt = u$, the clock reading will be proportional to

$$\text{(MS56)} \quad {}_1\!\int^2 dt(1 - u^2/c^2)^{1/2} = (t_2 - t_1)\sqrt{1 - u^2/c^2} = (\delta t)\beta$$

where β is the *Lorentz transformation.*

Hence if the clock travels with *finite* speed *(u)* it moves slowly (compared to conventional (ours) measurement), a phenomenon called *time dilation.*

As a consequence it also follows that length and mass alter in this moving system (relative to us):

$$\text{(MS57)} \quad L' = L(1 - u^2/c^2)^{1/2}$$

$$\text{(MS58)} \quad M' = M/(1 - u^2/c^2)^{1/2}$$

and the contraction in length observed is called the *Lorentz-Fitzgerald contraction,* a phenomenon which was a forerunner of the celebrated Einstein special theory of relativity.

Note that the modifier term in these equations takes a form similar to that in curvature calculations and, indeed, this is why the theory leads to description of curved space-time. This curved system can be approximated using *Regge Calculus* in which flat segments are used to form an approximate model, a process identical to the *Finite Element Method* which is introduced in the final chapter.

Conclusion

As promised our relativity exercise used many of the concepts earlier in the chapter and, in the end, was none too difficult. What makes the exercise so special, however, is that the argument seems a little suspect, if not wrong, at least to this author. Nevertheless there have been a few experiments which seem to support the theory to some extent. While we are at it, however, why not speculate about the possibility of having two time dimensions as some have suggested?

The foregoing is a very simplified approach (due to Eddington), however, and such things as Mohr's *large curvature correction* in numerical calculation of curvatures of deformation of beams undergoing 'finite' deformation complicate the numerical modeling of physical problems where 'second order' effects are introduced to classically simple linear problems (Mohr's 'LCC' is briefly discussed in Appendix D of Chapter 14).

MS13. A Computer Program for the Poisson Distribution

In the following exercise we use the fact that if $z_0, z_1, z_2,$ - - is a sequence of random numbers between zero and unity with uniform or flat distribution then the smallest integer k for which

$$\text{(MS59)} \quad x_k = z_0\, z_1\, z_2 - - - z_k \leq \exp(-\lambda)$$

is a Poisson distributed variable with mean λ, that is the number of occasions in N trials upon which k numbers (in addition to the first) must be used before their chain product is less than $\exp(-\lambda)$ is given by

$$\text{(MS60)} \quad Np(k) = N\exp(-\lambda)\lambda^k/k!$$

Proof

If $x_0 = z_0$ and z_1 are independent with frequency distribution $g(z_0)$, $h(z_1)$ then the frequency function $f_1(x_1)$ for $x_1 = z_0 z_1$ is given by differentiating

$$ {}_{x_1}\int^{'} f_1(x_1)\, dx_1 \;=\; {}_{z_1}\int^{1} {}_{z_0}\int^{1} g(z_0)h(z_1)\, dz_0 dz_1 $$

with respect to x_1, giving if we note that $dz_0/dx_1 = 1/z_0 = 1/x_0$, $dz_0 = dx_0$,

$$ f_1(x_1) \;=\; {}_{x_1}\int^{1} g(z_0)h(z_1)\, dx_0/x_0 \;=\; -\ \ln(x_1) $$

as $g(z_0) = h(z_1) = 1$ (flat distribution) and the limits are chosen (rather than x_1 and 0) to avoid $ln(0) = ?$. Then by induction

$$ \text{(MS61)} \quad f_k(x_k) = (-1)^k \ln^k(x_k)/k! $$

Using integration by parts to integrate Eqn MS61 $p(x_k \leq$ exp (-l)) is given by

$$ (MS62) \quad I_k \;=\; {}_0\int^{\exp(-\lambda)} f_k(x_k)\, dx_k \;=\; \{(-1)^k/k!\}[x_k \ln^k(x_k)]_0^{\exp(-\lambda)} \;+\; I_{k-1} $$
$$ =\; \exp(-\lambda)\lambda^k/k! \;+\; p(x_{k-1} \;\leq\; \exp(-\lambda) $$

and by induction (applied to the last term of Eqn MS62 this result is seen to be the sum of the first $k+1$ Poisson probabilities, that is the cumulative probability. Therefore if

$$ x_k \;\leq\; \exp(-\lambda) \ \text{ but } \ x_{k-1} \;\geq\; \exp(-\lambda) $$

then k is Poisson distributed.

Exercises

{1] Try the program QBASIC program QUESIM (in \MBS1 on the course BASICS disc). This uses the RND function to simulate a single queue, plotting the queue over time. It is easily extended to two or more queues. The coding is:

```
5 REM Queue Simulation Program
6 REM p$=chr$(27)+"t"+"1" ["0" = off]
7 REM ! #1,P$,chr$(219)*10 [to turn on graphics characters @ printer]
a$ = CHR$(219) + CHR$(219) + CHR$(219) + CHR$(219) + CHR$(219)
10 L = 2: t1 = 0: T2 = 0: r = 0
20 S = 5: q = 0: g1 = 0: G2 = 0
25 PRINT "input sequence flag: >0 = same; <0 = new )": INPUT i
30 FOR T = 1 TO 20
40 IF g1 > 0 THEN 60
50 r = 100 * RND(i): r = INT(r) / 100: g1 = L * r: t1 = t1 + g1: X = RND(i)
60 IF T < t1 THEN 65
q = q + 1: g1 = 0
65 IF G2 > 0 THEN 80
70 r = 100 * RND(i): r = INT(r) / 100: G2 = S * r: T2 = T2 + G2: X = RND(i)
```

```
80 IF T < T2 THEN 85
q = q - 1: G2 = 0
85 IF q < 0 THEN q = 0
90 FOR k = 1 TO q: PRINT a$; : NEXT: PRINT " "
95 NEXT T
96 PRINT T, q
100 END
```

[2] The following program (POISSON in \MBS1) generates a Poisson distribution using Eqn MS59 as a basis and should be reasonably transparent to the reader.

```
10 DIM NOBS(50): REM Program to generate Poisson distribution
20 INPUT "input n,lambda", N, LAMBDA
25 PRINT "N = ", N, "   LAMBDA = ", LAMBDA
30 KMAX = 1
50 FOR I = 1 TO 50: NOBS(I) = 0: NEXT
60 C = EXP(-LAMBDA)
70 FOR I = 1 TO N
80 K = 0: X = 1
90 IF X <= C THEN 110
100 X = X * RND(.5): K = K + 1: GOTO 90
110 IF K > KMAX THEN KMAX = K
120 NOBS(K) = NOBS(K) + 1
130 NEXT I
140 F = 1
150 FOR K = 1 TO KMAX
160 FK = K - 1: F = F * FK: IF K = 1 THEN F = 1
170 TH = N * C * LAMBDA ^ (K - 1) / F
180 PRINT FK, NOBS(K), TH
190 NEXT K
200 END
```

For N = 1000 and LAMDA = 2 the results are given in the following table (but note that with other languages or versions of BASIC the results will vary slightly with as random number generators vary slightly).

Results for numerically approximated Poisson distribution:

k	Program	Poisson distribution
0	125	135.335
1	279	270.671
2	252	270.671
3	197	180.447
4	101	90.224
5	33	36.089
6	11	12.030
7	2	3/437

MS References

Abramowitz M. and Stegun I. *A Handbook of Mathematical Functions.* Dover Publications, New York. 1965.
Bajpai AC, Mustoe IR and Walker D *Engineering Mathematics.* Wiley, Chichester. 1974.
Battersby A. *Mathematics in Management.* Pelican, Harmondsworth. 1966.
Bennet AA, Milner WE and Bateman H. *Numerical Integration of Differential Equations.* Dover Publication, New York. 1956.
Bernstein J. *Einstein.* Fontana, Glasgow. 1973.
Carnaham BA, Luther HA, Wilkes JD, *Applied Numerical Methods.* Wiley, NY NY, 1969.
Chirgwin BH, Plumpton C. *A Course of Mathematics for Engineers and Scientists, vol. 1.* Pergamon, London. 1961.
Coulson AE. *An Introduction fo Matrices.* Longman, London. 1965.
Copi IM. *Introduction to Logic,* 3rd edn. MacMillan, New York. 1968.
Crossley et al. *What is Mathematical Logic?* OUP, Oxford. 1972.
Eddington AS. *The Mathematical Theory of Relativity.* CUP, Cambridge. 1924.
Einstein A. *The Meaning of Relativity.* Methuen, London. 1922.
Fairbank RE, Shultheis R, Piper EB. *Applied Business Mathematics,* 10th edn. South-Western, Cincinnati OH. 1975.
Gross D, Harris CM. *Fundamentals of Queueing Theory.* Wiley, New York. 1974.
Kaye D. *Boolean Systems.* Longman, London. 1968.
Keppel G. *Design and Analysis, a Researcher's Handbook,* 2nd edn. Prentice-hall, Englewood-Cliffs NJ. 1982.
Kirk RE *Statistical Issues: a Reader for the Behavioural Sciences.* Brooks/Cole, Belmont CA. 1972.
Massey, H.S.W. and Kestelman, H. *Ancillary Mathematics.* Pitman, London. 1958.
Mohr, G.A. and Milner, H.R. Finite element analysis of large displacements in flexural systems. Computers & Structures, vol. 13, p 533. 1981.
Mohr, G.A. and Argyris, J.H. The large curvature correction in finite element analysis. Int. J. Arts & Sciences, vol. 1, n1. 2001.
Mohr, G.A. and Argyris, J.H. The large curvature correction in finite element analysis. Int. J. Arts & Sciences, vol. 1, n2. 2001.
Mohr GA, *Elementary Thinking for the 21st Century,* Xlibris (2014).
Mohr GA, Richard Sinclair & Edwin Fear, *The Evolving Universe, Relativity, Redshift and Life from Space,* Xlibris (2014).
Mohr, G.A. and Argyris, J.H. The large curvature correction in finite element analysis - II. Computer Methods in Applied Mechanics & Engineering, to appear. Neter J, Wasserman W, Whitmore GA, *Applied Statistics,* Allyn & Bacon, Boston MA 1978.
Newbold P, Bos T. *Introductory Business Forecasting.* South Western, Cincinnati OH. 1990.
Northrop EP, *Riddles in Mathematics.* Pelican, Harmondsworth. 1960.
O'Brien, DT, Lewis, DE, Guest, JF, *Mathematics for Business and Economics,* Harcourt Brace Jovanovich, Sydney. 1989.
Panico JA. *Queueing Theory.* Prentice-Hall, Englewood Cliffs, NJ. 1969.
Paul, RS, Haeussler, K. *Introductory Mathematical Analysis for Students of Business and Economics.* Reston Publ. Reston VA. 1985.
Robson C. *Experiment, Design and Statistics in Psychology.* Penguin, UK 1974.
Shavelson RJ, *Statistical Reasoning for the Behavioural Sciences,* 2nd edn. Allyn & Bacon., Boston MA. 1988.

BUSINESS FINANCE (BF)

The farmer is the only man in our economy who buys everything retail, sells everything wholesale, and pays the freight both ways. John F. Kennedy.

Business finance as a study primarily involves considering where to obtain finance and, given choices, which to make. For example whether to seek funding through *equity* (by issuing shares) or through *debt* (by borrowing from banks etc.) is an important decision requiring a sound knowledge of 'BF.' In practice some knowledge of accounting is also required and this is briefly introduced, whilst other pertinent material on such matters as accounts reporting were dealt with in BL (Business Law).

BF1. Introduction

Business finance involves several different types of activity which, though related, will often be carried out by different personnel or departments of a company. These include:

1. *Financial management.* This occurs at executive level and involves decisions on when and how to obtain finance, how to dispose of profits and on adjustments to company operations to improve profitability.

2. *Managerial accounting.* This is usually done at senior management level and involves 'overview accounting' of the company operations to provide the board and members (for example at the AGM) with information upon which to base financial management decisions.

3. *Departmental accounting.* This involves only the productivity, sales, inventory etc. figures and periodic control of these. At this level such matters as finance and taxation are not considered.

Sometimes there might be a further lower level dealing with 'over the counter' operations and day to day operations at this level. Such 'front line' data is passed up to (3), which in turn reports to (2), and so on.

Discussion of (1) commences in Sec. BF2 and examples of (2) can be found in BF4 and elsewhere (for example legal accountability requirements are discussed in BL).

Often, of course, accounting is not done in house. Taxation accounting, for example, is an important speciality beyond the scope of the present text. Moreover, tax matters vary considerably between countries, of course, and even in a given country a very up to date knowledge of current taxation requirements is important and cannot be given in an overview text such as the present one.

Accounting software

Massive amounts of software are now available for PCs, principal accounting applications including:

[1] Spreadsheets

The impact of the computer has been considerable and spreadsheets for cash flow, accounts receivable, financial statements (of assets and liabilities), profit and loss accounts and balance sheets are much used and changes in figures at any point in a large accounting system are instantly transferred throughout the system.

Many financial functions are available, along with 'math' options such as *regression, what-if?, distribution* and *automatic graphing* (the reader should try these) and some programs (e.g. Quattro) include optimization of both linear and non-linear problems.

[2] Databases

Databases, of course, are primarily intended for storing and retrieving data and consequently require such features as efficient searching and sorting routines. Common applications relating to accounting involve long term storage of company accounts and storage of customer information files (including address for invoicing, accounts owing etc.).

[3] Statistical analysis packages

The most common of these are for analysis of variations in share, currency and commodity prices etc. In the case of players on the currency market, for example, decisions must be made very quickly (literally 'before breakfast') and software for this is often developed in house by private and government organisations interested in currency matters.

Applications of accounting via PCs, of course, also include packages for personal or household budgeting. At the other end of the spectrum, package programs for large computer networks are now widely used.

Introduction to financial mathematics

Simple interest

For this the *accumulated value* is given by $S = P(1 + ni)$ where P is the *principal*, I is the interest rate and n is the number of periods (usually years).

Then the *present value* of a sum (S) n years hence is $PV = S/(1 + ni)$.

Compound interest

(BF1) $S = P(1 + i)^n$

(BF2) $PV = S/(1 + i)^n$

Annuities

For these S accumulates via a *geometric progression:*

(BF3) $S = a + ar + ar^2 + - - - - - + ar^{n-1}$ where $r = 1 + i$

giving $Sr = ar + ar^2 + - - - - + ar^{n-1} + ar^n$

when Eqn BF3 is multiplied by r. Subtracting Eqn BF3 from this result we obtain

(BF4) $S = a(r^n - 1)/(r - 1)$

(BF5) and $PV = S/r^n = a(1 - 1/r^n)/(r - 1) = a/(r - 1)$ $\quad n \to \infty,\ r > 1$

the last result being for a *perpetual annuity.*

Example: As an example of the latter, suppose a philanthropist wishes to give a scholarship of *$1000* p.a. How much capital is needed at $i = 8\%$? The answer is given by $PV = a/(r - 1) = 1000/0.08 = \$12,500$.

General annuities. These involve such variations as interest (at a *nominal rate i)* compounded m times per year and payments made monthly. Two common examples are:

[1] The compounding period is made equal to the payment period, when an *effective* rate of j is calculated using

$$1 + j = (1 + i/m)^m$$

Then if $i = 5\%$ we obtain $j = 5.0945\%$ for $m = 4$ and $j = 5.1162\%$ for $m = 12$.

[2] The payment period is made equal to the compounding period when an *equivalent 'a'* is calculated using

$$a' = a(r^{n'} - 1)/(r - 1) \text{ where } n' = m/p$$

where m = no. of interest payments per year and p = no. of annuity payments per year.

Continuous compounding

This corresponds to interest being calculated m times per year where m approaches infinity. Then to calculate the effective rate of interest we write

$$1 + j = (1 + i/m)^m \rightarrow e^i \text{ as } m \rightarrow \infty$$

giving $$j = e^i - 1 = 2.71829^i - 1$$

For example, when $i = 6\%$ *(0.06)* we obtain $j = 6.18365\%$.

Conclusion

Awareness of effective interest rates has every day application whilst Eqn BF2 is much used in calculating net present value of project proposals, in turn allowing the comparison of alternative schemes (see BF3).

BF2. Introduction to Financial Management

Financial management. Financial management involves such activities as

a. Raising capital (for example to acquire assets).
b. Setting the mix of debt and equity capital.
c. Studying alternative investment options.
d. Decisions on payment of dividends or reinvestment.
e. Valuing assets, liabilities, shares etc.
f. Decisions on amalgamations, takeovers etc.

Information required for such purposes includes a knowledge of:
1. Company objectives and strategies.
2. Accounting procedures and economics.
3. Analytical models such as the Capital Asset Pricing Model (CAPM).
4. The financial environment, that is economic trends, institutional (banks, government etc.) trends, legal restrictions, competitors and markets.

The role of the CFO

The role of the chief financial officer is to:
1. Maximize the value of the company by maximizing cash flow and balancing debt and equity (the optimum balance is called the *optimal capital structure (OCS)).*
2. Deal with the CEO, company planners (including the board), the MDs (for MR, HRM etc.) and other interested parties within the company.
3. Deal with banks, trusts, shareholders, stock brokers, market analysts etc.
4. Facilitate company growth by appropriate choices, timing etc.
5. Form financial strategy consistent with company objectives and management, shareholders etc. wishes and targets.
6. Set financial targets (both short and long term)

Analysing financial decisions

[1] *Investment decisions:* (a) A or B ?
(b) fits BP ?
(c) return on capital (ROC) ?

[2] *Capital management decisions:* (a) for operations.
(b) for investments.
(c) how much finance needed ?
(d) when needed ?

[3] *Financing decisions:* from cash flow, equity, debt ?

Cost of capital

In financial management the costs of various sources of capital are of crucial importance in decision making. Also of importance is the *weighted average cost of capital (WACC)* of a company and this is calculated as follows:

(BF6) $$WACC = k_0 = k_e(E/V) + k_d(1 - t_c)(D/V)$$

where k_e = WAC of equity, k_d = WAC of debt
E = monetary value of the company's equity
D = monetary value of the company's debt
$V = E + D$ = 'MV' of total capital
t_c = company tax rate

Then the *leverage* of the company is the ratio of D to the net worth of the company, whilst the OCS (optimal capital structure) is the optimum value of E/D.

When there are several debt sources these are summed in Eqn BF6, that is we use

$$\Sigma\ (k_d)_i\ (1 - t_c)(D_i V)$$

and likewise when there are various sources of equity capital (for example preferential shares, ordinary shares etc.).

Example: the following table gives an example of calculation of WACC.

(1) Source	(2) $(k)	(3) Proportion %	(4) Cost %	(5) WC = (3) x (4)
Bank O/D	200	10.26	7.10	0.728
Debentures	510	26.15	7.36	1.925
Pref. shares	190	9.74	13.68	1.332
Equity	1050	53.85	16.29	8.722
TOTAL	1950	100.00		12.707 = k_0

Interest rates

Some understanding of the behaviour of interest rates and the factors which lead to that behaviour is, of course, essential in financial management as such factors will also affect market conditions etc. Examples of how some logic can be seen in the behaviour of interest rates include the following:

[1] Historical trends in interest rates are important. For example Australian government 10 year bonds went from 3% in 1946 to 13% in 1986 with a peak of 16% along the way. From 13% in 1983, on the other hand, they went to 12% in 1988. Clearly, therefore, long term trends and short term ones are a very different matter.

[2] Factors affecting interest rates include:

a. *Demand* from the public sector, households etc.

b. *Supply* from savings, overseas funds etc.

c. Overseas rates (for example Australian rates are always higher but tend to follow the trends of US rates, but a little behind in time).

d. Balance of payments (current account).

[3] There is a process called the *transmission mechanism* whereby monetary policy affects interest rates etc., ultimately itself being affected by the results. This cycle has the following steps:

a. Government alters monetary policy.

b. Official cash rates affected.

c. Other short term rates affected.

d. General rates affected.

e. Demand for credit.

f. Spending alters (reduces/increases).

g. Inflation rates alter (up/down).

h. Back to (a).

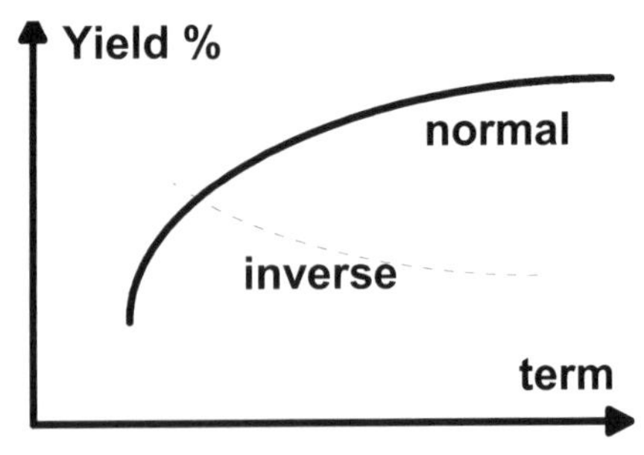

Fig BF1. Yield curves for interest rates

[4] The *yield curve* for interest rates of various terms (durations) of lending is usually upward sloping, as shown in Figure BF1.

Such upward sloping curves are *normal*. *Inverse* yield curves can occur, however, for example when there is strong expectation of a fall in official rates. When such expectation is of a rise, on the other hand, normal curves may become stronger.

Conclusion

In the foregoing introductory discussion of financial management and relevant matters three categories of financial decision were briefly discussed, namely investment, capital management and financing decisions. Each of these is considered in detail in the three sections that follow.

BF3. Investment decisions

Investment decisions (capital budgeting) are based on such considerations as:

a. **trategic fit.** Is the decision in line with business policy (BP) ?

b. **Economic return.** Is the return on capital (ROC) greater than the capital cost ? Here we define ROC as the cash flow from a project over its life span converted to present value. The present value calculation requires use of an appropriate *discount rate* such as the weighted average cost of capital (WACC).

c. **OCS.** Is the decision consistent with achieving/maintaining an *optimal capital structure* (the optimum proportions of debt and equity). Here considerations such as the greater tax deductions but also greater business risk associated with debt capital.

Generally it is advisable to base the company capital structures on that of similar companies ('twin companies'). Public utilities, for example, tend to have high debt which they can support because of their 'guaranteed' market whereas companies with highly variable/uncertain sales tend to have high equity.

Capital asset pricing model

In Sec. BF2 we say that k_0 or the WACC is given by

$$k_o = \%\ LT\ debt \times k_d\ +\ \%\ equity \times k_e$$

where k_d and k_e are respectively the weighted average costs of debt and equity. For example, when a company holds half its debt at two rates, 10 and 12%, and the company tax rate is 48% we obtain

(BF7) $k_d' = k_d\,(1 - t_c) = (10\% \times 0.5\ +\ 12\% \times 0.5)(1 - 0.48) = 5.7\%$

In the *capital asset pricing model (CAPM)* the cost of equity is given by

(BF8) $k_e = R(f) + \beta\,[R(m) - R(f)]$

where

$R(f)$ is the *risk free* rate for bonds etc. and this is approximately the inflation rate multiplied by a factor such as $x = 1.2$.

$R(m)$ is the *market rate*, that is the rate for market stock such as those of the top 100 companies (not atypical companies, of course).

β is the *risk factor* which = 1 for companies with average risk, is < 1 for 'safe' companies and, for example, » 2 for volatile stock.

For example, if $R(f) = 8\%$ and $R(m) = 10$ to 12% (use the higher figure) and $\beta = 1.2$ (a not uncommon value) then

$$k_e = 8\% + 1.2(12 - 8) = 12.8\%$$

so that if k_d' is as calculated in Eqn BP7 we obtain the WACC as

(BF9) $k_0 = 5.7 \times 0.5 + 12.8 \times 0.5 = 9.25\%$

if debt = equity = 50% of capital.

Discounted cash flow analysis

Discounted cash flow analysis (DCF) is one of the principal tools for investment decisions. It involves calculating the net present value (NPV) of a project as the present value of the sum of the projected cash flows minus the initial project cost.

For example, if we have $4,000 to invest and the estimated net annual cash flows which will result from two alternative projects are:

Project	year 1	year 2	year 3	year 4
A	-4,000	2,000	2,000	0
B	-4,000	500	-500	6,000

Calculating the NPVs using the WACC obtained in Eqn BP9:

(BF10) NPV of A $= - C + {}_{n=1}\Sigma^{N} R_n /(1 + k)^n$

$= - 4000 + 2000/1.0925 + 2000/1.0925^2 + 0$

$= - 4000 + 1831 + 1676 + 0 = - 493$

NPV of B $= - 4000 + 500/1.0925 - 500/1.0925^2 + 6000/1.0925^3$

$= - 4000 + 458 - 419 + 4601 = 640$

so that B is, though it may not have appeared so at first sight, in the longer term at least, the more profitable project.

Delegation process for DCF analysis

This is to first eliminate proposals that are not consistent with company strategy or BP. Then the NPVs of the remaining projects are compared to the initial outlays that they require and the preferred project(s) are chosen. If there is no project with a positive NPV result, however, then it may be decided to pay dividends, for example, rather than reinvest.

Valuing an acquisition

This involves the seller estimating a value $= S$ and the (potential) buyer makes an (initial) estimate $= B$. Assuming $S > B$ then both estimates are adjusted until $(S - B)/B$ is sufficiently small when the buyer is finally prepared to buy. This states the obvious but it is important to consider the question of possible overvaluation of assets in both financial decision making and accounting.

Retirement decisions

The foregoing DCF analysis assumed a project period of $N = 4$ *years.* Some projects, however, are indefinite or up to some *retirement* date. For example, in the case of machinery with a salvage value S_N at retirement the NPV is given by

(BF11) $NPV = \Sigma R_n/(1 + k)^n - C + S_N/(1 + k)^N$

If, for example, the machinery is 6 years old and has an estimated life of another 2 years then the retirement decision can be based on the following data:

Retirement end year	6	7	8
Net cash inflow	-	8,000	5,000
Salvage value	12,000	6,000	0

Assuming $k = 10\%$ the NPVs are calculated as

$$NPV(7) = - 12000 + 8000/1.1 + 6000/1.1 = 727$$

$$NPV(8) = - 12000 + 8000/1.1 + 5000/1.1^2 = -595$$

so that retirement at the end of year 7 is the preferred option.

Replacement

If items need to be replaced, rather than retired, then we substitute $(S_N - C_N)$ where $C_N > S_N$ for S_N in Eqn BP1, noting that here C_N is the capital replacement cost at year N which may differ from the initial cost C. Alternatively, where there is no salvage value, C_N must be subtracted from the cash flow for the year of replacement.

Projects with different lives

As an example, let A have a 1 year life and B a three year life. Then with replacement of A the NPVs for A and B are given by

Year	0	1	2	3	NPV
A (life = 1)	-20,000	24,000	0	0	1,818
B (life = 3)	-20,000	10,000	10,000	10,000	4,868
A (replace)	-20,000	-20,000 24,000	-20,000 24,000	- 24,000	4,976

Hence A (with replacement) is the preferred option. Note that B here has the same initial cost but much longer life with lesser resulting output or annual cash flow. This is based on the assumption that A is operated more intensely but, as a result, over a shorter period.

Capital rationing.

In practice available capital is limited and this limits project selection. Suppose, for example, that there are several alternative projects and we wish not only to establish which has the best NPV, but also to include as many as possible additional projects, but keeping within some capital limit or *constraint.* Then the following example illustrates alternative selection processes that may be used:

Project	A	B	C	D	E	F
C_i ($ 000)	200	200	200	200	400	400
NPV	28	20	15	35	45	23
NPV/C_i	0.14	0.1	0.07	0.17	0.11	0.05

The capital constraint is $\Sigma\ C_i \leq 600$ k ($)

By inspection we might choose projects A, B and D, giving a total NPV of 83k with total outlay of 600k, just satisfying the capital limit.

Comparing on the basis of NPV/C_i, however, we would choose project D first, then A and then E. The latter violates the capital limit, however, so that we make B the third choice instead. The same solution has been obtained, but with a little more conviction. In addition we have given priorities to the projects and are better positioned to alter our decision if, for example, the capital limit is changed.

The foregoing problem can be stated in the general form

(BF12) Maximize $\sum NPV_i\, x_i$ $x_i = 0$ or 1 only

subject to the constraints: (i) $\sum C_i\, x_i \leq C_{lim}$ (ii) $x_A + x_B \leq 1$

where constraint (ii) stipulates that projects A and B are *mutually exclusive* and there may be other such constraints.

This is an *Integer Programming problem,* a special case of *linear programming* which is dealt with in detail later in the text (in OT, that is Optimisation Techniques).

Conclusion

In making investment decisions acronyms abound and WACC, OCS, CAPM and NPV are important tools. In particular DCF (discounted cash flow) analysis using NPVs is important in project selection and also may include such considerations as retirement and replacement and capital constraints.

BF4. Capital Management decisions

When investment decisions have been made we know our capital requirements but next planning is needed to determine *when* capital is required. This is done by preparing *pro forma* income and balance sheets for the projected cash flow and capital requirements. In different companies this may be done anything from daily up to every few years to calculate the level of assets, expenses, debts etc. to be financed.

Pro forma statements

These take the form:	Year 1	Year 2	Year 3	Year 4
sales - cost of goods sold				
gross profit - operating expenses				
earnings - interest expenses				
profit before taxes - taxes				
profit after taxes - dividends				
change in retained earnings				

Then the forecast change in retained earnings is included in a pro forma balance sheet, a simple example of which might look as follows:

	Year 1	Year 2
Assets		
cash	- estimate cash needs	
accounts receivable	- estimate sales	
inventory	- estimate stock	
net fixed assets	- present assets + projected capital expenditures - depreciation - projected asset sales	
other assets	- e.g. secured patents, loans to affiliate companies	
Total assets (a)		
Liabilities and equity		
accounts payable	- projected owing on inventory etc.	
accrued expenses	- operating expenses	
long-term debt	- present +/- projected repayments/new loans	
shareholders' funds	- present + projected new issues	
retained earnings	- from pro forma income statement	
Total liabilities and equity (b)		

Other funding required: (b) - (a) gives this.

Here the 'out of balance' projected for each year ((b) - (a)) is the amount of money required to finance all the company's planned activities (assuming (b) - (a) is positive - if not then profit disposal decisions are required).

Sensitivity analysis

The term *sensitivity analysis* refers to experimental changes in a system to gauge their effect. In the case of pro formas for projected cash flow and finance requirements, for example, it is useful to prepare both best and west case statements. Then if the worst case statement is still a viable proposition the associated plan of company activities can proceed with greater confidence.

Example accounts

Tables BF1 and BF2 give examples of (a) a balance sheet, (b) a profit and loss account and (c) a statement of financial position. These, of course, are more formal than those required for planning purposes only, as above.

Table BF1

	Balance sheet as at June 30 1999		
1998	Assets		1999
$	*Current assets*	$	$
10,000	Cash	10,000	
110,000	Marketable securities	150,000	
180,000	Net accounts receivable	200,000	
350,000	Inventories (at lower of cost or market)	340,000	
650,000	Total current assets		700,000
	Fixed assets		
1,500,000	Fixed assets	1,600,000	

350,000	*less* Accumulated depreciation		400,000		
1,150,000	Total fixed assets				1,200,000
	Liabilities				
	Current liabilities				
30,000	Bank overdraft		40,000		
50,000	Commercial bills		40,000		
130,000	Accounts payable		120,000		
120,000	Provision for taxes		100,000		
330,000	Total current liabilities				500,000
	Long term liabilities				
300,000	Debentures		400,000		
150,000	Mortgages		100,000		
450,000				500,000	
	Total liabilities				
780,000				800,000	
	Shareholders' funds				
1,000,000	2,000,000 ord. shares par value 50c				
				1,000,000	
200,000	Issued and paid-up capital	200,000			
300,000	Share premium reserve	300,000			
120,000	General reserve	150,000			
400,000	Retained earnings	450,000			
1,020,000	Total shareholders' funds			1,100,000	
1,800,000	Total liabilities + shareholder's funds			1,900,000	

Profit & loss a/c - year ended 30/6/1999

1999			1998
$		$	$
3,100,000	Net sales		3,100,000
2,640,000	*Less* Cost of goods sold		2,700,000
460,000	Gross profit		400,000
	less operating expenses		
50,000	Selling	70,000	
50,000	Administration	60,000	
60,000	Finance (Interest)	70,000	
160,000	Total operating expenses		200,000
300,000	Operating profit (taxable income)		200,000
150,000	*less* Tax (at 50%)		100,000
150,000	Operating profit after tax		100,000

Table BF2. Statement of financial position

Statement of financial position as at 31 May 1999				
	Thousands of dollars $ 000			
	Consolidated		Parent company	
Funds provided	**1999**	1998	**1999**	1998
Shareholder's equity				
Paid up capital of IBC shareholders	**441,506**	441,506	**441,506**	441,506
Reserves & unappropriated profits	**1,567,237**	1,427,959	**719,694**	671,501
Total IBC shareholders' equity	**2,008,743**	1,869,465		
Equity of shareholders in subsid. cos	**39,013**	36,790		
Total shareholders' equity	**2,047,756**	1,906,255	**1,161,200**	683,319
Non-current liabilities	**951,439**	942,972	**693,041**	683,319
Current liabilities				
Provisions	**309,150**	304,187	**41,043**	48,523
Loans repayable within twelve months	**63,825**	33,855	**28,259**	23,395
Creditors	**230,558**	317,626	**156,051**	127,389
	603,533	655,668	**225,353**	199,307
Total funds provided	**3,602,728**	3,504,895	**2,079,594**	1,995,633
These funds are represented by				
Fixed assets	**2,110,868**	2,054,359	**581,363**	582,633
Investments	**273,600**	250,211	**856,138**	749,470
Other non-current assets	**28,202**	30,034	**25,801**	25,700
Current assets				
Inventories	**648,294**	619,792	**176,590**	183,356
Debtors	**228,762**	188,863	**217,148**	203,544
Net liquids	**233,201**	281,535	**222,554**	248,930
	1,110,257	1,090,190	**616,292**	637,830
Intangibles	**79,801**	80,101		
Total assets employed	**3,602,728**	3,504,895	**2,079,594**	1,995,633

BF5. Financing decisions

Having planned company activities (for example using DCF analysis to choose projects) and then determined the funding requirements of the company we must then decide how to raise this funding. At this point it is important to realize that funds can be generated internally as well as externally.

Internally generated funds

This involves careful asset and liability management. Means by which funds can thus be generated internally include:

a. Hasten accounts receivable collection (this involves the risk of disenchanting some customers).

b. Speed up production and inventory turnover.

c. By asset sales, for example of property or equipment.

d. Slow accounts payable settlement (this too involves a risk, such as banks foreclosing on loans, debenture holders applying for receivership etc.)
e. Extend the terms of bank loans.
f. Increase prices.
g. Reduce expenses.
h. Reduce or defer dividends.

The list could go on and some of the points are all too obvious but others may not be, indicating that indeed internal generation of additional funds is usually possible, though time is needed to do to.

Externally generated funds

These fall, of course, into the two categories

1. *Debt.* This includes bank or other institutional loans, loans from other companies and debenture stock. This may be short (≤ 1 year), medium (1 to 5 years) or long term (> 5 years) and loans may be *senior* (giving a primary claim on cash flow or assets for repayment) or *subordinated* (with secondary claim for repayment.
2. *Equity.* This includes ordinary shares, preferred shares and *hybrid* shares such as convertible (to preferred stock) bonds or shares with options (priority in buying new issues which may be exercised if, for example, the share price is to low).

A company is in a position to increase debt if:

a. Earnings are greater than interest payments.
b. It has strong and steady cash flow.
c. It has enough assets to cover (or secure) the debt.
d. Its debt levels are less than those of the OCS.

On the other hand equity might be more appropriate if:

a. The company needs to reduce debt.
b. Finance is required for long term projects.

Analyzing financial decisions

In appraising funding options a useful basis is the following mnemonic:

F **Flexibility:** options available, e.g., issue equity now and increase debt later.
R **Risk:** how much debt can be afforded ?
I **Income:** can the interest payments be met ?
C **Control:** issuing equity dilutes the current ownership whilst debt is often secured against assets etc. which may be lost if debt payments are defaulted.
T **Timing:** predictions for interest rates, share values etc. should be taken into account in funding plans.

Then in forming a financial plan these characteristics of proposed sources of funding should be compared to the company's BP (business policy), liquidity, OCS (optimal capital structure) and future cash needs.

Financing programs

These should include the following information:

1. A summary of the recommended program and its advantages.
2. A summary of why this program has been chosen.
3. A recommendation and rationale for an OCS.

4. Projection of amounts of funds required and when (based on a cash flow pro forma).
5. Sensitivity analysis of (4) - at least for the pessimistic case.
6. Detailed financing program giving the sequence of debt, equity or hybrid funding and the rationale for this.
7. A DCF (discounted cash flow) analysis of the plan giving the NPV of the company assuming the program is adopted.

Conclusion

Financing programs require careful comparison of the merits of internally and externally generated funds and of debt v. equity. Such programs should be in line with policy and the means of the company and be flexible.

BF6. Statistics and Share Values

Financial management decisions affect the value of a company's shares. Generally we hope to maximize the share value in the long term. In the short term, however, we would obviously prefer our actions to result in higher value.

In this context the *efficient market hypothesis (EMH)* is worth note. This takes three forms:

a. Weak form: current prices follow previous trends and historical factors.

b. Semi-strong form: current prices follow public information.

c. Strong form: current prices follow all information (that is including inside information etc.).

Of these it is usual to assume (b) and, indeed, somewhere between (a) and (b) would be a more realistic assumption for 'blue chip' stocks.

Risk and return

As an example suppose that for company A the statistical data for one $10 share held for one year is:

Return, R_{ai}	$9	10	11	12	13
Probability, P_{ai}	0.1	0.2	0.4	0.2	0.1

Then the mean or expected return and the associated standard deviation are

(BF13) $(R_a)_{av} = \Sigma\, R_{ai}P_{ai} = \$11$

(BF`14) $\sigma_a = \sqrt{\Sigma(R_{ai} - (R_a)_{av})^2\, P_{ai}}$

$= \sqrt{[(-2)^2 0.1 + (-1)^2 0.2 + (0)^2\, 0.4 + (1)^2\, 0.2 + (2)^2\, 0.1]} = \sqrt{(1.20)} = \$\,1.095$ (10.95%)

Therefore zero profit is 1/1.095 = 0;.913 standard deviations away from the mean. From a normal distribution table (or input 0.913 into program NUMINT in \MBS1 on the course Basic disc) we see that the probability of this is 32% (mid way between the figures boxed in the table). Hence the probability of zero profit is 18%.

For comparison consider a company B with $(R_b)_{av} = \$11$ and $s_b = 7.12\%$.

Now zero profit is 1/0.712 = 1.404s from the mean and the probability of this is 42% so that p(0 profit) = 8%.

As an exercise the reader should confirm that p(> 20% profit) is 18% for A and 8% for B, illustrating that because it has greater σ or 'spread' A is more likely to make no profit but also more likely to make a profit.

Portfolio theory

In this the following assumptions are made:

1. Expected returns are normally distributed, an acceptable assumption for a portfolio but not necessarily for some members.
2. Investors are *risk factors* (as distinct from risk neutral or risk seeking).

Then the mean and standard deviation for the portfolio are given by:

(BP15) $(R_p)_{av} = \sum x_i \ (R_{ii})$

(BF16) $\sigma = \sqrt{\sum\sum x_i x_j r_{ij} \sigma_i \sigma_j}$ (include i = j cases)

where $X_i = MV$ of share i/(∑ MV) (∑ MV = market value of portfolio)

r_{ij} = coefficient of correlation of returns on I, j ($r_{ij} = r_{ji}$, $r_{ii} = 1$)

For example, suppose the portfolio consists of two stocks and we have:

$X_1 = 60\%$, $(R_1)_{av} = 0.08$, $\sigma_1 = 0.04$

$X_2 = 40\%$, $(R_2)_{av} = 0.12$, $\sigma_2 = 0.06$

Then we obtain for the portfolio

$(R_p)_{av} = 0.6(0.08) + 0.4(0.12) = 0.096$

$\sigma_p = \sqrt{[(0.6)^2(0.04)^2 + (0.4)^2(0.06)^2 + 2r_{12}(0.6)(0.4)(0.04)(0.06)]}$

= 0.048 for $r_{12} = 1$ (perfect correlation + risk averaging)

= 0.04157 for $r_{12} = 0.5$ (risk is reduced)

= 0.03394 for $r_{12} = 0$ (risk is further reduced)

= 0 for $r_{12} = -1$ (perfectly negative correlation + zero risk)

calculating the standard deviation for various values of r_{12}, showing that the less the correlation between the two share values the less the risk (smaller σ) and the greater the advantage of a portfolio.

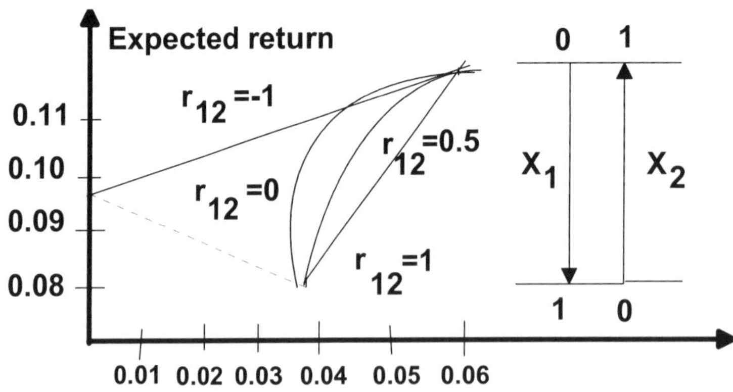

Fig. BF2 Effect of correlation coefficient

Fig BF2 shows the effects of varying the ratio of X_1 and X_2 and of various values of the correlation coefficient. It can be seen that for a given level of risk (σ) lower the correlation coefficient the higher the expected return. For the dashed line parts of the r_{12} curves an alternative point (at same risk) with a better rate of return exists, corresponding to a more profitable portfolio (with a higher proportion of X_2 which has a higher expected return).

Conclusion

Calculation of mean and S.D. (standard deviation) for a single share is, or course, a simple matter but may nevertheless be worthwhile. For portfolios the covariance terms are dominant in contributing to the S.D. of the portfolio. For a portfolio of 50 stocks, for example, these terms make up 90% of the S.D.

Thus when a new stock is added to a portfolio the covariance

$$C_{ip} = r_{ip}\,\sigma_I\,\sigma_p$$

is of paramount importance and there is no risk reduction and hence point in adding a new stock for which $r_{ip} = 1$. Furthermore, for portfolios of more than 15 stocks the possible risk reduction in adding a new share is normally small.

BF7. Statistics and CAPM

In the capital asset pricing model (CAPM) the cost of equity is calculated as a function of the rate for risk free bonds (R_f) and the market rate (R_m), shown in Eqn BF8.

For the purposes of the present discussion the market is a large portfolio and we assume:

1. All investors can borrow/lend at the risk free rate R_f.
2. All investors have available to them the same estimates of R_{av}, σ and C for shares and the same *time horizon* for their investments.
3. A *perfect market* in which there are no constraints such as transaction costs.

Fig. BF3 shows the line corresponding to $r = 0$ in Fig. BF2. This is the envelope of all points representing particular shares and is called the *efficient frontier* of the market as shares positioned on it have the best available return for given risk.

Fig. BF3 also shows the *utility function* for a particular investor. This is a curve representing investor expected returns (hypothetical) for given risk. When this curve touches the efficient frontier the investor is prepared to buy at that point (and many others if the curves cross). The shape of the utility function shown is that for a risk averse investor.

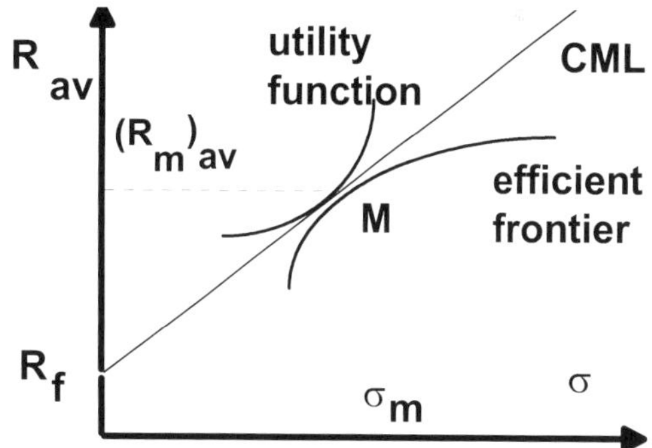

Fig. BF3 Market and investor curves

Capital market line

This is the line drawn from R_f tangential to the efficient frontier (at point M which is the risk-return point for the market portfolio of risky stocks). The equation of the CML is

$$(R_p)_{av} = R_f + [\,(R_m)_{av} - R_f\,]\,(\sigma_p / \sigma_m) \qquad \text{(BF17)}$$

The CML shows the trade-off between return and risk for efficient portfolios. For individual stocks or inefficient portfolios the *security market line* is used and the equation of this (in the *R-β* plane) is

$$(R_i)_{av} = R_f + \beta_i\,[(R_m)_{av} - R_f\,] \qquad \beta_i = C_{im} / \sigma_m^2 \qquad \text{(BF18)}$$

The beta value of the market portfolio is unity and stocks with a value less than one have lower risk whilst stocks with $\beta > 1$ have higher risk. As an example of this, Table BF4 shows values for some of Australia's largest companies.

Table BF4. Example Beta values.

Name	Beta	*Industry*
ACI International	0.651	Pap & pack
ANZ Banking Group	0.854	Banks
BHP	0.958	Div. res
Boral	1.088	Building materials
BTF Nylex	1.402	Div. ind.
CRA	1.458	O metals
CSR	1.004	Div. ind.
Coles-Myer	0.940	Retail
Comalco	1.339	O metals
Elders IXL	1.268	Enrep.
Goodman Fielder	0.848	Foor & hse
Lend Lease	1.243	Dev. & cont.
MIM	1.427	O metals
National Australia Bank	0.816	Banks
News Limited	1.606	Media
Pacific Dunlop	0.96	Div. ind.
Pioneer Concrete	1.197	Building materials
TNT	1.535	Transport
Western Mining Corp.	1.502	Gold
Westpac Banking Corp.	0.896	Banks

The characteristic line

This is obtained by subtracting R_f from both sides of Eqn BF18, giving

(BF19) $\delta R_i = (R_i)_{av} - R_f = \beta_i\,[(R_m)_{av} - R_f\,] = \beta_i\,(\,\delta R_m)$

which is a straight line through the origin with δR_i = 'excess' return on asset *I* and δR_m = 'excess' return on market portfolio.

The characteristic line represents the *systematic risk* and this cannot be diversified away from because it depends upon factors which affect the whole market such as drought, war etc. Points not on this line, therefore, represent *unsystematic risk.*

Beta, therefore, is a measure of the systematic risk of an asset. Its values are more reliable if obtained from long term data and values for a large portfolio, rather than a single stock, are more stable, as might be expected.

Unsystematic risk

Actual data may, of course, be dispersed and linear regression is used to fit a characteristic line to observed data. The slope of this line is then the estimate of β_i.

The equation of the regression line can be written as:

(BF20) $$(R_i)_{av} - R_f = \sigma_i + \beta_i [(R_m)_{av} - R_f] + e_i$$

where e_i is an error term which corresponds to the scatter of the individual observations from the regression line.

The beta value for a portfolio of assets is given by

(BF21) $$\beta_p = \Sigma X_i \beta_i$$

where X_i = MV of asset *i*/MV value of portfolio.

Then the S.D. of the possible returns of the portfolio is given, assuming no correlation of individual stock returns, by:

(BF22) $$\sigma_p = \sqrt{[\beta_p^2 \sigma_m^2 + \Sigma X_i^2 \sigma^2(e_i)]}$$

Then, as the number of stocks in the portfolio increases the size of the X_i^2 terms decreases and the contribution of the unsystematic risk (the second term on the right side of Eqn BF22) decreases. This term tends to become negligible when there are 15 or more stocks, when the advantages of diversification have been achieved.

Empirical studies of CAPM

These have suggested that a slightly greater value than R_f should be used (in its place) but that additional non-linear terms are not needed in Eqn BF8 (or BF18). Hence modified models in which R_f is replaced by $(R_z)_{av}$, for a portfolio of risky assets with $C_{zm} = 0$ are sometimes used. This variation is sometimes called the *two factor model.*

Another modification is to replace k_e in Eqn BF6 with $k_e/(1 - f)$ where f is a factor based on the costs of share transactions.

Conclusion

The CAPM is a simple means of estimating the cost of equity where the beta factor is crucial as values of this vary considerably. CAPM is easily applied to portfolios and simple modifications which improve its accuracy are easily included.

BF8. Statistics and Project Evaluation

Here we include statistical considerations into the DCF (discounted cash flow) analysis of projects. Here the net cash inflows produced by a project for a given period are subject to *uncertainty* and there are a number of possible outcomes and to each of these we attach a probability. Doing this for three annual outcomes for a hypothetical case we obtain.

Table BF5.

	Year 1		Year 2		Year 3	
	p( )	income	p( )	income	p( )	income
	0.1	2,500	0.2	2,500	0.3	2,500
	0.25	5,000	0.25	5,000	0.35	5,000
	0.3	7,500	0.3	7,500	0.2	7,500
	0.35	10,000	0.25	10,000	0.15	10,000
$(R_t)_{av} = \Sigma R_p$	7,250		6,500		5,500	
$s_t = \sqrt{(R - R_{av})_p{}^2}$	2,487		2,670		2,570	

Then the mean and standard deviation for each period *t* are calculated:

$$\text{(BF23)} \quad (R_t)_{av} = \Sigma R_t p_t(\,), \quad \sigma_t = \sqrt{\Sigma(R_r - R_t)^2 p(t)}$$

and the results are shown with the tabulation of the raw data for the annual outcomes.

Then the expected NPV of the project is given by

$$\text{(BF24)} \quad \text{NPV} = -C + \Sigma(R_t)_{av}(1 + k_f)^{-t} = -12000 + 7250/1.1 + 6500/1.1^2 + 5500/1.3^2 = 4095$$

for which the standard deviation is given by

$$\text{(BF25)} \quad \sigma = \sqrt{\sigma_f^2(1 + k_f)^{-2t}} = \sqrt{2487(1.1)^{-2} + 2760^2(1.1)^{-4} + 2750(1.1)^{-6}} = 3700$$

if the cash flows in each period are independent of those in others. In practice this is unlikely as most projects have overall budget constraints.

Then the S.D. when the cash flows are perfectly correlated (giving the greatest degree of dispersion) is given by

$$\text{(BF26)} \quad \sigma = \Sigma\sigma_t(1 + k_f)^{-t} = 2487(1.1)^{-1} + 2670(1.1)^{-2} + 2570(1.1)^{-3} = 6398$$

and the S.D. where the cash flows are less than perfectly correlated lies between the two values given by Eqns BF25 and BF26.

Alternative approaches

Alternative methods of approaching this type of problem include:
[1] *Simulation.* In this approach values of each variable (for example the income in year 1) are selected randomly and the known pdf for this variable 'consulted' to determine the probability of the value. Carrying out such *perturbations* many times (say 100) an approximate pdf for the NPV of the project can be determined. An example of a simulation exercise is given in Sec. OR9.
[2] *Sensitivity analysis.* In this selected variables are perturbed to give an idea of the sensitivity of the model to these variables. This in turn may suggest which variables should be more carefully constrained in planning and controlling a project.

Investment decisions

Knowledge of the risk or uncertainty of a project is particularly useful in decision making. For example, suppose that we have for two projects A and B the following data:

Project	NPV	σ	σ/NP V
A	5,000	2,000	0.4
B	1,000	1,000	0.5

On the basis of this simple information we should choose project A as the preferred project as it gives a higher return with lower relative risk.

The CAPM and project evaluation

We have seen that uncertainty in stocks can be represented by plots with *risk-return* coordinates, that is *R* v. σ, as shown in Figs BF2 and BF3. Equivalently, and more convenient in practice, we can use coordinates *R* and β (see Eqn BF18). Then when market equilibrium exists all risky securities plot on the *security market line (SML).*

Then, as an example, assume a company A is contemplating a project Z and the risk return coordinates for this and the company are as shown in Fig. BF4.

When A undertakes project Z the risk-return point of the company will lie on line ZA, the exact point depending upon the scale of the project relative to the size of the company. As this is above the SML, giving higher return for given risk than the market, investors will bid up the shares in A until 'A+Z' plots on the SML.

This implies that projects should be accepted if they plot above the SML, the equation for which is

$$(R_i)_{av} = R_f + \beta\,[\,(R_m)_{av} - R_f\,]$$

from which it follows that the discount rate, k_z for the project Z is

$$k_z = R_f + \beta_z\,[(R_m)_{av} - R_f] \qquad \text{(BF27)}$$

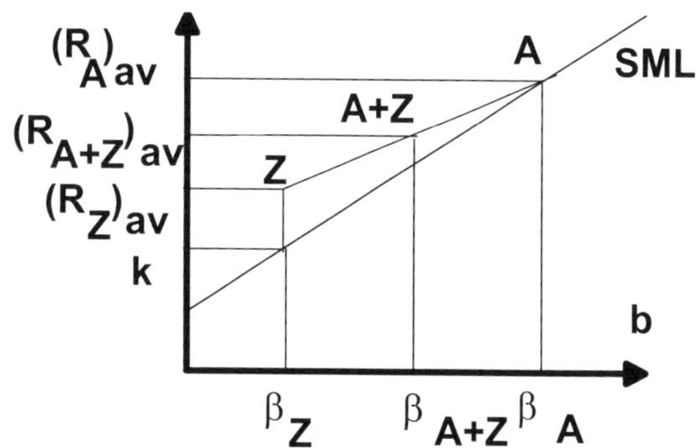

Fig. BF4. R-beta plot for co. A and project Z

This is the rate necessary to compensate investors for a risk β_z and it is because $(R_z)_{av} > k_z$ that the project is acceptable.

This provides a useful means of evaluating risky projects. For example if project Z has $\beta = 1.25$, the risk-free rate is 8% and the market premium is 4% then the required rate of return for the project is:

$$k_z = 8 + 1.25(4) = 13\%$$

and the NPV of the project is calculated using this rate.

Conclusion

The CAPM provides an important modification for DCF analysis, the discount rate k_z which gives more realistic NPVs than, for example, k_f.

Note that when there are variations in k_f these can be included in the k_z and in turn NPV calculations and that combinations of risky projects are usually assumed risk independent and their NPVs calculated separately.

BF9. Current Asset Management

We have discussed investment in shares or long term projects. A priority financial consideration, however, is current asset management and this too involves investment or funding. As a crude analogy here, it is important to keep the ship going as well as to decide upon it's destination!

Current assets and the operating cycle

The operating cycle by which assets are 'turned over' is illustrated in Fig. BF5 for the case of a company which offers credit terms on its sale.

This is for the case of a manufacturer who 'transforms goods in kind' and, of course, the objective is to minimize delays in the cycle and to maximize the quantities involved in it (subject to certain limits or constraints).

When credit is not issued the accounts receivable in a 'triangular cycle' and for the case of a retailer the finished products and raw material activities are merged into 'goods', resulting in a 'line cycle'.

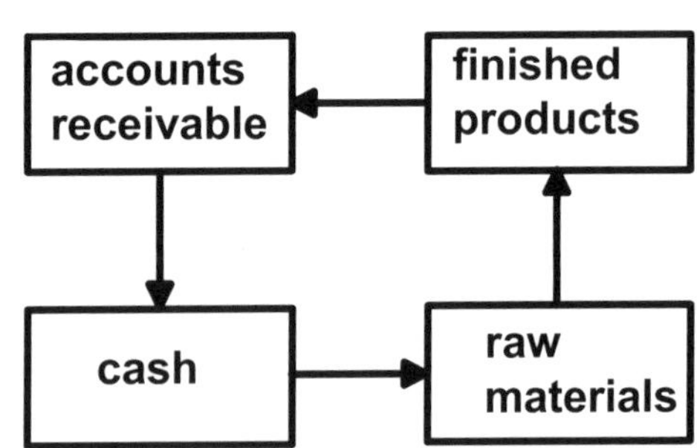

Fig. BF5 Credit based operating cycle

The importance of current assets is illustrated by the proportion of current assets to total assets shown for Australian companies in Table BF6.

Clearly current assets are a very significant part of a company's assets. In managing current assets we seek to:

1. Determine optimum levels of assets to be held. Adding a 'safety margin' to this we obtain the amount of current assets to be held.
2. Finance this asset holding, first distinguishing between the minimum or permanent current asset holding required (which should be as little as possible) and temporary asset holdings required to deal with such factors as seasonal variations in trade.

Table BF6. Current assets as a percentage of total assets for industry groups during 1973-74 to 1976-77.

Current assets	Manufact-uring	Wholesale	Retail	Services	All industries
Inventory	23.1	29.2	27.9	22.8	23.8
Cash	0.94	0.76	1.34	2.41	1.2
a/c's receivable	16.2	24.3	14.2	15.4	16.3
Total	40.4	54.7	44.9	40.4	41.3

These and other considerations, such as company policy in relation to current assets and, for example, credit sales, form the agenda for management of current assets and the financing of them.

Inventory management

Inventory management involves stocking raw material, work in progress (some proportion of which can be classed as inventory for accounting purposes) and holdings of finished goods.

Quantities of inventory required depend upon demand levels, the production process ('high tech' processes for example, may have different requirements to those of basic 'hands on' processes) and its duration, and also upon the price and durability of the goods (for example holdings of perishable goods, must, of course, be minimized rigorously).

The costs of inventory management include the following:

1. Acquisition costs, that is costs of 'set-up' of warehouses etc., the costs of the ordering process (staff time etc.), shipping and handling costs and, in some cases, foregone costs when quantity discounts offered by a supplier are not utilized (this is called an *opportunity cost*).

2. Carrying costs. These include the foregone interest income associated with the cost of inventory held, rent paid for storage space (and also rent forgone for space owned by the company which could have been rented out), interest charges, costs of deterioration and obsolescence and, in the case where prices are falling, the surplus price paid.

3. Stockout costs. These are the cost of lost sales and loss of customer goodwill (if not loss of long term customers) and production hold ups.

Hence the costs of inventory are often somewhat hidden costs more associated with non-productive use of funds which we should seek to minimize.

Economic order quantity

As carrying costs of inventory are directly proportional to the quantity held whereas the acquisition costs decrease when inventory is ordered in larger lots, the total of these two costs has a minimum called the *economic order quantity*, as shown in Fig. BF6.

The economic order quantity is easily determined by defining Y as the demand per unit time for the product and P as the unit price of the product. then the total cost of inventory purchase is = YP per period.

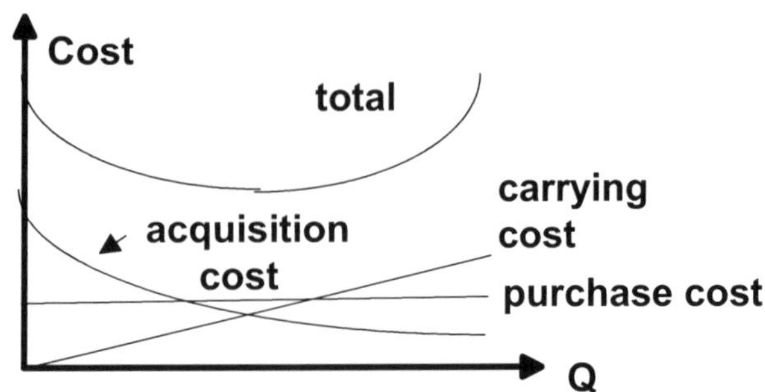

Fig. BF6. Economic order quantity.

Then if X is the order size (the number of units ordered at a time) the number of orders per period (month, year etc.) = Y/X.

If the cost per order is A, then the total acquisition cost per period is = AY/X.

Finally, if carrying cost per unit is , then the total carrying cost = $(X/2)C$, that is the cost for the average number of units stocked.

Then summing these purchase, acquisition and carrying costs per period we obtain:

(BF28) $$T = YP + (Y/X)A + (X/2)C$$

Taking the first derivative, that is dT/dX, and putting this equal to zero we obtain:

$$X = \sqrt{(2YA/C)} = \text{EOQ}$$

In turn we can now calculate Y/X, the associated order frequency.

Equation BF28 can also be applied to production processes when, if A = cost of setting up for production, the value $\sqrt{(2YA/C)}$ is the *optimum production run* size (and Y is now the 'production demand' and C the unit production cost).

Note, however, that in practice the EOQ has a range, as does, of course, the demand Y. In addition, when quantity discounts apply, the EOQ should be calculated for both the normal and discount prices.

Liquid asset management

Liquid assets are moneys held in currency or bank accounts, that is *cash,* and short term securities and other assets that can be converted to cash immediately. Liquid assets must be held for day to day operations, for example for transactions such as payments of accounts owing. Some proportion of liquid assets held should be as a precaution against unexpected cost increases etc. and sometimes it is advantageous to use such liquid assets for speculation on the stock market as a means of increasing company revenue.

Liquid assets involve costs such as those of issuing shares, overdraft charges and forgone interest (accounted for as the WACC k_0). Thus liquid assets behave in the same way as inventory, periodically requiring 'top up', as shown in Fig. BF7.

Here initial liquid asset holdings are R dollars in cash and one or more 'bundles' of short term securities worth C dollars. Then, when the \$$R$ has been spent a bundle of securities is sold to replenish the cash supply.

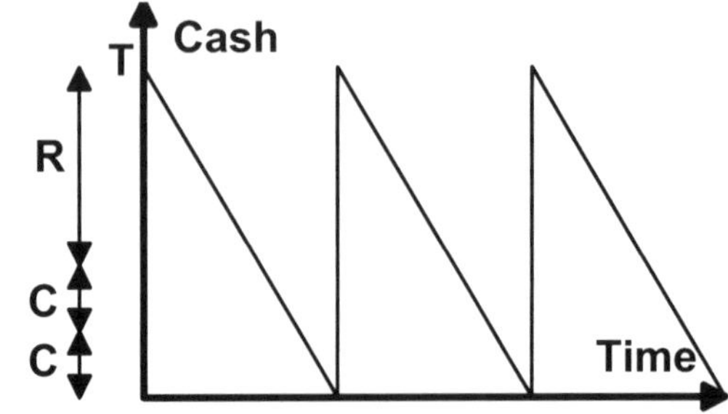

Fig. BF7 Cycling of liquid assets

Then the bundles of securities correspond to order size in Eqn BF28 so that C is given by

(BF29) $C = \sqrt{(2Tb/i)}$

where i is the short term interest rate and b is the transfer cost of converting $\$C$ of short term securities into cash, and R is given by

(BF30) $R = C + T(k_w + k_d)/\, i$

where k_w = cost (cents) of withdrawing $1 of invested funds and k_d = cost of investing $1 in short term securities.

Note that this result does not allow for cash stockout, which should in any case be avoided, or uncertainty in cash requirements, though of course it would be counterproductive to attach uncertainty to more variables than necessary in financial management.

It is also argued that the simple model here is unrealistic in many countries where companies usually use a bank overdraft rather than hold liquid assets to finance part of their operations. Some middle course, at least, on this point is probably preferable.

Accounts receivable management

Accounts receivable is money owed to the company from sale of goods or services on credit. Here it is necessary to distinguish between *trade credit,* which is often on more favourable terms than *consumer credit,* often involving quantity discounts and no interest charges or service fees, whereas consumer credit may involve cash discounts or interest charges and service fees in providing credit.

Costs of accounts receivable management include accounting costs, forgone interest on cash held in accounts receivable, cost of bad debts which must be written off (the accounts), cost of delinquent (late) debts (forgone interest etc.) and establishment costs for customer accounts.

It is important to have a clear *credit policy* which must include such matters as acceptance criteria (for giving credit), credit limits and terms and collection policy (installments v. lump sum etc. and measures taken on late payments).

Commonly credit is given by a *factoring company* which charges from two to four % interest on the total accounts held in the name of the company issuing credit and factoring companies usually required a minimum credit parcel of $M0.5. Usually a *non- notification agreement* is entered into whereby accounts are sent out under the selling company's name. The factoring company then holds the debtors' ledger and takes the risk for bad debts.

An alternative means of financing credit is by *accounts receivable financing* whereby finance is via a loan, usually form a finance company which is pledged the receivables as security. Finance companies will usually lend up to 70% of any bad debts (if the full amount were repaid there would be little incentive to collect the debt).

Credit cards are a means by which a limited factoring service is offered to retailers at a service charge ranging from 1.5 to 5%. The use of these is a satisfactory proposition for a retailer if the resulting increase in sales is greater than the cost of credit and if it is cheaper to use credit cards than to provide one's own credit.

Commonly used financial ratios

In the field of financial management many financial ratios are used as a measure of company liquidity, profitability etc. These include:

1. *Current ratio* = total current assets/total current liabilities. This is used as an indication of ability to pay short term debts.
2. *Quick ratio* = (cash+securities+a/c's receivable)/(total current liabilities - overdraft). This is a better indicator of immediate needs than (1)
3. *Inventory turnover* = annual sales/average inventory.
4. *Average collection period* = average receivables/average daily credit sales.
5. *Total asset turnover* = sales/total tangible assets.
6. *Debt to total assets* = total liabilities/total assets.
7. *Earnings coverage ratio* = EBIT/interest costs. Here EBIT is 'earnings before interest and taxes'.
8. *Profit margin on sale* = net profit after taxes/sales($).
9. *Return on shareholders' funds* = net profit after taxes/shareholder's funds.
10. *PE ratio* = price/earnings (per share) ratio for shares.

Conclusion

Current asset management is a very important part of company management and determination of such quantities as the 'EOQ' is vital as significant savings may result in the long term. In addition the means by which assets are held and credit given, for example, are important considerations and the alternatives should be carfully considered.

BF10. Sources of Finance

There is a market for finance called the *capital market* and the principal finance providers in this are:

1. *The Reserve Bank.* This has limited powers but can affect the capital market considerably by its actions. Its funds are the *statutory reserve deposits* it holds from the trading banks.
2. *Trading banks.* The dominance of these in the market is not what it once was and these now hold only about 20% of the total assets of financing institutions in Australia. The reserve Bank can control the trading banks to some extent by the amount of the statutory reserve deposits (SRDs) it requires of them and by requiring them to maintain a specified *LGS ratio* or proportion of liquid assets to total deposits (usually about 18%).
3. *Authorized short term money market dealers.* These are mostly insurance companies or overseas companies. There are as many of these as trading banks.
4. *Merchant banks.* There are mostly subsidiaries or offshoots of broking houses, life assurance companies, subsidiaries of trading banks or overseas companies. There are about 100 such companies.
5. *Finance companies.* These have the same origins as (4) and there are about 100 such companies at present. Some, for example, are allied with particular motor car manufacturers.
6. *Life assurance companies.* These are made up of insurance companies, investment funds, superannuation funds and overseas companies. The latter require government approval to commence operation in Australia. There are about 50 'life' companies.

Each different type of 'player' in the capital market has a particular role and good financial management demands a familiarity with the different services and options for finance which they provide.

Short term finance

Companies require short term finance principally to fund current assets when these require boosting for a limited period. Short term finance is often called *bridging finance* as it is frequently used to allow a project to commence or continue while long term finance arrangements are being negotiated. Then, as soon as the LT finance becomes available, the bridging loan is redeemed.

The principal means of short term finance are:

1. *Trade credit.* This accounts for roughly 15% of a typical company's liabilities + equity and nearly 50% of its short term finance. Whilst trade credit is not negotiated etc. it is a de facto form of finance. Wholesale companies, for example, use more trade credit (about 40% of their ST finance) than do manufacturing companies (about 30%) because they need to hold more current assets.

2. *Trading banks.* These provide ST finance in:

(a) *Overdrafts.* Banks issue an overdraft facility with an account with a limit and a rate penalty (calculated daily) and usually require some asset security and that a company have a satisfactory current ratio.

Overdrafts are often used to buy assets at bargain prices or loans on call and banks prefer that overdrafts are *fully fluctuating* (between 0 and L/2 where L is the limit).

When funding requirements are medium term banks may lend via a *fully drawn account*, rather than an overdraft, and these require slightly higher rates and regular repayments for a fixed period of, say, five years.

Another alternative arrangement is a *bill acceptance facility* whereby the bank agrees to act as an acceptor of bills issued by the company up to a specified amount.

(b) *Short term mortgages.* These are given at a higher rate than the overdraft rate and are usually to finance property or industrial development.

(c) *Lease finance.* This is at a significantly higher rate than overdraft rates but the use of lease finance has grown considerably in the last decade or so.

3. *Merchant banks, finance companies and authorized dealers.* These are sources of short term loans or mortgages. They also act as factoring agents, deal in the commercial bills market (that is sale of bills held under a bill acceptance facility between financial institutions), and are particularly active in lease financing and installment credit (to companies which sell goods on installment terms to cover their current asset needs).

4. *Intercompany loans.* Some companies with seasonal cash surpluses, for example, lend to companies with temporary cash needs. Later in their business cycle such companies may also need to borrow on the intercompany market and such arrangements are often semi-permanent.

Long term finance: equity

Companies usually fund themselves initially through issuing of shares. This provides long term finance which may be supplemented when the need arises by debt finance. Initial equity finance is obtained by *floating* a new or existing proprietary company. This is done by applying for stock exchange listing and this is granted subject to conditions such as minimum numbers of shares and shareholders required. It is further required that the public hold a substantial proportion of the issue.

Floats are sometimes private, that is funded by institutional investors, but it is usually necessary to 'go public' to attract sufficient investors to qualify for listing. Floats, therefore, are nearly always a public issue of ordinary shares, and this is one of several ways in which equity finance can be obtained. These include:

[1] *Initial issue of ordinary shares.* Usually with the advice of financial institutions the total value of the company is decided upon. Then the share price is set, from which the number of shares to be issued follows.

In setting the share price the price/earnings ratios of similar companies should be considered. If, for example, the company is expected to earn 10 cents per share and the PE ratio of similar companies is between 10 and 15, a share price of between $1.00 and $1.50 is indicated.

The cost of a public float is substantial, including advisory services, preparation of prospectus, legal fees for the latter, accounting fees, printing etc. and stock exchange charges. In addition, however, the issue should be underwritten, usually by the advisory financial institution, typically a merchant bank or broking house. Here, for a fee usually from 1 to 4% of the issue price the issue is guaranteed and the underwriter will take up any unsold shares, sometimes by enlisting sub-underwriters, these then being sold to their institutional clients.

[2] *Subsequent issues of ordinary shares.* When a company requires additional equity finance it can make a further issue of ordinary shares. Such issues may take several forms, including:

a. *Rights issues.* Here each shareholder is entitled to an additional number of shares proportional to his current holding. Usually the issue price is below the current market price to ensure that shareholders are keen to take up the rights. They are then able to resell the rights to obtain a short term gain. If the issue price is close to the market price, however, it is usual to have the issue underwritten.

As an example, suppose a company makes a one in four rights issue, that is N = 4 shares entitles to one additional share, and that the issue is at a subscription price S = $1.50 whilst the market share price = M = $2,00. Then the value of one right is given by

(BF31) $R = N(M - S)/(N + 1) = \$0.40$

Then if a shareholder has 1000 shares he can sell his rights for 1000 x 0.4/4 = $100 or exercise his right and take up 250 shares at a cost of $375. If he takes the first option it would seem that he has made money for nothing, but in practice the share price is likely to fall. If it falls to $1.90, for example, the loss in the value of his holding is exactly balanced by the value of his rights. Thus there is still motivation to exercise his right to increase his share holding at a 'bargain' price.

b. *Private issues.* A private issue of ordinary shares is a 'placement' of shares with institutional investors such as life companies, pension funds and investment companies. Such issues can be accomplished quickly, cheaply and at a price close to (but still less than) the market price. As the market price will be affected, however, private issues should be made only with the approval of shareholders except where expediency and urgency demand funding.

c. *Bonus issues.* When a company has spare funds, for example as a result of asset revaluation, it may make a bonus share issue. If this is, say, a 'one for one' issue we should expect the market value of the shares to halve. Such a share split does not alter the paid-up capital of a company and requires only a book entry in the balance sheet. Usually, however, the share value is not reduced in proportion to the 'dilution' of the shares resulting from the bonus issue and hence the company's market value is increased. Thus, whilst the issue has not raised equity, it has raised the value of the existing equity.

d. *Share options.* These are an option to buy a specified number of shares at a stated price by a given date. Then, if the share price of the company increases, option holders stand to gain by exercising their options.

Options are sometimes issued to employees as an incentive to greater participation and productivity and sometimes they are attached to an equity or private debt issue as a 'sweetener', in the latter instance in return for better interest rate terms, for example.

e. *Internal equity finance.* The equity sources of long term finance discussed thus far are all external. Internal equity finance is also important. This is moneys resulting from profits (after tax and dividends, if any), to which may be added depreciation charges (in some cases upward revaluation makes these a positive contribution), the final result being *retained earnings.*

Such retained earnings provide a 'free' source of long term finance when reinvested but there is an associated opportunity cost (interest rates etc. which could have been charged by investing the funds elsewhere).

Long term finance: debt

Debt finance is less costly than equity finance because interest is paid before dividends are considered and loans are usually secured against assets. Hence lenders are subject to less risk than shareholders and consequently will accept a lower rate of return. The cost advantage of debt is increased by its tax deductibility. The disadvantage of debt funding, however, is the greater risk and, if repayments are defaulted, creditors may seek liquidation

Debt finance can be obtained in various ways, some of these being:

[1] *Short to medium term loans (up to ten years).*

a. *Bank term loans.* Trading banks provide term loans for periods of up to 10 years for capital expenditure needs of rural, industrial, commercial and export development. The rates are usually slightly higher than the overdraft rate and fixed for an initial period and variable thereafter. Security in the form of charges over assets or the guarantee of an overseas bank or parent company is usually required.

b. *Term loans from government agencies.* Such agencies of government as the Australian Resources Development Bank (ARDB), created to assist major mining and other development projects, the Australian Industry Development Corporation (AIDC), which assists industrial development, and the Commonwealth Development Bank, which was initially intended to assist smaller primary producers and manufacturers, provide alternative sources of term loans for special purposes.

c. *Eurodollar loans.* A Eurodollar loan is negotiated in US dollars and channelled to Australia through the European banking system. Other currencies may be dealt with in the same way or via their country of origin. Increasing numbers of companies use overseas finance which is sometimes cheaper, though an interest rate penalty is involved and exchange rate fluctuations can affect the repayments required.

d. *Other financial institutions.* Term loans may also be obtained from merchant banks (or a consortium of these), finance companies (at a fairly high rate) and life companies (from which more favourable terms may be obtained if the company holds the company superannuation fund, for example).

[2] *Long term debt finance* (more than ten years).

a. *Mortgage loans.* The major sources of mortgage loans are life assurance companies, pension funds and trustee companies. Typically companies use such loans to finance their own buildings and plant. Rates and terms of such loans vary considerably and, for example, initial repayments of principal may be delayed for a number of years until the project develops a cash flow.

b. *Debenture and unsecured notes.* Debentures are issued in units (usually $100) and sold in bundles and are secured against specified assets. Unsecured notes are issued in the same way but without security but usually at a higher rate of interest than debentures (in turn marginally less than mortgage funds).

Debentures are secured either by a *fixed* or *floating charge* over assets. The latter is usually preferred by companies as stamp duties involved in specifying the assets over which a fixed charge is made are avoided. In addition they are free to dispose of assets and replace them with other, perhaps more attractive ones.

Debenture issues are usually made for one of three maturity dates, what is short term (2 - 4 years), medium term (5 - 8 years) and long term (10 -15 years).

When debentures are issued a *trust deed* stating the terms of interest and principal repayment, the security for the loan (usually a floating charge), restrictions requiring of the borrowing company such as limits on its further borrowing, sale of assets and the limits of liability of the company. A trustee is then appointed to hold the deed and oversee company operations to ensure that the terms of the deed are met.

c. *Negative pledge lending.* To avoid the restrictions of trust deeds unsecured loans are often obtained with a negative pledge provision which prohibits future loans on a secured basis without offering the holder of the negative pledge the same security. The terms of such loans often involve restrictions on dividend payments and financial ratios such as the current asset ratio. As these are in the company interest, however, they are less inhibiting than the asset restrictions of trust deeds.

Hybrids of debt and equity

[1] *Preference shares*

Preference shares receive priority in payment of dividends and in capital payments in the event of liquidation. Three conditions that may be attached to preference shares are:

a. *Redeemable* or *non-redeemable.* Redeemable shares are equivalent to debentures and may be automatically redeemable or at the company's option. Irredeemable preference shares are similar to ordinary shares.

b. *Cumulative* or *non-cumulative.* If the shares are cumulative the company is obliged to pay preference dividends not paid in previous years before paying ordinary shareholders. Such arrears payments are not required if they are non-cumulative.

c. *Participating* or *non-participating.* Participating shares entitle their holders to a dividend greater than the preference dividend rate in a very profitable year. Non- participating shares do not participate in profit sharing other than by the prescribed dividend rates.

In practice preference shares are usually irredeemable, cumulative and non- participating.

Preference shares are usually issued at a higher dividend rate than the debenture interest rate because debentures have priority of payment. This high cost has discouraged the use of preference shares in Australia in the past.

[2] *Convertible notes.*

These are unsecured notes that can be converted into shares at maturity, carrying a fixed interest rate in the interim, and if the holder does not convert he must be repaid at face value. Conversion is at a price specified in the notes and, assuming that the ultimate market price of the company's shares will be higher than this convertible notes do involve a value which may be attached to the option to convert.

Conclusion

There are many sources and types of equity and debt finance and study of the various options is often well worthwhile. The balance of a company's equity and debt financing, along with many other factors such as policy, it also important and the question of optimal capital structure is discussed further in the next section.

BF11. Capital Structure Decisions

The market value of a company (V) is the sum of the total market value of its equity (E) and debt (D), that is

(BF32) $V = E + D = NOI(1 - t_c)/k_0$

where NOI is the company's net operating income and k_0 and t_c are defined with Eqn BF6 which was

(BF33) $k_0 = k_e(E/V) + k_d(1 - t_c)(D/V)$

Then the *optimal capital structure* is that value of D/E which minimises k_0 (the weighted average cost of capital or WACC) and maximises V.

As an example consider a company with NOI = \$10,000 which is 'unlevered' (that is D = 0). This income is to be distributed to shareholders who hold 100,000 shares of 50 cents (hence the earnings per share are 10 cents) at a rate k_e = 13%. Then the value of the company is calculated in column (a) of Table BF7, assuming $t_c = 0$.

In this case, because D = 0, the required rate of return on equity capital (k_e) is equal to k_o, that is:

$$k_0 = NOI / V = 10{,}000/76{,}923 = 0.13$$

Now assume that, rather than issuing shares only, 60,000 shares at 50 cents and \$20,000 worth of 8% debentures are issued. Assuming the market value of the debt remains at the issue price and the shares increase in value to \$1 (from 77 cents in case (a)), then if the rate of return required by shareholders is 14% the value of the company is as calculated in column (b) of Table BF7.

The WACC of the company is now given by

$$k_0 = 0.14(60/80) + 0.08(20/80) = 0.125$$

showing a slight decrease from case (a).

Table BF7. Examples of different equity/debt mixes.

	(a)	(b)	(c)
NOI	10,000	10,000	10,000
k_d (Σ debts)	0	1,600	2,000
Σ dividends	10,000	8,400	8,000
k_e	0.13	0.14	0.2
E	76,923	60,000	40,000
D	0	20,000	25,000
V	76,923	80,000	65,000

Finally, if the company issues 50,000 shares at 50 cents and $25,000 worth of debt at 8% and the shareholders require a rate of return of 20% then the market value of the company is as calculated in column (c) of Table BF7. Here, as a result of the increase in debt funding, it is assumed that the share price has dropped to 80 cents (from $1 in case (b)).

Now the WACC of the company is given by

$$k_0 = 0.20(40/65) + 0.08(25/65) = 0.154$$

and the market value of the company has decreased whilst the cost of capital has increased as a result of a further increase in debt, as illustrated in Fig. BF8.

Here the cost of capital is reduced by the cheaper debt finance diluting the equity finance. The cost of equity increases, however, resulting in an optimum capital structure (OCS).

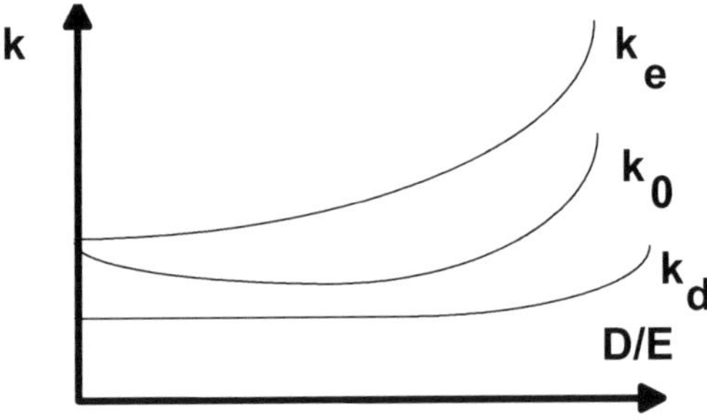

Fig. BF8 Optimum capital structure

Modified models

Modified models which seek to better reflect the behaviour shown in Fig. BF8 have been proposed, for example in which it is proposed that k_0 in Eqn BF33 should be a constant which is a measure of a company's risk and that the cost of equity should be calculated as

$$\text{(BF34)} \qquad k_e = k_e^* + (k_e^* - k_d)(1 - t_c)(D/E)$$

where k_e^* is the required return on equity when the company is financed only by equity (that is, $D = 0$). Neither such modified models nor the original CAPM model take into account the tax advantages of using debt or the risk factors associated with increased debt, however, but the original model of Eqn BF33 is, for conceptual purposes at least, still preferred.

Conclusion

The CAPM model of Eqn BF33 is, conceptually at least, still very useful and Table BF7 provides a good example of how a minimum value of the WACC and an associated maximum value of the company might occur at some optimum value of *D/E* corresponding to the optimal capital structure.

Indeed companies and sometimes share markets act as though an OCS exists though the assumption that the cost of equity rises as D/E rises is not entirely logical.

Nevertheless the search for the OCS is a worthwhile one and it should be based on earnings before interest and taxes, earnings per share, ability to service debt and like factors with a view to maximizing the market value of the company and the ROI of investors.

BF12. Share Price and Curve Plotting

In this final section an example of a simple but widely used technique for plotting day by day share prices to determine appropriate 'buy and sell' points is discussed. Then examples of how data for simple curves may be tested by linear plots are given. These are intended as exercises at this point but may initiate some thinking about whether share prices and the like can have determinable turning points or asymptotes.

Plotting share prices

A simple example of a commonly used method of plotting share values is the *three point reversal* method, originally employed with the New York market (appropriate adjustment to 'x', rather than three, points is therefore needed in application to other share markets).

This involves plotting a *point and figure* chart as shown in Fig. BF9. In this a new column is used when there is a reversal in price and dates can be marked on the time axis for, say, each month.

Then in the three point reversal method a reversal is when there is a price change equal to three squares on the chart, the chart being plotted as one square = $1 for prices above $20, one square = 50 cents for prices less then $20 and so on.

Then, with a little experience it is possible to identify patterns which indicate good points at which to buy or sell shares. There are many such patterns, however, and such techniques require a great deal of experience.

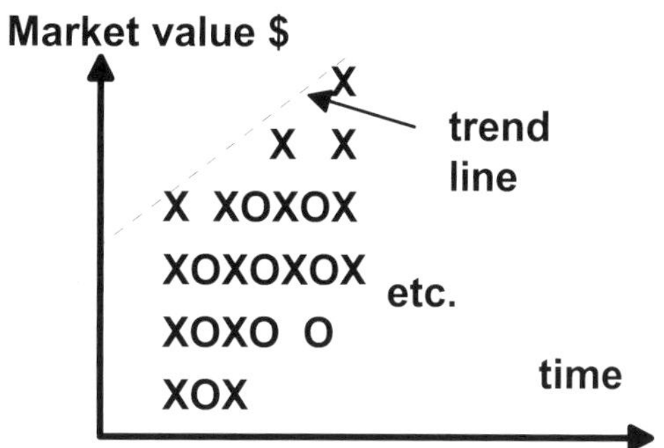

Fig. BF9 Three point reversal method

Such study of reversals and their pattern is usually applied to industrial shares. For commodities, on the other hand, trend lines like that shown in Fig. BF9 are generally used to indicate likely outcomes. These, however, only signal 'up' and not 'how far?' and such techniques as those discussed in the remainder of the chapter are potentially useful.

Curve plotting techniques.

In the MR chapter the method of linear regression (by least squares) is demonstrated.

In this, a line of best fit is fitted to observed data.

Many spreadsheet packages (e.g. Quattro, 123 and Excell) do this for you and the reader should try them on the data (x,y) = (1,20), (2,30), (3,40) when they should find the coefficient of correlation (c.c.) to be 1, the 'intercept' = 10 etc., i.e. we have a straight line.

In the interim, however, two useful examples of how this may be achieved graphically are given.

[1] **Rectangular hyperbola**

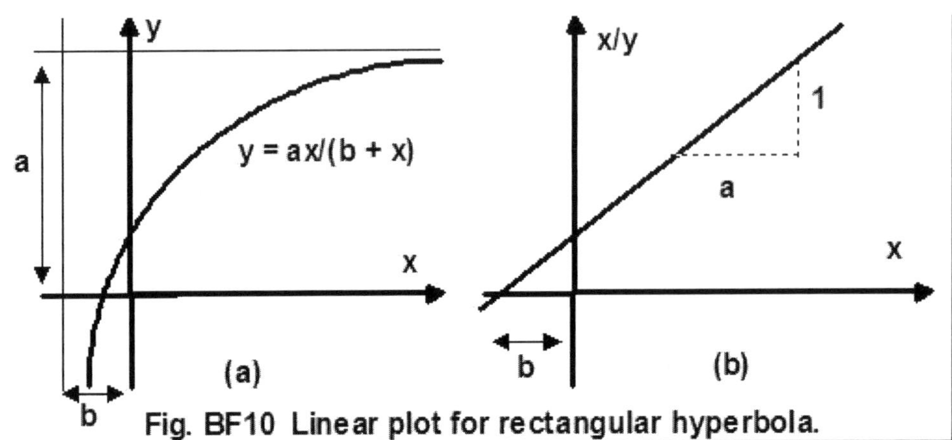

Fig. BF10 Linear plot for rectangular hyperbola.

The equation of this hyperbola is $y = ax/(b + x)$ which can easily be rearranged to give

$$x/y = (b + x)/a$$

so that if we plot (x/y) against x the straight line of Fig. BF10(b) is obtained and the magnitude of the intercept with the x axis = b whilst, or more interest, the inverse slope of the line equals the asymptote of the hyperbola.

This, the *Mohr plot*, is useful in estimating an asymptote or 'ceiling' value towards which it may be suspected that some variable is converging.

[2] **Parabola**

Fig. BF11(a) shows a parabola passing through the origin, turning at (x_p, y_p) and passing through the x axis again at $2x_p$. The equation for this parabola can be written as

$$y/x = (y_p/x_p)(2 - x/x_p)$$

so that if we plot (y/x) against x the straight line shown in Fig. BF11(b) is obtained.

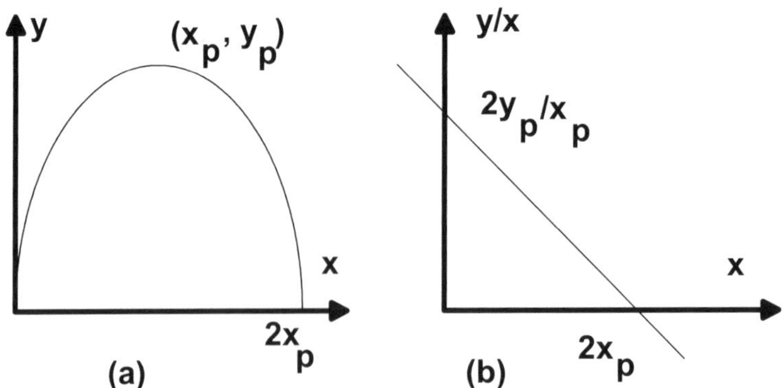

Fig. BF11. Linear plot for a parabola

Then the intercept of this line with the x axis = $2x_p$, the intercept with the y axis = $2y_p/x_p$ whilst the slope of the line is equal to $- y_p/x_p^2$. Therefore this type of plot is useful in estimating a turning point in a variable when one is suspected.

[3] **Other possible curves**

Many other possible curves might be considered but in econometrics, for example, where attempts are made to fit functions to economic variables, it is found that for most purposes functions of parabolic form are sufficient.

The reason for this might be understood if we examine an infinite polynomial, taking the exponential function as an example:

$$e^x \text{ or } \exp(x) = 1 + x + x^2/2! + x^3/3! + x^4/4! + - - - -$$

Then, within a range, square terms (or a parabola) are all that is needed to approximate a curve and practical functions in such fields as economics are not likely to rise much more steeply than $y = x^2$ or to oscillate like sin( ) or cos( ). Oscillations do, of course, occur, but not with sinusoidal regularity and we are more likely to study individual oscillations using plots such as that of Fig. BF11(b). Note too, in passing, that with suitable rearrangement of terms a linear plot can also be established for $y = \sqrt{x}$.

Conclusion

In a chapter on business finance where a good deal of discussion has been about share prices and uncertainty in these some mention, however brief, of the many techniques for plotting share price variations is appropriate though it is not possible to give recommendations on how such charts might be 'read'.

In this context graphical plots which reveal asymptotes and turning points are hopefully worthwhile.

Exercises

[1] Given the data: (x,y) = (1,7), (2,12), (3,15)
plot y against x and guess the peak or turning value of y_p. Repeat using another scale. Compare the two guesses. Then plot y/x against x and use the results in Fig. BF11 to find the turning point. (Ans: x = 4, y = 16).

[2] The exponential growth law was derived in Sec. MS. An application of this which has a similar spirit to the compound interest formula (which has been described as the very basis of capitalism) is *Mohr's Law of Money,* namely that if the rate of making money is given by

$$d\$/dt = (\text{constant} =)\,a$$

where a = *activity*, and if a = (constant = k)\$, the we obtain the exponential growth law:

$$\$ = (\text{constant})\ e^{kt}$$

and it is interesting to consider what values of the constant are comparable to substantial rates of interest in the compound interest formula.

BF References

Aitken M, Brown P, Izan H, Kua A, Walter T. An intraday analysis of the profitability of trading on the ASX at the asking price. Aust. J. Management, vol. 20, no. 2, 1995.
Aitken P. 10 Minute Guide to 1-2-3 97 for Windows. QUE, Indianopolis, IN, 1997.
Anthony RN, Govindarajan V. Management Control Systems, 8th ed. Irwin, Chicago, 1995.
Backer M, Jacobsen LE. *Cost Accounting.* McGraw-Hill Kogusaka, Tokyo, 1964.

Bruce R, McKern B, Pollard I, Skully M. Handbook of Australian Corporate Finance, 3rd edn. Butterworth, Sydney, 1989.
Bongiorno C. The Australian Dividend Handbook. ANz/McCaughan Research, Melbourne, 1993.
Cunningham C, Nikolai LA, Bazley JD. *Accounting: Information for Business Decisions.* Dryden Press, Orlando FA, 2000.
Cohen AW. Three Point Reversal Method of Point and Figure Stock Market Trading, 8th edn. Chartcraft Inc., Larchmot NY, 1982.
Day JX. Your Money and Your Life. Lothian. Melbourne, 1989.
______. Shares, Jan. 1999. Fairfax publications, Melbourne, 1999.
Fiske WP, Beckett JA. Industrial Accountant's Handbook. Prentice-Hall, Englewood Cliffs NJ, 1954.
Garrety MD. Making Money in The Futures Market in Australia. M.D. Garretty, Toorak, Melbourne, 1979.
Green I, Murray B. Test Questions in Accounting with Suggested Solutions, 8th edn. VCTA Publishing, Melbourne, 1990.
Hewat, T. The Intelligent Investors Guide to Share Buying. Wrightbooks, Melboure, 1988.
Lang T, McFarland WB, Schiff M. Cost Accounting. Ronald, New York, 1953.
Lewis M. Liar's Poker: Two Cities, True Greed. Hodder & Stoughton, London, 1989.
Magnus A, Scorgie ME Financial Management, Concepts and Calculations. LaTrobe University, Melbourne, 1998.
Microsoft Excel Users Guide, V 3.0. Microsoft, Redmond VA, 1991.
Microsoft Excel Function Reference, V 3.0. Microsoft, Redmond VA, 1991.
Microsoft Excel Database Access User's Guide, V 4.0. Microsoft, Redmond VA, 1992.
Mohr GA. Analysis and Design of Plate and Shell Structures using Finite Elements. PhD thesis, Univ. of Cambridge, 1976.
Mohr GA. A simple membrane element including the drilling freedom. Computers & Structures, vol. 13, p 483, 1981.
Mohr GA, *The War of the Sexes: Women Are Getting On Top,* Xlibris (2012).
Mohr GA, *The Pretentious Persuaders, A Brief History & Science of Mass Persuasion,* Horizon Publishing Group, Sydney, 2012 (edn 1), 2014 (edn 2).
Naish PJ. Summit Book of Investment. Evans Bros, London. 1968.
Newbold P, Bos T, Introductory Business Forecasting. South-Western, Cincinnati OH, 1990.
O'Leary TJ, Williams BK, O'Leary LI. McGraw-Hill Microcomputing Labs. McGraw-Hill, New York. 1992.
Peirson G, Bird R, Brown R. Business Finance, 4th edn. McGraw-Hill, Sydney, 1985.
______. Proc. Australian Society of Accountants 1980 State Congress. Aust. Soc. Accountants, Melbourne. 1980.
______. RSA Computer Literacy and Information Technology. Heinemann, Oxford. 1988.
Seiler RA. Principles of Accounting: A Managerial Approach. Charles E. Merrill, Columbus OH. 1967.
Wilkinson-Riddle GJ. Accounting Level III. McDonald Evans. Plymouth. 1982.
Williams LR. How I Made One Million Dollars Last Year Trading Commodities. Windsor Books, Brightwaters NY. 1979.
Wu FH. Accounting Information Systems. McGraw-Hill, New York. 1984.

MANAGEMENT PSYCHOLOGY (MP)

A long pull, and a strong pull, and all pull together. Charles Dickens.

Psychology has several branches, these including:

1. Behavioural psychology or behaviourism which deals with the observation of behaviour.
2. Psychoanalysis.
3. Development psychology which deals with juvenile development.
4. Social psychology which deals with the interaction of groups.
5. Cognitive psychology which deals with recognition.
6. Attitudinal psychology.

These branches are sometimes combined, for example combination of (1), (5) and (6) has important application in marketing and this is discussed in Secs MR8-10.

Here we begin with a brief introduction to some basic concepts of psychology, moving on to a more detailed discussion of human resource (or personnel) management (HRM), management development and leadership, personnel and productivity assessment and many other issues related to the psychology of management.

MP1. Some Basic Psychology Concepts

❖ *Accommodation.* This concept was developed by Piaget and describes the process by which an infant's brain adapts to information, striving for equilibrium or *balance* as it does so.

❖ *Acute/chronic.* A distinction much used in medical science. In psychiatry, for example, acute and chronic brain syndrome respectively refer to curable and incurable dementias.

❖ *Addictions.* Three basic models of addiction are chemical, psychodynamic and social learning. Sometimes addiction is a result of a combination of all three mechanisms.

❖ *Advertising.* Here the psychology of attitudes is very relevant (see Secs MR8 - 10) and psychologists have worked in the US advertising industry since 1910.

❖ *Ageing.* Geriatric psychology is a specialist area and includes study of such syndromes as *senile dementia of the Alzheimer type (SDAT).*

❖ *Binet.* Binet developed what became known as the *Stanford-Binet* test from which *intelligence quotient (IQ)* is measured.

❖ *CAT scan.* Computerized axial tomography, also known as CT scan. Computer mapping of densities of a body (usually the brain) from X-ray views to provide a 3-D representation of the body.

❖ *Conditioning.* Also termed reinforcement, the most famous experiments on this were conducted by Pavlov on dogs.

❖ *Double blind test.* Much used in testing of drugs when a third party gives the drug to the patient, neither party knowing which drug is being given. This procedure is used to eliminate the *placebo effect.*

❖ *Ego/id/superego.* The ego is the 'external' entity of Freud's trinity which faces the world, the id being its hidden desires and the superego its conscience, the id and superego thus being in competition.
❖ *Factor analysis.* Statistical analysis using correlation to determine the factors which account for most of the variations in data. Much used in the study of traffic and other accidents.
❖ *G factor.* A 'general factor' extracted from IQ tests of verbal, maths, music and other skills to account for most of the variation in these. Regarded as the most accurate intelligence measure.
❖ *Group dynamics.* The processes within groups. An application is group therapy but explanation of group behaviour in general depends much upon leader personality, the task at hand and threats to the group.
❖ *Industrial psychology.* Also termed occupational psychology this studies job satisfaction, stress and the like. *Time and motion study* (with a view to improved productivity) is a related study and *occupational therapy,* where tasks (usually menial) are given to patients is also related.
❖ *Interviews.* Interviews are much used for personnel selection though it is widely held that they are of little value and that observation of how well trainees do on the job is preferable.
❖ *Marxist psychology.* This highlights the concepts of *class* and *alienation,* the latter supposedly leading to lower IQ and problems at school and elsewhere.
❖ *Networking,* a term applicable to both business and social groups.
❖ *NLP.* Neuro-linguistic programming. A recent term concerned with persuasion but not involving anything new.
❖ *Organizational behaviour.* How organisations behave and how people in them behave. Recent focus in this area has been upon executive stress resulting in a tendency to reduce the hierarchical nature of many company structures.
❖ *Personality tests.* There are now over 5000 of these, ranging from tests for extroversion/introversion to tests of whether you will be good at a certain sport. These are discussed in Sec. MP4.
❖ *REM sleep.* Rapid eye movement sleep is necessary, though doubts exist about what for, but is has been suggested that insufficient REM sleep will result in diminished IQ, for example. REM sleep occurs about 80 minutes after sleep commences and recurs at similar intervals thereafter.
❖ *Social skills.* The skills needed to interact socially which include the use of language, *body language* and the like.
❖ *Transactional analysis* (TA). A form of therapy in which assumes that life involves acting in a child, adult or parent mode and that we are not one of these all the time.

Experimental psychology

This is worth special mention. Related to this we have already mentioned conditioning and time and motion study. Market research can also provide an example of the use of experiments and measurement of the results.

An notable example was the 'blue geese experiment' conducted in the 1950s in which parent geese and their offspring were dyed blue. It was then found that these blue offspring tended to mate with other 'blue geese'.

Other notable experiments have been those conducted by NASA on *stimulus deprivation* in the 1950s and those in which rat populations become self destructive beyond a certain population density.

Conclusion: Psychology is important, especially in advertising as we see later.

MP2. Introduction to Human Resource Management

Human resource management (HRM) or personnel management is a subset of management psychology which involves a broad range of activities which will involve personnel at all levels in an organization. In addition a basic knowledge of psychology (and hence sociology or social psychology which is a subset) and many other areas such as industrial relations is also important.

HRM issues

Some current HRM issues of particular note are:

1. Increasing worker participation in decisions (in contrast to 'top-down' management by objectives (MBO)).
2. Encouragement of workers to hold company shares.
3. Company HRM departments are traditionally run by women and deal only with routine matters. This has changed a somewhat, whilst separate recruitment companies are often run mostly by men.
4. New legislation such as that for equal opportunity (EO).
5. New technology implementation in HRM, for example use of MISs and databases.

HRM objectives

The principal objectives of efficient and effective HRM include:

1. Ensure that company employees are competent for their assigned work.
2. Development of commitment of company staff.
3. To improve the cost-effectiveness of the company.
4. To resolve conflicts over remuneration, conditions, personal matters or duties.
5. Dealing with the issue of workplace bullying.

In addition, good HR managers will deal with any problems which may present themselves concerning the well being of personnel.

Flow of human resources

Generally there is a 'flow' of human resources through and within an organization. This involves HRM in the following tasks:

1. Recruitment, training and career counseling.
2. Performance assessment, career paths, promotion policies and termination policies.
3. Promotion should be as a result of objective criteria known by all.
4. Movement of people parallel in an organization, that is to new duties.
5. Out placement of staff made redundant.

Reward systems

Employees may be rewarded in many ways, including wages and salaries, bonuses, merit increases, fringe benefits, titles, share issues and perks and privileges. Other less tangible benefits include environmental improvements, improved offices or facilities, improved treatment of staff etc.

Work systems

Whether business is carried out via hierarchical structure or a team approach is important and affects how HRM staff must approach their task of dealing with members of this structure or team.

Safety

Matters of industrial safety and insurance are a key concern of HRM staff.

Redundancy

HRM staff, of course, must also deal with superannuation packages and early retirement schemes or redundancy packages.

Conclusion

The tasks of human resource management are many and varied in nature and can do much to ensure more harmonious and profitable operation of an organization. Equally, HRM can do much to ensure that individual staff are more satisfied and productive.

MP3. HRM Activities

HRM departments have many activities. The following list shows how much (as a percentage) of each activity HRM departments are typically responsible for.

(90 %) Personnel records/reports/information systems.
Wages, injury compensation, leave scheduling, worker insurance.
Preemployment tests.
Job evaluation (skills levels etc. and hence appropriate wages).

(80 %) Retirement preparation, health/medical services.
Promotion/transfer/separation.
Induction/orientation.

(70 %) Counseling/recreation programs.
Recruiting/interviews/hiring.
Complaints/disciplinary procedures.

(60 %) Attitude surveys, out placement programs.
Union/labour relations.
Employee meetings/publication/performance evaluation.

(50 %) Safety programs/compliance.
HR planning, supervisor training.
Suggestions systems/performance evaluation.

(40 %) Management development.
Executive compensation administration.
Career planning and development.

(30 %) Security measures/property protection.
Payroll processing.
Productivity/motivation programs.

(20 %) Thrift/savings plan administration.
Skill training.
Public relations.

(10 %) Library.
Administrative services (mail, phone etc.)
Maintenance (cleaning etc.)

Just how many of these duties fall to HRM will depend upon the structure of the organization, that is, whether it has a pyramid or beaurocratic structure or an 'organic' or team structure. In either case, it is in part the task of HRM to assist staff to work within such structures by making them aware of who their immediate supervisor is, the chain of command and what duties they are responsible for.

Job design

Jobs can be based on the 'engineering' approach where each person is given a few simple tasks to perform repetitively. This is the production line approach to which time and motion study and the like especially apply.

The more contemporary approach, however, is to vary the tasks of personnel by *job enlargement* (horizontal changes in duties), *job enrichment* (vertical changes in duties) or *job rotation.* This is aimed, of course, at improving worker satisfaction. Whether it improves productivity may be doubtful in the short term but perhaps not so much so in the long term.

Job analysis

Job analyses are often prepared by HRM staff or, at least, dealt with by HRM in the course of other duties. Typical job analysis includes:

1. Job description. The title, duties and responsibilities of a job.
2. Job specification. The educational qualifications and skills required for the job.
3. Applicable EO and other requirements.
4. Rate of remuneration, including applicable bonuses etc.
5. In house training requirements and plans.
6. Term of employment contract.
7. Conditions of possible promotion (usually in the long term).
8. Any special safety requirements.

Many of these details, of course, are included in advertisements for positions and are also used as criteria in the selection process.

HR planning

HRM involves not only the short term tasks of recruitment and the like, but also requires long term planning which will be required to take into account such factors as:

1. Economic trends, new legislation and labour market trends.
2. Technological advances that may require new skills.
3. Business policy that may involve enlarging certain areas.
4. New projects planned.

Fig. MP1 shows an example of the layout for a long term HRM plan. Such HR plans, of course, should have an implementation schedule.

Fig. MP1. Long term human resource planning.

DIVISION	AREA			MANPOWER REQUIREMENTS REPLACEMENT	RECRUITMENT
SALES	DEMAND RE-QUIREMENTS	PRESENT	EXISTING PRODUCTS	PRESENT STAFF - LEAVERS	
			NEW PRODUCTS		ADDITIONAL STAFF
		NEW	EXISTING PRODUCTS		ADDITIONAL STAFF
			NEW PRODUCTS		
DISTRIBUTION	AREA COVERED	PRESENT		PRESENT STAFF - LEAVERS	
					ADDITIONAL STAFF
		NEW			ADDITIONAL STAFF
PRODUCTION	AVAILABLE CAPACITY	PRESENT	EXISTING TECHNIQUES	PRESENT STAFF - LEAVERS	
					ADDITIONAL STAFF
			NEW TECHNIQUES		ADDITIONAL STAFF
		NEW	EXISTING TECHNIQUES	PRESENT STAFF - LEAVERS	
					ADDITIONAL STAFF
			NEW TECHNIQUES		ADDITIONAL STAFF
ADMIN	SERVICE LEVEL	PRESENT		PRESENT STAFF - LEAVERS	
					ADDITIONAL STAFF
		NEW			ADDITIONAL STAFF

Conclusion

The large range of activities of human resource management is apparent and the level of detail required in some of these activities, for example job design and analysis, is quite considerable. In addition there is often a need for long term HR plans associated, in part, with long term company policy as well as other factors.

MP4. Recruitment and Selection

A human resource management function that requires special attention is that of recruitment and selection of personnel. For these activities appropriate policies and procedures are required and aspects of these are discussed in the following section.

Recruitment policy

Aspects of recruitment policy may include the question of whether recruitment should be by priority internal or external, what selection standards should be used and whether relatives of present personnel should be considered. In addition, of course, EO legislation and such factors must also be taken into account.

Internal recruitment

For this a skills inventory is useful whilst measures such as posting vacancies on notice boards are virtually cost free.

External recruitment

External recruitment may be conducted through various avenues, some of these including:

1. Employment agencies (for example for temporary staff).
2. Government unemployment agencies and welfare services.
3. Unsolicited applications and enquiries.
4. Unions and professional associations.
5. Schools and Universities.
6. Advertisements.
7. Employee and other referrals.

Selection procedures

Selection procedures might, for example, involve forming a short list of 6 (for a single position) and sometimes it is desirable that this process is audited. This list is then forwarded to a selection committee which chooses a final two candidates for the final interview and other procedures.

Then the final selection process might involve:

1. Reception and preliminary interview.
2. Application form (this might involve questions to which scores might be attached, when it is said to be a *weighted application blank).*
3. Selection tests (for aptitude and/or personality).
4. Final selection interview by manager, supervisor or committee.
5. Background checks (referees etc.).

This is only a guide, however, as selection procedures vary from the quick simple informal interview to procedures taking several days of interviews, seminars, tours of the organization, meetings with members of the organization, dinners and the like.

Interviews

Interviews may be one to one, by panels, planned (the questions having been scripted) or involve a set pattern (the latter are termed patterned or structured). The terms unguided, guided and directed are also used to describe interview types. They may require the interviewee to fill in a questionnaire and sometimes *stress interviews* are used in which the interviewer is deliberately hostile. Indeed inclusion of at least one such hostile question from a member of a panel is, whether by accident or design, a common occurrence.

Questions posed in interviews usually include such standard ones as " "Why do you want to work for us ?", "What do you think are your best attributes ?" or "What do you think you can do for the company ?"

As noted in Sec. MP1, however, the effectiveness of interviews for selection of personnel is often doubted. Inclusion of other steps in the selection process, therefore, is worthwhile, especially if weights are given to these other steps and a total evaluation used.

Aptitude tests

The best known of these is the *Stanford-Binet* test in which a series of questions is asked, these covering a range of area such as arithmetic, language and visual perception skills. Then the score obtained by an individuals compared with that appropriate for an average person of a given age, yields the *intelligence quotient* as

IQ = (mental age/actual age) x 100

This statement, however, is more designed for assessment of mental retardation and, after all, what is a mental age of 37 ?

In practice IQ is (questionably) assumed to peak at around the age of 18 and a given IQ test has a score associated with each IQ level determined from extensive trials.

Better but more complex tests have been devised which use various 'sub-tests' for mathematical, language and music skills etc. and the *G factor* or general factor which accounts for most of the variation in the scores in the sub-tests is determined.

An example is the *Weschler intelligence scale* which uses such tests as:

a. Verbal tests: information, comprehension, memory, arithmetic and vocabulary.

b. Performance tests: block design, digit symbol coding, picture completion, picture arrangement and object assembly.

There are Weschler scales for pre-school children, children and adults and the Weschler scales have μ (mean) = 100 and σ (standard deviation) = 15 from which the reader will be able to deduce that about 68% of people should have a score between 85 and 115 on the WAIS (Weschler Adult Intelligence Scale).

Personality tests

Personality tests are a relatively recent innovation but are gaining in popularity in connection with certain occupations. Examples of these include:

1. Use of questionnaires with statements such as "I usually go to the movies alone" or "I often feel depressed" to which a yes/no or tick/X response is required.
2. The California Psychological Inventory (CPI) which involves 15 sub-scales for such traits as dominance, self-acceptance, responsibility, self-control and independence.
3. 'Check lists' of up to 300 adjectives from which response to certain proposed events (hypothetical) is chosen. Personality is then judged to be of from 3 to 10 types.
4. Projective tests. These include exercises in sentence completion, the Rorschack ink blot test and the 'Thematic Apperception Test' (TAT) in which response to a set of pictures is recorded.

To date personality tests have been mainly applied in psychiatric and other clinical applications but their use in the context of management is increasing and correlation of personality types with marketing policies is also widely practiced.

Conclusion

Some aspects of HRM recruitment and selection procedures seem relatively routine but there is a need for improvement in this area. Aptitude or ability tests are potentially very meaningful if they involve at least a few sub-tests whilst personality tests are of growing importance, as are attitude tests which are discussed in Secs. MR8 - 10.

Note that the third type of personality test mentioned above is similar to the propositions of Mohr's Law (see Sec. BP12). In the latter, however, it is not must measurement or judgment of personality that is of primary concern but the interactions between different personality types.

MP5. Aspects of ongoing HRM

In section MP4 we discussed matters relating to recruitment and selection in detail. Other aspects of HRM as an ongoing task which deserve special attention include performance appraisal, career development and training and these are considered in the present section.

Performance appraisal

Assessment of performance of front line workers may be with a view to determining whether wage increases are justified or with the aim of worker development and hence productivity improvement. Feedback from such assessments will, or course, be useful to supervisors and others for the purposes of job planning and delegation.

Method of performance assessment may include:

1. Use of rating scales for attitudes, satisfaction with job etc.
2. Use of 'job dimension scales', that is rating of excellent, good, OK, fair and poor for various components of the job.
3. MBO (management by objectives) in which goals are set jointly., for example to reduce lost days, the results being measurable.
4. Ranking, for example from best to worst in a group of workers.
5. Check lists in which performance is marked as one of tick/X or a multiple choice option for various components of the job. Weights may be attached to the responses in calculating a total score.
6. Informal talks or formal interviews.

More unusual assessments might be made from a short essay written by each of those assessed or observation of actions or workers in a critical or emergency situation (that is do they stay calm and sort out the problem and so on).

Career development

In respect of career development of personnel HRM staff should deal with the following:

1. Career development of a person within a company generally takes the stages (a) exploration/orientation, (b) establishment, (c) maintenance and (d) decline (towards retirement). HRM should assist with these stages as appropriate.
2. Career development actions should be integrated with HR planning.
3. Goals and career paths should be set by consultation with personnel.
4. Career information should be disseminated to personnel.
5. Promotion, training and other opportunities should be publicized.
6. Personnel should be assessed and advised on career progress.
7. Education and training.

In-house training

In the course of a company's operations training may be needed to deal with problems encountered, grievances (about difficulties with equipment and the like) and delays and thus eliminate recurrence of such difficulties as far as possible.

In-house training has the advantages of being quick, allowing personnel to learn while working (or in parallel), better able to be focused on actual operational problems (on which there is feedback) and of being able to bring about more immediate improvements. In addition it is easy to include attitude and motivation improvement programs along the way.

Training methods can include on-the-job instruction or classroom sessions which might take the form of lectures, seminars, role-play sessions, or conferences.

Employee orientation

This is really a part, though a special one, of in-house training but has some special requirements which include:

1. Introduction to company history and policy.
2. Introduction to company products and offices or plants.
3. Details of pay and conditions of employment.
4. Information on safety requirements and any training required to meet these.
5. Information on company promotion policy.
6. Introduction to other personnel (particularly supervisor(s)).
7. Details of responsibilities and duties.

In some respects some of these points are very important as all too often a new employee takes a decade to find out much about some of his fellow workers, if he does at all. A little effort on orientation of each new personnel member will do a great deal to smooth their path for the years to come and, ultimately, all will benefit.

Conclusion

Ongoing work involving existing staff and recruitment of new staff are two basic areas of HRM work. These are, perhaps, approximately equally important and if both are done well company profitability will ultimately be the better for it. Also of some value, company image will be much improved, as will staff morale.

MP6. Management Development

When management development is dealt with in-house there should be a management development program, essential ingredients of which are:

1. Analysis of organization needs.
2. Appraisal of management performance.
3. An inventory of management skills, qualifications etc.
4. Planning of individual development programs.
5. Establishment of training and development programs.
6. Evaluation of programs.

With the establishment of efficient programs individual and collective management can be much improved. In additions items (1) to (3) above might be beneficial in identifying a need for recruitment of new staff to provide an improved management structure.

Management training

Amongst the various means by which management training might be undertaken the following are amongst the most commonly employed:

1. Work experience which may be obtained: (a) as an understudy, (b) by job rotation, (c) through coaching, or (d) by using two or more people for a particular management role (this is referred to as 'multiple management').
2. Formal courses given by Universities, professional bodies or other appropriate organizations.
3. Management games (usually using computer simulations) which give feedback which assists in 'self-training'.
4. Transactional analysis. This involves role play in adult, parent or child modes (see Sec. MP1) and in relation to management training the objective is to inculcate confidence in delegation and leadership.

Organizational development

Organization development is a planned process designed to improve organizational effectiveness and health through modifications in individual and group behaviour, culture and systems of organization.

Organizational development should be a process led by executives who, therefore, should receive relevant training or at least counseling on OD from another executive responsible for OD.

Organizational development involves using surveys and consultations with and between staff to set goals, negotiate agreements on performance and behaviour and to adjust the structure of the organization to better meet its objectives.

The basic objectives of OD are to foster belief that staff need encouragement and support, that cooperation should always be given and that staff should be open and direct in carrying out their work.

The elements of the OD process are:

1. Diagnosis of problems.
2. Selection and design of interventions.
3. Implementation of intervention.
4. Evaluation of results.
5. Adjustment and maintenance of system.

Interventions will typically involve questions such as "How free do you feel to talk to the boss ?" or "Do members of your department cooperate readily ?" This feedback is then used to bring about improvements in the 'health' of the organization.

Principally, however, so far as managers are concerned, the primary goal of OD is to encourage managers to show high levels of concern for both people and productivity. In turn part of that concern for people can be usefully expressed by implementing the OD process with their staff.

Effectiveness of decisions

In any discussion involving management training it is, perhaps, worth pointing out that the effectiveness of decisions is sometimes expressed as a product of two quantities

$$\text{Results achieved} = (\text{Quality of decision}) \times (\text{Motivation to implement})$$

and it is important to have both of these factors as high as possible because when both are only = 0.5 the product is, of course, only 0.25. The subject of motivation, therefore, is discussed in the following section.

Conclusion

Management development and training and management with emphasis on organization development and quality decisions can do much to improve a company both qualitatively and quantitatively.

MP7. Motivation

Motivation is an important part of achieving results, as pointed out at the close of Sec. MP6. In management, therefore, some understanding of the psychology of motivation is important and useful. Not only can it be helpful personally, of course, but it may help in learning to motivate others.

Drive reduction theories

Drive reduction theories of motivation (briefly referred to in Sec. MP1) assume a hierarchy of human needs such as:

1. Physiological (hunger, thirst etc.).
2. Safety, stability and security.
3. Belonging ('love' etc.).
4. Self esteem.
5. Accomplishment.

Then motivation is based on the wish to reduce these needs, the level of motivation depending upon the position of them in the hierarchy.

Motivation-maintenance theory

Also called the Motivation-hygiene theory this recognizes two types of motivational factor:

a. *Motivators* (or intrinsic motivators). These include such factors as achievement, recognition, the work itself, responsibility and advancement.

b. *Maintenance* factors (extrinsic motivators). These include such factors as business policy, supervision, salary, interpersonal relations and work conditions.

The application of this theory is simply to realise that we should foster (a) which we can do at little or no cost, and do what we can to maximize (b) which we can do at relatively little cost.

Achievement motivation theory

This is that some people are basically more motivated than others and attempts have been made to measure such differences using such tests as the Thematic Apperception Test (see Sec. MP4) to assess to what degree a person is a risk taker and therefore ambitious.

This theory clearly does not replace the others but should be used to augment them. Note too that some studies have suggested that motivation is the main pointer to likely success in management.

Behaviour modification

With some understanding of the basic theories of motivation it is possible to apply them to motivate and hence modify the behaviour of personnel. This can be done using:

a. *Positive reinforcement,* that is, using praise, encouragement etc.

b. *Negative reinforcement,* that is, using criticism (which is removed when the cause of criticism is remedied).

c. *Extinction,* that is, ignoring errant behaviour such as showing off.

d. *Punishment.*

Generally (a) and (b) are to be recommended but in time personnel will take positive reinforcement in particular for granted and ignore it. The remedy is to apply (a) and (b) alternately in some fixed ratio.

Other combinations are, or course, possible and, for example, (a) and (b) could be alternated in equal proportions with occasional doses of (c), leaving (d) to be used only in exceptional circumstances.

Teacher expectancy effect

The teacher expectancy effect is based on the observation that students aware of the fact that the teacher considers them 'bright' tend to do better than they otherwise would if they are not actually exceptional. In addition, teachers tend to mark students they consider bright more favourably (perhaps we could call this 'teachers pet syndrome'). Thus we have a double barreled effect.

For the present discussion, however, we shall merely consider an *expectancy effect* for which we write

$$\text{Motivation} = (\text{Valence}) \times (\text{Expectancy})$$

where *valence* is the desire for marks (or in other spheres for $) and *expectancy* is the person's notion of the probability that he will obtain a certain mark (perhaps enhanced by the teacher or, just as likely, by knowledge of his own record).

This expectancy is of a first level outcome (obtaining certain marks) with a second level outcome expected to follow from the first outcome (such as approval by parents).

This theory emphasizes the different levels of motivation that will exist in different people and managers should, if possible, have some idea of the valence of their staff and, in addition, make some effort to enhance this by increasing their expectancy.

Morale and productivity

Surprisingly there is little mathematical correlation between morale levels and productivity and the coefficient of correlation between them is only 0.14 (see Sec. MR7 for an explanation of 'c.c.').

Some reason why this is so might be had by comparing a company with a highly 'engineered' plant to one with a 'country club' atmosphere. Clearly we would expect productivity to be higher in the first.

We run into the difficulty of the question "To what extent are morale and motivation related?" The moral, however, is that morale should be as high as possible (without going overboard) and that we should then focus on motivation using positive reinforcement and the like.

Applying motivational theory

To apply motivational theory we should set out to increase both intrinsic and extrinsic motivation:

a. To increase intrinsic motivation we should place emphasis on achievement involved in the job, attribute a measure of leadership to the doing of it, emphasize the prospects of career development and security and attempt to improve the job design, including occasional job enrichment.

b. To increase extrinsic motivation we should emphasize the money and other rewards, emphasize the participatory nature of the work (in part by participating a little), allow as much team management as possible and emphasize the need to compete with fellow workers and/or groups or companies.

c. In addition some priorities, for example safety, should be indicated in our efforts at motivation.

Frustration

We have discussed morale previously, noting that it may be related to motivation, or vice versa if relationship is taken to mean of the cause-effect type. Frustration may be caused by environmental factors beyond our control or personal limitations.

Frustration may also be caused by more subtle situations such as those involving conflicting goals. When there are two goals, for example, there are three possible situations:

1. Avoid - avoid, or two negative goals.
2. Approach - avoid, or one of the goals is desirable.
3. Approach - approach, if both of the goals are desirable.

Then if the negative goals (for example disliked tasks) are associated with a penalty for non-achievement each of the foregoing situations involves conflict.

In the motivation and management context, therefore, it is clear that in setting goals it cannot hurt to be aware of the potential goal conflict problems. These are not likely to be of the almost perfect dilemma type cited here, more likely some second goal will be a slight distraction, but at least the need for clear definition of goals with appropriate rewards is highlighted by considering cases (1) - (3).

Conclusion

The theories of motivation, behaviour modification, expectancy effect and goal frustration are both interesting and useful in management practice. Indeed knowledge of all these can be combined to potentially great effect.

MP8. Leadership and Group Performance

In the preceding section motivation theories were discussed and ways in which managers could apply these to obtain improved morale and productivity were suggested. In the present section productivity result variation as a function of management involvement, peer group loyalty and attitudes of both management and workers is considered.

Communication with management

Fig. MP2 shows the results of a study of the relationship between average performance (or productivity) and amount of contact with the group supervisor. Clearly relatively frequent and regular management contact improves productivity as we would expect.

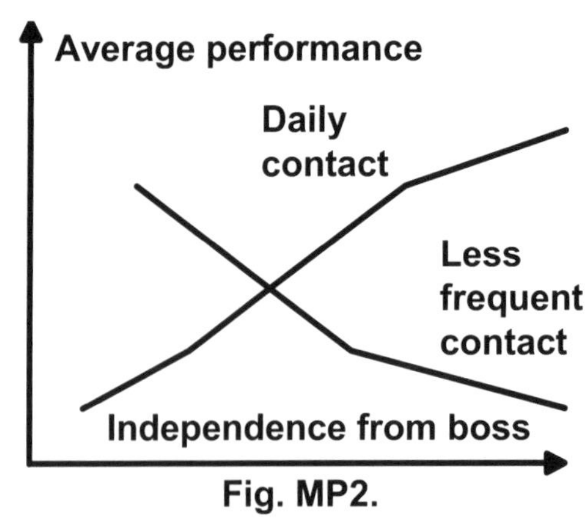

Fig. MP2.

Fig. MP3 shows the correlation between worker performance and group loyalty, indicating that productivity improves if group loyalty is high. In part this improvement results from the (necessary) emergence of 'team leadership'.

The study of Fig. MP3 also found that correlation between the proportion of workers who took their complaints to the boss and group loyalty took the same form (that shown).

In addition, the correlation between how easy the group found communication with the boss and group loyalty also took the same (ascending) form shown in Fig. MP3.

Fig. MP3. Performance and communication with boss v. group loyalty.

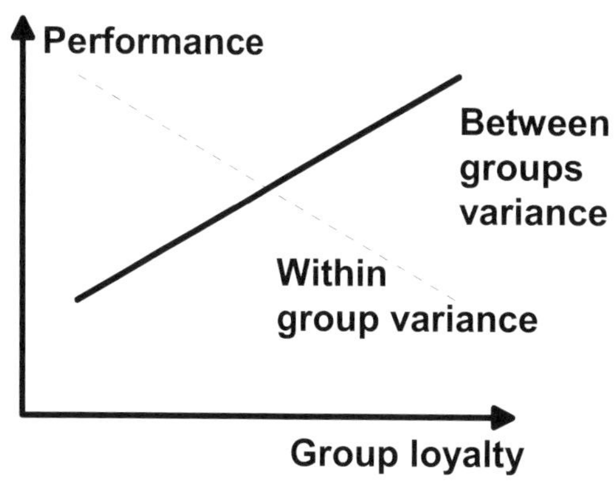

Effective communication (and hence loyalty) within the group and with the supervisor, therefore, both lead to improved productivity. In addition group loyalty improves communication with the supervisor, that is the factors of group loyalty, amount of supervisor communication, quality of supervisor communication and productivity are all interwoven in such a way as to suggest that if communication is optimized considerable improvements in productivity might result.

Expectancy and attitude

Fig. MP4.

Expected v. actual productivity

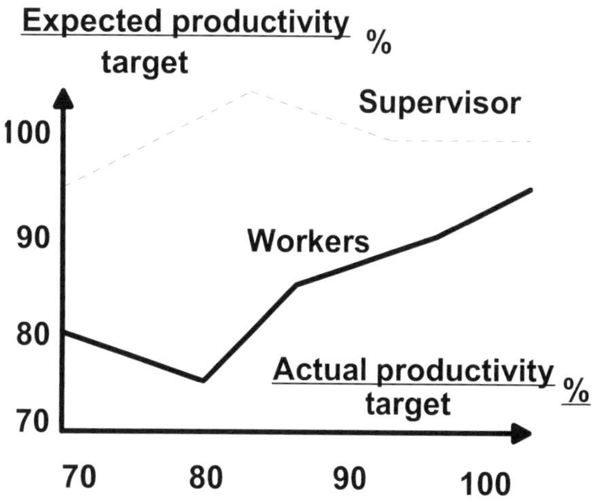

Fig. MP4 shows expected productivity compared to actual productivity for both the supervisor and the workers. Clearly the expectations of the supervisor are greater than those of the workers and are always fairly close to the target productivity.

The expectations of the workers, on the other hand, are for improvement when productivity is low and for slowing down when productivity is high and are perhaps, therefore, more realistic.

Unfortunately, however, there is no data from this study on the correlation between supervisor and worker expectations though this, of course, would depend on communications and, in any case, productivity variation is our main concern.

Fig. MP5 shows the results of a study of the effect of attitude of supervisor on productivity. There was a considerable spread in the results but there was sufficient correlation to support the finding that the more favourable attitude of the supervisor (to both the workers and the job) the greater the productivity, as we might expect.

Fig. MP5

Dependence of productivity on supervisor attitude.

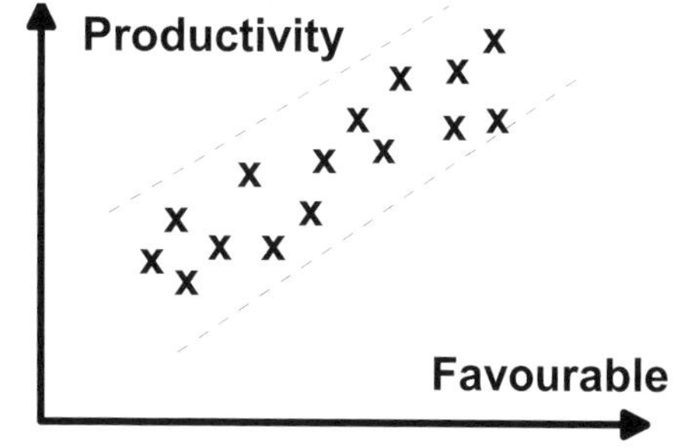

We might also expect that favourable supervisor attitude resulted in more favourable worker attitude and that the latter results in greater productivity.

Peer group loyalty

Fig. MP6 shows the relationship of peer group loyalty to productivity when motivation is towards accepting versus rejecting company goals. Clearly peer group loyalty towards company goals results in greater productivity as we would expect.

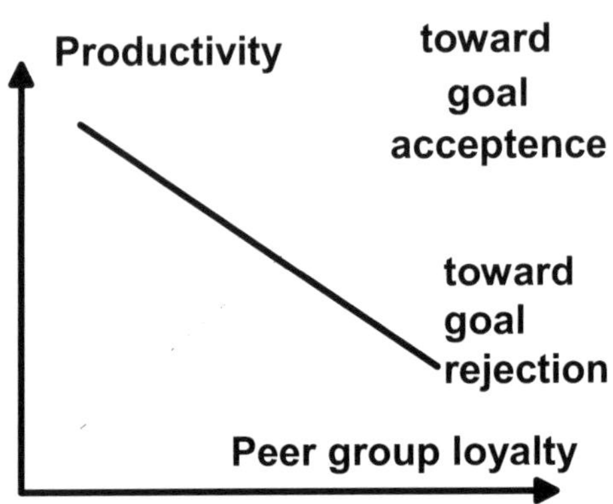

Fig. MP6
Loyalty towards company goals versus productivity

The results of Fig. MP6 are related to those of Fig. MP3, showing that group loyalty is a very important factor in productivity.

Conclusion

Besides those conclusions already made in the foregoing discussion, the following recommendations are suggested as worthwhile by the results of figs MP2 - 6:

1. There should be effective communication of productivity goals.
2. There should be thorough assessment of productivity results.
3. Groups or crews and tasks with low productivity should be identified.
4. Group loyalty should be encouraged and groups should be motivated to accept new staff and 'loners' in a group.
5. Leadership audits should be used.
6. Supervisors should exhibit favourable attitude and communicate frequently and regularly with their staff.
7. Group loyalty toward company goals should be sought.
8. Supervisors should make themselves freely available to staff with complaints and other feedback and make themselves easy to communicate with.

Generally, therefore, good leadership involving sufficient efficient communication of goals and team attitudes is likely to result in very considerable improvements in productivity.

It is also important, however, that measurements are made of productivity, group loyalty and management efficiency. The results will then be useful in identifying problems requiring correction and productivity results when favourable, for example, can be used as motivational information for supervisors and their groups.

MP9 Ancillary Issues

In the present section we consider the ancillary issues of wages and other benefits and safety and health, these respectively being motivational and security considerations. Such issues are a very important part of any discussion of management psychology.

Wage criteria

Criteria upon which wage rates may be based include the following:

1. Prevailing rates, applicable legislation and the cost of living.
2. Ability to pay and productivity of the company.
3. Whether work is done on flexitime, a compressed week, with RDO (rostered day off) or other basis.
4. Agreements with unions or individual agreements.
5. The requirements of the job, seniority or career path.

Job evaluation

Job evaluation might take into account such factors as:

1. Skill requirements, including experience, training and manual difficulty.
2. Knowledge requirements, including educational qualifications, experience, training and mental difficulty.
3. Responsibility for direction and safety of others.
4. Responsibility for materials and machines.
5. Working conditions and hazards.

Then weights can be attached to such factors and the weighted sum used as a guide to the level of remuneration appropriate.

Group incentives

Incentives which may be given to groups of workers include profit or other gains sharing and bonuses for productivity or methods improvements. Increasingly too workers are encouraged to participate in companies by becoming shareholders, for example by special options issues.

Management incentives

Special incentives given to management include bonuses, stock options, deferred compensation (in order to avoid tax) and perks such as company cars and other fringe benefits.

Benefits

The benefits, after wages, which may be given to workers include:

1. Overtime, holiday and sick pay.
2. Subsidized superannuation, safety insurance and life and/or health insurance.
3. Severance pay.
4. Leave loading
5. Cafeterias (at reduced prices), access to credit unions, moving expenses and recreational functions.
6. Purchase of company products at reduced prices.

Safety requirements

Legislation allows factory and health inspectors to check and report on business premises to ensure that safety regulations are satisfied.

The occupational health and safety act requires that accidents and illnesses of certain kinds should be reported. In addition, of course, companies should meticulously keep their own safety records.

Safety programs

Safety programs for large companies should be comprehensive and include such provisions as:

1. Statement of objectives and policies.
2. Details of organization of the program.
3. Persons responsible for the program such as medical officers, nurses and safety officers should be nominated.

4. Job safety analyses should be carried out for the various activities involved in the company operation.
5. Accidents should be fully investigated and analyzed.
6. Accident records should be kept and areas which are 'accident prone' should be identified (for example by using marked pins on a map of a large manufacturing plant).
7. Safety education and training programs.
8. Safety enforcement by nominated company officers.
9. First aid equipment should be kept.
10. The safety program should be disseminated through advertisements or articles in company magazines, notice boards etc.

Stress

As far as possible factors which increase stress should be minimized, for example:
1. Noise, smoke, heat, poor light and such factors.
2. Overcrowding.
3. Encouragement of group loyalty will help individuals cope with stress.
4. Communication of complaints regarding stress and factors causing it should be encouraged.

Managerial stress, of course, is increasingly a matter of concern and attendance at short courses in such areas might sometimes be worthwhile for many managerial staff.

Conclusion

There are many way, besides direct remuneration, in which companies can compensate both workers and management. In addition, proper safety programs and measures to reduce the stress of the working environment will contribute in the long run to company well being and profitability.

MP10. Management Leadership

Much discussion is had and many a course run on the somewhat intangible subject of management leadership. Some basic but useful observations can, however, be made on this subject. We begin with consideration of factors affecting the group which is to be managed, having noted the importance of group loyalty and communication with management in Sec. MP8.

Characteristics of a group

Characteristics of a group which a manager should take account of include common factors between its members, the organizational structure of the group (if any), the authority of particular members of the group and the group loyalty.

Such factors describe the internal nature of the group. Externally environmental factors which affect a group are the tasks assigned to it, the authority system assigning to it and the detailed organizational nature of the company to which the group belongs.

Finally, of course, it should be noted that any group usually has a leader and, if one is not appointed by management then the group will effectively find a leader on an informal basis.

Characteristics of a leader

Characteristics of a leader may include intelligence (which desirably is not greatly in excess of that of the group), social skills, a willingness to participate, drive and a need to achieve, and authority or 'power'.

Much of a leader's authority usually comes from appointment by persons higher in the organizational structure but whether a leader is convincing in the role, able to make good decisions and so on depends very much upon the nature of the individual.

Path-goal theory

The path-goal theory of leadership is based upon the expectancy model of motivation (see Sec. MP7) and recognizes four kinds of leader style or behaviour:

1. Directive leadership.
2. Supportive leadership.
3. Participative leadership.
4. Goal or achievement oriented leadership.

The theory then postulates that particular styles of leadership are more appropriate for particular assignments, for example:

a. (1) is good for ambiguous tasks but poor when clearly defined tasks are involved.
b. (2) is good when difficult tasks are involved.
c. (4) is good when 'one-off' tasks need to be done.

In addition, however, we would expect that some measure of (3) is always appropriate as the findings of Sec. MP8 suggest (as do countless other findings in the research literature).

Management participation

Management participation, as we have just noted once again, is beneficial and can be informal with individuals or groups or formal via committees, suggestion plans, 'quality circles', collective bargaining or regular meetings with group representatives.

Discipline

Discipline can be negative via the 'big stick' approach or, less drastically, criticism. It can also be positive, that is involving encouragement, or a combination of approaches may be used (see Sec. MP7). Useful recommendations on the subject of discipline include:

1. Disapproval should be of the error, not the person.
2. Discipline should be by way of a consistently applied and clear policy.
3. The punishment should fit the misdemeanor and there should be the options of oral warning, 'noted', written warning, suspension, discharge etc.
4. Right of representation and appeal should be advised and allowed.

Union effectiveness

When disputes arise, of course, unions may become involved. The effectiveness of unions as a function of their size is illustrated in Fig. MP7, showing that unions with about 3000 members are of considerable effectiveness whilst very small unions are relatively ineffective.

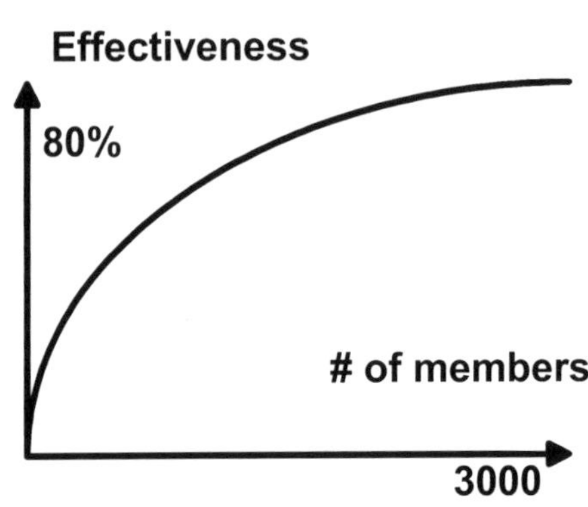

Fig. MP7
Union effectiveness versus size.

When personnel disputes are 'taken to the union' the responsible manager should negotiate in the first instance with the union representative in the company and, should industrial disputes be threatened, collective bargaining processes are needed to minimize or eliminate problems.

Leadership techniques

Any approach to leadership will involve a style which may be autocratic, democratic or laissez-faire, or one of the approaches of path-goal theory described above. It will also involve leader attitudes which may be those of empathy, objectivity or self-knowledge/confidence and, as shown in Fig. MP5, attitude is an important leadership factor.

Then two common leadership techniques are:

1. *Confidence building.* Here, after an initial orientation session, continued follow up is used to build confidence and a feeling of achievement, security and self-worth.
2. *Zeal building.* Here emphasis is based on inspiration and motivation. In this approach, in contrast to (1), the leader concentrates on strengthening himself, not the group (though it may not be realized by the group).

There are many other leadership techniques, of course, but the contrast between (1) and (2) is worth noting.

Conclusion

There is more to leadership than meets the eye and factors such as the nature of the group to be led (to which a leader can contribute), attitude, style or approach and participation are all important. In particular the path-goal theory described is useful in that it suggests that changes in leadership style are appropriate for different tasks.

MP11. Management Communication and Control

Superficially management communicates through the organization structures, that is, the types of networks illustrated in Secs BP5, 6 and 10. As we have seen in this chapter, however, there is much more to it than that and style, attitude and the like are important. In this section we include discussion of some basic principles of *direction* (or of communicating orders) and of the processes needed to control the resulting activities.

Principles of direction

Important principles for the direction of activities include consideration of:

1. The *purpose* of direction should be to make particular contributions to the objectives of the organization. This objective should be in harmony with the objectives of those carrying out the direction.

2. The *process* by which direction is given should involve each person having one superior for the purposes of objective supervision (as distinct from personal supervision whilst the direction is carried out).
3. The *efficiency* of communication which will depend upon its clarity, whether it gains attention and upon the standard and style of communication of the direction.
4. Whether the directions are specific or general.
5. Whether the directions are written or oral.
6. The appropriate degree of formality of the direction. Other than in the armed services, for example, orders will tend to be relatively informal, for example, "Suppose you do this."
7. The timing of the directions and whether they should be confidential.

Many other factors could be included but these are enough to demonstrate that just how orders are given is worth a little thought.

Control processes

Once directions have been given the resulting activities must be controlled and for this some of the following will be required:

1. Performance standards must be established appropriate to the type of activity involved.
2. Objective measurement methods for performance should be chosen.
3. Objective and prompt reporting of performance results should be established.
4. Reports should be audited internally and sometimes externally as well.
5. Deviations from required standards should be corrected.

Such control 'cycles' may be required for dealing with:

a. Physical standards of products.
b. Productivity of a manufacturing plant.
c. Scheduling of a construction project.
d. Costs and/or revenue from production/sales.
e. Inventory
f. Staff.

In dealing with inventory, for example, use is likely to be made of computer based information systems. In dealing with schedules, on the other hand, techniques such as CPM may be used and these are discussed later in the text.

Delegation

Directions or orders may take the form of delegation. This is a more general form of direction than issuance of orders to undertake a specific activity and involves authorizing somebody else to do the latter.

Delegation may be detailed or may pass on broad authority and a 'degree' of authority or control may be delegated, for example to an inexperienced manager. With such delegees, however, the responsibilities of direction and control then rest.

Conclusion

Direction and control procedures are important in management of companies, projects, individual activities and individual personnel.

In the present chapter we are concerned with the psychological aspects of management whilst in other chapters, such as Project Planning and Control (PP) or Operations Research (OR) more mathematical procedures for organizing and controlling activities are discussed.

MP12. An Example IQ Test and Real IQ

The following is a very short (6 minutes) example IQ test given by the author as a prelude to a full test, the example test having the answers filled in. This and the full test which followed it (and including a couple of other question types) was first used by the author over 20 years ago on a group of 'possible' engineering students and reasonable results were obtained. The full test was also short (15 minutes whereas 30 minutes is usual) and readers are not insulted by including it here. For those interest it was based on the well known book *Know Your Own IQ* by Hans Eysenck which I still see in the business shelves of bookshops.

Example test

In each question a missing number is to be deduced according to some logical arithmetic operation or sequence. In these example questions the answers are the numbers following a question mark and underlined. As part of a full test the time allowed for these 10 questions would be about 6 minutes.

Find the missing numbers:

[1] 6 7 9 13 21 ?37

[2] 447 (366) 254
262 (?512) 521

[3] 4 7 9 11 14 15 19 ?19

[4] 2 10 6
3 9 3

1 3 ?1

[5]

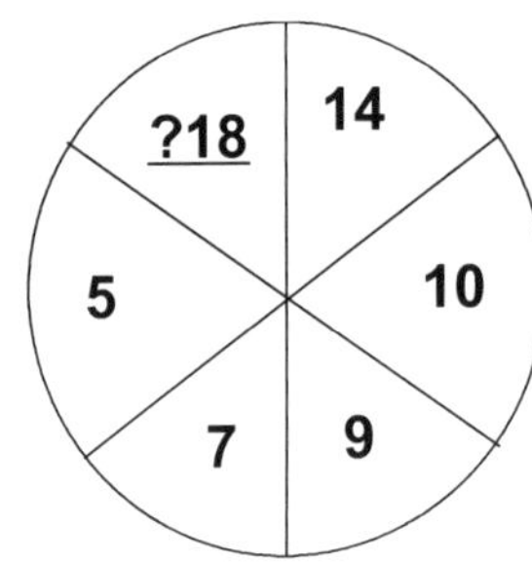

[6] 279 242 205 168 ?131

[7] 13 (78) 12
11 (?55) 10

[8] 126 62 30 14 ?6

[9]

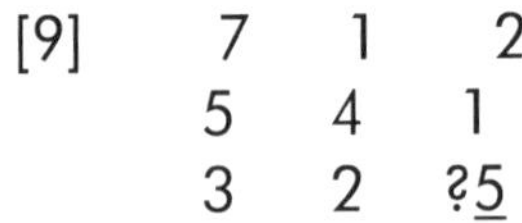

7 1 2
5 4 1
3 2 ?5

[10]

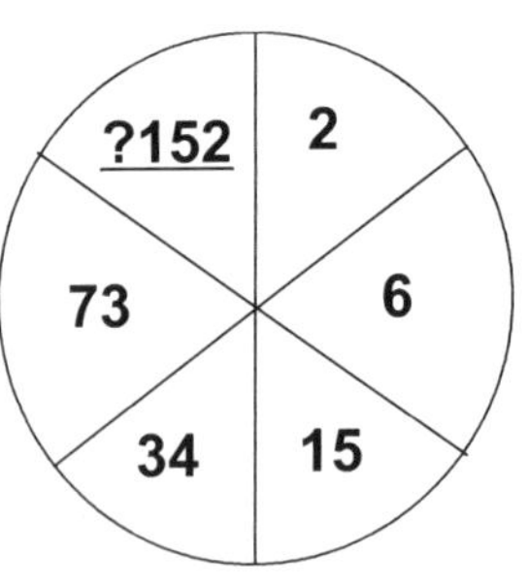

Keys to answers:
[1] The increments double.
[2] Middle number is twice the difference of the others.
[3] Alternate sequences (+3, +2, +1, +0) and (+2, +3, +4).
[4] 3rd # in row = 2nd - 2 x 1st.
[5] Diagonally opposite number is double.
[6] Decrements of -37.
[7] Middle number is half the product of the others.
[8] Next # = half x last # -1
[9] Sum of rows = 10
[10] Going around next # = 2 x last + 2 (then + 3, + 4 etc.).

Real IQ

The author invented 'Real IQ', which is calculated as

Real IQ = IQ(18) – a(disease/injuries)
+ b(years of learning since 18)
+ c(creativity) - d[(age -18) if over 18]

Here IQ(18) is that one develops, all going OK, by age 18 as a result of hereditary factors and education and 'a', 'b', 'c' and 'd' are constants, the values of which are discussed in a number of my recent books, and most recently *The Brainwashed* (2015) and *Human Intelligence, Learning & Behaviour* (2016 – with R. Sinclair & E. Fear).

This emphasizes that IQ can be improved by continued learning after all too many years at school (enough to decrease 'peak IQ' by 18 in some cases).

Newton, Bell and Edison are given as examples of people with high real IQ in the aforementioned book. Another might be Vladimir Putin, perhaps the smartest spy in history, whereas Kim Philby (who my father met in Cambridge), is now thought #1.

Some of the lowest IQ people, on the other hand include people 'hooked' on the 'pokies', gadjets very comparable with Harvard Psychologist B.F. Skinner's 'Skinner Boxes' in which 'enboxed' rats very quickly learnt to press a lever faster and faster to gain a food reward.

MP References

Beatty, R.H. *The Resume Kit*, 4th edn. Wiley, New York NY. 2000.
Belcher, D.W. *Compensation Administration,* 3rd edn. Prentice-Hall, Englewood Cliffs NJ. 1974.
Beach, D.S. *Personnel, The Management of People at Work,* 5th edn. MacMillan, New York. 1985.
Broom, L.H., Jones, F.L., McDonnell, P., Williams, T. *The Inheritance of Inequality.* Routledge & Kegan Paul, London. 1980.
Buchanan, J.M. and Tullock, G. *The Calculus of Consent.* Univ. Michigan Press, Don Mills, Canada. 1962.
Cohen, D. *Essential Psychology*. Bloomsbury, London. 1994.
Dabscheck, B. and Nilan, J. *Industrial Relations in Australia.* Allen & Unwin, Sydney. 1981.
Durkheim, E. *The Rules of Sociological Method,* 8th edn. The Free Press, New York. 1964.
Ekstrom, R.B. *Measurement, Technology and Individuality in Education.* Jowsey-Bass, San Francisco. 1983 (No. 17 of 'New Directions for Testing and Measurement')
Farkes, C.M. and Wetlaufer, S. The ways Chief Executive Officers lead. *Harvard Business Review,* May-June. 1996.
Flippo, KE.B. *Personnel Management,* 6th edn. McGraw-Hill, New York. 1988.
Ford, G.W., Hearn, J.M. and Lansbury, R.D. *Australian Labour Relations: Readings,* 3rd edn. MacMillan, Melbourne. 1980.
Hall, D.T. and Goodale, J.G. *Human Resource Management.* Scott/Foresman, Glenview IL. 1986.
Hampton, D.R., Summer, C.E. and Webber, R.A. *Organizational Behaviour and the Practice of Management,* 5th edn. Scott/Foresman, Glenview IL. 1987.

Hilmer, F.G. *When the Luck Runs Out: the Future of Australians at Work.* Harper & Row, Sydney. 1985.
Jackson, R.V. *The Population History of Australia.* McPhee Gribble/Penguin, Melbourne. 1988.
Jencks, C. *Inequality.* Peregrine/Penguin, Harmondsworth. 1975.
Lansbury, R.D. and Gilmour, P. *Organizations: an Australian Perspective.* Longman Cheshire, Melbourne. 1977.
Law, K.S. Estimating the dollar value contribution of human resource intervention programs: some comments on the Brogden utility equation. *Aust. J. Management*, vol. 20, no. 2. 1995.
Lien, A.J. *Measurement and Evaluation of Learning,* 3rd edn. Brown, Dubuque IL. 1976.
Lindzey, G., Hall, C.S. and Thompson, R.P. *Psychology,* 2nd edn. Worth Publishers, New York NY. 1978. + Carsrud, K.B. et al., *Study Guide for Lindzey, Hall, Thompson: Psychology,* 2nd edn. Worth Publishers, New York NY. 1978.
Kirk, R.E. (ed.) *Statistical Issues: A Reader for the Behavioural Sciences.* Brooks/Cole Publ. Co., Monterey CA. 1972.
Likert, R. *New Patterns of Management.* McGraw-Hill, New York. 1961.
Mann, L.. *Social Psychology.* Wiley, Sydney. 1969.
Mohr GA, *The Pretentious Persuaders, A Brief History & Science of Mass Persuasion,* Horizon Publishing Group, Sydney, 2012 (edn 1), 2014 (edn 2).
Mohr GA, *The History and Psychology of Human Conflicts,* Horizon Publishing Group, Sydney (2014).
Mohr GA, Richard Sinclair, & Edwin Fear, *The Evolving Universe: Redshift, Relativity, and Life From Space,* Xlibris, Sydney, 2014.
Mohr GA, Richard Sinclair & Edwin Fear, *Human Intelligence, Learning & Behaviour,* Inspiring Publishers, Canberra (2017).
Morgan, C.T., King, R.A. and Robinson, N.M. *Introduction to Psychology,* 6th edn. McGraw-Hill, Tokyo. 1979.
Pidgeon, D. and Yates, A. *An Introduction to Educational Measurement,* Routledge & Kegan Paul, London. 1968.
Pigors, P. and Myers, C.A. *Personnel Administration: a Point of View and a Method,* 9th edn. McGraw-Hill, New York. 1981.
Plowman, D., Deery, S. and Fisher, C. *Australian Industrial Relations.* McGraw-Hill, Sydney. 1980.
Robertson, I. *Sociology,* 2nd edn. Worth, New York. 1981.
Robson, C. *Experiment Design and Statistics in Psychology.* Penguin, Harmondsworth. 1973.
Tajfel, H. and Fraser, C. *Introducing Social Psychology.* Penguin, Harmondsworth. 1986.
Townsend, P. *The Concept of Poverty.* Heinemann, London. 1970.
Vernon, P.E. *Intelligence and Attainment Tests.* Univ. of London Press, London. 1960.
Weiss, M.L. and Mann, A.E. *Human Biology and Behaviour: an Anthropological Perspective,* 2nd edn. Little Brown & Co., Boston MA. 1987.
Windshuttle, K. *Unemployment.* Pelican, Harmondsworth. 1979.
______. *Course Evaluations,* Res. Report `3, Learning Resources Network (LERN), Manhattan KA. 1988.

MARKET RESEARCH (MR)

A straw vote only shows which way the hot air blows. O. Henry.

Marketing is the key to success in many a business, whether on a small or large scale. The first step of marketing must be to estimate the demand of a particular market, often through market research (MR). Then production and distribution must be designed to meet this demand whilst further marketing efforts are aimed at maintaining or enlarging market share. The present chapter is a brief introduction to market research and marketing and also introduces such topics as the *psychology of attitudes*, an area of study especially relevant to today's marketing techniques.

MR1. Introduction to marketing

At the outset of operations of any new company, management must define the purpose or *raison d'étre* of the company, that is the products that it aims to deal with. It is then necessary to make these products available by distributing them to supply points and, of course, the 'audience' must be informed of the availability of the products.

Market research

The principal purposes of marketing research are:

1. To feel out the market for a new product proposal.
2. Continuous or regular monitoring of customer views which may involve ad hoc studies or sampling, surveys and analyses.
3. To measure the effectiveness of marketing efforts.

Marketing management

Marketing management must be responsible for dealing with:

1. The product range and its packaging.
2. Prices and discounts.
3. Advertising through the media, whether by TV, radio, newspapers, the mail, letter boxing, signs etc. or some mix of such media.
4. Constraints set by funding limitations.
5. Target company profits which will depend greatly on the success of marketing efforts.

Marketing, therefore, involves a broad range of activities and takes up a large part of the budget of many companies and organizations, in some cases being the major reason for market share.

Marketing audits

Sometimes marketing audits, that is independent review of marketing operations or part thereof by senior management or consultants, are important. The purpose of these is to examine what is being done, make appraisals of this activity and to make recommendations on further marketing effort.

Marketing history

The image of a company and/or its products many have been built up over many years and it is sometimes worthwhile to consider whether this image should be maintained or whether a change is worthwhile. Three examples of such image might well be:

1. The hard working image which the Japanese enjoy, along with a reputation for product quality, quite the reverse of the situation in the 1960s.
2. The 'laid back' image of the US or Australian products, for example on the beer market, giving rise to a 'boozy' image in the case of Australians.
3. The 'class' image of products like the Dunhill range.

It is important in marketing, therefore, to decide what line of approach to take, tailoring one's message to the likely customers.

Conclusion

Company names don't need to be mentioned as examples of marketing or products which would barely exist without efficient almost saturation marketing campaigns which never let up. Marketing is also important, of course, in politics and in many other areas and, indeed, it may do much more than we realize to shape our lives and, more especially, those of our children. Whether this is a good thing or not is an important question, but there is no doubt that modern marketing techniques are an important instrument of change, hopefully for the better more often than not.

MR2. The Marketing Environment

In developing marketing operations it is important to consider the environment in which these are to be conducted as there are many environmental factors which cannot be influenced by marketing and these act as constraints which limit the potential marketing efforts. Some of these factors include:

1. Legal restrictions.
2. Community ethics and morals.
3. The economic system of the country of operation upon which income levels and distribution may depend, particularly disposable income.
4. The psychology and conditioning of the society which may play a part in individual attitudes.
5. The sociology of the community which may influence group attitudes.
6. The cultural nature of the society and, in turn, its interests and pursuits.
7. The demography of the population which determines the *retail gravitation* and hence the best product supply points.
8. Available distribution channels upon which the product distribution system may be based.

Clearly such factors are important considerations and careful consideration of them will reap long term rewards.

Market models

A key factor in developing marketing operations is the competitors in the market place and consideration of which of the basis economic market models shown in Table MR1 most nearly applies is worthwhile.

In case (a) entry is unrestricted but must be at the market price so that profits will be limited and the large number of competitors eliminates the possibility of concerted action to set prices. Examples of this situation include agricultural products or many raw materials. For such products there are considerable variations in production, price and profits and government intervention is sometimes necessary to cope with droughts and other problems.

Table MR1

Market model	# producers	Product	Entry
(a) pure (perfect) competition	many	homogeneous	unrestricted
(b) monopolistic competition	many	differentiated	unrestricted
(c) pure oligopoly	few	homogeneous	restricted
(d) differential oligopoly	few	differentiated	restricted
(e) monopoly	one	n/a	restricted

In case (b), that of monopolistic competition, product differentiation allows some latitude in prices able to be set by the producer and competition is via price and advertising. The retail industry is perhaps the best example of this situation.

In case (c), that of pure oligopoly, economies of scale necessary in some industries results in room for few competitors. In this situation prices are limited by the homogeneity of the products but there are often price consensuses or agreements to maintain prices at a profitable level. The raw materials industries sometimes exemplify this situation.

In case (d), that of differentiated oligopoly, price competition is sometimes fierce and companies are sometimes forced to the wall by price wars. It is here that marketing efforts tend to be greatest and non-price competition may be through brand advertising, product improvements and innovations etc. Examples of this area include the motor car industry, cigarettes or household detergents, though restrictions on cigarette advertising have altered the situation of late.

Finally, in case (e), that of monopoly, there is complete company control over production quantities and price of sale and hence profit levels. Examples include government controlled industries, such as gas and electricity or rail services in many countries though privatization of these has occurred to a considerable extent recently.

Whether a business fits wholly or partly into one of these categories, therefore, is important. Whether this be in an international market or simply a shop 'down the road', the way in which a market may be shared may be much the same except for the question of scale.

Conclusion

In marketing the nature of the community to which marketing efforts are directed may be important. Equally, the nature of the competition in the market place is important and care should be taken to identify the type of marketing situation which is likely to exist.

MR3. Preliminary Marketing Plans

Whether marketing is for a company, a political organization or for the purposes of publicizing social or environmental legislation, for example, the product concept must be carefully defined and a marketing brief established. This should include such details as:

1. The overall market as it stands and any segmentation of that market, for example by age, gender, socio-economic stratification (for example by way of income, education, occupation or location), personality and buyer behaviour (for example impulse buying) etc.
2. Important competitors in the market (at present) and other possible newcomers to the market.
3. The nature of the company and its products (initially).
4. Present and potential customers.
5. Distribution channels.
6. Advertising and promotion strategies.
7. Pricing policies.
8. Economic planning such as break-even production quantities.

Armed with such information it is possible to make judgments as to the viability of initial plans and modify any decisions which may have only been based on preliminary guesses.

Market analysis

From this basis (the preliminary marketing plan) preliminary market research can now commence, beginning by analyzing the market to determine:

1. How large is the market and at what rate is it likely to grow ?
2. Is the market segmented and, if so, how ? Is this likely to alter ?
3. What is the proposed company's share of the market or segment thereof and what is the share of competitors.
4. What are the key success factors in this market such as quality or diversity ?
5. What pricing, packaging and distribution is appropriate ?
6. What advertising and sales pitch is to be used ?
7. How may the company's market share be increased ? Where are the most likely new customers and is it possible to take market share from competitors ?

Such factors will help shape and refine the marketing policy to be used and greatly increase the chances of success.

Analysis of competitors

It is also important, of course, to study the competition, when such factors as the following should be considered:

1. Who are the competitors ? What are their strongest and weakest points ?
2. Compare the product quality, price, distribution, advertising and promotion of others in the market. How should one differ in approach ?
3. What are the strategies, resources and future products likely for the competitors ?
4. What is the history of the competition and thus what is it likely to do in the future ?

Then, given a knowledge of the competition it is easier to form marketing plans which will obtain the desired market share remembering, though, the financial constraints that must always be attached to such plans.

Self analysis

In addition a little introspection is useful in forming marketing plans, when a little thought should be given to such matters as

1. Desired market share ?
2. Company resources, finances and history. Are the plans in line ?
3. Objectives and strategy to get there ? What resources will be needed ?
4. Strengths and weaknesses of the company and/or its products.
5. Where and how much profit is to be made ?
6. What is the company/product image ? Can it be improved ?

Consideration of these and any other factors that will result in the company being a better player in the market, particularly building a lasting image that can be advertised with minimum effort.

Product analysis

Analysis of the product to be sold includes study of product quality, features, pricing and distribution. Important factors are whether the product is discretionary or a necessity and the sales force, advertising and other promotion to be used.

Preliminary recommendations

After consideration of these factors a preliminary recommendation should be made along the lines:

a. The current situation is - - - -
b. Key market factors are - - - -
c. The options are - - - -
d. The best plan is - - - -

Conclusion

Clearly even a preliminary marketing plan requires a good deal of work. Table MR2 summarizes some of the techniques which may be used to obtain data upon which more detailed marketing plans can be based.

Table MR2 Collection of Marketing Plan Information

Sampling:

Cheaper and quicker than a 100 per cent
A higher quality survey because of a smaller sample size
Sample size depends on degree of precision
Accuracy and power of the forecast required
Use past to estimate the future but gauge importance

Terms of reference

information required
time scale
budget
sources available
scope of survey
decisions to be made from survey

Conducting the survey

unstructured - uses only interview guide to analyze
useful for formulating and checking ideas
can omit significant questions and encourage irrelevancies
semi-structures - standard questions cope with most responses
ease of tabulation/analysis
ease of recording
questionnaire covers all points required
structured questionnaire
only for very simple information

Design questionnaire with:

space for easy recording of answers
stimulating and orientating early answers
important questions early on

Method of contact

Requirements of method chosen:
collect information speedily
produce information cheaply
cope with large volumes of information
generate quantitative information
produce new ideas
ask complex questions
probe in depth
give due weight to expert informants
protect against bias
check validity of the answers
explain divergence of opinions
ensure anonymity/confidentiality of individual opinions

Personnel interview
expensive
slow (1 hour per person)
answers can be checked
probing/follow up questions

Telephone interview:
speed
lower cost
small volumes of information
no complex questions
avoid being nuisance
difficult to check answers
difficult to establish rapport
relieves salesmen of routine tasks

Postal questionnaire:

low cost
low unpredictable response rate (5 to 10 %)
follow-up mailings
can provide blanket coverage
no interview control
sensitive information will not be given
only a few questions to be asked

Group discussions:
need six to ten people

MR4. Detailed Marketing Plans

Detailed marketing plans require more information on the market place, consumer motivations and buying patterns. This allows production and price targets to be set and a distribution chain to be chosen or developed. Then marketing policies must be adopted, for example *push strategies* which concentrate on availability of products, or *pull strategies* which promote the product in order to attract buyers. Then a marketing budget must be decided.

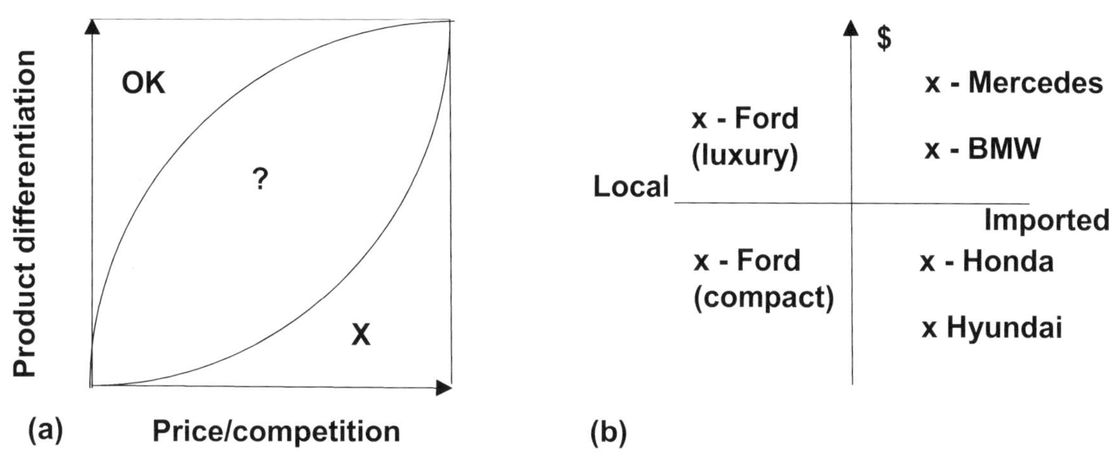

Fig. MR1 Product differentiation in the market

Fig. MR1 shows two simple ways of illustrating product positioning in the market place, here emphasizing product differentiation by way of features, quality, price, perceived value, image, reputation, reliability and prestige. In (a) when the product is highly differentiated and relatively cheap then all should be well but there is a transition zone in which outcomes are less certain.

Then in (b) Mercedes and BMW cars, for example, clearly have a loyal following whilst Hyundai, for example, occupy the bottom end of the market price wise. The point then, of course, is that Hyundai and Mercedes are not really competitors for market share, an important factor in estimating possible share.

Customer analysis

In analyzing the customers targeted by a product such factors as the following should be considered:

1. Sensitivity of customers to price changes and receptivity to advertising and promotional campaigns.
2. The types of shops these customers go to and the types of products they buy, for example do they buy well known products usually ?
3. The age and gender of customers for the product.
4. What knowledge do the customers have of the type of product ? What features and aspects of the product are they interested in ?

A knowledge of such factors is, of course, one of the most crucial factors in any marketing exercise.

Distribution analysis

Should distribution be by direct sales, manufacturer's representatives, distributors, wholesalers, mail order, vending machines or other? What profit margins should be allowed to the retailer to provide motivation to sell the product for you ? What advantages over competitors can be gained by better distribution?

Pricing policy

Price should be set within a tolerance, for example between the short or long term break even price and the perceived value of the product. Then an initial price can be set but plans should be made for future increases or decreases.

Financial analysis of production should include estimation of fixed costs, variable costs and projected revenue, break even production values etc.

Advertising and promotional strategy analysis

Analysis and planning of advertising should include consideration of such factors as:

1. The target audience: where are they, what age, are they married? What is their income, education, discretionary income? What type of suburb, town, city or region do they live in?
2. What medium should be used: TV, radio, newspaper, magazines, mail, flyers, salesmen, phone, movies, hoardings etc.
3. What short and long term effects are anticipated (presumably increased sales)?
4. What short and long term budget for promotion is allowed?

Obviously separation of long and short term targets is important and, for example, long term advertising budgets may be planned simply to maintain sales at a certain level, rather than initiate them.

Final marketing plan

Then the final marketing plan should include:

1. A summary of the key points in the plan.
2. A statement of the company's strengths and weaknesses.
3. A statement of the company's short and long term objectives.
4. A product strategy and rationale which is consistent with (2) and (3).
5. Demonstration that the plan is economically viable.

Recommended strategies and rationales for: (a) pricing policy,
(b) distribution, and (c) promotion.

Conclusion

A final marketing plan will be an important document which will do much to determine success or failure of product promotion.

Very often 'secondary' means of promotion might include T shirts, key rings, use of product in movies (by actors), spruikers and sales by subsidiary organizations, for example Coke via McDonald's and Pepsi via Pizza Hut.

Other aspects of primary promotion, for example through TV advertising, are the use of persons or organizations of repute to be associated with a product by endorsing it.

Finally, Table MR3 shows a check list of various types of advertising media and some of the funding, strategy and effectiveness considerations of a detailed marketing plan. In particular the importance of measuring the effectiveness of advertising should be noted as cost-effectiveness and tailoring advertising costs to a budget are necessary.

Table MR3. Advertising check list.

Types of media

- newspapers
- trade papers
- television
- radio
- cinema
- subscription journals
- business supplements
- posters
- placards
- direct mail
- exhibitions
- educational campaigns
- export journals
- institute publications

Reason for use:

- changes opinions and attitudes - level of` change depends on frequency and quality
- market share depends on opinions of product
- significantly improves level of sales closings (especially where no regular customer contact)
- reduces cost of selling - if adequate frequency
- advertising in well advertised market increases cost of selling

Allocation of funds:

- existing production capacity
- saturation point where resources become limited or expensive
- rate of market response to extra sales and marketing effort
- future market growth potential
- use contribution figures after direct costs instead of sales figures
- use true gross profit to net profit monetary values instead of % figures (relieves the considerable confusion created thereby)
- cost product groups down to net profit contribution (show marketing support costs in each group)

Media strategy

Is the market horizontal (everybody) or vertical (selective) ?

Where the primary objective of a press campaign is to enhance the reputation of the advertiser, large spaces in horizontal media are most likely to succeed.

When the primary objective is inquiries, small spaces in vertical media are usually more appropriate, particularly where a reader reply service is operated by the publisher.

Where advantages are in the price/ delivery/quality areas, a generalized customer-benefit approach is appropriate

Aim:

- to make advertising work harder and and more effectively
- to use professional and creative people
- assume you know your present and customers
- don't use a publication or program just because you like it
- don't approach advertising with preconceived ideas
- don't produce advertising that just pleases your boss
- remember it is the effects of advertising that are most important - these must be measured

MR5. Advertising and Public Relations

The purpose of advertising may be described as to 'persuasively communicate information (concerning a product or service) to its market.' This involves:

1. Market research
2. A creative brief
3. Visualization of the context of the advertisements
4. Writing of advertising copy
5. Art work
6. Purchase of media 'space'
7. Measurement of the penetration and effectiveness of the advertising

In particular, some market research to determine the likely effectiveness of an advertising campaign is worthwhile, even on the crudest basis, before funds are finally committed. Moreover, test marketing in a small area is also a possibility that should be considered.

Public relations

Public relations is a concern related to advertising but with a broader scope which may include:

1. Existing and potential customers.
2. Shareholders and other sources of capital (such as banks).
3. Employees.
4. Legislators, government organizations.
5. Pressure on the media for good comment about the company and/or its products.
6. Press releases, personal briefings.
7. In-house journals, meetings etc.
8. 'Events' which may include sport and other activities with which the company's name is associated.

Such public relations activities are often cost free and are complementary to advertising efforts.

Audience measurement

Measurement of audience size and type for a given medium is important but should also include in the case of magazine advertisements, for example, data on the 'level of reading' of the audience or whether particular pages such as sports pages are read or browsed (this is sometimes referred to as 'page traffic'). Hence the readership of an advertisement may not even remotely resemble the circulation of the publication that contains it.

TV audiences are measured by syndicating polling organizations whilst radio audiences are usually estimated by sampling via phone canvassing. The results, however, are important and do much to influence the prices charged for advertising.

A basic case study

A useful anecdotal example of advertising on a small scale to which any reader can relate is the following: the owner of a hair dressing and beauty salon in an outer suburb of a large city approached an advertising consultant for advice having:

a. Placed a $1500 advertisement in Vogue magazine with disappointing results.

b. The consultant suggested the objectives of advertising be defined, resulting in the information:

(i) Only from 3 to 5 new perms per week were required to fill idle time.

(ii) These were required on the quiet days, Monday and Tuesday.

(iii) The salon was in a small shopping centre in which only local clients could be expected.

(iv) The target audience was women.

(v) The advertising budget was 10 to 20% of the estimated sales increase of about $250, giving a figure of $25 to $50 per week.

The question was then what to say and how to say it ?

The answer was clearly along the lines

Special offer ! Monday and Tuesday only.

which could be placed in the local press as well as advertised on the shop window.

The alternative of letter boxing was briefly considered but decided to be too expensive and the local press was used for a small weekly ad. Whereas it was estimated that the original Vogue advertisement would have only reached from 2 to 3 people in the local area a $25 ad. in the local papers reached 22,000 homes every week !

Conclusion

This simple example illustrates the following points:

1. Estimate the increase in sales required, say as a result of slack capacity.
2. Determine when this increase is required.
3. Determine the location of the potential customers.
4. Determine the nature of the audience.
5. Determine the advertising budget.
6. Decide upon the message to be advertised.
7. Decide upon the medium for the message upon the basis of locality, target audience, budget etc.

Then, if such steps are followed sensibly, it will sometimes be fairly obvious how and where to advertise.

MR6. Market Research

The purpose of market research is to collect data upon which to base marketing decisions which may range from ad hoc decisions on how to market a new product to fine tuning the operational routine for long term advertising of a product. In the following section some of the stages of a market research campaign and the techniques that may be employed in these stages are discussed.

Stages of and techniques for market research

[1] Problem awareness and conceptualization. This may include monitoring of trade press, appraisal of current marketing practice, feedback from marketing efforts and 'related-area' reading in newspapers etc.

[2] Hypothesizing and qualitative problem refinement. This may include:

a. Group discussions
b. Motivational research
c. Unstructured interviews
d. Recorded observations
e. Laboratory experiments
f. Consumer 'clinics'

[3] Validation and quantification of marketing program. This may include:

a. Surveys
b. Retail audits
c. Consumer panels
d. Mass observation
e. Test marketing

These alternative means of measurement of the effectiveness of a campaign are discussed in the remainder of this section.

Market surveys

Market surveys are to determine the situation in a market at present, the performance of the competitors in the market and likely future trends. This may involve:

1. Collecting existing data ('desk research').
2. Collecting new data such as official figures such as trade statistics.
3. Usually a census of part of the relevant population is conducted.
4. Structured questionnaires may be used and the results collated to provide a final report.
5. Reports should include details of the sample, the time and the method by which the survey was conducted.

Sampling

Sampling may be by characteristics such as gender or variable features such as weight where matters of diet are concerned, for example. Some of the simple procedures of selection commonly used include:

1. Random sampling using random numbers, for example when the sample size is 1,000 out of a total population of 100,000 then the chance of selection is 1/100.
2. Systematic sampling, for example every n^{th} person is chosen, for example from the phone book.
3. Stratified sampling where a quota for each stratum of the population, for example for middle and low incomes, is set.
4. Cluster sampling. This simply involves choosing a street at random, for example, and then interviewing everybody in it.

Retail audits

These involved regularly checking stock levels at selected sites to give a measure of the effectiveness of distribution and sales for these sites.

Consumer panels

These are representative groups of people who provide continuous data, for example via a diary provided for this purpose. This approach is often used to test brand loyalty and switching.

Accuracy

If we are seeking data on population age distribution, for example, the preferred source would be birth records but generally verbal data is gathered for such purposes. This may involve *bias* $x_{av} = E(x_{av})$ where x_{av} is the *average* value of variable *x*, and *E( )* is the *expected value*, that is the average.

Sampling errors

These diminish with the size of the sample (whereas bias does not) and are measured by the *standard deviation* or error S (which is the square root of the variance) which is calculated as

$$S = \sqrt{\Sigma(x - x_{av})^2/(n-1)} = \sqrt{(\Sigma x^2 - (\Sigma x)^2/n)/(n-1)} \quad \text{(MR1)}$$

the second formula being called the *raw score formula.*

Conclusion

Marketing research involves many techniques for data collection and the following section discusses statistical correlation of such data.

MR7. Statistical Correlation

In the following section two methods of evaluating the statistical correlation between data sets are discussed. Typically, of course, these are used to compare observations with the assumed model and obtain a measure of the agreement between the two.

The Pearson correlation coefficient

The (Pearson) correlation coefficient is widely used to compare two sets of observations. If the coefficient (or *c.c.*) is close to one the two sets are strongly correlated, if it is zero they are not related and if it is close to minus one then the two sets of data are negatively correlated. It is calculated from the covariance between the two data sets as

$$c.c. = r_{xy} = \mathrm{Cov}(xy)/S_xS_y \quad \text{(MR2)}$$

where $\mathrm{Cov}(xy) = n\,\Sigma\, xy - \Sigma\, x\, \Sigma\, y$ (MR3)

$$S_x = \sqrt{(n\Sigma x^2 - (\Sigma x)^2} \quad \text{(MR4)}$$

$$S_y = \sqrt{n\Sigma y^2 - (\Sigma y)^2} \quad \text{(MR5)}$$

are the covariance and standard deviations of the two distributions.

As an example Table MR4 shows the expected marks *(x)* for a group of students and the actual marks *(y)* obtained in a test. Then the next three columns are used to calculate the value of the correlation coefficient according to Eqns (MR2) - (MR5).

Table MR4. Correlation coefficient calculation

x	y	x^2	y^2	xy
8	10	64	100	80
7	8	49	64	56
3	2	9	4	6
5	6	25	36	30
7	9	49	81	63
2	2	4	4	4
4	5	16	25	20
Totals: 36	42	216	314	259

Then we finally obtain the correlation coefficient as

$$r_{xy} = [7(259) - 36(42)] \,/\, [(\sqrt{7(216) - 36^2})\sqrt{7(314) - 42^2} = 0.98 \qquad \text{(MR6)}$$

and hence the expected and actual marks are strongly correlated.

The Pearson product-moment correlation coefficient is easy to calculate though some experience with this or any other method of correlation assessment is needed in order to ensure that proper judgments are made. An additional aid is to plot the data to obtain an idea of its scatter but the advantage of the correlation coefficient is that it gives a recognizable and quotable figure.

The Chi-squared test

The Chi-squared test is based on the skew Chi-squared distribution and is also called the *goodness of fit* or the *O-E* test.

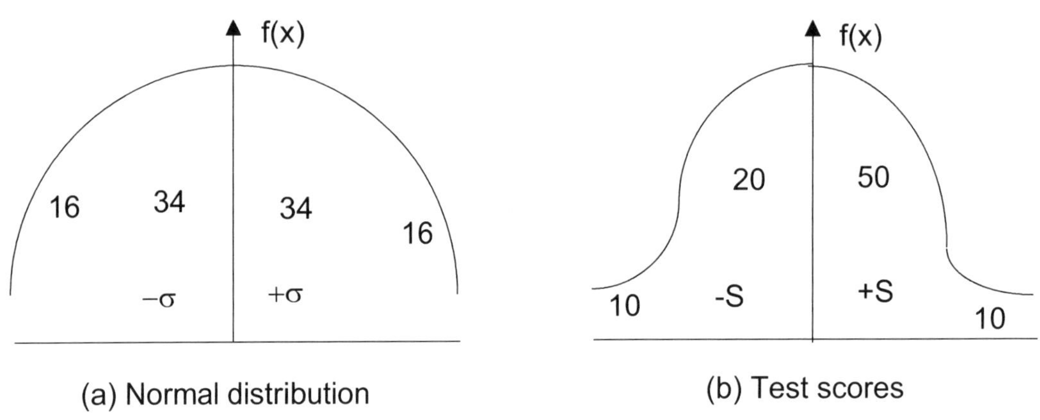

(a) Normal distribution (b) Test scores

Fig. MR2. Comparison of two distributions

Figure MR2 compares a normal distribution with the distribution of 100 student test scores. Then the data and calculation of the χ^2 variate $\Sigma(O - E)^2/E$ where O and E respectively denote observed and expected results is shown in Table MR5.

Table MR5. Calculation of Chi-squared value.

Category	O	E	$(O - E)^2/E$
1	10	16	2.25
2	20	34	5.76
3	50	34	7.53
4	20	16	1
Sum	100	100	16.54

Then we obtain the observed value of the Chi-squared variate as

$$\chi^2_{obs} = 16.54 \qquad \text{(MR7)}$$

and this is compared with the result for $\nu = (n - 1) = 3$ *degrees of freedom* and $\alpha = 0.05$ from standard statistical tables which is

$$\chi^2_{test}(0.05,\ 3\ d.f) = 7.81 \qquad \text{(MR8)}$$

and as the observed result exceeds the test result the test is failed so that the student marks are not normally distributed.

The test is said to have been failed at the *95% significance level* (i.e. with variable $\alpha = 0.05$ in the tables) and this is the criterion usually used with this test.

Conclusion

Both the Pearson correlation coefficient and the Chi-square test are widely used for the types of problems used as examples here and lead to simple tabular calculations. Such comparisons are sometimes useful in the market research context.

MR8. Introduction to the Psychology of Attitudes

As we noted at the beginning of chapter MP there are many branches of psychology. In the context of marketing, however, the psychology of attitudes is, of course, particularly important. A very brief introduction to this is therefore given in the following three sections. Attitudinal psychology has, besides applications in business, important application in such areas as politics and community health education.

Definition of attitude

Attitude can be defined as 'psychological *tendency* expressed by *evaluating* a particular entity with some degree of favour or disfavour.'

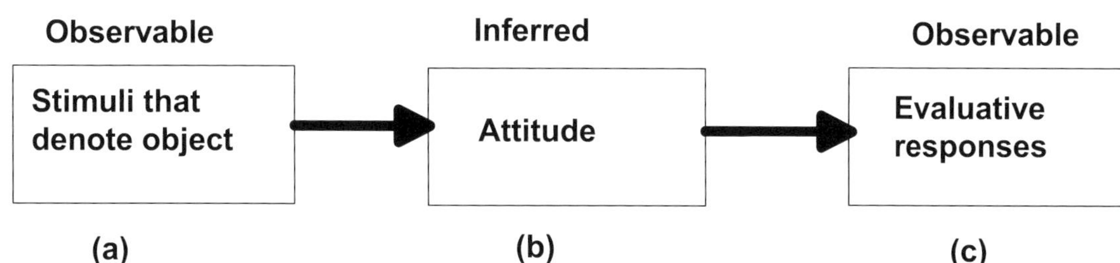

Fig. MR3. Psychological responses

Fig. MR3 simply illustrates the three types of response involved in attitudinal psychology. These are:

1. *Cognitive response.* This response is that of recognition of, for example, a name, a picture or other stimulus.
2. *Affective response.* This is a hypothetical construct and a latent variable. Here the sympathetic nervous system responds to (1) with feelings or emotions.

3. *Behavioural response.* This is the outward expression of (2) and may be a positive, neutral or negative response of some degree or intensity involving some observable action.

In this context, for example, conservatism, environmentalism or racism are objects. Then when we label a person a conservative, environmentalist or racist we infer an attitudinal position. Such attitudes are evidenced and also developed by the *'CAB* 'mechanism illustrated in Fig. MR3.

Schemas

Schemas are cognitive structures that represent a person's past experience in a stimulus domain by a higher order or abstract cognitive structure. Then attitude is a subset of such a schema.

Schemas have a selective effect on the retention, retrieval and remembering of information so that people have a better remembrance of stimuli that 'fit' their schemas and also for those that 'oppose.' This same selectivity applies to the 'input' of information as well as its output.

Functions of attitudes

Attitudes are necessary as part of our information processing system and have the following functions:

1. Knowledge function. Attitudes play an important role in summarizing past experience.
2. Adjustment or 'utilitarian' function. This proposed function has its roots in learning theory and enables people to maximize rewards in their environment and minimize punishment or losses.
3. Ego-defensive function. This has its roots in the idea of a defence mechanism and involves trying to avoid unpleasant realities.
4. Value-expressive function. This is related to the concept of the ego and social psychology and involves the expression of personal values and self-concept through attitude formation.

It follows from this theory that people like, and hence are motivated, to organize and simplify stimuli and collate related cognitions. Thus attitudes themselves energize and direct behaviour, that is, they motivate action as well as determine the form of reactions.

Conclusion

Attitudinal psychology and its fundamental *'CAB'* responses is very relevant to marketing where, for example, we seek to develop conditioned responses, brand loyalty and the like. It is also closely related to response development and learning of infants and hence an important branch of study.

MR9. Measurement of attitudes

In the present section *psychophysical scaling* or the measurement of reactions to a stimulus, sometimes referred to as 'stimulus-person scaling' (SPS), is discussed. This is related to the *'CAB'* mechanism introduced in section MR8 and is not to be confused with *psychometrics* or 'person scaling' which deals with IQ and like tests.

Scales of measurement

First it is useful to consider different types of scales of measurement that might be used to measure attitudes:

1. 'Nominal' measurement. Examples of this would be assigning the value one to male and zero to female or the numbers given to members of a sporting team.

2. Ordinal measurement. Here, for example, we simply establish an order such as A > B > C. Such scales can be subjected to a *monotonic transformation* when the relative positions on the scale are altered but they remain in the same order.
3. Interval scales. For these a *unit* is needed. When such scales undergo *linear transformation*, for example, the values on the scale might, say, be doubled, but points on the scale remain in the same relative positions.
4. Ratio scales. For these we need a fixed origin relative to which points are some ratio to each other.

Then ordinal scales are much used in measuring attitudes and sometimes, once these are established, interval scales can be formed.

Psychophysical scaling

Some of the more notable techniques developed for psychophysical scaling include:

1. *Method of successive intervals.* This was proposed by Thurston in 1937 and involves assuming reactions to stimuli are equivalent to a distance on the 'psychological scale' which assumes normally distributed responses and measures distance on this scale in terms of the standard deviation *S*.

2. *Method of equal-appearing intervals.* This was proposed by Thurston in 1929. In this approach responses are divided into 11 intervals each of size one. Then respondents are asked to place an item, for example the statement "I like - - " or item A, into one of the intervals. If the interval 5 is chosen this gives a score of 5 for A. Then the mean score for the item A is its scale value.

This procedure establishes a scale which is then used to measure attitudes by using a subset of the items scaled by the first (scaling) pool of judges. These items are presented in random order to persons to be tested and they are asked to place them on the scale, not according to their attitude, but according to their view of the score deserved by the item. Then the resulting test score is the sum of the scale values selected and this can be compared to the 'standard' values selected by the first pool of judges to measure the attitude of individual persons.

3. *Method of paired comparisons.* This approach was proposed by Thurston in 1928. In this approach the statements or stimuli are presented in pairs and placed in order. Hence the process is comparable to a 'bubble sort' (see IT12) and results in an ordinal scale. Then the number of times options A, B, C etc. were favoured is summed for each and the resulting score yields a scale. This process, however, requires very large numbers of judgments and is impractical except for a relatively small number of items requiring scaling.

4. *Guttman scaling.* This approach gives stimulus-person scaling simultaneously and results in a matrix of data called the *Guttman scalogram.* As an example imagine that we have five rods of from 5 to 7 feet in length (the exact lengths are not known). Then we ask each judge or respondent to place a one in the Guttman scalogram matrix Table MR6 when they are taller than a particular rod. This is then reorganized to give the result in Table MR6.

Table MR7 is obtained by placing the column with least ones at the left, the column with the most ones at the right, and so on. Then the row with the maximum number of ones is placed at the top (this is for Bill in our example and hence he is the tallest person) and that with the least ones is placed at the bottom.

	Stimuli (rods)				
Persons	C	E	B	D	A
2	1	1	1	1	0
4	0	1	0	1	0
3	1	1	0	1	0
6	0	0	0	0	0
5	0	1	0	0	0
1	1	1	1	1	1
* e.g. Jim is taller than C, E, B, D but not A					

Table MR6. Guttman scalogram for raw data.

The result is an upper diagonal matrix, as shown in Table MR7, and this results in a score for each person shown on the right side in Table MR7, this giving the ordinal ranking for each person.

	Stimuli (rods)					
Persons	A	B	C	D	E	Score
1	1	1	1	1	1	5
2	0	1	1	1	1	4
3	0	0	1	1	1	3
4	0	0	0	1	1	2
5	0	0	0	0	1	1
6	0	0	0	0	0	1

Table MR7. Reordered Guttman scalogram.

Application of Guttman scaling to attitudes

The preceding example of Guttman scaling was for physical stimuli, when a perfect upper triangular matrix resulted. Generally, however, this is not the case then attitudinal stimuli are considered.

An example is Bogardus' social stimulus scale, illustrated in Fig. Table MR8, in which respondents are asked to judge how closely they would relate to people of various nationalities or races.

	Acceptance level					
	Would marry	As a friend	Would give a job	Allow as citizen	OK as visitor	No contact
Armenians						
Bulgarians						
Canadians						
etc.						

Table MR8. Bogardus's social distance scale.

Such attitudinal stimuli do not yield a perfect upper triangular matrix but it has been suggested that when about 90% of the non-zero entries do appear on or above the diagonal that this *coefficient of reproducibility* value is acceptable.

Conclusion

Attitude scaling requires a certain amount of care, for example stimuli should not be ambiguous or irrelevant and responses to them should approximate a 'parabola distribution'. In actual research questions, electricity, light and sound have been used as stimuli. As we have noted, however, it is attitudinal stimuli of the type shown in Fig. MR6 which provide the greatest challenge and which are most relevant in market research.

Of the methods of scaling here the Guttman scalogram is appealing in nature whilst the rather obvious method of equal-appearing intervals is satisfactory for most purposes.

MR10. Person scaling

In Sec. MR9 we discussed stimulus-person scaling techniques. Person scaling techniques, however, make no attempt to locate responses on a scale and they are classified *a priori* as either favourable or unfavourable toward the attitude object. Then the location of persons on the attitude dimension is determined by the number of stimuli with which they agree and the extent of their agreement.

These person scaling methods are derivatives of the psychometric model traditionally much used for ability or IQ tests in which responses to items are viewed as indicators of a common latent ability.

Likert scaling

Likert's *method of summated ratings* was designed to be much easier to use than the method of equal-appearing intervals but to be at least as reliable. In this approach a large pool of items which are chosen intuitively for their relevance to the attitude object is used. These items usually consist of statements of belief but statements about behaviours or affective reactions can also be used.

Typically each item is presented to respondents in a multiple-choice format such as:

1. Strongly disagree.
2. Disagree.
3. Undecided.
4. Agree.
5. Strongly agree.

Then the response to each item is given a score such as 5 for strongly agree.

Then, for example, a survey on attitudes towards women might contain questions like:

(a) Swearing is more objectionable from a woman.
(b) Intoxication in women is worse than in men.

With scores from 1 - 5 given to each of perhaps a dozen or so such questions the total score is then obtained for each respondent.

Such a survey is much simpler than Thurston's method of equal-appearing intervals but usually the initial pool of items should be pilot tested on a group of people to eliminate ambiguous and nondiscriminating items which tend to result in neutral responses. This can be done by examining the *item-total score correlations*, each of which correlates the respondents' scores on an item with their scores summed over all the items. Then a good item will have a positive correlation and generally better items have higher correlations.

Reception-yielding model of attitude formation

In relation to marketing and advertising attitude measurement techniques are much used. It is also important, however, to have some understanding of how attitudes can be changed by cognitive and attitudinal processes.

The reception-yielding model of attitude change is illustrated in Fig. MR4 and postulates that the probability of attitude change is given by

$$P(C) = P(R) \times P(Y) \quad \text{(MR9)}$$

so that a maximum change is given where the reception and yielding curves intersect, as shown in Fig. MR4. The implications of this model are readily apparent and have wide application in marketing and elsewhere, such as in education.

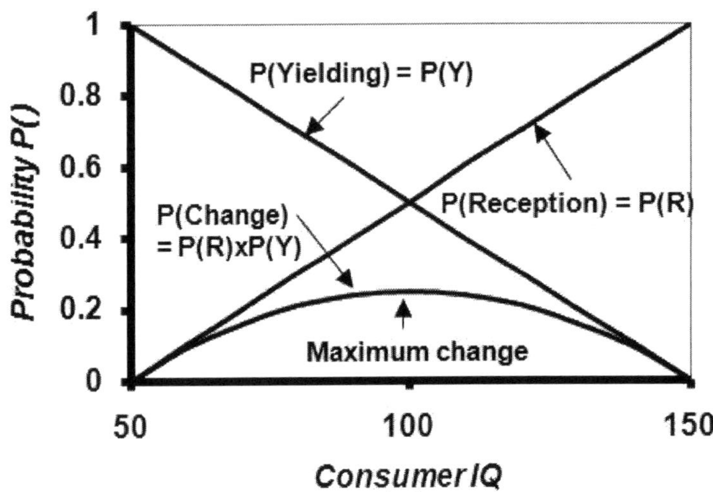

Fig. MR4 Probability of reception, yielding and attitude change.

The forgetting curve

Fig. MR5.
Forgetting curves for two messages.

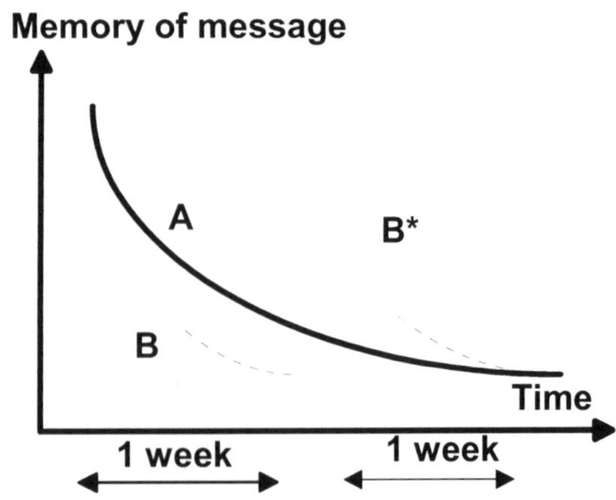

Also important in marketing and related areas is the 'forgetting curve' A shown in Fig. MR5 for a message. Curve B is for a second message and curve B* is the result after this second message is repeated.

Actual studies of ;such results suggest that:

a. *Recency* should be greatest with a long time interval between exposure to the two messages and a short time interval between exposure to the second message and the assessment (i.e. just after the end of the first week).

b. *Primacy* should be most evident with a short exposure interval and a long assessment interval (i.e. just before the end of the first week).

Here primacy refers to the relative 'strengths' of the messages, result (b) indicating primacy of greater strength of message A.

In such studies, however, correlation between retention and persuasion is by no means guaranteed. Nevertheless, they have obvious implications in the context of advertising and education.

Conclusion

Likert scaling, in addition to the method of equal-appearing intervals and Guttman scaling are all of interest and the reader will probably recognize at least the description of Likert scaling.

The reception-yielding and forgetting curve models are of obvious importance in many areas, the latter reminding us of the term *brain washing* which, of course, saturation advertising may be.

The discussion of attitude, response and measurement of Secs MR8 - 10 does not include, however, the question of group response (as distinct from a single individual) and this, of course, may be an important factor, bringing with it such factors as peer group pressure.

For the future, though, such work as *mere exposure research*, where subliminal advertisements or messages are used, promises to yield interesting results.

Finally, whilst the focus of the present chapter is market research the implications of some of the discussion of the psychology of attitudes for areas such as education are noteworthy.

MR11. New Trends in Marketing

There are many new trends at present or likely to become evident in the foreseeable future. This section begins with discussion of trends which some prophets of doom feel will make business increasingly more difficult as time goes by. It concludes, however, on a more optimistic note, in part taking encouragement from the notion that, whatever the trends might be, good business practice is to take advantage of them

Consumer resistance

In business circles there were fears of consumer resistance in the 1990s to such things as:

1. Product obsolescence.
2. Unnecessary products such as a second family car, swimming pools or oversized houses.
3. Capital expenditure on such items as houses or company shares.

There has always been concern, however, about such trends and, for example, in the case of housing there may again be a need for government intervention to ensure affordable housing loans as there was in the 1930s in the USA.

The car market, on the other hand, may be set to boom as electric cars become increasingly desirable as oil supplies become more costly.

In addition, however, while there are areas where a growth of consumer resistance may be feared there are, correspondingly, areas in which there is considerable growth in consumer spending.

Consumer spending

There is currently, especially in many large cities where house prices have tended to become unaffordable to new entrants to the market, a growing 'live for today' approach to consumer spending and this is seen in:

1. The growing fast food industry, including take-away food and packaged 'heat only' meals sold in grocery stores.
2. Increasing diversity in consumption of alcohol.
3. Increasing use of drugs which may perhaps be encouraged by the legalization of marijuana.160
4. Increasing use of leisure industries such as those involving gambling.
5. Increasing use of restaurants by young childless workers (who may remain childless).
6. Greater spending by young and independent working women on cosmetics, clothes, jewelry and other beauty and fashion products including hair dressing and magazines.
7. Greater spending on boundless ranges of magazines, videos, books, computer games, music and other home entertainment products.
8. Greater spending on cars, holidays and other major items by young childless couples or unattached persons.

In these and many other areas there seems to be a growing market in some communities but one or two of the following examples may be on the wane.

New trends

Some of the new trends of late include:

1. Vegetarianism.
2. Recycling.
3. Pollution free and environmentally friendly products.
4. Diets and weight watching.
5. Alternative therapies. Of these the list grows daily:

a. aroma therapy
b. herbal remedies
c. acupuncture and Chinese medicine
d. group therapy
e. exercise therapy, for example Yoga
f. transcendental meditation
g. reflexology - and so on.

In relation to such matters as (4) and (5) and market research some brief mention of Sheldon's *somatypes* might be of interest. These were proposed in 1940 and are:

i. Dominant endomorph
ii. Dominant mesomorph
iii. Dominant ectomorph

Then a scale of 1 to 7 was attached to each based on fat development (e.g. folds in skin etc.), muscular development and skeletal development. A truly 'middling' person, therefore, would be described as 4/4/4 in this system which was devised after much research because three basic body types were felt unrealistic for classification purposes. Such scaling systems might be of interest in some areas of market research.

New work trends

New technology has resulted in considerable changes in the number of workers in various industries in recent decades. In the agricultural industries, for example, automation has greatly decreased numbers employed. Correspondingly there has been an increase in the number of 'white collar' workers in the cities at the expense of the number of 'blue collar' workers. Such changes may sometimes by worth taking into account in marketing.

Consumer groups

In any chapter on marketing consumer groups are perhaps worth mention as consumer magazines, for example, are involved in a good deal of product and sometimes market research. In this connection the celebrity which Ralph Nader gained in the later 1960s from his book *Unsafe at Any Speed* is worth of note (in this book Nader pointed out that cars were made for everything but safety).

Politics

Politics, of course, is an increasing application of marketing and here such material as that of Secs MR8 - 10 is of note as such material was banned in the Soviet Union and may well still be elsewhere.

Certainly in the USA, at least, serious presidential candidates and the like are likely to have the odd advertising consultant in tow or vice versa.

Conclusion

Market research may often, if not usually, appear absolute drudgery, but with a little better appreciation of the subtleties of attitudinal psychology, for example, it becomes much more interesting.

In addition, those of a more mathematical bent may be able to find some measure of refuge in such material as that of Sec. MR7. As elsewhere in the course, however, those averse to mathematics are advised to pass over such sections or at least avoid becoming bogged down in them on a first reading.

MR12. Exercise: An Example of Likert Scaling

The present section gives an example of a type of questionnaire (below) which the author found useful some two decades ago for class evaluation of lecturing etc. The approach is, in fact, reminiscent of Likert scaling and students enjoyed the revenge [in advance] of giving a mark out of 100, especially as I asked them to also give marks (with different colour pen or ringed etc.) to the HOD who shared teaching of the subject with me. He scored pretty badly!

Though it looks a little formidable this survey worked well and I was pleased with the results. For other purposes, however, such as a questionnaire I took to 20 schools seeking views of students on a proposed 2 year tertiary course, fewer questions and a tick the box and fill in the dashed lines approach is more appropriate. In the latter instance, incidentally, I was particularly interested in whether allowance by the 2 year course for *progression* into longer courses significantly increased interest in the 2 year course. As expected it did.

Finally, try the program RYPLOT(.BAS) in \MBS1 on the course Basics disc. This simply plots the reception-yielding plot MR10, assuming a hyperbola and parabola for the two curves required.

Circle the appropriate number:	**Very good**	**Good**	**Aver -age**	**Fair**	**Poor**
Rate your lecturer's:					
1. Choice of material	5	4	3	2	1
2. Performance generally	5	4	3	2	1
3. Explanations of the theory	5	4	3	2	1
4. Use of practical examples	5	4	3	2	1
5. Development of the theory	5	4	3	2	1
6. Stressing of important points	5	4	3	2	1
7. Choice of tutorial examples	5	4	3	2	1
8. Time given to individuals	5	4	3	2	1
9. Choice of lab. experiments	5	4	3	2	1
10. Helping understand subject	5	4	3	2	1
11. Style	5	4	3	2	1
12. Teaching report writing	5	4	3	2	1
How well does lecturer do in:					
13. Getting you interested	5	4	3	2	1
14. Knowledge of subject	5	4	3	2	1
15. Motivating you to work well	5	4	3	2	1
16. Giving clear explanations	5	4	3	2	1
17. Lecturing at followable rate	5	4	3	2	1
18. Giving good lecture notes	5	4	3	2	1
Other:					
19. Are the tests useful to you ?	5	4	3	2	1
20. Course relevant to needs ?	5	4	3	2	1
Add the numbers you circled:	**Score/100:**				

References

______. *B&T Year Book: Advertising, Marketing and Media,* 35th edn. Thomson Publs, Sydney, 1992.

Blondel, J. *Voters, Parties and Leaders.* Pelican, Harmondsworth, Middlesex. 1965.

Brown, Linden, *Competitive Marketing Strategy,* 2nd edn, Helson ITP, Melbourne (1997).

Buchanen, J.M. and Tullock, G. *The Calculus of Consent.* Univ. of Michigan Press, Ann Arbor, MI. 1974.

Clarke, H.H. *Application of Measurement to Health and Physical Education.* Prentice-Hall, Englewood Cliffs, NJ. 1967.

Cohen, H, *You Can Negotiate Anything,* Angus & Robertson, Sydney. 1982.

Cutlip, S.M., Centre, A.H., Broom, G.M. *Effective Public Relations,* 6th edn. Prentice-Hall, Englewood Cliffs NJ. 1985.

Denes, P.B. and Pinson, E.N. *The Speech Chain.* Bell Telephone Labs (US). 1972.

Dillon, W.R, Madden, T.J. and Firtle, N.B. *Essentials of Marketing Research.* Irwin, Homewood IL. 1993.

Dunlevy, M. *Interviewing Techniques for Newspapers.* Deakin Univ. Press, Melbourne. 1980.

Eagly, A.H. and Chaiken, S. *The Psychology of Attitudes.* Harcourt Brace Jovanovich, Orlando, FA. 1992.

Foss, D.J. and Hakes, D.T. *Psycholinguistics, an Introduction to the Psychology of Language.* Prentice-Hall, Englewood Cliffs NJ. 1978.

Gerlach, V.S. and Ely, D.P. *Teaching and Media.* Prentice-Hall, Englewood Cliffs, NJ. 1971.

Jackson, R.V. *The Population History of Australia.* McPhee Gribble, Melbourne. 1988.

Jefkins, F. *Advertising Today.* International Textbook Col., London. 1977.

Keegan, W.J. *Global Marketing Management,* 5th edn. Prentice-Hall, Englewood Cliffs NJ. 1995.

Kendall, R. *Public Relations Campaign Strategies, Planning for Implementation.* Harper Collins, New York NY. 1992.

Kotler, P. *Marketing Management,* 8th edn. Prentice-Hall, Englewood Cliffs NJ. 1994.

Mason, Jim. *Advertising Without Tears.* MCCullock Publ. Lts, Carlton VIC. 1990.

McKee, Charles. *Winning the War for Market Survival.* Rydge Publ. Ltd, Sydney. 1979.

Mohr, G.A. and Power, A.S. *Tertiary Study Aspirations of Victorian School Leavers.* Aust. Jour. Ad. Ed., Melbourne. 1977.

Mohr GA, *The Pretentious Persuaders, A Brief History & Science of Mass Persuasion,* Horizon Publishing Group, Sydney, 2012 (edn 1), 2014 (edn 2).

Mohr GA, Edwin Fear, *The Brainwashed, From Consumer Zombies to Islamism and Jihad,* Inspiring Publishers, Canberra (2016).

Nurk, F. *Global Marketing Management, A Strategic Perspective,* 2nd edn. Allyn and Bacon., Boston MA. 1993.

Ostrander, S. and Schroeder, L. *Super Learning.* Delacorte Press, NY NY. 1979.

Postman, N. and Weingarter, C. *Teaching as a Subversive Activity.* Penguin, Harmondsworth, Middlesex. 1971.

Roberts ML, Berger PD, *Direct Marketing Management,* Prentice-Hall, Englewood Cliffs NJ, (1989).

Robertson, T.S. *Consumer Behaviour.* Scott/Foresman, Glenview IL. 1970.

Sargent, M. *Drinking and Alcoholism in Australia.* Longman Chesire, Melbourne. 1979.

Shavelson, R.J. *Statistical Reasoning for the Behavioural Sciences.* Allyn and Bacon, Boston, MA. 1978.

Shaw, W. and Day, G. *The Businessman's Complete Checklist.* Century Hutchinson, London. 1987.

Solomon, M.R. *Consumer Behavoiur.* Allyn and Bacon, Boston MA. 1992.

Stone, Bob. *Successful Direct Marketing Methods*, 6th edn. NTC Business Books, Chicago IL. 1997.

Strano, Z. *Communicating.* Harcourt Brace Jovanovicj, Sydney. 1984.

Terpstra, V. and Sarathy, R. *International Marketing,* 6th edn. The Dryden Press, Forth Worth TX. 1994.

R.R. Traill, *Mind and Micro-Mechanism, a Hunt for the Missing Theory.* Ondwelle Publications, Melbourne. 1999.

Wasserman, W. and Whitmore, G.A. *Applied Statistics.* Allyn and Bacon, Boston MA. 1978.

Weiss, D.E. *100% American.* Poseidon, New York NY. 1988.

Wells, W., Burnett, J. and Moriarty, S. *Advertising, Principles and Practice,* 2nd edn. Prentice-Hall, Englewood Cliffs NJ. 1992.

INFORMATION TECHNOLOGY (IT)

BASIC gave a kind of access to computers that had never existed before.
Robert L. Albrecht

The purpose of information systems and technology is, of course, to deliver information to those requiring it, of particular interest in the present text being *management information systems (MIS).* We are all aware, of course, of the impact of the personal computer (PC) in both the office and the classroom. There has also been, however, a great increase in the use of communications technology and it is this, combined with computer technology, that has led to what some call the 'Information age.'

IT1. Introduction

Information technology is a combination of computer and communication technology and, typically, this provides data which serves as the information upon which managers and others can base decisions.

Typical systems for this purpose involve at the simplest level a group of networked PCs which provide *real-time* management information (that is instantaneous MI which is immediately available to others without the need for further human invention).

History of information technology

The modern electronic computer as we know it stemmed from the invention of the transistor in 1948. This let to the development of *integrated circuits* circa 1960, that is, many transistors on a single *chip.* Next came very large scale integration (VLSI) circa 1970 which allowed more than 10,000 components to be placed on a single chip. Then came the *microchip* and with it the PC as we know it today.

In communication technology, on the other hand, *analogue* systems were, of course, the basis of the radio and telephone etc. In these communication is via wave forms or *tones*, or course, but now *digital* technology provides an alternative. Here a *pulse* replaces a tone and this is based on the binary system for digital computers where binary switches are used to store numbers in binary (or base two) form (for example ten is stored as 1010, that is $2^3 + 2$).

Now, therefore, with the two technologies thus combined it is easy to understand how computers can be linked via the telephone, providing the advanced communications systems that we know today.

The role of ergonomics

In the context of information technology the role of ergonomics, that is the study of human factors and limitations relevant to the design of machines, is worth note. Here we seek to design the man-machine interface optimally, for example seeking the maximum output from a system. Such interfaces involve *controls* (with which man controls machines) and *displays* (which give feedback to the human controller).

Some consideration of human limitations is, of course, important in the field of information technology, for example in limiting speed of information display.

Information theory

Information theory is the mathematical theory of information. If a character set has 100 characters, for example, a study of the relative frequency of use of each character allows us to estimate the speed at which we can transmit messages using this set,

The basic unit of electronic information storage in a computer is the *bit.* This is a binary switch equivalent to a binary number as it can have values 0/1. Then a *byte* is the smallest accessible unit in computer memory and is 6 or 8 bits. A computer *word* is then the common unit of information storage for a particular computer system, typically 16 bits for the early PCs, 32 bits for a mainframe and 64 bits for a super computer.

EBCDIC (Extended Binary Coded Decimal Interchange Code) uses 8 bits to store a single character. The letter A (capital), for example, is represented by 11000001 (in binary, or 193 in decimal). This system was much used by IBM but the ASCII (American Standard Code Information Interchange) code which uses 7 bits for each character is that used in PCs and more likely to be of interest to most computer users.

Number storage in computers then typically uses 4 bytes to store a 'real number' and 2 bytes to store an integer number, 4 bytes storing about 7 decimal places (actually 6.8). Many machines use different word lengths, however, whilst particular software uses different precisions as well.

IT2. Information Systems

In the following section a very brief introduction to a few of the countless variations in information systems that are possible is given, discussion of designing and running such systems following in later sections. Then a brief introduction to the functions of management information systems is given.

System modes and area

Information systems can combine text, data, voice and image modes and can be *local area networks (LANs)* or *wide area networks (WANs).* Such systems provide:

1. *Communication services.* These may be in transmission mode, which may be one-way or two-way, or switchable mode in which the particular audience is varied.
2. *Network services.* These may consist of LANs (of PCs) to which may be added video messaging, for example, or PABXs with voice messaging. Services with additional facilities such as messaging are sometimes called *value added services.*
3. *Value added services.* These include e-mail, ticket reservation, EFT (electronic funds transfer), management information systems, voice mail, fax and image mail.

Table IT1 shows some of the various ways in which such services can be combined, clearly illustrating the many options available.

Networks of computers etc. may take many forms, some basic examples being:

1. *Star network.* This simply consists of a central computer linked to several others (these being independent).
2. *Ring network.* Here each computer is connected only to two others.
3. *Multistar network.* Here the central computers of a number of star networks are connected together.

Of these (1) is, perhaps, the most common, occurring in many offices, whilst (3) is much used in the banking industry, for example.

		TEXT	DATA	VOICE	IMAGE
Commun-ication services	**1-W trans. (broadcast)**	Teletext	Teleswitch; telesoftware	Radio	TV
	2-W trans.	Teleprinter VDU/PC	Modems; mains born control	Telephone	CCTV fax typewriter
	Switched services	Telex teletext	Credit and load control Packet switching	Telephone network	Slow-scan TV Vido-phone Video conference
Commun-ications networks	**Now**	Telex LANs Packet switch sets	LANs Packet switch sets	PABXs	
	Future		Integrated services digital network (ISDN)	Cellular radio Public switched telepone network (PSTN)	Wideband
Value added networks		Teletext	Teletext	Voice messaging	Video messaging
Value added services		e-mail word processing Internet	Ticket reservation Database EFT, EFTPOS MIS etc.	Voice mail Telepone answering	Fax Security TV Image mail
		TEXT	DATA	VOICE	IMAGE

Table IT1 Examples of information systems

Management Information Systems

Management information systems (MISs) have three principal functions:

1. Operational control. Here information is provided to front-line managers for routine functions such as payrolls, stock control, invoicing and mailing lists. The systems used for such purposes are called *transactional processing systems (TPSs).*

2. *Management control.* For this *information provision systems (ISPs)* give information to middle-level managers for the preparation of routine or ad hoc reports, for example on sales or market trends.

3. *Strategic planning.* Here information is provided to top-level management for the purposes of executive decisions via:
(a) *Decision support systems (DSSs),* for example forecasting models or mathematical models of physical systems.
(b) *Programmed support systems (PSSs).* Here the mathematical model programmed is also programmed to provide decisions.

Clearly the requirements of the three functions and levels are very different, illustrating the broad role which MISs play in management.

Information system structures

The MISs for different levels of management described in the foregoing will usually be linked, for example:
a. The TPSs (1) feed information to the IPS (level (2)) which in turn feeds information to the DSS at level (3).
b. A central database feeds information to the TPSs, IPSs and DSS and vice versa.

Many other variations are, of course, possible, the important point to note being that MISs of different types and levels must generally be connected together.

Expert systems

These apply experience gained from 'feedback' and programmed 'rules' to make decisions and new rules and give reasons for them, giving rise to the term *artificial intelligence (AI)* which, for some applications at least, is regarded as potentially better than human intelligence.

Conclusion

Clearly a great many variations in information systems are possible but notionally, at least, it is practical to regard a network of computers as the basis or 'standard' system of which there are lesser forms (such as simply a PABX) and, or course, massive systems.

IT3. Organizing MISs

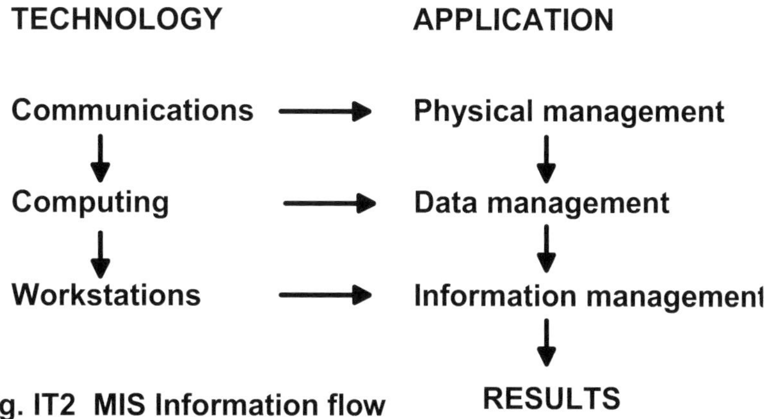

Fig. IT2 MIS Information flow

Information systems should be so organized that they facilitate the flow of information, as illustrated in Fig. IT2. Indeed Fig. IT2 illustrates the sort of information flow required by the different types of MIS in Sec. IT2.

Then to design a total information system a useful beginning is by setting up a table of the sort shown in Table IT1. Here the different modes of information transfer for each of many requirements is decided.

For each such decision, of course, sites for use of each component of the system must be selected and networking requirements decided upon.

Clearly, therefore, the detailed design of coordinated systems is a complex task, one which requires careful research and planning, costing, testing etc. at every stage.

Implementation of IS plans

In fully implementing a detailed information system plan the following stages are generally necessary:

1. Formulation of a five year overall plan.
2. Detailed system design using Table IT2, for example.
3. Feasibility study.
4. Refined plan.
5. Report to accompany plan (including business plan).
6. Project plan (including training etc.).
7. Implementation.
8. Appraisal.
9. Fine tuning.

Table IT2. Information system planning matrix.

IS requirements	Text	Data	Voice	Image
Collect				
Store				
Process				
Communicate				
MIS/TPS				
MIS/IPS				
MIS/DSS				
MIS/PDS				
MIS/Expert				
MIS/Expert				
Co/Intra-site				
Co/Inter-site				
Co/External				
Comms/Transmission				
Comms/Switching				
Comms/Value added				

In the case of a large company, therefore, building a MIS is a considerable task and, in the case of an international airline, for example, it is a massive one and a major factor in the success or otherwise of the enterprise.

Including the human communication

Discussion of information technology tends to forget the human element at times and in this context the following points are worthwhile:

1. Informal communication whether in the corridor or lunch room, is beneficial and should not be eliminated.
2. Provision should be made for formal 'non-electronic' communication, for example via memos, couriers etc.
3. Communication structures such as those noted in Sec. BP10 should also be considered as part of efficient functioning of a company.
4. Meetings, whether one to one or scheduled group meetings are, of course, important to business of any kind and, indeed, generally where decisions are actually made.

Conclusion

Detailed planning and implementation of information systems is important and can be as large task, there being a great many needs that need to be net as well as the need to connect MISs (Management Information Systems).

In applying IT to develop MISs, however, the human element should not be forgotten and provision must be made for 'non-electronic' communication for example via company memo forms, invoice sheets etc.

IT4 Information system design

In the preceding section we discussed selection of modes of communication for use by management and other information systems. This results in the hardware of the system.

As part of efficient use of the system it is then important to examine in detail the information requirements of different people and parts of the company. This may be necessary to design an information system and to ensure that it is used effectively.

The wrong approach

A common but inefficient IS approach is to set up a few independent systems (sometimes a single unattached PC), for example for:

a. Payroll, billing, stockholder lists etc.
b. General accounting, inventory etc.

This involves a wasteful duplication of information and a lack of efficient (automatic) interaction between (a) and (b).

The answer lies in setting up at least a small computer network with interactive files for accounting purposes, for example (such solutions are sometimes refereed to as 'integrated data processing' or 'total systems').

Information flow plan

A simple way of obtaining a detailed information flow plan is to first decide on the categories of information required, for example:

1. Financial information (F).
2. Personnel data (P).
3. Logistics information (Log).
4. Marketing information (M).

5. R & D information (R & D).
6. Operations data (Ops).
7. Executive observations (Exec).

Then a table is constructed using these categories as rows, the columns containing the following:

a. Specification of the information, that is, the types of information and their format.
b. Implementation, that is the hardware required.
c. Programming and/or software requirements.

This in part duplicates the functions of Table IT1, in that equipment decisions are made and hence the results may be used to augment those of Table IT2.

Finally, it is necessary to determine an operating structure for the system. Assuming the programmers control the system, for example, the hierarchical structure shown in Fig. IT3 might be used.

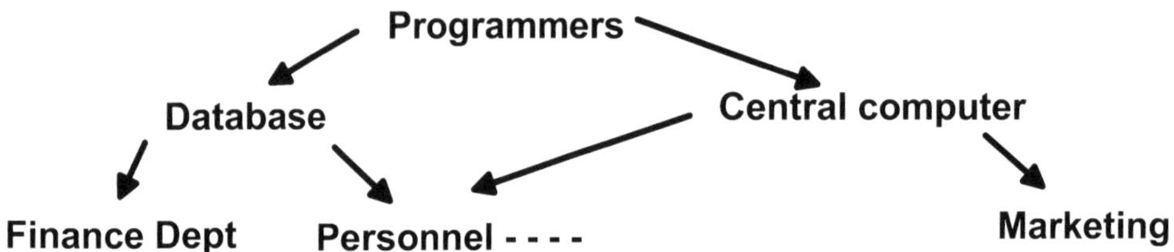

Fig. IT3. Control structure for IS

To then determine the information flow in the system a chart such as that shown in Table IT2b can be used to show what departments or people have access to particular information.

Table IT2b. Information flow chart (X = access)

Information	Directors	HOD/F	HOD/P - - -	Line mgnt - -	Sec/M - - -
Financial (F)	X	X	X		
Personnel (P)	X	X			
Logistics	X	X			X
Marketing (M)	X				
R & D	X				
Operations	X			X	
Executive	X	X	X		

This table, or course, would normally be stored in the computer files of the manager of the IS and perhaps a few other people, allowing them to check and alter access as required.

Conclusion

Information system design and operation have only been discussed at the crudest level here but, hopefully, this is a sufficient introduction to the average reader. In relation to computer networking, of course, suitable software must be used to operate the network and many packages are now available for this and these are, essentially, more important than the hardware used. The best of these packages permit quick orientation to a new network.

IT5. Database management

Strictly speaking a database need not be mounted on a computer and, of course, can exist as hard copy solely. They usually are stored on a computer system, of course, and vary from small collections of files for personal use to large DBs for an organisation requiring information about large numbers of people.

Database management systems (DBMSs)

Database management systems may have one or all of the following features:

1. Command mode.
2. Menu-driven systems.
3. Program mode in which particularly specified requirements are dealt with by a short 'application program.'

DBMSs can handle many types of interrelated data and are sometimes part of an integrated package, which, for example, might also include word processing, spread-sheeting, graphics output and telecommunications.

'File managers', on the other hand, use a simple menu to make additions or deletions in a file, generally the cursor being used to move through a 'window' to part of the file for this purpose.

Data models

DBMSs usually use one of the following systems or structures:

1. Hierarchical - this is a special case of (2).
2. Network where files are related by a network structure.
3. Relational.

Relational databases are the most generally useful type and have the following features:

a. A relational database consists of one or more two dimensional tables constructed from very simple rules.
b. Relationships by virtue of common data values exist between these tables.
c. Systematic methods can be used to generate tables from raw data in which data duplication is minimized and maintenance of the tables is simplified.
d. High level query languages are usually associated with RDBMSs for efficient searching and updating.

Such tables are said to be in the *first normal form* if they are two dimensional and contain single valued entries, for example the following two tables:

STUDENT-SUBJECT
TEACHER-SUBJECT

If we seek to find out what students a particular teacher had, however, we are faced with a tedious exercise. One solution might be to construct the table

STUDENT-SUBJECT-TEACHER

which could be searched quickly to obtain the required information.

This latter table is said to be in the *second normal form* because the data is not independent. A clearer example of this is the following:

CUSTOMER(NAME, STREET, CITY, STATE, ZIP, PHONE)

where ZIP follows from CITY and STATE and we could eliminate this dependency by creating the table

ZIPS(CODE,CITY,STATE)

which would allow us to remove CITY and STATE from the original table which would now be in the *third normal form.*

This example indicates some of the intricacies that could be involved with related databases but in practice tables in these and normal form are often more convenient and are those generally used in practice.

File storage

Computers usually store data files in either *sequential access* or *random access* mode. In sequential mode blocks of data can only be read in the order in which they were stored (or in reverse order using two 'backspace' commands before each read command).

With random access data can be read from anywhere in the file but this, of course, requires an address to be given to locate any particular piece of data required. A simple example of this process is included in Sec. IT11.

Typical DBMS commands

Typical DBMS commands are similar to a few of those encountered in Sec. IT11, taking the general (not literal - don't use these) form:

CREATE file name - to create an empty file with this name
USE file name - to use or go into this file
APPEND - to append
DISPLAY ALL - shows whole file
DISPLAY ALL FOR CITY =
DELETE ALL FOR CREDIT =
EDIT 08 - move to line 8 ready to amend it

and little difficulty is had in using such commands.

Formation of tables is accomplished by commands of general (only) form:

HEADER1 =
HEADER2 =
FIELD = NAME(5,25) - first number = column position
FIELD = CITY(30,25) - second number = field width
FIELD = BALANCE(60,.10)

and these too present little difficulty.

In practice, however, one need not fully type in commands in full SQL (Sequential Query Language) and most of the work of setting up databases and then producing reports from them is done with a few mouse clicks and typing the odd word here and there when prompted accordingly, for example to complete queries to select/sort records for a report.

Note too that Visual Basic (VB) is much oriented towards databases, having its own built in database viewer and 'Crystal Reports' for extracting reports from them. This is really only of much use to professional programmers, however, and for most users Approach, Access etc. are all that is needed, whilst for students Works is OK as an introduction, though it is probably better to go straight to Smartsuite or Office as soon as possible thereafter.

Uses of databases

Typical examples of the use of DBMSs include:

1. Searching, for example for details of a single person or a group of people.
2. Reporting. Reports may be written rapidly using the sort of commands given for formation of tables above. In addition sorting of entries to the reports, column totals and the like can, of course, be automatically included.
3. Compiling mailing lists (for example used to print mailing labels).
4. Merging tables. Some tables can be merged and this is referred to as the *union.* Along the same lines, therefore, tables can be *intersected, subtracted, projected* when some columns are eliminated) or *joined* (when columns of a second table are added).

Selection can also be used to form a subset of a first table.

Conclusion

In any brief chapter on information technology DBMSs are an important topic. The foregoing details give an introduction to the subject which, given a suitable package such as Approach or Access, should not prove too formidable to the reader.

IT6. Costs and benefits of IT

There is no doubting the usefulness of information technology and it would be tempting to some to use computers etc. wherever possible. In a large organisation, however, large scale use of IT involves massive expenditure. In the present section we briefly discuss how to evaluate the benefits of IT and thus assess what level of expenditures might be justified.

Table IT3. Computer usage in various industries (USA 1966).

	Insurance	Banks	Oil	Transport	Retail	Manuf-turing
Accounting	89	98	36	55	66	43
Decision	3	2	7	12	6	10
Sales forecast			5	2	2	8
Production control			3	9	4	13
Info. retrieval	4		3	12		8
Engineering			20	2		7
Simulation			17	1		1
Other	4		9	7	22	10

Table IT3 shows the levels of computer usage for various purposes by companies in various industry sectors. The figures in the table are the percentage of the activities which it was estimated were carried out by computer.

The figures for this table come from a survey carried out in 1966 and are chosen for inclusion here because of this. The reason is that 'now' figures would indicate, for example, all accounting done by computer.

In addition, these results relate to a relatively formative stage in IT and are, in some respects at least, more indicative of the situation faced when we contemplate new expenditures on IT.

The figures for accounting would not surprise us now, except that now they would be close to 100% right across. Similarly the figures elsewhere in the table would now, or course, be higher (where any figure at all is appropriate, that is).

The diverse usage of computers in the oil industry, as evidenced in Table IT3, is perhaps also worth remark and were no doubt a portent of what was to come in other industries.

Cost effectiveness

To judge the cost-effectiveness (and not the cost-benefit ratio or similar) of an IT system it can be assumed that given outputs (both in quantity and quality) are required from the system. Hence the system which achieves this cheapest is the 'most efficient' in that it gives the lowest 'input/output ratio.'

Assuming that the system is reliable this is a reasonably appropriate basis for evaluating ISs because the required output is data (and how well this is used is another matter). With computer systems, for example, other hidden costs such as documentation, training, ease of interfacing and so forth must, of course, be considered.

Such a lowest cost criterion seems a rather sweeping simplification but in conjunction with the following suggested steps in evaluation a sensible process emerges:

1. Identify all reports, including joint reports currently produced which could be tackled with a new IS.
Classify these as: (a) essential, or (b) nonessential.
2. Calculate the present cost of 2(a), \$a.
3. Calculate the cost with the new system, \$p, making due allowance for initial capital cost written off over an appropriate period.
4. If \$p < \$a the new system is cost effective (we can stop here).
5. If \$p > \$a can the incremental cost be justified on cost-benefit grounds?
That is, is the \$(benefit) of 2(b) > (\$p - \$a) ? Here only a qualitative judgement is used of the benefit and if we are satisfied the new IS is now justified.
If we are not yet satisfied we can attempt an approximate estimate of the benefit of 2(b), including such intangibles as company image, work satisfaction and the like.

The procedure outlined is, for simplicity, a crude one and, generally, costs associated with the eventual replacement of the old IS must be taken into account (in the above statement it is assumed that a new application presently done without an IS is contemplated).

Nevertheless, naive as it may seem, cost-effectiveness is an appropriate criterion for judging applications of IT such as MISs, in the first instance at least.

Conclusion

IT has been with us a long time and only relatively recently has it spread to somewhere approaching the full potential impact and level of usage. Nevertheless, indeed perhaps more than ever, new applications of MISs and the like, over and above those already existing in a company might required careful thought and consideration of their cost-effectiveness.

IT7. Application of Computer in Business

In the preceding section usage of computers in industry and evaluation of the cost effectiveness of information systems were briefly discussed. In the following section we consider the effectiveness with which computers have been used in industry and discuss some of the factors which may lead to improved efficiency of computer applications.

A comment on computer utilization

Once again we indulge in a little archaeology and quote from the McKinsey report on computer utilization in 36 large US and European companies. The report was conducted in 1968 as a follow up to an earlier 1963 one and one comment it contains is:

> *In terms of technological achievement, the computer revolution in US business is outrunning expectations. In terms of economic payoff on new applications, it is clearly losing momentum.*
>
> *From a profit viewpoint, our findings indicate computer efforts in all but a few exceptional companies are in real, if often unacknowledged, trouble. Faster, costlier, more sophisticated hardware; larger and increasingly costly computer staffs; increasingly complex and less ingenious applications; these are in evidence everywhere. Less and less in evidence, as these new applications proliferate, are profitable results. This is the familiar phenomenon of diminishing returns. But there is one crucial difference: as yet, the real potential of the computer has barely begun to be tapped.*

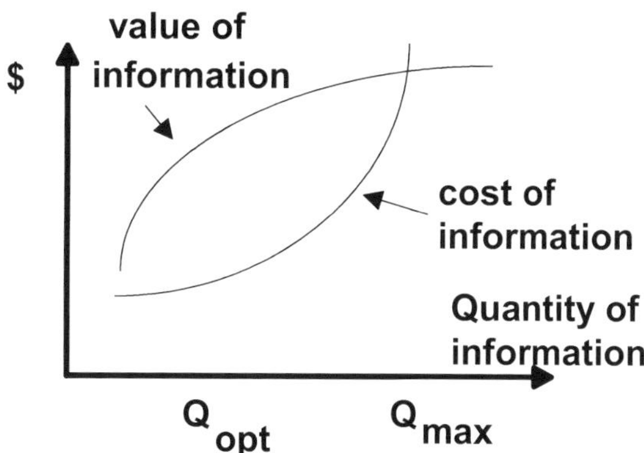

Fig. IT4. Optimum information system

The McKinsey report might still be a useful warning today and, at the very least it is a useful introduction to Fig. IT4. Here Q_{max} is for the maximum feasible system and Q_{opt} is where the ratio of information value to cost is a maximum.

At Q_{opt}, therefore, the IS has maximum cost-effectiveness. In practice of course, a more detailed analysis is required, perhaps based on NPV calculations.

Information system applications

We have discussed MISs, databases and distribution of information to various personnel and departments (such as finance, marketing and so on) to this point. Table IT3 is suggestive of other applications and still further applications are the following:

1. Models of distribution systems for products.
2. Sales reporting systems.
3. Consolidation of data from interstate and/or overseas branches of a company.
4. Regular manufacturing plans for various plants of a company with various sites.
5. Cost schedules for the plans of (4).
6. Central recording of all changes in plant and processes.
7. Cumulative records of labour efficiency.
8. Cost projections for +2 and +5 years, say, for the relative profit of different product markets and the expected costs and revenues of moving into those markets.

These and countless other examples can be found, as the latter were, in actual practice. A useful exercise in just where the savings might really be (rather than in the accounting department) is given in Table IT4.

Table IT4. Comparison of cost changes.

% of earnings	As is	-10% admin.	-10% goods
Admin. I general	15	13.5	15
Profit (before tax)	20	21.5	26.5
Cost of goods sold	65	65	53.5

Here the effect of a 10% reduction in administration costs increases profit by 7.5% whereas a 10% reduction in manufacturing costs increases profit by 27.5%. The example is a little trivial but the point is often neglected as we associate computers and industry so heavily with accounting and like activities.

Successful information systems

Many relatively unsuccessful ISs result from little or no use of feasibility studies, cost-effectiveness and consultation with staff, particularly executive staff.

More successful systems, on the other hand, tend to have:

1. Executive involvement in defining objectives, criteria and priorities.
2. Proper planning and costing.
3. Executive involvement in ensuring plans and strategies are followed.
4. High expectations of success.
5. Diversified applications.
6. Effective ongoing control and accountability for results.
7. Bugs are eliminated and the system is fine tuned where possible.
8. New application opportunities are identified.

Such checklists are bound to appear often in any book on business, but one moral of these points is simply that of good management practice.

Conclusion

The cautionary note of the very dated McKinsey report is probably still worthwhile, as is that implied in Fig. IT4. Simple though it is, the point made in Table IT4 is well worth note and highlights the area where savings are still to be had in most industries. The final bottom line, however, is that good management helps ensure a successful IS.

IT8. Data Collection and Security

An important consideration in some information systems is data collection and integrity. Another is the effectiveness with which the system copes with data changes and testing it for such aspects of its performance. Finally, IS security is, of course, important and this is briefly discussed, concluding with an interesting example of a cipher, these having long been used in history and being, in fact, an exercise in information technology.

Data collection

Data required for accounting systems, for example, develops naturally in the course of business. Elsewhere, however, it must be collected, for example feedback on product quality. Such data collection is sometimes referred to as *scanning* and often valuable, if not essential, information is not collected. The remedy is to coordinate scanning through:

1. Explicit assignment of responsibility for data collection.
2. Planning to define information needs.
3. Encouragement of internal communication via meetings and the like to provide feedback.
4. Check that the quantity of data is as it should be.
5. Allocate priorities in data collection.

Testing information systems

Some simple tests of information systems include:

1. Comparison of accounts and other data using especially written short test programs.
2. Random sampling (for example to check mode of data storage).
3. Extraction of specific data (for example to check its accuracy).
4. Perturbations in data, for example add $100 somewhere in the accounting system and check if the change 'flows through' correctly.

There are many others of course but the main point is to remind the reader of such tests and that MISs, like most things, require regular check ups.

Computer security

Some of the measures which should be considered in relation to security of computer systems include:

[1] Minimize errors by: (a) Testing new systems and software.
(b) Checking replacement software against the old software.
(c) Eliminate i/o errors by checking.

[2] Limit access to: (a) Hardware using keys and passwords
(b) Software by issuing only compiled programs.
(c) Allow read only access to those who need only this.

[3] Keep backup copies (perhaps in another location).

[4] Variable passwords (for example based on codes or ciphers).

[5] Insurance.

[6] Separation of duties so that fewer personnel have access to any particular data and any particular person has a lesser range of access.

[7] Test the IS with a hypothetical mini-model to check correct access and functioning before permitting anyone access to real data.

Many of these precautions are mandatory whilst the last is, of course, also a useful exercise in the staff training stage.

Code and ciphers

Codes and ciphers abound through history and, for example, Julius Caesar had a personal one (and probably needed it) as did many others in his line of work. Modern examples that are household names are Morse code and Pitman shorthand, the latter originally being intended as a code.

The table of Fig. IT5 is the key to a simple code of a type once quite popular because of the ease with which it can be changed (by using a new key word which might also be included in a message).

In Fig. IT5 the top row and LH column word (smokingcap) is the *keyword* for the code. Then the letter *a* is represented by *ss, og* or *no* by using the first letter as the row in the table and the second as the column.

	S	M	O	K	I	N	G	C	A	P
S	a	b	c	d	e	f	g	h	i	j
M	k	l	m	n	o	p	q	r	s	t
O	u	v	w	x	y	z	a	b	c	d
K	e	f	g	h	i	j	k	l	m	n
I	o	p	q	r	s	t	u	v	w	x
N	y	z	a	b	c	d	e	f	g	h
G	i	j	k	l	m	n	o	p	q	r
C	s	t	u	v	w	x	y	z	*	*
A	*	*								
P										

Fig. IT5 Cipher for a simple code

Notice that the alphabet has been written three times (sufficient) and the following * entries are positions used to denote the end of a word (that is *ca, cp, as* and *am*).

Then the reader can verify that the code

scsso msica ogcpm ksaso ksass knooi

translates into 'have a nice day.'

Such a code can be complicated a little further by including a key number, say 7, when every seventh letter of the coded message is ignored. Then, with regular changing of the keyword, a not too simple code is obtained.

Conclusion

In the preceding section some note of the term scanning in relation to data collection is worthwhile, as are the examples of tests for ISs. Some of the points suggested regarding computer security are really mandatory whilst the example code is, hopefully, interesting and may stimulate ideas in that area which might eventually prove useful.

IT9. A Case Study

The principle objective of the new global British Airlines system was increased *asset utilization* with, in turn, a reduction in the cost of assets. This was achieved by greater usage of scheduled flights and hotels involved in package deals. In turn inventory was able to be reduced and greater debtor control was achieved as an additional bonus of the system.

Communications

The communication network involved the following major features:

1. Telecommunications were handled by 40 PABX systems distributed globally and operation of these was optimized by the computer system resulting in considerable savings.
2. VHF communications at 70 airports.
3. In flight communications and navigation aids.
4. Closed circuit TV, flight information services and PA systems at each airport.

Computer system

The centralized computer system included the following activities in its operation:

1. Seat reservation system. This took hundreds of man years to develop and deal with alternate flights, connecting flights and waiting lists.
2. Inventory records of scheduled flights for BA and other airlines were kept up to a year ahead.
3. The system was directly linked to other airlines, this linkage requiring no human intervention.
4. Check-in and luggage weights were recorded, this data being used to adjust aircraft trim and fuel load.
5. Flight plans were adjusted in line with weather and other conditions and the results were available for reservation purposes.
6. Cargo scheduling etc. was controlled.
7. Stock and maintenance forecasts for engineering.
8. In-flight data analysis included evaluation of aircraft components.
9. Accounting.
10. Maintenance of personnel selection, development and skills inventories.
11. Statistical records of component defects, personnel and commercial data.
12. Planning data including timetables, payloads, budgets and mathematical models.

Thus a massive system with enormous capabilities was developed.

The results

The system was, of course, very successful and was emulated by other airlines so that their linked systems resulted in even greater improvements in airline operations globally.

On the cost side it was estimated that a 1% increase in 'load factor' per annum would recover 4% of the initial outlay. On this basis it was expected that there would be an 18% return on investment in the system after 10 years. In addition qualitative benefits such as improved service to both the public and management, not to speak of improved conditions for staff, were derived.

Conclusion

The foregoing was a spectacular example of the implementation of information technology for its times and remains of interest today. It is also a useful example of the sort of project for which a discounted cash flow analysis to calculate NPV and future cash flows is used for a project producing long term benefits and revenue.

IT10. BASIC programming

BASIC was developed by Kemeny and Kurtz at Dartmouth College (New Hampshire) in the early 1960s and was much used on minicomputers (which typically had 16 terminals, each being allowed 16 kb of RAM, the amount required by the then versions of BASIC) in the 1970s. In 1975 the first microcomputer was sold, a clumsy box + switches affair with storage of only 256 bytes. In the same year Tiny BASIC, consisting of just 20 pages of code, was written and many versions of this quickly appeared and, also in 1975, Gates and Allen launched Microsoft Corporation with their version, this being marketed with the Altair microcomputer. In the early 1980s IBM quit their almost monopoly of the electric ('golfball') typewriter market, switching to production of PCs, the first IBM PC having 16 kb of RAM.

BASICJ, BASICA and GW ('Gee Whiz") BASIC appeared. All used about 64 kb and the latter is quite powerful. QBASIC, using a rudimentary GUI (graphic user interface) followed and was shipped with DOS 5 whilst Quick BASIC, the first fully compiled BASIC appeared around the same time, and Visual Basic (VB) for Windows shortly thereafter, this having compilation as an option. VB4 was still somewhat clumsy to use, but VB5 is very user friendly though very complicated. VB5 is quite quick, but not as quick as the original computer language, FORTRAN, or the later C++.

VB6, however, is about as quick as C++ when compiled so that it is once again competitive. The great attraction is the original basic feature of being having a command interpreter which allows programs to run on an almost 'line by line basis without full, compilation, i.e. you don't type the whole program in, compile and receive a long list of cryptic error messages which don't even tell you where the program stopped. Instead mistyped lines produce an immediate error as you type the program in so when you do run the program there will be only one error message at a time, telling you when the program stopped and you go to that line and correct the usually obvious error, and thus work your way through what should be only a few errors.

Recently another compact version YABASIC ("Yet Another' -) appeared and this is 'ported' to Sony Play Station Twos.

Here we will use QBASIC, which takes only about 500 kb (c.f. VB5/6 takes about 100 MB and the Pro version is very expensive). Half of this being its HELP file which gives a fairly good, concise introduction to BASIC, though if the reader can track down an old GWBASIC manual that is some help. Alternatively a recent book by Greg Perry in the SAMS series (see IT ref. list) gives a good overview of programming, concentrating on QBASIC to introduce the reader to programming via several simple examples. QBASIC programs read directly into a VB 'module' (i.e. subroutine).

The most elementary BASIC commands are:

RUN - to run a program
SAVE - to store a program
ENTER - to add lines
REN - to renumber program lines (with default 'gaps' of 10)
LIST - to list the program (on screen)
BYE - to leave BASIC

Arithmetic operations

The following program determines the square toot of a number using Newton's method (see Sec. NM1) in which the root is given by iterating the recursion relation

$$x_{new} = (x_{old} + num/x_{old})/2$$

where num = number for which the square root is required

x_{old} = initial estimate of the square root

Then, using a tolerance number TOL as a termination criterion the program is:

```
10 Rem SQRT using Newton's method
20 Input "input, xold, num,tol", XOLD, NUM, TOL
30 XNEW = 0.5*(XOLD+NUN/XOLD)
40 DIFF = ABS(XNEW-XOLD)
50 IF DIFF<TOL THEN GOTO  80
60 XOLD = XNEW
70 GOTO 30
80 PRINT "SQRT =", NEW
```

and to test the program typical input is 1,4,0.001 to obtain $\sqrt{4} = 2$.

Note that ABS( ) is a library function for the absolute value and that in some versions of BASIC a final line, 90 END is required (and in VB a first line Sub MYPROG( ) is needed to declare a subroutine). In early versions of BASIC line numbers were necessary and in very early versions of BASIC variable names were restricted to a single alphabetic character plus a single optional digit.

In QBASIC (and VB) line numbers are not necessary and variable names can be many characters but statements are upper case (converted thus if typed otherwise). Then when computation is redirected by a GOTO (or THEN GOTO, for which only the GOTO is actually required) statement the target line must have a *label* (e.g. LAB1:) which is given in the GOTO statement. Thus the foregoing example can be written more briefly as

```
INPUT xold, num, tol
lab1: xnew = (xold + num/xold)/2 : diff = ABS(xnew-xold)
IF diff<tol GOTO lab2
xold = xnew: GOTO lab1
lab2:PRINT xnew
```

where a semicolon is used as a *statement separator.* The author, however, generally uses line numbers throughout his programs, one reason being that, having put many BASIC programs in books, they are very handy in this situation to help describe the program (i.e. "lines 110 - 160 do - - - ').

Strings

Ease of string handling is one of the traditional advantages of BASIC. The following program reads three names (given in the DATA statements at the end) and prints them (on screen) with three spaces between. It then prints an integer and a real number using PRINT USING to *format* these.

```
10 READ a$, b$, c$
20 x$ = SPACES$(3)
30 PRINT A$;x$;b$;x$;c$
40 P$="#####" : Q$ = "#####.##"
```

```
50 n = 2 : c = 14/3
60 PRINT USING P$ ; n ; : PRINT USING Q$;c
70 DATA 'Bob", "Jim", "Ted"
```

Note that a ; follows the first PRINT USING statement to print both numbers on the same line, otherwise the second number will appear on a second line. Here in line 40 P$ is in *integer* format and Q$ is in *real number* format. Strictly variables should be *declared* at the start of the program as *integer, real, double precision* etc. but the author has worked mostly with Chris Cochran's MegaBasic (about twice as fast as QBASIC) which does not do this, instead running a different version of the program for double precision computation.

Arrays and Loops

The following program dimensions, i.e declares the size of, *arrays,* then using a *loop* (on i) to read names and ages and print them out, right justifying the names using the LEN function.

```
10 DIM names$(10),num(10)
FOR i = 1 to 3
READ names$(i), num(i)
j = LEN(names(i)) : x$ = SPACE$( j )
PRINT x$;names$(i),num(i) : NEXT
DATA "Jane" , 25
DATA "June" , 35
DATA "Caroline" , 15
```

Subroutines

This program demonstrates the formation of subroutines using the GOSUB command. In this approach, however, the subroutine is still stored with the program (in the same file) and a superior approach is discussed in Sec. IT11 in which subroutines are kept in workspaces (which in turn are saved as separate files) and accessed from a main or 'calling routine'.

```
10 PRINT "main"
20 GOSUB 50
30 PRINT "main"
40 END
50 PRINT "sub"
60 RETURN
```

Functions

Finally we give a simple example of a user defined function to calculate the square of a number. Note the way the variable X is passed to the function as an *argument* and the function result is returned as R.

```
10 DECLARE FUNCTION SQ(Z)
20 Z=2
30 Y = SQ(Z)
40 PRINT Z
100 FUNCTION SQ(Z)
110 Z=Z*Z
END FUNCTION
```

Note that QBASIC automatically stores the function as a *subroutine* in a separate *workspace* accessed via the VIEW menu from the menu bar (at the top of the screen).

Standard functions

Standard arithmetic, mathematical and string functions used in BASIC include

INT( ) - gives the integer (truncated) value of a number

ABS( ) - gives absolute value of a number (unsigned)

RND(x) - gives a random number [x <0 gives same number, > 0 (or x not given) gives the next number in the sequence, = 0 gives the last number

SQR - gives square root

SIN( ) - gives SIN( ) of an angle in radians

LEN(A$) - see example program in "Arrays and loops" earlier in this section

CHR$(n) - gives the ASCII character corresponding to integer n (e.g. n = 65 gives A)

Conclusion

The brief introduction given here assumes that the reader is familiar with a little BASIC and the very simple programs for strings and arrays hint at how easy it is to write a simple database program of your own, for example.

IT11. Files and workspaces

In the following section files for main or 'calling' routines of programs and separate files for subroutines called by the main program are illustrated. Such files are usually stored directly on your hard disc and backed up on on floppy discs etc.

The following program is called MAIN and is one of the 50+ QBASIC programs given with the DBS/MBS course (in directory \MBS1 on the 'BASICS" disc). It has a subroutine 'datin' which is called and numbers passed to it, omitting one number so that it prints as zero when the number list is printed while in the subroutine:

```
DECLARE SUB datin (X!(), M!, Y!())
REM MAIN
DIM X(41), Y(41), G(40, 40)
DIM KODE(40), H(40, 40)
COMMON SHARED N, L, LEC, IMPN, G(), KODE(), H(), Y()
X(1) = 5: Y(2) = 3: N = 10: M = 10: Z = 2.5
datin X(), M, Y()
PRINT "main", X(1), Y(2), N, M, Z
END

SUB datin (X(), M, Y())
PRINT "sub", X(1), Y(2), N, M, Z
END SUB
```

Here the COMMON SHARED statement allows the listed variables to be accessed from other subroutines (not actually needed here).

Data files

Here we give an example of a date file (as distinct from a program file) using the following program:

```
OPEN "c:\basic\temdat" FOR OUTPUT AS #7
OPEN "c:\basic\gmdata" FOR RANDOM AS #8 LEN = 100
x = 2: y = 3
PUT #8, 1, x :PUT #8, 2, y
WRITE #7, x, y
CLOSE #7
OPEN "c:\basic\temdat" FOR INPUT AS #7
GET #8, 2, z
PRINT z
INPUT #7, z
PRINT z
```

Here two files are used for *sequential access* and *direct access*, in the second case generally overestimating the *record* length and reading back only the second number written to it.

Searching and comparing data

The following code is a very simple example of comparing data, in this case string data. In conjunction with search, therefore, such comparisons can be used to locate specific data.

```
10 a$ = "jim"
20 b$ = "jim"
30 IF a$ = b$ THEN PRINT "OK"
40 b$="ted"
50 IF a$ = b$ THEN PRINT "OK" ELSE PRINT "NO"
```

In the previous example program such comparisons might be used to extract negative numbers (perhaps corresponding to negative account balances) and the associated personal details from a file.

Conclusion

In the examples of subroutines, data files etc. we have discussed much of the work involved with databases and other aspects of information is encountered, providing a brief introduction to the kinds of applications programs used in MISs.

The following section gives a few further examples and exercises for the reader, of particular relevance being sorting routines, in particular a quick sorting routine which uses recursive programming.

IT12. Programming Exercises and Sorting Routines

The reader is urged to try out some of the simple programs in Sec. IT11 and also some of those in the following section.

Transcendental functions

The following pair of exercises carry over from Sec. MS2. The first is simply based on the question: "How many terms of the series for exp(x) do I need?" and provides the answer.

```
10 INPUT, "Input x",x
20 EXPS = 1 : F = 1
30 FOR I = 1 TO 20
40 F = F * X / I
50 EXPS = EXPS + F
60 PRINT " i = ", I+1, "exps = ",EXPS,"exact = ",exp(X)
```

and with QBASIC which uses 7 figure computation (for single precision), the number of terms needed in the series to obtain the exact result is 10 when x = 1 and 19 when x = 4.

The second exercise is simply to use a screen (or printer, when LPRINT replaces PRINT) as a crude plotter, for example plotting part of a SIN( ) curve:

```
10 X = 0 : PI = 4 * ATAN(1)
20 FOR J = 1 to 21
30 Y = SIN(X)
40 X = X + PI/10
50 x$=SPACE$(40+INT(Y*35))
60 PRINT X$ ; X
70 NEXT
```

using an 'x' to plot each point and limiting the loop on J to the depth of the screen.

Things are a lot different, of course, using built in graphics or graphics packages but it is useful to remember that simple but practical plots can be done straight from a program like that used here.

Random numbers

Random numbers were used in the exercise of Sec. MS13 and will be needed again in the *simulation* exercise of Sec. OR9. Another simple exercise using random numbers is that of estimating the value of π by counting the number of randomly plotted points that fall within a circle and comparing this number to the total number of points. This is done in the following program (which is also program PIPLOT>BAS in \MB1 on the course 'BASICS' disc).

```
5 REM Simple exercise - random number plot gives estimate of pi
8 CLS
10 INPUT "i/p N ", N
20 C = 0: SCREEN 1: COLOR 4, 1: COLOR 4, 1: A = 2 * ATN(1): T = 1
30 CIRCLE (0, 200), 200, 1, 0, A, T: LINE (0, 0)-(0, 200): LINE (0, 199)-(300, 199)
40 FOR I = 1 TO N: X = RND: Y = RND: R = SQR(X * X + Y * Y)
50 IF R < 1 THEN C = C + 1
60 X = 200 * X: Y = 200 * Y: CIRCLE (X, Y), 1, 1
70 NEXT
80 LOCATE 22, 26: PRINT "pi= "; 4 * C / N
```

Using 100 random numbers (N = 100 in line 10) the estimate of pi was 3.24 and, of course, the accuracy of the result increases as more points are used.

Sorting routines

As a final exercise we briefly consider *sorting routines*, that is, routines for sorting a list of randomly ordered numbers into ascending or descending order (there are also *shuffling routines* which do the opposite).

The simplest type of sort is a *bubble sort* in which we successively pass down through the numbers, interchanging pairs of numbers when the second exceeds the first. Eventually the numbers fall into descending order. The program BSORT.BAS in \MBS1 on the 'BASICS' program disc does this, taking over 2000 calculations to sort 100 numbers.

More efficient is *search sorting* which seeks out the maximum number of those remaining to be sorted and places this at the top of these. The program SSORT.BAS in \MBS1 does this, taking over 400 calculations for the 100 number sort. The listing for this is:

```
0 DIM V(100): REM Search sort - needs approx 400 calcs
15 FOR I = 1 TO 100: VALUE = RND(.5) * 100: V(I) = INT(VALUE): NEXT
18 CALCS = 0
20 FOR N = 1 TO 100: MAXN = 0
30 FOR I = N TO 100
40 IF V(I) <= MAXN THEN 60
45 CALCS = CALCS + 1
50 MAXN = V(I): POSN = I
60 NEXT I
70 V(POSN) = V(N): V(N) = MAXN
80 NEXT N
90 FOR I = 1 TO 100: PRINT V(I); : NEXT
100 PRINT "Calcs = ", CALCS
```

More efficient are *hybrid* sorting routines which combine the two approaches. The program NSORT is a crude and inefficient attempt at this. More efficient routines use *recursion* (i.e. the subroutine calls itself) and take only about 200 calculations for the 100 number sort. QBASIC, however, will not permit such recursion so instead the listing for the program QSORT from \MBS1 is given below

This uses the *Quick Sort* method and is relatively sophisticated. It lives up to its name, however, and takes about 167 calculations for the 100 number test.

```
DIM H, L, ii AS LONG
DECLARE SUB quicksort (a(), L, H)
DECLARE SUB partition (L, H, ii, a())
DIM a(101)
FOR i = 1 TO 100: VALUE = RND(.5) * 100: a(i) = INT(VALUE): NEXT
calcs = 0
CALL quicksort(a(), 1, 100)
FOR i = 1 TO 100: PRINT a(i); : NEXT
PRINT "Calcs = ", calcs

SUB partition (L, H, ii, a())
SHARED calcs: DIM i, j AS LONG
piv = a(L): i = L: j = H + 1: REM Choose pivot as first element in range
```

```
DO
 DO
  i = i + 1: REM From start look for larger # (if there is)
 LOOP UNTIL a(i) > piv OR i >= H
 DO
  j = j - 1: REM From end look for smaller # (if there is)
 LOOP UNTIL a(j) < piv OR j <= L
        REM If they haven't crossed swap them
 IF i < j THEN
  temp = a(i): a(i) = a(j): a(j) = temp: calcs = calcs + 1
 END IF
LOOP UNTIL j <= i: REM Swap pivot with the split in the array
a(L) = a(j): a(j) = piv: calcs = calcs + 1
ii = j: REM Return index of # in correct location for next 'split sort'
END SUB
SUB quicksort (a(), L, H)
REM If the range is valid then sort
IF L < H THEN
REM Split the array & return index of the item in the correct location
CALL partition(L, H, ii, a())
REM Sort the lower portion
CALL quicksort(a(), L, ii - 1)
REM Sort the upper portion
CALL quicksort(a(), ii + 1, H)
END IF
END SUB
```

General

[1] Try the program PLOTX4 in \MBS1 on the course Basics disc. This uses the statements WINDOW SCREEN and VIEW which will give some idea on the origins of 'Windows' as a GUI (Graphical User Interface).

[2] Try out a DB package, and in particular the following exercises:

(a) Write a small DB of addresses.

(b) Write another DB of *accounts payable* and JOIN it to the address DB, using these addresses to produce *form letter*s.

(c) Produce (perhaps using a standard *template*) an invoice form and set this up as a form letter connects to the DBs formed in (a) and (b).

(d) Try producing a *report* from a small DB (using a *query* to select records).

(e) Include a date *field* in the DB and select records between two dates.

(f) Include a field *cost* (of inventory items) in the DB and obtain a column total for the selected records in the report.

(g) Add a field *price* (of sale) to the DB and form a *derived field, profit* = (price - cost) in the DB.

(h) Include the profit field in your report and obtain a column total for it.

Conclusion

In this chapter we had a brief look at IT (strictly ITC), concentrating mostly on guidelines for the design of ISs, noting that these are generally a combination of many modes of communication and computer technology. *Cost effectiveness* of systems is given a little thought and BASIC programming is introduced concisely.

Note that the 1995 first edition of the DBS/MBS used DOS and MegaBasic, the second Windows 3.1 and QBASIC, the third Windows 97B and QBASIC, the fourth Windows XP service pack 2 and QBASIC, and the fifth and final edition used Windows XP, Windows Vista, and Windows 7 together with QuickBasic and VB5.

IT References

W.W.R. Ball, *Mathematical Recreations and Essays,* McMillan, London 1922

K.S. Braithwaite, *Information Engineering,* vol. 1, CRC Press,Boca Raton FA 1992.

S. Brown, *Visual Basic in Record Time,* Sybex, Alameda CA 1998.

I.G. Burch, F.R. Strater, G. Grudnitski, *Information Systems: Theory and Practice,* 3rd edn, Wiley, New York 1983

H.L. Capron, B.K. Williams, *Computers and Date Processing,* Benjamin Cummings, Menlo Park CA 1982.

J.D. Carrabis, *Hard Disc Management Techniques for the IBM,* Sams, Indianapolis IN 1988.

C. Cochran, *MegaBasic Users Manual,* American Planning Corp., Alexandria VA 1984.

E.J. Desautels, *Symphony for the IBM PC and Compatible Computers,* Brown, Dubuque IO 1985.

D. Fox, *Pure Visual Basic,* Sams 1999.

C.B. Kreitzberg, B. Scheidman, *The Elements of FORTRAN Style,* HBJ, New York 1972.

J. Krutch, *Experiments in Artificial Intelligence for Small Computers,* Sams, Indianopolis IN 1981.

D.A. Lien, *The BASIC Handbook* 3rd edn, Microtech, Dubai UAE 1989.

G.M. Litton, *Database Management*, Brown, Dubuque IO 1987.

G. Masters, *DOS 5: A-Z,* Sybex, Singapore 1992.

D. McCracken, W.S. Dorn, *Numerical Methods and FORTRAN Programming*, Wiley, New York 1964.

T.W. McCrae, *Management Information Systems,* Penguin, Harmondsworth 1971.

G.A. Mohr, H.R. Milner, *A Microcomputer Introduction to the Finite Element Method,* Pitman, Melbourne 1986; Heinemann, London 1987.

Mohr GA, *Elementary Thinking for the 21st Century,* Xlibris (2014).

T.J. O'Leary, B.K. Williams, L.I. O'Leary, *McGraw-Hill Microcomputing Labs, 1992 annual edition*, McGraw-Hill, New York 1992.

Perry, G, *Introduction to Computer Programming,* SAMS, New York 2001.

M.J. Powers, D.R. Adams and H.D. Mills, *Computer Information Systems Development: Analysis and Design,* South Western, Cincinnati OH 1984.

W.T. Price, *Fundamentals of Computers and Data Processing with BASIC,* Holt Rinhart and Winston, New York, NY. 1983.

J. Sachs, *Your IBM PC Made Easy,* Central Book Co., Taipe, 1984.

P. Schnaidt, *Enterprise-Wide Networking,* SAMS, Carmel IN. 1992.

Time-Life (eds), *Computer Languages,* Time-Life Inc. 1986.

D. Will-Harris, *Wordperfect: Desktop Publishing in Style* 2nd edn, Peachpit, Berkeley CA 1990.
F.R. Wu, *Accounting Information Systems*, McGraw-Hill, New York 1984.
S.M. Zimmerman, L.M. Conrad, *Understanding and Using Microcomputers,* West, St Paul MN 1986.
Abacus StatView Manual (for MAC), Abacus Concepts Inc., Berkeley CA 1992.
Aldus Freehand User's Manual (for MAC), Aldus Corp. 3rd edn, Seattle WA 1991.
Aldus Persuasion V2.0 User Manual, Aldus Corp., Seattle WA 1991.
Borland Quattro Pro V4.0 Functions and Macros, Borland, Scotts Valley CA 1992.
Borland Quattro Pro for Windows V5.0, Borland, Scotts Valley CA 1993.
DEC FORTRAN Language Reference Manual, DEC, Maynard MS 1992.
Disk Operating System, Command Reference and Error Message, V6, IBM 1993.
FileMaker II (for MAC), Claris Corp., Mountain View CA 1988.
Lotus Word Pro 96: Exploring Word Pro, Lotus Dev. Corp., Atlanta GA 1995.
MacIntosh System Software User's Guide V 6.0.4, Apple Computer Corp., Cupertini CA 1989.
MS Excel User's Guide etc. V3.0 (for MAC), MS 1991.
MS GW-BASIC User's Guide and User's Reference, MS Corp. 1987.
MS-DOS User's Guide and User's Reference V4.0, Microsoft 1988.
MS-DOS 6 User's Guide V6.0, Microsoft 1993.
MS Powerpoint V2.0 User's Manual, MS 1988.
MS Windows V3.1 User's Guide, MS 1992.
Networking Essentials, 2nd edn, Microsoft Press, Redmond, Washingon, 1997.
Norton Utilities V2.0 (for MAC), Symantec, Cupertino CA 1992.
Nisus User's Guide V3.0 (for MAC), Paragon Concepts Inc., Solana Beach CA 1991.
123 for Business, Lotus
Planix Office User Manual V1.0, Foresight Resources Corp., Kansas City KS 1993.
Wordperfect 5.1 Reference vols 1 and 2, Wordperfect Corp., Orem UT 1990.

Sundry: many computer magazines over two decades.

NUMERICAL METHODS (NM)

You are now number one, John Argyris, To author on phone from Stuttgart 2001.

Earlier, basic mathematics topics, including statistics, were introduced as this material was required in later chapters. Here numerical methods much used in computer applications are introduced and these are needed in following chapters. An example is numerical solution of matrix equations and an important application of this, *input-output analysis,* is given in at the close of subject ME, and this is an excellent demonstration of the application of numerical methods to economic problems.

NM1. Iterative and Search Techniques

In the following section a number of simple techniques for solving problems in a *stepwise* fashion are discussed. These are often used in conjunction with matrix methods of analysis, for example to provide powerful general techniques of tackling complex mathematical modeling problems.

Recurrence formulas

A simple example of a recurrence formula is *Newton's formula* for determining the square root of a number:

$$\text{(NM1)} \quad Lim_{n \to \infty}(x_n + A/x_n)/2 = \sqrt{A}$$

for which the recurrence relation is

$$\text{(NM2)} \quad x_{n+1} = (x_n + A/x_n)$$

where A is the number for which the square root is sought, x_n, is the last estimate of the root and x_{n+1} is an improved estimate.

For example, to obtain √4 we put $A = 4$ and begin with $x_o = 1$, giving

$$x_1 = (1 + 4/1)/2 = 2.5$$

$$x_2 = 2.5 + 4/2.5) = 2.05 \text{ etc.}$$

so that clearly *convergence* is very rapid.

The reader is encouraged to write a short computer program of a few lines for this formula, including a tolerance number to test whether the root has been found with sufficient accuracy, if so terminating iteration. (or try the code given in Sec. IT10).

Basic iteration

Basic iteration is a simple means of determining the solution of a problem by rearranging its equation and iterating the result in an attempt to obtain a solution. As an example suppose we wish to find the roots of the equation

(NM3) $x^2 - 5x + 4 = 0$

By factorization it is obvious that the roots are $x = 1$ and $x = 4$, but a more general method of solution is obtained by writing

(NM4a) $x_{n+1} = (x_n + 4)/5 = F(x)$

(NM4b) $\boldsymbol{x}_{n+1} = \sqrt{(5x_n - 4)}$

Then (a) with $x_o = 1$ gives the root $x = 1$, whilst with $x_o = 5$ the solution *diverges.* The recurrence relation (b), on the other hand, gives the root $x = 4$ with $x_0 = 2$, 3, or 5 but gives an imaginary solution when $x_0 = 0$ (which a computer program is should not allow).

Here we notice the first of three important properties of basic iteration, these being:

[1] Only one root can be obtained from any particular arrangement.

[2] Convergence is guaranteed if $| F'(x) | < 1$ near the root.

[3] The method has *first order convergence*, that is dx is proportional to $(x - x^*)$ where x^* is the exact solution. In other words the rate of convergence is proportional to the distance from the solution.

Basic iteration can be used to solve nonlinear matrix equations, for example, by placing the nonlinear terms on the right hand side and retaining a left side of the form $A\{x\}$ where A is a matrix of constant entries and $\{x\}$ is a vector of variables x, y etc., for which a solution is sought.

Search methods

Search methods involve using successive *trial values* to 'locate' the solution to a problem. For example suppose we week the solution of

(NM5) $f(x) = x^3 - x - 1 = 0$

then we assume trial values of x and calculate the resulting value of $f(x)$. Beginning with $x = 0$ we obtain

$$f(0) = -1, \quad f(1) = -1, \quad f(2) = 5$$

and with $x = 2$ we observe a change in sign, indicating that $f(\ ) = 0$ has been passed. Then we use *bisection* of the interval $x = 1 \rightarrow 2$, that is use $x = 1.5$ to give $f(1.5) = 0.875$.

Then, the sign having changed, we bisect the interval $x = 1.25 \rightarrow 1.5$ using $x = 1.375$ to give $f(1.375) = -0.225$.

Continuing in this fashion the solution is more closely bracketed but the solution can be obtained more quickly by using *linear interpolation* rather than bisection in the intervals in x.

This can be written as

(NM6) $x' = x + \delta x/\delta t$

so that in place of the first bisection (with $x = 1.5$) we use

$$x' = 1 + 1/6 = 1.167$$

giving $f(x') = -0.579$.

Interpolating again

$$x' = 1.167 + (2 - 1.167)/(5 - (-0.579)) = 1.3163$$

giving $f(x') = -0.0356$ which after two interpolations is much closer to the solution than we were after three bisections.

Note that Eqn NM5 has two other roots and to obtain these other trial values of x some distance from the first root must be used. Sometimes this is achieved by *shifting* the origin of the problem using the substitution $(x - x^*)$ where x^* is the first root (estimate) for x in Eqn NM5. Then the search is for the distance of the next root from the first.

Fig. NM1 illustrates Newton's method of finding the roots of an equation. Here in seeking the root of $f(x) = 0$ we *extrapolate* along the tangent to the curve $y = f(x)$ at the current point x_n to obtain an improved solution x_{n+1}, so that the change in x is given by

$$\delta x = -(\text{residual error})/(\text{slope})$$

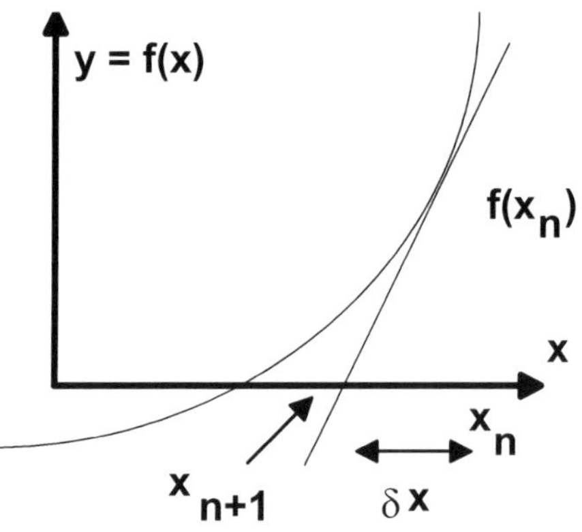

Fig. NM1 Illustration of Newton's method of finding the roots of equations

where the *residual* or residual error is the distance of $f(x_n)$ from the required value of zero and the *slope* is the derivative of the function $f(x)$ with respect to x evaluated at $x = x_n$.

Then the recurrence relation for Newton's method is written as

(NM7) $x_{n+1} = x_n - f(x_n)/f'(x_n)$

and this might be described as the *tangent slope method.*

If, for example, we seek the roots of Eqn NM3, then we have

$$f(x) = x^2 - 5x + 4 \text{ and } f'(x) = 2x - 5$$

so that the recurrence relation is

$$x_{n+1} = x_n - (x_n^2 - 5x_n\ 4)/(2x_n - 5) = (x_n^2 - 4)/(2x_n - 5)$$

which with $x_o = 5$ gives the successive results $x = 4.2, 4.012, 4.000$ so that convergence is a good deal faster than with basic iteration in Equations NM4. Then $x_0 = 2$ quickly leads to the other root ($x = 1$) whilst $x_0 = 3$ will yield the first root again (i.e. $x = 4$).

Here we notice the first of three characteristics of Newton's method (sometimes referred to as the Newton-Raphson method), these being:

1. The root obtained depends upon the starting point.
2. The method has *second order convergence*, that is dx is proportional to $(x - x^*)^2$ (whereas basic iteration had only first order convergence).
3. No simple criterion for convergence exists (as it does for basic iteration).

Often search techniques are used to approximately locate a root (which may be of $f'(x) = 0$ when we are seeking turning points) and then Newton's method is applied to efficiently find an accurate solution.

The initial slope method

In some types of problem calculation of the new value of $f'(x)$ required by Newton's method is laborious. In such cases we can use only the first or *initial value* of this slope, that is $f'(x_0)$ in Eqn NM7, giving

$$\text{(NM8)} \qquad x_{n+1} = x_n - f(x_n)/f'(x_0)$$

and this method must work as iteration will continue as long as there is a residual (value of $f(x)$).

Convergence is a good deal slower than with Newton's method (first order convergence, in fact) but numerous *acceleration* techniques have been proposed to remedy this in part. The simplest of these multiply the increment in x suggested by Eqn NM8 by a *convergence factor* which typically ranges from 0.8 to 1.5.

Conclusion

In econometrics, for example, the search and other techniques described here have obvious application, as they do in many areas of modern computer analysis of physical systems, including, of course, those in business.

NM2. Predictor-Corrector Methods

From their name predictor-corrrector methods sound like something we might be grateful to see used in the governance of our national economy and, indeed, such methods do have wide potential application. In such methods a prediction is made by such techniques as Newton's method and then we correct our 'aim' on the basis of the result of this prediction.

Euler's method involves taking steps in some variable x, say δx, to calculated the value of a function $y = f(x)$ at some value of x several steps δx away.

To explain this procedure we write a *linear interpolation* in terms of a *dimensionless coordinate* $s = dx/\delta x$ which varies from zero to one in the interval δx, that is the interpolation for x is written as

$$\text{(NM9)} \qquad x = (1 - s)x_i + (s)x_{i-1}$$

and the functions in brackets are called *interpolation functions.*

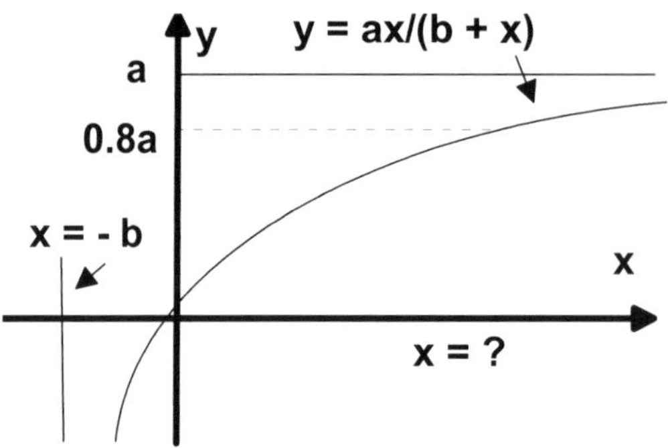

Fig. NM2 Rectangular hyperbola with asymptotes y = a and x = -b.

Then for a function y = *f(x)* like that shown in Fig. NM2 we can write

(NM10) $$\delta y x' = \delta y (dx/dy) = \delta y (dx/ds)(ds/dy) = dx/ds = -x_i + x_{i-1}$$

using the chain rule of differentiation and noting that $dy/ds = \delta y$.

Then rearranging this result we have

(NM11) $$x_{i+1} = x_i + \delta y (dx/dy)$$

which is Euler's method.

Applying this to the rectangular hyperbola shown in Fig. NM2 we obtain the recurrence relation

$$x_{i+1} = x_i + \delta y (b + x_i)^2/ab$$

(NM12) or $$x_{i+1}/b = x_i/b + (\delta y/a)(1 + x_i/b)^2$$

in dimensionless form, yielding the results shown in Table NM1 when eight equal steps in *y* are taken up to 0.8*a*.

Table NM1. Solutions to the problem of Fig. NM2

y/a	x/b Euler	x/b Runge-Kutta	x/b Exact
0.1	0.1000	-	0.1111
0.2	0.2210	0.2400	0.2500
0.3	0.3701	-	0.4286
0.4	0.5578	0.6607	0.6667
0.5	0.8005	-	1.0000
0.6	1.1247	1.4874	1.5000
0.7	1.5761	-	2.3333
0.8	2.2397	3.8164	4.0000

The results for the Euler method (sometimes called the *continuation method*) are poor, illustrating the need for an improved method such as the following one.

Predictor-corrector method

An improved method is obtained by replacing the linear interpolation of Eqn NM9 by the *quadratic interpolation*

$$x = (1/2)(s^2 - s)x_{i-1} + (1 - s^2)x_i + (1/2)(s^2 + s)x_{i+1}$$

in which the dimensionless coordinate s ranges from minus one to one (this interpolation is derived later in this chapter). Then the result of Eqn NM10 is now

(NM13a) $\delta y x'' = (1/2)(2s - 1)x_{i-1} - 2sx_i + (1/2)(s^2 + 1)x_{i+1}$

from which

(NM13b) $\delta y x'_i = (x_{i+1} - x_{i-1})/2$

using $s = 0$ in Eqn NM13a. Eliminating x_{i-1} from these two results gives

(NM14) $x_{i+1} = x_i + \delta y(1 - 1/2s)x'_i + \delta y(1/2s)x_{i+1}$

which is the second order Runge-Kutta predictor-corrector formula. Using this we obtain the following solution strategy:

(NM15) $x_1 = x_0 + \delta y(dx/dy)_0$ - first predictor

(NM16) $x_{i+1} = x_{i-1} + 2\delta y(dx/dy)_i$ - subsequent predictors

(NM17) $x_{i+1} = x_i + (1/2)\delta y\,[(dx/dy)_i + (dx/dy)_{i+1}]$ - corrector

where Eqn NM15 results from Eqn NM14 when $s = \infty$ (this is also the Euler formula), Eqn NM16 is a rearrangement of Eqn NM13a and Eqn NM17 results from Eqn NM14 when the dimensionless coordinate $s = 1$.

This gives much better results than the Euler method using only half as many steps, as shown in Table NM1 (where to make the comparison fair half as many steps are used but two gradient calculations are required for each step, namely the predictor and corrector).

This approach can also be used to modify Newton's method (see Fig. NM1) but in this case convergence is already sufficiently rapid for most purposes.

Conclusion

The Euler or continuation method is rather inaccurate in highly nonlinear problems and the predictor-corrector method described gives considerably better results. It is, perhaps, best understood in words than from Eqns NM15 - 17:

a. Use the last tangent at the present point to extrapolate from the last point to the next point (equivalent to using a chord approximation).

b. Calculate the slope at this *estimate* of the next point and use the average of this and that used to obtain the estimate to extrapolate to the next point.

Then this 'correct the aim' approach is much more accurate and much more logical than the Euler method.

NM3. Solution of Matrix Equations

In the following section two important methods of solving matrix equations of the form $A\{x\} = \{b\}$ are described. A concise program for one of these is then given in Sec. NM4.

Gauss-Seidel Iteration

Gauss-Seidel iteration can be described by the *algorithm*

(NM18) $$a_{ii}x_i^* = b_i - {}_{j=1(j\neq 1)}\Sigma^n\, a_{ij}x_j$$

and such algorithms can be coded almost literally. This method, however, is best understood from a simple example such as solution of the two simultaneous equations:

(NM19) $$2x_1 + x_2 = 7, \quad x_1 + 2x_2 = 8$$

which are rewritten as $x_1 = (7 - x_2)/2, \; x_2 = (8 - x_1)/2$

Then beginning with $x_1 = x_2 = 1$ and iteratively using the rearranged Eqns NM19 we obtain

Iteration	x_1	x_2
1	3	2.5
2	2.25	2.875
3	2.063	2.969
Exact	2	3

and the results are converging fairly well.

Note, however, that if the equations are first written in the form

(NM20) $$x_1 + 2x_2 = 7, \quad 2x_1 + x_2 = 8$$

then the results diverge (try this as an exercise).

Then for convergence we require the magnitude of the *pivot* (the diagonal coefficient in the matrix expression of the equations) to be equal to or greater than the magnitude of the other coefficients for each row or equation.

A slight variation in the Gauss-Seidel method is *Jacobi* or *simultaneous iteration* where all the x_i are evaluated at each iteration or 'pass' through the values before being used for the next evaluation or iteration. Generally convergence will be slightly slower and this method is rarely used.

Boolean matrices

(NM21) $$\begin{bmatrix} 1 & 0 & 0 \\ 0 & 0 & 1 \\ 0 & 1 & 0 \end{bmatrix}\begin{bmatrix} 1 & 2 & 3 \\ 4 & 5 & 6 \\ 7 & 8 & 9 \end{bmatrix} = \begin{bmatrix} 1 & 2 & 3 \\ 7 & 8 & 9 \\ 4 & 5 & 6 \end{bmatrix}$$

The first matrix of Eqn NM21 *premultiplies* the second, causing rows two and three to be swapped. Such matrices are called Boolean matrices and only have zero or 'one' entries.

If this same matrix had been used to *postmultiply* the second matrix then its second and third columns would have been swapped.

Such matrices are rarely used in practice but the concept of a matrix which operates on another matrix, swapping or subtracting rows and/or columns is helpful in understanding many matrix techniques.

Gauss-Jordan reduction

Gauss-Jordan reduction is a practical numerical method of finding the inverse A^{-1} of a matrix *A*. Then the solution of the matrix equation $A\{x\} = \{b\}$ is given as $\{x\} = A^{-1}\{b\}$, where here $\{x\}$ = a one column matrix or *vector* of the unknowns or *variables* x_i and $\{b\}$ is a vector containing the right hand side values of the set of simultaneous equations whose coefficients are stored in matrix *A*.

This method involves performing such operations on matrix *A* so as to reduce it to an identity matrix (i.e. with entries = 1 on the *leading diagonal* running from top left, and = 0 elsewhere), expressing these operations as a matrix *B* (a complicated extension of the idea of a Boolean matrix). Then if matrix *A* is first *augmented* by an identity or unit matrix we can write:

(NM22) $$B[\,A,\ I\,] = [\,I,\ C]$$

then *A* has been reduced to a unit matrix and we have

$$BA = I \quad \text{so that} \quad B = A^{-1}$$

and $$C = BI = A^{-1}$$

so that the premultiplying matrix *B* was the required inverse (though we did not know it) and all the operations performed on matrix *A* to reduce it to a unit matrix (various row subtractions to produce the zero off-diagonal entries required) are recorded as matrix *C*.

Then it turns out that the operations required to reduce *A* to a unit matrix are straightforward so that, using these at the same time on a unit matrix, the inverse A^{-1} is obtained and this is done on an example in Table NM2.

Table NM2 Gauss-Jordan reduction *tableau*.

	2	2	2	1	0	0
	2	3	4	0	1	0
	2	4	3	0	0	1
row1/pivot → r1*	1	1	1	1/2	0	0
r2 - 2r1*	0	1	2	1	1	0
r3 - 2r1*	0	2	1	-1	0	1
r1(last) - 1 x 2r2	1	0	-1	3/2	-1	0
r2(last)/pivot → r2*	0	1	2	-1	1	0
r3(last) - 2 x r2*	0	0	-3	1	-2	1
r1(last) - (-1) x r3*	1	0	0	7/6	-1/3	-1/3
r2(last) - 2 x r3*	0	1	0	-1/3	-1/3	2/3
r3/pivot → r3*	0	0	1	-1/3	2/3	-1/3

Here r2 denotes row 2 and so on, and r2* denotes the row after it has been divided by the pivot (the first operation of each reduction).

Here three reductions (of successive columns from left to right) have been performed, the first operation of each being division by the pivot (entry on the diagonal) of matrix *A*. This is followed by the operation

(NM23) new row = old row - pivot row* x *row multiplier*

where * denotes having been divided by its pivot and the *row multiplier* is the entry in each row directly above or below the pivot.

This method can easily be written as an *algorithm* and this will directly correspond to the key lines of the program given in Sec. NM4. In this program the matrix is not actually augmented by a unit matrix but overwritten by the forming inverse.

Note that problems will occur when a pivot is zero is close to it and routines which use *pivotal condensation* or *pivoting* are used to overcome such difficulties. In these columns are swapped to obtain the largest possible pivot (from the columns remaining unreduced). These column swaps are recorded in a one dimensional array and corresponding rows are swapped at the conclusion of Gauss-Jordan reduction (reversing the swaps). This is necessary because swapping any two columns of a matrix results in a corresponding swap in the rows of the inverse.

A program including pivoting is given in Sec. NM12 and a simpler program which does not is given below.

NM4. Solution of Matrix Equations (cont.)

Gauss reduction

Gauss reduction is a method of *direct solution* of matrix equations, that is a solution is obtained without calculating the inverse of the connecting matrix *A*. This method is also called *triangular elimination* because it reduces the matrix *A* to an 'upper triangular' matrix *(U)*. The operations required to achieve this are exactly the same as in Gauss-Jordan reduction except that the 'row subtraction' operations are only carried out below the pivotal position. Thus, returning to the example of Table NM2 we obtain:

Table NM3 Example of Gauss reduction

(a) forward reduction

		Matrix A		{b}
	2	2	2	12
	2	3	4	20
	2	4	3	19
r1/pivot r1*	1	1	1	6
r2 - 2 x r1*	0	1	2	8
r3 - 2 x r1*	0	2	1	7
OK	1	1	1	6
r2(last)/pivot r2*	0	1	2	8
r3(last) - 2 x r2*	0	0	-3	-9
OK	1	1	1	6
OK	0	1	2	8
r3(last)/pivot	0	0	1	3

(b) back substitution

$b_3 = x_3 = 3$

$b_2 - 2x_3 = x_2 = 8 - 2(3) = 2$

$b_1 - x_2 - x_3 = x_1 = 6 - 2 - 3 = 1$

Here in the forward reduction to reduce matrix *A* to upper triangular form the same operations are carried out on the RHS vector *{b}* (that is, *{b}* replaces *I* on the LHS of Eqn MN22).

Then the back substitution yields the solutions of the equation *A{x} = {b}* in reverse order as

(NM24) $$x_i = b_i - \sum_{j=i+1}^{n} a_{ij}(last) \times x_j$$

and Eqn NM24 is, in fact, equivalent to inverting the upper triangular matrix to which *A* was reduced and premultiplying the RHS vector by it (it must be as it yields the solution!). Inversion of triangular matrices, therefore, is a very simple exercise numerically.

Gauss reduction requires roughly n^3 operations (+, -, x, /) to obtain the solution whereas Gauss-Jordan reduction takes about twice as many operations when the inverse of *A* is calculated (but not the same number if A^{-1} is not formed as can be seen in the program given in this section). The classical Laplace expansion (see Sec. MS5), on the other hand takes *n*! operations and hence is only practical for $n \leq 4$.

Coding of matrix operations

Computer coding of most matrix operations is relatively straightforward and, for example, multiplication of two matrices *A (M x L)* and *B (L x N)* to obtain a matrix *C* (which will be *M x N*) can be coded as

```
10 FOR I = 1 TO M: FOR J = 1 TO N
20 C(I,J) = 0 : FOR K = 1 TO L
30 C(I,J) = C(I,J) + A(I,K)*B(K,J)
40 NEXT : NEXT : NEXT
```

and here it is clear why for the matrices to be *compatible* (for the purposes of multiplication) the number of columns of the first must be equal to the number of rows of the second (so that rows and columns can be multiplied together in the required fashion).

Gauss-Mohr reduction subroutine

The following BASIC subroutine uses Gauss-Jordan reduction to form the inverse of a matrix *S,* overwriting it by its forming inverse. Underlining and [ ] are to indicate modifications discussed later but are not actual code. This incredibly short ten line routine was the basis of Mohr's *PC Finite Element Solution System (PC FESS),* first developed for teaching on a 8 terminal 'midi computer' in 1983 and used on a Spectravideo PC in 1984. Version 2 was a far longer and more complex affair developed using MegaBasic and an XT PC in 1987.

```
10 FOR I = 1 TO N
20 X = S(I,I) : Q(I) = Q(I)/X [: S(I,I) = 1]
30 FOR J = 1 TO N
40 S(I,J) = S(I,J)/X : NEXT
50 FOR K = 1 TO N
60 IF K = I THEN 100
70 X = S(K,I) : [S(K,I) = 0 : ] Q(K) = Q(K) - X*Q(I)
80 FOR J = 1 TO N
90 S(K,J) = S(K,J) - X*S(I,J) : NEXT J
100 NEXT K : NEXT I
```

Then if the two underlined statements are added the reduction operations are also applied to a RHS vector {Q} so that, at the completion of 'GJR' this vector contains the solution of the equation *S{x} = {Q}*.

In Gauss-Mohr Reduction (GMR) the bracketed statements are removed and the lower limits in lines 30 and 80 are changed from 1 (one) to I+1 so that reduction operations are carried out only to the right side of the pivot and the inverse of *A* is not formed but the solution of *S[x] = [Q]* is still obtained with the amount of computation almost halved.

Note that before this program segment is entered matrix *S* and vector *{Q}* (if used) must be appropriately dimensioned and filled, for example using

```
2 INPUT "INPUT N",N
4 DIM S(N,N), Q(N)
6 FOR I = 1 TO N
8 READ S(I,J) : NEXT : NEXT
9 FOR I = 1 TO N : READ Q(I) : NEXT
110 END
120 DATA 5/8, -1/2, 1/8
130 DATA -1/2, 1, -1/2
140 DATA 1/8, -1/2, 5/8
150 DATA 1,2,3
```

Here the data is for a 3 x 3 matrix of the form shown in Eqn NM25 so that the inverse should take the simple form shown (PRINT lines need to be added to print the results). Then the RHS vector is given by line 150, so that the solution of *S{x} = {Q}* (which will be contained in array Q( ) will be (10, 14, 14).

$$\text{(NM25)} \quad \begin{bmatrix} \frac{n+2}{2n+2} & -1/2 & 0 & - & - & \frac{1}{2n+2} \\ -1/2 & 1 & -1/2 & - & - & 0 \\ 0 & -1/2 & 1 & - & - & 0 \\ - & - & - & - & - & - \\ 0 & 0 & - & -1/2 & 1 & -1/2 \\ \frac{1}{2n+2} & 0 & - & 0 & -1/2 & \frac{n+2}{2N+2} \end{bmatrix}^{-1} = \begin{bmatrix} n & n-1 & n-2 & - & 2 & 1 \\ n-1 & n & n-1 & - & 3 & 2 \\ n-2 & n-1 & n & - & 4 & 3 \\ - & - & - & - & - & - \\ 2 & 3 & 4 & - & n & n-1 \\ 1 & 2 & 3 & - & n-1 & n \end{bmatrix}$$

The form of matrix used here (that is a *tridiagonal matrix* with unit diagonal, -1/2 for all the off-diagonal entries on either side of the diagonal and exceptional corner values as shown in Eqn NM25) is very useful for testing matrix inversion or solution routines.

Conclusion

Gauss reduction is the fundamental means of solving matrix equations though there are a few minor and major variations on the theme. Gauss-Jordan reduction, however, can also be used for direct solution of matrix equations (when the inverse of the connecting matrix is not formed) as the short program given shows.

NM5. Eigenvalues

Eigenvalue problems are an oft neglected type of problem but a brief introduction to them here is worthwhile as some of the suggested applications at the close of the section suggest. In plain English eigenvalues are unique scalar numbers the various values of which result in the determinant of a 'compound matrix' being zero (and hence the matrix is singular or cannot be inverted).

Eigenvalues defined

The eigenvalues of a matrix A are defined by the statement

$$\text{(NM26)} \quad | A - \lambda I | = 0$$

and the values λ_i which cause Eqn NM26 to be satisfied are the eigenvalues.

Considering simple 2 x 2 matrix as an example we obtain:

$$\text{(NM27)} \quad \left| \begin{bmatrix} 1 & -1 \\ -1 & 1 \end{bmatrix} - \lambda \begin{bmatrix} 1 & 0 \\ 0 & 1 \end{bmatrix} \right| = 0$$

for which the LaPlace expansion is

$$(1-\lambda)^2 - 1 = 0 \rightarrow \lambda_1 = 0 \text{ and } \lambda_2 = 2$$

In practice the LaPlace expansion is not used and numerical techniques based on Gauss reduction are used to evaluate the determinant of the compound matrix for successive values of l. Approximate estimates of the eigenvalues are then those values of λ for which the determinant is close to zero.

Eigenvectors

For every eigenvalue of a (compound) matrix there is a corresponding eigenvector $\{e_i\}$ which satisfies the equation

$$\text{(NM28)} \quad | A - \lambda I | \{e_1, e_2\}$$

(here assuming a 2 x 2 matrix as in our example problem).

The eigenvectors are determined by substituting the eigenvalues into Eqn NM29 and then solving the resulting matrix equation. First, however, the first entry (typically, it can be any other one) in the eigenvector is put = 1. This is an arbitrary *datum* value (and it also acts like a boundary condition and, in many practical problems, the compound matrix is singular without this condition) and the remaining entries in the eigenvector relative to this describe a *mode* or shape.

Then putting $e_1 = 1$ and substituting $\lambda_1 = 0$ and $\lambda_2 = 2$ the corresponding eigenvectors for the problem of Eqn NM27 are obtained as

$$\text{(NM29)} \quad \{e_1\} = \{1, 1\} \quad \text{(the rigid mode)}$$

$$\text{(NM30)} \quad \{e_2\} = \{1, -1\} \text{ or } \{e_2{}^*\} = \{1/\sqrt{2}, -1/\sqrt{2}\}$$

where in the rigid mode (characterized by a zero eigenvalue) the variables all move in unison. The second form of the second eigenvector is the *Euclidean norm* which is obtained by dividing each entry by the square root of the sum of the squares of all entries (so that the 'S.S' of $\{e^*\}$ =1).

Note in passing the identity

$$\text{(NM31)} \quad \Sigma\, \lambda_1 = trace(A) = \Sigma\, a_i$$

that is, the sum of the eigenvalues equals the sum of the diagonal entries of matrix A. This provides a very useful check of the accuracy of eigenvalue calculations.

Chio's method

Chio's method of determining the value of the determinant of a matrix is based on Gauss reduction and is simply

$$\text{(NM32)} \quad \det(A) = {}_{i=1}\Pi^{\,n}\, a_{ii}^* = a_{11}^* a_{22}^* a_{33}^* \text{ - - - } a_{nn}^*$$

where a_{ii}^* are the pivots encountered during Gauss reduction.

For example the pivots for the matrix of Table NM3 were 2, 1 and -3 so that det(A) = (2)(1)(-3) = -6 which is the correct result.

Hence the program given in Sec. NM4 can be used to calculate determinant values since Gauss-Jordan reduction will have exactly the same pivots as Gauss reduction.

Eigenvalue search techniques

Now that we have a practical numerical method of evaluating determinants (Chio's method) search can be used to determine eigenvalues by:

a. Incrementing λ gradually from a trial value until det$(A - \lambda I)$ changes in sign.

b. Using bisection (or interpolation) to estimate the eigenvalue that has now been bracketed.

This process is then repeated, first using the shifting described in Sec. NM1, to determine the other eigenvalues.

Then the eigenvectors can be determined by inserting the eigenvalues in Eqn NM28 and using a routine such as that given in Sec. NM4 to obtain the corresponding eigenvectors (first remembering to put e_1 =1).

Inverse iteration

Another means of determining *eigenpairs* (eigenvalues and their corresponding eigenvectors) is inverse iteration where the recurrence relation

$$\text{(NM33)} \quad \{e\}^{n+1} = (\lambda)\, A^{-1}\, \{e\}^{n}$$

is used (here (λ) denotes that the eigenvalue is taken to be absorbed into $\{e\}^n$) beginning with an initial trial trial eigenvector (typically {I}, a unit vector).

Then iteration will result in the eigenvector for the *lowest* eigenvalue and the value of λ is given by the ratio of the first (or any other) entries in $\{e\}^{n+1}$ and $\{e\}^n$. This value is then used to 'shift' matrix A and the procedure used to calculate the next eigenpair.

Vector iteration

This is exactly the same as inverse iteration except that matrix A is not inverted so that we use the recurrence relation

(NM34) $\{e\}^{n+1} = (1/\lambda)\, A\, \{e\}^n$

and again $(1/\lambda)$ denotes that the eigenvalue is taken to be absorbed into $\{e\}^n$. Now, however, iteration gives the eigenvector for the *highest* eigenvalue.

For the matrix A of Eqn NM27, for example, beginning with a trial eigenvector {1, 0} we obtain

(NM35) $\begin{bmatrix} 1 & -1 \\ -1 & 1 \end{bmatrix} \begin{Bmatrix} 1 \\ 0 \end{Bmatrix} \rightarrow \begin{Bmatrix} 1 \\ 1 \end{Bmatrix} \rightarrow \begin{Bmatrix} 2 \\ 2 \end{Bmatrix} \rightarrow \lambda_2 = 2$

(NM36) $\begin{bmatrix} -1 & -1 \\ -1 & -1 \end{bmatrix} \begin{Bmatrix} 1 \\ 0 \end{Bmatrix} \rightarrow \begin{Bmatrix} -1 \\ -1 \end{Bmatrix} \rightarrow \begin{Bmatrix} 2 \\ 2 \end{Bmatrix} \rightarrow \lambda_1{}^* = -2$

where we write $\lambda_1{}^*$ as a reminder that matrix A has been 'shifted' in Eqn NM36 by $\lambda_2 = 2$ (i.e. using this value in Eqn NM28 so that 2 is subtracted from the diagonal entries) so that the actual eigenvalue is given by

(NM37) $\lambda_1 = \lambda_1{}^* + \lambda_s$

Applications of eigenvalue techniques

Some of the many applications of eigenvalues include:

1. Analysis of physical systems which can be modeled as eigenvalue problems, common examples being natural frequencies of (unforced) vibration, buckling loads and shapes of engineering structures and 'modes' in any problem expressed in the form of Eqn NM27.
2. In economics eigenvalues of input-output matrices (see Sec. ME12) indicate natural modes of variation of 'money flow' between nations or simply companies.
3. The *rank* of a matrix is equal to the number of non-zero eigenvbalues which it possesses and this indicates the number of independent equations which the rows of the matrix correspond to (note that when Gauss-Jordan reduction is used to evaluate the determinant of a matrix by Chio's method a zero pivot, corresponding to a zero eigenvalue, will 'blow up' the process. Hence zero pivots require the use of pivoting, i.e. column/row swapping).
4. The most common form in which physical eigenvalue problems occur is

(NM38) $(A - \lambda B)\{e\} = \{0\}$

Then if vector iteration is to be used to determine the eigenpairs, for example, we simply replace A by $B^{-1}A$ in Eqn NM34. Indeed in many problems involving vibrations of some kind it is possible to use a *lumped* matrix to approximate matrix B as a diagonal matrix (for which the inverse is given simply by the reciprocals of the diagonal elements in this lumped matrix). Typically this lumped B matrix is obtained by summing the entries in each row and placing the result on the diagonal (putting zeroes elsewhere).

Conclusion

Eigenvalue problems are one of a number of the more mathematical areas of this course text that can be skipped by some readers, at least on a first reading. Indeed until some familiarity with matrices has been gained and then with the input-output problem of Sec. ME12, for example, eigenvalue problems can sensibly be ignored by those not familiar with them.

NM6. Finite differences

The finite difference method has been around for about 150 years and it really comes into its own with the availability of computers as it is essentially a method of *numerical differentiation.* Thus any differential equation can immediately be expressed in finite difference form. Applying this at several points in a *domain* the resulting simultaneous equations can be solved using the techniques discussed in Secs NM3 and NM4.

Difference tables

Table NM4 gives a finite difference table for $f(x) = x^3$, the results being those characteristic of this simple function (for example a point of inflexion at $x = 0$ and no turning points).

Table NM4 Finite difference table for $f(x) = x^3$

n (of dx)	x	f(x)	Differences			
			first	second	third	fourth
0	-3	-27				
			19			
1	-2	-8		12		
			7		6	
2	-1	-1		6		0
			1		6	
3	0	0		0		0
			1		6	
4	1	1		6		0
			7		6	
5	2	8		12		
			19			
6	3	27				

The even numbered differences can be related to particular values of *n* and *x* but the odd numbered differences cannot. Then for the first differences we can therefore relate each value shown in the table to the start, the middle or the end of the interval to which it corresponds, resulting in the definitions:

(NM39) $\Delta f_n = f_{n+1} - f_n$ or the *forward difference* for point n

(NM40) $\delta f_{n+1/2} = f_{n+1} - f_n$ or the *central difference* for the interval

(NM41) $\nabla f_{n+1} = f_{n+1} - f_n$ or the *backward difference* for point n+1

Then the values of the first differences do not alter (and are as in Table NM4, for example) but their point of reference alters.

Generally central differences are the *natural* choice and they are also more accurate, involving a *truncation error* of the order of δx^2 whereas forward and backward differences involve a truncation error of order δx. In some cases, however, forward differences result in simpler mathematical models of certain types of problems and are therefore preferred.

Central difference formulas

Denoting $\delta x = h$ the central difference formulas for the second and fourth differences can be deduced from Eqn NM40, giving

(NM42) $$(df/dx)_{n+1/2} = f'_{n+1/2} = (f_{n+1} - f_n)/h$$

(NM43) $$f''_n = (f'_{n+1/2} - f'_{n-1/2})/h = [(f_{n+1} - f_n)/h - (f_n - f_{n-1})/h]/h = (f_{n+1} - 2f_n + f_{n-1})/h^2$$

(NM44) $$f^{IV}_n = (f''_{n+1} - 2f''_n + f''_{n-1})/h^2 = [f_{n+2} - 2f_{n+1} + f_n - 2(f_{n+1} - 2f_n + f_{n-1}) + f_n - 2f_{n-1} + f_{n-2}]/h^4$$
$$= (f_{n+2} - 4f_{n+1} + 6f_n - 4f_{n-1} + f_{n-2})/h^4$$

and these formulas can be extended into two or more dimensions, for example.

Eqn NM43 is used in Sec. NM10 to establish a recurrence relation for a vibration problem and thence determine the vibrations that result after a transient excitation.

Conclusion

The finite difference method (FDM) is a very important one and it is also the predecessor of the finite element method (FEM) and the boundary element method (BEM). Respectively these methods tackle any differential equation of the nth order (involving derivatives of that order) by

1. Using n^{th} derivatives (the original DE) (FDM)
2. Reducing the DE to order *n/2.* (FEM)
3. Reducing the DE to zero order. (BEM)

and these methods are discussed in the FM chapter.

NM7. Numerical integration

Numerical integration has important applications in modern mathematical analysis. In the economics an obvious example might be calculation of the areas under supply and demand curves to determine the associated revenue. At present we shall restrict attention to one dimensional integration but like analytical integration, numerical integration is readily extended to deal with two or more dimensions.

Mid-ordinate and trapezoidal rules

Fig. NM3 shows the two most basic rules for numerical integration. With the first of these, the mid-ordinate rule, the area under the curve $y = f(x)$ is estimated as

(NM45) $$I = h \ {}_{i-1}\Sigma^n \ y_i$$

that is, as the sum of the rectangles of width h and height y_i, the height of the curve at the middle of each strip, there being n such strips.

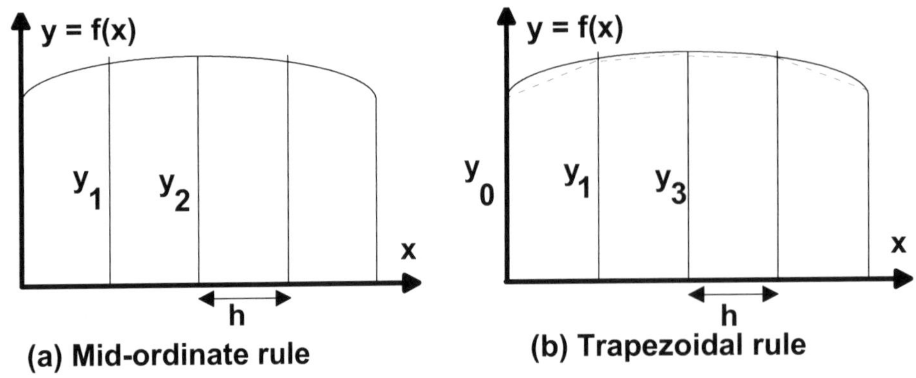

Fig. NM3 Simple rules for numerical integration

The trapezoidal rule, on the other hand, averages the ordinates on each side of each strip, equivalent to calculating the area of a trapezoid. Then for *n* such strips we obtain the formula

(NM46) $I = (h/2)[y_0 + y_n + 2\sum_{i=1}^{n-1} y_i]$

so that summation of ordinates involves halving the first and last and adding the remaining (internal ordinates).

Thus rule gives a linear approximation (in each strip) to $y = f(x) = a_1 + a_2x + a_3x^2$- - (in general), so that the *truncation error* is of the order of the square of h which we denote as $O(h^2)$.

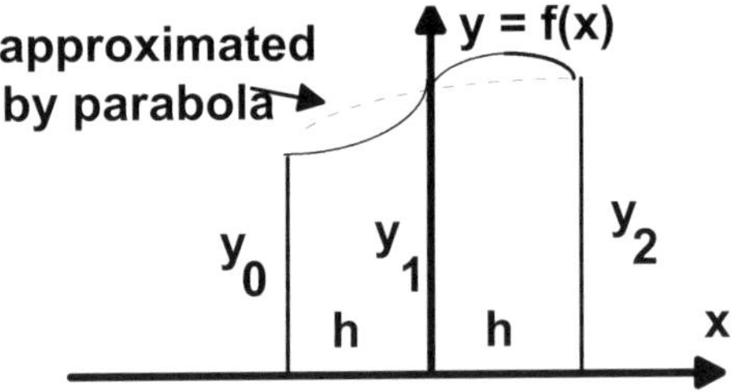

Fig. NM4 Simpson's rule

Fig. NM4 illustrates the idea of Simpson's rule. Here a pair of strips is used to exactly integrate the quadratic approximation shown (dashed line).

Then we can write the exact integral of this quadratic curve as

(NM47) $I = \int_{-h}^{h} (a + bx + cx^2)dx = [ax + bx^2/2 + cx^3/3]_{-h}^{h} = 2ah + 2ch^3/3$

The numerical integration is written as

(NM48) $\sum_{i=0}^{2} w_i f(x_i)(2h)$

where w_i are *weights* for each point, $f(x_i)$ is the ordinate at each point and $2h$ is the *subdomain size*. Then noting that $w_0 = w_2$ from symmetry the numerical result can be written as

(NM49) $I = [w_0(a - bh + ch^2) + w_1(a) + w_0(a + bh + ch^2)](2h) = 2ah(2w_0 + w_1) + 2ch^3(2w_0)$

As the results of Eqns NM47 and NM49 must be identically equal it quickly follows from term by term comparison of the right hand sides that $w_0 = 1/6$ and $w_1 = 1 - 2w_0 = 4/6$ so that the formula for integration of the double strip shown in Fig. NM4 is

(NM50) $I = (2h/6)(y_0 + 4y_1 + y_2)$

so that combining several such strip pairs Simpson's formula can be written in the mnemonic form

(NM51) $I = (h/3)[y_{first} + y_{last} + 4\Sigma y_{odd} + 2\Sigma y_{even}]$

even numbered ordinates generally being involved in two adjoining 'double strips' so that a factor of two is attached to the summation of these, the factor four for the 'middle' ordinates in the strip pairs following from Eqn NM50.

Because of symmetry considerations, in fact, Simpson's rule exactly integrates a cubic function as is easily shown by adding a term dx^3 before integrating in Eqn NM47. Therefore it has a truncation error $O(h^4)$ and is thus much more accurate than the trapezoidal rule but is no more difficult to use.

Gauss quadrature

This exploits the symmetry property observed with Simpson's rule to generate a series of numerical integration rules. The first is the two point rule which exactly integrates a cubic function. The *optimum* integration point coordinates (-*s* and *s*) and weights *w* are given by

(NM52) $I = (2h)]wf(x = -s) + wf(x = s)]$

$= (2hw)(a - bs + cs^2 - ds^3) + (2hw)(a + bs + cs^2 + ds^3)$

$= (2hw)(2a + 2cs^2)$

This result should be identically equal to that of Eqn NM47 and thus comparing them term by term it quickly follows that $w = ½$ (as expected by symmetry with only two weights) and $s^2 = h^2/3$ or $s = +/- (h/\sqrt{3})$ for a double stip like that shown in Fig. NM4.

Hence Gauss quadrature for this double strip is written as

(NM53) $I = \Sigma w_i f(s_i)(2h) = (2h)\{f(-1/\sqrt{3})/2 + f(1/\sqrt{3}/2)\}$

and integration for several such double strips is accomplished in the same way as with Simpson's rule. Once again the truncation error is $O(h^4)$ but now this is accomplished with two rather than three points.

Example

As a simple example suppose that we wish to calculate

(NM54) $I = {}_0\int^{\pi/2} \cos(x)dx = 1$

using two strips (or one double strip) using the four rules discussed:

[1] Mid-ordinate rule (with three ordinates)

$I = (\pi/6)[\cos(15^0) + \cos(45^0) + \cos(75^0)] = 1.0115$ (error = 0.0115)

[2] Trapezoidal rule (2 strips/3 ordinates)

$$I = (\pi/8)[\cos(0) + 2\cos(45^0) + \cos(90^0)] = 0.9481 \qquad \text{(error = - 0.0519)}$$

[3] Simpson's rule (1 double strip/3 ordinates)

$$I = (\pi/12)[\cos(0) + 4\cos(45^0) + \cos(90^0)] = 1.0023 \qquad \text{(error = 0.0023)}$$

[4] Two point Gauss rule (1 double strip/2 ordinates)

$$I = (\pi/4)[\cos(45^0 - 45^0/\sqrt{3}) + \cos(45^0 + 45^0/\sqrt{3})] = 0.9985 \quad \text{(error = -0.0015)}$$

and the two point Gauss rule clearly gives the most accurate result.

In like fashion to the two point rule, Gauss rules for from 3 to 100 points have been calculated, an *N* point rule exactly integrating a polynomial of order *(2N - 1)* so that is has a truncation error of $O(h^{2N})$.

Conclusion

Numerical integration is a straightforward process and of the basic rules Simpson's rule is the preferable. Generally, however, the Gauss rules are 'optimal' and though these involve coordinates with irrational values this is no obstacle in the computer age.

NM8. Lagrangian interpolation.

Numerical integration has many important applications. In the present section Lagrangian interpolation of values of a function at two or more points is discussed. We restrict attention to one dimensional interpolation but extension to two or more dimensions is straightforward.

Lagrange interpolation formula

The Lagrange interpolation formula for interpolation of *N* equally spaced values of a function *u = f(x)* is

$$\text{(NM55)} \qquad u = {}_{i=1}\Sigma^N f_i u_i \text{ where } f_i = {}_{k=1(k\neq i)}\Sigma^N (x - x_k)/(x_i - x_k)$$

using *interpolation functions* f_i corresponding to each point value u_i.

Applying Eqn NM55 to the linear interpolation of Fig. NM5 gives

$$\text{(NM56a)} \quad f_1 = (x - x_2)/(x_1 - x_2) = (x - L)/(-L) = 1 - x/L$$

$$\text{(NM56b)} \quad f_2 = (x - x_1)/(x_2 - x_1) = (x - 0)/L = x/L$$

$$\text{(NM57) or} \quad u = (1 - x/L)u_1 + (x/L)u_2$$

L

1 2

(x = 0) x (x = L)

Fig. NM5 Linear interpolation

and writing the interpolation of Eqn NM57 in terms of a *dimensionless coordinate s = x/L* which varies from zero to one we obtain

$$\text{(NM58)} \qquad u = (1 - s)u_1 + (s)u_2 = \Sigma f_i u_i = \{f\}^t\{u\}$$

where *{f }* is a vector of interpolation functions and *{u}* is the vector of point of *nodal* values of the function $u = f(x)$.

The linear interpolation could have been established by inspection, of course, but it provides a useful introduction to the Lagrange formula. Then use of this to form the interpolation functions for higher order interpolation functions follows without difficulty.

Fig. NM6 shows three equally spaced points for which we seek to establish a quadratic interpolation. Rather than use the Lagrange formula we shall use matrix inversion to establish the interpolation functions because this approach can be applied to interpolations of different types of variables, as we shall see in Sec. NM9.

Again using a dimensionless coordinate (originating at the centre of the domain) we write a quadratic interpolation polynomial

(NM59) $$u = a_1 + a_2 s + a_3 s^2 = \{M\}^t\{s\} = [1,\ s,\ s^2]\begin{Bmatrix} a_1 \\ a_2 \\ a_3 \end{Bmatrix}$$

L/2 L/2
1 (s = -1)
2 (s=0)
3 (s = 1)
s = 2x/L

Fig. NM6 Quadratic interpolation

where *{M}* is a vector of *modes* and *{a}* is a vector of their *amplitudes.*

Then substituting the nodal values of u on the LHS of Eqn NM59 and their corresponding dimensionless coordinates *(s)* on the RHS we obtain

(NM60) $$\{u\} = \begin{Bmatrix} u_1 \\ u_2 \\ u_3 \end{Bmatrix} = \begin{bmatrix} 1 & -1 & 1 \\ 1 & 0 & 0 \\ 1 & 1 & 1 \end{bmatrix}\begin{Bmatrix} a_1 \\ a_2 \\ a_3 \end{Bmatrix} = A\{a\}$$

Then, inverting the matrix A the amplitudes are obtained as

(NM61) $$\{a\} = \begin{Bmatrix} a_1 \\ a_2 \\ a_3 \end{Bmatrix} = \begin{bmatrix} 0 & 1 & 0 \\ -1/2 & 0 & 1/2 \\ 1/2 & -1 & 1/2 \end{bmatrix}\begin{Bmatrix} u_1 \\ u_2 \\ u_3 \end{Bmatrix} = A^{-1}\{u\}$$

Then combining Eqns NM59 and NM61 we obtain

(NM62) $$u = \{M\}^t\{a\} = \{M\}^t A^{-1}\{u\} = \{f\}^t\{u\}$$

so that the required interpolation functions are given by

(NM63) $$\{f\}^t = \{M\}^t a = [1,\ s,\ s^2]\begin{bmatrix} 0 & 1 & 0 \\ -1/2 & 0 & 1/2 \\ 1/2 & -1 & 1/2 \end{bmatrix}$$

giving the final interpolation as

(NM64) $$u = (1/2)(s^2 - s)u_1 + (1 - s^2)u_2 + (1/2)(s^2 + s)u_3 = \Sigma\, f_i\, u_i$$

The reader should check this result by putting s = 1, 0, 1 into Eqn NM64 when the required results $u = u_1, u_2, u_3$ are obtained.

This interpolation is, of course, much more accurate than linear interpolation when curved functions are involved. Extension of the inversion procedure to establish a cubic Lagrangian interpolation for four points is straightforward.

NM9. Hermitian interpolation

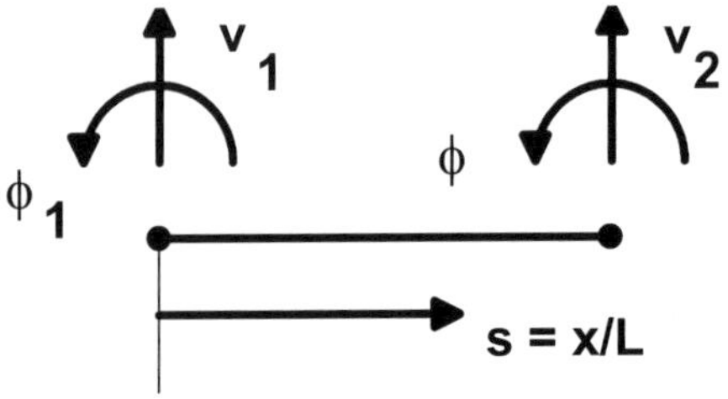

Fig. NM7 Cubic Hermitian interpolation

Fig. NM7 shows two nodes with *freedoms* v_1 and v_2 in a translational variable v and also two rotational freedoms ϕ_1 and ϕ_2 where

$$(NM65) \quad \phi = dv/dx = (dv/ds)(ds/dL) = (1/L)(dv/ds)$$

$$\text{or} \quad \phi* = dv/ds = L\phi$$

and ϕ is the derivative or slope of v and ϕ^* is the *dimensionless derivative* of v with respect to the dimensionless coordinate s and this is the more useful form for the present purposes as it allows us to form a dimensionless interpolation matrix A^{-1} using the inversion procedure used in Sec. NM8.

Then writing and differentiating a cubic interpolation polynomial gives

$$(NM67a) \quad v = a_1 + a_2 s + a_3 s^2 + a_4 s^3 = \{f\}^t\{a\}$$

$$(NM67b) \quad \phi^* = dv/ds = a_2 + 2a_3 s + 3a_4 s^2$$

and substituting nodal values on the left and right sides we obtain

$$(NM68) \quad \{v, \phi^*\} = \begin{Bmatrix} v_1 \\ \phi_1{}^* \\ v_2 \\ \phi_2{}^* \end{Bmatrix} = \begin{bmatrix} 1 & 0 & 0 & 0 \\ 0 & 1 & 0 & 0 \\ 1 & 1 & 1 & 1 \\ 0 & 1 & 2 & 3 \end{bmatrix} \begin{Bmatrix} a_1 \\ a_2 \\ a_3 \\ a_4 \end{Bmatrix} = A\{a\}$$

Then inverting A gives the interpolation functions as

$$(NM69) \quad \{f\}^t = \{M\}^t A^{-1} = [1,\ s,\ s^2, s^3] \begin{bmatrix} 1 & 0 & 0 & 0 \\ 0 & 1 & 0 & 0 \\ -3 & -2 & 3 & -1 \\ 2 & 1 & -2 & 1 \end{bmatrix}$$

so that the final interpolations for v and its derivatives can be written as

$$(NM70) \quad v = f_1 v_1 + L f_2 \phi_2 + f_3 v_2 + L f_4 \phi_4 = f_1 v_1 + f_2 \phi_1{}^* + f_3 v_3 + f_4 \phi_2{}^*$$

$$\text{where } f_1 = (1 - 3s^2 + 2s^3),\ f_2 = (s - 2s^2 + s^3),\ f_3 = (3s^2 - 2s^3),\ f_4 = (s^3 - s^2)$$

and

(NM71) $\phi = dv/dx = (1/L)(dv/ds) = (1/L)(d\{f\}^t/ds)\{v, \phi\}$

$$= (6s^2 - 6s)v_1/L + (1 - 4s + 3s^2)\phi_1 + (6s - 6s^2)v_2/L + (3s^2 - 2s)\phi_2$$

The reader should check these results by putting $s = 0$ and 1 into Eqns NM70 and NM71 when $v = v_1$, v_2 or $\phi = \phi_1$, ϕ_2 should be obtained.

Conclusion

Both Lagrangian and Hermitian interpolations are much used in mathematical modelling of physical systems. They might also be of interest in econometric problems where values and their rates of change are known. In addition the inversion procedure used to establish the cubic Hermitian interpolation can, with little modification, be used to fit cubic *splines* in a 'piecewise' fashion to model complicated curves and shapes (essentially the known values and slopes are used to determine the amplitudes *{a}* of Eqn NM67a.

NM10. Time Stepping Techniques

In this section central finite difference approximations are used to model a problem of *transient boundary excitation.* Here the finite difference equations are rearranged so that *time stepping* can be used to calculate the system response as the time is gradually incremented (this process is sometimes referred to as numerical integration).

First order time dependent problems

First order time dependent problems are governed by differential equations with first order derivatives (with respect to both space and time). Such problems have a 'creep' character, the solution creeping towards an equilibrium state from an initial state. The numerical equations for such problems take the general form

(NM72) $C\{f'\} + K\{f\} = \{Q\}$

and the entries in the vector *{f'}* are approximated using first order finite differences, that is

(NM73) $\{f'\} = [\{f\}_{n+1} + \{f\}_n] / \delta t$

for a time increment δt. then this expression is substituted into Eqn NM72 and the result rearranged with only $\{f\}_{n+1}$ on the left side (including its multiplying matrix *C*), the exact form of the right side depending upon whether forward, central or backward differences are used.

Then the small steps in time are used to calculate updated vectors $\{f\}_{n+1}$ and this procedure of time stepping is illustrated for a second order problem below.

Second order problems

Second order time dependent problems involve differential equations with second order derivatives with respect to time (accelerations or equivalent quantities). Such problems have a vibration or oscillation character which may be a *steady state* forced vibration (by a cyclic loading) or a result of *transient boundary excitation* in which vibrations resulting from a temporary loading gradually die down.

Assuming that damping effects associated with velocity terms can be neglected (that is, the $C\{f'\}$ term in Eqn NM72) numerical matrix models of second order problems take the form

(NM74) $$M\{f''\} + K\{f\} = \{Q\}$$

where the RHS load vector can be time dependent.

Then using a time increment $\delta t = h$ and using the central difference approximation of Eqn NM43 in Eqn NM74 we obtain the recurrence relation

(NM75) $$M\{f\}_{n+1} = h^2\{Q\}_n + (2M - h^2K)\{f\}_n - M\{f\}_{n-1}$$

Omitting the loading term and partitioning the matrices M and K into 'free' and boundary related terms denoted by the subscript 'b' gives

(NM76) $$\begin{bmatrix} M & M_b \\ M_b^t & M_{bb} \end{bmatrix}\begin{Bmatrix} f \\ f_b \end{Bmatrix}_{n+1} = \begin{bmatrix} 2M - h^2K & 2M_b - h^2K_b \\ 2M_b^t - h^2K_b^t & 2M_{bb} - h^2K_{bb} \end{bmatrix}\begin{Bmatrix} f \\ f_b \end{Bmatrix}_n - \begin{bmatrix} M & M_b \\ M_b^t & M_{bb} \end{bmatrix}\begin{Bmatrix} f \\ f_b \end{Bmatrix}_{n-1}$$

assuming that the matrices M and K are symmetric.

The bottom row of Eqn NM76 can be deleted because the 'boundary' values $\{f_b\}$ are known and assuming the matrix partition M_b is null (zero entries, as is the case when a 'lumped' or diagonal approximation for the M matrix is used to simplify the analysis) we obtain the recurrence relation

(NM77) $$M\{f\}_{n+1} = -h^2K_b\{f_b\}_n + (2M - h^2K)\{f\}_n - M\{f\}_{n-1}$$

Here 'loading' occurs via specified values of $\{f_b\}_n$, for example loadings applied cyclically by machines to their mountings or transient excitation of buildings subjected to earthquakes. A simple example of the latter type of problem is shown below.

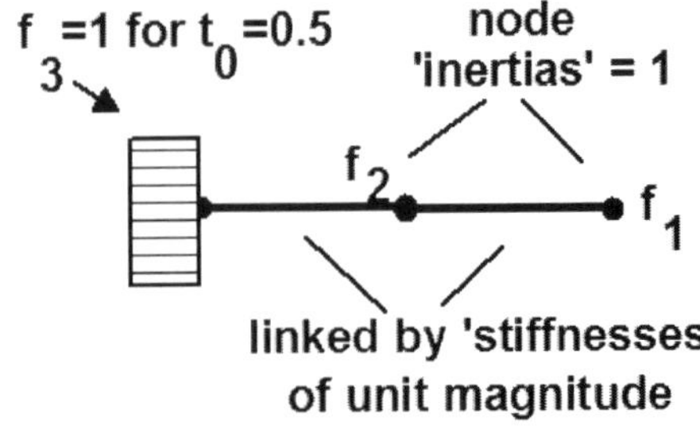

Linking each pair of nodes by a 'stiffness' matrix

(NM78) $$k = \begin{bmatrix} 1 & -1 \\ -1 & 1 \end{bmatrix}$$

these are added to a 3 x 3 *system matrix* giving

(NM79) $$K = \begin{bmatrix} 1 & -1 & 0 \\ -1 & 2 & -1 \\ 0 & -1 & 1 \end{bmatrix}$$

This summation is, in fact, the basis of the finite element method (FEM) and this is discussed further in subject/chapter FM. Partitioning this matrix as required by Eqn NM76 the matrices required for Eqn NM77 are

$$\text{(NM80)}\qquad K=\begin{bmatrix}1 & -1\\ -1 & 2\end{bmatrix}\qquad K_b=\begin{bmatrix}0\\ -1\end{bmatrix}\qquad M=\begin{bmatrix}1 & 0\\ 0 & 1\end{bmatrix}$$

and substituting these into Eqn NM77 we obtain

$$\text{(NM81)}\qquad \begin{Bmatrix}f_1\\ f_2\end{Bmatrix}_{n+1} = s\begin{Bmatrix}0\\ 1\end{Bmatrix}(f_3)_n + \begin{bmatrix}2-s & s\\ s & 2-s\end{bmatrix}\begin{Bmatrix}f_1\\ f_2\end{Bmatrix}_n - \begin{Bmatrix}f_1\\ f_2\end{Bmatrix}_{n-1}$$

where $s = 50h^2$.

Then imposing the transient excitation $f_3 = 1$ for $t_0 = 0.5$ and using a time step length $h = 0.1$ we obtain

$$\text{(NM82a)}\qquad (f_1)_{n+1} = (1.5f_1 + 0.5f_2)_n - (f_1)_{n-1}$$

$$\text{(NM82b)}\qquad (f_2)_{n+1} = 1(t \le 0.5) + (0.5f_1 + f_2)_n - (f_2)_{n-1}$$

These are easily plotted by the BASIC program VIBPLOTon \MBS1 of the course 'Basics' disc, the listing of which is:

```
5 REM Time stepping vibration program
10 A1 = 0: B1 = 0: A2 = 0: B2 = 0: XL = 0: SL = 0
20 SCREEN 1: COLOR 4, 1: LINE (0, 0)-(0, 200): LINE (0, 100)-(300, 100)
30 FOR T = 0 TO 2.5 STEP .1
40 S = 0: IF T <= .5 THEN S = 1
50 A3 = 1.5 * A2 + B2 / 2 - A1: B3 = S + A2 / 2 + B2 - B1: X = 120 * T
60 Z = 100 - 20 * SL: Y = 100 - 20 * S: LINE (XL, Z)-(X, Y)
65 Z = 100 - 20 * B2: Y = 100 - 20 * B3: LINE (XL, Z)-(X, Y)
67 Z = 100 - 20 * A2: Y = 100 - 20 * A3: LINE (XL, Z)-(X, Y)
70 A1 = A2: B1 = B2: A2 = A3: B2 = B3
80 XL = X: SL = S: NEXT
```

The screen output takes the form shown in Fig. NM8 and it is instructive to see how results vary when different 'stiffness/mass' ratios are used, for example this is very low there is 'pudding like' response rather than the 'tauter' elastic vibration here.

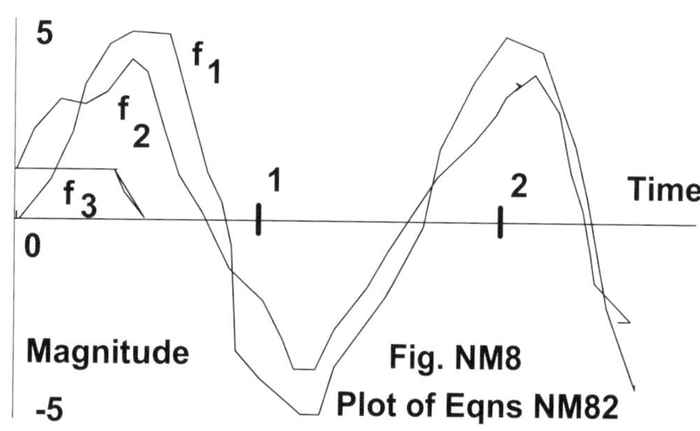

Fig. NM8
Plot of Eqns NM82

Considering the simplicity of the final equations Fig. NM8 yields a good deal of information (in the original context the problem was the lateral movements at three levels of a two story building with transient ground movement).

Whilst the foregoing formulation appears complicated at the outset (for example Eqn NM76) the matrices of such lumped *M* models (Eqn NM80) can be written down immediately with practice and the recurrence relations of Eqns NM82 follow without difficulty.

Conclusion

In practice we might begin immediately with Eqn NM81 and determine the required values for it from those in Eqns NM80 which, with experience of the particular class of problem at hand is straightforward. Programming the resulting recurrence relations for only a few degrees of freedom is a simple task which can yield important results and hence time stepping procedures have considerable potential for application in economics, for example, as we shall see in the IE chapter.

NM11. Applying constraints to matrix problems

Eqn NM83 is a hypothetical input-output analysis problem (see Sec. ME12) with the constraint $x_1 = 0.3x_3$ imposed using the *Lagrange multiplier* method:

$$\text{(NM83)} \quad \begin{bmatrix} 1 & -0.2 & -0.1 & -0.05 & 1 \\ -0.3 & 1 & -0.2 & -0.1 & 0 \\ -0.4 & -0.3 & 1 & -0.2 & -0.3 \\ -0.5 & -0.3 & -0.4 & 1 & 0 \\ 1 & 0 & -0.3 & 0 & 0.000001 \end{bmatrix} \begin{Bmatrix} x_1 \\ x_2 \\ x_3 \\ x_4 \\ \lambda \end{Bmatrix} = \begin{Bmatrix} 1 \\ 7 \\ 12 \\ 17 \\ 0 \end{Bmatrix}$$

The inclusion of the extra row and column corresponding to the Lagrange multiplier λ presents no difficulty and Mohr's *small slack variable* $1/\beta, \beta = 10^6$, is included on the diagonal so that pivoting is not required by the solution routine (normally a zero appears in this position).

Without this constraint the solution is *{x}* = {10, 20, 30, 40}, but with it we obtain (to 3 dp)

$$\text{(NM84)} \quad \{x\} = \{8.839, 19.448, 29.462, 39.039, 0.949\}$$

and this satisfies the constraint to 5 dp, i.e. it is satisfied to the accuracy imposed by β (note that β must be 2-3 dp less than the precision of the computation).

Now, however, the original equations are only satisfied approximately (we have in effect altered them), for example substituting the values of Eqn NM84 into the first we obtain

$$\text{(NM85)} \quad x_1 - 0.2x_2 - 0.1x_3 - 0.05x_4 = 0.051$$

not =1 as required, so that the value of λ must be included as well to obtain the correct result. The degree of approximation, and in turn the severity of the constraints, is then indicated by the magnitude of the Lagrange multiplier(s).

Such problems can be written in the general form

$$\text{(NM86)} \quad \begin{bmatrix} S & G^T \\ G & -I_m\beta \end{bmatrix} \begin{Bmatrix} x \\ \lambda \end{Bmatrix} = \begin{Bmatrix} q \\ q_c \end{Bmatrix}$$

where G is a matrix of m constraint equations and I_m is a unit matrix of order m. Using the second row of Eqn NM86 we can write

$$\text{(NM87)} \quad \{x_c\} = \beta G\{x\} - \beta\{q_c\}$$

and substituting this result into the first row of Eqn NM86 gives

$$\text{(NM88)} \quad [S + \beta G^T G]\{x\} = \{q\} + \beta G^T\{q_c\}$$

and this *λ–β transformation* was discovered by Mohr. Now β acts as a *penalty factor* (so that the small slack variables might be described as inverse penalty factors).

These are the preferred means of imposing such constraints because the original matrix is not increased in size, instead being augmented by the 'penalty matrix' $\beta G^T G$.

This method (the penalty method) is easy to program, in the present example reading in a constraint row 1, 0, -0.3, 0, 0 where note that the last entry is the RHS or 'load' value (corresponding to q_c in Eqn NM88).

Using the penalty method (again with $\beta = 10^6$) the solution of Eqn NM84 is again obtained but there is no Lagrangian multiplier value to remind us of the degree of approximation (in relation to the unconstrained original equations), But if we calculate

$$\text{(NM89)} \quad \beta\,(x_1 - 0.3x_3) = 0.949 \text{ (not zero)}$$

we see that that an implicit Lagrange multiplier value is revealed (the same as that obtained in Eqn NM84).

As noted above, RHS values for the constraints must be given (as indeed is the case for Lagrange multiplier constraints) and, for example, constraints such as $x_1 = x_3 + 10$ are easily imposed, the solution to our example then being (this replacing the original constraint)

$$\text{(NM90)} \quad \{x\} = \{31.326, 25.549, 21.326, 48.858\}$$

Note that such constraints as the latter can be added to any matrix solution routine such as that given earlier by adding

$$\text{(NM91)} \quad \beta \begin{bmatrix} 1 & 0 & -1 & 0 \\ 0 & 0 & 0 & 0 \\ -1 & 0 & 1 & 0 \\ 0 & 0 & 0 & 0 \end{bmatrix} = 10\beta \begin{Bmatrix} 1 \\ 0 \\ -1 \\ 0 \end{Bmatrix}$$

to the reduced/problem (without row/column 5) problem of Eqn NM83, giving the same result as Eqn NNM90 (given the same β).

Note that in the special case where we want to suppress a variable to zero (the most common *boundary condition* in physical problems) we simply add a large (penalty) factor to the diagonal location in the coefficient matrix corresponding to that variable (i.e. in position (3,3) if it is the third variable).

Finally a third way of enforcing matrix is constraints is *basis transformation* (the 'basis' in any problem being the set of variables used model it). If for example we wish to enforce the constraint $x_2 = x_4$ in our example problem we use the transformation

$$\text{(NM92)} \qquad \{x'\} = \begin{Bmatrix} x'_1 \\ x'_2 \\ x'_3 \\ x'_4 \end{Bmatrix} = \begin{bmatrix} 1 & 0 & 0 & 0 \\ 0 & 1 & 0 & -1 \\ 0 & 0 & 1 & 0 \\ 0 & 0 & 0 & 1 \end{bmatrix} \begin{Bmatrix} x_1 \\ x_2 \\ x_3 \\ x_4 \end{Bmatrix} = T\{x\}$$

to transform the problem variables, using the *congruent transformation*

$$\text{(NM93)} \qquad T^T ST\{x\} = \{q\}$$

to transform the coefficient matrix to that for the new variables.

Basis transformation is much used by Mohr's *method of nested interpolations* for *finite element* formulation to transform a *global* set of element variables to a more convenient *local* set corresponding to a known (convenient) interpolation and an example of this method is given in Appendix B of subject FM.

Conclusion

A short program that uses all three methods is given in the following section. As noted above the penalty method is preferable to and equivalent to the Lagrange multiplier method (first proved by Mohr), whilst the basis transformation method is generally used for *transforming*, not constraining, variables. Indeed trying to use all three methods at once, as the program given in the following section does is quite confusing and using the 'BT' method does not give the same results as for the other two methods because, in Eqn NM91, for example, it does not effectively *eliminate* variables from the solution (as the other methods do) but 'rescales' them'. At this point only some attention to the penalty method is recommended, and particularly the 'big number on the diagonal' method of suppressing variables to zero.

NM12. Exercises and Programs

[1] Try the PCMETH(.BAS) program in \MBS1 on the course Basics disc. This uses the predictor-corrector method of Sec. NM2.

[2] Try the NUMINT program. This uses three point Gauss quadrature and Bode's rule (the formula for this is given at program start - both rules are of quintic accuracy) to estimate the area under a Normal distribution curve (= probability).

[3] Try coding the Gauss-Jordan reduction program of Sec. NM4 and inverting the matrix of Table NM2. Also try out the following (.BAS) programs (in \MBS1):

a. GJRED - simple Gauss-Jordan reduction routine

b. GJRBS - Gauss-Mohr reduction, i.e. direct solution with GJR, including simple banding
c. GDRBS - Gauss-Doolittle reduction (also with banding) - this is a simple variation in which row division is done after row subtraction, this having advantages when parallel processing is used.
d. RESOL - this carries out Gauss reduction, dealing with an additional RHS vector or 'load' case during forward reduction. Then only the back substitution calculation need be repeated for the additional case.
e. MATINV - includes an inversion routine with pivoting.
f. INVERTM - another inversion routine with pivoting (by Kris Sweiger).
[4] The program IOAFEX.BAS in \MBS1 combines all three constraint methods described in Sec. NM11, using Gauss-Mohr reduction for solution. The listing is

```
5 REM Example of Lagrange Multiplier, Penalty & Basic constraints at once !
10 DIM C(20, 20), V(20), G(10, 20), F(20): a$ = "####": B$ = "#######.###"
20 DIM T(20, 20), S(20, 20): B = 100000
30 RESTORE 420
40 READ NV, NC, NS, IB
50 FOR I = 1 TO NV: FOR J = 1 TO NV
60 READ C(I, J): NEXT: NEXT
70 FOR I = 1 TO NV: READ V(I): NEXT
80 FOR I = 1 TO NC: FOR J = 1 TO NV
90 READ G(I, J): NEXT: READ F(I): NEXT
100 IF IB = 0 THEN 160
110 FOR I = 1 TO NV: FOR J = 1 TO NV: READ T(I, J)
120 S(I, J) = C(I, J): NEXT: NEXT
130 FOR I = 1 TO NV: FOR J = 1 TO NV: C(I, J) = 0
140 FOR K = 1 TO NV: C(I, J) = C(I, J) + S(I, K) * T(K, J)
150 NEXT: NEXT: NEXT
160 FOR I = 1 TO NV: FOR K = 1 TO NC
170 V(I) = V(I) + B * G(K, I) * F(K): NEXT: NEXT
180 FOR I = 1 TO NV: FOR J = 1 TO NV
190 FOR K = 1 TO NC
200 C(I, J) = C(I, J) + G(K, I) * G(K, J) * B: NEXT K
210 NEXT J: NEXT I
220 FOR K = 1 TO NS
230 READ N, SP
240 FOR I = 1 TO NV
250 C(N, I) = 0: V(I) = V(I) - SP * C(I, N)
260 C(I, N) = 0: NEXT I
270 V(N) = SP: C(N, N) = 1: NEXT
280 FOR I = 1 TO NV: X = C(I, I): V(I) = V(I) / X
300 FOR J = I + 1 TO NV: C(I, J) = C(I, J) / X: NEXT
320 FOR K = 1 TO NV
330 IF K = I THEN GOTO 370
340 X = C(K, I): V(K) = V(K) - X * V(I)
350 FOR J = I + 1 TO NV
360 C(K, J) = C(K, J) - X * C(I, J): NEXT J
```

```
370 NEXT K
380 NEXT I
390 PRINT "Node     Value"
400 FOR I = 1 TO NV
410 PRINT USING a$; I; : PRINT USING B$; V(I): NEXT
420 DATA 5,1,0,1
430 DATA 1,-.2,-.1,-.05,1
440 DATA -.3,100000,-.2,-.1,0
450 DATA -.4,-.3,1,-.2,-1
460 DATA -.5,-.3,-.4,1,0
470 DATA 1,0,-1,0,.000001        : REM L CONSTRAINT X1 = X3
480 DATA 1,7,12,17,0
490 DATA 1,-1,0,0,0,0           : REM PENALTY CONSTRAINT X1 = X2
500 DATA 1,0,0,0,0              : REM BASIS TRANS. MATRIX For X2 = X4
510 DATA 0,1,0,-1,0
520 DATA 0,0,1,0,0
530 DATA 0,0,0,1,0
540 DATA 0,0,0,0,1
```

The data is for the problem of Eqn NM83 and line 420 = 5 equations, 1 penalty constraint, no *specified (boundary)* values for the variables (if any these would be the last data lines, being read in line 230). The solution routine is Gauss-Mohr reduction, that is the GJR routine of Sec. NM4 modified for *direct solution* to operate only to the right of pivot and on the right side (i.e. the inverse matrix is not formed).

Note also the programs IOABAN and IOABANST in \MBS1. These use Gauss reduction and now handling banded matrices is more complicated, whilst the second of these is designed for large problems, only storing part of the (banded) system matrix at a time and reducing the equations and 'funneling' them through an array at least just larger than the band width. Some of the data for these programs corresponds to sets of data for two IOA type problems connected together and this work is ongoing research.

NM References

Arfken, G. Mathematical Methods for Physicists. Academic Press, New York NY. 1968.

Bajpai, A.C., Mustoe, L.R. and Walker, D. Engineering Mathematics. Wiley Chichester. 1974.

Carlaw, H.S. and Jaeger, J.C. Operational Methods in Applied Mathematics. OUP, London. 1945.

Crandall, S.H. Engineering Analysis: A Survey of Numerical Procedures. McGraw-Hill, New York. 1956.

Goettzel, G. and Tralli, N. Some Mathematical Methods of Physics. McGraw-Hill, New York. 1960.

Kempner, T. (ed). The Penguin Management Handbook, 4th edn. Penguin, Harmondsworth. 1987.

Klein, L.R. The World Economy - a Global Model. Perspectives in Computing, vol.2 , no. 2. May 1982.

Lee, J.A.N. Numerical Analysis for Computers. Reinhold, New York. 1966.

Leontief, W.W. The Structure of the American Economy, 1919-1939, 2nd edn. OUP, Fair Lawn NJ. 1951.
Mohr, G.A. A contact stiffness matrix for finite element problems involving external elastic restraint. Computers & Structures, vol. 12, p 189. 1980.
Mohr, G.A. Finite element analysis of viscous fluid flow. Computers & Fluids, vol. 12, p 217. 1984.
Mohr, G.A. and Caffin, D.A. Penalty factors, Lagrange multipliers and basis transformation in the finite element method, IEAust, vol. CE27, p 174. 1985.
Mohr, G.A. Finite Elements for Solids, Fluids, and Optimization. OUP, Oxford. 1992.
Mohr, G.A. Numerical procedures for input-output analysis. Appl. Maths and Computation, vol. 101, p 89. 1999.
Mohr GA, Elementary Thinking for the 21st Century, Xlibris, Sydney, 2014.
Przemieniecki, J.S. Theory of Matrix Structural Analysis. McGraw-Hill, New York. 1968.
Smith, L.P. Mathematical Methods for Scientists and Engineers. Dover, New York. 1953.
Steinberg, D.I. Computational Matrix Algebra. McGraw-Hill Kogusaka, Tokyo. 1974.
Swokowski, E.W. Calculus with Analytic Geometry, 3rd edn. Prindle, Weber and Schmidt, Boston MA. 1984.
Theil, H., Boot, J.C.G. and Kloek, T. Operations Research and Quantitative Economics. McGraw-Hill, New York. 1965.

INTERNATIONAL ECONOMICS (IE)

Protectionism is the institutionalization of economic failure. Edward Heath.
A democracy exists whenever those who are free and are not well-off, being in the majority, are in sovereign control of government, an oligarchy when control lies with the rich and better-born, these being few. Aristotle.

In this chapter we discuss *macroeconomics.* This is usually concerned with the national economy of a country but necessarily includes consideration of *international economics* (the 'big E' as it is sometimes called). In contrast *microeconomic* deals with economics at corporate level, that is with *managerial economics,* and this is discussed in the following level.

IE1. Introduction

In this section we shall introduce a few introductory economic principles and concepts which are generally pertinent in any discussion of economics.

Economic progress.

Economics these days is generally discussed in much the same fashion as the weather and with similar pessimism. It is worth noting that since 1900 production per capita has increased fourfold and the length of the working week has been reduced by 30% in industrialized countries.

Economic problems

Current economic problems include unemployment, inflation, the poor, the environment and 'undesirable production', that is, production of goods and services which are socially and economically destructive.

The role of government.

There are various schools of though on just how great a role government should play in economics. Adam Smith (1776), the pioneer of modern economics, favoured a totally free market with no tariffs etc. Keynes (1936), on the other hand advocated government creation of jobs and a greater government role in the economy. This was a relatively moderate position, however, compared to that of Marx who advocated ownership by the workers (not by the state as is commonly supposed).

Today, however, some mix of these three points of view exists. There must be some element of social policy for the disadvantaged whilst debate over the relative merits of *Keynesian economics* versus those of the *monetarists* (who hold that the government should only 'fine tune' the controls of a free market economy) continues.

Economic goals.

What are our economic goals? These are likely to include dealing with high unemployment, achieving price stability, production efficiency, equitable distribution of income and economic growth. Additional qualitative factors which should also be considered are the environment and individual economic freedom and security.

Specialization.

It is because individuals specialize their work that we need *exchange* and hence money. This introduces economies of scale into our activities. Here a simple example of *comparative advantage* is relevant.

Suppose a doctor who earns $50 per hour takes one hour to mow the lawn. To have a gardener do it, on the other hand, costs $5 per hour but the gardener takes two hours to do the job. Which is the best option?

At first sight some would say that the doctor should mow the lawn himself and save $10. This involves an *opportunity cost*, however, of $50 which the doctor could have made by staying in his office another hour and has forgone. The example is somewhat trivial but does demonstrate *comparative advantage.*

Resource constraints.

As an example of the application of *resource constraints* suppose we wish to maximize the total production P of a product by two processes, x and y, and that these processes cost $4 and $5 per unit respectively. Then if this is subject to the constraints (i) that the total cost be not more than $32 and (ii) that not more than 6 units can be produced using process x, we state the problem mathematically as

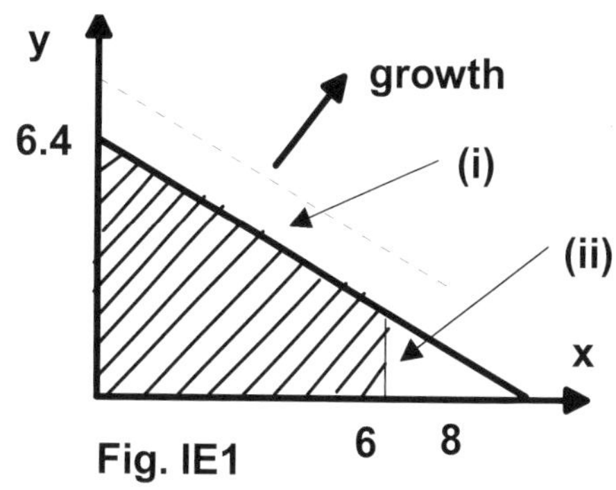

Fig. IE1

(IE1) Maximize $P = x + y$

subject to $4x + 5y \leq 32$ (i)

$x \leq 6$ (ii)

This is, in fact, a *linear programming* (LP) problem and the solution is obtained graphically in Fig. IE1. Here the shaded area is the *feasible region* and this is bounded by the axes and the two constraints.

The solution will be one of the corner points of the *simplex* formed by the constraints and it is easily found that the maximum occurs at $x = 6$, $y = 1.6$ (giving the maximum $P = 7.6$).

Generally, the boundary given by (i) and (ii) is called the *production possibilities curve* (PPC) which grows as shown in Fig. IE1 if allowed.

Economic planning.

In economic planning it is, of course, important to consider both short and long term goals and frequently some balance must be struck between these. For example, a fundamental question is whether it is better to encourage spending on capital goods (for example building factories etc.) or permit spending on consumption goods (output from existing factories).

The former (capital goods expenditure) will provide long term growth in the economy at the price of short term deprivation. Generally, therefore, some balance between the two extremes must be struck.

Conclusion

Economics is the study of how people, company's and countries make a living and of the problems associated with so doing. Much progress has been made and much remains to be made and definition of economic goals should be made with sensible constraints in mind, as well as due consideration of both short term and long term effects.

Finally, whilst the mathematical details of economics are important tools, some of the fundamental questions such as the degree to which government should be involved remain matters of debate.

IE2. Supply and Demand

The law of *supply and demand* is well known and is usually stated along the lines "supply rises to meet demand" and this, as far as it goes, is true. This does not, however, tell us why this happens. In the following section supply and demand curves are discussed along with the effects on these of imposed controls, government and business policies and other considerations.

Fig. IE2 shows typical supply and demand curves for which it is frequently assumed that there is *perfect competition*, that is there are many buyers and sellers and none are able to influence the price individually. Then the result is called a *competitive market.*

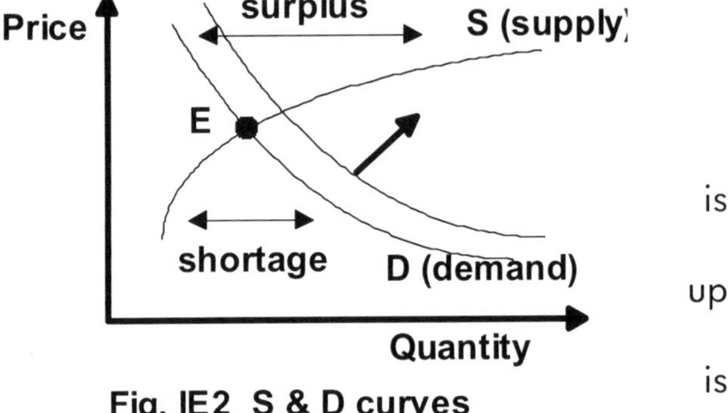

Fig. IE2 S & D curves

Here the supply goes up as the price goes up because the supplier is more motivated to produce more goods. The S curve, therefore, is drawn from the point of view of the *supplier.*

The demand curve, on the other hand, goes down as the price goes down because with a greater quantity of goods available competition forces the price down (or conversely shortages result in increased prices). Hence the D curve is drawn from the point of view of the buyer.

Then the point of intersection of the two curves, E, is called the *equilibrium point.* Below this point demand exceeds supply and there is a shortage and above it supply exceeds demand and there is a surplus, as shown in Fig. IE2.

If there is an increase in demand, as shown in Fig. IE2, then there is an increase in the equilibrium price P_E. Clearly, therefore, S & D curves show a good deal of information.

Introduction of controls

What happens if arbitrary price controls are introduced? This provides a useful example of the application of S & D curves. Suppose, for example, a ceiling price P_C is placed on the product. Then, as shown in Fig. IE3, we move down the (short term) supply curve S_S to a point A and there is a short term shortage.

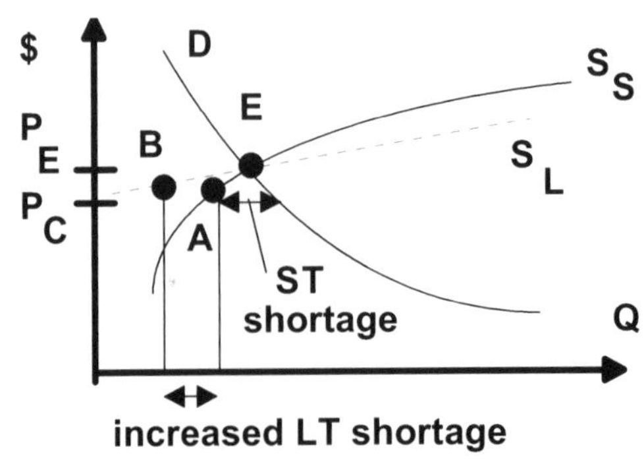

Fig. IE3

Further, in the long term suppliers will reduce supply for given price giving a new and 'flatter' supply curve S_L. Operation then moves to a point B in Fig. IE3, so that the shortage increases in the long term.

Note that the foregoing version of 'S&D' dates back to Adam Smith (1723-1790) and strictly applies only to *commodities*. For mass produced products Mohr proposes that an 'inverse' form of S&D applies, as indeed it clearly does (Mohr, 2012/ 2014, 2016).

Elasticity of supply and demand

The *elasticity* of supply or demand is given by the slope of the corresponding curve, that is by

(IE2) $$e = (\delta Q/Q)/(\delta P/P)$$

and is comparable to the definition of many similar quantities in science.

A particular example is the aggregate labour market which is often assumed to have a vertical supply line, there being a fixed number of available workers (or zero elasticity). When the size of the work force increases, therefore, so that this labour supply line moves to the right, it quickly follows that wages *(P)* will fall.

Optimum production

In the present context it should be noted that there are limits to which production can be increased as well as optimal production rates which must be considered.

Fig. IE4 shows the profit (per item) v. quantity produced *(Q)* curve for a production process. Here P increases at first as set up costs etc. are 'spread' until constraints come into play and P decreases. Then a maximum marginal profit occurs when the production quantity = Q_{opt}.

As the marginal profit P = marginal revenue (MR) - marginal cost *(MC)* clearly P_{max} is obtained when $MC = MR$.

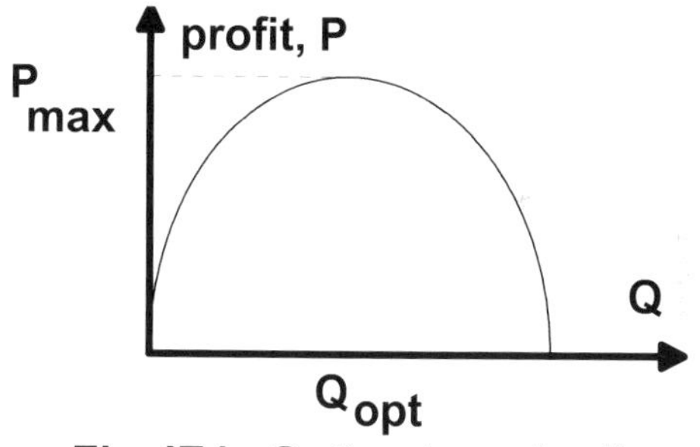

Fig. IE4. Optimal production

Then in a very competitive market (in which the elasticity e is high), it can be seen from the well known result

(IE3) $$P - MR = P/e$$

that $P = MR = MC$. Hence we can conclude that in a very competitive industry production is close to MC (exceeding it slightly by P/e).

Effect of government

Government affects supply and demand in various ways, including:

1. It purchases goods and services.
2. Through *transfer payments* (welfare etc.) which are largely spent, thereby increasing demand.
3. Through taxes, including federal, property, sales, personal and company taxes. Such *receipts* take money out of the system.
4. Through *expenditure* on education, welfare, roads etc.
5. Through regulations and controls which affect interest and tax rates etc.

Effects of business

The business sector affects supply and demand in the economy in such ways as the following:

1. By purchasing goods and services, thus creating demand.
2. By production, creating supply.
3. Through imports and exports.
4. Through the stock market, levels of activity influencing economic growth, currency exchange rates etc.
5. Through the capital market, levels of activity influencing exchange rates, interest rates and economic stability.

Conclusion

Supply and demand curves have useful application as we have already seen and many more applications will be seen later. Consideration of factors such as labour supply and efficient production rates is, in this context, of vital importance, as is an understanding of the various ways in which government and the business sector can influence supply and demand.

IE3. National product and national income

National product is the dollar value of goods and services in a year and national income is the sum of all income derived from providing these goods and services, including wages and salaries, rents, interest and company profits. These are discussed in detail and applications of these measures are discussed in the following section.

Gross national product (GNP)

GNP is one of the most widely publicized economic yardsticks and is defined as the sum of several terms, namely:

(IE4) $$GNP = C + G + I_g + X - M$$

where C = NP = personal *consumption* and expenditures
G = government purchases of goods and services (not including transfer payments such as social security benefits)
I_g = gross domestic investment (plant and equipment, including inventories)
X = exports of goods and services
M = imports of goods and services

Because of the need to allow for depreciation a net national product is defined as

(IE5) $$\text{NNP} = \text{GNP - depreciation} = \text{GNP} - (I_g - I_n)$$

where I_n = net private domestic investment = I_g - depreciation.

Then national income (NI) is given by

(IE6) $$\text{NI} = \text{NNP - sales taxes}$$
$$\approx \text{PI} = \text{NI - (co. + soc. sec. taxes) + transfer payments}$$
and $$\text{DI} = \text{PI - personal taxes}$$

where PI = personal income and DI = disposable income (spent on interest payments or consumption or saved).

Finally, defining the *consumer price index* (cpi) as the weighted average price increase through the whole economy (%), the *'real GNP'* is given by

(IE7) real GNP = (nominal GNP)/(1 + cpi/100)

Example

As an example consider the effect on GNP of the Keynes proposition that increased government expenditure should be used to reduce unemployment.

This is illustrated in Fig. IE5. Here increased government spending has resulted in an increase in demand which shifts us from point A to an equilibrium point E (hence we have shifted to another demand curve).

There may then, however, be a further increase in demand as a result of increased competition (by those now employed etc.). This will result in an increase in price and we move to point B in Fig. IE5. Hence inflation has resulted and moves to curb this will reduce employment, the by now all too familiar cycle.

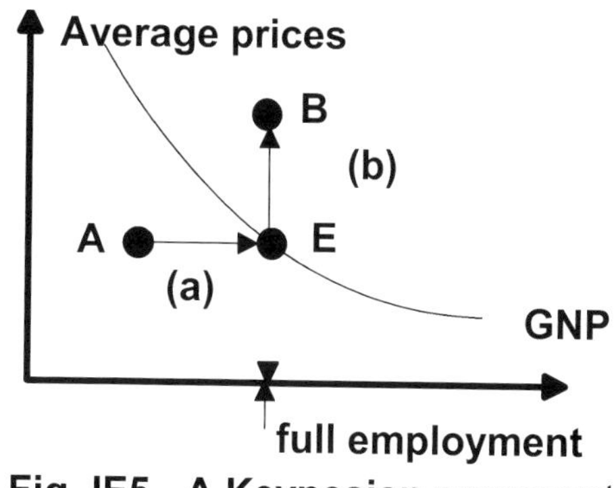

Fig. IE5. A Keynesian argument

To give a measure of step (a) in Fig. IE5 Keynes defined a *consumption function C,* from which follows the *marginal propensity to consume (MPC)* and *marginal propensity to save (MPS):*

(IE8) $MPC = \delta C/\delta DI, \; MPS = \delta S/\delta DI$

and *MPC* is the slope of the consumption function whilst $MPC + MPS = 1$.

Then, supposing we have $MPS = 0.2$, and increase in government spending (δG) of \$M100 will result in $\delta GNP = \delta G/MPS$ = \$M500 (using the second of Eqns IE8). This *multiplier effect* of savings is very important, though hard to believe from the simple equations given here. The point is, however, that if $MPS = 1$ there is no such effect and it is consumption which brings about the effect in question.

Fiscal policy

The foregoing discussion of GNP considers only variation of *G* and its effect. To generalize how government *fiscal policy* affects the GNP we write the budget *(B)* in terms of revenue *(R)* and expenditure *(G)* as

(IE9) $B = R - G$

and if $R > G$ (surplus), for example as a result of higher taxes, then demand is reduced and the cpi drops.

If $R < G$ (deficit), on the other hand, the deficit spending may stimulate the economy in the short term at the expense of greater government debt.

If this increase of $G = \delta G$ = \$M100 and the tax rate is t = 25% (i.e., 0.25) we amend the multiplier effect calculated above to

(IE10) $\delta GNP = \delta G/[MPS(1 - t) + t]$ = \$M333

so that inclusion of tax (or an increase therein) reduces the effect on the economy (this phenomenon is called *fiscal drag).*

Then in formulating fiscal policy the aim should be to 'juggle' R and G in such a way as to achieve full employment and then balance the budget (so that $R = G$) when that objective has been attained.

Conclusion

GNP is a simple quantity but less simple are the supply and demand considerations involved in fiscal policy which involve questions of employment levels, government spending, tax rates and inflation, to name a few.

On the question of government spending it is probably worth noting as an aside that costs of security (defence, police etc.), education, welfare (social security and health) and infrastructure are, of course, very high indeed, not to speak of administration costs both internal and external to these. In economies where government is largely responsible for these activities, therefore, it should be able to control events to a considerable extend by fiscal policy.

IE4. The Financial System

The financial system of banks, stock exchanges etc. is the machinery by which the economy runs. Important parts of this machinery include the following:

The Money Stock.

The money stock in the economy is the total currency *in circulation* (that is, in public hands) plus the total of *demand deposits* (that is cheque accounts etc.). This total is denoted M_1 and a second total $M_2 = M_1$ + the total of savings/business accounts = M_1 + 'near money' is also defined as a measure of the money stock.

Liquid assets.

A liquid asset is one which can be converted into money *(M_1)* readily at little cost at its 'proper' value.

The Reserve Bank.

The reserve bank might be termed the 'banks' bank' as it holds the *statutory reserve deposits (SRDs)* of the trading banks, a set ratio called the *reserve ratio (R)* of their total deposits. Its excess reserves are its total reserves less the SRDs.

Suppose, for example, $R = 0.2$ and \$M10 is deposited by a customer in a bank. The bank now has excess reserves and can create \$M10/0.2 = \$M50 worth of additional demand deposits.

This occurs because the bank can lend \$M8 to a customer who passes this (by cheque) as payment for property etc. to a customer of another bank who deposits the cheque. This second bank can now lend 80% of this amount and so on, so that we obtain a series of demand deposits resulting:

(IE11) δD = original deposit + 80& of latter + 80% of latter - - - -

$$= 1/[1 - (1 - R)] = 1 + (1 - R) + (1 - R)^2 + - - - -$$

This then is the crux of how the banking system works and the reason why the multiplier effect discussed in Sec. IE3 does actually occur.

Interest rates.

The reserve bank can affect interest rates by buying government bonds, decreasing their supply and thence forcing up their price. This in turn reduces their interest rate and banks may follow suit and cut their *prime rate* (the rate on their safest loans).

The discount rate.

This is the rate the reserve bank charges the trading banks when it makes loans to them. By increasing this or the reserve ratio to tighten the money supply the reserve bank might seek to slow down an 'overheated' economy, for example.

The stock market.

The reserve bank can influence the stock market by, for example, increasing the discount rate, in turn leading to a general increase in rates which in turn may lead to a fall in the stock market.

Common examples of such policy are:

a. Expansive monetary policy.

Here the reserve bank buys bonds causing reduction in interest rates and in the MPS (marginal propensity for saving). Thus greater demand is stimulated causing an increase in the GNP (which includes the multiplier effect of Eqn IE10).

b. Restrictive monetary policy.

Here the reserve bank sells bonds causing an increase in rates and in the MPS. Thus demand is reduced, causing a decrease in the GNP (again including the multiplier effect).

Note here that increase in price of securities is assumed to cause a reduction in their interest rate. This is because for a $100 bond with a yield of 8% the present value if it has a ten year term is given by

$$PV = 8/r + 8/r^2 + 8/r^3 + - - - - + (100 + 8)/r^{10}$$

where $r = 1 + i$ and i is the market interest rate. From this it is clear that if the market rate increases then PV decreases and vice versa.

Conclusion

The multiplier effect related to Eqns IE8 is of importance not only in the overall economic system as Eqn IE10 shows, but also in the banking system, as shown by Eqn IE11. In turn, this part of the sequence of events, which the reserve bank can trigger off by intervention in the securities market etc. Such monetary policy, the 'monetarists' (as distinct from the 'Keynesians') argue, should be the limit of government powers in what should otherwise be a free market economy.

IE5. Aggregate demand

We have now seen two ways of controlling the economy, one being fiscal policy, that is a positive δG acting as an 'injection' to stimulate the economy, as illustrated by Eqn IE10. This is the Keynesian approach. In the opposition camp are the monetarists such as Friedman who argue that only monetary policy is necessary to fine tune what should otherwise be a free market economy. Here we shall briefly discuss both approaches.

Monetary policy

The aim of monetary policy is to control the economy by controlling the money supply, in turn affecting interest rates which in turn affects investment *(I)* and hence aggregate demand *(C + I)*.

Fig. IE6 shows the marginal efficiency of investment or investment demand curve, that is the amount businesses will invest at various interest rates.

Then, as described in Sec. IE4, expansive monetary policy, as it causes a reduction in interest rates, leads to an increase in investment demand and hence in aggregate demand and we move down the 'MEI' curve.

The classical economic theory of the *velocity of money (V)* is in line with this approach. This theory is based on an *equation of exchange*

(IE12) $$MV = PQ$$

where

M = the quantity of money in public hands
P = average level of prices
Q = quantity of output
V = velocity of money = number of times M is spent to buy Q during the year

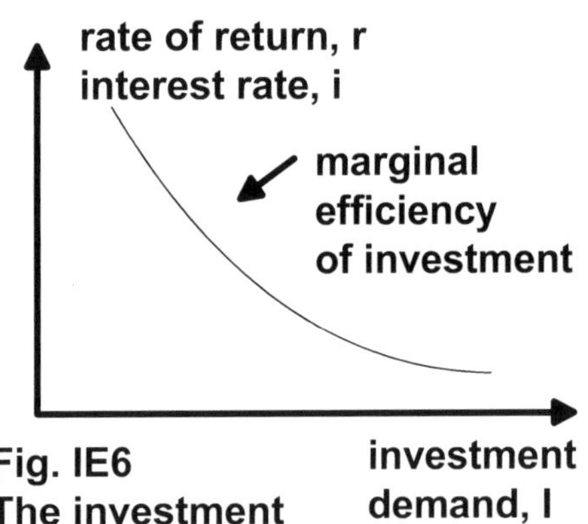

Fig. IE6
The investment demand curve.

and V is defined as equal to PQ/M and taken to be approximately constant (so that Eqn IE12 is a tautology).

Then monetarists argue that the authorities should increase the value of M by a fixed percentage each year (and figures from 2 to 4% are suggested). This will give a corresponding growth in Q and hence GNP.

Fiscal policy

Fiscal policy was discussed in Sec. IE3 where it was shown that an increase in government spending δG leads to a 'multiplier effect' increase in GNP.

Those who have doubts about this approach, however, argue that deficit budgeting (via an increase in G or reduced taxes) and borrowing to finance that deficit will decrease I (domestic investment) and hence aggregate demand. In the case of an increase in G (as advocated by Keynesians) this result is called *crowding out*, that is government investment displaces private investors from the market.

Monetary policy v. fiscal policy

The best policy would seem to be to use a combination of both approaches and to thus have a 'two pronged' approach. For example we might choose to have:

a. Fiscal expansion (an increase in G)
b. A low growth in M (giving some restraint)

using 'unused' growth in M and borrowing part of the finance for δG from the private sector, thereby aiming for lesser increases in I (and hence growth in GNP) and a more stable system.

Exercise

As an exercise discuss the following propositions concerning reducing unemployment:

1. Income splitting between spouses before tax when there is only one bread winner.
2. Keeping tariff barriers for certain areas of activity.
3. Reduce the average working week to, say, 35 hours &/or 4 days
4. Export incentives (taxe breaks or other).
5. Lower interest rates to promote business.
6. Making first home mortgages part tax deductible to stimulate business in the building industry.
7. Reduce the retirement age:
(a) Across the board
(b) In certain industries (hazardous etc.), circumstances (injury etc.)
8. Add any others that come to mind.

As an example of (1) consider:

a. husband income = \$60k, tax = \$20k
wife income = \$30k, tax = \$10k
total net income = \$60k
b. husband income = \$60k, tax = \$10k (\$10k spouse allowance)
total net income = \$50k (+ expenses of spouse working saved)

This doesn't sound too bad from the point of view of the family but the government now collects only a third as much tax from this couple but will collect tax from another worker replacing the wife in the workforce and, in addition will save social security payments for that worker. There is also a social benefit to the family and the person taken off the dole.

Conclusion

A study of aggregate demand has provided a means of comparing the classical monetarist and Keynesian (fiscal) points of view on economic policy.

It would seem clear that some middle course might be the best one, making the best use of whatever controls that we have.

In speaking of growth in GNP etc., it is perhaps worth remembering that oft quoted growth rates of 2% and the like (by politicians etc.) are really only treading water in the face of population increase, if that, and with unemployment an enduring problem in what were once the strongest economies there is a need for a reappraisal of such matters as taxation and deficit budgeting to support greater demands by 'green', educational, business or other groups. In addition such measures as a shorter working week, less tax for single bread winners (supporting spouses) and tax and other incentives for industries that are likely to create sought after employment might help.

IE6. Aggregate Supply.

The backward 'L' result AEB in Fig. IE5 can be taken as a supply function because as employment/output increase so does price.

If the steps of this Keynesian *aggregate supply* function are plotted on axes rate of inflation (%) and unemployment (%), respectively vertical and horizontal, we obtain a special L shaped case of the *Phillips curve*. In other words, we reverse the GNP axis in Fig. IE5 and relabel it unemployment, also reversing AE by moving A to the right of E.

The Phillips curve was based on nearly 100 years of statistical data (up to 1957) for the UK and takes the form shown in Fig. IE7(a). Calculations based on this data suggested that with unemployment at about 2.5% wage inflation would remain in the range 2.5% to 3%, just offsetting growth in GNP so that price inflation would be zero.

For a decade (until 1966) the Phillips curve held well but thereafter began to come adrift and in 1968 Friedman developed the concept of the *expectations augmented Phillips curve* shown in fig. IE7(b). Here we begin at point A, the 'natural' rate of unemployment (of which estimates range from 4% to 10%). Now if the government increases money supply, causing greater aggregate demand which in turn increased prices, then unemployment is reduced and we move to point B.

Now inflation is around 2% and p_e = expected inflation = 2% causing pressure for increase in 'real wages' and we move to point C, the increase in wages causing increased unemployment.

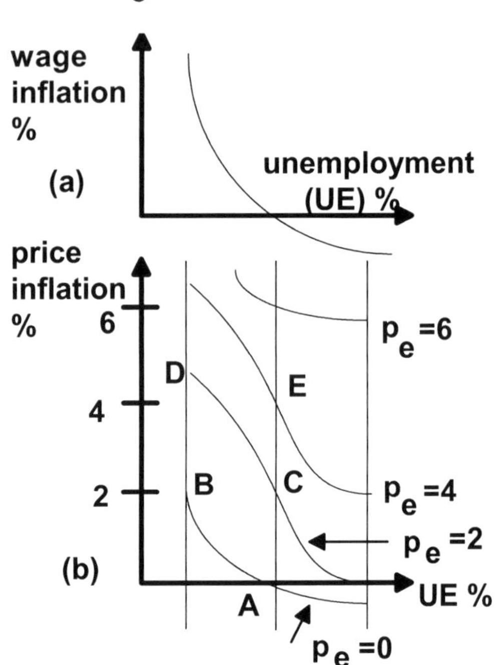

Fig. IE7. Phillips curves

Then if another injection of funds into the money supply occurs the process is repeated and we move from point C to point D, and thence to point E, and so on. Hence a *cost-push* (prices and wages) or *demand-pull* (high demand) cyclic behaviour results called an *inflationary spiral.* As this phenomenon did occur for many years in some countries the augmented Phillips curve does work well in showing how continued monetary policy of a 'catch up' kind can cause even more trouble.

Conclusion

Solutions to the sorts of problems illustrated by Fig. IE7 might include wage indexation (to the cpi), freer markets (elimination of monopolies etc.), price surveillance, and tariff reductions. Some would have it, however, that we must be prepared to accept that a 'natural' rate of unemployment of near 10% may be appropriate in modern economies and that it is cheaper to pay people the dole than create government jobs of a relatively unproductive nature in offices which would be more costly to provide than dole payments.

This is to forget the problems of the 'boom and bust' nature of the system whereby *recessions* (decline in GNP for two consecutive quarters in seasonally adjusted terms) and *depressions* (greater than 10% unemployment for two consecutive years) are accepted too easily. The latter question is discussed in Sec. IE7 and the question of unemployment is returned to in Sec. IE12.

IE7. Economic Instability

Economic instability, witnessed by bearish and bullish markets, slumps, recessions, depressions and booms is an all too familiar fact of life. In the following section we briefly outline the nature of the business cycle and examples of factors which contribute to it. Discussion of alternative approaches to smoothing out economic cycling is then given in the following section.

The four phases of the business cycle

As an example consider a manufacturer whose sales are shown in column (1) of Table IE1. Suppose that a new assembly line is required to produce 10,000 units of produce. Then the required number of lines is shown in column (2). The net investment required is then the *change* in column (2) and this is shown in column (3). Finally, supposing that equipment replacement requirements are that two lines are replaced each period. Then the *gross investment* required is then column (3) + 2 and this result is shown in column (4).

Table IE1. Illustration of the *acceleration principle.*

Period	Phase	(1) Sales (thousands)	(2) Lines = (1)/10,000	(3) $\delta(2)$ = net investment	(4) (3) + 2 = gross inv.
1	steady	200	20	0	2
2	steady	200	20	0	2
3	expansion	220	22	2	4
4	expansion	240	24	2	4
5	peak	250	25	1	3
6	peak	250	25	0	2
7	recession	230	23	-2	0
8	recession	210	21	-2	0
9	trough	200	20	-1	1
10	trough	200	20	0	2

Then, as Table IE1 shows, a smallish increase in sales (typically 3 to 10%) doubles gross investment, a phenomenon called the *acceleration principle*. It is such phenomena that give rise to instability in the economic system.

In the case of investment, therefore, some 'lag' in funding tends to smooth out such problems. In other words when an increase in sales occurs it is desirable to assume that it will only partly be sustained in basing investment decisions on that increase.

Factors contributing to fluctuations

Factors which affect the business cycle and its stability include:

1. Changes in consumer spending or saving.
2. Changes in net exports (X - M).
3. Changes in government spending (remember the multiplier effect).
4. Fiscal and monetary policy.
5. Interest rate changes (and in turn inflation rates).
6. Political factors, such as 'election budgets'.

As an example, Fig. IE8 shows the yield rate of Australian government bonds for the period 1946 - 86. Whilst over the long term there is a general upward trend the shorter term fluctuations are on occasions very sharp.

Particular events during that period were the OPEC initiated oil crises of 1973 and 1979 in which a large and sudden increase in oil price forced importers of oil to borrow heavily from banks, it turn causing inflation, in turn raising the oil price. Arguably the effects of these can be seen in Fig. IE8.

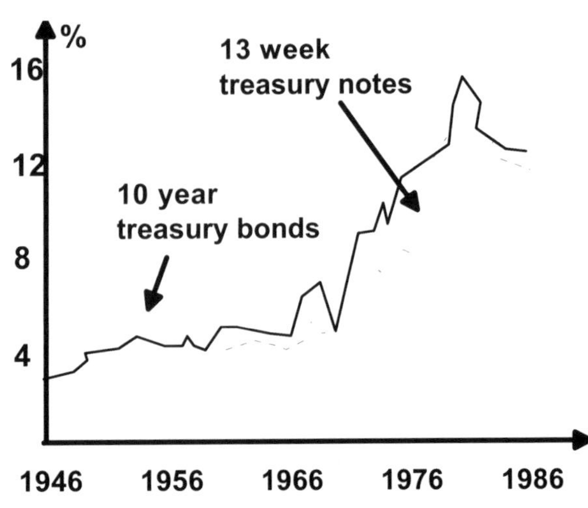

Fig. IE8. Australian government bond yields

Beneficiaries of fluctuations

At the national level boom and bust behaviour of the economy and its market benefits certain people, for example:

a. Currency exchange dealers knowingly benefit from instability.
b. Import/export companies may unwittingly benefit.

Both parties may also contribute to instability, as may politicians etc. via wars and other disruptions.

At the international level major economies such as those of the USA, UK, Germany and Japan have a major influence, as do organizations such as the IMF and EEC, of course.

Whether 'globalization' of economics will result in a more stable system is a moot point, however, and it seems unlikely that individual countries can ever be guaranteed stability.

Conclusion

Economic instability is much discussed and in much the same vein as the weather. Nevertheless the question of satisfactory control mechanisms is an important one and this is taken up again in the following section.

Having mentioned the 1973 and 1979 oil shocks, however, one cannot help but wonder what further events of a similar, if not related, kind are in store in the future. By then, hopefully, a better insulated system will be in place.

IE8. Fine tuning or stable policy settings ?

Whether we choose to use fiscal (Keynesian approach) of monetary policy or a combination of the two to regulate the economic system it is still important to decide whether this should be done using periodical 'fine tuning' adjustments or by putting in place fairly rigid policy rules

The fiscal or Keynesian approach is to increase aggregate demand ($C + I$) and thereby stimulate the economy via the multiplier effect of Eqn IE10 with a view to creating full employment.

Then periodic fine tuning is used to eliminate the GNP gap shown in Fig. IE9, this being the shortfall from a target GNP (set, for example, with the aim of full employment). Setting such targets, however, requires the use of forecasts which in turn require appropriate data and techniques for evaluating it.

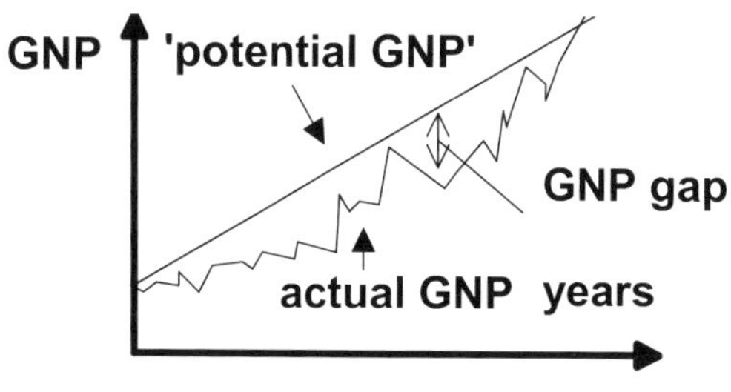

Fig. IE9. The GNP gap.

Forecasting

Forecasting techniques may include linear regression, which is discussed in Sec. IE11, or simple graphical techniques such as those suggested in Sec. BF12.

In examining data to make forecasts likely *turning points* are of interest and these may be inferred from *leading indicators* such as orders for durable goods, housing construction or movements in the currencies of other countries when a historical tendency to follow them is known to exist.

Policy rules

If the monetary policy approach us used, however, simple rules such as

1. Increase money supply (M_1 or M_2) by 4 to 5% per annum.
2. Balance a full employment budget each year.

are all that may be required according to the monetarists.

Such an approach involves no real government decision or action and supposedly permits a much freer market economy. It seems rather optimistic, however, to assume that such simple rules can be put in place and that the system will then run itself without interference. After all, even where there is minimal government interference, wars, plagues, famine or commodity crises may still require policy alteration.

Conclusion

Whatever approach, be it Keynesian (fiscal) or monetary, or a combination of these, the following points should be noted in connection with its implementation:

1. Smoothing of economic behaviour should be done by prompt action in line with policy.
2. Abrupt changes in policy should be avoided.
3. Policy should be based on long term objectives.

With these precautions, therefore, whichever approach is used the short term disturbances resulting from its implementation will be minimized.

IE9. Exchange rates

Currency exchange rates, of course, are an important factor in macroeconomics and not only affect importers and exporters but, in turn, the whole national economy as well. Indeed they also have direct effects, for example upon the stock market and interest rates. In the present section we briefly discuss the foreign exchange market and the exchange rate system.

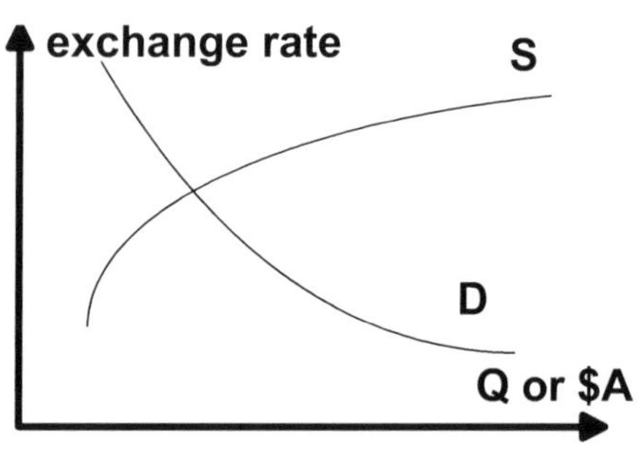

Fig. IE10. S & D curves for the Australian dollar.

Fig. IE10 shows hypothetical supply and demand curves for the Australian dollar. These are part of a foreign exchange market which may be likened to a stock market so that the price or exchange rate of the $A is governed by the demand for it and the supply of it.

Such demand is caused when overseas companies buy Australian goods or assets or overseas tourists spend in Australia. On the other hand Australians touring overseas, for example, add to the supply of $As by their spending. This then, is the market mechanism by which exchange rates are now flexible and able to fluctuate daily.

Such fluctuations, however, are able to be limited to some extent by the reserve bank which holds *foreign exchange reserves* of other currencies and can use these to intervene in the market.

For economies highly dependant upon exporting commodities, it is best to peg the exchange rate (Caves et al., 1990). For many years, however, China has pegged its exchange rate, much to the detriment of the US and other economies, and during the 2016 US election campaign Donald Trump frequently railed against China for this. This, and a number of other apparent errors in modern economic theory are dealt with by Mohr in a number of books in chapters entitled *Econobabble* (Mohr, 2012/14, 2014, 2016).

A brief history of the exchange system

Until the end of the Second World War currencies were based on the *gold standard* which equated each unit of a given currency to a certain number of ounces of gold. The gold standard was, in fact, introduced by Isaac Newton in 1717 as one of his first acts as treasurer of the Royal Mint.

During the Great Depression of the 1930s, however, countries began to abandon the gold standard system. In 1945, therefore, the Bretton-Woods system (named after the town in New Hampshire where representatives of the Allies met in 1944 to establish a new system) of foreign exchange was established. In this the *par value* of a currency was stated in gold or $US and values were *pegged* by each individual government.

Then, however, when currencies were *devalued* or *revalued* excessive trade in currency or speculation tended to occur.

Countries were required to maintain a reserve deposit with the *International Monetary Fund* as well as maintain sufficient *international liquidity* by holding reserves in cash and gold. The USA, however, was required to hold its entire reserves in gold and was faced with propping up the IMF system, making it impossible to deal with its own deficits.

Hence the IMF/Bretton Woods system began to break down in 1971 and in 1973 a system of flexible exchange rates was established.

This allows countries to concentrate on budgeting for full employment and stable prices without being preoccupied by the balance of payments (X - M). In the latter regard it was no longer necessary to decide where to 'peg' a currency and the foreign exchange market of *floating* currencies automatically adjusted itself.

Fig. IE11 shows variations in the valuation of three other currencies against the Australian dollar over nearly a decade. This is given to simply illustrate the short term fluctuations but the long term trend should also be noticed.

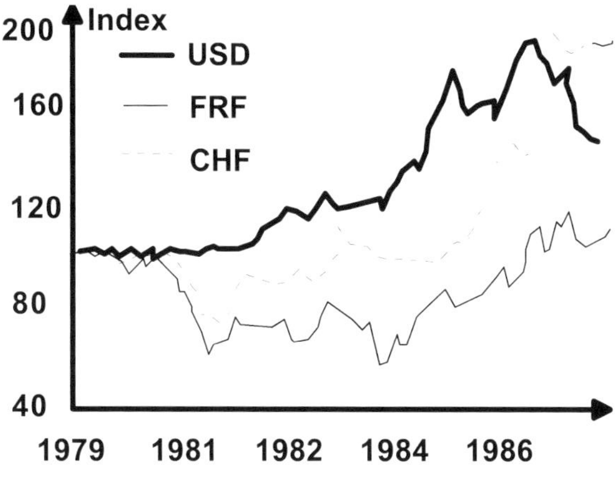

Fig. IE11. Fluctuations against $A

For small open countries, especially those heavily dependent on commodity prices, the advantages of a pegged exchange rate are particularly great, and the great depreciation of the Australian currency since 1970 might remind us of this.

Conclusion

The foreign exchange, like any other market, is subject to supply and demand pressures. The resulting variations in rates is one of many factors which complicate international trade, others including tariffs and quotas.

As elsewhere, however, there is a general trend towards reducing such restrictions and freeing up markets. As with most aspects of the economic system, however, we cannot be certain that there will not be some degree of reversal in such trends in the future.

IE10. Socialist systems

In a chapter on macroeconomics entitled International Economics it is perhaps appropriate to briefly discuss socialist systems as these have had a major influence in the USSR and Yugoslavia, for example, and still continue to do so elsewhere. It is also of interest, therefore, to briefly discuss the history of the *Westminster system* of government upon which government in much of the 'west' is based.

What is Socialism?

It is important at the outset to note that *socialism* refers to the 'means of production' being owned by the state whereas *communism* refers to the means of production being owned by the people. The two terms are often confused but in a complex and highly technological modern society it is doubtful that communism is practical.

It is doubtful, for example, that the very large companies required in some industries, many of these now multinational ones, can be owned and run by the 'people', taking people to mean those in a particular community.

What is clear, however, is that the Marx-Engels manifesto was anti-capitalist and this was the real spirit of the 1917 Russian revolution, a spirit which many believed would eventually spread globally. This revolution created a socialist state with a long term view towards forming a communist society.

Marx v. the Critics

Marxists will argue that the capitalist *class* accumulates increasingly more capital or a 'surplus value' in fact created by the workers. The working class, therefore, are left to accumulate misery, that is *"In proportion as capital accumulates, the lot of the labourer be his payment high or low, must grow worse"* as Karl Marx put it.

Critics of this view will point out that in practice state ownership leads to totalitarian government which makes the people worse off, rather than better.

Marxists will also argue that in capitalism monopolies or oligopolies must eventually develop, in turn influencing the political system so that something akin to totalitarianism can result.

In defence against this view critics of Marxism will argue that it is better to reform the capitalist system, not replace it, for example by introducing anti-monopoly laws.

The USSR System

Though the USSR has been more or less dismantled, some aspects of its system remain whilst socialist systems operate elsewhere in the world. Moreover, the communist party in Russia, for example, still has a good deal of support. Hence some discussion of the USSR system as it was is still worthwhile, principal features of that system being:

1. In the USSR policy was based on five year plans. Critics would argue that this was too inflexible and did not allow for adjustments.
2. Without a free market coordination was difficult. Supposing we wished to increase steel production, for example, then we needed extra plant to make it and in turn extra steel to make the plant. In other words it is difficult to be self sufficient as a single entity despite a perhaps massive size.
3. In the USSR investment (*I*) ran at about 30% of GNP (about the same figure as Japan at the time and twice that for the USA), this funded by a 30% general sales tax (GST).
4. This high level of investment was aimed at building industry but resulted in excessive restrictions in consumption and chronic shortages in goods.
5. In the USSR system there was effectively no such thing as unemployment as everyone could be given a job, however unproductive.

The Westminster system

A brief history of the Westminster system is:

1. Pre 1066 (Saxon times). The barons and King met each year at Easter, Whitsun and Christmas.
2. 1258 (in the reign of Henry III). A meeting of the barons of England at Oxford was the origin of the *House of Lords.*
3. 1264. Simon de Montfort, on the King's behalf, organized a meeting of two knights from each county.

4. 1265. Two citizens from each county were included in the latter meeting, constituting the origin of the *House of Commons.*
5. In the reign of Elizabeth I the puritans became the first party and were the opposition to the crown.
6. In the reign of James I the cavaliers and roundheads emerged as two opposing political forces.
7. 1681. The origin of the names *Whig* and *Tory.*

What of the future?

Not long ago some economics texts asked the question about socialism and capitalism: "Are the systems converging?".

About the USSR, at least, it is now safe to say that its system has changed and some aspects of socialism, such as centralization of power, have been much reduced. Before the USSR was dismantled, however, there had long been changes such as a greater tendency to pay highly skilled workers more, less interventionist government and slow opening up to outside (and hence not state) capital.

About the future in the USSR, or China, for example, it therefore seems safe to say that there has been a move in the direction of capitalism (and democracy, but this is not necessarily synonymous with any particular economic system).

What can we say about the USA and like countries? Clearly there is some disenchantment with the two party system. This has been around for 20 to 30 years but may begin to crystallize somewhere. In Australia, for example, a third party holds the balance of power in the upper house or senate but has no influence in the legislative lower house. In the USA, on the other hand, it is not impossible to imagine a (rich) independent being elected president.

And finally, what can we say about China? What influence will such a potentially powerful country have in the future? Presumably it will increasingly join the global economy and consequently move a little to the right politically.

Conclusion

The politico-economic systems of both the 'east' and the 'west' will doubtless continue to change slowly. Whilst current trends are towards freer capitalist markets it is possible that this trend may be slightly reversed at some point.

IE11. Econometrics

Econometrics is the estimation and refinement of *a priori* relationships between economic quantities. As an example suppose we wish to represent the quantity of a product demanded at time t as

(IE13) $$q(t) = a + bp(t) + ci(t) + d(t)$$

where $p(t)$ = price function (for product)
$i(t)$ = income function (for consumers)
$d(t)$ = disturbance or error function

and a, b and c are parameters and in this case we expect $b < 0$ and $c > 0$.

Then we use observed data and such techniques as linear regression to determine the values of the parameters *a, b* and c which most closely fit the function *q(t)* to the observed values of demand at various times.

Armed with this result we are than able to use the model of Eqn IE13 to *forecast* demand when such estimates are required.

Linear regression

Linear regression fits a line of 'best fit' to observed data on a *least squares basis* (usually), that is we minimize the sum

$$\Sigma \text{ distance(points - regression line)}^2$$

For example, suppose we are given two sets of marks for students, *x* and *y*, respectively expected (from previous results) and actual results for a test. Then these marks are shown in the first two columns of Table IE2, followed by two further columns obtained from them which are used to allow quick calculation of the required line.

As shown, the sum of each column is obtained, the first two summed giving

$$x_{av} = \Sigma\, x/N = 36/7 \quad \text{and} \quad y_{av} = \Sigma\, y/N = 6$$

Table IE2.

	x	y	x^2	xy
	8	10	64	80
	7	8	49	56
	3	2	9	6
	5	6	25	30
	7	9	49	63
	2	2	4	4
	4	5	16	20
S	36	42	216	259

Then the slope of the line

(IE14) $y = y_{av} + b(x - x_{av})$

is given by

$$b = \{N\,Sxy - Sx\,Sy\}/\{N\,Sx^2 - (Sx)^2\} = \{7(259) - 36(42)\}/\{7(216) - 1296\} = 1.39$$

so that the required line is

$$y = 6 + 1.39(x - 5.14)$$

Then when we want to establish whether such data fits a parabola, for example, we should seek a regression line for *x* v. $y/x = y^*$ in the same manner, replacing *y* by y^* above.

Exercise

As an example of the latter situation determine the regression line for the data

$$(x, y^*) = (1,7), (2,6), (3,5)$$

Then, noting that $y^* = y/x$ find the equation relating y and x.
[Ans: The result corresponds to Fig. BF11a with $x_p = 4$, $y_p = 16$].

Conclusion

Linear regression is a simple matter, as the example of Table IE2 shows. It is customary to use a least squares basis but, for example, a linear basis would simply involve a third column:

$$(y - y_{av})/(x - x_{av}) = \delta y/\ \delta x$$

and dividing the sum of this column by N we obtain an estimate of b (where δy or $\delta x = 0$ such points are ignored and N reduced by one). A least squares basis, however, is more accurate and no more difficult to use.

IE12. Mohr's time stepping of economic models

Klein modeled the performance of the US economy in the years 1921 - 1941 using three *structural equations* (in $B US):

(IE15) $C = 16.8 + 0.02P + 0.23P_L + 0.8(W + S)$

(IE16) $I = 17.8 + 0.23P + 0.55P_L - 0.15K_L$

(IE17) $W = 1.6 + 0.42X + 0.16X_L + 0.13|t - 1931|$

where $|t - 1931|$ is a heavy side step function (i..e. = 0 of $t < 1931$ and = 1 if $t > 1931$) and subscript 'L' denotes 'last value/year', and adding three *definitive equations*

(IE18) $X = C + I + G$

(IE19) $P = X - W - T$

(IE20) $K = K_L + I$

where C = total consumption, I = total investment, W, S are the private/public sector wages, X is the private sector production, P is the profits (nonwage income), K = stocks (capital goods at end of year), G = government spending, T = business taxes and subscript L denotes value for the previous year. In the above, t, S, G, T are exogenous, that is, a set of independent variables.

We can make the model more 'self contained' by assuming tax rate $t = 0.2$ so that

(IE21) $S = (1 - t)\ G = 0.8G$ and $T = t\,(W_L + P_L)$

and including these in Klein's equations.

Then the equations can be rearranged and written in the matrix form

$$A\{V\} = \begin{bmatrix} 1 & 0 & -0.8 & 0 & -0.02 & 0 \\ 0 & 1 & 0 & 0 & -0.23 & 0 \\ 0 & 0 & 1 & -0.42 & 0 & 0 \\ -1 & -1 & 0 & 1 & 0 & 0 \\ 0 & 0 & 1.0 & -1 & 1.0 & 0 \\ 0 & -1 & 0 & 0 & 0 & 1 \end{bmatrix} \begin{Bmatrix} C \\ I \\ W \\ X \\ P \\ K \end{Bmatrix} = \begin{Bmatrix} Q_1 \\ Q_2 \\ Q_3 \\ G \\ 0 \\ K_L \end{Bmatrix}$$

where $Q_1 = 16.8 + 0.23P_L + 0.8S$ (and $S = 0.8G$)

$Q_2 = 17.8 + 0.55P_L - 0.15K_L$

$Q_3 = 1.6 + 0.16X_L + 0.13|t - t_0|$

Now they can be coded and Mohr's *time stepping* method and the GJR routine given in Sec. NM4 used to solve for the variables *{V}* after each of a succession of one year steps.

This is done in the program KEPLOT in \ MBS1 on the course 'Basics' disc, the coding being:

```
5 DIM A(6, 6), Q(6), R(6), v(6), S(6), F(6), PR(100, 2), FR(6)
10 FOR j = 1 TO 6: S(j) = 0: F(j) = 1: L(j) = 0: NEXT j:SCREEN 1:COLOR 4, 1:COLOR 4, 1
15 F(6) = 2: REM S(2)=100:S(3)=100:S(5)=100
20 n = 6: z = 0: D = 0: K1 = 100: X1 = 100: P1 = 10: W1 = 25
25 FOR I = 1 TO n: FOR j = 1 TO n: READ A(I, j): NEXT j: NEXT I: GOSUB 100
30 T = .2: G = .8: z = z + 1: IF z > 30 GOTO 85
32 IF z = 10 OR z = 11 THEN G = 1.5 AND T = .5
33 REM ? "IP - if 99 then end":input g,t:if g=99 goto 85
35 R(2) = 17.8 + .55 * P1 - .15 * K1: R(3) = 1.6 + .16 * X1 + .13 * D: R(6) = K1
40 R(5) = -T * (W1 + P1): R(4) = G * R(5): S = .8 * R(4): R(1) = 16.8 + .23 * P1 + .8 * S
45 FOR I = 1 TO n: Q(I) = 0: FOR K = 1 TO n
50 Q(I) = Q(I) + A(I, K) * R(K): NEXT K: NEXT I
55 FOR j = 1 TO n: v(j) = (2 * Q(j) + S(j)) / F(j)
60 A = 10 * (z - 2): B = 150 - L(j)
65 X = 10 * (z - 1): y = 150 - v(j): LINE (A, B)-(X, y): v = INT(y / 8.5) + 2
66 IF z < 30 GOTO 68
67 LOCATE v, 38: PRINT j
68 NEXT j
70 P1 = Q(5): X1 = Q(4): K1 = Q(6): W1 = Q(3)
75 FOR j = 1 TO n: L(j) = v(j): NEXT j: IF z > 10 THEN D = D + 1
80 PR(z, 1) = P1: PR(z, 2) = K1
82 GOTO 30
85 FOR I = 1 TO n: FR(I) = Q(I): NEXT I
86 DRAW "bm0,150 m300,150 bm0,0 m0,200"
90 END
100 FOR I = 1 TO n: X = A(I, I): A(I, I) = 1
105 FOR j = 1 TO n: A(I, j) = A(I, j) / X: NEXT j
110 FOR K = 1 TO n: IF K = I GOTO 120
112 X = A(K, I): A(K, I) = 0
115 FOR j = 1 TO n: A(K, j) = A(K, j) - X * A(I, j): NEXT j
120 NEXT K: NEXT I
125 RETURN
130 DATA 1,0,-.8,0,-.02,0
135 DATA 0,1,0,0,-.23,0
140 DATA 0,0,1,-.42,0,0
145 DATA -1,-1,0,1,0,0
150 DATA 0,0,1,-1,1,0
155 DATA 0,-1,0,0,0,1
```

Here the initial values of *P* etc. are set in line 20 and the values chosen in Eqns IE21 are set in line 30. In line 32 a temporary disturbance is introduced and here, instead, D = D + 1 can be set after the tenth iteration/year (z in the program) to activate Klein's original 'after 1931 term'.

Another version of this program, GNPEQNS(.BAS assumed) in \MBS1 also given and this does not use screen graphics, simply plotting numbers to form the time curves for the six variables, useful for continuous plotting via a printer.

APPENDIX: A Concise but Complete Macroeconomic Model

The following is a very brief summary of the book by Vernon which should now be followable with a little study. Herein the basic GNP equations (in simple form) are developed into a fairly complete model which can be used to estimate magnitudes of actions required attain objectives such as full employment.

Extending Vernon's equations for the LMS (liquid money supply) and ISE (interest sensitive expenditure) curves slightly, I showed that *increasing interest rates increases inflation,* as intuition suggests, but economists think the opposite, one reason why in the author's recent books *The Pretentious Persuaders* and *The Brainwashed,* this proof is included in a chapter called *Econobabble* (Mohr, 2012/ 2014, 2016).

1. FISCAL MODEL

Equilibrium:

Aggregate supply/output $Q = E$ the aggregate real demand/expenditure

$= C + I$ or consumption + investment

$$= a + bQ^* + I = 50 + 0.8Q^* + 70 \qquad (1)$$

where Q^* = real private disposable income = Q assumed here

$\delta C/\delta Q^* = b$ = marginal propensity to consume (MPC)

giving

$Q = (a + I)/(1 - b) = (50 + 70)/0.2 = 600$ with $1/(1 - b)$ = consumption multiplier

Full employment constraint:

$Q_f = 1000$ = full employment output

Consider three cases:

(a) With I = 70 (as above) Eqn (1) gives $E = 50 + 0.8(1000) + 70 = 920$
- this is greater than the equilibrium demand (600) so we have shortfall (in production) unemployment

(b) $I = 150$ gives $Q = (a + I)/(1 - b) = (50 + 150)/(1 - 0.8) = 1000$
giving: full employment
$E = 50 + 0.8(1000) + 150 = 1000$
so that we have equilibrium and thus constant prices (or zero inflation)

(c) $I = 230$ gives $E = 50 + 0.8(1000) + 230 = 1080$
giving an expenditure gap $= E - Q_f = 80$ with demand > supply and prices rise

Note: (1) MPC reduces with income level: e.g

Income (after tax)	Consumption	MPC
3,000	5,000	1.67
30,000	24,000	0.80

and MPC also tends to decrease with time (i.e. we 'get wise')

(2) Time series analysis gives results for the regression line such as:

$C = 1.51$ (\$B) $+ 0.91Q^*$ with b in the range 0.88 to 0.92

Government purchases:

$E = C + I + G$ with $C = a + b(Q - T + D)$ (2)

a= 50, I = 70 still and let G = 80

T = real Gov. tax receipts = 200

D = real Gov. transfer payments = 100

giving $C = 50 + 0.8Q + 0.8(-200 + 100) = -30 + 0.8Q$

so that we have $E = C + I + G = 120 + 0.8Q$ (3)

Considering the same three cases:

(a) Q = E (equilibrium ignoring the full employment constraint)

gives Q = 120/0.2 = 600

and shortfall unemployment with C = -30 + 0.8(600) = 450, I = 70, G = 80

(b) using *discretionary fiscal ease* to obtain full employment we

(i) use $\delta G = 80$ giving from Eqn (3) $E = 200 + 0.8(Q_f = 1000) = 1000$

and $Q = (a - bT + bD + I + G)/(1 - b)$ from Eqn (2) with E = Q

$= (50 - 160 + 80 + 70 + 160)/0.2 = 1000$

(ii) or $\delta T = -5$ or $dD = 5$ gives $dE = 4$

so that we need change in T or D of magnitude 100 for full employment

(c) using *discretionary fiscal restraint* we do the reverse of (b), that is

we have $\delta G = -80$

or $\delta T = 100$ or $\delta D = -100$

which when I = 230 so that E = 50 + 0.8(1000) + 230 = 1080 gives the required change (in the original case (c) above).

Including tax rate:

$Q = E$ (for equilibrium) $= a + b[(1 - t)Q - T + D] + I + G$

where disposable income Q* (assumed = Q) is reduced by tax rate t, and now T is a tax constant,

giving $\delta Q/\delta I = 1/[1 - b(1 - t)] = 2.5$ (not 5 as before) with t = 0.25

and $\delta Q/\delta T = -b/[1 - b(1 - t)] = -2$ (not -4 as before)

$\delta Q/\delta D = b/[1 - b(1 - t)] = 2$ (not 4 as before)

and these multipliers are reduced further when monetary policy is included.

2. MONETARY MODEL

Money supply MS = MD the money demand (both real)

where MS = M/P with P = price level factor = 1 assumed

MD = f(Q, r); I = f(r); C = f(Q*, r) (r = interest rate)

For demand we have $E = C + I^* + G$

with C = consumption expenditure function = $a + bQ^* - sr$

where s = interest responsiveness of C

$= 50 + 0.8Q^* - 1000r$ with $Q^* = Q(1 - t) - T + D = Q - 50 + 75$

where T = tax constant and t = tax rate

I* = investment expenditure function = I - ir where i = interest responsiveness of I

(early versions of the Fed-MIT model take s approx. = i)

= 200 - 1000r

G = 230

so that

$E = E^* + b(1 - t)Q - (i + s)r$ with $E^* = a - bT + bD + I + G$

$= 50 - 40 + 60 + 200 + 230 = 500$

so that $E = Q$ for equilibrium gives

$$r = \{E^* - [1 - b(1- t)]Q\}/(i + s) = (500 - 0.4Q)/2000 = 0.25 - 0.0002Q \qquad (4)$$

nd this is the *interest sensitive expenditure curve* (ISE curve) - a 'down' demand curve (with r the up/price axis and Q the across/quantity axis)

For supply $MS = M/P = 200/P = 200$

$= MD = L + kQ - qr$ with L = money demand constant = 50

k = income responsiveness of money demand = 0.2

and q = interest responsiveness of money demand = 1000

giving

$$r = (L - M/P + kQ)/q = -0.15 + 0.0002Q \qquad (5)$$

and this is the *liquid money supply curve* (LMS curve) - an 'up' supply curve

and summing the two equations gives $2r = 0.10$ or $r = 0.05$ whence $Q = 1000$ *(check this graphically as an exercise in S-D diagrams).*

Then $\delta C/\delta r = - s = - 1000$ and $dI/dr = - i = - 1000$

so that an increase of 1% in r gives decrease of 10 $B in both C and I

Note: we have here $kQ = M/P$ (if $r = 0$, $L = 0$) or $M(V = 1/k) = PQ$

if we compare with the classical velocity of money theory, whence velocity = 1/k

Then if we have $\delta I = 80$ so that $I = 280$ (giving an expenditure gap = 80)

this gives IS curve $r = 0.29 - 0.0002Q$

and if $P = 1.25$ the LMS curve is $r = - 0.11 + 0.0002Q$

Solving the two equations (by summing them to give $2r = 0.18$) gives

$r = 0.09$ and $Q = 0.2/0.0002 = 1000$ as the point of intersection (and equilibrium)

and the gap is removed.

Aggregate savings approach:

Define aggregate saving = $S = Q - (C + G)$ (= I at equilibrium)

$= SP + SG$ where SP = private = $Q^* - C = Q - T + D - C$

SG = govt = $T + tQ - D - G$

giving $S = Q - \{a + b[(1 - t)Q - T + D] - sr\} - G$

$= - a + bT - bD - G + [1 - b(1 - t)]Q + sr$

$= - 50 + 40 - 60 - 230 + 0.4Q + 1000r$

$= - 300 + 0.4Q + 1000r$

and $SP = Q - T + D - \{a + b[(1 - t)Q - T + D] - sr\}$

$= Q - 50 + 75 - \{50 + 0.6Q - 40 + 60 - 1000r\} = - 45 + 0.15Q + 1000r$

$SG = T + tQ - D - G = 50 + 0.25Q - 75 - 230 = - 255 + 0.25Q$

and these sum to give S as required

Then $I = 200 - 1000r$ (from previously)
$= -300 + 0.4Q + 1000r$
giving $r = 0.25 - 0.0002Q$ or the original ISE curve of Eqn. (4) with $r = .05$ and $Q = 1000$ at the equilibrium point and $S = 150 = I$; $SP = 155$
so that $SG = -5$ (in deficit).

IE References

Aarons, R. and Loftus, A. The Secret War Against the Jews, Mandarin Press, Melbourne, 1999.

Attiyek, R., Lumsden, K. and Bach, G.L. Macroeconomics: A Programmed Book, 2nd edn. Prentice-Hall, Englewood Cliffs NJ. 1970.

______. Transcripts on the Poltical Economy of Development. Australian Broadcasting Commission, Sydney. 1977

Benham, F. Economics, 6th edn. Pitman, London, 1960.

Black, E. IBM and the Holocaust. Little Brown, London, 2001.

Booker, M. The Last Domino: Aspects of Australia's Foreign Relations. Sun Books, Melbourne, 1978.

Caves, RE, Frankel, JA, Jone, RW, World Trade and Payments, An Introduction, 5th edn. Scott, Foresman/Little, Brown, Glenview IL, 1990,

Clark, G. In Fear of China. Lansdown Press, Melbourne, 1972.

Crough, G., Wheelwright, T. and Wiltshire, T. Australia and World Capitalism. Penguin, Ringwood VIC, 1980.

David, A. and Wheelwright, T. The Third Wave. Left Book Club Co-op. Ltd, Sydney, 1989.

Gilpin, R. War and Change in World Politics. CUP, Cambridge, 1981.

Gilpin, R. The Political Economy of International Relations. Princeton Univ. Press, Princeton NJ. 1987.

Hunt, E.K. and Sherman, H.J. Economics: An Introduction to Traditional and Radical Views, 4th edn. Harper & Row, New York. 1981.

Jay, P. The Crisis of Western Political Economy. Australian Broadcasting Commission, Sydney, 1980.

L.R. Klein, *Economic Fluctuations in The United States, 1921-1941*, John Wiley & Sons, New York, 1950.

Klein, L.R., Pauly, P. and Voison, P. The world economy - a global model. Perspectives in Computing, vol. 2, no. 2, 1982.

Levinson, M. Capitalism with a safety net ? Harvard Business Review, Sept-Oct. 1996.

Leontief, W.W. The Structure of the American Economy, 1919-1939, 2nd edn. OUP, Fair Lawn NJ. 1951.

Lindert, P.H. Prices, Jobs and Growth: an Introduction to Macroeconomics. Little Brown, Boston MA, 1976.

MacKenzie, K. The English Parliament. Pelican, Harmondsworth, 1963.

Mintzberg, H. Managing government, governing management. Harvard Business Review, May-June 1996.

Mohr, G.A. Time Stepping of Macroeconomic Models. Appl. Maths Comput., Vol. 102, pp 273-278, 1999.

Mohr G.A., *The Pretentious Persuaders,* Horizon Publishing Group, Sydney, 2012, 2014.

Mohr G.A., *Elementary Thinking for the 21st Century,* Xlibris, Sydney, 2014.

Mohr G.A., *The Brainwashed, From Consumer Zombies to Islamism and Jihad,* Inspiring Publishers, Canberra, 2016.

Sampson. The Arms Bazaar. Coronet, Sevenoaks, Kent, 1977.

Shavelson, R.J. Statistical Reasoning for the Behavioural Sciences, 2nd edn. Allyn & Bacon, Boston MA, 1976.

Smith, A. Paper Money. Summit Books, New York NY. 1981.

Sweezy, P.M. The Theory of Capitalist Development. Dennis Dobson, London, 1946.

Tarshis, L. Modern Economics. Houghton Mifflin, Boston. 1967.

Vernon, J. Macroeconomics. Dryden Press, Hinsdale IL, 1980.

Wells, S.J. International Economics. Allen & Unwin, London, 1969.

Wonnacott, P. and Wonnacott, R. Economics. McGraw-Hill, New York, 1979 + Howitt, P. Study Guide to Accompany Wonnaccott/Wonnacott: Economics. McGraw-Hill, New York, 1979.

MICROECONOMICS (ME)

A society in which consumption has to be artificially stimulated in order to keep production going is a society founded on trash and waste, and such a society is a house built upon sand. Dorothy Sayers.

In the preceding chapter we discussed macroeconomics is, that is national and international economic matters such as the foreign exchange market. In this chapter we discuss *microeconomics*, that is, economic management of the local market and corporations, sometimes referred to as managerial economics.

ME1. Elasticity

In the preceding chapter we introduced the concept of supply and demand and the associated S & D curves were much used to explain economic phenomena. By consideration of the *elasticity* of supply and demand many more useful applications of the theory of supply and demand are found.

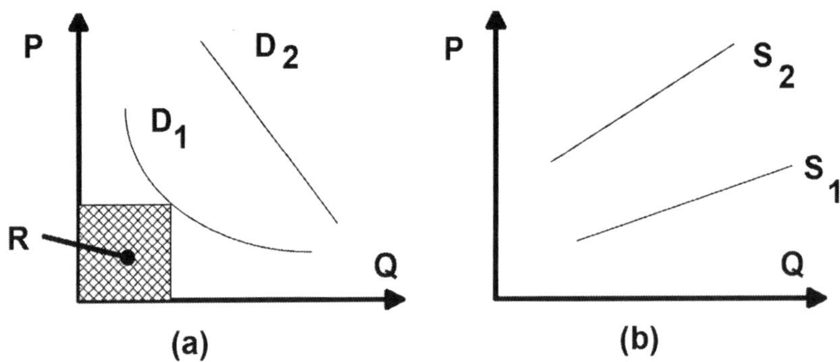

Fig. ME1. Elasticity of supply and demand.

In Eqn IE2 we defined elasticity as

(ME1) $e = (\delta Q/Q)/(\delta P/P)$

so that it is the quotient of the fractional or percentage changes in Q and P.

When we are dealing with a curve and $dQ = Q_2 - Q_1$, $dP = P_2 - P_1$ for two points which values of Q and P should we use in calculating elasticity ? The answer is to define e as:

(ME2) $e = (\delta Q/Q_{av})/(\delta P/P_{av})$

where $Q_{av} = (Q_1 + Q_2)/2$, $P_{av} = (P_1 + P_2)/2$

That is, e is calculated as the *inverse slope of the chord* between the two points on the curve. In the limit, therefore, $e = dQ/dP$ ïis the *inverse slope* of the curve at a point.

Fig. ME1(a) shows two demand curves:

(a) D_1 is for *elastic* demand ($e < -1$) and $\delta P \rightarrow -\delta R$

(b) D_2 is for *inelastic* demand ($e > -1$) and $\delta P \rightarrow +\delta R$

where R is the *revenue* which is given by the shaded area shown in Fig. ME1(a) for a given point. Hence when demand is elastic and increase in price gives a decrease in revenue.

Fig. ME1(b) shows two supply curves. The curve S_1 is *elastic* ($e > 1$) and hence 'flat' whilst S_2 is *inelastic* ($e < 1$) and 'steep'.

Application of the elasticity concept

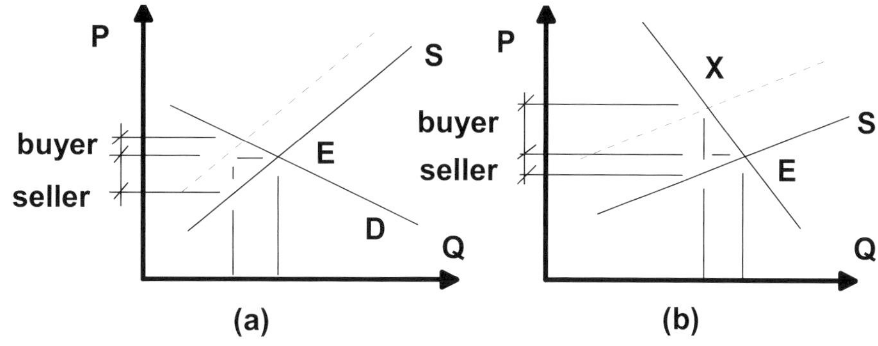

Fig. ME2. Price changes with (a) elastic D, (b) elastic S.

Fig. Me2(a) shows the effect of an increase in price, for example as the result of imposition of a tax, when demand is elastic (or 'flat'). Then operation moves to point X and the seller bears most of the burden of the price increase, as shown.

When the supply is elastic, on the other hand, the buyer bears most of the price increase, as shown in Fig. ME2(b).

Clearly, therefore, elasticity is very important in considering the effect of price increases as the effects on revenue and whether the sellers of buyers bear the burden of such increases depends upon the elasticity of supply or demands.

Factors in elasticity of demands

Examples of factors which affect elasticity of demand include:

1. Luxury items (for example hats) tend to have elastic demand whereas essentials (such as electricity) have inelastic demand.
2. Cost and hence proportion of available funds is an important factor and, for example, expensive items such as cars have elastic demand while cheap (and perhaps essential) items such as toothpaste have inelastic demand.
3. Availability of alternatives is another factor. When alternative products exist, for example competing types of confectionary, demand is elastic but when there are almost no alternatives (for example salt) demand is inelastic.
4. Whether items are required immediately or for use in the long term is another key factor. Ski equipment, for example, will tend to have elastic demand whereas items like car parts have inelastic demand.

Factors in elasticity of supply

Similarly there are many simple factors which affect the elasticity of supply, examples being the following:

1. Products with low storage cost will tend to have elastic supply whereas those for which storage cost is high, for example food, will have inelastic supply.
2. Products for which storage is of limited feasibility, such as perishable goods, will have inelastic supply whilst goods which have no such constraints will have elastic supply.
3. When substitute products can be produced when necessary, for example substitute crops for farming, then supply is elastic but when substitution is not possible supply is inelastic.
4. When goods must be disposed of in the short term (for example perishable or other goods with a limited shelf life) then supply is inelastic whereas where goods need only be sold in the long term then supply is elastic.

Special problems of agriculture

Discussion of factors affecting elasticity of supply and demand has already considered problems such as those of perishable goods and the essential nature of food products. Other special problems of agriculture include:

1. Seasonal fluctuations in supply.
2. Boom crops which shift the supply curve S to the right in Fig. ME2(b) and thus cause a drop in price.
3. Droughts which have the opposite result of (2), that is a shortage occurs along with an increase in price.
4. 'Food mountains' stored over years to maintain prices are then difficult to dispose of.
5. Global surpluses can lead to a local surplus being exacerbated.

In general, indeed, agriculture is more prone to fluctuations in supply and demand and it is often difficult to cope with the problems that result.

Conclusion

The degree of elasticity of supply and demand curves has an important influence on the effect of changes in supply and demand. There are many factors which determine whether supply or demand is elastic or inelastic. Both supply and demand of agriculture products, however, tend to be inelastic and agriculture has many special problems as a result.

ME2. Demand and Supply Variations

In the following section we introduce the concept of *utility* and then of *marginal* utility and cost. These are very important quantities used in determining quantities of goods to supply.

Marginal utility

We define utility as the satisfaction a customer gains from buying a unit of a particular product. Then the *marginal utility* is the satisfaction from buying one additional unit. Expressing this in dollars and assuming that satisfaction (or usefulness, and hence price the buyer is prepared to pay) decreases with each further unit bought, that is the 'law of diminishing utility', the result being equivalent to a demand curve.

Fig. ME3 shows an example in which D is the utility function for a buyer. If the market price is as shown then the area A_2 represents purchase at utility exceeding market price and is the *consumer surplus.* When utility is less than purchase price, however, the consumer surplus represented by area A_1 is negative.

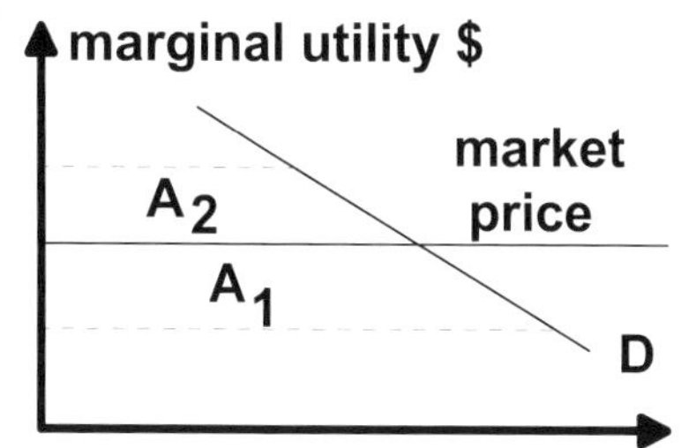

Fig. ME3. Consumer surplus.

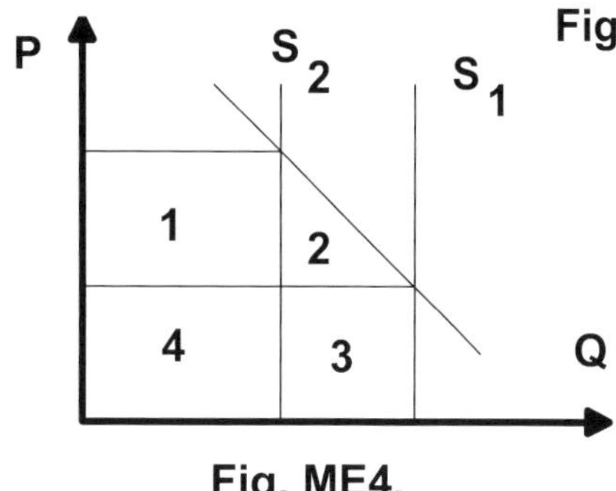

Fig. ME4.

Fig. ME4 shows an example of this surplus concept. Suppose there is a drought and the (inelastic) supply of an agricultural product drops from S_1 to S_2. Then the areas 1 and 2 represent a negative consumer surplus or consumer deficit. Similarly area 3 is a negative producer surplus (producer surplus is discussed at the end of this section).

Then the losses and gains may be summarized as follows:

Consumers	lose 1	lose 2	
Producers	gain1		lose 3
Σ= nation		lose 2	lose 3

leading to the conclusion that as a result of the price rising the consumers lose (as expected), whereas the producers might with a little luck gain a little but the nation as a while loses in terms of lost GNP.

The marginal cost (MC) or producing an item is the increase in total cost involved in producing one additional item. Fig. ME5 shows a typical example where marginal cost increases as Q increases (that is the 'law of diminishing returns').

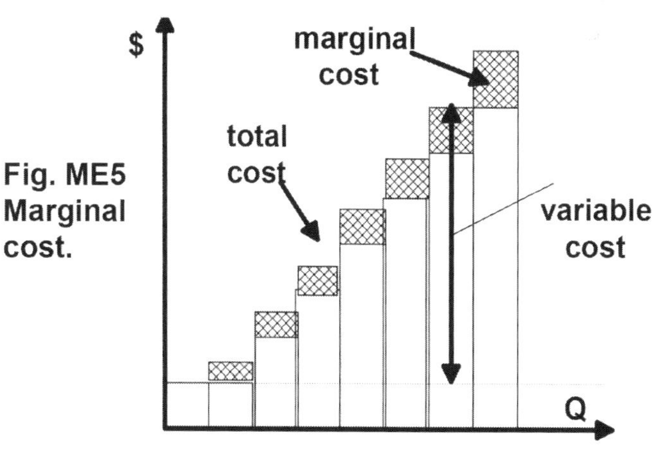

Fig. ME5 Marginal cost.

This increasing marginal cost is shown in Fig. ME6 where the point of intersection with the marginal return (MR), here a constant price, gives the optimum production quantity and the maximum profit (see Sec. IE2).

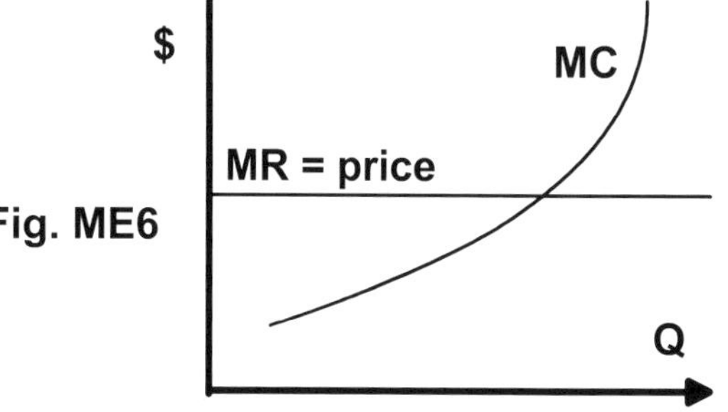

Fig. ME6

Short run supply curve

If we define average cost as total cost divided by output and average variable cost as total variable cost divided by output the curves AC and AVC are obtained in Fig. ME7.

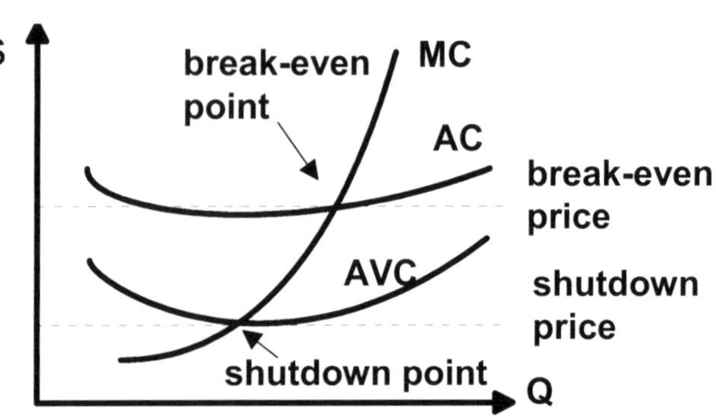

Fig. ME7. Short run supply curve.

Then the MC curve intersects the AVC cost at the *shutdown point* and output *Q* below this level does not cover variable costs (or fixed costs) and the short run supply curve is the portion of the MC curve above this point.

The MC curve then intersect the AC curve at its minimum (because to the left of the intersection point MC < AC and MC 'pulls the AC curve down' and to the right MC > AC and MC 'pushes the AC curve up') and this is the *break-even* price and output at above this level is profitable.

Example. As a simple example suppose you own a second house for which the fixed costs of your mortgage etc. are \$200 pw and the variable costs are \$40 pw, whereas you rent it for only \$100 pw. Should you keep renting it ? The answer is yes in the short term as this will at least help cover your costs. At least until you can sell it, that is, which is what you should do in the long term unless considerable capital gains are expected.

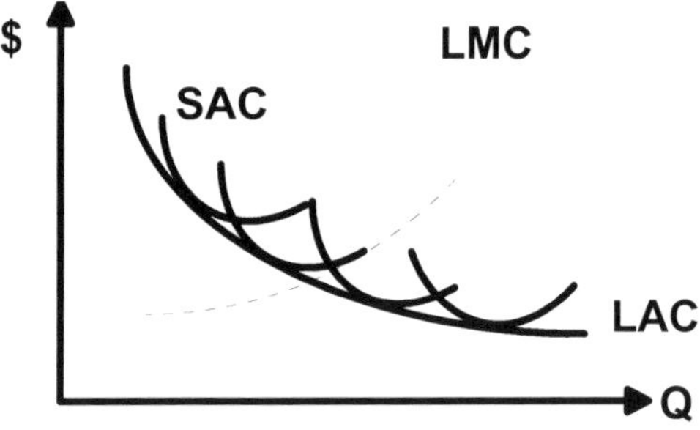

Fig. ME8. Long run supply curve

Long run supply curve

The short run supply curve deals with a particular 'level' or 'range' of operation. When there are several different ranges, for example corresponding to several factories or production lines (some of which can be shut down), we draw short run average cost curves (SAC) for each level of operation as shown in Fig. ME8.

Then the locus of these is the long run average cost curve (LAC) and this intersects the long run marginal cost curve (LAC) at the *long run break even point* and the *long run supply curve* is the part of the LMC curve above this point.

Producer surplus

Fig. ME9 shows the MC curve for a producer. If there is a price increase *dP*, as shown, then areas 2 + 3 give the increase in revenue, area 2 being a cost so that area 3 is the *producer surplus.*

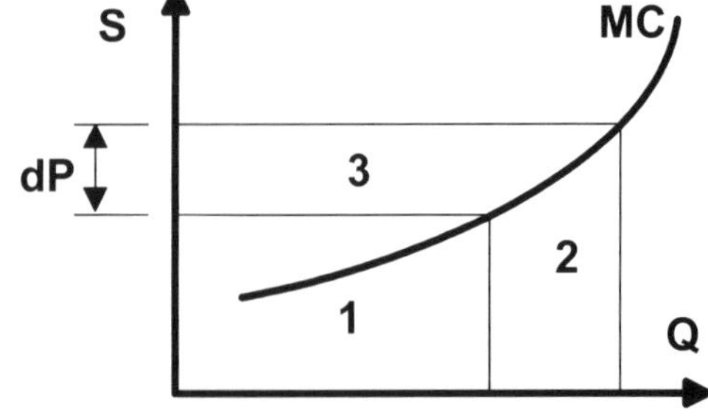

Fig. ME9. Consumer surplus

Conclusion

Marginal utility/cost curves are equivalent to supply and demand curves and once again such curves are shown to have very useful applications in illustrating the effects of price changes and critical points such as break-even points in cost-quantity studies.

ME3. Competition and Monopoly

In assuming demand and supply curves to this point we have assumed a perfectly competitive market, that is, the prices are determined by market forces and not by arbitrary means. In the following section we discuss the notion of a competitive market and associated problems.

Perfect competition

In a (perfectly) competitive market it is assumed that:

1. Social benefit = private benefit, so that marginal benefit of a product to society = marginal utility (to the user), i.e. MU.
2. Social cost = private cost, so that marginal cost of a product to society = marginal cost (of production), i.e. MC.

Then in a competitive market:

consumers purchase until MU = P
companies produce until P = MC
so that MU = MC

and this result applies to both private and public production and consumption.

When production is at levels other than for MU = PC there are efficiency losses such as that shown by the shaded areas in Fig. ME10. In case (a) fewer potentially beneficial units are produced than required and in case (b) each unit produced has MC > MU.

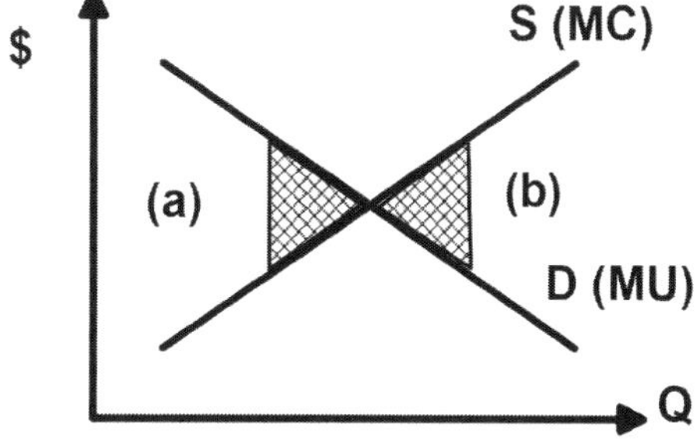

Fig. ME 10. Efficiency losses.

Markets, of course, are not perfect and are affected by such things as:

a. Distribution of income, the demand curves of different individuals depending on their income.
b. Market information will be unequal and sometimes misleading.
c. Speculative buying (for resale, not consumption).
d. Government subsidies (which considerably affect agricultural supply, for example).
e. Monopolies, cartels etc.

Discussion of the latter, the other points being discussed at other points in the text, follows in the remainder of this section.

Monopoly

Monopolies arise in such situations as the following:

1. A company has control over an input or technique required to make a product.
2. Through the law, for example where postal services are run by government or bus services are given exclusive contracts to operate routes.
3. Natural monopoly, that is, where no other company can match the cost efficiencies of an established company.
4. Collusion, for example where two or more companies form a cartel.

Fig. ME11 shows the demand (= average revenue) curve for a monopoly. If we move from point B at which 1 unit was sold for \$50 to point C were 2 units are sold for \$45 the marginal revenue for the firm

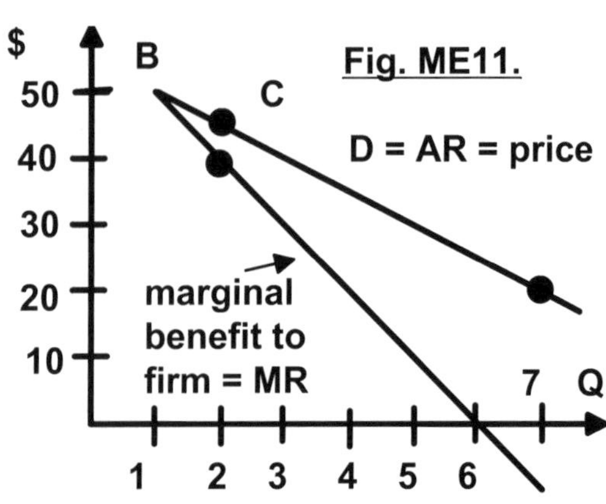

$$= 2(45) - 50 = \$40$$

Continuing such calculation for the full range of Fig. ME11 the results shown in Table ME1 are obtained.

Hence for a monopoly the MR and D curves differ and MR < *P* (price). This has followed from the assumption that D = AR = price. This is so for monopolies because the demand for a single firm is the market demand.

Table ME1. Derivation of MR for Fig. ME11

Q	P = AR	P x Q	MR
1	50	50	50
2	45	90	40
3	40	120	30
4	35	140	20
5	30	150	10
6	25	150	0
7	20	140	-10

Monopoly output and price

In Eqn ME3 it is shown that efficient operation is at the intersection of marginal cost and marginal utility or benefit. For a monopoly MU = MR so that point A in Fig. ME12 is chosen, giving output Q_A.

Then the price to sell at follows from the demand (= AR = P) curve, giving point B which is referred to as the profit-maximizing point on the demand curve. This profit = Q_A x BC = shaded area in Fig. ME12.

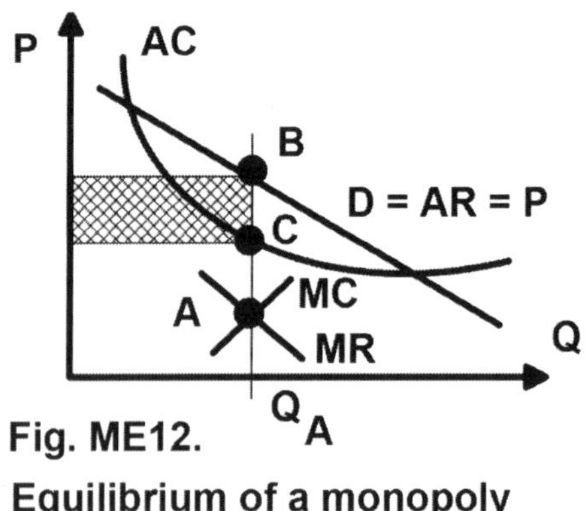

Fig. ME12.
Equilibrium of a monopoly

Conclusion

Monopolies involve the following disadvantages:

1. Prices are greater than they would be in a competitive market.
2. Production will tend to be less than in a competitive market.
3. They tend to be inefficient as their 'price freedom' allows this.

Hence antimonopoly policies and legislation are common along with price regulation and auditing to alleviate such difficulties.

ME4. Oligopoly

Oligopoly is domination of a market by a few companies. The degree to which this occurs is measured by the *concentration ratio,* that is, the proportion of the market that is captured by (say) four companies. The most obvious example is the car industry but others occur in the packaged food industry, for example.

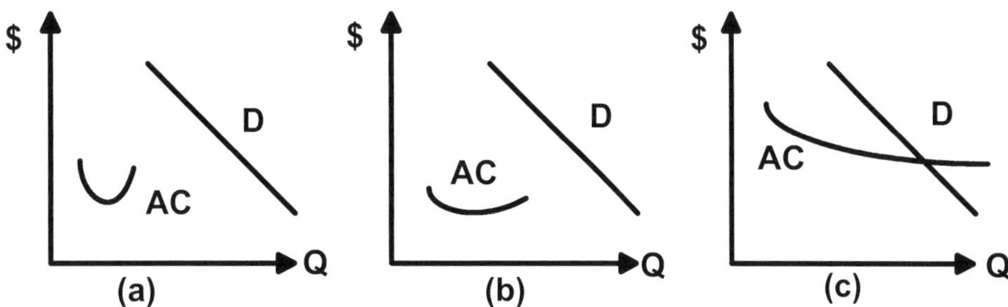

Fig. ME13. Perfect market, oligopoly and monopoly.

Fig. ME13(a) illustrates the situation in a competitive market. Here the 'cost range' of a firm is such that many firms are needed to supply the market. Many agricultural products are examples of this situation.

Fig. ME13(b) illustrated the situation of *natural oligopoly,* that is where the AC curves of individual firms fall over a large range so that only a few firms are needed to meet demand.

Natural oligopoly often occurs as a result of economies of scale in certain industries such as the car industry where mass production is particularly beneficial in reducing cost.

Fig. ME13(c) illustrates the situation of *natural monopoly,* that is where the AC curve for a single firm may only bottom close to the demand curve or even after it. An example is the steel industry.

Companies of case (b) are not required to expand by market forces but may seek *market power,* leading to movement towards monopoly. Alternatively, oligopoly companies may collude to fix prices, for example the OPEC cartel and its actions in the 1970s.

Bilinear demand

Fig. ME14 shows the demand curve for a company which is one of three forming an oligopoly, each having an equal market share of 10 units. The company is operating at point E but wishes to increase price to P_2.

If, however, the competitors hold their prices the company will lose market share by the amount δ shown and will be forced to sell at price P_3 to maintain this reduced market share, so that the actual demand function takes the bilinear form shown (i.e. D-E-X).

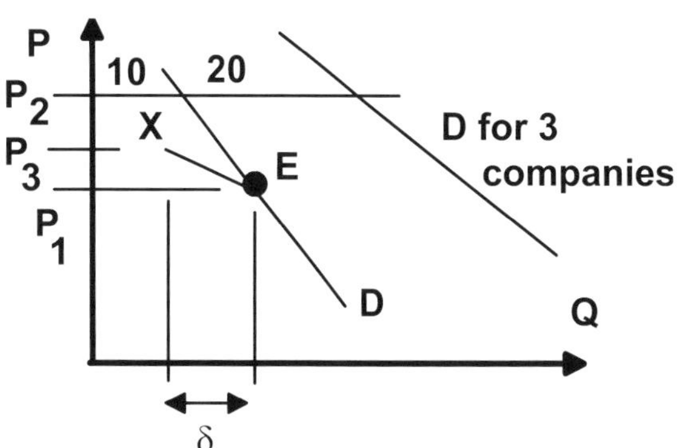

Fig. ME14. Bilinear demand function

Non-price competition

Not all competition in markets is simply by way of price, which has dominated the discussion to this point. Companies may also compete, of course, by advertising etc. or through research and development to refine products and production. When very large amounts are spend on such activities over a long period it can form a *barrier* to new entrants to the market.

Conclusion

Oligopoly occurs naturally when economies of scale favour it and then it offers a price advantage to the consumer. It also has the advantage of often involving large research and development budgets which lead to product improvements and development of new products, thus giving additional benefit to consumers and to industry.

ME5. External Costs and Benefits

In recent decades we have become increasingly aware of external costs which result from production such as pollution (requiring prevention and/or clean up costs) and congestion (freeways and high rise buildings are more costly than their counterparts on a 'unit usage' basis). Equally it is important to realize that some public services provide external benefits, that is benefits to certain people regardless of who paid for them.

Pollution

Pollution of the air, water, or noise pollution involve two types of costs, namely

1. *Internal costs* of prevention, cleanup etc.
2. *External costs* (or downstream costs) of cleanup, damage repair, compensation etc.

Suppose a free market is operating in equilibrium at point E_1 with output Q_1 and that a tax is implemented to provide for the costs of pollution cleanup forcing operation to move to point E_2 on the MC* curve which is the marginal cost curve for society. Then in relation to MC* (and not MC) there is an efficiency gain = E_1XE_2.

If, however, there was, in addition, a production limit Q_3 imposed to limit pollution there would be an efficiency loss E_2FG.

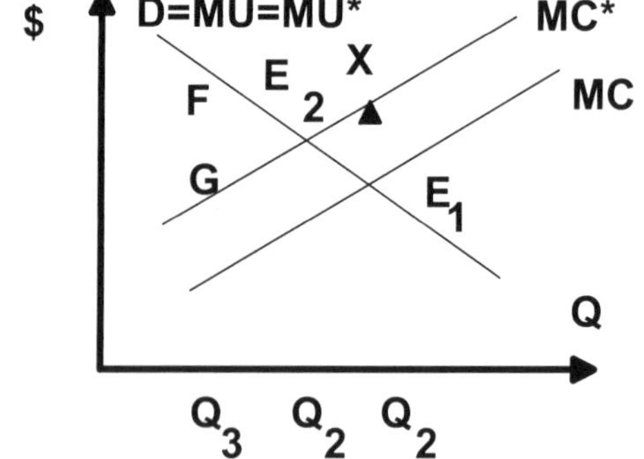

Fig. ME15. External costs or limits

If allowance for cleanup costs is included in determination of economic formulation of operating points and allowance made for social costs then from the broader point of view optimum production is possible.

Recycling

Recycling, as well as cleanup, reduces pollution and can be allowed for in budgeting. In addition recycling reduces consumption, of course, so that it provides two benefits.

Congestion

Traffic congestion can be reduced by, for example, small tolls which act like the tax in Fig. ME15 and will reduce peak flows and in turn reduce the need for further freeway construction.

In some cases lower public transport fares in peak periods can actually prove more economical, the increased revenue reducing the deficit caused by unprofitable off peak services. This in turn reduces traffic congestion.

Price, of course, need not be the only incentive for public transport. Provision of bus only lanes and the like can give public transport a comparative advantage in congested areas.

Public services

Suppose a free market is operating at equilibrium at point E_1 with output Q_1 but the product involved has a 'general social benefit', that is the community at large as well as the customers.

Then when this social benefit is taken into account the marginal utility curve is MU*. Then if a subsidy is paid by the government to move output to level Q_2 and hence operation to point E_2 there is an efficiency gain (in relation to MU*) of E_1E_2X.

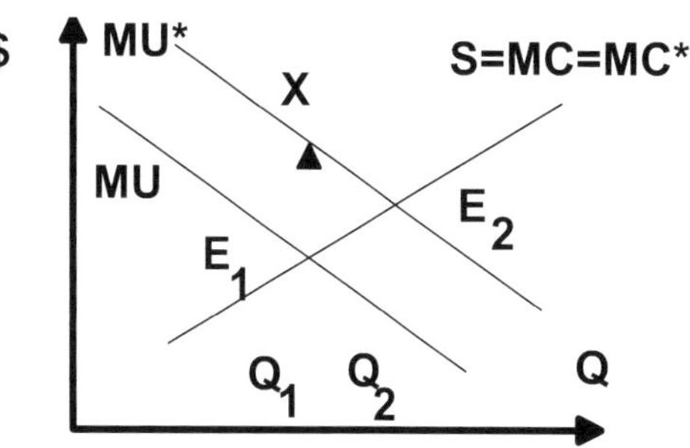

Fig. ME16. Efficiency gain with a public service.

Once again, therefore, we see how allowance for social factors in utility (or return) and cost can lead to rational economic models which, in relation to these factors are efficient.

Benefit-cost analysis

Benefit-cost analysis is a well known technique in which simple tables of costs and benefits of alternative schemes are used to determine preferred plans for public works, choosing first those projects which have the largest *benefit-cost ratio.*

Such techniques can readily include social factors in their benefit calculations whilst demand and supply and marginal utility and cost information can provide data for their application.

An example benefit-cost analysis is given in Sec. OT10.

Conclusion

Pollution and public services have been used respectively as examples of the use of adjusted marginal cost and utility functions, interpreting these as examples of social cost or benefit. The adjustments used here to allow for tax (or price) and quota impositions can, of course, be used in any context.

ME6. International Trade

Some of the advantages of international trade to local markets include:

1. It provides increased competition.
2. Economies of scale are encouraged locally in order to compete with overseas markets.
3. It introduces foreign industries with 'comparative advantage' which can produce at lower 'opportunity cost' (see IE1) into the local market, in turn encouraging local producers with such advantage to export.
4. Technological change is often introduced, boosting local production and in turn overall international trade.

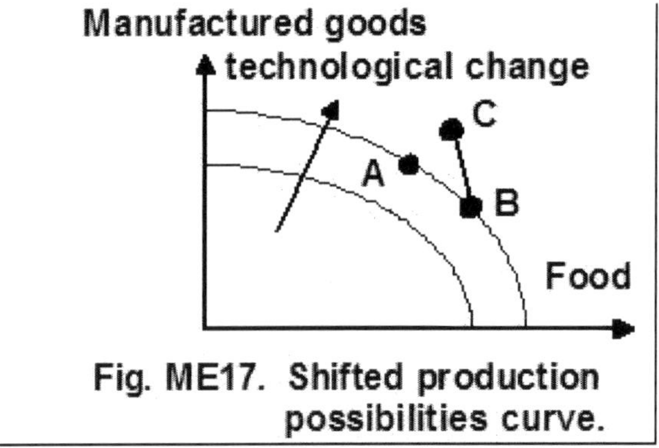

Fig. ME17. Shifted production possibilities curve.

Fig. ME17 shows an example of the effect of technological change introduced by international trade. Here new technology shifts the production possibilities curve (PPC, see Sec, IE1) outwards so that total production and consumption may be increased.

Then the effect of specialization can also be shown by, for example, an increase in food production in moving from point A to B. Then through international trade the shortfall in production of manufactured goods is made up by moving from point B to C, beyond the PPC curve and yielding greater total production and consumption than would be possible in the local market.

Effect of imports and exports on costs and production

Fig. ME18 illustrates the effect of exports. Here there is a fall in local consumption Q_0 - Q_1 but an increase in production Q_2 - Q_0 to provide the required exports. With the fall in local consumption there is an increase in demand and price rises to P_e.

Then the efficiency gain of these changes resulting from exports is the sum of areas 3 and 4 in Fig. ME18.

With imports, on the other hand, price decreases to P_i and there is a decrease in local production Q_0 - Q_1, and there is an increase in consumption Q_2 - Q_0.

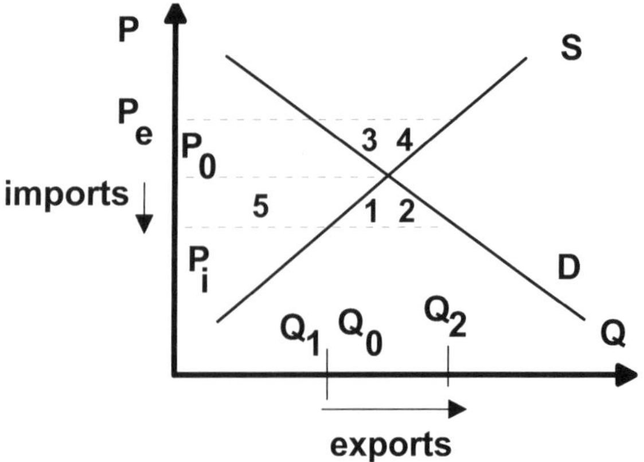

Fig. ME18. Effects of imports & exports

Hence the producers lose the revenue of area 5 but the consumers gain an increase in consumption and corresponding benefit equal to areas 5 + 1+ 2. Thus there is an overall efficiency gain of areas 1 + 2 transferred from the producers to the consumers.

Note, however, that in the case of imports we might be concerned about loss of employment resulting from the decrease in local production. As a result of the fall in prices, though, there may be an overall increase in real income.

The effects of tariffs etc.

The effects of tariffs, quotas, subsidies etc. on local and international trade involve such issues and effects as:

1. Tariffs and other 'protectionist' measures are often deemed necessary in the case of 'essential' industries such as the defence industry.
2. Such protection may be used to maintain employment levels and in turn is sometimes an issue of 'electoral sensitivity' so that timing of protection measures may not be desirable from the economic point of view.
3. Advertising campaigns to encourage buying of local products to protect local jobs are common and, indeed, 'buying local' does have this effect.
4. Local industry often campaigns against imports of 'cheap labour' goods.
5. Removal of protection tends to force local prices to match lower import prices.
6. Restriction of trade doesn't result in cheaper imports but may help diversify local trade.
7. Protection may be used to allow development of new industries but the question of how long to maintain it is a difficult one.

Multinational corporations.

Multinational corporations (MNCs) can affect monopoly and even affect government policy in host countries and consequently they are regarded by many as undesirable.

On the other side of this coin, however, the overseas operations of MNCs have the effect of a loss of jobs in the 'home' country (with a flow-on effect to other industries) where their funds could have been invested. There is also a corresponding loss of technology advantage over the host countries.

Trade blocs

Trade blocs such as the EEC have become important players in international trade and their actions can result in price and access barriers to outsiders.

On the other hand such agreements as the GATT (General Agreement on Tariffs and Trade) agreement, first set up in 1947, have had a considerable effect in signatory and other countries in reducing international tariffs.

Conclusion

International trade is generally beneficial and over recent decades there has been a general tendency to reduce tariffs and a movement towards a global market economy. Locally the effects of international trade on employment are still of concern and integrated domestic and international trade policies are needed to alleviate such concerns.

Recently, however, there is an increased interest in developing *regional trade*, that is trade within a 'world region' such as SE Asia where there is an ASEAN treaty, or, or course, Europe. Such trade is a subset of total international trade in which special agreements concerning particular areas of trade are sometimes reached.

Finally, trade agreements are sometimes reached between two neighbouring counties, for example Australia and New Zealand or Canada and the USA and these are another subset of total international trade.

ME7. The Labour Market

We now turn our attention to applying supply and demand considerations to the labour market. Here such considerations as productivity, wage rates, statutory minimum wages and the like can be examined using the concepts of marginal cost and marginal benefit.

Marginal productivity of labour

The marginal physical product of labour is the additional number of units of output a firm can produce when it hires one additional worker. The dollar value of this product is the *marginal productivity of labour (MPL)* and the curve of this is the demand curve for labour, as shown in Fig. ME19. As expected this has a 'diminishing' returns character.

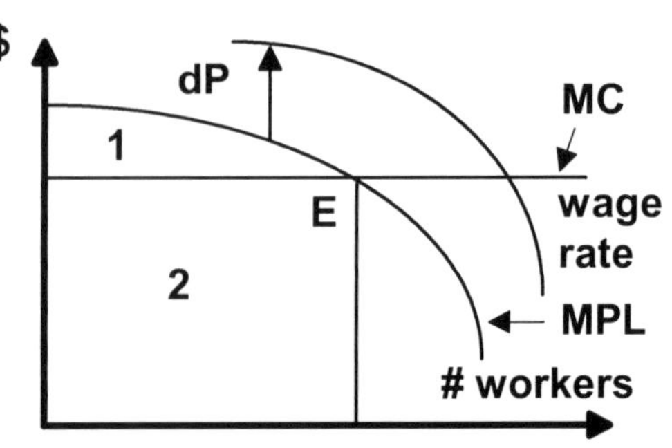

Fig. ME19. Demand for labour.

Then the cost of labour is, or course, the wage rate and this is the marginal cost to the firm of employing one more worker. Then the intersection of the MPL and MC curves gives the number of workers required and thus a company should hire until MPL = wage rate.

Then at the equilibrium point E the total labour cost of production is equal to area 2 and area 1 is the cost of other factors of production.

If the product being manufactured increases in price then the MPL curve rises by an amount dP as shown in Fig. ME19. Thus the equilibrium point moves to the right and the demand for labour is increased.

Effect of a minimum wage

Fig. ME20 shows the effect of increasing a minimum wage form W_1 and W_2, shifting operation from E_1 and E_2 (here assuming that the labour supply curve is a vertical line and hence point E_1 was at full employment).

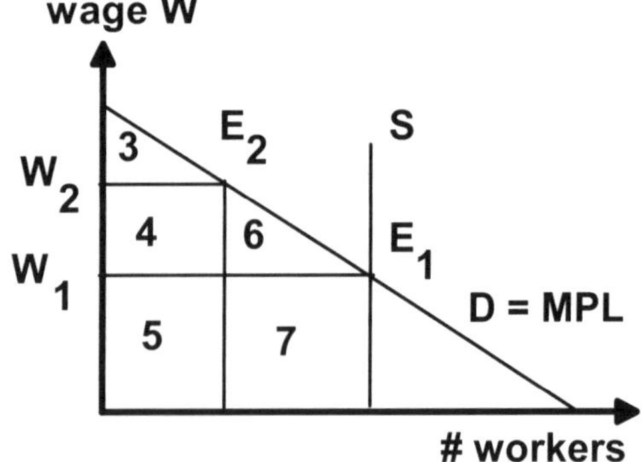

Fig. ME20. Effect of increase in minimum wage.

Then workers still employed gain the revenue of area 4 but those losing their jobs lose the revenue of area 7. Other factors of production lose the revenue of areas 4 and 6. Then the net loss of efficiency is the sum of areas 6 and 7.

Thus the overall effect is a loss of productivity and, of course, wages on the part of those who lose their jobs. Only a minority, therefore, those still employed gain (and consumers lose also from higher prices).

The effect of unions

Until now we have considered the case of a perfectly competitive market. Now suppose a *monopsonist* (single buyer) controls the labour market and, when operation is at equilibrium point E, reduces the wage rate to W_1.

Then, as shown in Fig. ME21 there is an efficiency loss EE_1E_3. If a union then negotiates a wage W_2 between the two previous rates some of the lost efficiency is regained. But, on the other hand, if the union is able to set a higher wage W_3 the same efficiency loss obtained with wage reduction to W_1 occurs.

In practice, or course, a result between the two extremes is expected as a result of collective bargaining etc.

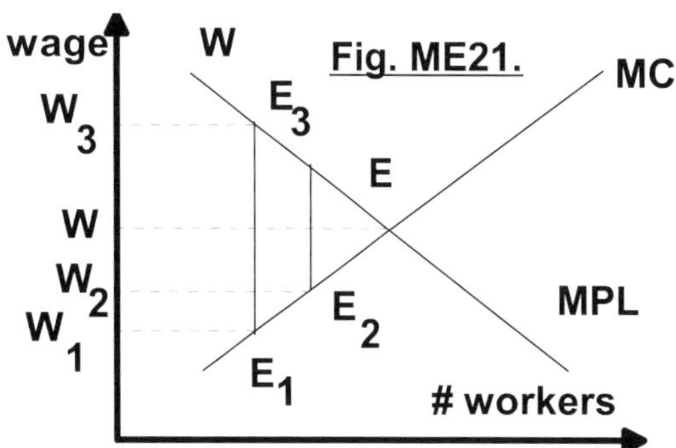

Industrial action

Industrial action (usually strikes) seeking better wages and conditions may result in a compromise that will suit both parties better in the long term.

Such action can have a flow-on effect to other companies and industries which may be adversely affected (for example an auto workers strike might result in closure of a small parts supplier). Such effects may then rebound on the origin of the action.

Strikes in certain public service areas are electorally sensitive (such as in the health area) and can have wide effects, perhaps impacting other public service areas.

Finally, it should be noted that strikes do not always affect a company as adversely as might be expected. Sometimes, for example, it allows time to run down overstocked inventory. Indeed companies have been known to 'engineer' strikes to this end.

Conclusion

The labour market provides yet another example of supply and demand at work. Here productivity and wage increases are amongst the major considerations and once again S & D curves provide useful insights into the effects of these.

Generally, however, wage increases need to be treated with caution, as Fig. ME20 shows, because sometimes only a relatively small number of people stand to gain if heavy job losses result or the rest of the community is affected.

Finally, special situations such as *bilateral monopoly* can occur when an employer has monopsony power and the union has monopoly power. Outcomes may then depend upon the bargaining skills of the parties as well as upon economic considerations.

ME8. Income From Capital Assets

Around 75% of national income is from wages and salaries. The remainder is made up of income from such assets as capital (debt or equity capital) and property and land. These make up an important part of the overall economic system.

Debt capital

Fig. ME22 shows the S & D curves for loan capital, the latter being the *marginal efficiency of investment (MEI)* line, that is another 'law of diminishing returns' type of function. Then operation is at the equilibrium point E shown.

Then if an interest rate ceiling i_1 is arbitrarily imposed, demand is theoretically Q_1 but supply is limited to Q_2 and thus operation moves to point E_2 and fewer loans are given. There is also a loss of efficiency E_2EX which is transferred from borrowers to lenders (who retain their funds), that is there is a loss of efficient projects etc. which are not funded.

If, on the other hand, the supply of loans was fixed by a vertical line as in Fig. ME20, then an entirely different result is obtained and, in fact, there is a loss of efficiency in raising interest rates.

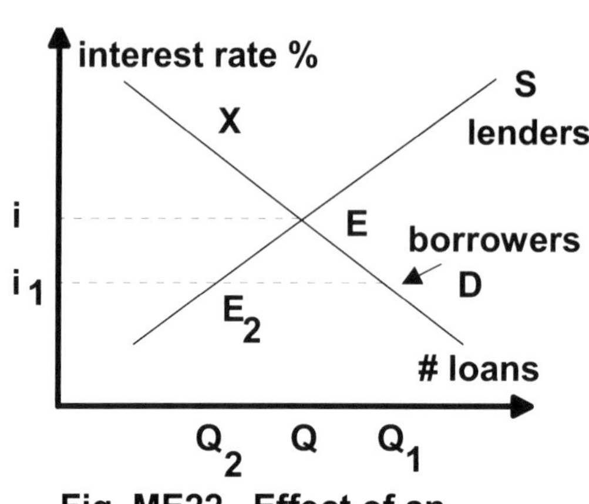

Fig. ME22. Effect of an interest rate ceiling

Equity capital

The same arguments for debt capital apply to the supply and demand of equity capital (that is shares in public companies). In addition, rates of return are based on a risk free rate (for the safest stocks) plus a premium based on the market's general rates and a multiplying beta factor for the risk of the individual company and its shares. This is discussed in the BF (Business Finance) chapter.

Human capital

Human capital refers to the investment costs of education and training and the value of skills thus acquired.

One of the key questions this raises is who should pay for such training? Generally, in fact, a mixture of payment methods exist and often the employee *contributes* to the costs by direct or deferred payment, employers contribute through taxes and assistance with employee costs whilst the government provides the initial and major ongoing funding.

Recent trends in this area have seen a narrowing of the salary gap between university and high school graduates in some countries (but a widening in others, particularly in certain specializations) and an increase in private training courses of a relatively short duration along with an increase in 'vocational' training via one or two year courses.

Rent

Rental rates depend upon a number of factors. As shown in Fig. ME23, for example, rates may increase with proximity to the CBD of a city (for dwellings and offices, the reverse might be true for farming land).

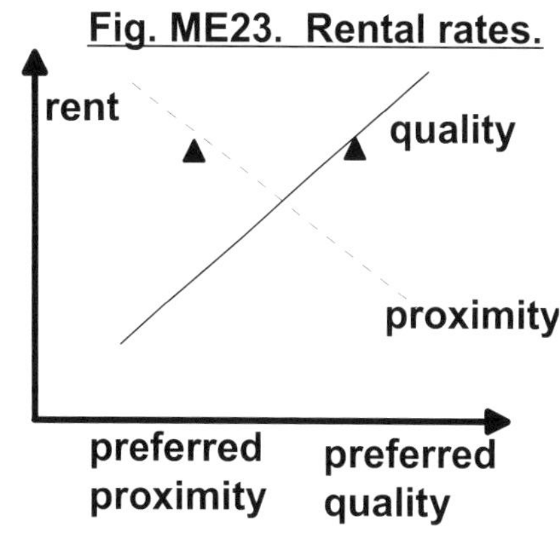

Fig. ME23. Rental rates.

They may also increase with the 'quality' of the individual area in question (for example its fertility in the case of farming land) and also with the quality of the location or general surrounding area (for example 'posh' suburbs, or course, command a higher rental).

Note that increases in rent are 'capitalized in the present value of the asset' (see chapter on Business Finance for definition of NPV or net present value), that is properties are partly valued on the basis of the rent they can command.

Conclusion

Once again S & D curves prove useful in illustrating the behaviour of capital markets. Markets for property, of course, behave in much the same way. To a lesser extent 'human markets' of various types of workers can also be represented by S & D curves or, at the very least, demand and supply arguments apply.

ME9. Economic Growth and Resource Conservation

In our discussions of economics much has been said about economic growth (in GNP etc.) and the views on economic control of the Keynesians and monetarists, both camps holding particular views on how growth should be managed. In the long term, however, it has to be born in mind that we have only finite resources and that, partially in response to such constraints, population should stabilize around 2020+. These issues are briefly discussed in the following section.

Market for natural resources

Fig. ME24 shows the S & D curves for the market for a natural resource which is common property. For such a resource we define a *reservation price* which is the price of obtaining the resource plus an amount sufficient to compensate for reduction of the resource in future.

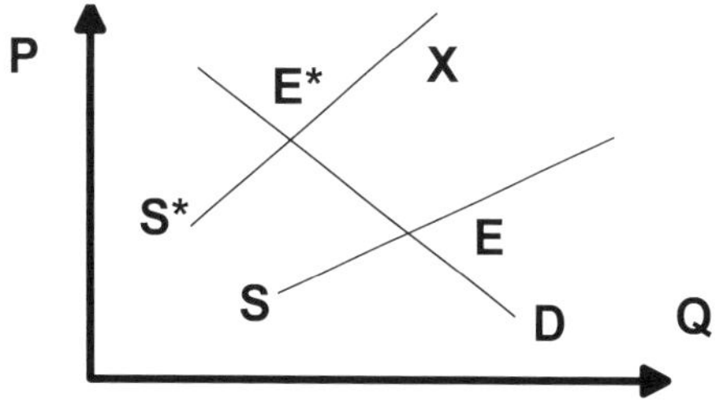

Fig. ME24. Market for natural resource which is common property

Allowing for the reservation price the realistic supply curve is S* and operation moves to E*. Hence operating at point E entailed an efficiency loss equal to the area E*EX.

Whether the additional funds obtained by using the reservation price could have been obtained by other means, for example, by a special tax, does not alter the basic argument here, namely that it is inefficient (in the long run) not to make such allowance for depletion.

Renewable resources

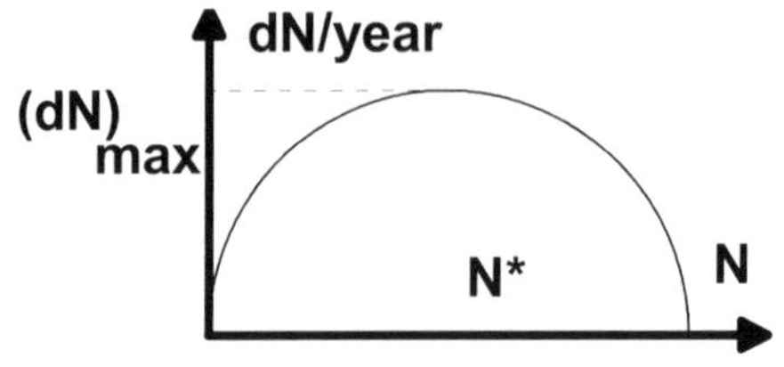

Fig. ME25. Sustainable yield curve.

Fig. ME25 shows the sustainable yield curve for a renewable resource, for example a fish population *N*. For this the curve for the increase per year in this population *(dN)* is shown, having a maximum $(dN)_{max}$ when $N = N^*$.

The maximum value of *dN* is the *maximum sustainable yield* and operation at this point will maintain the resource in constant quantity.

When harvesting is depleting such a resource, however, it is important to determine N^* and $(dN)_{max}$ and take appropriate action (such as harvesting at less than $(dN)_{max}$ until the population is restored to N^*).

Non-renewable resources

In the case of non-renewable resources such as oil it is important to have a long term policy. Actions that can be taken in such instances include:

1. Encourage consumption of alternative resources.
2. Produce alternative resources.
3. Develop alternative resources (through R & D, exploration etc.).
4. Encourage responsible usage of limited resources.

Further, as depletion increases the cost of limited resources such changes in consumer behaviour will be encouraged by price pressure.

Overall, or course, it is necessary to control the global population as soon as possible. The majority of this, of course, is not likely to own a car (certainly not a petrol driven one at least), but increasingly depletion of many other resources will be of concern.

Finally, a fine example of the success of policy (3) was the development of synthetic lubricating oils. In the future we might be able to rely on electric cars but they will still need lubricants!

Economic goals

Generally the 'complete overview' figure used for an economy is economic growth (in GNP) and figures often suggested for this were 4%. Lesser figures are appropriate in some economies now, and much larger ones in others.

In fully developed economies the future standard of living is guaranteed by technology (given population stabilizes) and growth economically is not needed in the long term. Indeed in some cases the point has already been reached at which it is necessary to limit growth.

Conclusion

Proper planning is, or course, vital in dealing with limited but renewable resources and with nonrenewable resources. In the latter instance much in the way of alternative product use and development needs to be done. In addition economic growth should be limited in developed economies and population growth must be curtailed globally.

ME10. Income distribution

If we are to have a capitalist or at least free market society then it is necessary to address the question of income distribution or inequality. Clearly there must be, at least apparently. such inequality and the following section discuses this and related issues briefly.

Human Capital

Human capital (investment in education etc.) is the basis of any sensible argument about income distribution, along with net present value (NPV) of income in different occupations.

As an example, suppose we compare the income potential of Mr A and Mr B assuming a discount rate of 10%:

1. A studies to be a surgeon to age 30, then has income \$100k til age 55.

2. B becomes a plumber at 20, then has income \$20k, increasing at the discount rate to a little over \$50k until age 30 and then stabilizing at at \$50k til age 55.

Comparing their total incomes over time we obtain:

NPV for A at age 30 = $100/(1.1 - 1) = 1000$ (\$k)

NPV for B at age 30 = $20(1.1^{10} - 1)/(1.1 - 1) + 50/(1.1 - 1) = 819$ (\$k)

so that B is not so badly off at all. Indeed if he invested some of his earnings when young and relatively uncommitted he could well be ahead.

Hence it is difficult, to say the least, to compare rates of remuneration but equally certain that they cannot be equal at any particular point in time. The long term view must be taken and, moreover, there must be some incentive for those who commit to long studies etc.

Distribution of income

Fig. ME26 shows typical income distribution curves and the complete equality line:

(i) = complete equality line
(ii) = after tax and transfers
(iii) = actual (Lorentz curve)

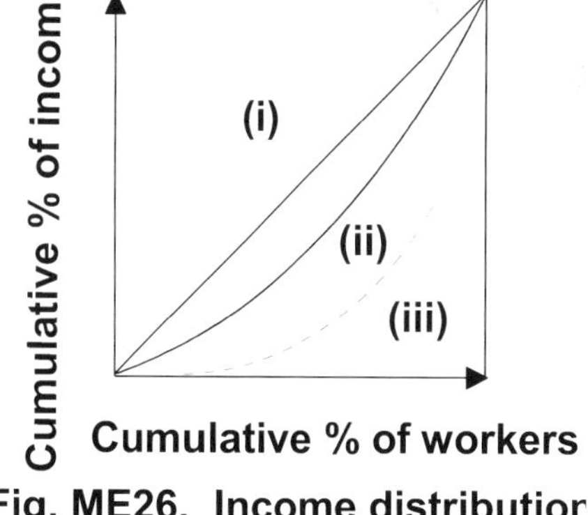

Fig. ME26. Income distribution

It demonstrates that tax and transfer payments (pensions etc.) reduce income equality significantly.

Note, however, that *equality* and *equity* are not synonymous and that equity means 'fair' and that this would should not the basis of income policy. Some occupations requiring exceptional skill and effort, for example, should be remunerated at a higher level than others. Just how high is the real question.

Equal opportunity laws

Equally opportunity, affirmative action and other legislation of similar intent is now commonplace. This is generally intended to give equal access to employment and equal pay where appropriate, but it is not intended to ensure equal pay in general, only to give an 'fair race' so far as competition for remuneration goes.

Poverty

Poverty is unavoidable in any society. Thus to deal with poverty the following things are needed:

1. It is important to define a poverty line to help address the problem more effectively by knowing its magnitude. For this purpose the *Engels coefficient*, that is the proportion of low incomes that is spent on food, is useful (and it takes values of from 0.25 for single persons to 0.33 for small families).
2. Adequate social security arrangements, including child allowances.
3. An infrastructure of emergency and other aid organizations.
4. Training courses for all in need.
5. Subsidized housing.
6. Means of dealing with the welfare trap.

The poverty problem, of course, is much dependent upon unemployment and this has been discussed at a number of points in the text.

Negative income tax?

Fig. ME27 shows the effect of what may seem a novel idea, that is, a negative income tax. With this in region (i) the poor are given a minimum income and this subsidy is tapered and given to all incomes in region (ii). Finally tax proper occurs in region (iii).

In fact this is much the same as the system in place in several countries but the version suggested here might lead to much more drastic leveling of incomes.

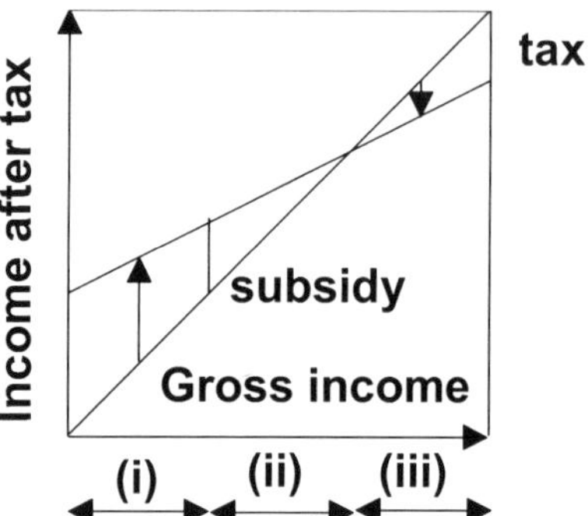

Fig. ME27. Effect of a negative income tax.

The rich

In many counties much effort has been directed at closing tax loopholes and preventing improper business practices. Factors such as company tax rates have to be considered carefully as excessive rates would discourage business expansion and development and hence job creation.

Conclusion

The question of income distribution is a vexatious one. As the example of Mr A and Mr B shows, just what is equitable is not easy to determine. The poverty question too is vexatious, along with that of unemployment. With proper planning, however, much can be done to alleviate these problems.

ME11. Cost functions

In the following section the determination of actual cost functions such as supply and demand curves is discussed. Then examples of such functions are given and the simple mathematical manipulations required to use them are demonstrated.

Determination of cost functions

To determine the data for a function $y = f(x)$ of a production process cost (y) where x is the number of units produced the following guidelines are useful:

1. x and y must be related (by such a function).
2. Production should be observed when production is 'constant' or steady.
3. Sufficient observations must be made to give a reasonable spread of data (in fact the range of production is often underestimated).
4. Observations of variation in y as a result only of those in x are required (and not as a result of other contributing factors).

Then a suspected form for the function must be established. Usually a polynomial function with unknown coefficients is used and the values of the coefficients can be determined by linear regression (see Sec. IE11).

Short and long run supply curves

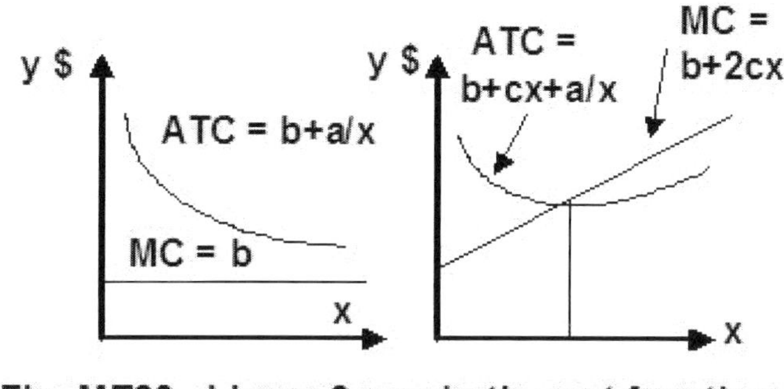

Fig. ME28. Linear & quadratic cost functions

Suppose the long run supply curve for a production process has been found to be of the form

(ME24) $y = a + bx - cx^2 + dx^3$

where a minus sign for c is often the suspected form for such curves.

Then the average total cost (ATC) and marginal cost (MC) are immediately given as

(ME5) $y/x = \text{ATC} = a/x + b - cx + dx^2$

(ME6) $dy/dx = \text{MC} = b - 2cx + 3dx^2$

In practice, in fact, linear and quadratic cost functions are generally satisfactory and examples of these are shown in Fig. ME28.

Finally, for the minimum in ATC shown in Fig. ME28(b), we have the *marginal average cost* given by the quotient rule of differentiation (Eqn MS6),

(ME7) $d(y/x)/dx = (xy' - y)/x^2$

(ME8) $= 0 \text{ when } y' = y/x$

so that the minimum in the ATC curve occurs when marginal cost (MC) equals average cost (ATC), that is the MC curve intersects the average (total) cost curve at its minimum point, as assumed in Sec. ME2. As pointed out there, this is the break-even point for production.

Demand functions

As an example assume that demand x and price S are related by

(ME9a) $2x + S^2 - 12000 = 0$

giving

(ME9b) $p(x) = \sqrt{(12000 - 2x)}$

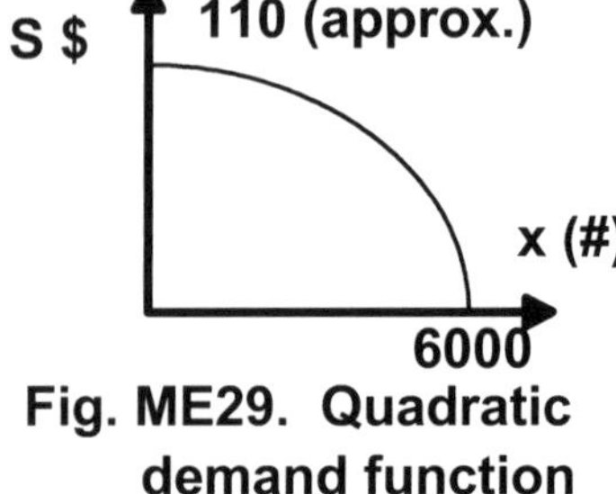

Fig. ME29. Quadratic demand function

as the demand function and this is shown in Fig.ME29.

Then it follows immediately that

(ME10) marginal demand function = $p'(x)$

(ME11) (total) revenue function = $R(x) = xp(x)$

(ME12) marginal revenue function = $R'(x) = (12000 - 3x)/\sqrt{(12000 - 2x)}$

and setting the latter to zero gives $x = 4000$ as the number of units produced for maximum revenue, each at price $p(x)$ = \$ 63.25, so that the maximum revenue is $R(x = 4000)$ = 4000(63.25) = \$ 235,000.

Profit functions

Profit functions are given by subtracting the production cost function $y = C(x)$ from the revenue function $R(x)$:

(ME13) $P(x) = R(x) - C(x)$

and the marginal profit function is given by

(ME14) $P'(x) = R'(x) - C'(x)$

so that profit is maximum when

(ME15) $R'(x) = C'(x)$

so that maximum profit occurs when marginal revenue and marginal cost are equal and, it then follows from Eqn ME8, these are both then equal to the average cost y/x.

As an example let $C(x) = x^3 - 3x^2 - 80x + 500$ and S = 2800 so that R(x) = 2800x. Then equating $C'(x)$ and $R'(x)$ we obtain

(ME16) $3x^2 - 6x - 80 = 2800;\ \ x^2 - 2x - 960 = 0;\ \ (x - 32)(x + 30) = 0$

giving the roots $x = 32$ and $x = -30$.

Then with the 'sensible' solution $x = 32$ we test the nature of the turning point:

(ME17) $p''(x) = R''(x) - C''(x) = 0 - (6x - 6) = -6(32) + 6 < 0$

so that the turning point is a maximum and the value of the profit at this maximum is given by

$$P(32) = 2800(32) - [32^3 - 3(32)^2) - 80(32) + 500] = \$\ 61{,}964$$

Conclusion

Once they have been determined (for example by regression) cost functions are easy to use to determine intersection points and maxima, such points having the applications described in preceding sections of this and the preceding chapter.

ME12. Input-Output Analysis (IOA)

One of the major purposes of the Numerical Methods (NM) chapter was to introduce matrix techniques necessary for input-output analysis. This important technique was developed by Wassily Leontief at Harvard in 1931 and his study of the US economy with it gained a Nobel Prize and later Laurence Klein applied IOA to the world economy, also receiving a Nobel Prize.

At a basic level IOA analyses the interdependence of various industries. Consider, for example, three companies X, Y and Z that sell/buy products/materials to/from each other, the value of these transactions over some regular period being shown in Table ME2.

Table ME2. Input-output analysis data

	Purchases				Total
	X	Y	Z	External	Output ($)
Sales					
X	-	60	40	100	200
Y	40	-	100	260	400
Z	50	100	-	50	200
Labour	110	240	60	-	410
Total input	200	400	200	410	1,210

This table also includes labour costs for the period, as well as *external* sales (other than to the other two companies). Then company Y, for example, sells $40 of goods to X and $100 to Z, the remaining $260 of its total output ($400) being sold externally.

To produce this output Y purchases $60 in goods from X and $100 from Z, also spending $240 on labour costs.

Then from Table ME2 we can easily calculate *input coefficients* by dividing the three X,Y,Z columns by their totals, giving the results shown in Table ME3.

Table ME3. Input coefficients

	X	Y	Z
X	-	0.15	0.2
Y	0.2	-	0.5
Z	0.25	0.25	-
Labour	0.55	0.6	0.3

Then for company Y, for example, Table ME3 shows that for each $1 of output produced 15 cents is spent on purchases from X, 25 cents on purchases from Z and 60 cents is spent on labour costs.

Then using the coefficients of Table ME3 we can write the outputs *x,y,z* for companies X, Y,Z as

(ME18a) $x = 0.15y + 0.20z + 100$

(ME18b) $y = 0.20x + 0.50z + 260$

(ME18c) $z = 0.25x + 0.25y + 50$

Now suppose we wish to determine the effect of increasing the external sales of X to $120 (from $100). Then we change the last number in Eqn ME18a and rearrange the equations to give:

$$\text{(ME19)} \quad \begin{bmatrix} 1 & -0.15 & -0.20 \\ -0.20 & 1 & -0.50 \\ -0.25 & -0.25 & 1 \end{bmatrix} \begin{Bmatrix} x \\ y \\ x \end{Bmatrix} = \begin{Bmatrix} 120 \\ 260 \\ 50 \end{Bmatrix}$$

and solving these equations using a routine such as that given in Sec. NM4 we obtain

$$x = \$223, \;\; y = \$408, \;\; z = \$208$$

From these results we are then, for example, able to calculate the increased labour costs resulting for each company as:

X: 223 x 0.55 = 122.7 (increase of $12.7)
Y: 408 x 0.60 = 244.8 (increase of $4.8)
Z: 208 x 0.30 = 62.4 (increase of $2.4)

Here a 'flow through' effect to other companies is immediately apparent (a more superficial approach would predict the increase in labour cost for X as increase in external output (20) multiplied by 0.55 = $11 and effects on other companies would be neglected).

Conclusion

Input-output analysis is an important technique and a program (whose inversion routine uses pivoting) for solving IOA problems is given in the following section.

ME13. Exercises

[1] Work through the cost function exercises of Sec. ME11 carefully.

[2] Check in your local papers to see if you can find evidence of the variation in rentals with proximity to the CBD shown in Fig. ME23. (Suggestion: do this for office space as 'quality' of suburb will have less effect. A comparison of residential and office rental rates per square metre is also interesting; sometimes they are similar).

[3] Try yourself out on the following T-F questions:

1. Output per person in industry is higher now than in 1900.
2. Output per person rises every year.
3. The average working week is shorter than in 1900.

4. The average working week has fallen more rapidly since 1940 than it did from 1900 to 1940.
5. Keynes was an advocate of no government intervention.
6. Karl Marx was an economist.
7. From 1931 to 1940 unemployment in the USA was above 14%.
8. When prices rise through inflation everyone suffers from that rise.
9. Renewable resources can be harvested at any rate without depletion.
10. Homeowners with large mortgages tend to benefit from inflation.
11. S & D curves are elastic if they are fairly 'flat.'
12. The poverty line is higher in the country that in the city.
13. Since 1950 the proportion of national income going to the poorest 20% had increased.
14. Economic growth and equitable income distribution are complementary economic goals.
15. Most profitable production occurs when marginal cost is equal to marginal revenue.

{Ans: 2,4,5,8,9,12 are all the same of the two (T-F) options so try the questions first to compare the result.]

[4] The following program (PHMIOEX in \MBS1 on the course Basics disc) solves the IOA problem example of Sec. ME12 using an inversion routine (INVERTA) which includes pivoting, using a *flag vector* M( ) to record column/row swaps and another vector (i.e. column matrix) is used to store columns during swapping.

```
DECLARE SUB inverta (A!(), n!)
   n = 3: DIM M(n, n), X(n), B(n)
   B(1) = 120: B(2) = 260: B(3) = 50
   FOR I = 1 TO n: FOR J = 1 TO n
   READ M(I, J): NEXT: NEXT
   inverta M(), n
   FOR I = 1 TO 3: FOR J = 1 TO 3
   X(I) = X(I) + M(I, J) * B(J): NEXT: NEXT
   PRINT "Solution"
    FOR I = 1 TO 3: PRINT I, " = ", X(I): NEXT: END
    DATA 1,-0.15,-0.2
    DATA -0.2,1,-0.5
    DATA -0.25,-0.25,1

SUB inverta (A(), n)
REM Inversion routine with pivoting
   DIM M(n), COL(n): AMIN = 1E-20
   FOR I = 1 TO n: M(I) = -I: NEXT
   FOR II = 1 TO n: D = 0
   FOR J = 1 TO n: IF M(J) > 0 THEN 100
   FOR I = 1 TO n: IF M(I) > 0 THEN 90
   IF ABS(D) >= ABS(A(I, J)) THEN 90
   L = J: K = I: D = A(I, J)
90 NEXT I
100 NEXT J
    TEMP = -M(L): M(L) = M(K): M(K) = TEMP
    FOR I = 1 TO n: COL(I) = A(I, L): A(I, L) = A(I, K)
```

```
   A(I, K) = COL(I): NEXT I
   IF ABS(D) <= AMIN THEN PRINT "SINGULAR"
   FOR J = 1 TO n: A(K, J) = -A(K, J) / D: NEXT
   FOR I = 1 TO n: IF I = K THEN 180
   FOR J = 1 TO n: A(I, J) = A(I, J) + COL(I) * A(K, J): NEXT J
180 NEXT I
   COL(K) = 1
   FOR I = 1 TO n: A(I, K) = COL(I) / D: NEXT
   NEXT II
   FOR I = 1 TO n: IF M(I) = I THEN 270
   FOR L = 1 TO n: IF M(L) = I THEN 240
   NEXT L
240 M(L) = M(I): M(I) = I
   FOR J = 1 TO n: TEMP = A(L, J): A(L, J) = A(I, J)
   A(I, J) = TEMP: NEXT J
270 NEXT I
END SUB
```

The data used in the listing is that for the IOA problem of Sec. ME12.

Note that the programs IOBAN and IOBANST are banded solution routines, the second using file storage to handle matrices larger than the dimensions coded for the system matrix, thus 'funneling' equations though this limited 'work matrix'. Both these programs experiment with combining separate IOA 'sub-problems'.

Note too that the program IOFEX tests the Lagrange multiplier, penalty factor and basis transformation *constraint* techniques applied by Mohr to input-output analysis and described in Sec. NM12 on a simple matrix of form of the IOA type.

ME References

Batra R, Surviving the Great Depression of 1990, Bantam/Schwartz, Sydney/Melbourne 1989.

Bowman, RG, Buchanan J, The efficient market hypothesis - a discussion of institutional, agency and behavioural issues, Aust. J. Management, vol. 20, n2, 1995.

Cipolla CM, The Economic History of World Population, 6th edn, Penguin, Harmondsworth 1974.

Cole CL, Microeconomics: A Contemporary Approach, Harcourt Brace Jovanovich, New York 1973.

Cole CL and Baumol WJ, Microeconomics: A Contemporary Approach, Harcourt Brace Jovanovich, New York 1973.

Davies JR, Hughes S, Managerial Economics, MacDonald & Evans, Plymouth 1977.

Elkan W., An Introduction to Devlopment Economics, Penguin, Harmonsworth 1973.

Galbraith, JK, The Liberal Hour, Pelican, Harmondsworth 1963.

Gibson G, Hermann A, Kirkwood L, Swiericzuk J, The Australian Economy: An Overview, Pitman, Melbourne 1977. Management and Policies, Pitman, Melbourne 1979. Problems and Issues, Pitman, Melbourne 1978.

Hicks JR, The Social Framework, 3rd edn, OUP, Oxford 1960.

Meadows DH, Meadows DL, Randers J, Behrens WW, The Limits to Growth, Pan, London 1972.

Hocking A (ed.), Investigating Economics, 2nd edn, Longman Cheshire, Melbourne 1980.

Mohr GA, Numerical procedures for input-output analysis, Applied Mathamatics & Computation, vol. 101, pp 89-98, 1999.

Mohr GA, *The Pretentious Persuaders,* Horizon Publishing Group, Sydney, 2012, 2014.

Mohr GA, *Elementary Thinking for The 21st Century,* Xlibris, Sydney, 2014.

Mohr GA, *The Brainwashed,* Inspiring Publishers, Canberra, 2016.

Nankervis FT, Descriptive Economics: The Australian Economic Structure, 2nd edn, Longman, Green & Co., Melbourne 1956.

Packard V, The Waste Makers, Pelican, Harmondsworth 1963.

Pearce DW, Turner RK, Economics of Natural Resources and the Environment, Harvester Wheatsheaf, Hemel Hempstead 1990.

Quayle M, Robinso T, McEachem W, Microeconomics: A Contemporary Introduction, Nelson, Melbourne 1994.

Noble CE, Australian Economic Terms, 2nd edn, Longman Cheshire, Melbourne 1980.

Sweezy PM, The Theory of Capitalist Development, Dennis Dobson Ltd, London 1946.

Reineck I, The Money Masters: Banks, Power and Economic Control, Heinemann, Melbourne 1988.

Waud, RN, Microeconomics, 3rd edn, Harper & Row, New York, NY 1986.

Williams M, Stevenson K, Australia, A Mixed Economy, Longman Cheshire, Melbourne 1981.

Wonnacott P, Wonnacott R, Economics, McGraw-Hill, New York 1979.

OPTIMIZATION TECHNIQUES (OT)

We all of us live too much in a circle. B. Disraeli.

In any discussion of business science optimization techniques play an important part as with these we seek to obtain improved solutions to a wide variety of problems ranging from those of design of business systems, manufacturing and construction systems and of products that are more economical, efficient and not only produce a better business bottom line but also a better product so that customers benefit as well in the long run.

OT1. Introduction

Mathematical optimization of systems generally involves some or all of the following steps:

1. A mathematical *model* of the system is constructed. This may take the form of a governing differential equation, a governing equation or law which may be linear, quadratic etc. or simultaneous equations which may be formed by applying a governing D.E. or law at several points (or coordinates in one or more problem variables.
2. The *objective* must be decided, for example minimum cost, maximum profit, maximum quantity produced or qualitative benefits to the community (to which we would normally assign a monetary value).
3. We then form an *objective* or *merit function* which would typically take the form

(OT1a) Σ (costs) = $f(x, y - - -)$

4. We then identify any *constraints* applying to variables in this objective function and these would typically take the form

(OT1b) $x + y \leq 100$

where x, y are numbers of components or their costs and 100 is a limit in supply of components or funds.

5. Then we would normally seek to express the problem in a form that can be dealt with by one of the standard techniques available, for example the *linear programming (LP)* method or the *steepest descent* method.
6. Having obtained an optimum (or at least improved) solution using such methods a *sensitivity analysis* is carried out in which the effects of changes in the values of the design variables x, y etc. (from the values for the optimum solution), their associated costs or the limit values involved in constraints are gauged by systematically varying these quantities and observing the changes in the objective function that result.

In a production plant operation, for example, we might desire the maximum quantity of production for given inputs, the minimum inputs for a given quantity of production, minimum production time or minimum cost per item produced.

Generally, in fact, we seek to maximize the *benefit/cost* ratio which might involve maximizing output, minimizing cost or both.

Conclusion

Mathematical optimization techniques involve a logical well ordered approach to problems. Once the problem has been 'set up' the number crunching techniques are relatively simple. For example linear programming problems can be solved using a slight variation in the Gauss-Jordan reduction routine given in Sec. NM4.

OT2. Classical Theory of Optimization

The classical theory of optimization is based on the elementary calculus of curves, that is a stationary or turning point in $y = f(x)$ is given by $dy/dx = 0$ and this is a relative maximum when $d^2y/dx^2 < 0$. In the case of a maximum we picture this as the slope dy/dx being positive or up to the left of the T.P. and changing to negative or down to the right of the T.P. so that dy/dx is decreasing and hence its derivative (d^2y/dx^2) is negative.

Multivariate problems

In speaking of the calculus of curves we are dealing with *univariate problems.* In the case of multivariate problems stationary points with respect to a particular variable x_i are defined by

$$\text{(OT2)} \quad \partial f/\partial x_i = 0 \quad i = 1 \rightarrow n$$

and in optimization problems this is our objective. Here the derivatives are *partial derivatives* with respect to each of the x_i and these are simply obtained by differentiating $f(x_1, x_2 - -)$ with respect to each of the x_i in turn, treating the function as if the particular x_i were the only variable (which for the purposes of calculating a partial derivative it is).

Then if a point is stationary with respect to all the problem variables x_i it is a relative minimum if

$$\text{(OT3)} \quad |H| = |\partial^2 f/\partial x_i \partial x_j| > 0 \quad \partial^2 f/\partial x_i \partial x_j \neq 0, \ i,j = 1 \rightarrow n$$

where H is a *Hessian* matrix of second order partial derivatives. The point is thus a relative maximum when $|H| < 0$ and is a *saddle point* when $|H| = 0$.

Including constraints

Inequality constraints are written in the form

$$\text{(OT4)} \quad c_j(x_i) + y_j = 0 \quad i = 1 \rightarrow n, \ j = 1 \rightarrow m$$

where the y_j are *slack variables.*

Then the extrema of $f(x)$ are the turning points of the *Lagrangian function*

$$\text{(OT5)} \quad \phi(x, \lambda) = f(x) + {}_{j=1}\Sigma^m \lambda_j c_j(x_i)$$

where $\{\lambda_i\}$ are *Lagrange multipliers*. The extrema are thus unconstrained solutions of

$$\text{(OT6)} \quad \{\partial f/\partial x_i + {}_{j=1}\Sigma^m \lambda_j \partial c_j/\partial x_i = 0 \mid c_j + y_j = 0\} \quad j = 1 \rightarrow m, \ i = 1 \rightarrow n$$

Then when the Lagrangian function is a minimum for variations in $\{x\}$it is a maximum for variations in $\{\lambda_i\}$(if some $y \neq 0$, and this second problem is called the *dual problem),* that is we have a *saddle point* in the Lagrangian function.

Conclusion

Formal statement of optimization of multivariate problems appears a little formidable at first but simple examples such as that given in Sec. OR4 do much to overcome the difficulty. For now, however, we move on to linear programming problems, the special case in which there are no turning points and the solution is determined by intersection of the constraints.

OT3. Linear Programming

In the following section we introduce the linear programming (LP) problem. We begin with graphical solution of a problem with only two variables and this illustrates many of the intricacies of the LP problem.

Graphical solution of the LP problem

Fig. OT1 shows the linear programming problem:

(OT7) Min/Max $z = 2x_1 + 7x_2$

where $z = f(x_1, x_2)$ is the objective or merit function in which z is the total cost and 2, 7 are the *unit costs*, subject to the constraints

(OT8) $x_1 - 2x_2 \geq -14$ (1)

(OT9) $5x_1 + 2x_2 \leq 50$ (2)

(OT10) $x_1 + 2x_2 \geq 18, \quad x_1, x_2 \geq 0$ (3)

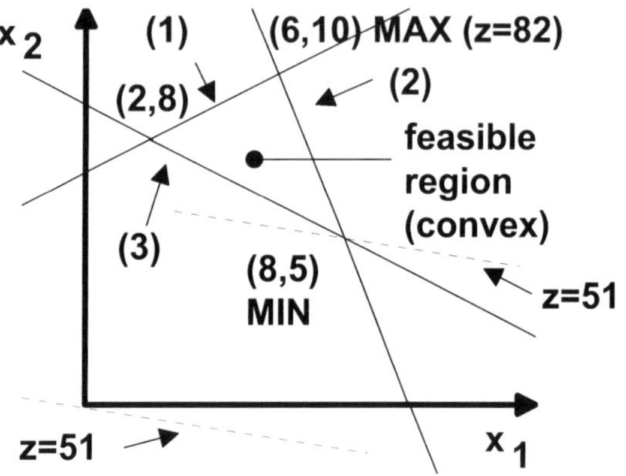

Fig. OT1. Graphical solution of the linear programming problem

and the variables x_1 and x_2 are assumed to be positive. Then, as shown in Fig. OT1, the feasible region is bounded by the three constraints and the vertex at which the line of Eqn OT7 first touches this gives the minimum point ($z = 51$) and the maximum is given by another vertex ($z = 82$).

This, then, is a key feature of the LP problem, namely that the solution is determined by the constraints and, indeed, it is these that really define the problem largely.

Poorly posed problems

Examples of poorly posed LP problems include:

1. If Eqn OT10 is replaced by

(OT11) $x_1 + 2x_2 \geq -1$

then the third constraint does not lie in the positive quadrant so that the minimum is the trivial solution $x_1 = x_2 = 0$.

2. If the objective function is

(OT12) $z = x_1 + 2x_2$

which is parallel to the third constraint then the minimum solution is indeterminate and lies on the line of Eqn (OT10) between the vertices (2,8) and (8,5).
3. The problem is infeasible if all three constraints are such that the feasible region is not in the positive quadrant.
4. If the second constraint is, for example,

(OT13) $5x_1 + 2x_2 \geq -20$

so that it passes to the left of point (2,8), the intersection of the other two constraints, then the feasible region is unbounded and there is no maximum solution to the optimization problem.

When there are many constraints, however, such difficulties are relatively unlikely but, of course, numerical methods of solution are then needed as in most cases there will be more than two variables.

The Simplex Method

The Simplex Method of solving LP problems was developed by Danzig circa 1947. In this slack variables are added to inequality constraints and the problem is written

(OT14) Min/Max $z = \{c\}^t\{x\}$

(OT15) subject to $A\{x\} + I\{y\} = \{b\}$

Then if we apply Gauss-Jordan reduction to Eqn OT15, premultiplying both sides by a matrix *B* which is equal to the inverse of *A*, we obtain

(OT16) $I\{x\} + A^{-1}\{y\} = A^{-1}\{b\}$

where we write A^{-1} symbolically only (in fact this applies strictly only when the constraints are all equality constraints equal in number to the number of variables $\{x\}$ so that *A* is a square and hence invertable matrix, when the solution is the RHS of Eqn OT16.

Generally, however, there are some inequality constraints to which slack variables must be added. Then there are usually more variables than there are constraint equations and the solution procedure must determine which are the 'critical' or *active* constraints and solve to determine the optimum solution in terms of these.

This means that, in practice, we replace A^{-1} in Eqn OT16 by a matrix *B* which *reduces* the augmented matrix *(A,I)* partially using Gauss-Jordan reduction on a column by column basis. Then variables which take a non-zero value at any point in the solution process are said to be in the *basis* (noting that generally some variables will be zero, in particular slack variables associated with constraints intersecting at the optimum point).

This procedure then has useful application to problems of *constrained linear estimation* in which each variable has a range such as

(OT17) $x_i^* - \alpha \leq x_i \leq x_i^* + \beta$

such constraints being a special case of the LP problem.

Conclusion

The LP problem has a very simple graphical solution in the case of only two variables. Generally, however, numerical methods must be used and these are discussed in the following section.

OT4. The Simplex Method

The Simplex method of tackling LP problems was briefly described in Sec. OT3. Here we give a simple numerical example of the 'standard' Simplex Method using a problem with only two variables shown in Fig. OT2.

Fig. OT2 shows the graphical solution to the LP problem

(OT18) Max $z = 5x_1 + 4x_2$

subject to the constraints

(OT19) $2x_1 + x_2 \leq 6$

(OT20) $4x_1 + 5x_2 \leq 20$

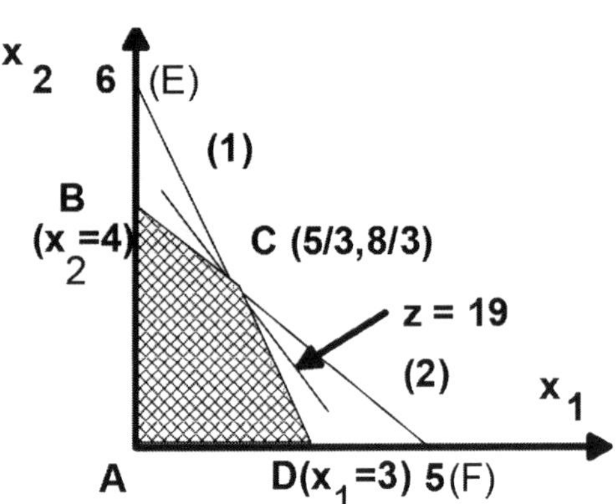

Fig. OT2. LP with 2 variables.

Including two slack variables there are four variables and the optimum solution will involve non-zero values of two of these so that the number of possible solutions is

(OT21) $^4C_2 = 4!/(2!2!) = 6$

these being the points A, B, C, D, E, F shown in Fig. OT2, that is the intersections of the constraints and/or the axes (also constraints as we allow all variables must be positive).

Writing the simplex *tableau* of the problem as

Table OT1. Simplex tableau for Eqns OT18-20 (pivots underlined).

$\underline{2}$	1	1	0	6	
4	5	0	1	20	
5	4	0	0	0	
1	1/2	1/2	0	3	
0	$\underline{3}$	-2	1	8	
0	3/2	-5/2	0	-15	
1	0	5/6	-1/6	5/3	$x_1 = 5/3$
0	1	-2/3	1/3	8/3	$x_2 = 8/3$
0	0	-3/2	-1/2	-19	z= 19

Then the problem is solved by using the pivot selection rule:

1. The pivot column is chosen as that with the maximum positive cost. When no positive cost remains (in the bottom or objective function row) the required maximum has been obtained.
2. The pivot row is then chosen as that with the minimum value of b/a (b being a RHS value for a constraint and a being a coefficient in the pivot column).

Then in Table OT1 the first tableau has max $c = 5$ and min $b/a = 3$, giving the underlined pivot = 2 shown. Using Gauss-Jordan reduction to reduce this column (to 'unit' form with zeroes for all but the pivot position) we obtain the second tableau shown.

Then in the second tableau the max $c = 3/2$ and the min b/a for this column is 8/3, giving the underlined pivot shown (= 3). Then GJR with this pivot yields the third tableau shown. As no positive costs remain this gives the solution for the maximum z (= 19 with $x_1 = 5/3$ and $x_2 = 8/3$).

Note that choosing the row using the 'min b/a ' rule is equivalent to moving along the axis for this variable (for the pivot column) until a constraint is first encountered, the resulting pivot choice being the 'safest'.

Reversed constraints

In the latter exercise we have only dealt with $\leq$ constraints (by adding slack variables). To deal with $\geq$ constraints the constraint is simply reversed in sign and once again we add slack variables.

Equality constraints

Equality constraints must be enforced. One way of ensuring this is adding an *artificial variable* y^* and ensure that a pivot is chosen in the row for this constraint to force y^* out of the basis (i.e. to zero). Pivots must thereafter be disallowed in the column for y^*.

An alternative approach is to replace each equality constraint by a pair of $\leq$ and $\geq$ constraints (reversing the signs for the $\geq$ constraint as described above).

Sensitivity analysis

This involves varying some of the variables, their costs or the limits for the constraints to ascertain the effect upon the optimum solution.

In the case of changes in unit costs the amount of such change which does not alter the optimum solution is of particular interest. Generally, however, we will be at least equally interested in a possible new solution which is easily obtained by rerunning the computer program.

Another change, of course, is to add further constraints and once again the simplest approach is to add another data line to the computer program data for each of these.

Conclusion

Solution of LP problems using the tableau procedure described above is, of course, limited to cases with few variables, otherwise computer programs are required. To this point we have only applied the Simplex Method to maximization and pivoting rules that also deal with minimization are discussed in Sec. OT5.

Then section OT6 deals with the dual LP problem. Here the original and slack variables interchange roles. Note, however, that the dual LP problem can also be solved by tackling the original problem using dual pivoting rules (that is, when the problem is that of maximization, a dual pivoting rule will give the minimum).

OT5 Alternative Pivoting Rules for the Simplex Method

An alternative pivoting rule to the 'max *c*, min *b/a*" rule used in Sec. OT4 is for minimization to *search* the whole A matrix for the *optimum pivot,* that is that pivot which gives the maximum change in the objective function but which does not cause any entry in the cost row (other than the last for *z*) to become negative (otherwise we would have overshot the minimum). Indicating the sign requirements for *a,b,c* in pivot search and selection we can write this and a *dual pivoting rule* for maximization as:

$$\text{(OT22)} \quad \text{Min:} \quad a_{ij} \rightarrow \max\{(-b)(+c)/(-a) \mid \text{all } c' > 0\} \text{ until all } b > 0$$

$$\text{(OT23)} \quad \text{Max:} \quad a_{ij} \rightarrow \max\{(+b)(+c)/(+a) \mid \text{all } b' > 0\} \text{ until all } c < 0$$

and these rules can be applied successively when required, that is, after obtaining the minimum solution the second rule is applied to obtain the maximum solution.

In the first of these we choose pivots corresponding to negative RHS values as the presence of these indicates that we are not inside the feasible region and then the negative pivots used eliminate negative RHS values.

Once the minimum solution has been obtained the second pivot selection rule can be used to obtain the maximum solution, now choosing the pivot which gives the maximum change in the objective function but does not cause any RHS value to become negative (corresponding to leaving the feasible region).

Then using these rules for the example of Eqns OT7-10 we obtain:

Table OT2. Application of dual pivoting rules.

-1	2	1	0	0	14	
5	2	0	1	0	50	
-1	-2	0	0	1	-18	
2	7	0	0	0	0	
0	4	1	0	-1	32	
0	-8	0	1	5	-40	
1	2	0	0	-1	18	
0	3	0	0	2	-36	
0	0	1	1/2	3/2	12	y_1 =12
0	1	0	-1/8	-5/8	5	x_2 = 5
1	0	0	1/4	1/4	8	x_1 =8
0	0	0	3/8	31/8	-51	z = 51
0	0	2/3	1/3	1	8	y_3 = 8
0	1	5/12	1/12	0	10	x_2 = 10
1	0	-1/6	1/6	0	6	x_1 = 6
0	0	-31/12	-11/12	0	-82	z = 82

The solutions correspond to those obtained graphically in Sec. IT3 and a computer program using the first of these rules is given later in the text.

When search for the pivot using Eqn OT22 proves tedious for manual solution minimization can be achieved using the dual of the 'max *c*, min *b/a* ' rule used in Sec. OT5, this being to choose the pivot row as that with the worst *-b* (constraint violation causing infeasibility) and then the column with the minimum $c/|a|$ value, with $a < 0$ to eliminate this negative RHS value.

Then the standard rule ('max *c*, min *b/a* ') is used for maximization. Indeed the simpler rules result in the same pivot choices in the example of Table OT2. In larger problems, however, the rules of Eqns (22) and (23) will result in solution with fewer reductions though there is a trade-off in savings in time doing reductions against time taken searching for and checking pivots.

As a further example consider the problem:

(OT24) Min/Max $z = x_1 + 2x_2 + 4x_3$

subject to:

(OT25) $x_1 + x_2 + x_3 \leq 6$

(OT26) $2x_1 + 2x_2 + 4x_3 \geq 8$

(OT27) $2x_1 + x_2 \leq 4$

for which the resulting tableau and solution are given in Table OT3.

Table OT3. Successive solution for Min/Max

1	1	1	1	0	0	6	
-2	-2	-4	0	1	0	-8	
2	1	0	0	0	1	4	
1	2	4	0	0	0	0	
0	0	-1	1	1/2	0	2	
1	1	2	0	-1/2	0	4	
0	-1	-4	0	1	0	-4	
0	1	2	0	1/2	0	-4	
0	1/4	0	1	1/4	-1/4	3	$y_1 = 3$
0	1/2	0	0	0	1/2	2	$x_1 = 2$
0	1/4	1	0	-1/4	-1/4	1	$x_3 = 1$
0	1/2	0	0	1	1/2	-6	Min
0	1	0	4	1	-1	12	
0	1/2	0	0	0	1/2	2	
0	1/2	1	1	0	-1/2	4	
0	-1/2	0	-4	0	3/2	-18	
2	2	0	4	1	0	16	$y_2 = 16$
2	1	0	0	0	1	4	$y_3 = 4$
1	1	1	1	0	0	6	$x_3 = 6$
-3	-2	0	-4	0	0	-24	Max

The pivots selected are underscored in Table OT3 and the solution proceeds without difficulty. Then in Sec. OT6 the solution of the dual form of this problem is obtained and compared with this result. This will show that the costs and RHS entries are interchanged between the two problems and that the maximum of one is the minimum of the other.

The Dual LP Problem

If we state the primal LP problem as

(OT28) Min: $z_P = \{ c \}^T \{ x \}$

(OT29) subject to $A \{ x \} \geq \{ b \} \quad \{ x \} \geq 0$

then the dual LP problem is

(OT30) Max: $z_D = \{ b \}^T \{ y \}$

(OT31) subject to $A^T \{ y \} \leq \{ c \} \quad \{ y \} \geq 0$

As an example consider the problem of Eqns OT24-27. Reversing the signs of the first and third constraints the primal problem is

(OT32) Min/max: $z_P = x_1 + 2x_2 + 4x_3$

subject to

(OT33a) $-x_1 - x_2 - x_3 \geq -6$

(OT33b) $2x_1 + 2x_2 + 4x_3 \geq 8$

(OT33c) $-2x_1 - x_2 \geq -4$

Then 'tranposing' the problem according to Eqns OT28-31 the dual problem is obtained as

(OT34) Min/Max $z_D = -6y_1 + 8y_2 - 4y_3$

subject to

(OT35a) $-y_1 + 2y_2 -2y_3 \leq 1$

(OT35b) $-y_1 + 2y_2 - y_3 \leq 2$

(OT35c) $-y_1 + 4y_2 \leq 4$

Then the dual problem is solved using a simplex method tableau in Table OT4. First the maximum solution is obtained using the 'max *c,* min *b/a* ' rule. Then, before minimization can proceed the signs of the units costs and the RHS constraint limits must be reversed. This is because the maximum solution is infeasible from the point of view of the minimum solution (which has already been overshot).

This is done in the fourth tableau in Table OT4 and then the minimum of the dual problem is obtained using the 'worst -b, min c/| a |' rule.

Comparing Tables OT4 and OT3 we see that for the maximum of the dual problem (z = 6, corresponding to the minimum of the primal) we have y_2 = 1, x_2 =1/2 and y_3 = 1/2. These correspond to the cost values for the primal problem, demonstrating the information value of these.

Table OT4. Solution of the dual LP problem.

-1	2	-2	1	0	0	1	
-1	2	-1	0	1	0	2	
-1	4	0	0	0	1	4	
-6	8	-4	0	0	0	0	
-1/2	1	-1	1/2	0	0	1/2	
0	0	1	-1	1	0	1	
1	0	4	2	0	1	2	
-2	0	4	-4	0	0	-4	
-1/4	1	0	0	0	1/4	1	y_2 = 1
-1/4	0	0	-1/2	1	-1/4	1/2	x_2 = 1/2
1/4	0	1	-1/2	0	1/4	1/2	y_3 = 1/2
-3	0	0	2	0	1	-6	Max
-1/4	1	0	0	0	1/4	-1	Reverse
-1/4	0	0	-1/2	1	-1/4	-1/2	signs of
1/4	0	1	-1/2	0	1/4	-1/2	b's &c's
3	0	0	2	0	1	-6	
1	-4	0	0	0	-1	4	
0	-1	0	-1/2	1	-1/2	1/2	
0	1	1	-1/2	0	1/2	-3/2	
1	-4	0	0	0	-1	4	y_1 =4
0	-2	-1	0	1	-1	2	x_2 =2
0	-2	-2	1	0	-1	3	x_1 =3
0	16	4	0	0	0	-24	Min

Then for the minimum of the dual problem (z = 24, corresponding to the maximum of the primal) we have y_1 = 4, x_2 = 2 and x_1 =3. Again these correspond to the cost values for the primal problem.

Thus the primal problem can be either minimized or maximized, or both, and complete information is obtained. The only advantage of the dual problem, therefore, is when it results in a more economical solution, perhaps when there are many constraints with few variables, for example, a situation which will be reversed when the problem is posed in its dual form.

Conclusion

The linear programming problem is an important one which has a simple graphical solution when there are only two variables and this illustrates the part which the constraints play in forming the solution.

Numerical solution can be achieved using Gauss-Jordan reduction applied to a tableau for the problem. The standard pivoting rule for maximization is the 'max *c*, min *b/a* ' rule and for minimization the dual of this can be used, that is the 'worst *-b*, min $c/|a|$' rule.

Two more complex pivoting rules are given in which the maximum permissible change in the objective function is found by searching the whole of the augmented *A* matrix. This may be a little tedious to apply manually but is readily incorporated into computer programs.

Two computer programs for the simplex method are given in Sec. OR12 after further applications of the method have been discussed in that chapter.

OT7. Unconstrained Non-linear problems

Non-linear problems are governed by the fundamentals stated in Sec. OT2, and when there are only one or two variables analytical calculus can be used, as demonstrated in Sec., but generally numerical methods must be used, as for LP problems. Most of these have a search character so that the techniques discussed in Secs NM1 and NM2 are useful.

Univariate problems

For problems involving very complicated expressions with only one variable, for example, search with a computer program of only a handful of lines can be useful. Here trial values are used until the function to be optimized passes a turning point. Then bisection or interpolation can be used to home in upon the solution.

The method of steepest descent

For multivariate problems the method of steepest descent is one of the most fundamental methods available. This is a *first order gradient method* which is based on allowing a *perturbation*

$$\text{(OT37)} \qquad |\,\delta x\,| \;=\; \sqrt{(\Sigma\ \delta x^2)}$$

in the vector of (design) variables, resulting in the objective function altering by an amount

$$\text{(OT38)} \qquad \delta f = \Sigma\ (\partial f/\partial x_i)(\delta x_i) + \lambda(\Sigma(\delta x^2 - \Delta^2)$$

where Δ is the optimum perturbation, that is, that for which

$$\text{(OT39)} \qquad \partial(\delta f)/\partial(\delta x_i) = 0 = \partial f/\partial x_i + 2\lambda\,(\delta x_i) \qquad i = 1 \rightarrow n$$

from which it follows that

$$\text{(OT40)} \qquad \{\delta x_i\} = -\{\partial f/\partial x_i\}/2\lambda = -\ (\text{constant})\{g\}$$

so that the greatest change in the objective function results from search in the direction of the gradient vector $\{\,g\,\}$.

The method is comparable to Newton's method for finding the roots of equations (see Sec. NM1). Indeed for nonlinear optimization of multivariate problems the *second order gradient methods* in which the search direction is given by an equation of the form

$$\text{(OT41)} \qquad \{\delta x_i\} = -\ H^{-1}\{g\}$$

have their mathematical basis in Newton's method. Modern numerical methods, however, begin by assuming $H = I$ (the unit matrix) and gradually form an improved approximation for the Hessian matrix using products of the changes in the gradient vector $\delta\{\,g\,\}$.

Numerical calculation of the gradient vector

In practice numerical methods are usually used to calculate the gradient vector approximately, perturbing each variable in turn by an amount δx_i and noting the change in the objective function δf_i. Then the gradient vector is estimated by the first order finite difference approximations

$$\text{(OT42)} \qquad (g) = \{\delta f_i / \delta x_i\}$$

this being a simple example of the 'vector search methods', many of which use a combination of $\{ g \}$ and the vector normal to it as a search direction.

An example of steepest descent

As a simple example of the steepest descent method suppose we wish to minimize the function

$$\text{(OT43)} \qquad f = (x_1 - 2)^2 + (x_2 - 1)^2$$

The minimum is very obvious but assuming otherwise the steepest descent search procedure is written using a step length S as

$$\text{(OT44)} \qquad \begin{Bmatrix} x_1 \\ x_2 \end{Bmatrix} = \begin{Bmatrix} x_1 \\ x_2 \end{Bmatrix}_{n-1} - S \begin{Bmatrix} \partial f / x_1 = 2x_1 - 4 \\ \partial f / \partial x_2 = 2x_2 - 2 \end{Bmatrix}$$

where here the required partial derivatives are known explicitly (but in general would be calculated by the perturbation process of Eqn OT42).

Then beginning at the point (3,3) with $S = 0.2$ Eqn OT44 becomes:

$$\text{(OT45)} \qquad \begin{Bmatrix} x_1 \\ x_2 \end{Bmatrix} = \begin{Bmatrix} 3 \\ 3 \end{Bmatrix} - 0.2 \begin{Bmatrix} 2 \\ 4 \end{Bmatrix} = \begin{Bmatrix} 2.6 \\ 2.2 \end{Bmatrix}$$

yielding $f = 1.80$. Continuing with gradually increased step lengths the results shown in Table OT5 are obtained.

Table OT5. Steepest descent example

S	x_1	x_2	f
0	3	3	5
0.2	2.6	2.2	1.8
0.4	2.2	1.4	0.2
0.6	1.8	0.6	0.2
0.8	1.4	-0.2	1.8
0.5	2	1	0

Here with $s = 0.6$ we might suspect something but we proceed with $s = 0.8$ just to make sure. Now it is clear that a turning point has been passed, if not earlier, and bisection is used with $S = 0.5$ which, in this simple case, yields the correct solution.

Though this problem appears trivial it makes a useful computer exercise if the gradient vector is calculated numerically using perturbations in x_1 and x_2.

In the following section, however, the same example is given with the addition of constraints. Then penalty factors are used in sequence to obtain a solution and Sec. OT12 gives a computer program which carries out the numerical solution.

Conclusion

The steepest descent method is a fundamental and powerful method of numerical solution of non-linear optimization problems. The required gradient vector is easily calculated using perturbations in each of the variables in turn to give a finite difference approximation of the search direction. In the simple example given only one search direction was needed but generally several must be used successively.

OT8. Constrained Nonlinear Problems

Constrained nonlinear optimization problems are sometimes solved by stepwise application of the Simplex Method but this is a relatively tedious process. In the present section we describe the SUMT or *sequence of unconstrained minima technique* in which constraints are factored by *penalty factors* and added to the objective function. Then search techniques are used with a gradually increased value of the penalty factor to locate the optimum solution with increasing accuracy.

Exterior point methods

In these calculations begin from an exterior point (from the feasible region) and we seek to minimize the function

$$(\text{OT46}) \qquad F(x) = f(x) + \beta\,\Sigma \;|\; c_i(x)\;|^2 \;+ \beta\;\Sigma\,[e_i(x)]^2 \qquad \beta \to \infty$$

where | | denotes a *step function* which is zero when the inequality constraints $c_i(\,x\,)$ are not violated, $e_i(\,x\,)$ denotes an equality constraint and β is a penalty factor.

Then the SUMT technique involves solving the problem as though it were unconstrained using, for example, the steepest descent method with a sequence of gradually increasing values of the penalty factor.

If we begin with β = 0, for example, we would first obtain the unconstrained minimum. Then as $\beta \to \infty$ the constraints would take control of the solution if appropriate (in view of the use of a step function for the inequality constraints).

Interior point methods

With these SUMT is first applied to the task of minimizing

$$(\text{OT47}) \qquad C = \Sigma\; s_i + \Sigma\;[e_i(x)]^2$$

where s_i are slack variables associated with the inequality constraints. This finds a feasible point and then we seek to minimize the function

$$(\text{OT48}) \qquad F(x) = f(x) + \beta\;\Sigma[1/c_i(x)] \;+ \beta^{-1/2}\;\Sigma\;|\;e_i(x)\;|^2 \qquad \beta \to 0$$

and now the inverted form of the term for the inequality constraints provides a *response surface* which prevents access to infeasible regions.

Many such slight variations of the SUMT approach have been suggested but we shall restrict attention to the basic form of Eqn OT46.

An example problem

Suppose we add two constraints to the problem of Eqn OT43, giving the constrained nonlinear optimization problem

(OT49) Min: $f = (x_1 - 2)^2 + (x_2 - 1)^2$

subject to the constraints

(OT50) $1 - x_1^2/4 - x_2 \geq 0$

(OT51) $x_1 - 2x_2 + 1 = 0$

Then the SUMT problem is stated as

$$\text{(OT52)} \quad \text{Min:} \quad F = f(x_1, x_2) + \beta \mid 1 - x_1^2/4 - x_2 \mid^2 + \beta(x_1 - 2x_2 + 1)^2 \quad \beta \to \infty$$

Then using steepest descent with

$$\text{(OT53)} \quad \{x\}_n = \{x\}_{n-1} - S\,\{\partial F/\partial x_1,\, \partial F/\partial x_2\}$$

the solution progresses towards the optimum in the typical fashion shown in fig. OT3.

Here the solution is beginning near (2,2), close to the unconstrained optimum at (2,1), and cross-crosses the equality constraint in a relatively inefficient way. This is because the steepest descent direction is influenced by the parabolic constraint and a component tangential to this will be involved in the search direction.

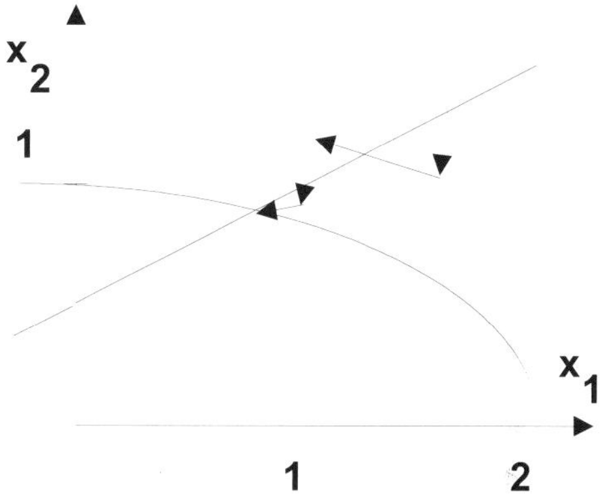

Fig. OT3. Steepest descent method

Improved procedures which incorporate the predictor-corrector method of Sec. NM2, therefore have been devised. In these the search directions are averaged with those used in the previous search and this sort of approach does much to smooth out the convergence shown in Fig. OT3.

In the method proposed by Mohr, for example, allowance is made for the scaling effect of the penalty factors in writing the predictor step as:

$$\text{(OT54)} \quad \{x^*\}_n = \{x\}_{n-1} - (1/2)S\,\{(\beta_n/\beta_{n-1})(g_{n-1})_{av} + g_{p0}\}$$

where β_n, β_{n-1} are the current and previous penalty factors
$(g_{n-1})_{av}$ is the gradient vector used for the last corrector step
g_{p0} is the gradient vector calculated at the beginning of this predictor step

and the corrector step is calculated as

$$\text{(OT55)} \quad \{x\}_n = \{x\}_{n-1} - S\{g_n)_{av} = \{x)_{n-1} - (1/2)S\{g_{pe} + g_{p0}\}$$

where g_{pe} is the gradient calculated at the end of the predictor step.

Then the 'adjust the aim' approach of predictor-corrector methods is clearly evident in the last term of Eqn OT55.

Conclusion

The steepest descent method in conjunction with SUMT is an example of state of the art optimization techniques for nonlinear problems with constraints.

For simple problems with few variables and constraints it may be of wider interest and the strategy involved is certainly an interesting one.

In Sec. OT12 a short computer program is used to solve the problem of Eans OT49-51 and plot the 'landing on the moon' result shown in Fig. OT3.

OT9. Benefit-cost Analysis

Benefit-cost analysis is much used in economics and management and its basis is rooted in the fundamentals of optimization theory. This theory is briefly outlined in the present section and a detailed example of benefit-cost analysis is then given in Sec. OT10.

Output from a process

Fig. OT4(a) shows the production output curve for a process with a single input x_1. Then the slope of this curve is given by

(OT56) $r_1 = dq/dx_1$

and this production rate is shown in Fig. OT4(b) and, as shown, the usual operating region desired is at or just after the turning point in this rate.

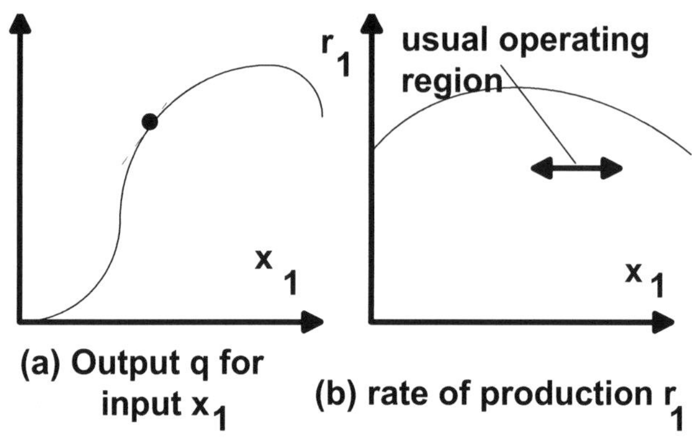

Fig. OT4. Output for a single input x_1

Multiple inputs

Fig. IT5(a) shows curves for q vs x_1 and x_2 and between these a 'shell' shape is formed. For a given production quantity the corresponding plane intersects this shape giving a curve called an *isoquant.* Then Fig. OT5(b) shows a series of isoquant contours. From these we can define a *substitution rate*

$$s_{12} = dx_1/dx_2$$

calculated assuming all other inputs are fixed. Then as this relates to an isoquant contour we can write

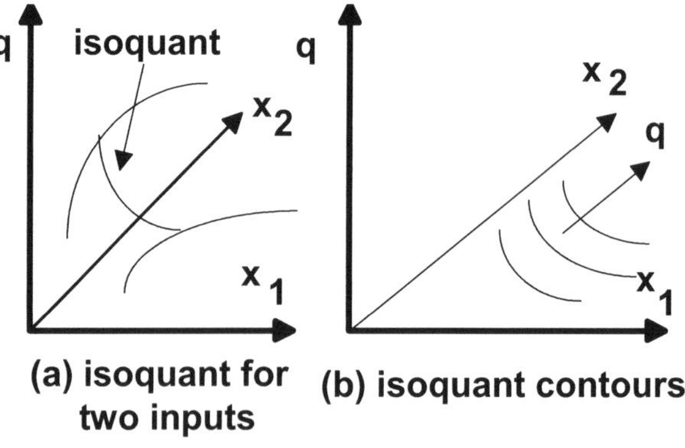

Fig. OT5. Multiple inputs and outputs

$$\delta q = (dq/dx_i)\delta x_i + (dq/dx_2)\delta x_2 = 0$$

from which it follows that

(OT57) $s_{12} = dx_1/dx_2 = - r_2/r_1$

so that the substitution rate depends on the relative production rates pertaining to the two inputs.

Optimization

For the purposes of optimization the objective function is written as

(OT58) $z = V(q) - C(x)$

where $V(q)$ gives the value of the output and $C(x)$ gives the cost of the inputs, noting that production is a function of the inputs, that is

(OT59) $q = q(x)$

is a constraint.

For a constant level of output we can write

(OT60) $dz/dx_u = - dC/dx_i = - c_i$

where c_i is the unit cost for input *i.*

Then to obtain the optimum solution we seek a stationary point of the Lagrangian function

(OT61) $dF/dx_i = dz/dx_i + \lambda\{q - q(x)\}$

so that we write

(OT62) $dF/dx_i = dz/dx_i + \lambda(dq/dx_i) = 0$ for all i

so that for a constant level of output we have

(OT63) $- c_i + \lambda r_i = 0$ or $r_i/c_i = 1/\lambda$ for all i

which we interpret as indicating that the optimum condition is when the *benefit-cost ratio is constant.*

This is an important result which recurs in other guises in other areas of science, for example in the work of Michell (1904) in which he concludes that structures (that is buildings etc.) are optimal when the strain in all components is equal to some constant value. General application of such *optimality criteria* are discussed in Sec. OT11.

The optimum result given by Eqn OT63 corresponds to tangency of an isoquant with a cost contour, as shown in Fig. OT6. Then for different levels of output the locus of all such tangency points defines the *expansion path* for production.

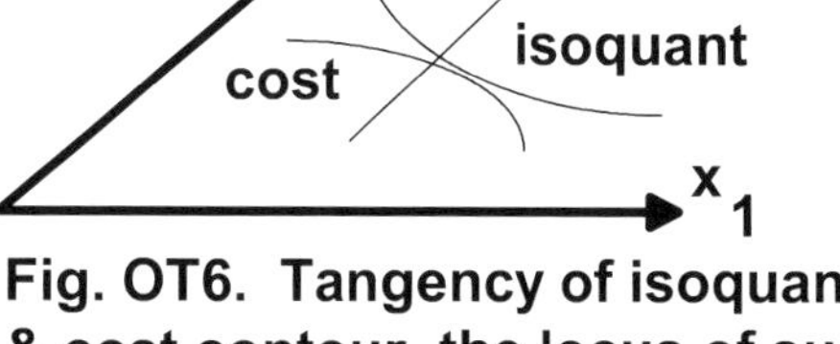

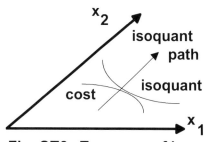

Fig. OT6. Tangency of isoquant & cost contour, the locus of such points being the expansion path.

Then repeating the step leading to Eqn OT57 for a cost contour we have

$$\delta C = 0 = (dC/dx_1)\delta x_i + (dC/dx_2)\delta x_i$$

from which it follows from Eqn. OT57 that

(OT64) $dx_1/dx_2 = - c_2/c_1 = - r_2/r_1$

Cost benefit function

Then if we plot the quantities and costs that occur along the expansion path we obtain the cost-benefit function shown in Fig. OT7. If we express this result as a cost function $C'(q)$ we can write the objective function as

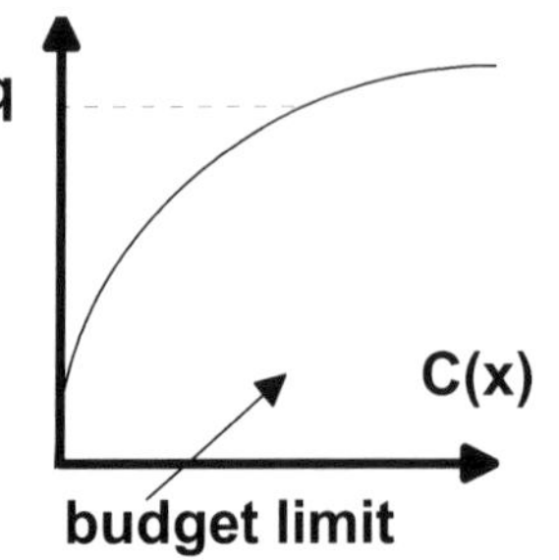

Fig. OT7 Use of budget limit and cost-benefit functioı **to determine output**

(OT65) $z = V(q) - C'(q)$

so that for the optimum when $dz/dq = 0$ we have

(OT66) $dV/dq = dC'/dq$

that is, the *marginal revenue* is equal to the *marginal cost*, a result which we have encountered earlier in the context of economics.

Procedure

The foregoing results are used as the basis of the following benefit-cost analysis procedure:

1. Establish an initial feasible solution $q = q(x)$.
2. Calculate the r_i and c_i values for this.
3. Check the r_i/c_i rations and:

(a) increase the x_i with high r_i/c_i
(b) decrease the x_i with low r_i/c_i

In practice r_i values are easily determined by a perturbation in each x_i giving $r_i = \delta q/\delta x_i$. Realistic cost data, however, presents a more difficult problem as it is usually given on a fixed cost per unit basis which does not take into account fixed costs or non-linearity.

Note that in establishing a feasible production solution when alternative products or projects are available we choose those with the highest r_i/c_i ratios as a matter of priority, continuing the selection process until the budget limit has been reached.

Conclusion

Benefit-cost analysis is widely used and the fundamental result of Eqn OT63 is of particular note and has wide application.

A simple but useful example of such analysis is given in the following section where only constant r_i and c_i values are used.

OT10. A Benefit-Cost Analysis Example

In the following section a simple benefit-cost analysis example is given. This involves only constant values of the production/benefit rates and costs but nevertheless provides a useful illustration of how to logically develop a production program.

Developing the best work program

The example is that of a road repairs program for which the costs of the various levels of repairs or reconstruction are shown in Table OT6.

Table OT6. Cost of road operations

Operation	$k /lane km
P Patching	10
T Flush topseal (25 mm)	20
S Reseal (50 mm)	50
F Reconstruction	100
R Reconstruction	200

Table OT7 shows the various types of road works to be carried out and the years of service provided by the treatments of Table OT6.

Table OT7. Required works and longevity of the options

Road type	Lane km to repair	Years of service P	T	S	F	R
A Residential	30	2	5	10	20	50
B Residential feeder	20	1.5	4	8	15	45
C Signaled arterial	10	1	3	5	10	30
D Freeway	5	0.5	2	3	5	10

Then the years of service in Table OT7 are divided by the corresponding costs of Table OT6 to give the *r/c* results of Table OT8.

Table OT8. r/c ratios for the various options.

Road type	Operation P	S	T	F	R
A (30)	0.20	0.25	0.20	0.20	0.25
B (20)	0.15	0.20	0.16	0.15	0.225
C (10)	0.10	0.15	0.10	0.10	0.15
D (5)	0.05	0.10	0.06	0.05	0.05
	(10)	(20)	(50)	(100)	(200)

Then, choosing the larger *r/c* ratios in Table OT8 the construction program is determined, as shown in Table OT9. For the first step of the program the two largest *r/c* ratios (both 0.25) are considered, that is the A/T and A/R options (where A = row and T = column) in Table OT8. For these the δC values are given by multiplying the figures in brackets for the appropriate rows and columns in Table OT8. Then the δq values are given by multiplying the 'km' and 'YOS' values in Table OT7.

Then the A/R option is rejected as too costly, so that stage 1 of the program is A/T.

Table OT9. Works program selection.

Stage	Option	δC	δq	C	q
1	A/T	600	150	600	150
	A/R	6,000	2,500		
2	B/R	4,000	900		
	B/T	400	80	1,000	230
3	C/T	200	30	1,200	260
	C/R	2,000	300		
4	D/T	100	10	1,300	270
	D/S	250	15		

Next we choose the B/R and B/T options, respectively with r/c = 0.225 and 0.20, finally selecting the second, the first being too costly.

Now, assuming we desire a spread of activity over all types of road (A - D), we next compare C/T and C/R, both with r/c = 0.15, choosing the cheaper option again for stage 3. Now requiring a D component for stage 4 we select D/T with the maximum r/c values for this road type.

Fig. OT8 shows the benefit-cost curve for the program selected in Table OT9 and this takes the required form (that is, the slope diminishes gradually).

Such approaches may seem relatively tedious and mathematically trivial at first sight but in practice the data of Tables OT6 and OT8 is generally constant, the main variable being the quantities or work required in Table OT7.

Mathematically, on the other hand, the criterion established in Eqn OT63 is of considerable importance and its 'constant rate' nature has wide application in other areas of mathematics and science. As for complexity or elegance, the reader will observe that the mathematics of this chapter or the chapter on Operations Research, for example is relatively simple and indeed this is fortuitous as it encourages use in such areas as business science and economics, a key purpose of the present text.

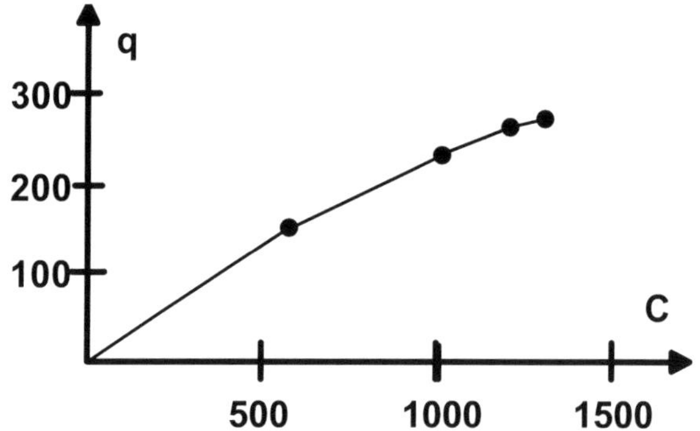

Fig. OT8 Benefit-cost curve for the program of Table OT9.

Conclusion

Benefit-cost analysis is a simple process to apply and has very wide potential application. In choosing a works program the form of Fig. OT8 is of note (and note also that it corresponds to a supply curve in the economics context).

OT11. Optimality Criterion Methods

In the following section a simple approach to optimization problems called *optimality criterion methods (OCM)* is discussed. In these methods analysis to determine the values of the variables of a mathematical model is iterated, adjusting chosen parameters of the model according to some *optimality criterion.* Generally such methods do not obtain an optimum solution in the mathematical sense but they do yield improved solutions which are often close to the optimum solution and, in some cases, may prove a more practical result.

Fully stressed design

In Eqn OT63 we obtained the basis for benefit-cost analysis as the result

$$r_i/c_i = \text{constant}, \quad \text{for all } i$$

Similar results apply elsewhere in mathematics, for example the pioneering paper by Michell (1904) in which it is shown that optimal truss structures (for buildings etc.) will have all their components equally stressed. The optimal solutions obtained by Michell involved structures consisting of orthogonal sets of curves (that is intersection at right angles) but it has since been shown that with relaxed boundary conditions the solutions are trusses with straight members as generally used in practice.

Then in other types of structures this criterion is often used, this process being called *fully stressed design (FSD)* and after each analysis of the structure to determine the member stresses the sizes of the members are adjusted. Repeating this process iteratively a convergent FSD solution is usually obtained.

This same approach is useful in many other contexts, but retaining the FSD case as an example, the steps are:

1. Establish an optimality criterion. In FSD this is that stress S = force/cross section area (for the example of a rod in tension or compression) should be approximately the same value, say some limiting value S^* for safety, in every part of the system.
2. Analyse the structure and determine the stress in every member. Then:
(a) where member stress > S^* increase the member cross section
(b) where member stress < S^* decrease the member cross section
3. Continue repeating step (2) until member stresses are all approximately equal to S^* and/or the structure weight $W = \Sigma A_i L_i$ stops changing (converges), here denoting A_i = cross section areas of members and L_i = their length.

This approach is sometimes called the *stress ratio method* and with such methods of iterative solution many other slight refinements to help guide us towards a realistic and sensible solution can be included, such as the following:

a. *Move limits* which limit the changes in member areas (in the FSD example) allowed in any one step.
b. *Section limits* A_{min}, that is minimum and perhaps maximum allowed values of A.
c. *Convergence factors* which multiply the amount by which a member area is changed (compared to the value suggested by calculation).

Convergence factors

With some types of iterative numerical method an *overconvergence factor* greater than one is used (common values range from 1.2 to 1.8, for example making the change in member area in FSD 1.5 times the amount suggested by its stress ratio S^*/S with a view to speeding up the solution).

In other (rather more exceptional) cases an *underconvergence factor* less than one is used to prevent oscillation in the solution.

As an example consider the Gauss-Seidel iteration problem given in Sec. NM3:

Solve: $2x_1 + x_2 = 7$
$x_1 + 2x_2 = 8$

For 'GSI' we rewrite these equations as $x_1 = (7 - x_2)/2$
$x_2 = (8 - x_1)/2$

and using a convergence factor = f a new value in x_1 is written as

$$x_1^* = x_1 + f(x_1' - x_1) = (1 - f)x_1 + fx_1'$$

where x_1^* = new value, x_1 = old value and x_i' = value calculated at this iteration using GSI.

Then using $f = 1.2$ we obtain the recurrence relations

$$x_1^* = -0.2x_1 + 0.6(7 - x_2)$$

$$x_2^* = -0.2x_2 + 0.6(8 - x_1)$$

and beginning with $x_1 = x_2 = 1$ we obtain the successive results

$x_1 = 3.4$ $x_2 = 2.56$
$x_1 = 1.984$ $x_2 = 3.0976$
$x_1 = 1.9446$ $x_2 = 3.0137$

giving a slightly faster convergence than without a convergence factor but from this point on we should put $f = 1$ (it is common procedure to gradually diminish a convergence factor as the solution proceeds).

In such a small example a slight improvement in convergence rate might not seem to matter much but in the case of large systems of simultaneous equations such as in finite element analysis of a substructure of an aircraft, for example, such slight improvements in solution efficiency are valuable.

Conclusion

Optimality criterion methods are a useful subset of the techniques used for (approximate) optimization. They are very easy to understand and can usually be added to an existing numerical model by looping it with adjustments based on comparison with the optimality criteria at the end of the loop.

In particular FSD is an example that is easy to visualize and understand and, indeed, the same technology is useful in some other applications of optimality criterion (OCM) methods.

OT12. Steepest Descent Exercise

As an exercise we tackle the SUMT problem of Eqns OT49-51 using steepest descent. Restating the problem for clarity we have:

$$\text{Min:}\ f = (x_1 - 2)^2 + (x_2 - 1)^2$$

subject to the constraints: $1 - x_1^2/4 - x_2 \geq 0$
$x_1 - 2x_2 + 1 = 0$

Then the SUMT problem is

(OT67) $\text{Min:}\ F = f(x_1, x_2) + \beta\ |\ 1 - x_1^2/4 - x_2\ |^2 + \beta(x_1 - 2x_2 + 1)^2 \quad \beta \to \infty$

and using steepest descent the gradients of this augmented function are calculated as

(OT68) $g_1 = 2x_1 - 4 + 2\beta C(-x_1/2) + 2\beta(x_1 - 2x_2 + 1)$
$g_2 = 2x_2 - 2 + 2\beta C(-1) - 4\beta(x_1 - 2x_2 + 1)$

where $C = (1 - x_1^2/4 - x_2)$, and if C > 0 then we put C = 0 as this constraint is not violated.

The gradients of Eqn (OT68) are used in the program SDPLOT (in \MBS1 on the course Basics disc) to obtain solutions by trial search (with additional programming this can be automated, for example using bisection [see Sec. NM1]).

Better results are obtained, however, by using perturbations of each *design variable* in turn (by about 5 or 10%) and calculating approximate gradients from the *finite difference* approximation:

$$g_i = (F_2 - F_1)/\delta x_i \quad \text{for each variable } i$$

This is done in the program FDPLOT (listing follows) and the simple coding can be generalized to deal with many variables and problems in any context.

Then by using only two searches at $\beta = 1$ (with searches S = 0.082 and S = 0.14) and also two searches at β = 100 (S = 0.0047 and S = 0.00035) a reasonably good solution can be obtained as

$$x_1 = 0.7321 \text{ and } x_2 = 0.8660 \text{ with } F = 1.6242$$

whereas the exact solution is $x_1 = \sqrt{(3)} - 1$, $x_2 = \sqrt{(3)}/2$ and $F = 13.75 - 7\sqrt{3}$.

If exact gradients are used for β = 1, 10, 100, 1000, 10^4, 10^5, 10^6 six or so searches can be used with each β to obtain a no more accurate result.

This is because use of FD gradients is comparable to using a *predictor-corrector method* (the greater accuracy of which was demonstrated in Sec. NM2). This is because using exact gradients is like following tangents on a curve looking for a turning point - the results can be 'miles off'. The approximate FD gradients, however, act like a 'chord approximation' and give much better results, the chord (at reasonable intervals) giving a much better idea where a curve is going than the slope.

Program FDPLOT.BAS

The following short program uses Eqns OT67 and OT68 to calculate the gradients and objective function for our example problem. For each trial search the penalty value is input first (B in line 40) and then the trial search length (S in line 90), successive searches 'overwriting' the previous one. Thus when the objective function F (printed in line 110) is seen to 'turn' (i.e. increase) repeat the previous trial - then use (B = current, S = 0) to terminate that search. Continue with the next search (at least two with any B), using a new value of B when search is approaching a 'steady result' or make it 'policy' to use, say, 4 searches with each B. Repeat the process with the next B (preferably 100 times the last one, not 10). When (if) the solution seems OK/converged use B = 0 and S = 0 to terminate work and progress of the solution is plotted.

Exercise: Try the 4 step solution with B/S as noted above (i.e., B =1, S = 0.082 for first search - note that the stated search lengths are termination values with which a search of many shorter steps was conducted to arrive at these values).

```
10 DIM C(10, 10): I = 0: M = 1.05
20 PRINT "input x1,x2": INPUT X1, X2: C(1, 1) = X1: C(1, 2) = X2
40 PRINT "input b": INPUT B
45 I = I + 1: C(I, 1) = X1: C(I, 2) = X2: S1 = 0: IF B = 0 THEN 155
60 GOSUB 200: F1 = F: X1 = X1 * M: GOSUB 200: F2 = F: X1 = X1 / M
70 G1 = (F2 - F1) / (X1 * (M - 1))
80 X2 = X2 * M: GOSUB 200: F2 = F: X2 = X2 / M: G2 = (F2 - F1) / (X2 * (M - 1))
90 PRINT "Input S ": INPUT S: IF S = 0 THEN 40
100 X1 = X1 + (S1 - S) * G1: X2 = X2 + (S1 - S) * G2
110 GOSUB 200: PRINT X1, X2, "F= ", F
150 S1 = S: GOTO 90
155 SCREEN 2: x = 200 * C(1, 1): y = 150 - 100 * C(1, 2): LINE (x, y)-(x, y)
156 FOR J = 1 TO I: x = C(J, 1): y = C(J, 2)
157 x = 200 * x: y = 150 - 100 * y
158 LINE -(x, y): NEXT J
159 x = 0: y = 50: LINE (x, y)-(x, y)
160 FOR Z = 0 TO 2 STEP .01
170 x = Z: y = 1 - x * x / 4: x = 200 * x: y = 150 - 100 * y
180 LINE -(x, y): NEXT Z
190 LINE (0, 100)-(400, 0): LINE (0, 150)-(600, 150): LINE (0, 150)-(0, 0)
195 END
200 G = 1 - X1 * X1 / 4 - X2: E = X1 - 2 * X2 + 1: IF G > 0 THEN G = 0
210 FU = (X1 - 2) ^ 2 + (X2 - 1) ^ 2
220 F = FU + B * G * G + B * E * E
230 RETURN
240 REM search x 4: .082 & .14; .0047 & .00035
```

OT References

Bersekas DP, Constrained Optimization and Lagrange Multiplier Methods, Academic Press, New York, 1982.

Box Mj, Davies D, Swann WH, Nonlinear Optimization Techniques, ICI Monograph No. 5, Oliver & Boyd, Edinburgh, 1969.

Budnick FS, Mojena R, Vollmann TE, Principles of Operations Research for Management, Irwin, Homewood IL, 1977.

Eckstein O, Water Resource Development: The Economics of Project Evaluation, Harvard Univ. Press, Cambridge MA, 1958.

Fiacco AV, McCormick GP, The sequential unconstrained minimization technique for nonlinear programming, Management Science, vol. 10, p 360. 1964.

Hillier FS, Lieberman GJ, Introduction to Operations Research, 3rd edn, Holden Day, Oakland CA, 1980.

Mohr GA, Analysis and Design of Plates and Shells using Finite Elements, PhD thesis, Univ. of Cambridge, 1976.

Mohr GA, Elastic and plastic predictions of slab reinforcement requirements, Proc. Instn Civil Engrs (London), part 2, vol. 67, p 851. 1979.

Mohr GA, Design of shell shape using finite elements, Comput. Struct., vol. 10, p 127. 1979.

Mohr GA, Finite Elements for Solids, Fluids and Optimization, OUP, Oxford, 1992.

Mohr GA, Optimization of critical path models using finite elements, Aust. Civil Engng Trans, vol. CE36, no. 2, p 851. 1994.

Mohr GA, Finite element optimization of structures, part I (solids problems), Comput Struct., vol. 53, p 1217. 1994; part II (fluids problems), Comput. Struct., vol. 53, p 1221. 1994.

Mohr GA, Approximate numerical nonlinear optimization, Int. J. Arts & Sciences, paper 97/7, 1977.

Mohr GA, A predictor-corrector method of constrained nonlinear optimization, Int. J. Arts & Sciences, Vol. 2, No. 2, pp 38-48, 2002.

Mohr GA, Cook PL, Dual pivoting rules for the Simplex Method, Int. J. Arts & Sciences, Vol. 2, No. 2, pp 49-60, 2002.

Rust BW, Burrus WR, Mathematical Programming and the Numerical Solution of Linear Equations, Elsevier, New York, 1972.

Wang C, Computer Methods in Advanced Structural Analysis, Intext, New York, 1973.

Whittle P, Optimization under Constraints, Wiley, London, 1971.

OPERATIONS RESEARCH (OR)

In the Soviet Army it takes more courage to retreat than to advance. Joseph Stalin.

Operations research is a branch of mathematics of great interest in the study of business. Generally the mathematical models set up to simulate a real system are aimed at optimization of the system, at least approximately. In the first section we outline areas covered earlier in the text which could be considered operations research topics. Indeed, it should be noted in passing, that throughout the text a philosophy of approach is that topics in two or more subjects contribute to the total pool of material in a given area, another example being mathematics itself, the MS (Maths & Stats), being complemented by many other chapters, including this one.

OR1. Introduction

As noted above, many operations research topics which are a subset of that subject (itself a subset of mathematics) have already been covered in other subjects of the course. Examples include the following:

1. *Decision trees* - Sec. BP4. See also probability trees in Sec. MS8.
2. *Linear programming* - Secs BF3, IE1 and OT3-6.

Further study of this in this chapter is in Secs OR5-6 and OR11-12.

The *Finite Element Method* is introduced to the *distribution problem* in the final chapter (FM).

3. *Calculus* (to determine turning points) - see Secs MS3 and OT2.
4. *Queueing Theory* - MS11.
5. *Numerical methods* - NM1 and NM2 (search methods).
6. *Nonlinear optimization* - unconstrained - OT7.
   - constrained - OT8 and OT12.
7. *Cost-benefit analysis* - OT9-10.
8. *Optimality criterion methods* - OT11.
9. *Critical Path Method (CPM)* - Secs PP2-5 and 11-12.
10. *Flow line methods* - Sec. PP6.
11. *Assembly line balancing* - Sec. PP7.
12. *Group Technology* - Sec. PP8.
13. *Line-of-balance systems* - Sec. PP9.
14. *Control charts* - Sec. PP10.

It will be noticed, however, that most of this material is in the two immediately preceding and following chapters on Optimization Techniques and Project Planning and Control and these two chapters can be bracketed with the present one.

Conclusion

Operations research is a large subject of considerable importance in business science. Many OR topics have already been covered earlier in the text so that this material, together with that of the present chapter, should give the reader a reasonable acquaintance with OR.

OR2. Classical Deterministic Models

In the following section we discuss problems which can be solved by simple classical calculus. In these a simple objective function is formed and differentiation used to establish turning points. Though they are very simple and often neglected in favour of larger scale 'number crunching' techniques, the examples given here are, in fact, amongst the most useful OR exercises, often giving a 'one-off' one line answer that can be used in the long term.

(1) Police patrol sectors

Fig. OR1 shows a section of a city in which a single patrol car is assigned duties of surveillance. Then, when an incident occurs we seek to minimize the travel time to it which can be expressed in terms of speeds v_x and v_y as

(OR1) $T = dx/v_x + dy/v_y$

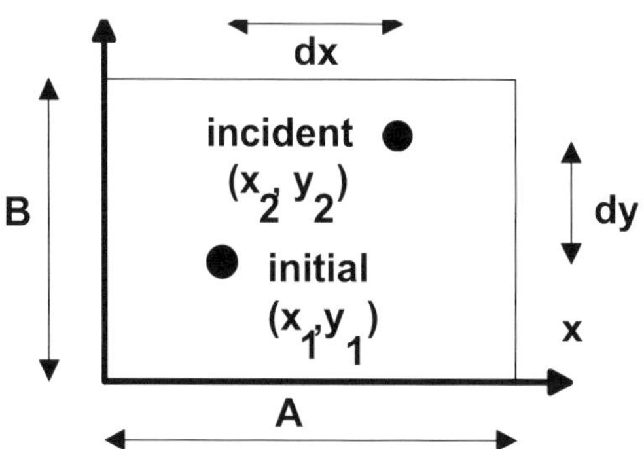

Fig. OR1. Police patrol problem.

Intuition is enough to tell us that the average distance in each direction (through a grid of city blocks) that the car will have to travel are given by

(OR2) $(dx)_{av} = A/3, \quad (dy)_{av} = B/3$

where A and B are the dimensions of the patrol sector.

Then, assuming the sector area = AB = 4 and an average speed in both coordinate directions = 10, we seek to minimize

(OR3) $T = (1/3)[(4/B)/10 + B/10]$

Taking the first derivative gives the simple solution

(OR4) $d(T)/d(B) = - 4/30B^2 = 1/30$, giving $B = \sqrt{4} = 2$

and checking the second derivative we have

(OT5) $d^2(T)/d(B)^2 = 8/30B^3 = 1/30 > 0$

so that we do indeed have a minimum solution. Though the problem is almost trivial, however, it does provide a good example of setting up such problems.

This problem is also a reminder that traffic flow problems can be dealt with as a two dimensional flow problem and, indeed, this is one of the reasons for dealing with 2-D flow analysis in the Finite Methods (FM) chapter.

(2) Setting off-peak fares

Suppose we seek to increase demand for off-peak usage of a public transport facility and that studies of passengers as a function of price using linear regression gives the following demand function

(OR6) $f = -2q + 5$

where f is the fare (\$) and q is the off-peak demand (thousands of passengers).

Then if we seek to maximize the total revenue R we write

(OR7) $R = fq = 2.5f - f^2/2$

and calculating the first derivative we obtain

(OR8) $dR/df = 2.5 - f = 0$, giving $f = 2.5$

and checking the second derivative we have

(OR9) $d^2R/df^2 = -1 < 0$

so that we do have a maximum solution as required and this is $f = 2.5$ which gives $q = 1.25$ (thousand) and $R = 3{,}125$ ($) as revenue.

Note that the revenue function (Eqn OR7) is a parabola passing through the original and intersecting the f-axis again at $f = 5$ and this gives a useful though little unrealistic model which can, however, be refined without great difficulty.

(3) Advertising periods

Suppose that the *response function* for an advertisement is

(OR10) $r = 1 - \exp(-0.02t)$

and this is the proportion of a target population which buys a product at time t after an advertisement.

Suppose the market size of the target population reached is 100,000 people and the unit profit for the product is $2 then the revenue function is

(OR11) $R = 200{,}000\{1 - \exp(-0.02t)\}$

Then if the advertising costs are given by the function

(OR12) $C = 2000t + 2500$

the profit function can be written (in $1,000s) as

(OR13) $P = R - C = 197.5 - 200\exp(-0.02t) - 2t$

and calculating the first derivative we obtain

(OR14) $dP/dt = 4\exp(-0.02t) - 2 = 0$

from which $\exp(-0.02t) = 2/4 = 1/2$, giving $-0.02t = \ln(1/2) = -0.6931$

giving $t = 34.66 = 35$ days for which the maximum profit is given as

(OT15) $P_{max} = 197.5 - 200(1/2) - 70 = 27.5$ (k$)

In this case the profit function is an 'exponential parabola' which intersects the time axis at $t = 1.28$ and $t = 77.54$ (this is most easily verified numerically using search).

Indeed the exponential model for the response function proposed here is of considerable usefulness though, of course, the problem requires more detailed study in practice as advertising campaigns will have to be repeated periodically, response function parameters may vary owing to seasonal factors or for different media and so on.

OR3. Deterministic models (cont.)

(4) Replacement models

Fig. OR2 shows the depreciation in capital value of a machine or plant with time as well as the increasing operating cost as the machine gets older, resulting in a total cost function with a distinct minimum, as shown. Writing this total cost as

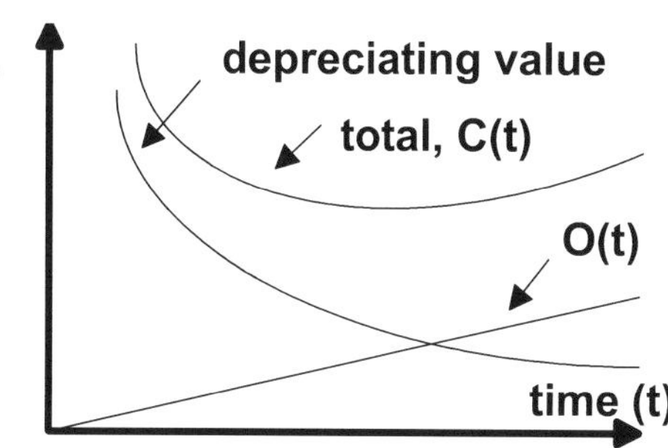

Fig. OR2. Total cost for a machine or plant

(OT16) $C(t) = K(t)/t + O(t)$

where $K(t) = P - S$ is the capital value expressed as the difference of the principal P and the salvage value S.

Then if the operating cost function $O(t) = a + bt$ we have

(OR17) $C(t) = (P - S)/t + (a + bt)$

and taking the first derivative we have for the optimum replacement time t^*,

(OR18) $C(t) = -(P - S)/t^2 + b = 0$, giving $t^* = \sqrt{\{(P - S)/b\}}$

If, for example, P = \$k 100, S = \$k 20, a = \$k 5/year and b = \$k 1/year then we obtain the time for replacement as $t^* = 8.94$ years and the associated total cost = $C(t^*)t^*$ = \$k 204.63.

Once again a potentially very useful result is obtained relatively easily and, not for the first time, a combination of a 'down curve' and a linear cost function appears in Fig. OR2 to provide a problem with an optimum point.

(5) Sale of an asset

Suppose we have an asset whose present value is given by

(OR19) $P = R(t)\exp(-rt)$

where $R(t)$ is a monotonically increasing function for which the rate of increase decreases. If the capital investment on the asset was C then the net present value is given by

(OR20) $N = R(t)\exp(-rt) - C$

Taking the first derivative we obtain

(OR21) $dN/dt = R'(t)\exp(-rt) + R(t)(-r)\exp(-rt)$
$= \{R'(t) - rR(t)\}\exp(-rt) = 0$, giving $R'(t) = rR(t)$

as the condition for the maximum NPV.

Taking the second derivative gives

(OR22) $d^2N/dt^2 = \{R'(t) - rR(t)\}(-r)\exp(-rt) + \{R''(t) - rR'(t)\}\exp(-rt)$
$= \{R''(t) - rR'(t)\}\exp(-rt) < 0$

because $R'(t) = rR(t)$ from Eqn OR21 and $R''(t) < 0$, $r > 0$ and $R'(t) > 0$ are assumed at the outset, so that we have a maximum as required.

As an example consider the *return function* to be of the form

(OR23) $R(t) = 500(1 + t^{0.6})$, $r = 0.08$

and substituting this into the result of Eqn OR21 gives $500(0.6)t^{-0.4} = 0.08\{500(1 + t^{0.6})\}$ and multiplying through by $t^{0.4}$ and dividing by 40 we obtain

(OR25) $t + t^{0.4} - 7.5 = 0$

Solving this result using Newton's method (see NM1) we have

(OR26) $t_{n+1} = t_n - f(t)/f'(t) = t_n - (t + t^{0.4} - 7.5)/(1 + 0.4t^{-0.6})$

and beginning with $t = 1$ this recurrence relation yields the results

$t_o = 1$ gives $t_1 = 1 - (1 + 1 - 7.5)/(1 + 0.4) = 4.9286$

and then $t_2 = 5.4190$, $t_3 = 5.5035$ and so on until we obtain $t = 5.5196$ or $t = 5.52$ for which the return function value is $R(t) = 1{,}894$ so that the net present value is

(OR27) $N = 1{,}894\exp(-0.08(5.52)) - 700 = 1218 - 700 = 518$

if the capital outlay was $700, yielding a profit of $518.

Once again a very simple mathematical model yields a useful result but, of course, the parameters need adjustment for real applications. In addition a useful example of the use of Newton's method results.

Conclusion

Deterministic models involving a single variable can model many operations research problems readily. With the use of classical calculus simple optimum solutions to such problems can be obtained.

Finally, the last example given provides a useful application of one of the techniques (Newton's method) discussed in Sec. NM1, reminding us that numerical methods are complementary to classical techniques.

OR4. Multivariate Deterministic Models

In the last two sections we dealt only with deterministic OR models with a single variable and these are, of course, immediately amenable to basic calculus. In the present section we consider two variable problems and then generalize the discussion to problems with more than two variables.

Two variable problems

For these we presume an objective function

(OR28) $z = f(x,y)$

and this is a turning point with respect to both variables if

(OR29a) $\partial f/\partial x = 0$

(OR29b) $\partial f/\partial y = 0$

and the simultaneous Eqns OR29 are solved to find *(x,y)* at the turning point.

Then to determine the nature of the turning point we calculate the determinant

(OR30) $D(x^*, y^*) = f_{xx} f_{yy} - (f_{xy})^2$

where $f_{xx} = \partial^2 f/\partial x^2$, $f_{yy} = \partial^2 f/\partial y^2$, $f_{xy} = \partial f/\partial x \partial y$ are second partial derivatives.

Then (a) if $D > 0$ we have a maximum if $f_{xx}, f_{yy} < 0$
or we have a minimum if $f_{xx}, f_{yy} > 0$
(b) if $D < 0$ we have *a saddle point* (for example a maximum with respect *to x* and a minimum with respect to *y*)
(c) if $D = 0$ the test is indeterminate (in this unlikely event more investigation is needed to determine the nature of the stationary point.

Examples

As a simple introduction suppose we wish to maximize the revenue function

(OR31) $R = -3x_1^2 - 2x_2^3 + 20x_1x_2$

subject to the constraint

(OR32) $x_1 + x_2 = 100$

Using the latter to eliminate x_1 from the objective function *R* we have

(OR33) $R = -25x_2^2 + 2600x_2 - 30{,}000$

Calculating the first derivative gives

(OR34) $R'(x) = -50x_2 + 2600 = 0$, giving $x_2 = 52$

and since $R''(X) = -50 < 0$ the turning point is a maximum with $x_1 = 48$, $x_2 = 52$ and $R = 37{,}600$.

Here, however, the constraint allowed us to reduce the problem to a single variable again (but well worthwhile when possible). Now consider the problem of two products with related demand functions (of their prices):

(OR35) $q_1 = 100 - 4p_1 - p_2, \quad q_2 = 90 - 2p_1 - 3p_2$

where q_1, q_2 are their demands and p_1,p_2 their prices. The total revenue from the two products is then

(OR36) $R = p_1q_1 + p_2q_2 = p_1(110 - 4p_1 - p_2) + p_2(90 - 2p_1 - 3p_2)$

$$= 110p_1 - 4p_1^2 - 3p_1p_2 + 90p_2 - 3p_2^2$$

Taking the first partial derivatives we obtain

(OR37a) $\partial R/\partial p_1 = 110 - 8p_1 - 3p_2 = 0$

(OR37b) $\partial R/\partial p_2 = -3p_1 + 90 - 6p_2 = 0$

which are easily solved (for example by subtracting the second from twice the first) to give $p_1 = p_2 = 10$.

Now taking the second partial derivatives we obtain

$$\partial^2 R/\partial p_1^2 = -8, \quad \partial^2 R/\partial p_2^2 = -6, \quad \partial^2 R/\partial p_1 \partial p_2 = -3$$

so that Eqn OR30 yields D( ) = $(-8)(-6) - (-3)^2 = 39 > 0$ so that the point is a maximum as required and the demands and revenue are $q_1 = 60$, $q_2 = 40$ and r = \$1000 (for a given period).

Problems with *n* variables

For a function of n variables

(OR38) $z = f(x_1, x_2, x_3 - - -)$

we have a turning point if

(OR39) $\partial f/\partial x_1 = 0, \quad \partial f/\partial x_2 = 0, \quad \partial f/\partial x_3 = 0$ etc.

and these simultaneous equations are solved to determine the coordinates of the turning point $(x_1^*, x_2^*, x_3^* - - -)$.

Calculating the second partial derivatives we can form a *Hessian matrix*

(OR40) $$H = \begin{bmatrix} f_{x_1x_1} & f_{x_1x_2} & - - & f_{x_1x_n} \\ f_{x_2x_1} & f_{x_2x_2} & - - & \\ - & - & - - & \end{bmatrix}$$

and the determinants of the 1 x 1, 2 x 2 etc. matrices H_1, H_2 - - formed beginning at the top left corner are called the *principal minors* of this matrix.

Then if:
a. All principal minors are > 0 then H is positive definite and the turning point is a minimum
b. The principal minors alternate in sign (starting with a minus) then H is negative definite and the turning point is a maximum.

In general, however, turning points will be maxima with respect to some variables and minima with respect to others and investigation of the values of their individual second derivatives will reveal which situation applies. This allows the variables to be divided into two groups for further study of the problem.

The Lagrangian function

For problems with constraints the Lagrangian function can be used to augment the objective function with the constraints, each multiplied by a *Lagrange multiplier* In the example of Eqns OR31 and OR32 this gives

(OR41) $L(x_1,x_2,\lambda) = -3x_1^2 - 2x_2^2 + 20x_1x_2 - \lambda\{x_1 + x_2 - 100\} = f(x,y) - \lambda g(x,y)$

Calculating the first partial derivatives

(OR42a) $\partial L/\partial x_1 = -6x_1 + 20x_2 - \lambda = 0$
(OR42b) $\partial L/\partial x_2 = -4x_2 + 20x_1 - \lambda = 0$
(OR42c) $\partial L/\partial x_3 = -x_1 - x_2 + 100 = 0$

which are solved simultaneously to give $x_1 = 48$, $x_2 = 52$ and $\lambda = 752$.
Calculating the determinant of the *bordered Hessian matrix* we obtain

(OR43) $$|H| = \begin{vmatrix} 0 & g_x & g_y \\ g_x & L_{xx} & L_{xy} \\ g_y & L_{yx} & L_{yy} \end{vmatrix} = \begin{vmatrix} 0 & 1 & 1 \\ 1 & -6 & 20 \\ 1 & 20 & -4 \end{vmatrix} = 50 > 0$$

so that the turning point is a maximum (and had det(H) been less than zero the turning point would have been a minimum).
We can proceed in the same way in the case of inequality constraints and the signs of the Lagrange multipliers will indicate whether the constraints are *binding* or not.
When there are more than two variables, however, numerical solution is generally necessary using such techniques as the SUMT method for which an example program is given in Sec. OT12.

Conclusion

In the case of only two variables nonlinear optimization problems present no great difficulty and constraints can easily be included. Here an equality constraint effectively reduced the problem to a single variable, such reduction being important in larger problems too. Such simple exercises, however, provide useful models in their own right as well as an understanding of the behaviour of multivariate systems.

OR5. Linear Programming

Linear programming was discussed in Secs OT3-6 in a good deal of detail. There we dealt with graphical solution for the case of two variables, slack variables, inequality constraints (both $\le$ and $\ge$) and pivot selection rules in the simplex tableau for both minimization and maximization (including dual rules and search rules which maximize the change in the objective function).

Finally, in Sec. OT6, we dealt with the dual form of the LP problem in which the primal and dual (or slack) variables interchange roles.

In the present section we include a simplex method example in which an equality constraint is dealt with by splitting it into two constraints (one $\le$ and one ≥ 0). This artifice is used in two of the LP programs given at the close of the chapter.

The problem is to minimize and maximize

(OR44) $z = 15x_1 + 5x_2$ subject to

(OR45a) $x_1 + 2x_2 \le 10$

(OR45b) $x_1 - 3x_2 = 0$

(OR45c) $x_1 + x_2 \ge 6$

Splitting the second constraint into two, the simplex tableau obtained is shown in Table OR1. First using the 'worst -b, min c/|a|' rule, the minimum solution is obtained. Then the standard 'max c, min b/a' rule is used to obtain the maximum solution ($x_1 = 6$, $x_2 = 2$ and $z = 100$).

Table OR1. Simplex tableau for Eqns OR44-45.

1	2	1	0	0	0	10	
1	-3	0	1	0	0	0	
-1	3	0	0	1	0	0	
-1	-1	0	0	0	1	-6	
15	5	0	0	0	0	0	
-1	0	1	0	0	2	-2	
4	0	0	1	0	-3	18	
-4	0	0	0	1	3	-18	
1	1	0	0	0	-1	6	
10	0	0	0	0	5	-30	
0	0	1	0	-1/4	5/4	5/2	
0	0	0	1	1	0	0	
1	0	0	0	-1/4	-3/4	9/2	$x_1 = 4.5$
0	1	0	0	1/4	-1/4	3/2	$x_2 = 1.5$
0	0	0	0	5/2	25/2	-75	MIN
0	0	4/5	0	-1/5	1	2	
0	0	0	1	1	0	0	
1	0	3/5	0	-2/5	0	6	
0	1	1/5	0	1/5	0	2	
0	0	-8	0	5	0	-100	
0	0	4/5	1/5	0	1	2	
0	0	0	1	1	0	0	
1	0	3/5	2/5	0	0	6	$x_1 = 6$
0	1	1/5	-1/5	0	0	2	$x_2 = 2$
0		-8	-5	0	0	-100	MAX

Note that the last pivot is for the unusual case of minimum RHS value = 0 (the only other apparent alternative, the entry 1/5 two rows below in this column, results in an infeasible solution with a negative RHS entry).

Conclusion

The split constraint approach is used for transportation problems of the type described in the following section to allow them to dealt with by the programs given at the end of the chapter.

OR6. Transportation Problems

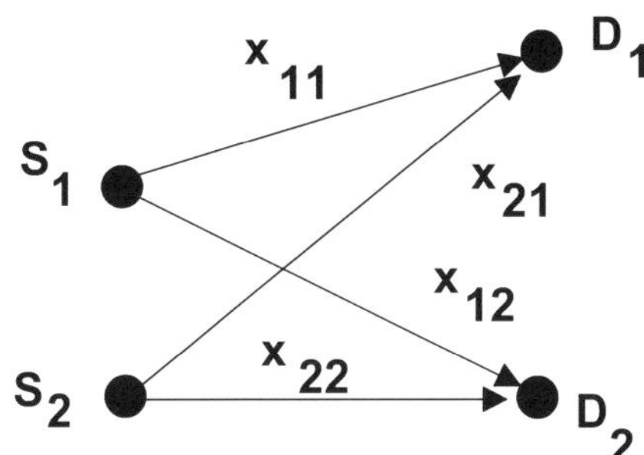

Fig. OR3. Distribution network

	Destination		
Origin	1	2	Supply
1	2	1	30
2	1	2	60
Demand	40	50	90/90

Table OR2. Distribution tableau.

Fig. OR3 shows a simple distribution network with two supply points S_1 and S_2 and two demand points D_1 and D_2. The flows between the points are the x_{ij} values shown and the costs per unit for these flows are shown in Table OR2 where the supplies and demands generated by the two points is also given.

Then the *distribution* (or *transportation) problem* is the optimization problem

(OR46) Min. $z = \Sigma \Sigma c_{ij} x_{ij}$

subject to

(OR47a) $x_{11} + x_{12} + 0 + 0 = 30$
(OR47b) $0 + 0 + x_{21} + x_{22} = 60$
(OR48a) $x_{11} + 0 + x_{21} + 0 = 40$
(OR48b) $0 + x_{12} + 0 + x_{22} = 50$

where Eqns OR47 are the supply constraints and Eqns OR48 are the demand constraints.

Then the problem can be solved by:

1. The simplex method when the last constraint is omitted. This makes allowance for the fact that the sum of demands equals the sum of supplies so that this last constraint is not required. Use of the simplex method for such problems is demonstrated in Sec. OR12.
2. Tabular methods such as the *Northwest Corner Method.* Computer methods are obligatory in practice, of course, but this method is briefly described in the present section as in introduction to distribution problems.

Northwest corner method

Table OR3. Northwest corner method.

	Destination		
Origin	1	2	Supply
1	(2) ↓ 30	(1)	30
2	(1) 10	(2) → 50	60
Demand	40	50	

Table OR3 illustrates the northwest corner method for the problem of Fig. OR3 and the data of Table OR2, showing the route unit costs in ( ).

Here, commencing at the 'NW corner' of the table the RHS supply is satisfied. Then we step down to the next row and make that flow the lesser of the two flows sufficient to satisfy the RHS supply or bottom row demand constraints. Then we step to the right to make the flow there as large as the 'closer' of the two S & D constraints.

With larger tables there will be a 'step-like' path through the table and when we read the bottom of the table we should have an *initial feasible solution.*

Table OR4 Stepping stone algorithm

	1	2
1	(2) [−1]↓ 30	(1) ←[+1]
2	(1) 10 →[+1]	(2) [−1]↑ 50

Now we shall seek to improve this solution using the *stepping stone algorithm.* With this we begin in an empty cell and test the effect of adding one unit to this, then developing an anticlockwise loop with alternate -1 and +1 entries in the table, as shown in Table OR4.

Now we calculate the *improvement index* for this path by multiplying the flow changes by their associated unit costs [in ( )], giving in the example

$$-1(2) + 1(1) - 1(2) + 1(2) = -2$$

so that each unit shifted using this path will reduce costs by two and we should shift as many units in this way as possible.

	1	2
1	(2) 0	(1) 30
2	(1) 40	(2) 20

Table OR5. Final solution.

Observing Table OR4 we can shift 30 units out of cell 1-1 and doing this we obtain the final (optimal) solution shown in Table OR5 and for this

$$z = 40(1) + 20(2) + 30(1) = 110$$

compared with the initial solution (Table OR3) of $z = 170$.

The problem is, for clarity, a very small one and generally larger loops are tested, comparing different alternatives according to their improvement indexes.

Modifications of the distribution problem

Many modifications and variations of the distribution problem are possible, some of these including:

1. In the special case when the right hand sides of Eqns OR47 and OR48 reduce to unity the problem is the *assignment problem*, that is one route is assigned to each supply point. Such problems involve flows of only zero or unit and are sometimes called *integer programming problems.*
2. When supply is surplus to demand dummy demand points with a high route cost (so supply to 'real' demand is preferred) are specified to model the situation.
3. In entering data for computer solution of a problem routes can be eliminated with minimal data change by specifying a very high *penalty* cost for them
4. Such analyses often include *transfer points* at which there is both input and output. There are modeled by a pair of supply and demand points with appropriate S & D values and zero route cost between them
5. As such problems tend to involve large numbers of constraints the dual problem may be more economical to solve (see Sec. OT6).

Conclusion

The NW corner method and the stepping stone algorithm are useful to introduce transportation problems and some aspects of them are perhaps useful elsewhere. For the distribution problem, however, at first sight Eqns OR46-48 suggest linear programming and programs for this are given in Sec. OR12.

OR7. Dynamic programming

Dynamic programming is a process of *recursive optimization* in which steps toward the optimum solution are taken using information from previous steps, typically for time dependent problems.

The general procedure used in dynamic programming is:

1. Divide the problem into stages, a process referred to as *decomposition.*

2. At each stage decisions are made based on an optimization objective. This objective is called the *recursion equation.*

3. The results are combined to yield a solution, a process referred to as *composition.* Sometimes the 'summation' of decisions made at each stage may be said to form a *policy.*

A common example is the critical path method (CPM) where when the schedule is revised at various stages in the calendar for the project. The overall process is then referred to as PERT, or Program Evaluation and Review Technique, noting that in 'full PERT' statistical time estimates are given for the elements of the project.

Fig. OR4 shows the shortest route or 'stagecoach problem. Here the nodes are towns and the distances between them are shown on the arrows between nodes. We seek to determine the shortest route systematically and this can be done using a tabular dynamic programming approach

Table OR6 shows dynamic programming of the problem broken into three stages at which distance totals to each node are compared.

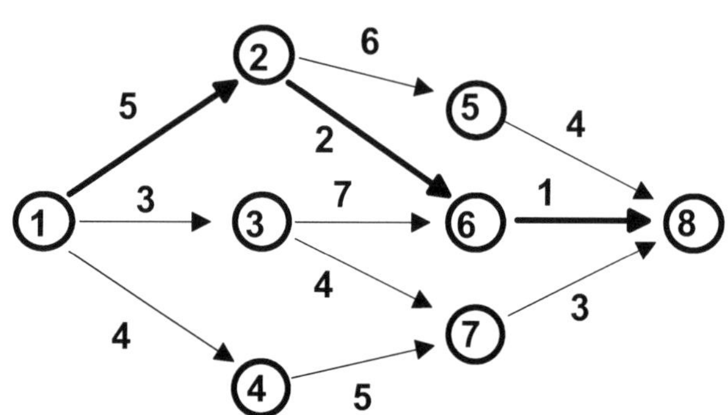

Fig. OR4. Shortest route problem.

Table OR6. Dynamic programming solution for Fig. OR4.

Stage	Travel to node	Travel from node			Decision	ΣDistance
		1				
I	2*	5			1	5
	3	3			1	3
	4	4			1	4
II		2	3	4		
	5	5+6			2	11
	6*	5+2	3+7		2*	7
	7		3+4	4+5	3	7
		5	6	7		
III	8	11+4	7+1	7+3	6*	8 (min)

Then the distances to nodes 2, 3 and 4 in stage I are carried through as data for stage II. Here choices are made of the shortest cumulative distances to nodes 6 and 7 and the cumulative distances (the shortest values having been chosen) are carried through to stage III. Here node 6 is found to have given the shortest cumulative distance to node 8 (a distance = 8 units).

This completes the *forward pass*. Now we carry out a *backward pass* in Table OR6, moving through the points marked with an asterisk (*). Thus from stage III we note that it was node 6 which gave use the shortest distance and move back to the row for this at stage II. There we note that node 2 gave the shortest distance to node 6 and we move back to the row for node 2 at stage I.

Finally, we have found the nodes giving the shortest distance to be 1, 2, 6 and 8.

This particular problem is similar to the critical path problem except that we seek the shortest route rather than the longest time. Indeed, as we shall now show it is easily solved by a computer program using a similar approach to that used to program CPM.

The tabular approach of Table OR6, however, can, with a little ingenuity be applied to almost any type of capital budgeting, inventory or like problem. In the former case alternative projects would correspond to nodes, their NPVs then correspond to the stages (of the capital program) and their individual costs correspond to the route times between nodes. Then we use a tabular approach like that of Table OR6 to determine the cheapest program (to gain a certain total NPV).

Program for the shortest route problem

The following BASIC program for the shortest route problem is similar to the CPM program of Sec. PP11, reading in the number of nodes (Z) and the number of links between them (E) at line 20. Then the node number pairs and distances for each of these links or elements is read in line 30.

The data included in lines 180 - 200 is for the problem of Fig. OR4 and the output (from line 160) will simply be the node numbers of the shortest route in reverse order (excluding node 1), that is 8, 6 and 2.

```
5 REM Program for Shortest Route Problem
10 DIM N(20, 20), D(20), T(20), P(20, 3), B(20)
20 READ Z, E: PRINT "Shortest route is:"
30 FOR I = 1 TO E: READ N(I, 1), N(I, 2), D(I): NEXT
40 FOR I = 1 TO E: FOR J = 1 TO 3: P(I, J) = 0: NEXT: NEXT
50 FOR K = 1 TO E: J = N(K, 2): I = 1
60 FOR M = 1 TO 3: IF P(J, M) = 0 THEN 70
I = I + 1: NEXT
70 P(J, M) = K: NEXT
80 FOR I = 1 TO Z: B(I) = 0: T(I) = 100: NEXT: T(1) = 0
90 FOR K = 1 TO E: I = N(K, 1): J = N(K, 2): T2 = T(I) + D(K)
100 IF T2 < T(J) THEN T(J) = T2
105 NEXT
110 FOR K = Z TO 1 STEP -1: F = 100
120 FOR M = 1 TO 3: IF P(K, M) = 0 THEN 150
130 L = P(K, M): N1 = N(L, 1): N2 = N(L, 2): T2 = T(N1) + D(L)
140 IF T2 < F THEN B(N2) = N1: F = T2
150 NEXT: NEXT: K = Z
160 PRINT K: K = B(K): IF K = 1 THEN END
170 GOTO 160
180 DATA 8,11
190 DATA 1,2,5, 1,3,3, 1,4,4, 2,5,6, 2,6,2
200 DATA 3,6,7, 3,7,4, 4,7,5, 5,8,4, 6,8,1, 7,8,3
```

As in CPM, a *precedence matrix* is formed in lines 50 to 70 and this stores the element numbers leading to each node. Then a *forward pass* is used in lined 80 to 105 to find the shortest distance to the nodes.

Then a *backward pass* is carried out in lines 110 to 150. Here the precedence matrix is used to find and store the node which gives the shortest distance to each node in array B( ).

Then, finally, in line 160 the shortest route is output. Such programs, of course, are a more attractive approach to dynamic programming problems than tables such as Table OR6 which, except for the simplest of problems, quickly become rather cumbersome.

Conclusion

Dynamic programming in practice may simply mean procedures of regular review and adjustment of project and other schedules. Sometimes, however, very useful tabular methods of solution can be devised for capital budgeting problems.

For problems like the shortest route problem, on the other hand, simple programs such as that given here solve the problem readily.

OR8. Inventory models

Inventory models, like queueing models discussed in MS (Maths & Stats), may be deterministic or *stochastic.* In addition, they may have some of the following features:

1. A *lead time* t_L is specified for ordering and this is the time taken to receive goods after ordering.
2. Inventory systems may be fixed-order or variable-order quantity systems.
3. Inventory systems may use a continuous inventory record or use a periodic review system giving a discontinuous inventory record.
4. The system may be single or multi-tier, involving different 'levels' of storage.
5. The system may hold single or multiple items.
6. If stockouts are allowed there may be provision for *backordering,* that is orders are taken and filled at a later data to avoid loss of sales.
7. The system may have a continuous time horizon (as in the classical deterministic/analytical models) of a finite or discrete horizon in time.
8. Costs of purchase or production of items may be fixed or variable.
9. Ordering, shortage and other secondary costs may be taken into account (shortages involving an opportunity cost).

EOQ model

Fig. OR5 illustrates the economic order quantity (EOQ) inventory model for a vendor. This deterministic model was briefly discussed in Sec. BF9 and has a single level of stock of a single item with fixed cost, zero lead time and a continuous time horizon.

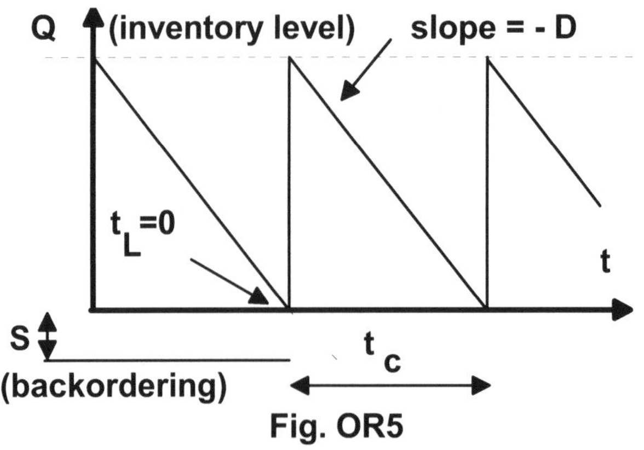

Fig. OR5

This uses a regular inventory cycle time t_c as shown in Fig. OR5. The slope of the falling stock level = $-D$ where D is the demand per unit time, as shown.

If we let the ordering or setup cost = C_0 and the holding or carrying cost = C_h the total cost per nit time is as shown in Fig. OR6.

Here the total cost is given by the function

(OR49) $C(Q) = f_1(Q) + f_2(Q) = (D/Q)C_0 + (Q/2)C_h$

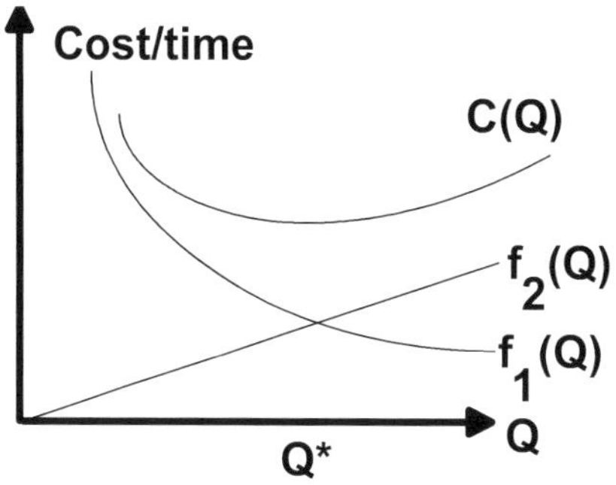

where the holding cost is assumed directly proportional to the quantity held and the ordering cost is taken as inversely proportional to this quantity.

Fig. OR6. Minimum cost stock level Q*

Then, as shown in Fig. OR6, there is a quantity Q^* for which the total cost is a minimum. By differentiating Eqn OR49 with respect to Q this is obtained as

(OR50) $Q^* = \sqrt{(2DC_0/C_h)}$

and the corresponding inventory cycle time is $t_c^* = Q^*/D$.

Other inventory models

Many other inventory models can, of course, be devised, some of these including:

1. EOQ with lead time. For these the lead time demand is calculated as

(OR51) $R = t_L D - \text{Int}(t_L/t_c^*)Q^*$

the second term on the RHS allowing for the situation $t_L > t_c^*$ when stocks are replenished by earlier orders. Then orders must be placed when stocks drop to the 'reserve' amount R.

2. EOQ with backordering. For these we include a cost of shortage C_s per unit time (of shortage). Then the EOQ is given by

(OR52) $Q^* = \sqrt{\{(2DC_0/C_h)[(C_h + C_s)/C_s]\}}$

and the maximum permitted shortage quantity is given by

(OR53) $S^* = \sqrt{[2C_0DC_h/(C_hC_s + C_s^2)]}$

3. EOQ with lost sales and models with deterministic periodic review. For these the EOQ is still that given by Eqn OR50.

4. Production inventory models. For these the EOQ approach can be used but is really not designed for the production situation. For this dynamic programming or the MRP approach discussed below are more helpful.

5. EOQ with discounts. When discounts for large orders are available a term DP where P = purchase cost, is added to Eqn OR49. Then Q^* is calculated with P as both the normal and discount value and decisions made on the basis of these results.

6. Stochastic demand can be dealt with approximately by using a mean value of the demand D when again Eqn OR50 gives the EOQ.

Material requirements planning (MRP)

This approach is useful in complex production situations and involves the following steps:
a. A master production schedule is made.
b. This is *exploded* to give schedules for the 'ingredients' of the 'recipe' with which the total product is made up. Sometimes a *bill of materials* is used for this purpose.
c. These individual material schedules are used to determine the gross material requirements.
d. Comparing these results with the existing inventories the net materials requirements are determined.

Establishing and maintaining such records requires a considerable effort sometimes but the resulting databases ultimately result in economies of operation in the long run.

Periodic maintenance scheduling

Maintenance scheduling can be considered a special case of the inventory problem. Then if we write a cost function for maintenance as

(OR54) $$C(M) = (D/M)C_b + (M/2)C_p$$

where M is the quantity of maintenance activity, C_b is the cost of breakdown and C_p is the cost per unit time of periodic maintenance, we obtain the same form of result as in Fig. OR6.

Then an economic maintenance quantity (units per year, for example) and associated cycle time can be established as for inventory in Eqn OR50.

Conclusion

The classical EOQ inventory model is both simple and useful and applies, sometimes with slight modification, to a wide range of inventory problems and also to such problems as maintenance scheduling.

In complex production situations such models as the EOQ model may be applied to a range of components and computer data bases are frequently used to cope with inventories.

OR9. Simulation

In the following section we briefly discuss (mathematical) simulation, paying particular attention to *stochastic simulation* using the well known *Monte Carlo method.* In this random numbers are used to generate data for a particular distribution so that its parameters can be estimated or to generate a random distribution.

Example

The observed distribution of replacement times for cars in a car pool are shown in Table OR7.

Then the right hand column of Table OR7 shows the cumulative frequency range associated with each replacement time and this interval is used to 'capture' random numbers (1 - 100), each capture simulating a car requiring replacement at the corresponding time.

Table OR7. Car replacement data.

Replacement time (months)	Frequency %	Random number range
12	4	1-4
16	7	5-11
20	13	12-24
24	17	25-41
28	27	42-68
32	11	69-79
36	7	80-86
40	6	87-92
44	5	93-97
48	2	98-100

Then using random numbers the simulation is summarized in Table OR8. Here we wish to determine the number of replacement cars for a pool of ten cars that will be needed in a period of 12 years. The Table shows the random numbers used for trial 1 of the simulation, using only the first two digits of these numbers.

Table OR8 Car pool replacement simulation.

Car	Random number	Trial:	1	2	3	4	5	6	7
			Months to replacement						
A	96(268)		44	20	24	16	28	36	
B	03(550)		12	16	24	32	32	24	20
C	22(188)		20	44	16	28	28		
D	63(759)		28	36	28	28	28		
E	55(006)		28	20	28	24	28		
F	81(972)		36	28	28	28	44		
G	06(344)		16	24	24	32	28	32	
H	92(363)		40	20	44	16	28		
I	96(083)		44	40	24	44			
J	92(993)		44	36	28	20	24		

Then trials are ceased for each each car (or row) of the table when the next entry would cause that total number of months for that car to exceed 144 (or 12 years). Then finally the total number of cars needed is 53.

Note that in practice such a simulation should be repeated several times to obtain an averaged result.

Other applications

The Monte Carlo process may be applied to queueing problems. For example, the times could be gap times between customer arrivals and/or the service times.

For such applications the program given in Sec. MS13 to simulate a Poisson distribution can be used to simulate arrivals and service completions and queueing models with any number of servers, constraints and queue size limits can be modeled.

Once again, however, note that such simulation exercises need to be repeated a number of times to gain an accurate picture of the problem under study.

Random number generator

A sound method of generating random numbers is the *multipicative congruential method* which generates a sequence of uniformly distributed pseudo-random integers. This uses the recursion routine

(OR55) $x_i = \mathrm{MOD}(ax_{i-1}, m)/m$

where MOD(X,Y) is the smallest non-negative remainder of *R* such that *X-R* is exactly divisible by Y (e.g. MOD(34,17) = 0, MOD(13,5) = 3 and MOD(-13,5) = 2). This function is calculated in the following program listing (RAND.BAS from Basics disc \MBS1).

The *modulus m* is usually expressed in the form 2^L, and a common choice is $L = 2L_{max}/3$ where L_{max} is the largest value tolerated by the machine and language used. Then a good choice for *a* is close to $2^{L/2}$.

```
5 REM Generates flat random distribution - checks  flatness of 2 x 100 nos
10 DIM C(200), H(10), H2(10)
20 FOR I = 1 TO 10
30 H(I) = 0: H2(I) = 0: NEXT
40 B = 2 ^ 16: X = 5663879: M = 2 ^ 8 + 3
45 INPUT "input seed x", Y: REM If x=0 then use value in line 40
46 IF Y = 0 THEN 50: X = Y
50 FOR K = 1 TO 200
60 A = M * X: X1 = A / B: X2 = X1 - INT(X1)
70 X = INT(X2 * B): Z = X / B: C(K) = Z: NEXT
80 FOR K = 1 TO 100
90 X = C(K): Y = C(K + 100)
100 I = INT(10 * X + 1): J = INT(10 * Y + 1)
110 H(I) = H(I) + 1: H2(J) = H2(J) + 1: NEXT
120 FOR I = 1 TO 10: PRINT I, H(I), H2(I): NEXT
```

Here L (= B in code) = 16 is used (7 digit computation), so the value for *a* is taken as $2^8 + 3$ (line 40). Then the remainder corresponding to the use of a MOD( ) function is calculated in statements 2 & 3 in line 60 and statement 1 in line 70.

The resulting random numbers are stored in the array C( ). Then to test the flatness of their distribution two 'batches' of 100 numbers are grouped according to their rounded up values in the range 0 - 10. The results are sometimes 'flatter' than built in functions.

Finally note that the maximum period before the numbers start repeating with the above procedure is about *m*/20.

Conclusion

The Monte Carlo simulation procedure is very simple and versatile and, for example, in conjunction with the Poisson distribution generator given in Sec. MS13 can model an almost unlimited range of queueing problems.

The random number program given here may also be of interest, if not usefulness, in such applications.

OR10. Network Problems

We have already encountered network problems such as shortest route problem. In the present section we discuss two further network problems which may be of interest.

Minimal spanning tree

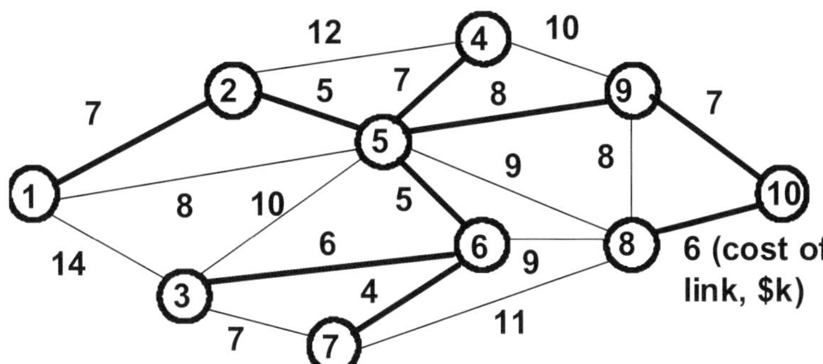

Fig. OR7 Minimal spanning tree problem

Fig. OR7 shows a minimal spanning tree problem where we seek to minimize the total distance of the links between the nodes (or the total cost associated with these connections) without leaving any node 'hanging' without a link to another (an example of such a situation might be a water supply or irrigation system).

A procedure for solving this problem is as follows:

1. Select *any* node and connect it to the closest node, breaking any links that are crossed in the process.
2. Connect any unconnected nodes to the nearest node, breaking any links that are crossed in the process.
3. Repeat the process until all nodes are connected.

Repeating this process and beginning at node 1 in Table OR7 we obtain the results shown in Table OR9.

Table OR9. Steps taken for the problem of Fig. OR7

Step	Nodes connected	Cost ($k)	Σ Cost
1	1-2	7	7
2	2-5	5	12
3	5-6	5	17
4	6-7	4	21
5	6-3	6	27
6	5-9	6	33
7	5-4	7	40
8	9-10	7	47
9	10-8	6	53

Then the steps used in Table OR9 give the minimal spanning tree shown in Fig. OR7 (the heavier lines). The reader can easily verify that this result does indeed give the minimal total cost of linkage of the points.

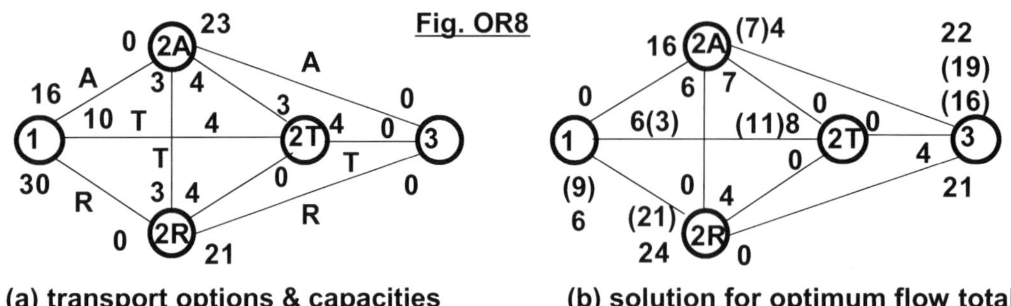

Fig. OR8

(a) transport options & capacities

(b) solution for optimum flow total

Fig. OR8 shows a maximal flow problem. Here we wish to deliver the maximum amount of mail from node 1 (the source or origin) to node 3 (a sink) by a combination of air, truck and rail transport and the links using these are marked A, T and R in Fig. OR8(a). Nodes 2A, 2T and 2R are air, truck and rail terminals and the capacities for flow *away* from each node are shown in Fig. OR8 for each link, having different values at each end.

Then the problem is solved using the following procedure (known as the Fulkerson-Ford algorithm):

1. Find any path from origin to sink with positive flow capacities (C) on each link. If no such path exists we have the optimum solution.
2. Find the maximum positive capacity C* for this path and increase the flow along the path by this amount.
3. Compensate for this flow increase by:

(a) Subtracting C* from all outgoing flows along this path.
(b) Adding C* to all ingoing flows along this path.

Then following this procedure for the problem of Fig. OR8(a) the steps involved are:

Step	Path	Flow Change
1	1-2A-3	16
2	1-2R-3	21
3	1-2T-3	4
4	1-2T-2A-3	3
5	1-2R-2A-2	3

and the maximum total flow obtained is 47 (units/time).

Once again a remarkably simple procedure is involved as is typical of network problems, though these are often of crucial importance in business science.

Conclusion

We have now encountered an interesting variety of network problems, whilst CPM/PERT is dealt with in PP (Project Planning) and the distribution problem is given the 'works' in FM (Finite Methods).

OR11. Foulkes algorithm

This interesting algorithm forms a Boolean matrix in which, for 8 items A, B, C, D, E, F, G, H which have to be dealt with in a certain order, the constraint A must precede B, D and G is written A < B, D, G and the first row of the matrix represents this. 'Before or after' constraints are written >< and 'not before' as I<. In this problem the constraints are:

A < B, D, G; B < C; B>< D, F; C < E;
D < C; E >< H; FI< G; G< C< H.

giving the matrix M_1:

$$M_1 = \begin{array}{c} A \\ B \\ C \\ D \\ E \\ F \\ G \\ H \end{array} \begin{bmatrix} 1 & 1 & 0 & 1 & 0 & 0 & 1 & 0 \\ 0 & 1 & 1 & 1 & 0 & 1 & 0 & 0 \\ 0 & 0 & 1 & 0 & 1 & 0 & 0 & 0 \\ 0 & 1 & 1 & 1 & 0 & 0 & 0 & 0 \\ 0 & 0 & 0 & 0 & 1 & 0 & 0 & 1 \\ 0 & 1 & 0 & 0 & 0 & 1 & 1 & 0 \\ 0 & 0 & 1 & 0 & 0 & 0 & 1 & 1 \\ 0 & 0 & 0 & 0 & 1 & 0 & 0 & 1 \end{bmatrix} \qquad M_4 = \begin{bmatrix} 1 & 1 & 1 & 1 & 1 & 1 & 1 & 1 \\ & 1 & 1 & 1 & 1 & 1 & 1 & 1 \\ & & 1 & & 1 & & & 1 \\ & 1 & 1 & 1 & 1 & 1 & 1 & 1 \\ & & & & 1 & & & 1 \\ & 1 & 1 & 1 & 1 & 1 & 1 & 1 \\ & & 1 & & 1 & & 1 & 1 \\ & & & & 1 & & & 1 \end{bmatrix}$$

Then the matrix is multiplied by itself using *Boolean multiplication* (in which performing matrix multiplication normally we then only accept results = 0 or, if >1, = 1). After four such multiplications the matrix stays the same, telling us that their are at most *three* items in a group (as can be seen from the original matrix). The resulting matrix is M_4, showing only the non zero entries.

Now by swapping rows and columns so that in each column all the ones are above the zeroes, we obtain matrix M^*,

$$M^* = \begin{array}{c} A \\ B \\ D \\ F \\ G \\ C \\ E \\ H \end{array} \begin{bmatrix} 1 & 1 & 1 & 1 & 1 & 1 & 1 & 1 \\ 0 & 1 & 1 & 1 & 1 & 1 & 1 & 1 \\ 0 & 1 & 1 & 1 & 1 & 1 & 1 & 1 \\ 0 & 1 & 1 & 1 & 1 & 1 & 1 & 1 \\ 0 & 0 & 0 & 0 & 1 & 1 & 1 & 1 \\ 0 & 0 & 0 & 0 & 0 & 1 & 1 & 1 \\ 0 & 0 & 0 & 0 & 0 & 0 & 1 & 1 \\ 0 & 0 & 0 & 0 & 0 & 0 & 1 & 1 \end{bmatrix}$$

with the row/column swaps indicated by the order now shown on the LHS of the matrix. This is the *path* the solution of the ordering problem follows, except that we must swap B and D because there is no constraint 'link' between them. In the form of the matrix we see four 'steps' in the number of zeroes per row (i,e, between 0, 1, 4, 5, 6) and correspondingly there are five subgroups of items, namely A, (BDF), G, C, (EH) in the solution path.

The program FOULKES in \MBS1 on the course Basics disc performs the multiplications for the foregoing example and this not very widely known algorithm is certain to interest some readers.

OR12. LP programs

Program for sequential MIN + MAX

The following program (NEWLP in \MBS2 on the course Basics disc) uses the 'worst -b/min c/|a|' rule to find the minimum solution and then the standard 'max c/min b/a' rule to find a maximum solution.

Note that the program uses the '10 line' GJR coding given in Sec. NM4 (in lines 180-230) as a basis for *partial* reduction of the matrix for each pivot choice.

Pivot selection and dealing with both MIN and MAX is a little messy but note that the program was first written on an HP85 PC, when most readers had never seen a PC hardly, This the author got it for $10 not long ago but it had no cartridges so the program had to be typed in each time !

```
10 REM LP program: Q=1 for MAX, Q=2 for MIN & Q=3 for MIN then MAX
20 RESTORE 450
30 DIM A(10, 15): T = 10 ^ -6: READ N, M, Q
40 FOR I = 1 TO N + 1: FOR J = 1 TO M + 1: READ A(I, J): NEXT: NEXT
50 C1 = 0: FOR J = 1 TO M: C2 = A(N + 1, J)
60 IF C2 > C1 THEN C1 = C2: C = J
NEXT
70 IF C1 = 0 THEN 250
80 F = 0: B1 = 10 ^ 10
90 FOR I = 1 TO N
100 IF A(I, M + 1) < 0 THEN F = 1
110 IF ABS(A(I, C)) < T THEN 150
120 B2 = A(I, M + 1) / A(I, C)
130 IF B2 < 0 THEN 150
140 IF B2 < B1 THEN B1 = B2: R = I
150 NEXT I
160 IF F = 1 THEN GOSUB 330
170 IF F = 0 AND Q >= 2 THEN 250
180 X = A(R, C)
190 FOR J = 1 TO M + 1: A(R, J) = A(R, J) / X: NEXT
200 FOR I = 1 TO N + 1
210 IF I = R THEN 230
X = A(I, C)
220 FOR J = 1 TO M + 1: A(I, J) = A(I, J) - X * A(R, J): NEXT
230 NEXT I
240 GOTO 50
250 PRINT "Z = ", -A(N + 1, M + 1)
260 FOR I = 1 TO N: FOR J = 1 TO M
270 D = ABS(A(I, J) - 1)
280 IF D < T AND ABS(A(N + 1, J)) < T THEN K = J
NEXT J
290 PRINT "X"; : PRINT USING "##"; K; : PRINT " = "; : PRINT USING "######.###"; A(I, M
+ 1)
300 NEXT I
310 IF Q = 3 THEN Q = 1: GOTO 50
320 END
```

```
330 B1 = 0: FOR I = 1 TO N
340 B2 = -A(I, M + 1): IF B2 < 0 THEN 360
350 IF B2 > B1 THEN B1 = B2: R = I
360 NEXT I
370 C1 = 10 ^ 10
380 FOR J = 1 TO M
390 IF ABS(A(R, J)) < T THEN 430
400 IF A(R, J) > 0 THEN 430
410 C2 = -(A(N + 1, J) / A(R, J))
420 IF C2 < C1 THEN C1 = C2: C = J
430 NEXT J
440 RETURN
450 DATA 4,6,3
460 DATA 1,2,1,0,0,0,10
470 DATA 1,-3,0,1,0,0,0
480 DATA -1,3,0,0,1,0,0
490 DATA -1,-1,0,0,0,1,-6
500 DATA 15,5,0,0,0,0,0
510 DATA 6,10,3
520 DATA 1,1,0,0,1,0,0,0,0,0,30
530 DATA -1,-1,0,0,0,1,0,0,0,0,-30
540 DATA 0,0,1,1,0,0,1,0,0,0,60
550 DATA 0,0,-1,-1,0,0,0,1,0,0,-60
560 DATA 1,0,1,0,0,0,0,0,1,0,40
570 DATA -1,0,-1,0,0,0,0,0,0,1,-40
580 DATA 2,1,1,2,0,0,0,0,0,0,0
```

The dimensioning limits to nine constraints and fourteen variables (line 30) and data is included for two problems:

a. The problem of Table OR1 (lines 450 - 500) which is solved for both the minimum and maximum without difficulty.

b. The distribution problem of Eqns OR46-48 using the 'split constraint artifice demonstrated in Sec. OR5 (lines 510-580). The solution will agree with Table OR5 but if you ask for the MAX solution as well the initial feasible solution of Table OR3 is obtained. A more efficient 'direct' LP method program for distribution problems is given in Sec. OR12.

The data is read in simply as a line giving # constraints (N), total # variables (M) + Q = 1,2,3 (see line 10 for explanation), followed by the constraints (in $\leq$ form and including their columns for slack variables and their RHSs) and finally the 'cost row'. That is, for simplicity the full simplex tableau is read in.

MIN program with search for optimum pivot

The following program (LPMIN2 in \MBS2) uses the pivoting rule of Eqn OT22 to obtain the MIN solution for the problem of Eqns OT7-10. This is read in as the number of design variables (D) and slack variables (S) in line 20, followed by constraints (in $\leq$ form) and the cost row.

Here a full 'augmented' matrix is not stored (or read in !) and pointer matrices B( ) and Z( ) are used to indicate which of the variables are in the basis.

```
10 REM LP Program - MIN using Min(bc/a) rule
20 DIM A(9, 5), X(12), B(8), Z(4)
30 READ D, S: M = D + 1: N = S + 1
40 FOR I = 1 TO N: FOR J = 1 TO M: READ A(I, J): NEXT: NEXT
50 REM initialization of variables and pointer matrices
60 L = 0: V = D + S
70 FOR I = 1 TO D: X(I) = 0: NEXT
80 FOR I = M TO V: X(I) = A(I - D, M): NEXT
90 FOR I = 1 TO S: B(I) = D + I: NEXT
100 FOR I = 1 TO D: Z(I) = I: NEXT
110 I1 = 0: J1 = 0
120 IF L = 20 THEN 460
130 REM pivot selection
140 FOR J = 1 TO D: IF A(N, J) = 0 THEN 460
NEXT
150 FOR I = 1 TO S: IF A(I, M) < 0 THEN 170
NEXT
160 GOTO 460
170 Q = -1
180 FOR I = 1 TO S: FOR J = 1 TO D
190 IF A(I, J) = 0 OR A(I, M) > 0 THEN 280
200 T = A(N, J) * A(I, M) / A(I, J)
210 IF T <= Q THEN 280
220 FOR K = 1 TO D
230 IF J = K THEN 260
240 T1 = A(N, K) - A(N, J) * A(I, K) / A(I, J)
250 IF T1 < 0 THEN 280
260 NEXT K
270 I1 = I: J1 = J: Q = T
280 NEXT J: NEXT I
290 IF Q <= O THEN 460
300 REM Gauss Jordan reduction
310 IF I1 = 0 OR J1 = 0 THEN 460
320 L = L + 1
330 T = B(I1): X(T) = 0
340 B(I1) = Z(J1): Z(J1) = T
350 P1 = 1 / A(I1, J1): A(I1, J1) = 1
360 FOR J = 1 TO M: A(I1, J) = A(I1, J) * P1: NEXT
370 FOR I = 1 TO N
380 IF I = I1 THEN 420
390 T = A(I, J1): A(I, J1) = 0
400 FOR J = 1 TO M
410 A(I, J) = A(I, J) - A(I1, J) * T: NEXT
420 NEXT I
430 FOR I = 1 TO S
440 T = B(I): X(T) = A(I, M): NEXT
450 GOTO 110
460 PRINT L, " reductions required."
470 PRINT "Min = ", -A(N, M)
480 FOR I = 1 TO S: PRINT B(I), X(B(I)): NEXT
490 END
500 DATA 2,3, -1,2,14, 5,2,50, -1,-2,-18, 2,7,0
```

OR13. Direct LP method program for distribution problems

The following program (DISTP in \MBS2) uses the 'direct' method of Mohr to solve distribution problems. In this a pivot is taken in each (constraint) row in turn in the column with the minimum value of $c_j/|a_{ij}|$ and GJR applied to this column, yielding an initial *infeasible* solution to the problem. The minimum solution is then obtained by choosing pivots using the 'worst -b/min $c/|a|$ rule (note $a < 0$ to eliminate the infeasible - b on the RHS).

Once again the full constraints are read in but the second program of Sec. OR11 can be used to overcome this, building in the 'in turn' initial pivoting used here to do so.

```
10 REM Distribution Problem Program - 'Direct solution' - for MIN
30 DIM A(20, 20), B(20), NV(20)
40 READ NC, NX
50 FOR I = 1 TO NC + 1: FOR J = 1 TO NX: READ A(I, J): NEXT
60 READ B(I): NEXT
70 FOR I = 1 TO NC: C = 10 ^ 6
80 FOR J = 1 TO NX: IF ABS(A(I, J)) < .000001 THEN 110
90 F = A(NC + 1, J) / ABS(A(I, J))
100 IF F < C THEN C = F: COL = J
110 NEXT J
120 GOSUB 320
130 NEXT I
140 I = O: C = 0: FOR K = 1 TO NC: IF B(K) < C THEN I = K: C = B(K)
145 NEXT
150 C = 10 ^ 6: FOR J = 1 TO NX: IF A(I, J) >= 0 THEN 170
160 F = A(NC + 1, J) / ABS(A(I, J)): IF F < C THEN C = F: COL = J
170 NEXT
180 IF I = 0 THEN 240
190 FOR J = 1 TO NX
200 F = A(NC + 1, J) - A(I, J) * A(NC + 1, COL) / A(I, COL): IF F < 0 THEN PRINT "OVER"
210 NEXT
220 GOSUB 320
230 IF I > 0 THEN 140
240 REM
250 FOR J = 1 TO NX
260 C = 0: FOR I = 1 TO NC: IF ABS(A(I, J)) < .000001 THEN C = C + 1
265 NEXT
270 IF C <> NC - 1 THEN 290
280 FOR I = 1 TO NC: IF ABS(A(I, J)) = 1 THEN K = I
285 NEXT: NV(K) = J
290 NEXT J
300 FOR I = 1 TO NC + 1
305 PRINT "  X"; : PRINT USING "##"; NV(I);
306 PRINT " = "; : PRINT USING "##########"; B(I): NEXT
310 END
320 P = A(I, COL): B(I) = B(I) / P
330 FOR J = 1 TO NX: A(I, J) = A(I, J) / P: NEXT
340 FOR K = 1 TO NC + 1
350 IF K = I THEN 390
360 M = A(K, COL): B(K) = B(K) - M * B(I)
370 FOR J = 1 TO NX
380 A(K, J) = A(K, J) - M * A(I, J): NEXT J
390 NEXT K
```

```
400 RETURN
410 DATA 5,9
420 DATA 1,1,1,0,0,0,0,0,0,110
430 DATA 0,0,0,1,1,1,0,0,0,160
440 DATA 0,0,0,0,0,0,1,1,1,150
450 DATA 1,0,0,1,0,0,1,0,0,140
460 DATA 0,1,0,0,1,0,0,1,0,200
470 DATA 50,100,100,200,300,200,100,200,300,0
```

The data lines appended are for the problem described by the 'data table':

	Unit costs			Supplies
( ) = node #	50	100	100	110 (1)
	200	300	200	160 (2)
	100	200	300	150 (3)
Demands	140 (4)	200 (5)	80 (6)	

for which the solution (MIN) is route flows 15 = 110, 25 = 80, 26 = 80, 34 = 140 and 35 = 10 (others zero) with total cost 670,000.

The program DISTP2 (in \MBS1) solves for the MAX of distribution problems, a worthwhile exercise from some standpoints!

OR14. An interesting distribution problem

This is where the S & D points are periods of time, e.g. ACME Co. makes a chemical for which demand is seasonal and production follow this approximately. The sales forecast is: 1st quarter 60,000 mg; 2nd quarter 97,000 mg; 3rd quarter 118,000 mg; 4th quarter 95,000 mg [total = 370,000].

Production scheduled is: 51,000, 80,000, 119,000 and 100,000 for the respective quarters [total = 350,000 so that 20,000 mg must be bought from outside at $70 per 1000 mg - but this price is falling at an estimated $1 per quarter].

Internal production cost is $50 per 1000 mg - to this is added $1 for storage for a quarter if kept for later sale and $2 for two quarters storage, when $10 is also needed for filtering and re-testing of the material. If kept for three quarters some reprocessing is required and cost, including storage, is $30 per 1000 mg.

If orders are held over for one quarter cost in administration and loss of customers is $5 (per 1000 mg), for two quarters this is $9 and $13 for three. Thus the S & D Tableau is, with costs as $/1000 mg and sales/production in units of 1,000 mg:

Costs/1,000 mg	1st quarter	2nd quarter	3rd quarter	4th quarter	Production capacity (S)
1st quarter	50 [51]	51	62	80	51 (S1)
2nd quarter	55	50 [80]	51	62	80 (S2)
3rd quarter	59	55 [1]	50 [118]	51	119 (S3)
4th quarter	63	59 [5]	55	50 [95]	100 (S4)
Buy outside	70 [9]	69 [11]	68	67	20 (S5)
Sales fore-cast	60 (D1)	97 (D2)	118 (D3)	95 (D4)	Total: 370

Check that this table describes the problem OK and then solve it using DISTP.PGM.

Note that we would expect to buy outside in the fourth quarter when that is cheapest but that is not the optimum solution. Interpretation of the solution is also a little confusing - essentially flows above the diagonal in the table are 'holds' and those below are 'delay in filling order.'

The solutions are shown in [ ] in the table, giving a total revenue of $18,939 (x1000).

Conclusion

As Sec. OR1 lists, we are building up an impressive list of numerical/OR problems and this continues in PP (Project Planning) and FM (Finite Methods) where we return to the distribution problem.

LP is clearly important and, at least so far as relatively modern (computer) techniques go, it dominates many OR books. Our approach has been much simpler (for example we have not used *surplus* (for $\geq$ constraints) or *artificial* variables (for = constraints), in the former case reversing constraint signs instead and in the latter case one would simply use 'forced pivoting' as in the latter program, barring return to these rows for these constraints thereafter).

Goal programming is an application of LP worth note for the interested reader to follow up. In fact GOALP(.BAS) in \MBS2 is the same program as the first of Sec. OR11 with the data for 'a GP' problem which it handles OK.

In the end, however, the FEM modeling (and optimization) of networks introduced in FM is the preferred approach to network problems.

OR References

Ackoff RL (ed.), Progress in Operations Research, vol. 1, Wiley NY, 1961.

Ackoff RL, Sasieni MW, Fundamentals of Operations Research, Wiley NY, 1968.

Battersby, A, Mathematics in Management, Penguin, Harmondsworth UK, 1966.

Budnick FS, Mojena R, Vollmann TE, Principles of Operations Research for Management, Irwin, Homewood IL, 1977.

Churchman CW, Ackoff RL, Arnoff EL, Introduction to Operations Research, Wiley NY, 1968.

Enrick NL, Management Operations Research, Holt Rinehart & Winston, NY, 1965.

Hillier FS, Lieberman GJ, Introduction to Operations Research, 3rd edn, Holden Day, Oakland CA, 1980.

Kaufman A, Faure R, Introduction to Operations Research, Academic, London, 1968.

Gilmour P, Logistics Management, An Australian Framework, Longman Cheshire, Melbourne, 1993.

Makower MS, Williamson E, Operations Research, 3rd edn, Hodder & Stoughton, Sevenoaks, Kent, 1975.

Mohr GA, A bilinear rule for macroscopic traffic flow, *Australian Road Research,* Vol. 13, No. 1, pp 38-40, 1983.

Mohr GA, *Finite Elements for Solids, Fluids, and Optimization,* Oxford University Press, Oxford, 1992.

Mohr, GA, Numerical procedures for input-output analysis, Applied Maths & Computation, vol. 101, p 98, 1999.

Mohr, GA, Finite element modelling of distribution problems, Applied Maths & Computation, vol.. 105, pp 69-76, 1999.

Mohr, GA, Optimization of primal and dual network models of distribution, Computer Methods in Applied Mechanics & Engineering, vol. 188, p 135, 2000.

Mohr GA, Optimization of primal and dual network models of distribution, Comp. Meth. Appl. Mech. Engng, vol. 188, p 135, 2000.

Mohr GA, Flow ratio design of primal and dual network models of distribution, *Int. J. Arts & Sciences,* Vol. 1, No. 1, pp 10-18, 2001.

Mohr GA, Optimization and finite element modelling of input-output analysis problems, *Int. J. Arts & Sciences,* Vol. 2, No. 1, pp 23-29, 2002.

Mohr GA, Finite element modelling and optimization of traffic flow networks, *Int. J. Arts & Sciences,* Vol. 2, No. 2, pp 30-37, 2002.

Mohr GA, A predictor-corrector method of constrained nonlinear optimization, Int. J. Arts & Sciences, Vol. 2, No. 2, pp 38-48, 2002.

Mohr GA, Cook PL, Dual pivoting rules for the Simplex Method, Int. J. Arts & Sciences, Vol. 2, No. 2, pp 49-60, 2002.

Mohr GA, Flow ratio design of primal and dual network models of distribution, *ANZIAM Journal,* Vol. 45, pp 573-583, 2004.

Paul, RS, Haeussler, Introductory Mathematical Analysis for Students of Business and Economics, Reston Publ. Co, Reston VA.

Rust BW, Burrus, WR, Mathematical Programming and the Numerical Solution of Linear Equations, Elsevier, NY NY, 1972.

Sasieni M, Yaspan A, Friedman L, Operations Research, Wiley, NY, 1959.

Schmenner, RW, Production/Operations Management: Concepts and Situations, 4th edn, McMillan, NY, 1990.

Singh J, Operations Research, Penguin, UK, 1971.

Theil H, Boot JCG, Kloek T, Operations Research and Quantitative Economics, McGraw-Hill, NY, 1965.

PROJECT PLANNING & CONTROL (PP)

I am not sure I should have dared to start;
but I am sure I should not have dared to stop. Winston S. Churchill

In the following chapter approaches to planning projects are discussed including network techniques such as the *critical path method* and its variants, and *flowline* techniques, respectively much used in the construction and manufacturing industries.

PP1. Introduction

At the outset it is important to emphasize the distinction between project planning and project or production control, the first often being an exercise undertaken only once while the latter involves the business of overseeing the day to day operation of some enterprise. In addition we can make a distinction between the planning of projects, taking these to be a 'one-off' task generally, and planning of production processes, these having a relatively continuous and long term nature.

Project planning

In project planning we are dealing with, for example, construction of a building, a ship or factory. We may also be planning the advertising campaign to launch a new product or, not unrelated, a political campaign for election.

For such purposes we should carefully decide what steps the project requires (the planning phase being one of them) and then determine how these steps should be scheduled. For this such techniques as the critical path method (CPM) are very useful as they provide a systematic framework with which to tackle scheduling of complex projects.

Then such schedules are analysed to determine the start and end times for each activity or element of the project and *bar charts* are then prepared to fit them to a calendar which is then used to help guide the project towards a timely completion.

Note, however, that the decision tables and trees discussed in Sec. BP4 and the discounted cash flow analysis discussed in Sec. BF3 are examples of many other techniques that may be used in project selection and planning.

Production planning

Production planning involves devising production processes that will be used for long term manufacture of items and commonly we are dealing with what might be described as mass production, on some scale at least.

For this purpose the elements of the process should be identified and analysed using suitable diagrams or other means of visualization or simulation. Then such techniques as the flow line method are used to schedule the process so that interruptions are avoided and the process is made as efficient as possible.

Consider, for example, the two production procedures shown in Fig. PP1 for two hamburger chains. In the first, Fig. PP1(a), the ingredients are combined via a simple 'tree' structure while in the second, Fig. PP1(b), a production line approach is used for hamburgers made to order and re-heating may therefore be required.

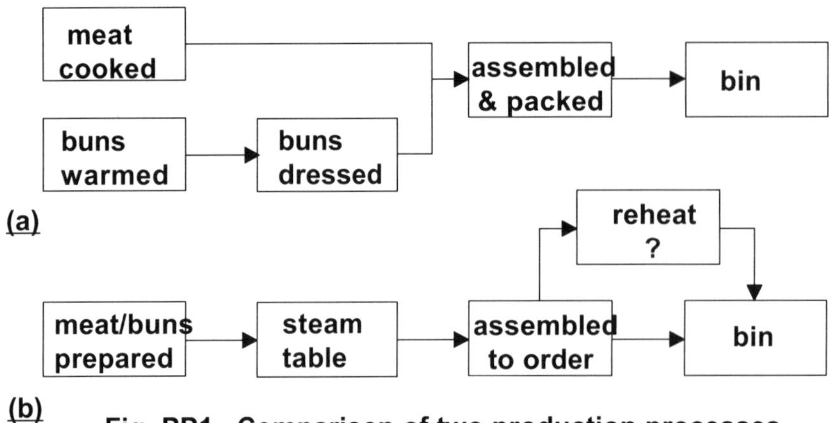

Fig. PP1. Comparison of two production processes

The second process is likely to be more costly so that a premium will have to be charged for the made to order facility.

Then, analyzing such processes, the times for each step, the 'throughput' times and the costs of inputs at each stage must be evaluated to fully cost the process and determine a profitable price for the product.

Production control

Once a project has been planned and production has commenced such aids as bar charts and control charts are useful in helping control work on a regular basis. Then compliance with scheduling requirements, quality and quantity of production and possible improvements in procedures must be considered.

In some cases alterations in schedules or processes will require a return to the planning stage to form a new schedule for a building project, for example, or to introduce new procedures and perhaps technology into a production process.

Conclusion

Project planning, production scheduling and production control are all crucial activities in business science and each is discussed in greater detail in following section.

PP2. The Critical Path Method

The principal objective of the critical path method is to ensure greater profitability in construction. To this end we are mainly concerned with the controllable elements of the project which are time dependent, in particular the use of labour or labour related services. Other costs such as interest charges or material costs, on the other hand, we usually have no control over but accurate estimation of unit costs and quantities required is still, however, important.

Flow charts

Fig. PP2 shows a *flow chart* using classical 'arrow notation' (or *activity on* arrow) to show the way in which *activities* or *elements* of a project are connected. For each element a duration is shown and the footings element has been split into two parts to provide a more efficient schedule.

Element 56 is a *dummy element* which is needed to help enforce the proper sequence of work (and analysis using a computer program will not work without it as *node* 5 will be ignored in the backward pass of the program).

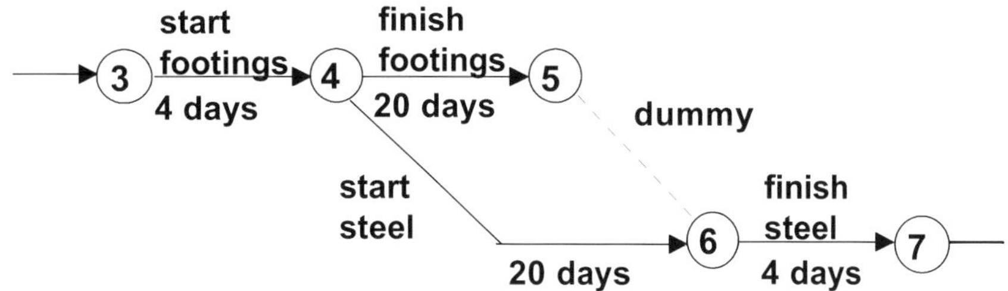

Fig. PP2. Flow chart using arrow notation.

An alternative notation for flow charts is *precedence notation* (*activity on node*) and this is illustrated in Fig. PP3 Here a *lag factor* is used to more concisely describe the overlap in activities shown in Fig. PP2. In addition the earliest start and finish and latest start and finish times are sometimes shown on each element in the locations shown.

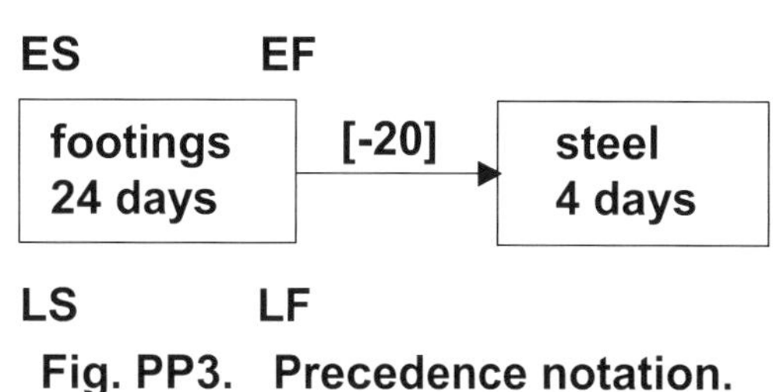

Fig. PP3. Precedence notation.

Precedence notation can be set up on a regular grid using standard preprinted sheets. The results are often much simpler and clearer and many fewer elements are used as a result of such artifices as lag factors as is seen by comparing Figs. PP2 and PP3.

This approach is then of particular usefulness for multistory buildings, for example, the columns being able to be used for repetition of elements at each floor level, as illustrated in Figure PP4.

Then in Fig. PP4 the first digit of each element number is the floor number. Note that multi-storey buildings can be scheduled effectively using the flow line technique described in Sec. PP6.

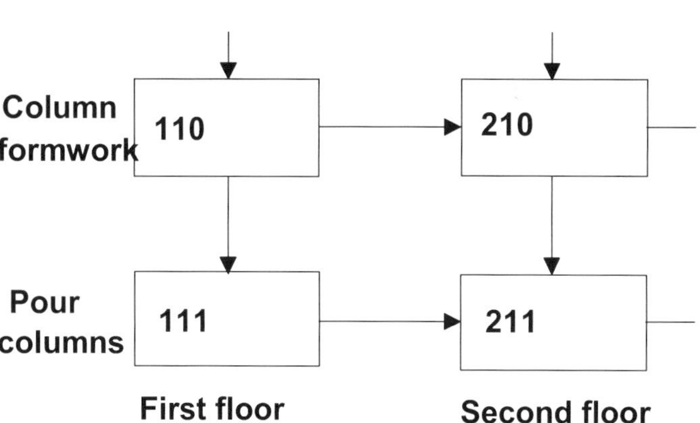

Fig. PP4. Precedence notation for multistorey building

Fig. PP5 shows a simple network for which the critical path is shown by heavier lines. Here there is no node 4 but this could be inserted to provide a dummy element at the tail of element 3 so that elements 2 and 3 then had unique node numbers (as may be preferred by some computer programs).

To determine the critical path Table PP1 is constructed with all the path times leading to each node calculated. Then the latest of these times is the earliest start (ES) time for elements which follow this node. Then in relation to particular elements we can call this the earliest start time for this node (given that it takes different values).

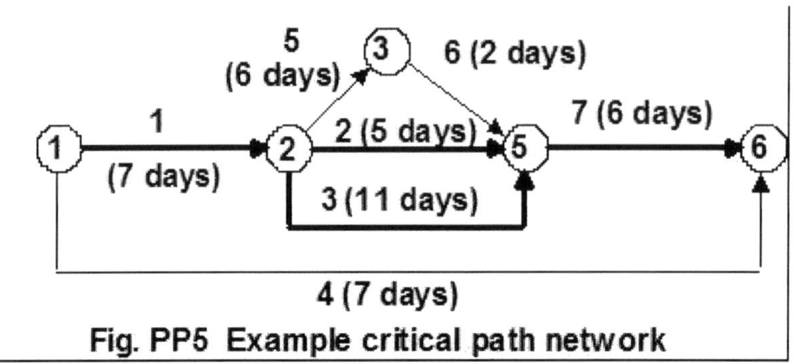

Fig. PP5 Example critical path network

The longest path time for the last node is the job time for the project and elements whose path times to any node in Table PP1 were the latest times for that node are *critical elements* and these lie on the critical path.

Table PP1. Determination of critical path

Node	Path times	Latest time
1	0	0
2	7	7
3	12	12
5	14,12,18	18
6	21,18,24,7	24

The operations of Table PP1 are called a *forward pass* and when this is complete and the job time is known a *backward pass* is commenced. In this we work back through the network subtracting element times for each element from the latest time for their end nodes to give the latest times for their start nodes. Comparing these with the node times established in Table PP1 the earliest start and finish (ES and EF) and latest start and finish (LS and LF) times for each element are calculated.

Then elements on the critical path have ES = LS and EF = LF, that is they have zero *slack* or *float.* Various types of float can be defined, as shown in Fig. PP6. These are:

1. *Total float.* This is the amount of delay an element may have without delaying the completion of the project.
2. *Free float.* This is the amount of delay an element may have without affecting following elements (including their float). This applies only to elements which are the last of an independent chain of events, for example element 6 in Fig. PP5.
3. *Dependent float.* This is part of the total float associated with the path upon which an element lies and usage of this float by an element reduces float available to following elements.

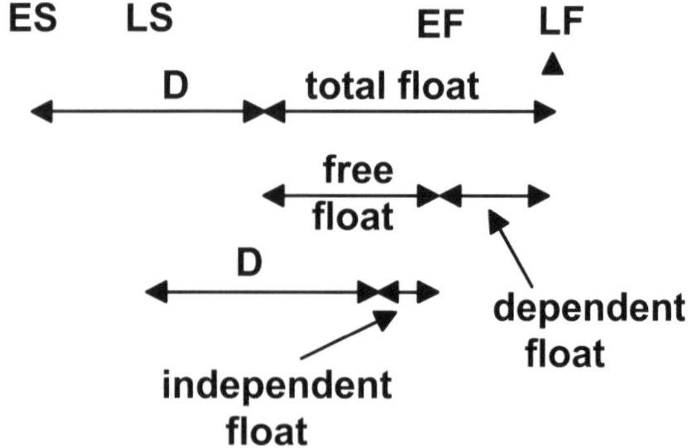

Fig. PP6. Various types of float.

4. *Independent float.* This is an irreducible amount of float available which has been 'built in' to the analysis to allow for contingencies.

In practice independent float is perhaps best allowed by way of dummy activities. This clarifies the definition of float for which we can then write

(PP1) Total float (TF) = Free float (FF) + Dependent float (DF)

as shown in Fig. PP6.

Conclusion

The critical path method is a very widely used technique for project scheduling, perhaps because it is the natural, if not obvious, approach.

The critical path can be found using the tabular scheme of Table PP1 and from this the ES, LS, EF and LF times for each element follow. Simple programs which also accomplish this are given later in the chapter.

PP3. Bar Charts

Bar charts, sometimes called *Gantt charts*, are the means by which the results of a CPM analysis are used to coordinate the progress of a project. Of particular importance, *resource scheduling*, in which bars are shifted judiciously in order to smooth out fluctuations in resource usage can be accomplished with the aid of bar charts.

Application of bar charts

Once an analysis of a network has been carried out to determine the critical path and then the ES, LS, EF and LF times for each element these are used to construct a bar chart. Typically classical CPM computer printouts used such notation as:

XXX	critical element
VVV	non-critical element
000	free float
DDD	dependent float
SS	Saturday or Sunday (no work)
H	public holiday
---	miscellaneous

and so on, so that a great deal of information is set to a calendar.

Fig. PP7 shows a simple example of a bar chart for the use of a particular resource (hence many possible bar charts can be constructed for different resources, including materials and labour, and for parts of the project). Then, as shown by the dashed lines, bars can be shifted in order to smooth out resource usage and this process is referred to as *resource scheduling*.

Clearly use of the resource has been leveled out, three units being used for an initial period and two units for the remainder.

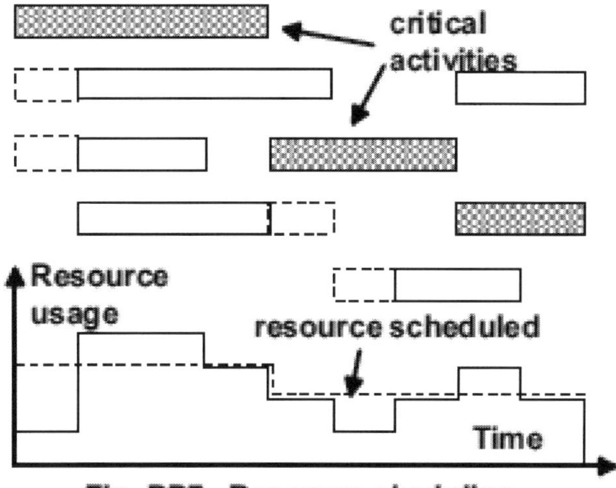

Fig. PP7. Resource sheduling.

Conclusion

Bar charts and applications such as resource scheduling are an important part of project scheduling using CPM. They are also important in managing the day to day running of a project. Note too that schedules are frequently altered as the result of actual times taken for elements of a project. When the CPM analysis is repeated at a number of stages with this new information the general process involved is referred to as *dynamic programming.* Further examples of dynamic programming are given in Sec. OR7.

PP4. Crashing a project

In critical path analysis 'crashing' a project refers to compressing elements on the critical path as much as possible. Generally this will raise the costs of these elements but the total cost of the project may be reduced as a result of savings in overheads and other fixed costs such as interest rates payable on finance for the project, avoidance of penalties for late completion and bonuses for early completion.

Fig. PP8 shows an example. The normal project time is that for the minimum cost neglecting overheads etc. When overheads and penalties are taken into account, however, the total cost curve gives a minimum somewhere between the crash and normal project times. Hence whilst a project might only be crashed fully when there is considerable pressure to do so, some degree of compression of times on the critical path is generally worthwhile.

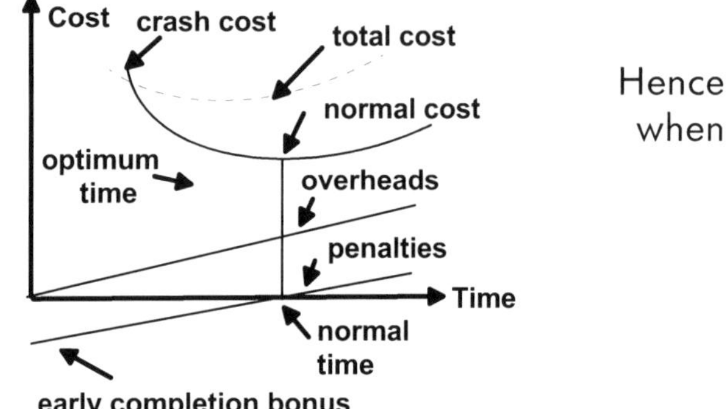

Fig. PP8. Effect of overheads and penalties/bonuses on project cost

Then this result affects the cost curve for the project, as shown in Fig. PP9 where the higher costs for the compressed critical elements raise the project cost curve to the dashed result.

This is shown for the earliest start curve for the sake of clarity. In practice, however, we would generally prefer to use the LS curve and then make any adjustments by compressing critical elements of this. This is because the LS curve delays payments associated with non-critical elements as much as possible, thereby reducing interest charges for the project.

Fig. PP9. ES & LS cost curves and effect of compressing critical elements

Conclusion

Whilst crashing of critical elements is generally attempted only in extreme circumstances, some compression of the critical path, however, may reduce total project costs as a result of reduced overhead costs and the like. It is also important to use LS times for non-critical elements as this will generally reduce interest charges for the project. It is then possible to combine these two measures to reduce project cost.

Note that the effect shown in Fig. PP8 can be included in a cost curve for each element and this modification and the PERT technique is discussed in the next section.

PP5. Modifications of the Critical Path Method

In this section we discuss two modifications of the critical path method. The firsts is *PERT* (Program Evaluation and Review Technique) and the second is a modification of CPM in which each element is given a cost versus time curve. Then the steepest descent method is used to obtain an optimum solution for the resulting critical path problem.

PERT

This is a simple modification of CPM in which three time estimates are provided for each element, these being:

1. An optimistic time (*a*) which is the best result that could be achieved in, say, 10 attempts.
2. A median or most likely time (m) which is the time most likely to be obtained in a number of attempts.
3. A pessimistic time (*b*) which is the worst result that could be achieved in, say, 10 attempts.

Then the expected time for each element is calculated as

(PP2) $t_e = (a + 4m + b)/6$

and this is equivalent to assuming a parabolic frequency distribution.

Then according to the *central limit theorem* the distribution of the total time T for n sequential tasks is approximately normal (that is, random and symmetrical) with a mean equal to the sum of the individual means and a variance equal to the sum of the individual variances as $n \rightarrow \infty$ regardless of the distribution of the individual tasks.

Then the probability of completing the job in a time T is given by the Normal probability

(PP3) $P(\{T - T_e\}/\sigma > 0)$

where

(PP4) $T_e = \Sigma\, t_e$ and $\sigma^2 = n\, \Sigma\, \sigma_i^2$

and

(PP5) $\sigma_i = (b - a)/6$

for the standard deviation of the individual elements.

Then analysis proceeds as with CPM using a forward pass but now this gives an earliest time, a latest time and a scheduled or chosen time for each node and we can attach a probability to this scheduled time. Following with a backward pass expected, latest and scheduled times of completion are obtained for each element and probabilities are attached to the scheduled times.

In practice simplified PERT (or CPM as we have described it) is usually used but some attempt to provide probabilities of elements completing on schedule is useful in making management decisions.

It should also be noted, however, that PERT makes no attempt at optimizing anything. It simply forms a schedule in which three (rather than two) times are attached to each element, attaching a probability to the likely actual completion time for an element.

It is nevertheless worthwhile to use formulas such as those of Eqns PP3-5 to estimate the variance for typical elements and thus for the entire project without actually including this data in the CPM analysis.

Optimization of the critical path

Fig. PP10 shows the quadratic cost function assumed by G.A. Mohr for elements of a CPM network. Here three durations D_1, D_2 and D_3 are specified along with their associated costs, $D_3 = (D_1 + D_2)$ being the median time.

Then fitting a quadratic interpolation to these three points the duration D_4 which gives the minimum cost C_4 is given by

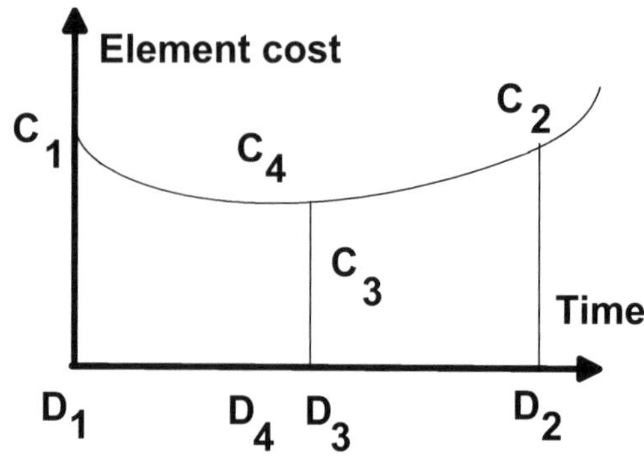

Fig. PP10. Element cost function.

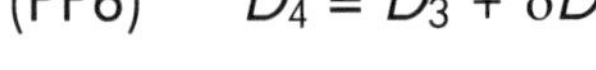

(PP6) $D_4 = D_3 + \delta D$

where

(PP7) $\delta D = (D_2 - D_1)/(C_1 - C_2)/4(C_1 - 2C_3 + C_2)$

and the minimum cost occurring with this duration is given by

(PP8) $C_4 = C_1(1 - 3x + 2x^2) + 4C_3x(1 - x) + C_2(2x^2 - x)$

where

(PP9) $x = (D_4 - D_1)/(D_2 - D_1)$

is a dimensionless coordinate for this interpolation.

Then providing the three point data for each element the optimum time for each is calculated and critical path analysis is carried out in the usual way, also calculating the total project cost as

(PP10) $P = \Sigma\, C_i + F\, T_{proj}$

by summing the element costs and adding a term for the fixed costs shown in Fig. PP8. This is the product of a fixed cost per unit time (F) and the total project time (T_{proj}) which is the time for the last node of the network.

Then, applying the steepest descent method to each critical element, its duration is increased by an amount δD, giving a perturbed value

(PP11) $D^* = D_4 + \delta D$

Then using the quadratic interpolation of Eqn PP8 with

(PP12) $x = (D^* - D_1)/(D_2 - D_1)$

the corresponding element costs C^* are calculated.

Collecting the results for all critical elements gives a gradient vector

$$\text{(PP13)} \qquad \{g\} = \{(C^* - C_4 + F\delta D)/\delta D\}$$

Then trial step lengths S are used to search in this direction for the optimum solution and the optimum durations for the critical elements are calculated as

$$\text{(PP14)} \qquad \{D^*\} = \{D\} - S_{opt}\{g\}$$

where S_{opt} is the step length which gives the minimum total project cost (using Eqns PP8 and PP12) to calculate the element costs) the trial values of which are calculated as

$$\text{(PP15)} \qquad P^* = P + \Sigma_{cr}(C^* - C_4 + \delta D\, F)$$

Finally the critical path analysis is repeated and, if the critical path is unchanged the procedure is complete. If not, the steepest descent procedure is repeated to determine a new optimum solution for this new critical path.

The potential savings resulting from this procedure are not large, in part because minimum element costs D_4 are used at the outset and this is where the main savings lie. In the case of small networks that represent the operations in the mass production of some item, however, these savings would be substantial over time.

Conclusion

The simple estimates of probability required for the PERT method are well worth making, even if they are not used in the CPM analysis. Then, summing variances along the critical path, for example, the variance for the whole project is easily estimated.

The quadratic cost function approach illustrated in Fig. PP10 is of potential value in providing small savings in networks representing mass production processes. In addition Eqns PP6-9 are useful as a means of providing improved data for standard CPM analyses.

PP6. The Flowline Method

In the following section we describe the flowline method of production scheduling. For this a project or part thereof is broken into sections which are carried out at similar rates. This approach is usually applied to mass production lines but it is especially useful in the case of multi-storey building projects or construction of 'project' homes, for example. The method is easily understood by considering three contrasting production systems which are discussed in this section.

Parallel production

Fig. PP11 illustrates production in which all 'sub-projects', for example a number of houses, are built at the same time.

For parallel production the total project time is given by

$$\text{(PP16)} \qquad T_p = \Sigma\,(K_i + t_i)$$

where K_i is called the *production module* for steps i and t_i are waiting times (for delivery, holidays etc.).

In the case where all rates are the same the total production time when there are m steps and no waiting times is

(PP17) $T_p = K\,m$

This approach gives the shortest total time but requires maximum usage of resources and its only logical use is for one-off situations, not for ongoing business.

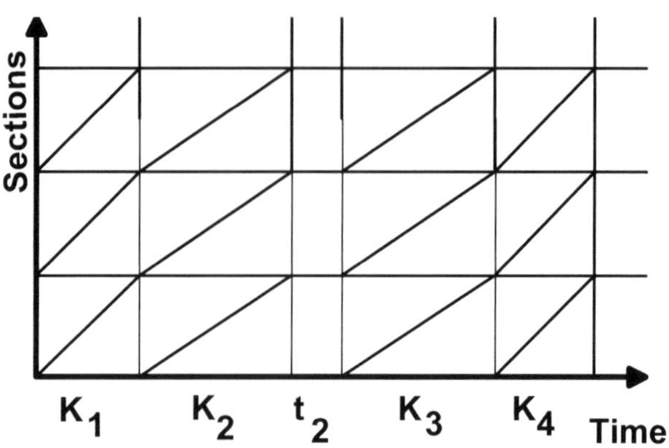

Fig. PP11. Parallel production

Sequence production

Fig. PP12 illustrates sequence production in which each sub-project is completed before starting the next. This gives the total project time as

(PP18) $T_s = n\,\Sigma\,(K_i + t_i)$

when there are n sections or sub-projects. Then when the modules for the steps in these are equal and there are no waiting times the total time is given by

(PP18b) $T_s = K\,m\,n$

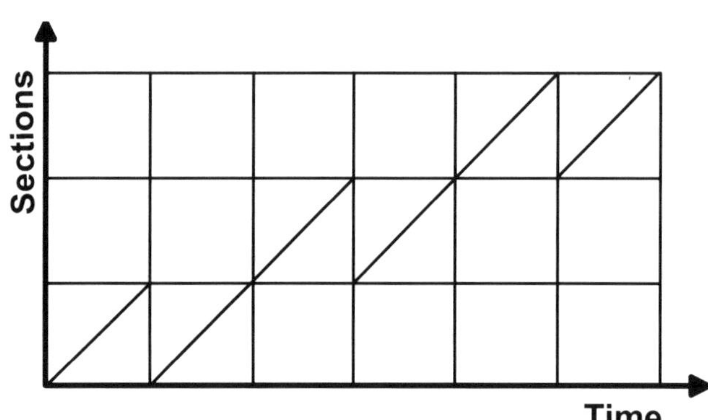

Fig. PP12. Sequence production

where we have $m = 2$ and $n = 3$ in the example of Fig. PP12.

This approach results in the longest total time and delaying one activity does not affect others. This again represents an extreme situation in relation to the flow line approach and both Figs PP11 and PP12 are of little practical value except as an introduction to the flow line production model.

Flowline production

Fig. PP13 shows an example of flow line production where, for example, line A might be excavation for footings, B for pouring footings, C for brickwork and D for roof framing in the case of house construction.

Then for flowline production the total production time is given by

(PP19) $T_f = K(m + n - 1)$

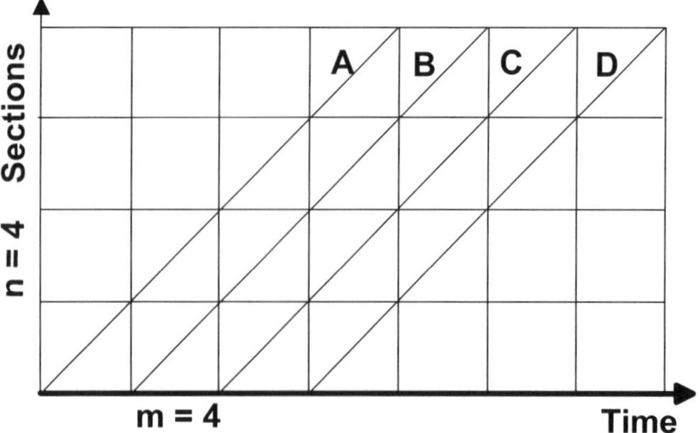

Fig. PP13. Flowline production

where the production modules or rates are equal, as must be the case to prevent lines interfering (unless there are gaps between the lines and still only a temporary difference in the 'general' rate is permitted as flow lines cannot cross).

Then in Fig. PP13 the time until all lines are in operation is given by

(PP20) $K(m - 1)$

and this is called the *running in time* and is equal to the *running out time*, that is the time for cessation of production after the first line finishes.

Hence the *time of full production* can be calculated as

(PP21) $K(m + n - 1) - 2K(m - 1) = T_{full} = K(n - m + 1)$

and in practice it is desirable to maximize the ratio

(PP22) $T_{full}/T_f = K(n - m + 1)/K(n + m - 1)$

so that the larger the number of sections the more efficient the process, for example in mass production where $n >> m$.

Conclusion

The flowline method is an important tool for production scheduling and can also be used elsewhere when a number of similar projects are undertaken or when a project can be broken into sections of similar nature, as in construction of a multi-storey building, for example. Then, as flow line method emphasizes, the work on these sections should be overlapped as much as possible to maximize the efficiency of operations.

Finally, flowline diagrams provide many interesting exercises when some lines are sped up or slowed down, adjusting others to prevent overlapping. The changes in results of the form of Eqn PP21 then clearly indicate the effect of such changes, generally emphasizing that the ideal form of Eqn PP19 with $n >> m$ should be the objective.

PP7. Assembly lines

Having discussed the flow line method of production scheduling, observing that this can be applied to any situation where a number of lines of similar nature have to be produced, we now discuss assembly lines and some of the specific details of these that must be considered in designing and operating mass production systems.

Assembly line balancing

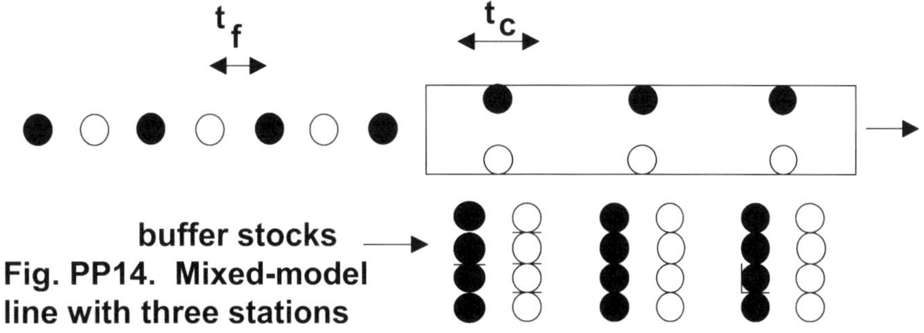

Fig. PP14. Mixed-model line with three stations

Fig. PP14 shows a mixed-model assembly or flow line with $N = 3$ stations. Here two products are assembled using components fed to the stations as well as *buffer stocks* of components.

When the line uses or is modeled on the principle of using a belt or other mechanical conveyor the gap time for component inputs t_f is called the *feed time* and the time components are available for access at a station is called the *tolerance time.*

In such a line the *cycle time* is given by

(PP23) $t_C = t_S + t_L$

where t_S is the *service time* and t_L is the lost time (non-productive work and idle time).

Ideally *rigid pacing* in which t_C is assumed constant can be attained but in practice *pacing with margin* is used and this requires buffer stocks.

Now in balancing the line we seek to minimize the sum of the idle times at the stations (the *balancing loss*), that is we minimize

(PP24) $L = {}_{i\text{-}1}\Sigma^N t_L = {}_{i\text{-}1}\Sigma^N(t_C - t_S)$

where

(PP25) $t_S = \Sigma\, t_E$

is the sum of the *work element* times at a station.

Statistical variations

In designing balanced lines, estimates of cycle times should not be unreasonably small as ultimately this may result in greater losses in efficiency than those desired in making 'tight' estimates.

One solution is to take the variance of the work element times into account, giving the standard deviation of the service time as

(PP26) $S_S = \sqrt{(\Sigma\, \sigma_E^2)}$

and in balancing the line we then seek to minimize

(PP27) ${}_{i=1}\Sigma^N (t_C - t_S - zS_S)$

where z is an appropriate value of the variate for the normal distribution, for example 1.96 at the 97.5% level (that is work at a station would be completed within the cycle time provided 97.5% of the number of occasions).

Double lines

Fig. PP15 illustrates a double line. These are, when practical, more efficient than single lines because stations other than the first two are fed by two stations, reducing the likelihood of starving or blocking of stations. Rotary lines are an example of another such variation.

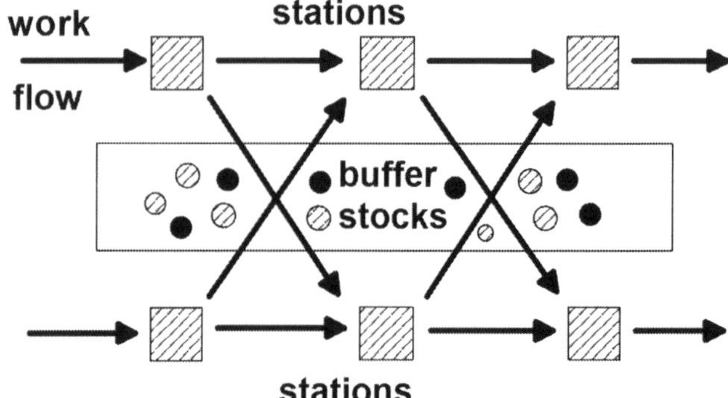

Fig. PP15. A double line.

Mixed model lines

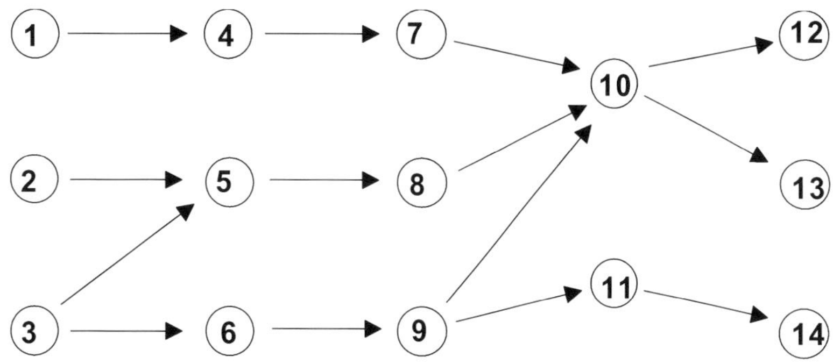

Fig. PP16. Mixed-model line

Fig. PP16 shows the layout of a more complex form of mixed-model line where three products move between the stations:

Product A: stations 3, 5, 8, 10, 13 or 3, 6, 9, 11, 14

Product B: stations 1, 4, 7, 10, 12

Product C: stations 2, 5, 8, 10, 13

Here products share only some processes and balancing work loads at the different stations, the product flows and minimizing time losses requires careful tabulation of the number of operations required at each station, its service time (which may vary for the different products) and hence the total work time required at each station. Then iteration using a simple computer program is the only way of practically modeling the problem with a view to maximizing its efficiency.

Line efficiency

In practice a 5% balancing loss is a good result and cycle times (or tolerance times in the case of belt lines) should be set close to the mean unpaced service times (which may require measurement). Then feed times should be set within a margin from the cycle times, depending upon such factors as the availability of buffer stocks and the variance in the service time.

Conclusion

The flow line method of production scheduling is based on an overview of the different stages of production, each being classified merely by a name (of the activity) and a number (its module).

Assembly line balancing then takes an 'inside' look at the processes involved in production and resulting improvements in efficiency will reduce the K value applicable in flow line analysis.

Many of the systems considered here, however, are more concerned with mass production in a factory situation only. Then when production takes the form shown in fig. PP16, for example, the group technology approach described in Sec. PP8 is also useful.

PP8. Group Technology

Group technology is an approach more suited to such applications as engineering manufacture where grouping components into families by identifying common manufacturing requirements is more important than an assembly line approach. In this approach some of the key considerations are:

1. Group technology is directed at *batch production* and more emphasis is placed on dealing with *components.*
2. Components are grouped into families in which they have similar manufacturing requirements to other family members.
3. Machines or production units are grouped into *production cells* which deal with *component families.*
4. These production cells are the approximate equivalent of a flow line in assembly line models and the component families are comparable to the sections or 'sub-projects' in Sec. PP6.

Component families

For each component a *component-process-routing (CPR)* program can be established. Then where grouping of components into families is not obvious comparison of their CPR programs to determine whether they visit similar sequences of production cells may help in component grouping.

Sometimes a component's CPR program may be 'all over the place' and this may be indicative of a need to rearrange the factory layout.

Design problems

In designing an efficient production system component quantities and production cell capacities must be balanced approximately and some manipulation of component families and grouping of facilities may be needed to achieve a reasonable balance.

In some cases physical layout corresponding to the product flow shown in Fig. PP16 may require rearrangement to improve overall efficiency.

Process sequencing

Using the CPR program data the *travel chart* shown in Table PP2 can be constructed for the component flows for a period of time.

Table PP2. Travel chart.

		Operation								
r/c	Opn	1	2	3	4	5	6	7	8	r
5	1		20	10	5	5	10			50
1.6	2	2		10	10	5			10	40
1	3				5	5	15			25
1m2	4	4		3		5	10			25
0.5	5				→→	**To**	5	5		10
0.8	6		6		**From**			15	15	35
0.6	7						5		10	15
0.14	8							5		5
	c	10	25	25	20	20	45	25	34	

Then for flowline assembly Table PP2 should yield an upper triangular matrix. To improve the sequencing we sum the row and column entries, as shown, and then calculate the ratio of these sums on the left side of Table PP2.

Then operations with high values of this ratio should be placed earlier in the sequence and operations with low values placed later. Such rearrangement will maximize in-sequence movement and minimize 'back-tracking.'

Then, observing the extreme left column of Table PP2 the required order of operations is:

Operation sequence: 1, 2, 4, 3, 6, 7, 5, 8

and the travel chart provides a convenient means of improving the sequencing. Note, however, that the criterion for this must be the ratio of the row and column totals and not the individual totals.

In addition, a limitation of the travel chart is that it cannot take into account the possibility of 'U-lines', for example, where shortcuts alter the situation considerably.

Conclusion

For certain types of production, typically engineering manufacturing of a range of related products, the group technology approach is useful. A good deal of judgment is required in grouping products and processes but the travel chart, for example, is one of many techniques which assist in obtaining a more efficient production operation.

PP9. Line-of-balance systems

Line-of-balance systems are especially useful for certain manufacturing situations where emphasis is based on *assembly* of a product from components. The lines of production of the various components are drawn backwards from the LOB to schedule the operations on these.

LOB flow chart

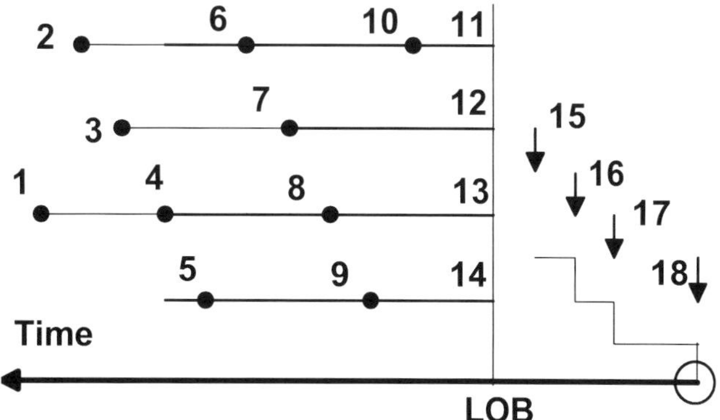

Fig. PP17. LOB flow chart

Fig. PP17 shows a simple example of a LOB flow chart, time originating at the extreme right hand side. Then flow lines for four components are drawn back from the LOB, the nodes in these corresponding to completion of some stage of their manufacture.

Then to the right of the LOB the assembly stages are scheduled, as shown, completion occurring when $t = 0$.

The LOB approach corresponds to parallel production in the flow line method whilst as in CPM float can easily be introduced into LOB flow charts.

Then, as shown in Fig. PP18, progress can be checked at any point on the LOB calendar and checked against the schedule (here the dollar value of progress of work on each flow line is summed).

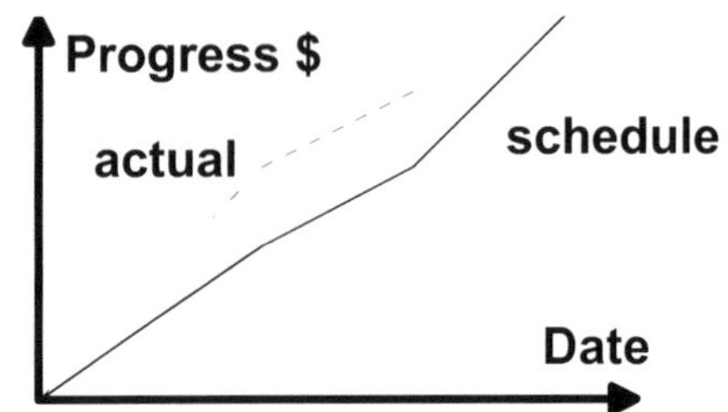

Fig. PP18. LOB Production schedule

Conclusion

LOB flow charts are a very simple means of scheduling and are particularly appropriate where emphasis is on assembly of a product. This situation corresponds to that of parallel production in flow line analysis (except that the lines will have different starting points).

PP10. Project Control and Assessment

In the following section we discuss observations of production processes with a view to quality control, data being recorded on *control charts*. Brief mention is then made of the results that are typically obtained from *time and motion* or *method studies.*

Control charts

Control charts are a very simple means of monitoring production variations and are widely used. These take the appearance shown in Fig. PP19 where daily observations of the mean of sample variables relating to a product are plotted and compared with the required mean value for the product.

Consider for example the case of a pharmaceutical company manufacturing aspirin tablets with a mean weight of M = 0.441 and variance V = 0.008 and suppose that small samples of 5 tablets are taken to measure the mean weight x_{av}. Then the expected mean and standard deviation are:

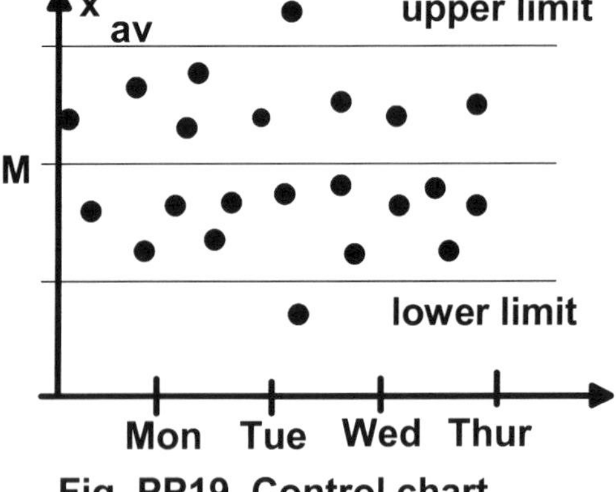

Fig. PP19. Control chart.

(PP28) $E(x_{av}) = M = 0.441$

(PP29) $V(x_{av}) = V/\sqrt{n} = 0.008/\sqrt{5} = 0.00358 = S$

Then assuming that a deviation from the mean of 3*S* is allowable the upper and lower limits for the control chart are:

(PP30a) Upper limit = $M + 3S = 0.452$

(PP30b) Lower limit = $M - 3S = 0.430$

Then the observer notes any measurement falling outside these limits, recording the time (and date) and any reasons that might be thought responsible for it (if any). Later, therefore, trends in the deviant result might help locate the source of the problem or at least suggest what remedial action should be taken.

Assuming a Normal Distribution, the limits +/- 3*S* should be satisfied 99.4% of the time (hence the reason for taking note if they are not). These limits are fairly 'wide', however, and limits +/- 2*S* are also commonly used (95.4% for normal distribution).

In addition it is also of interest to plot the frequency distribution of the sample data to get an idea of its variance and any skew, for example.

Fig. PP20 shows examples of the many results obtained from analysis of task performance. Case (a) shows that pace relative to a standard pace is asymptotic to a value somewhat above the standard value after a large number of learning repetitions. The learning curve is then found to be a little lower as the length of the task increases

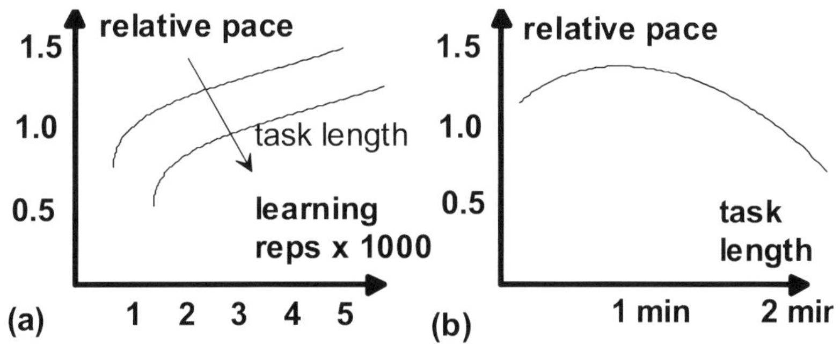

Fig. PP20. Pace/standard vs learning reps & task lenç

Then case (b) shows that the relative pace achieved ultimately peaks at task lengths of around one minute.

Other factors that might contribute to the results of such studies include:

1. The complexity of the task.
2. The similarity of the task to known tasks (i.e. its familiarity).
3. The level of skill required by the task.
4. Operator attitude, motivation etc.
5. Operator turnover (i.e. replacement through retirement etc.).

Many other factors can be involved on the human side, such as group empathy, managerial style and the like and some of these were discussed in MP (Management Psychology).

Conclusion

Control charts and the like are an important aid to production control. These may also be used for behavioural studies wherein, of course, some production problems will lie.

PP11. Simple CPM program

The listing for a simple program (CPM.BAS in \MBS2 on the DBS Basics disc) follows. Note that the precedence matrix is P(,), the coding being very transparent. The data is for the problem shown in Fig. PP21, the first line being the number of nodes and elements. The remaining lines each give the pair of node numbers, the duration, a unit cost and a wastage or tolerance figure giving the possible fractional cost overrun. Note the dummy element G* (with zero duration) to enforce a precedence.

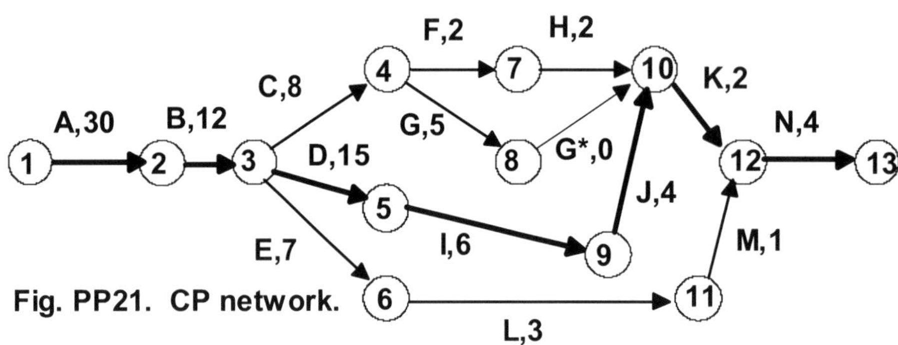

Fig. PP21. CP network.

Output gives the ES, EF, LS and LF times for each element (they are input in 'alphabetical' order and output in the same order) and these will correspond to the critical path shown in Fig. PP5.

```
5 REM CRITICAL PATH METHOD PROGRAM
6 RESTORE 500
10 DIM N(20, 2), D(20), C(20), W(20), T(20), P(3, 20)
20 DIM S1(20), F1(20), S2(20), F2(20)
30 A$ = "        ": READ Z, E: REM INPUT NO. NODES AND ELEMENTS
40 FOR I = 1 TO 3: FOR J = 1 TO 10
50 P(I, J) = 0: NEXT: NEXT: REM INTITIALIZE PRECEDENCE MATRIX
60 FOR I = 1 TO E
70 READ N(I, 1), N(I, 2), D(I): REM ,C(I),W(I) ; Rem I/P ELE DATA - N.B> ELEMENTS
80 NEXT: REM MUST BE IN NUMERICAL ORDER
90 Q = 0: Q2 = 0: REM INITIALIZE TOTAL PROJECT COSTS
100 FOR K = 1 TO Z: T(K) = 0: NEXT: REM INITIALIZE LF TIMES FOR NODES
110 FOR K = 1 TO E: J = N(K, 2): I = 1
120 FOR M = 1 TO 3: IF P(M, J) = 0 THEN GOTO 140
130 I = I + 1: NEXT M: REM COLLECT PRECEEDING ELEMENT
140 P(I, J) = K: NEXT K: REM NUMBERS FOR EACH NODE
150 FOR K = 1 TO E: REM COMMENCE FORWARD PASS **********
160 I = N(K, 1): J = N(K, 2): S1(K) = T(I): REM S1(K)=ES TIME FOR ELEMENT
170 F1(K) = T(I) + D(K): REM F1(K)=EF TIME FOR ELEMENT
180 IF F1(K) > T(J) THEN T(J) = F1(K): REM INCREASE NODE LF TIME IF NECESSARY
190 Q = Q + D(K) * C(K): Q2 = Q2 + D(K) * C(K) * W(K)
200 NEXT: REM END FORWARD PASS       **********
210 PRINT "JOBTIME = ", T(Z): PRINT "JOBCOST = ", Q:
PRINT "PESSIMISTIC COST VARN = ", Q2
220 FOR I = 1 TO E: F2(I) = 1000: NEXT: REM INTITIALIZE LF TIMES
230 FOR K = 1 TO E: REM COMMENCE BACKWARD PASS %%%%%%%%%
```

```
240 R = E - K + 1: I = N(R, 1): J = N(R, 2): REM MOVE BACWARDS THROUGH ELEMENTS
250 IF J = Z THEN F2(R) = T(Z): REM LF TIME FOR LAST ELEMENT
260 S2(R) = F2(R) - D(R): REM LS = LF - DURATION
270 FOR M = 1 TO 3: S = P(M, I): IF S = 0 THEN GOTO 290
280 IF F2(S) > S2(R) THEN F2(S) = S2(R): REM LF OF PREC ELES = LS OF THIS ELEMENT
290 NEXT
300 IF S1(R) = S2(R) THEN F = F + D(R) * W(R): REM INCREMENT PROJECT DELAY
ESTIMATE
310 NEXT: REM END BACKWARD PASS     %%%%%%%%
320 PRINT "PESSIMISTIC JOB DELAY = ", F
PRINT A$, "ES", A$, "EF", A$, "LS", A$, "LF"
330 FOR K = 1 TO E: PRINT USING "##########"; S1(K); F1(K); S2(K); F2(K): NEXT
340 END
 REM DATA FOR PROBLEM OF FIG PP21
500 DATA 13,15
510 DATA 1,2,30, 2,3,12, 3,4,8, 3,5,15, 3,6,7
520 DATA 4,7,2, 4,8,5, 8,10,0, 7,10,2, 5,9,6, 9,10,4, 10,12,2
530 DATA 6,11,3, 11,12,1, 12,13,4
```

The output will be (program does not print element 'tags', as noted OP being in same order as IP, but could easily be modified to do so).

Element	A	B	C	D	E	F	G	G*	H	I	J	K	L	M	N
ES	0	30	42	42	42	50	50	55	52	57	63	67	49	52	69
EF	30	42	50	57	49	52	55	55	54	63	67	69	52	53	73
LS	0	30	54	42	58	63	62	67	65	57	63	67	65	68	69
LF	30	42	62	57	65	65	67	67	67	63	67	69	68	69	73

Then we see that critical elements do indeed have ES = LS and EF = LF and the dummy element has ES = EF and LS = LF. Of course printout of the floats could easily be added when zero float quickly indentifies a critical element.

Conclusion

This short program is useful for small exercises and it is extended in Sec. PP12 to optimize a network whose elements have quadratic time functions.

PP12. CPM Program with Quadratic Elements

The following program (CPMOP.BAS in \MBS2) deals with elements with quadratic cost functions and uses steepest descent to optimize the solution, as described in Sec. PP5. The data is for the problem of Fig. PP5 and is:

Element	Nodes	D_1	D_2	C_1	C_2
1	1,2	7	14	10	6
2	2,5	5	10	10	6
3	2,5	11	11	10	10
4	1,6	7	14	10	6
5	2,3	6	12	10	6
6	3,5	2	4	10	6
7	5,6	6	12	10	6

The minimum durations D_1 correspond to the original data in Fig. PP5 for which the project cost result is P = 440 and the project time is 24. Including the fixed cost F of Eqn PP10 (= FC in program, read in line 50) with value = 1, this increases P by 24 (i.e. to 464). Note that F = 1 seems a small value but is not totally unrealistic, adding about 5% to the total project cost and larger values simply crash the project to a minimum time solution . The program listing:

```
10 REM CRITICAL PATH METHOD PROGRAM - opt S = - 2.1
20 TOL = .1: REM ACCURACY LIMIT ON TIMES
30 DIM N(10, 3), D(10, 4), C(10, 4), T(10), P(3, 10), G(10)
40 DIM S1(10), F1(10), S2(10), F2(10): REM ES,EF,LS,LF TIMES
50 A$ = "        ": READ NN, NE, FC
60 FOR I = 1 TO 3: FOR J = 1 TO 10
70 P(I, J) = 0: NEXT: NEXT: REM INTITIALIZE PRECEDENCE MATRIX
80 FOR I = 1 TO NE
90 READ N(I, 1), N(I, 2), D(I, 1), D(I, 2), C(I, 1), C(I, 2)
100 NEXT: REM MUST BE IN NUMERICAL ORDER
110 PC = 0: REM INITIALIZE TOTAL PROJECT COST
120 FOR K = 1 TO NN: T(K) = 0: NEXT: REM INITIALIZE LF TIMES FOR NODES
130 FOR K = 1 TO NE: J = N(K, 2): I = 1
140 FOR M = 1 TO 3: IF P(M, J) = 0 THEN GOTO 160
150 I = I + 1: NEXT M: REM COLLECT PRECEEDING ELEMENT
160 P(I, J) = K: NEXT K: REM NUMBERS FOR EACH NODE
170 FOR I = 1 TO NE
180 C1 = D(I, 1) * C(I, 1): C2 = D(I, 2) * C(I, 2): REM MIN & MAX TOTAL COSTS
190 D(I, 3) = (D(I, 1) + D(I, 2)) / 2: REM MEDIAN DURATION
200 DC3 = D(I, 3) * (C(I, 1) + C(I, 2)) / 2 - (C1 + C2) / 2
210 C3 = (C1 + C2) / 2 - DC3: REM MEDIAN TOTAL COST
220 C(I, 1) = C1: C(I, 2) = C2: C(I, 3) = C3
230 DT = .25 * (D(I, 2) - D(I, 1)) * (C(I, 1) - C(I, 2))
240 DEN = C(I, 1) - 2 * C(I, 3) + C(I, 2)
250 IF DEN = 0 THEN DT = 0: IF DEN = 0 THEN 270
260 DT = DT / DEN
270 D(I, 4) = D(I, 3) + DT: REM DURATION FOR MIN COST (EQN 22.31)
280 IF D(I, 1) = D(I, 2) THEN DT = 0: IF D(I, 1) = D(I, 2) THEN 310
290 DT = (D(I, 4) - D(I, 1)) / (D(I, 2) - D(I, 1))
```

```
300 REM NEXT LINE GIVES MIN COST FOR ELEMENT (EQN 5.11)
310 C(I, 4) = C1 * (1 - 3 * DT + 2 * DT * DT) + 4 * C3 * DT * (1 - DT) + C2 * (2 * DT * DT - DT)
320 NEXT I
330 PC = 0
340 FOR I = 1 TO NE: N(I, 3) = 0: NEXT
350 FOR I = 1 TO NN: T(I) = 0: NEXT
360 FOR I = 1 TO NE: S1(I) = 0: F1(I) = 0: S2(I) = 0: F2(I) = 0: NEXT
370 FOR K = 1 TO NE: REM COMMENCE FORWARD PASS
380 I = N(K, 1): J = N(K, 2): S1(K) = T(I): REM S1(K)=ES TIME FOR ELEMENT
390 F1(K) = T(I) + D(K, 4): REM F1(K)=EF TIME FOR ELEMENT
400 IF F1(K) > T(J) THEN T(J) = F1(K): REM INCREASE NODE LF TIME IF NECESSARY
410 PC = PC + C(K, 4)
420 NEXT: REM END FORWARD PASS      **********
430 PC = PC + FC * T(NN)
440 PRINT "JOBTIME = ", T(NN); : PRINT " JOBCOST = ", PC
450 FOR I = 1 TO NE: F2(I) = 1000: NEXT: REM INTITIALIZE LF TIMES
460 FOR K = 1 TO NE: REM COMMENCE BACKWARD PASS %%%%%%%%%
470 R = NE - K + 1: I = N(R, 1): J = N(R, 2): REM MOVE BACWARDS THROUGH ELEMENTS
480 IF J = NN THEN F2(R) = T(NN): REM LF TIME FOR LAST ELEMENT
490 S2(R) = F2(R) - D(R, 4): REM LS = LF - DURATION
500 FOR M = 1 TO 3: S = P(M, I): IF S = 0 THEN GOTO 520
510 IF F2(S) > S2(R) THEN F2(S) = S2(R): REM LF OF PREC ELES = LS OF THIS ELEMENT
520 NEXT
530 IF ABS(F2(R) - F1(R)) < TOL THEN N(R, 3) = 1
540 NEXT K: REM END BACKWARD PASS
550 PRINT "Critical flags: "; : FOR I = 1 TO NE: PRINT N(I, 3); : NEXT
555 PRINT "   Element times follow:"
560 FOR K = 1 TO NE: PRINT S1(K), F1(K), S2(K), F2(K): NEXT
570 TC = -1: REM ELEMENT DURATION INCREMENT
580 FOR I = 1 TO NE: REM COMMENCE GRADIENT CALC. (CRIT. ELES ONLY)
590 IF N(I, 3) = 0 THEN 680
600 ET = D(I, 4) + TC
610 IF ET < D(I, 1) THEN ET = D(I, 1)
620 IF ET > D(I, 2) THEN ET = D(I, 2)
630 IF D(I, 1) = D(I, 2) THEN DT = 0: IF D(I, 1) = D(I, 2) THEN 660
640 DT = (ET - D(I, 1)) / (D(I, 2) - D(I, 1))
650 REM NEXT LINE IS NEW ELEMENT COST (EQN 5.11)
660 EC = C(I, 1) * (1 - 3 * DT + 2 * DT * DT) + 4 * C(I, 3) * DT * (1 - DT) + C(I, 2) * (2 * DT * DT - DT)
670 G(I) = (EC - C(I, 4) + FC * TC) / 1
680 NEXT I
690 REM: NEXT LINE INPUTS TRIAL SEARCH STEP LENGTH (CNTRL C TO STOP)
700 INPUT SN: IF SN <> 0 THEN S = SN: IF SN = 99 THEN END
710 PC2 = PC
720 FOR I = 1 TO NE
730 IF N(I, 3) = 0 THEN 850
740 ET = D(I, 4) - S * G(I): REM NEW ELEMENT TIME
750 IF ET < D(I, 1) THEN ET = D(I, 1)
760 IF ET > D(I, 2) THEN ET = D(I, 2)
770 IF D(I, 1) = D(I, 2) THEN DT = 0: IF D(I, 1) = D(I, 2) THEN 800
780 DT = (ET - D(I, 1)) / (D(I, 2) - D(I, 1))
790 REM NEXT LINE GIVES NEW ELEMENT COST (EQN 5.11)
```

```
800 EC = C(I, 1) * (1 - 3 * DT + 2 * DT * DT) + 4 * C(I, 3) * DT * (1 - DT) + C(I, 2) * (2 * DT * DT -
DT)
810 TC = ET - D(I, 4)
820 PC2 = PC2 + EC - C(I, 4) + TC * FC: REM ADJUST PROJECT COST
830 IF SN = 0 THEN D(I, 4) = ET: REM STORE ELE DURATION IF SEARCH ENDED
840 IF SN = 0 THEN C(I, 4) = EC: REM STORE ELE COST IF SEARCH ENDED
850 NEXT I
860 PRINT PC2
870 IF SN = 0 THEN 330: REM RETURN TO CPA IF SEARCH ENDED
880 GOTO 700: REM CONTINUE SEARCH
890 DATA 6,7,1              : REM DATA FOR TEST PROBLEM
900 DATA 1,2,7,14,10,6
910 DATA 2,5,5,10,10,6
920 DATA 2,5,11,11,10,10
930 DATA 1,6,7,14,10,6
940 DATA 2,3,6,12,10,6
950 DATA 3,5,2,4,10,6
960 DATA 5,6,6,12,10,6
```

Now running the program, the project time is 27.25 and the total cost is P = 459 with the initial minimum element costs and their associated durations (given by Eqns PP6 - 9). After printing this initial solution the program prompts for a *search length* S (with ?) and careful trial with a succession of incremented values is needed to locate a turning point. Note that when a TP is located (P increases) conclude the search with the most successful previous search length to leave the model at that point. In this case the TP is found with search length = -2.1, giving P = 458.1895.

To try a further search now use a zero search length. The program the calculates a new gradient vector (by the usual perturbation, applied only to the critical elements) and again gradually increasing search lengths are tried. In this no reduction in P occurs with a very small S so this is the usual cue to end, which is done by entering S = 99.

Our tiny example problem is relatively 'rigid' in terms of P and project time, but the project schedule is significantly altered. Not surprisingly the CP is not altered.

Conclusion

The techniques described in this chapter all have their place in project and production scheduling and control. Of particular note, however, are the widely used CPM (in which statistical values can easily be included), the flow line method and the LOB method. Group technology is also of interest (note a table equivalent to a matrix yet again) and, of course, control charts and the like are important too, as are the behavioural aspects of production efficiency which we have barely touched upon.

PP References

Ackoff RL, Sasieni MW, Fundamentals of Operations Research, Wiley, NY, 1968.

Enrick, NL, Management Operations Research, Holt Rinhart & Winston, NY, 1965.

Hillier FS, Lieberman GJ, Introduction to Operations Research, 3rd end, Holden-Day, Oakland CA, 1980.

______, A Programmed Introduction to PERT, ITT/Federal Electric Corp., Wiley, NY, 1963.

Mohr WE, Bawden AE, Network Analysis Reference Manual, 6thedn, EPAC P/L, Melbourne, 1974.

Mohr WE, Flowline Reference Manual, EPAC P/L, Melbourne, 1977.

Mohr WE, Project Management and Control, 3rd edn, Dept. of Architecture and Building, Univ. of Melbourne, 1981.

Mohr GA, *Finite Elements for Solids, Fluids, and Optimization,* Oxford University Press, Oxford, 1992.

Mohr GA, Optimization of critical path models using finite elements, Trans Aust. Instn Civil Engrs, vol. CE35(2), p 123, 1994.

Mohr GA, *Elementary Thinking for the 21st Century,* Xlibris, Sydney, 2014.

Neter, J, Wasserman, W, Whitmore, GA, Applied Statistics, Allyn and Bacon, Boston MS, 1978.

Powers MJ, Adams DR, Milles, HD, Computer Information Systems Development: Analysis and Design, South-Western, Cincinnati OH, 1984.

Schmenner RW, Production/Operations Management: Concepts and Situations, 4th edn, MacMillan, NY, 1990.

Smith KM. Critical Path Planning: A Practical Guide, MacDonald, London, 1971.

Wild R, Mass Production Management, Wiley, London, 1972.

Note: most OR books (see OR ref. list) deal with CPM and sometimes one or two ot the other topics in the foregoing chapter.

FINITE METHODS (FM)

Tis best to do a little well and leave the rest to those that follow. Isaac Newton

At many points we have encountered concepts which contribute to the present chapter, including *discrete* probability distributions, the *finite difference method, numerical integration, interpolation functions* and *numerical* and *matrix methods.* In addition we have encountered problems such as network problems like CPM or the shortest route problem in which *elements* are linked to make up the mathematical model.

In Sec. PP12 many of these concepts were combined when quadratic interpolation was applied to elements of CPM networks. Numerical methods involving a forward and backward pass and the use of a precedence matrix were then used to solve the problem, then using the steepest descent method to provide an optimum solution to the CPM problem. In fact this was an application of the increasingly important *finite element method* and this and two related methods are discussed in what follows.

FM1. The Three Finite Methods

Three powerful 'finite methods' have developed and been widely applied relatively recently in mathematical history. These are:

1. The *Finite Difference Method (FDM).* FDM has been around for over 100 years but really only came to prominence with the advent of the electronic computer. Finite differences were introduced in Sec. NM6 and used in Sec. NM10 to form the recurrence relation for a vibration problem.

2. The *Finite Element Method (FEM).* FEM was developed in the mid 1950s to analyse aircraft structures. Since then it has been applied in a very wide range of areas of mathematical modeling and we have already seen application of FEM in Secs NM10 and PP12.

3. The *Boundary Element Method (BEM).* This developed in the late 1970s and can be viewed as a subset of the finite element method (whilst FDM can be viewed as a special case in which each time we calculate a difference for, say, a time interval, then that interval and the points at each end of it can be regarded as an *element* in time).

The mathematical bases of these three methods are compared in Sec. FM2. Before that, however, we shall briefly outline the finite element method and its application to *continuum* problems.

The intuitive origins of FEM

The finite element method was based on matrix method of structural analysis in which 'stiffnesses' of 'lumps' of a continuum (for example a panel of an aircraft shell) were treated in the same way as discrete elements such as columns and beams of a building. Then *element* matrices for these are formed and placed in a *system* matrix for the whole structure, being located in that matrix according to the order of their end or corner nodes, a process we have already seen in Sec. NM10 (and Sec. FM3 gives a better example of FEM for those new to it).

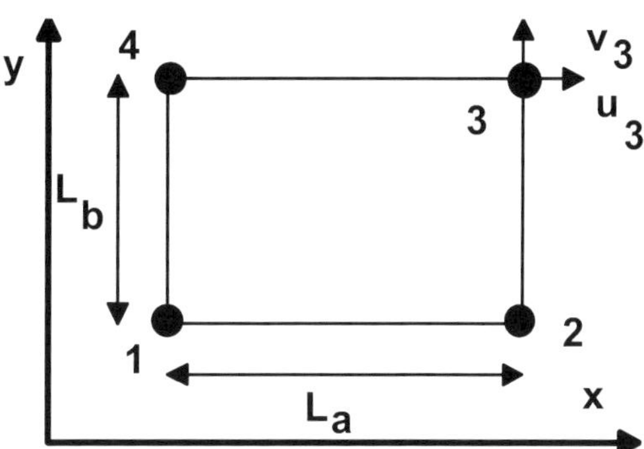

Fig. FM1. Finite element with freedoms u, v at six nodes

Fig. FM1 shows an example, a two dimensional rectangular finite element with four nodes, each with two *degrees of freedom (df)* at each node, these being the displacements *u, v* in the directions of the coordinates *x, y*. Then if the element is stretched towards the right, for example, the *u* values for the RHS nodes will be greater than those on the left, that is, the element is stretched or in *tension.*

Then if we form an 8 x 8 stiffness matrix for this element the *element stiffness matrixes (ESMs)* for many elements can be combined to model complex structures such as panels with cutouts.

Explicit formulation of the ESM for this element is possible but unwieldy but the task can be accomplished numerically with relative ease, as demonstrated for a very elegant *isoparametric* element in Sec. FM9.

For a rectangular element with one freedom (such as a *potential* function) at each corner the element matrix takes the form

$$\text{(FM1)} \qquad k = (1/12)\begin{bmatrix} 4\lambda+4/\lambda & -4\lambda+2/\lambda & -2\lambda-2/\lambda & 2\lambda-4\lambda \\ & 4\lambda+4/\lambda & 2\lambda-4/\lambda & -2\lambda-2/\lambda \\ & & 4\lambda+4/\lambda & -4\lambda+2/\lambda \\ & & & 4\lambda+4/\lambda \end{bmatrix}$$

where $\lambda = L_a/L_b$ and L_a, L_b are the dimensions of the rectangle, as shown in Fig. FM1

Such simple matrices can be used to model pretty well any problem of physical science, for example that of *rectilinear flow* (e.g. of fluid, traffic) in a two dimensional field, as illustrated in Fig. FM2.

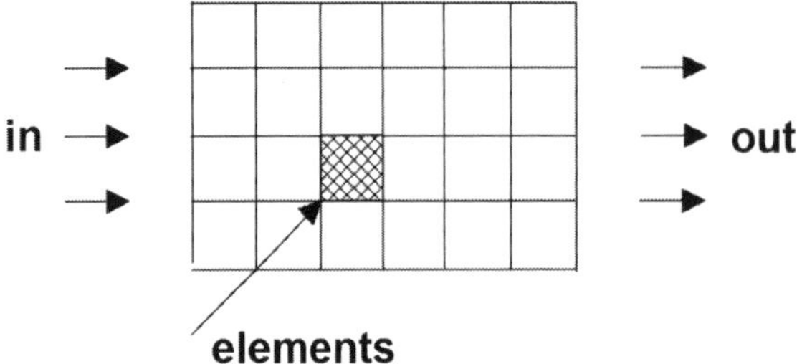

Fig. FM2. 2-D flow problem

Here there are input and output fluxes, as shown, and the problem might be one in which the *permeabilities* differ in the *x* and *y* directions.

FEM analysis of *potential flow* is discussed in Sec. FM10 and a program for it given in the following section.

Conclusion

We have already encountered and used FDM and FEM earlier in the text. In the next section we discuss the mathematical bases of these. In the remainder of the chapter numerous examples are given to demonstrate the usefulness of these methods.

FM2. The FDM, FEM and BEM Methods

In the following section we briefly discuss the three finite methods immediately being able to show how a finite difference *cell* is able to be formed for two dimensional problems. Then the mathematical basis of FEM is briefly discussed and this is employed later in the chapter. Finally, BEM is very briefly discussed.

Finite difference method

In the finite difference method the equations governing the problem are replaced by finite difference expressions at a number of points. Then collecting the resulting equations for a number of *nodes* they are solved simultaneously to find the values of the problem variables at these nodes.

As a two dimensional example consider the partial differential equation (*LaPlace's equation)*

$$\text{(FM2)} \qquad \nabla^2 \phi = \partial^2\phi/\partial x^2 + \partial^2\phi/\partial y^2 = 0 \qquad \phi = \phi(x, y)$$

where ϕ is a two dimensional function and $\nabla^2(\ )$ is called the *Laplacian function* or *operator.* Noting that a partial derivative with respect to *x* involves considering *y* to be constant, we apply the result of Eqn NM43 in both the *x* and *y* directions in the finite difference *cell* shown in Fig. FM3.

Then we obtain for the x direction

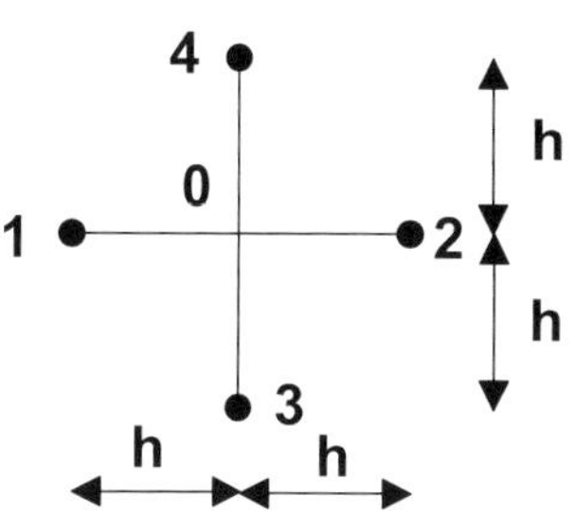

Fig. FM3
Finite difference cell

$$(FM3) \quad \partial^2\phi/\partial x^2 = [(\partial\phi/\partial x)_{02} - (\partial\phi/\partial x)_{10}]/h$$
$$= [(\phi_2 - \phi_0)/h - (\phi_0 - \phi_1/h]/h$$
$$= [\phi_1 - 2\phi_0 + \phi_1]/h^2$$

and similarly for the y direction

$$(FM4) \quad \partial^2\phi/\partial y^2 = [\phi_3 - 2\phi_0 + \phi_4]/h^2$$

so that we can express the LaPlacian operator as

$$(FM5) \quad \nabla^2 \phi = [\phi_1 + \phi_2 - 4\phi_0 + \phi_3 + \phi_4]/h^2$$

Then 2-D problems involving this operator are solved by the following procedure:

1. A grid of nodes is formed for the problem domain.
2. The boundary conditions, that is, the known values of ϕ, are set.
3. Then we solve for the remaining ϕ values by:

(a) Iteration at each node using Gauss-Seidel iteration.
(b) Assembling the equations in the form $K\{\phi\}$€= $\{f\}$ and solving them using Gauss reduction or like techniques.

An example of such a problem is solved in Sec. FM6 and this illustrates the simplicity of FDM for problems governed by relatively complicated partial differential equations.

Finite element method

The finite element method can be applied to some naturally skeletal problems by inspection but, in general, the following procedure is used:

1. In each element an interpolation function of the nodal values is formed:

$$(FM6) \quad \phi = \{f\}^{\tau}\{\phi\}$$

2. This interpolation is substituted into the governing PDE, giving if this is Eqn FM2

$$(FM7) \quad \int[\{f_{xx}\}^t + \{f_{yy})^t]\{\phi\}\, dV = R\ (\simeq 0)$$

where f_{xx} and f_{yy} are the second partial derivatives of the interpolation functions and the PDE is approximately satisfied (leaving a small *residual R*) over the volume *V* of the element.

3. Then the *method of weighted residuals (MWR)* is used, multiplying the residuals for each element by a weighting factor. In the *Galerkin method* the interpolation functions themselves are used as weights so that we obtain

$$(FM8) \quad \int\int \{f\}\,[\{f_{xx}\}^t + \{f_{yy}\}^t]\, dxdy\, \{\phi\} \simeq 0$$

4. Applying *integration by parts* to this result (writing $f = \{f\}$ to simplify the resulting expressions) we obtain

(FM9) $\int\int\{f\}[\{f_{xx}\}^t dxdy = \int f f_x^t\, dy \mid - \int\int f_x f_x^t\, dxdy$

(FM10) $\int\int\{f\}[\{f_{yy}\}^t dxdy = \int f f_y^t\, dy \mid - \int\int f_y f_y^t\, dxdy$

where the first terms on the right sides are boundary forcing terms for the problem.
Then combining Eqns FM9 and FM10 we obtain element equations of the form
(FM11) $k\{\phi\} = \{q\}$

5. These element equations are summed to give system equations of the form
(FM12) $K\{\phi\} = \{Q\}$

and, first setting the boundary conditions or known values of ϕ, these equations are solved to determine the unknown ϕ values at the nodes.

A simple example of the *assembly* of element equations to obtain and solve the system equations is given in the following section whilst numerical calculation of the matrices given by Eqns FM9 and FM10 is described in detail in Sec. FM10.

Boundary element method
In the boundary element method integration by parts is used twice in step (4) above. This 'forces the equations to the boundary' and reduces the order of the derivatives involve in the mathematical model to zero. BEM system equations take the general form

(FM13) $H\{\phi\} - G\{\partial\phi/\partial n\} = \{0\}$

where $\partial\phi/\partial n$ denotes a derivative in the direction normal to the boundary.
In most cases, however, simple approximate boundary matrices can be added to FEM models in the exceptional cases when they are required and BEM is thus generally used only for specialized problems in physics.

Conclusion
For a differential equation of order *n*:

(a) FDM uses approximation of derivatives of order *n*
(b) FEM reduces the order of derivatives to *n*/2
(c) BEM reduces the order of derivatives to zero.

Of these three FEM is the most widely used, one reason being that when Galerkin weighting is used in step (3) above this gives a *least squares* character to the solution which results in greater accuracy (and is mathematically equivalent to the intuitive 'energy' methods originally used in structural analysis applications of FEM).

Then when boundary effects require the addition of special matrices to the system matrix these can be included in the analysis without difficulty. Then for time dependent problems, for example, finite difference methods are often used to form recurrence relations with which the problem is solved by *time stepping* (e.g. see Sec. NM10). In this way, therefore, aspects of all three methods can be combined.

FM3. Simple FEM Flow Problem

In the following section we introduce a simple example of FEM, namely analysis of current flow in a direct current (DC) network. This, however, illustrates many of the basic techniques used in the finite element method very well.

The element equations

Fig. FM4 shows a typical element *n* with resistance *R* and connecting nodes *i* and *j*. Assuming flow into a node is positive we can use Ohm's law (that is drop in voltage or *potential* δV = current x resistance = *CR*) to write

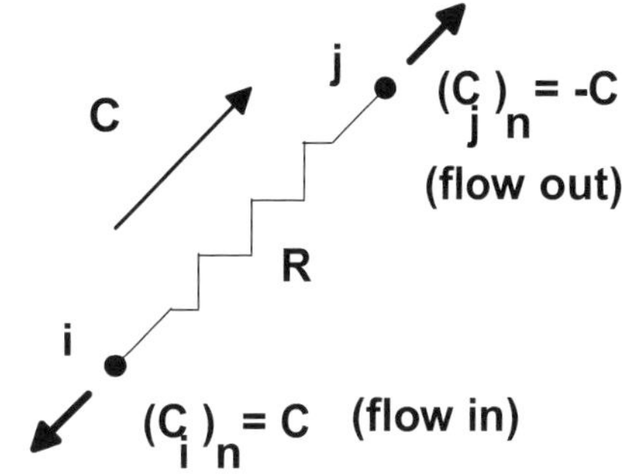

Fig. FM4. Typical resistance element n connecting nodes i and j.

(FM14) $G\delta V = GV_i - GV_j = C = (C_i)_n$

(FM15) $-GV_i + GV_j = -C = (C_j)_n$

where $G = 1/R$ is the *conductance* of the element. Combining Eqns FM14 and FM15 into matrix form we obtain

$$\text{(FM16)} \quad \begin{bmatrix} G & -G \\ G & G \end{bmatrix} \begin{Bmatrix} V_i \\ V_j \end{Bmatrix} = \begin{Bmatrix} (C_i)_n \\ (C_j)_n \end{Bmatrix}$$

(FM17) or $k_e \{ V \} = \{ C_n \}$

where k_e is the element *conductance matrix.*

For the simple network of Fig. FM5, deploying the entries from the element matrices in the system matrix according to the element node numbers, this takes the form

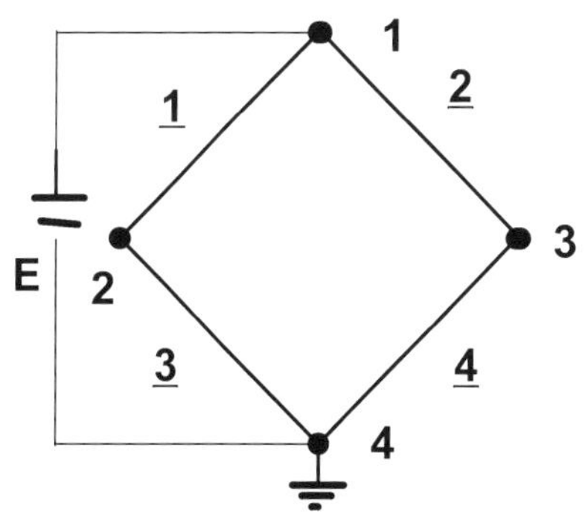

Fig. FM5 DC network problem

$$\text{(FM18)} \quad C = \begin{bmatrix} G_1 + G_2 & -G_1 & -G_2 & 0 \\ -G_1 & G_1 + G_3 & 0 & -G_3 \\ -G_2 & 0 & G_2 + G_4 & -G_4 \\ 0 & -G_3 & -G_4 & G_4 + G_3 \end{bmatrix}$$

and note that that as currents at a node must sum to zero (i.e. no 'leakage', this being Kirchoff's current law) the RHS or 'load' vector of Eqn FM17 will be zero, or we have a 'nothing happening' problem until we deal with the boundary conditions shortly.

This 'summation' or assembly of the element matrices can in this case be simply coded in a program as
(FM19a) C(I,I) = C(I,I) + G
(FM19b) C(I,J) = C(I,J) - G
(FM20a) C(J,I) = C(J,I) - G
(FM20b) C(J,J) = C(J,J) + G
where *I,J* are the node numbers for the element being dealt with and *G* is its conductance.

Solution of the system equations

Then to solve the system equations we first apply the boundary conditions $V_1 = E$ and $V_4 = 0$ using the following procedure:

1. Multiply the columns corresponding to these values by these boundary values and transpose the results to the right side.
2. Remove the corresponding rows and columns on the left side, leaving a one on the diagonal.
3. Place the boundary condition values on the right side.

Doing this in our example problem we obtain

$$\text{(FM21)} \quad \begin{bmatrix} 1 & 0 & 0 & 0 \\ 1 & G_1+G_3 & 0 & 0 \\ 0 & 0 & G_2+G_4 & 0 \\ 0 & 0 & 0 & 1 \end{bmatrix} \begin{Bmatrix} V_1 \\ V_2 \\ V_2 \\ V_2 \end{Bmatrix} = \begin{Bmatrix} E \\ G_1 E \\ G_2 E \\ 0 \end{Bmatrix}$$

giving the solution $V_2 = G_1E/(G_1 + G_3)$ and $V_3 = G_2E/(G_2 + G_4)$.

Note in passing that if we connect a Galvanometer between nodes 2 and 3 we have a Wheatstone bridge and we can easily show using the latter result that for $V_2 = V_3$ (no flow between 2 and 3) we require $R_1/R_3 = R_2/R_4$.

The following program, DCNETQ from \MBS1 on course Basics disc carries out these operations. Data for the present problem is in the simpler program DCNET and DCNETB is the same as DCNETQ with alternative data. The first data line is the number of nodes (NP), elements (NE) and points at which voltage is specified (NS). Then the element node numbers and conductances are read and used to form the system matrix. Finally the specified voltages (the boundary conditions) are read and the simple Gauss-Mohr reduction procedure of Sec. NM4 is used to solve the problem (for the nodal voltages), after which the element currents are calculated (all = 0.5). Note that the program includes calculation of *boundary reactions*. For this purpose boundary conditions rows are not 'zeroed' but kept and -(boundary row) x nodal voltages = boundary reaction, in this case the currents at nodes 1,4 (= +/- 1).

```
5 REM FEM model of distribution networks
7 REM RESTORE 600
10 DIM C(20, 20), V(20), IB(20): A$ = "#": B$ = "######.###"
20 READ NP, NE, NS
100 FOR K = 1 TO NE
110 READ I, J, R
115 IF R = 0 THEN 170
130 C(I, I) = C(I, I) + 1 / R
140 C(I, J) = C(I, J) - 1 / R
150 C(J, I) = C(J, I) - 1 / R
160 C(J, J) = C(J, J) + 1 / R
```

```
170 NEXT
180 FOR K = 1 TO NS
190 READ N, S: IB(N) = 1
200 FOR I = 1 TO NP
205 IF IB(I) = 1 THEN 220
210 V(I) = V(I) - S * C(I, N)
220 NEXT I
230 V(N) = S: NEXT
232 READ NQ, Q
234 IF NQ = 0 THEN 238
235 IF IB(NQ) = 1 THEN 232
236 V(NQ) = V(NQ) + Q: GOTO 232
238 REM
240 FOR I = 1 TO NP
245 IF IB(I) = 1 THEN 340
250 X = C(I, I): V(I) = V(I) / X
260 FOR J = I + 1 TO NP
270 C(I, J) = C(I, J) / X: NEXT
280 FOR K = 1 TO NP
285 IF IB(K) = 1 THEN 330
290 IF K = I THEN GOTO 330
300 X = C(K, I): V(K) = V(K) - X * V(I)
310 FOR J = I + 1 TO NP
320 C(K, J) = C(K, J) - X * C(I, J): NEXT J
330 NEXT K
340 NEXT I
350 PRINT "Node    Potential"
360 FOR I = 1 TO NP
370 PRINT USING A$; I; : PRINT USING B$; V(I): NEXT I
375 PRINT "Flows"
380 FOR I = 1 TO NP
381 IF IB(I) <> 1 THEN 386
382 Q = 0: FOR K = 1 TO NP
383 Q = Q + C(I, K) * V(K): NEXT
385 PRINT USING A$; I; : PRINT USING B$; Q
386 NEXT I
390 RESTORE 400
391 TC = 0: TQ = 0
392 FOR K = 1 TO NE: READ I, J, R: F = 0: IF R = 0 THEN 394
393 F = (V(I) - V(J)) / R
394 PRINT USING A$; I; J; : PRINT " Route flow = ";
PRINT USING B$; F: TC = TC + F * R: TQ = TQ + F: NEXT
396 PRINT "TC = ", TC, " TQ = ", TQ
399 DATA 4,4,2
400 DATA 1,2,1
410 DATA 1,3,1
420 DATA 2,4,1
430 DATA 3,4,1
440 DATA 1,1
450 DATA 4,0
451 DATA 0,0
```

Conclusion

DC networks provide a useful introduction to the finite element method and the simple program given for these illustrates some basic techniques used in programming FEM. As we shall see in Sec. FM6, replacing Ohm's Law by Mohr's Law of Distribution the same program, can be used to model *distribution* problems, as was first discovered with the foregoing program.

FM4. One dimensional flow problem

In this section we study a very simple one dimensional heat flow problem using both the finite element method and the finite difference method, giving a useful comparison of the two methods.

Finite element method

The equation governing steady state anisotropic heat flow is

$$\text{(FM22)} \qquad \partial(\kappa_x \partial T/\partial x)/\partial x \;+\; \partial(\kappa_y \partial T/\partial y)\partial y \;+\; G \;=\; 0$$

where $T = T(x,y)$ is the temperature distribution, κ_x and κ_y are the thermal conductivities in each axial direction and G is the heat generation per unit volume.

Reducing the problem to one dimension with $G = 0$, substituting an interpolation for T, integrating over the element volume and using Galerkin weighting (with the interpolation functions) we obtain

$$\text{(FM23)} \qquad A\kappa \int \{f\}\{f_{xx}\}^t\, dx\, \{T\} \;=\; \{0\}$$

where A is the cross-sectional area of the element. Applying integration by parts to this result gives

$$\text{(FM24)} \qquad A\kappa \int \{f_x\}\{f_x)^t\, dx\, \{T\} \;=\; A\kappa\{f\}\, \partial T/\partial x \;\; |$$

Then using a linear interpolation (of two nodes) we have

$$\text{(FM25)} \qquad \{f\} \;=\; \{1 \,-\, x/L,\; x/L\} \;\text{ and }\; \{f_x\} \;=\; \{-1/L,\; 1/L\}$$

and substituting Eqns FM25 into Eqn FM24 we obtain

$$\text{(FM26)} \qquad (A\kappa/L)\begin{bmatrix} 1 & -1 \\ -1 & 1 \end{bmatrix}\begin{Bmatrix} T_1 \\ T_2 \end{Bmatrix} = A\kappa\begin{Bmatrix} \partial T/\partial x_1 \\ \partial T/\partial x_2 \end{Bmatrix}$$

noting that the presence of the interpolation on the RHS of Eqn FM24 indicates simply that the nodal values of the variable interpolated are used for this boundary term. The resulting terms on the RHS of Eqn FM26 are the *interelement reactions* or fluxes and, like the currents in the problem of Sec. FM3, these sum to zero between elements.

Fig. FM6 shows a simple 1-D heat flow example with only two elements. Then using Eqn FM26 the equations for the system are

$$\text{(FM27)}\quad \begin{bmatrix} 1 & -1 & 0 \\ -1 & 2 & -1 \\ 0 & -1 & 1 \end{bmatrix} \begin{Bmatrix} T_1 \\ T_2 \\ T_3 \end{Bmatrix} = \begin{Bmatrix} 0 \\ 0 \\ 0 \end{Bmatrix}$$

Dealing with the specified temperature at the wall (T_w = T_1 = 1000) in the manner described in Sec. FM3 we obtain the reduced equations

$$\text{(FM28)}\quad \begin{bmatrix} 2 & -1 \\ -1 & 2 \end{bmatrix} \begin{Bmatrix} T_2 \\ T_3 \end{Bmatrix} = \begin{Bmatrix} 100 \\ 0 \end{Bmatrix}$$

yielding the expected results $T_2 = T_3 = 100$ and, if we had put $T_3 = 0$ then the result would have been $T_2 = 50$, again the expected result.

The problem is, though almost trivial, a good example of FEM at its simplest though some of the mathematics involved when we begin with a differential equation will worry some readers. As with the DC network problem of Sec. FM3, however, results such as Eqn FM26 are in fact obvious with very little experience.

Finally, the program FLOW1D in \MBS2 on the course Basics disc is aimed at the foregoing example, adding values corresponding to conductivity at the nodes, if required, to alter the solution. This corresponds to the 'infinity conditions' discussed at the close of the chapter.

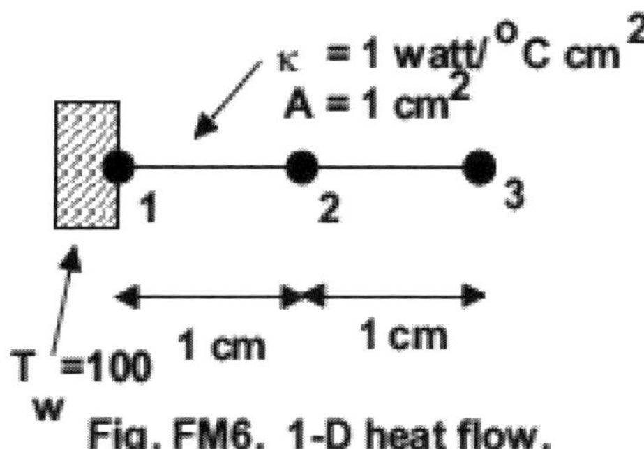

Fig. FM6. 1-D heat flow.

Finite difference method

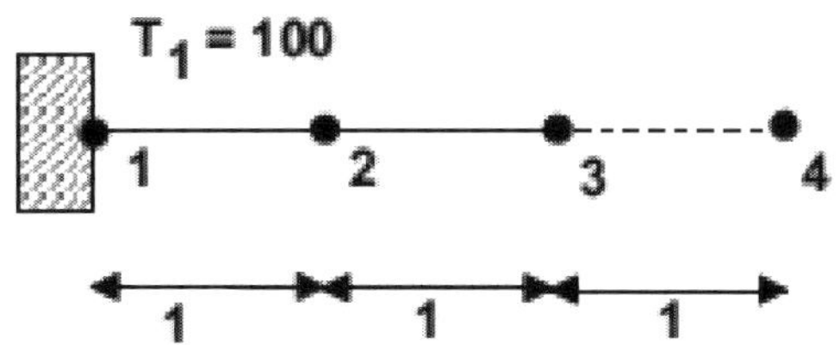

Fig. FM7. Nodes for FDM solution

If we use the finite difference method to solve the problem of Fig. FM6 then, as shown in Fig. FM7, an extra 'dummy node' must be included, as shown.

Then applying Eqn FM3 at node 2 we obtain

$$\text{(FM29)}\quad \partial^2 T/\partial x^2 = (T_1 - 2T_2 + T_3)/h^2 = 0$$

and applying Eqn FM3 at node 3 and combining the results we have

$$\text{(FM30)} \quad \begin{bmatrix} 1 & -2 & 1 & 0 \\ 0 & 1 & -2 & 1 \end{bmatrix} \begin{Bmatrix} T_1 \\ T_2 \\ T_3 \\ T_4 \end{Bmatrix} = \begin{Bmatrix} 0 \\ 0 \end{Bmatrix}$$

Then dealing with the boundary condition $T_1 = 100$ in the usual way (multiplying the corresponding column by this value and transposing the result to the RHS) we also impose the condition $T_3 = T_4$ for a *free boundary.* This is done by adding the column for T_4 to the column for T_3, so that we now have

$$\text{(FM31)} \quad \begin{bmatrix} -2 & 1 \\ 1 & -1 \end{bmatrix} \begin{Bmatrix} T_2 \\ T_3 \end{Bmatrix} = \begin{Bmatrix} -100 \\ 0 \end{Bmatrix}$$

from which we obtain the expected results ($T_2 = T_3 = 100$).

Direct substitution in the differential equation is very straightforward. The disadvantage of FDM, however, is the artifices needed to deal with free boundaries and boundary conditions for the differential equation have to be dealt with to obtain the forcing terms on the RHS of Eqn FM26.

Conclusion

If we begin with a flow law $q = A(dT/dx)$ the element matrix of Eqn FM26 can be written down immediately by analogy with the DC network problem. Then, given the experience of the formal derivation of Eqn FM26, we will know that flux terms are needed on the RHS of the element equations. Then, indeed, FEM solution of flow problems becomes a simple matter.

FM5. 2-D FDM EXAMPLE AND EXTRAPOLATION

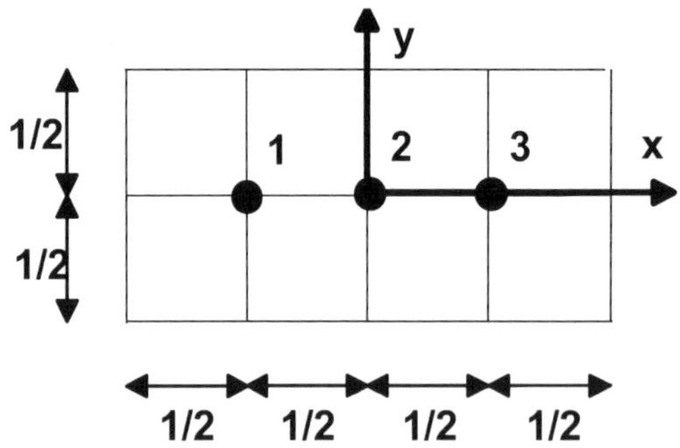

Fig. FM8. Electromagnetic wave guide problem

Fig. FM8 shows the finite difference grid with only three internal nodes for a rectangular wave guide in which the vibrations are governed by the Helmholtz equation, the *transverse electric wave* being given by

$$\text{(FM32)} \quad \nabla^2 \psi + \lambda\psi = 0, \ \ \partial\psi/\partial n = 0 \ \text{ on boundary}$$

this being a *Neumann problem,* and the *transverse magnetic wave* is given by

$$\text{(FM33)} \quad \nabla^2 \phi + \lambda\phi = 0, \ \ \phi = 0 \ \text{ on boundary}$$

and this is a *Dirichlet problem* (named after the type of boundary condition).

We shall deal with the latter so that, with ϕ vanishing on the boundary, we need only determine its values at the three nodes shown in Fig. FM9 for this coarse grid.

Then using the finite difference expression of Eqn FM5 for the Laplacian operator the equations for this problem are

$$\text{(FM34)}\quad \left[(1/h^2)\begin{bmatrix} -1 & 1 & 0 \\ 1 & -4 & 1 \\ 0 & 1 & -4 \end{bmatrix} + \lambda \begin{bmatrix} 1 & 0 & 0 \\ 0 & 1 & 0 \\ 0 & 0 & 1 \end{bmatrix}\right]\begin{Bmatrix} \phi_1 \\ \phi_2 \\ \phi_3 \end{Bmatrix} = \begin{Bmatrix} 0 \\ 0 \\ 0 \end{Bmatrix}$$

where $h = 1/2$ and solving this result for the *eigenvalues* we obtain

$\lambda_1 = 10.343$ (exact = 12.337)
$\lambda_2 = 16$ (exact = 32.067)
$\lambda_3 = 21.657$ (exact = 71.555)

and the exact solutions are shown in parentheses.

Repeating this exercise with $h = 1/4$, requiring 21 internal nodes, the result for λ_1 is 11.846, still some distance from the exact solution but a much improved estimate can be obtained using extrapolation.

h^2 extrapolation

Such processes as the foregoing where accuracy depends on the fineness of the grid or mesh (that is $1/h$) will have a *truncation error* of the order of h^n which we denote as $O(h^n)$.

Then we can write for an approximation of a variable d by two meshes with spacings h_i and h_j ($h_i > h_j$)

(FM35) $d_i = d^* - (\text{constant})h_i^n$

(FM36) $d_j = d^* - (\text{constant})h_j^n$

and eliminating the constant we obtain the extrapolation formula

(FM37) $d^* = d_j + (d_j - d_i)/[(h_i/h_j)^n - 1]$

For the finite difference method the truncation error is *always* of the order $n = 2$, the same result applying for many simpler, lower order finite elements.

Substituting the results for λ_1 with $h = 1/2$ and $h = 1/4$ in the wave guide problem we obtain the estimate

(FM38) $\lambda_1^* = 11.846 + (11.846 - 10.343)/(2^2 - 1) = 12.347$

which is close to the exact solution (12.337), illustrating the importance of extrapolation in connection with numerical approximation procedures.

Conclusion

For certain special problems, such as that of the magnetic wave form in the wave guide problem, FDM is particularly easy to apply. More important here, however, is the extrapolation formula of Eqn FM37 as this has very wide application.

FM6. FEM DISTRIBUTION MODELS

Fig FM9 shows a distribution network for which the data is given in Table FM1.

Table FM1. Distribution problem data

Unit costs			Supplies
5	10	10	110
20	30	20	160
10	20	30	150
140	200	80	
Demands			

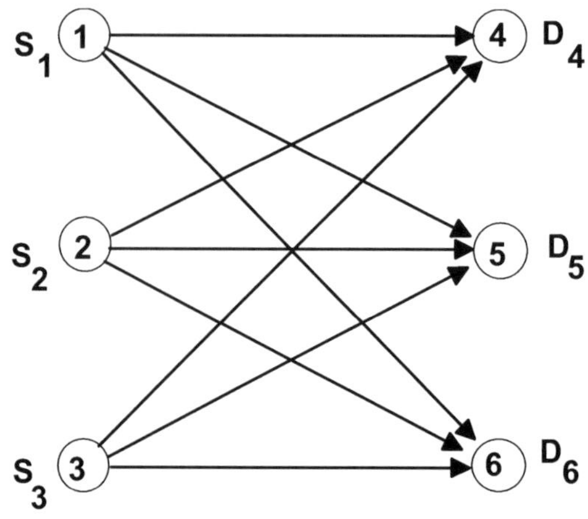

Fig. FM9. Distribution nework

Observing Eqns OR46 - 48 such problems can clearly be solved as linear programming problems using the split constraint technique for 'equality constraints' and one of the simple LP programs or the 'direct LP' method programs for distribution problems given in that chapter. Then the optimum solution (giving minimum total transportation cost, $T = 6700$) has route flows:

(FM39) 15 = 110, 25 = 80, 26 = 80, 34 = 140, 35 = 10

and the number of non zero route flows = (# supply points + # demand points) -1, as is always the case in this type of problem.

Writing this solution in matrix form as

$$(\text{FM40}) \qquad A\{q\} = \begin{bmatrix} 1 & 0 & 0 & 0 & 0 \\ 0 & 1 & 1 & 0 & 0 \\ 0 & 0 & 0 & 1 & 1 \\ 0 & 0 & 0 & 1 & 0 \\ 1 & 1 & 0 & 0 & 1 \\ 0 & 0 & 1 & 0 & 0 \end{bmatrix} \begin{Bmatrix} q_{15} \\ q_{25} \\ q_{26} \\ q_{34} \\ q_{35} \end{Bmatrix} = \begin{Bmatrix} 110 \\ 160 \\ 150 \\ 140 \\ 200 \\ 80 \end{Bmatrix}$$

each route flow can be expressed, using *Mohr's first Law of Distribution*, as a function of the 'potentials' V_i , V_j at each node,

(FM41) $q_{ij} = (V_i - V_j)/c_{ij}$

Taking all $c_{ij} = 1$, we can write the *basis transformation*

$$(\text{FM42}) \qquad \{q\} = \begin{Bmatrix} q_{15} \\ q_{25} \\ q_{26} \\ q_{34} \\ q_{35} \end{Bmatrix} = \begin{bmatrix} 1 & 0 & 0 & 0 & -1 & 0 \\ 0 & 1 & 0 & 0 & -1 & 0 \\ 0 & 1 & 0 & 0 & 0 & -1 \\ 0 & 0 & 1 & -1 & 0 & 0 \\ 0 & 0 & 1 & 0 & -1 & 0 \end{bmatrix} \begin{Bmatrix} V_1 \\ V_2 \\ V_3 \\ V_4 \\ V_5 \\ V_6 \end{Bmatrix} = T\{v\}$$

Substituting Eqn FM42 into Eqn FM40, first reversing the signs of the bottom three rows of A (note that now $A = T^t$), we obtain

$$\text{(FM43)} \quad K\{V\} = AT\{V\} = \begin{bmatrix} 1 & 0 & 0 & 0 & -1 & 0 \\ 0 & 2 & 0 & 0 & -1 & -1 \\ 0 & 0 & 2 & -1 & -1 & 0 \\ 0 & 0 & -1 & 1 & 0 & 0 \\ -1 & -1 & -1 & 0 & 3 & 0 \\ 0 & -1 & 0 & 0 & 0 & 1 \end{bmatrix} \begin{Bmatrix} V_1 \\ V_2 \\ V_3 \\ V_4 \\ V_5 \\ V_6 \end{Bmatrix} = \begin{Bmatrix} 110 \\ 160 \\ 150 \\ -140 \\ -200 \\ -80 \end{Bmatrix} = \{Q\}$$

which is exactly the same result (for K) as obtained by summing element matrices of the form

$$\text{(FM44)} \quad k_{ij} = (1/c_{ij}) \begin{bmatrix} 1 & -1 \\ -1 & 1 \end{bmatrix}$$

(with all c_{ij} =1) for the optimum network (i.e. with only the five flows of Eqn FM39).

So it transpires that we can use the program given in Sec. FM3 to model distribution problems, in other words in exactly the same way as for DC networks by replacing resistance *(R)* by route unit cost c_{ij}. Then the 'loads' are the nodal supplies and demands (with inflow taken as positive), specified as such for each node, and the boundary condition is simply V = 0 at the last node (6 here) as a datum for V.

Modeling the optimum network (5 routes) it is found that the routes can now have any unit costs and the flows remain the same. If all c_i = 10 the nodal potentials turn out to be

(FM45) $V_1 = 300$, $V_2 = 1600$, $V_3 = -600$, $V_4 = -2000$, $V_5 = -800$, $V_6 = 0$

(the latter being the boundary condition) and the 'reaction' at node 6 = -80, as expected. That we can have any costs here corresponds to a *statically determinate structure* in structural mechanics. Here we shall call it a *minimum system.*

If all 9 original routes (with the costs of Table FM1) are included, however, the solution is that shown in Table FM2, with total cost $T = 7313$.

Table FM2. Flow in FEM model

	4	5	6
1	23.4	77.9	8.7
2	52.3	56.9	50.8
3	64.3	65.2	20.5

We now have a very useful means of modeling distribution problems, and using the steepest descent method they can then be optimized, as shown in Sec. FM7.

Indeed the FEM model can be used to obtain 'better than optimal' solutions. In Fig. FM9, for example, if supply at node 1 and demand at node 6 are increased by 20 unit, we obtain route flows: 14 = 130, 25 = 60, 26 = 100, 25 = 100, 34 = 140, 35 = 10
and total cost T is still = 6700, a more efficient result.

Conclusion

We have here perhaps the most important, yet most simple (of those serious), of the powerful finite element method as we could, for example model Internet usage etc.

FM7. OPTIMIZING FEM DISTRIBUTION MODELS

The FEM distribution models developed in Sec. FM6 can be optimized using the method of steepest descent, first defining an *element access* parameter A_{ij},, with initially $A_{ij}^0 = c_{ij}$ at the beginning of each search, the merit function being

(FM46a) $f = T = \Sigma\, c_{ij} q_{ij}$

Using perturbations of each A_{ij}^0 the gradient vector is given by

(FM46b) $\{ g_{ij} \} = \{\delta f / \delta A_{ij} \}$

where $\delta A_{ij} = (M - 1)A_{ij}$
with M a move limit for which the value 1.1 is used for the present application, solving the $K\{ V \} = \{ Q \}$ at each perturbation to determine δf.

Then trial search is conducted with a gradually increasing *search length S*, using

(FM47) $A_{ij}' = A_{ij}^0 - S\{ g \}$

seeking a turning point in f.

If during search a negative route flow is detected we set $c_{ij} = A_{ij} = 0$ for that route and omit it from the model, also setting a flag which returns to calculation of a new gradient vector, the model having changed. Note that such element omission is disallowed during calculation of the gradient vector using Eqn FM46.

Dual models and maximization

Now, quite remarkably, our simple model permits two immediate variations:

1. Simply by using a plus in Eqn FM47 we can obtain maximum solutions.
2. Simply by replacing using c_{ij} in place of $(1/c_{ij})$ as the constitutive parameter for the element matrices we obtain the *dual model.*

Now we can obtain both MIN and MAX solutions for FEM (primal) distribution models and for dual distribution models as well.

Then for the analysis of the dual model (that is with c_{ij} in place of $1/c_{ij}$) we obtain the route flows shown in Table FM3.

Table FM3. Flow in FEM model

	4	5	6
1	29.3	51	29.7
2	68..7	80.3	11
3	42	68.7	39.3

with a total cost $T = 7930$, *and* in place of the voltage values for the primal of Eqn FM45, we have 'nodal currents' (i.e. dual variables of the 'voltage/resistance' type). The values for the dual of the optimum primal network corresponding to Eqns FM47 are

(FM48) $\{ C^* \} = \{ 12.333, 4, 1.833, -12.167, 1.333, 0 \}$

for which the route flows are calculated using Eqn FM41 with c_{ij} replaced by its inverse, giving the expected values of Eqn FM39.

Thus, the nodal current values at nodes 2 and 5 are given by

(FM49) $C^*_2 = C^*_6 + q_{26}/c_{26}$
(FM50) $C^*_3 = C^*_2 - q_{25}/c_{25}$

and so on.

Then the four possible optimum results for the problem of Fig. FM9 are summarized in Table FM4.

Note that some flows are midway between the two possible 'exact' MIN and MAX solutions possessed by this problem shown in the table, these having been obtained using the direct LP method program given in Sec. OR12 (this for MIN) and a similar program for the MAX case. As noted in Sec. OT3, this is because the optimum solution lies on one side of the simplex, not at a node.

Table FM4.

Primal MIN					
S^*	0	0.4	0.7	0.7	
T	7,313	7198	6981	6700	
flows	0, 110, 0 / 45, 35, 80 / 95, 55, 0				
Exact (1)	0, 110, 0 / 0, 80, 80 / 140, 10, 0				
Dual MIN					
S^*	0	0.3	0.9	0.6	
T	7930	7792	7226	6700	
flows	0, 110, 0 / 69.3, 10.7, 80/ 70.7, 79.3, 0				
Exact (2)	0, 110, 0 / 80, 0, 80 / 60, 90, 0				
Primal MAX					
S^*	0	2.0	2.7	1.9	1.6
T	7317	7335	7770	7570	8850
flows	110, 0, 0 / 0, 160, 0 / 30, 40, 80				
Exact (1)	110, 0, 0 / 30, 130, 0 / 0, 70, 80				
Dual MAX					
S^*	0	0.4	0.7	1.1	
T	7930	8112	8495	8850	
flows	110, 0, 0, 27.1, 132.9, 0/2.9, 67.1, 80				
Exact (2)	110, 0, 0 / 0, 160, 0 / 30, 40, 80				

The coding for the program DISTOP (from \MBS2 from the course Basics disc) is as follows. This is an extension of the program given in Sec. FM3 and data input is the same as for this. Search is conducted by simply giving gradually increasing trial search lengths. When an element is omitted (for having negative flow) this is signaled by an additional OP line (giving value of T) and we know to begin a new search. When no more members can be omitted, that is we have a *minimum system,* the solution will not change with further search.

```
5 REM FEM model of distribution networks
10 M = 1.1: Y = .1: REM Lines 115, 150 & 350 are 'case change' lines
15 DIM C(20, 20), V(20), IB(20)
20 DIM RC(20), NN(20, 2), RA(20), SPEC(20), Q(20), G(20)
25 RESTORE 500
30 READ NP, NE, NS
35 FOR k = 1 TO NE
40 READ i, j, R: RC(k) = R: RA(k) = R
45 NN(k, 1) = i: NN(k, 2) = j: NEXT
50 FOR i = 1 TO NS: READ N, s: SPEC(N) = s: IB(N) = 1: NEXT
55 READ NQ, F: IF NQ = 0 THEN GOTO 65
60 Q(NQ) = F: GOTO 55
65 S1 = 0: FOR i = 1 TO NE: RA(i) = RC(i): NEXT: FLAG = 0: GF = 1: s = 0
67 REM Form1.Cls
70 cflag = 1: GOTO 135
72 F1 = TC: PRINT TC: Z = 0
75 Z = Z + 1: IF Z > NE THEN GOTO 102
77 IF RA(Z) = 0 THEN GOTO 100
80 RA(Z) = RA(Z) * M: cflag = 2: GOTO 135
82 RA(Z) = RA(Z) / M
85 REM If M <> 1 Then GoTo 90
87 REM G(z) = 0: GoTo 100
90 G(Z) = (TC - F1) / ((M - 1) * RA(Z))
95 REM ! "Gf",GF
100 GOTO 75
102 GF = 0
105 PRINT "I/P S": INPUT s: IF s = 99 THEN GOTO 295
107 PRINT "S = "; s; "  ";
110 FOR i = 1 TO NE: IF RA(i) = 0 THEN GOTO 125
115 RA(i) = RA(i) + (S1 - s) * G(i): REM + for min, - for max
120 REM If RA(I)<0 then [RA(I)=0:FLAG=1:RC(I)=0]
125 NEXT
130 cflag = 3: GOTO 135
132 S1 = s: F1 = TC: IF FLAG = 1 THEN GOTO 65
133 GOTO 105
135 FOR i = 1 TO NP: V(i) = 0: FOR j = 1 TO NP: C(i, j) = 0: NEXT: NEXT
140 FOR k = 1 TO NE
145 R = RA(k): i = NN(k, 1): j = NN(k, 2)
150 IF R = 0 THEN GOTO 175
152 R = R / 1: REM r/1 for primal
155 C(i, i) = C(i, i) + 1 / R
160 C(i, j) = C(i, j) - 1 / R
165 C(j, i) = C(j, i) - 1 / R
170 C(j, j) = C(j, j) + 1 / R
```

```
175 NEXT
180 FOR k = 1 TO NP: IF IB(k) <> 1 THEN GOTO 215
185 F = SPEC(k)
190 FOR i = 1 TO NP
195 IF IB(i) = 1 THEN GOTO 205
200 V(i) = V(i) - F * C(i, N)
205 NEXT i
210 V(N) = F
215 NEXT
220 FOR i = 1 TO NP: V(i) = V(i) + Q(i): NEXT
225 FOR i = 1 TO NP
230 IF IB(i) = 1 THEN GOTO 285
235 X = C(i, i): IF X = 0 THEN X = 10 ^ -6
237 V(i) = V(i) / X
240 FOR j = i + 1 TO NP
245 C(i, j) = C(i, j) / X: NEXT
250 FOR k = 1 TO NP
255 IF IB(k) = 1 THEN GOTO 280
260 IF k = i THEN GOTO 280
265 X = C(k, i): V(k) = V(k) - X * V(i)
270 FOR j = i + 1 TO NP
275 C(k, j) = C(k, j) - X * C(i, j): NEXT j
280 NEXT k
285 NEXT i
290 GOTO 345
295 PRINT "Node    Potential"
300 FOR i = 1 TO NP
305 PRINT i, V(i): NEXT i
310 PRINT "Flows"
315 FOR i = 1 TO NP
320 IF IB(i) <> 1 THEN GOTO 340
325 F = 0: FOR k = 1 TO NP
330 F = F + C(i, k) * V(k): NEXT
335 PRINT i, F
340 NEXT i
345 TC = 0: TQ = 0
350 FOR k = 1 TO NE: R = RC(k): F = 0: A = RA(k): IF A = 0 THEN GOTO 370
352 A = A / 1: REM a/1 for primal
355 i = NN(k, 1): j = NN(k, 2): F = (V(i) - V(j)) / A
360 IF GF = 1 THEN GOTO 370
365 IF F >= 0 THEN GOTO 370
367 RA(k) = 0: RC(k) = 0: FLAG = 1
370 IF s <> 99 THEN GOTO 374
372 PRINT NN(k, 1), NN(k, 2), " route flow = ", F: GOTO 375
374 IF s <> 0 THEN PRINT CINT(F * 100) / 100;
375 TC = TC + F * R: TQ = TQ + F: NEXT
380 IF s = 0 THEN GOTO 385
382 PRINT " TC = "; TC; " TQ = "; TQ
385 IF FLAG = 1 THEN GOTO 65
386 IF s = 99 THEN GOTO 400
387 IF cflag = 1 THEN GOTO 72
388 IF cflag = 2 THEN GOTO 82
```

```
399 IF cflag = 3 THEN GOTO 132
400 END
500 DATA 6,9,1
505 DATA 1,4,5
510 DATA 1,5,10
515 DATA 1,6,10
520 DATA 2,4,20
525 DATA 2,5,30
530 DATA 2,6,20
535 DATA 3,4,10
540 DATA 3,5,20
545 DATA 3,6,30
550 DATA 6,0
555 DATA 1,110
560 DATA 2,160
565 DATA 3,150
570 DATA 4,-140
575 DATA 5,-200
580 DATA 0,0
```

The data appended is for the problem of Fig. FM9, for which the solution shown in Table FM3 can be obtained with the searches used there. Note that these S^* are the optimum search lengths which were determined by trial with a gradually increasing S until a member is eliminated. Use of excessively large S will abort the process so a certain amount of trial is required.

An alternative approach using a simple iterative method is given in Sec. FM8.

FM8. Flow Ratio Design for Distribution Networks

In the present section we tackle the task of Sec. FM7, that is, optimization of FEM primal and dual distribution models using an *optimality criterion method (OCM).* Whilst less accurate than the already approximate (but often exact) results with steepest descent such, such iterative methods are easy to use and very widely applicable and might often be used very successfully to obtain 'better' solutions in situations were an optimum solution cannot even be defined, must less obtained,

Stress ratio design

The best known OCM method is *fully stressed design (FSD) in structural mechanics* (of materials), where, most easily visualized, a roof type truss is optimized by iterating a FEM analysis similar to that for DC networks in Sec. FM3, solving for the horizontal and vertical displacements under load at each node (or joint). Then the member stresses are calculated from these in much the same ways as the distribution flows in Eqn FM41. Then the member cross sectional areas are adjusted according to:

$$A_i^* = (\text{new stress/stress limit})A_i$$

where 'stress limit' is some limiting permissible stress for the material.

In the present context, essentially a flow problem, there is no flow limit, though we could tackle the problem that way.

We find a new approach, however, by adjusting the element units costs at each iteration using *Mohr's second (optimality criterion) law of distribution:*

(FM51) $c_{ij}{}^* = R\, c_{ij}$

where $R = (q_m / \mid q_{ij} \mid)$ is the 'flow ratio'
q_m is the 'median flow' $\approx q_{av}/2$
$q_{av} = Q/N$
where $Q = \Sigma\, q_{ij}$ is the total flow in the network of N routes.

Then to obtain the minimum solution lower and upper costs limits

(FM52) $c_L = c_{av}/40 \rightarrow c_{av}10, \quad c_U = 10^6$

where $c_{av} = \Sigma\, c_{ij}/N$.

Observing these limits iteration proceeds and some routes vanish as their costs approach the upper limit, resulting in very small flows, flows less than 0.001 being set to zero prior to calculating the total distribution cost

(FM53) $T = \Sigma \mid q_{ij} \mid (c_{ij})_0$

where $(c_{ij})_0$ are the initial costs for each route (these are kept, along with the 'new' values produced by iteration.

The iteration process is now very simple, routes simply dropping out one by one until there is no further change in the solution, when we have a *minimal system.*

Dual problem and maxima

Again the dual FEM model is formed by using c_{ij} instead of its reciprocal as the element parameter and to seek a MAX solution (of either the primal or dual model) we simply use the inverse of R in Eqn FM51.

Demonstration program

The following is the listing of a simple demonstration program which handles only MIN of the primal problem. Data is for the problem of Fig. FM9 and 12 iterations produces the exact MIN solution. Generally, however, one can only hope for solution 'close' to the MIN and for large problems this may take quite a few iterations for the primal MAX or dual MIN (as for these we have 'further to go').

The q_m value is coded in the program (line after line 22) and not read as data.

The changes required to use the dual problem or seek MAX solutions are very simple, as noted above,

Note that with the use of this simple program *Mohr's third (equality principle) law* of distribution is discovered, namely that in the minimum solution for the system the costs of the (remaining) elements will all (or nearly all) = c_L, whilst in the dual problem the cost will all = c_U. The equality in final costs (after iteration) is reminiscent of fully stressed design and thus Michell's classical (1905) 'equal strain' condition, but now we have a problem of an economic nature, so our discovery is clearly of great importance and we might even begin to wonder why the quality principle would not have almost universal application.

```
0 REM FSD (by iteration) of FEM distribution model
1 N = 20: DIM C(N, N), A(N), B(N), D(N), Q(N), V(N)
2 I = 3: J = 3: T = 0: G = 1000: N = I + J: E = I * J: A$ = "#########.#####"
3 FOR K = 1 TO I: FOR L = 1 TO J: M = (K - 1) * I + L
4 A(M) = K: B(M) = I + L: READ R(M): D(M) = R(M): NEXT: NEXT
5 FOR K = 1 TO N - 1: READ Q(K): NEXT K: Q(N) = 0
6 FOR I = 1 TO N: FOR J = 1 TO N: C(I, J) = 0: NEXT: NEXT
7 FOR K = 1 TO E: I = A(K): J = B(K): X = 1 / R(K)
8 C(I, I) = C(I, I) + X: C(I, J) = C(I, J) - X
9 C(J, I) = C(J, I) - X: C(J, J) = C(J, J) + X: NEXT
10 FOR K = 1 TO N: V(K) = Q(K): NEXT
11 FOR I = 1 TO N - 1
12 X = C(I, I): V(I) = V(I) / X
13 FOR J = I + 1 TO N: C(I, J) = C(I, J) / X: NEXT
14 FOR K = 1 TO N - 1: IF K = I THEN 17
15 X = C(K, I): V(K) = V(K) - X * V(I)
16 FOR J = I + 1 TO N: C(K, J) = C(K, J) - X * C(I, J): NEXT
17 NEXT K: NEXT I
18 FOR I = 1 TO N: PRINT I; : PRINT USING A$; V(I): NEXT
19 T1 = 0: T2 = 0: T3 = 0: T = T + 1
20 FOR K = 1 TO E: X = R(K)
21 F = (V(A(K)) - V(B(K))) / X
22 Y = ABS(F): IF Y < .001 THEN F = 0: GOTO 24
  Z = R(K) * 25 / Y
23 IF Z > 10 ^ 6 THEN Z = 10 ^ 6
  IF Z < 1 THEN Z = 1
  R(K) = Z
24 PRINT A(K); B(K); : PRINT USING A$; F; R(K)
25 Y = ABS(F): T1 = T1 + X * Y: T2 = T2 + Y: T3 = T3 + Y * D(K): NEXT
26 PRINT USING A$; T1; T2; T3: PRINT " Itns = "; : PRINT USING "#####"; T
27 INPUT X: IF X = 99 THEN END
  GOTO 6
28 DATA 5,10,10,20,30,20,10,20,30
29 DATA 110,160,150,-140,-200
```

FM9. THE QUADRATIC TRIANGLE ELEMENT

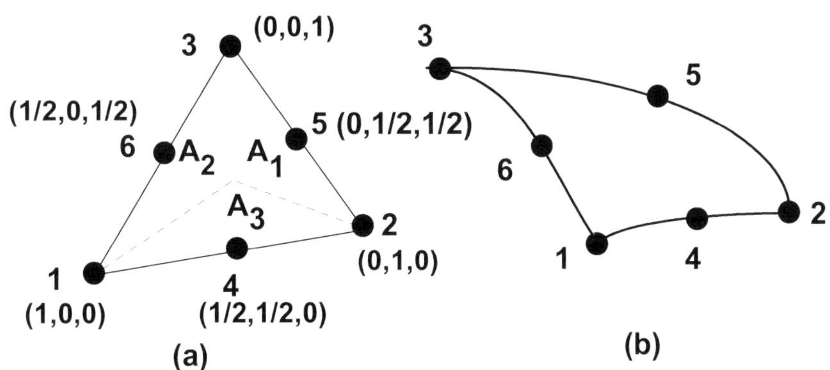

Fig. FM10. (a) Quadratic triangle element showing area coordinates of nodes; (b) mapped isoparametrically.

Fig. FM10 shows one of the most useful finite elements, a triangular element with six nodes, three of these at the mid-points of the sides. Using a process called *isoparametric mapping* the element can have the curved sides shown in Fig. FM10(b), making it particularly useful.

Area coordinates

For triangular elements it is useful to define *area coordinates* for any point in the element using the ratios of the areas shown in Fig. FM10(a) to the total area A of the element. After a little algebraic manipulation it can be shown that the area coordinates L_1, L_2, L_3 are given by

$$\text{(FM54a)} \quad L_1 = A_1/A = (a - y_{32}x + x_{32}y)/2A$$

$$\text{(FM54b)} \quad L_2 = A_2/A = (a - y_{13}x + x_{13}y)/2A$$

$$\text{(FM54c)} \quad L_3 = A_3/A = (a - y_{21}x + x_{21}y)/2A$$

where $a = 2A/3$ and $2A = x_{21}y_{32} - x_{32}y_{21}$ with

$$y_{32} = x_3 - x_2, \quad x_{13} = x_1 - x_3, \quad x_{21} = x_2 - x_1$$

$$y_{32} = y_3 - y_2, \quad y_{13} = y_1 - y_3, \quad y_{21} = y_2 - y_1$$

and the reader can verify that Eqns FM54 give the nodal coordinates shown in Fig. FM10a. From the nature of the definition of the area coordinates the identity

$$\text{(FM55)} \quad L_1 + L_2 + L_3 = 1$$

also follows.

Interpolation

To develop an interpolation for the element we begin by writing the interpolation polynomial in terms of a vector of modes { M } and modal amplitudes { c }

$$\text{(FM56)} \quad \phi = \{c\}^t\{M\} = c_1L_1^2 + c_2L_2^2 + c_3L_3^2 + c_4L_1L_2 + c_5L_2L_3 + c_6L_3L_1$$

and substituting the areal coordinates of the nodes we obtain

$$\text{(FM57)} \qquad \{\phi\} = \begin{Bmatrix} \phi_1 \\ \phi_2 \\ \phi_3 \\ \phi_4 \\ \phi_5 \\ \phi_6 \end{Bmatrix} = \begin{bmatrix} 1 & 0 & 0 & 0 & 0 & 0 \\ 0 & 1 & 0 & 0 & 0 & 0 \\ 0 & 0 & 1 & 0 & 0 & 0 \\ 1/2 & 1/2 & 0 & 1/2 & 0 & 0 \\ 0 & 1/2 & 1/2 & 0 & 1/2 & 0 \\ 1/2 & 0 & 1/2 & 0 & 0 & 1/2 \end{bmatrix} \begin{Bmatrix} c_1 \\ c_2 \\ c_3 \\ c_4 \\ c_5 \\ c_6 \end{Bmatrix} = C\{c\}$$

Inverting the matrix C (alternatively Eqns FM57 are easily solved by elimination) the interpolation functions $\{f\}$ for the interpolation

$$\phi = \{f\}^t(\phi\}$$

are given by

$$\{f\}^t = \{M\}^t C^{-1} = \{M\}^t \begin{bmatrix} 1 & 0 & 0 & 0 & 0 & 0 \\ 0 & 1 & 0 & 0 & 0 & 0 \\ 0 & 0 & 1 & 0 & 0 & 0 \\ -1 & -1 & 0 & 4 & 0 & 0 \\ 0 & -1 & -1 & 0 & 4 & 0 \\ -1 & 0 & -1 & 0 & 0 & 4 \end{bmatrix}$$

yielding the results

$$f_1 = L_1^2 - L_1L_2 - L_3L_1 = L_1(2L_1 - 1)$$

$$f_2 = L_2(2L_2 - 1), \quad f_3 = L_3(2L_2 - 1)$$

$$f_4 = 4L_1L_2, \quad f_5 = 4L_2L_3, \quad F_6 = 4L_3L_1$$

using the identity of Eqn FM55 to simplify the results for f_1, f_2 and f_3. These area coordinate functions are much simpler than the Cartesian formulas obtained by substituting Eqns FM54 into Eqns FM57.

Isoparametric mapping

Using the area coordinate interpolation functions we can now calculate the derivatives using the interpolation matrix

$$\text{(FM58)} \; S = \begin{Bmatrix} \partial(\;)/\partial L_1 \\ \partial(\;)/\partial L_2 \end{Bmatrix} = \begin{bmatrix} 4L_1 - 1 & 0 & 4L_1 + 4L_2 - 3 & 4L_2 & -4L_2 & 4 - 8L_1 - 4L_2 \\ 0 & 4L_2 - 1 & 4L_1 + 4L_2 + -3 & 4L_1 & 4 - 4L_1 - 8L2 & -4L_1 \end{bmatrix}$$

using the identity of Eqn FM55 to eliminate L_3.

Then the Cartesian derivatives are related to these local derivatives by

$$\text{(FM59)} \qquad \begin{Bmatrix} \partial\phi/\partial L_1 \\ \partial\phi/\partial L_2 \end{Bmatrix} = \begin{bmatrix} \partial x/\partial L_1 & \partial y/\partial L_1 \\ \partial x/\partial L_2 & \partial y/\partial L_1 \end{bmatrix} \begin{Bmatrix} \partial\phi/\partial x \\ \partial\phi/\partial y \end{Bmatrix}$$

and the connecting matrix is the *Jacobian matrix J.* This can be calculated numerically at each integration point (using numerical integration to form the element equations) using the matrix of Eqn FM58:

$$(FM60) \qquad J = S[\{x\} \ \{y\}]$$

so that the interpolation for the Cartesian derivatives is given by

$$(FM61) \qquad \begin{Bmatrix} \partial\phi/\partial x \\ \partial\phi/\partial y \end{Bmatrix} = J^{-1} S\{\phi\} = T\{\phi\}$$

and this process is easily coded in the program of Sec. FM11.

Numerical integration

The appropriate numerical integration when first derivatives of the interpolation functions are used to form the element equations is simply at the three midside nodes. This exactly integrates terms of the form $\int L_1^2$, as required, so that we calculate contributions to the element matrix which take the form

$$(FM62) \qquad \int\int\{f_x)\{f_x\}^t dxdy$$

as

$$(FM63) \qquad {}_{i-1}\Sigma^3 \; T_1 T_2^t \; |J|_{abs} \, \omega_i/2 \qquad \omega_i = 1/3$$

where T_i denotes row 1 of the matrix T obtained in Eqn FM61 and $|J|_{abs}$ gives approximately twice the element area as Eqn FM59 suggests.

Then to calculate finite element matrices for the quadratic triangle element an integration loop is required by Eqn FM63 and in this loop Eqn FM58 is coded literally and this result used to calculate the Jacobian matrix using Eqn FM60. The matrix T is formed numerically using Eqn FM61 and the result used in Eqn FM63 to calculate the terms required for the element matrices by equations like Eqns FM9 and FM10.

Conclusion

Using areal coordinates the interpolation functions for the quadratic triangle are much simplified. Then use of the numerically calculated Jacobian matrix at each integration point allows the element to have curved (quadratic) sides, greatly simplifying element formulation as well.

FM10. FEM Analysis of Potential Flow

In the following section we develop the equations required to form mathematical models of potential flow problems. Using the results of Sec. FM9 we are then able to use finite elements to analyse potential flow problems.

Potential flow

In potential flow the flow pattern is represented by *orthogonal* sets of curves (that is, intersecting at right angles) for the values of a *potential function* ϕ and a *stream function* ψ. In terms of these functions the velocities of flow are given by

$$\text{(FM64)} \quad u = -\partial\phi/\partial x, \quad v = -\partial\phi/\partial y$$

$$\text{(FM65)} \quad u = \partial\psi/\partial y, \quad v = -\partial\psi/\partial x$$

and the contours of the stream function are the *streamlines* of flow whilst the orgthogonal contours of the potential function are those of the *potential* of the flow. We will use the potential function approach as it is more appropriate for our present purposes (e.g. we have already defined a 'potential' in FEM distribution models).

Eqns FM65 already satisfy the *continuity condition*

$$\text{(FM66)} \quad \partial u/\partial x + \partial v/\partial y = 0$$

this ensuring conservation of matter as it states that for a control volume *dydy* 'flow in = flow out.'

Potential flow must also satisfy the *irrotationality condition*

$$\text{(FM67)} \quad \omega_z = (\partial v/\partial x - \partial u/\partial y)\hat{k} = 0$$

where ω_z = is the vorticity, being a vector with the direction of $\hat{k}$, the unit vector perpendicular to the plane.

Then substituting Eqns FM64 into Eqn FM66 we obtain the governing equation for the problem

$$\text{(FM68)} \quad \nabla^2 \phi = \partial^2\phi/\partial^2 x^2 + \partial^2\phi/\partial y^2 = 0$$

namely LaPlace's equation.

Finite element interpolation

Substituting the interpolation $\phi = \{f\}^t\{\phi\}$ into Eqn FM68 we obtain

$$\text{(FM69)} \quad \int\int\{f\}[\{f_{xx}\}^t + \{f_{yy}\}^t]\, dxdy\, \{\phi\} = \{0\}$$

using Galerkin weighting with the interpolation functions and integrating over the element volume (assuming the element has constant thickness = 1).

Then applying integration by parts to both terms on the left of Eqn FM69 the results of Eqns FM9 and FM10 are obtained so that the element equations are given by

(FM70) $k\{\phi\} = \{q\}$

where

(FM71) $k = \int[\{f_x\}\{f_x\}^t + \{f_y\}\{f_y\}^t]dxdy$

(FM72) $\{q\} = \int\{f\}\{f_x\}^t\{\phi\}dy + \int\{f\}\{f_y)^t\{\phi\}dx$

The forcing terms of Eqn FM72 can be simplified by transforming to the normal and tangential axes at the boundary shown in Fig. FM11. Then denoting

$c_x = \cos\alpha$ and $c_y = \sin\alpha$

we can write, assuming all *direction cosines* positive (an artifice used by Mohr to ensure that $\int ds$ around the boundary yields a positive result)

(FM73a) $dx/dn = c_x, \quad dy/dn = c_y$

(FM73b) $dx/ds = c_y, \quad dy/ds = c_x$

Using Eqns FM73b in Eqn FM72 we obtain

$$(FM74) \quad \{q\} = \int\{f\}[c_x\phi_x + c_y\phi_y]ds$$
$$= -\int\{f\}[c_x u + c_y v]ds$$

including the definitions of Eqns FM64 to obtain the final result.

Then the element matrices are obtained by using Eqns FM61 and FM63 to evaluate Eqn FM71 by numerical integration and a short program which does this is given in Sec. FM11.

Rectilinear flow

Fig. FM11 shows a finite element mesh for the rectilinear flow problem. To force the flow loads = 1 or 1/2 are specified at inlet and ϕ = 0 is set as a datum at outlet.

Then for this simple problem the results will be those expected, namely

(FM80) $u = -\partial\phi/\partial x = -1, \quad \phi_{in} = QL/H$

where $Q = \Sigma\, q_\phi$ at inlet, are obtained.

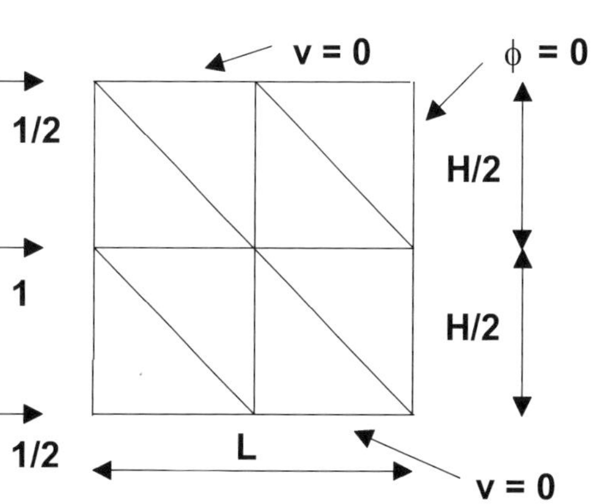

Fig. FM11. Rectilinear flow

The problem is simple but with the use of FEM irregular domains, sources and sinks etc. can be dealt with simply by the addition of a line or two of data and a program for this purpose is given in Sec. FM11.

FM11. Program for potential flow

The following program (PFMGUV in \MBS2 on the course Basics disc, where the alternative programs QBPOTF, QFLOW and SINKFL can be found, with alternative data) uses the 6 node isoparametric triangular element described in Sec. FM9 to solve potential flow problems.

It automatically generates the mesh (with the diagonals 'one-way' as in Fig. FM11) for a rectangular domain, given the dimensions of this. After obtaining the solution for the nodal potentials these are used to calculate the velocities (= the gradients of the potentials) at the nodes, then calculating average nodal velocities = sum of velocities calculated in the N elements impinging at the node (the *nodal valency*) divided by N.

Data is read as

Line 1: # nodes = NP, # elements = NE, # b.c. nodes = NB, # symmetry conditions = CN, half band width = BW = max value of (max node # - min node # + 1) for an element.

Line 2: # grid lines in X direction = NX, # grid lines in Y direction, domain size in X direction = XLIM, domain size in Y direction = YLIM

NB lines: number of set values for potential function

CN lines: read 'nodal connection conditions' (not used - these are to enforce symmetry - so that we model only half or a quarter of a problem)

Loads: nodal loads - terminate with a 0,0 line.

The first 3 data sets are meshes for a source and sink problem (+/- 10 at two interior points). The first of these has a REM line for possible use to model the rectilinear flow problem (here with potential set, not loads, at inlet).

The last data set is for the distribution problem of Fig. FM9 posed as a two dimensional problem.. In this node number sets are read in for 4 of the 8 elements to form a 'two-way' (re. the diagonals) mesh, and to allow this remove the REM in lines 112 and 113.

```
5 REM Potential Flow Program
10 UDL = 0: RESTORE 600
15 DIM CORD(90, 2), EM(6, 6), S(90, 90), Q(90), XY(6, 2), NOP(40, 6), SI(90, 90)
20 DIM CI(6, 2), DL(2, 6), TJ(2, 2), T(2, 6), IB(90), EV(6), NCN(90), U(90), V(90)
25 REM ***** Integration at midside nodes
30 CI(1, 1) = 1: CI(1, 2) = 0: CI(2, 1) = 0: CI(2, 2) = 1: CI(3, 1) = 0: CI(3, 2) = 0
35 CI(4, 1) = .5: CI(4, 2) = .5: CI(5, 1) = 0: CI(5, 2) = .5: CI(6, 1) = .5: CI(6, 2) = 0
40 READ NP, NE, NB, CN, BW
45 READ NX, NY, XLIM, YLIM
50 NEX = NX - 1: NEY = NY - 1: DX = XLIM / NEX: DY = YLIM / NEY
55 FOR I = 1 TO NX: FOR J = 1 TO NY: NN = NY * (I - 1) + J
60 CORD(NN, 1) = DX * (I - 1): CORD(NN, 2) = DY * (J - 1): NEXT: NEXT
65 NEX = (NX - 1) / 2: NEY = (NY - 1) / 2
```

```
70 FOR I = 1 TO NEX: FOR J = 1 TO NEY
75 NI = (I - 1) * 2 * NY + (J - 1) * 2 + 1: NJ = NI + 2 * NY
80 NS = NEY * (I - 1) + J: NN = 2 * NS - 1
85 NOP(NN, 1) = NI: NOP(NN, 2) = NJ: NOP(NN, 3) = NI + 2
90 NOP(NN, 4) = NI + NY: NOP(NN, 5) = NOP(NN, 4) + 1: NOP(NN, 6) = NI + 1
95 NN = 2 * NS
100 NOP(NN, 1) = NI + 2: NOP(NN, 2) = NJ: NOP(NN, 3) = NJ + 2
105 NOP(NN, 4) = NOP(NN - 1, 5): NOP(NN, 5) = NJ + 1: NOP(NN, 6) = NOP(NN - 1, 4) + 2
110 NEXT: NEXT
112 REM Read NN:For J=1 to 6:Read NOP(NN,J):Next:If NN=0 then 115
113 REM Goto 112      :Rem These two lines to make mesh '2-way'
115 FOR L = 1 TO NE: REM ####### LOOP ON ELEMENTS
120 FOR I = 1 TO 6: K = NOP(L, I)
125 XY(I, 1) = CORD(K, 1): XY(I, 2) = CORD(K, 2)
130 FOR J = 1 TO 6: EM(I, J) = 0: NEXT: NEXT
135 FOR IP = 4 TO 6
140 F1 = 4 * CI(IP, 1): F2 = 4 * CI(IP, 2)
145 GOSUB 510
150 F = ABS(DJ) / 6
155 FOR K = 1 TO 3: NK = NOP(L, K + 3): Q(NK) = Q(NK) + F * UDL / 3: NEXT
160 FOR I = 1 TO 6: FOR J = 1 TO 6
165 EM(I, J) = EM(I, J) + F * (T(1, I) * T(1, J) + T(2, I) * T(2, J)): REM EQN 7.18
170 NEXT: NEXT
175 NEXT IP: REM END NUMERICAL INTEGRATION LOOP *************************
180 FOR I = 1 TO 6: NR = NOP(L, I)
185 FOR J = 1 TO 6: NC = NOP(L, J)
190 S(NR, NC) = S(NR, NC) + EM(I, J): NEXT: NEXT: REM ADD k TO SYSTEM MATRIX
195 NEXT L: REM END LOOP ON ELEMENTS ####################################
200 FOR I = 1 TO NP: FOR J = 1 TO NP
205 SI(I, J) = S(I, J): NEXT: NEXT
210 FOR L = 1 TO NB: REM LOOP BOUNDARY CONDITION NODES
215 READ N, F: IB(N) = 1: Q(N) = F
220 FOR I = 1 TO NP
225 IF IB(I) = 1 THEN 235
230 Q(I) = Q(I) - F * S(I, N)
235 NEXT I
240 Q(N) = F: NEXT L
245 FOR I = 1 TO CN: READ N1, N2
250 FOR K = 1 TO NP
255 S(K, N1) = S(K, N1) + S(K, N2)
260 NEXT
265 S(N2, N2) = 1: Q(N2) = 99: NEXT
270 READ NQ, F
275 IF NQ = 0 THEN 290
280 IF IB(NQ) = 1 THEN 270
285 Q(NQ) = Q(NQ) + F: GOTO 270
290 REM 245 - 265 FOR = B.C.s & 270 - 285 FOR LOADS
295 FOR I = 1 TO NP
300 IF IB(I) = 1 THEN 360
305 X = S(I, I): Q(I) = Q(I) / X: REM X=PIVOT
310 J2 = I + BW: IF J2 > NP THEN J2 = NP
315 FOR J = I + 1 TO J2
```

```
320 S(I, J) = S(I, J) / X: NEXT J: REM ROW/PIVOT
325 FOR K = 1 TO J2: IF K = I THEN GOTO 355
330 IF IB(K) = 1 THEN 355
335 X = S(K, I): IF X = 0 THEN 355
340 Q(K) = Q(K) - X * Q(I)
345 FOR J = I + 1 TO J2
350 S(K, J) = S(K, J) - X * S(I, J): NEXT J: REM ROW SUBTRACTION OPERATION
355 NEXT K
360 NEXT I
365 PRINT "Nodal Stream Function Values"
370 FOR I = 1 TO NP
375 PRINT USING "#####"; I; : PRINT USING "#######.#####"; Q(I)
380 NEXT
383 INPUT ZZ
385 PRINT "Boundary Flows"
390 FOR I = 1 TO NP
395 IF IB(I) <> 1 THEN 420
400 F = 0: FOR K = 1 TO NP
405 F = F + S(I, K) * Q(K)
410 NEXT
415 PRINT USING "#####"; I; : PRINT USING "#######.#####"; F
420 NEXT I
425 REM
430 FOR I = 1 TO NP: NCN(I) = 0: U(I) = 0: V(I) = 0: NEXT
435 FOR I = 1 TO NE: FOR J = 1 TO 6
440 NN = NOP(I, J): NCN(NN) = NCN(NN) + 1: NEXT: NEXT
445 FOR EN = 1 TO NE
450 FOR I = 1 TO 6: K = NOP(EN, I)
455 XY(I, 1) = CORD(K, 1): XY(I, 2) = CORD(K, 2): EV(I) = Q(K): NEXT
460 FOR NL = 1 TO 6: N = NOP(EN, NL)
465 F1 = 4 * CI(NL, 1): F2 = 4 * CI(NL, 2): GOSUB 510
470 FOR J = 1 TO 6
475 U(N) = U(N) - T(1, J) * EV(J) / NCN(N)
480 V(N) = V(N) - T(2, J) * EV(J) / NCN(N): NEXT
485 NEXT NL: NEXT EN
490 PRINT "Nodal average velocities u,v"
495 FOR I = 1 TO NP
500 PRINT USING "#####"; I; : PRINT USING "#######.#####"; U(I); V(I): NEXT
505 END
510 DL(1, 1) = F1 - 1: DL(1, 2) = 0: DL(1, 3) = F1 + F2 - 3
515 DL(1, 4) = F2: DL(1, 5) = -F2: DL(1, 6) = 4 - 2 * F1 - F2: REM MATRIX OF EQN 7.15
520 DL(2, 1) = 0: DL(2, 2) = F2 - 1: DL(2, 3) = F1 + F2 - 3
525 DL(2, 4) = F1: DL(2, 5) = 4 - F1 - 2 * F2: DL(2, 6) = -F1
530 FOR I = 1 TO 2: FOR J = 1 TO 2: TJ(I, J) = 0: FOR K = 1 TO 6
535 TJ(I, J) = TJ(I, J) + DL(I, K) * XY(K, J): NEXT: NEXT: NEXT: REM J AS PER EQN 7.16
540 DJ = TJ(1, 1) * TJ(2, 2) - TJ(1, 2) * TJ(2, 1): DD = TJ(1, 1)
545 TJ(1, 1) = TJ(2, 2) / DJ: TJ(2, 2) = DD / DJ: REM INVERT JACOBIAN
550 TJ(1, 2) = -TJ(1, 2) / DJ: TJ(2, 1) = -TJ(2, 1) / DJ
555 FOR I = 1 TO 2: FOR J = 1 TO 6: T(I, J) = 0: FOR K = 1 TO 2
560 T(I, J) = T(I, J) + TJ(I, K) * DL(K, J): NEXT: NEXT: NEXT: REM EQN 7.17
565 RETURN
```

```
600 DATA 15,4,2,0,7
610 DATA 5,3,4,2
620 DATA 6,10
630 DATA 12,-10
635 REM Data 1,1, 2,1, 3,1, 13,0, 14,0, 15,0
640 DATA 0,0

700 DATA 45,16,2,0,11
710 DATA 9,5,4,2
720 DATA 15,10
730 DATA 35,-10
740 DATA 0,0

800 DATA 85,32,2,0,11
810 DATA 17,5,4,2
820 DATA 25,10
830 DATA 65,-10
840 DATA 0,0

900 DATA 25,8,1,0,11
910 DATA 5,5,4,4
911 DATA 3,3,13,15,8,14,9, 4,3,15,5,9,10,4
912 DATA 5,11,21,23,16,22,17, 6,11,23,13,17,18,12, 0,0,0,0,0,0,0
915 DATA 25,0
920 DATA 2,110
930 DATA 3,160
940 DATA 4,150
950 DATA 22,-140
960 DATA 23,-200
970 DATA 24,-80
980 DATA 0,0
```

If the last data set is used the flow rates obtained are those of Table FM5 and these reflect fairly well the supplies and demands of the original network problem of Fig. FM7.

Table FM5.

y	x =0	x = 2	x = 4
0	56.3	84.6	30
1	98.5	85.1	69.5
2	149	105	158.5
3	79.6	87.4	97.5
4	41.4	87.9	52.5

The resemblance would be even greater, of course, if we added *line elem*ents, giving these much less 'stiffness' than the 2- D (continuum) elements which would then serve to model the 'background flow' (e.g. minor streets in a road traffic problem).

Indeed if we attempted to optimize the 2-D model (with a fine mesh without line elements) it would tend to reduce to one of line elements, as in the usual network models of distribution.

FM12. Conclusions

In a wide ranging text which the author hopes is of value to readers, it is also hoped that the DBS/MBS course for which it is written is of comparable, if not greater value than the traditional MBA.

Naturally some background in maths and computing is required, preferably to graduate level in science, engineering, computing etc.

A weakness then is that, having to concentrate a good deal on numerical methods etc.. the usual concentration on 'non math' case study, business plan, proposal writing, discussion etc. is missed. It is hoped that readers/students will be able, in the fullness of time, to make up ground in these areas.

Then, perhaps, they will better prepared for the challenges of management in an increasingly computer/IT/numerical methods oriented world.

Appendix A: Finite element modeling of traffic flow

Extract from a paper on FEM modeling of traffic flow.

Abstract. The simple linear traffic flow rule is used to form simple 2 df line elements to model traffic flow networks.

1. Introduction

Recently Mohr developed simple a simple Finite Element Method (FEM) approach to analysis and optimization of distribution problems [1-3]. In these the inverse costs were used as the constitutive parameters in the primal problem and costs for the dual problem the both problems were optimized using the steepest descent method with a temporary *element access* parameter set equal to the unit cost transportation cost for each route at the start of each steepest descent search. Both problems were also able to be optimized, at least approximately, using an iterative optimality criterion methods with ratio of each route's current estimate of route flow to the average route flow in the network as an optimality criterion, it being found that the final solutions occurred with all non vanishing route costs equal to a limiting value, this *equality principle* corresponding to Michell's celebrated constant strain principle in structural mechanics.

In the case of the traffic flow problem the equations for each route are based on the linear traffic flow rule, that is

$$(1) \quad v_{ij} = V_{ij}(1 - k_{ij}/K_{ij})$$

k_{ij} and v_{ij} are the flow density and velocity for element ij and K_{ij} and V_{ij} are respectively the element jam density and free flow velocity. Then the equations for each element are

$$(2) \quad \begin{Bmatrix} q_i \\ q_j \end{Bmatrix} = (K_{ij}V_{ij}/L_{ij})\begin{bmatrix} 1 & -1 \\ -1 & 1 \end{bmatrix}\begin{Bmatrix} P_i \\ P_j \end{Bmatrix}$$

where q_i, q_j are the inflows at each end, L_{ij} is the route length and P_i, P_j are arbitrary potentials at the element nodes. Thus the problem is equivalent to that of a DC electrical network and is very simple to program for a computer [4],

2. A simple example problem

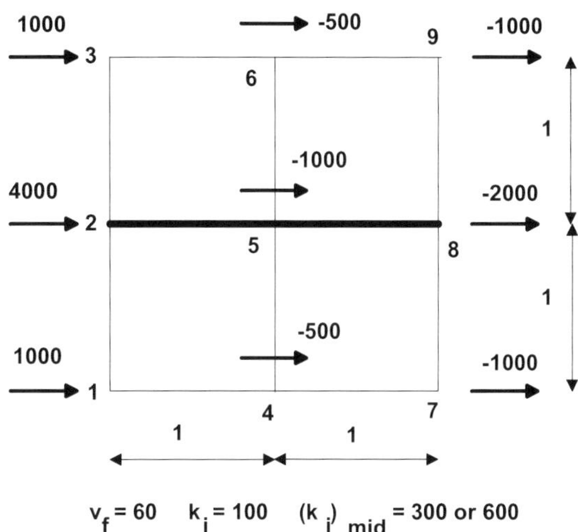

Figure 1. Simple traffic flow network

Fig. 1 shows an example network with the nodal flows shown, positive flows being inwards. The FEM solution for the element traffic flows, densities and velocities is given in Table 1, the flows being calculated using the linear traffic flow law

$$(3) \quad q_{ij} = k_{ij}v_{ij} = k_{ij}V_{ij}(1 - k_{ij}/K_{ij})$$

where k_{ij} and v_{ij} = element flow density &velocity. Rarranging Eqn (2) the density is the appropriate root of a quadratic equation, from which the velocity and route flow follow.

Table 1. Solutions for route flows in Fig. 2 using Mohr's law [$q_{ij} = (k_j v_f/L)(V_i - V_j)$]

Route	(a) mid k_j = 300			(b) mid k_j = 600		
	flow	k_2	v_2	flow	k_2	v_2
12	-178.6	3.07	-58.16	60.4	1.02	59.39
23	178.6	3.07	58.16	-60.4	1.02	-59.39
14	1178.6	26.85	43.89	939.6	19.44	48.34
45	-142.9	2.44	-58.54	-192.3	3.32	-58.01
36	1178.6	26.85	43.89	939.6	19.44	48.34
56	142.9	2.44	58.54	192.3	3.32	58.01
25	3642.9	84.54	43.09	4120.9	79.11	52.09
58	2357.1	46.49	50.70	2736.3	49.73	55.03
47	821.5	16.37	50.18	631.9	11.96	52.82
69	821.5	16.37	50.18	631.9	11.96	52.82
78	-178.6	3.07	-58.16	-368.1	6.57	-56.06
89	178.6	3.07	58.16	368.1	6.57	-56.06
Σtravel time	234.63 hours			213.44 hours		

In case (b) we have upgraded the centre routes 25, 58 and the flow changes are as expected, the flows in these centre routes increasing and the total travel time in the system decreasing. Note that the linear v-k rule is used here and that such rules as Mohr's bilinear rule [5] are more realistic.

3. Conclusion

Traffic flow networks are easily modeled using the same approach as that used by Mohr for distribution problems. As with the latter, it is then straightforward to optimize them, obvious objectives being minimum total travel time in the network, for example.

Appendix B: Mohr's Infinity Conditions

A section from the 2nd paper on Mohr's *infinity conditions,* here applied to potential flow. These conditions can be used to model distribution in infinite 2-D domains.

6. Infinite boundary modeling

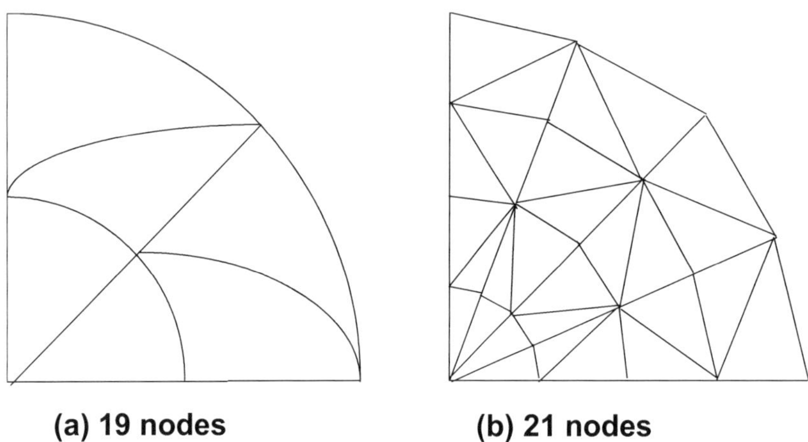

(a) 19 nodes **(b) 21 nodes**

Fig. 5. Two models of a quadrant of an infinite domain with point source at centre.

Fig. 5 shows a quadrant of a circular domain (of radius 4) with a point source at its centre modeled using (a) 6 node isoparametric elements [12], and (b) the present cubic element.

Then to simulate an infinite domain no boundary conditions other than $\phi = 1000$ at the centre are imposed but 'stiffnesses' equal to the angle (in radians) subtended by each node's 'share' of the boundary added to the pivot for each boundary node's ϕ freedom before final solution of the problem. In Fig. 5(a), for example, the added values (in degrees) are 11.25 for the two nodes at x = 0 and y = 0 and 22.5 at the other three nodes of the circular boundary.

Table 3 shows the results obtained. The expected results are obtained by fitting the appropriate decay function which is [16,17]

$$\phi = -(1/2\pi)\phi_0 \ln(r) + C \qquad (23)$$

and this is that much used in the boundary element method [18].

Then in case (3) (row 5) the constant C is calculated by substituting $\phi = 520$ at $r = 1$ in Eqn (23) and using the result to calculate ϕ for the other radii. Then for case (4) $\phi = 370$ and r = 2 is used to obtain row 6.

Table 3. Results for the problem of Fig. 5.

Case	r = 1	r = 2	r = 3	r = 4
6 node FE (1a)	525	367	276	210
6 node FE (1b)	520	365	275	209
Cubic FE (2a)	620	447	341	261
Cubic FE (2b)	520	374	284	218
Expected (3)	520	410	345	299
Expected (4)	480	370	305	259

Cases (1a) and (2a) are the FEM results with only 'elastic' boundary conditions. Here a 'natural' decay rate occurs in the meshes used but in general the desired rate of decay should be modelled by choosing an appropriate *C* value and setting a corresponding ϕ value as a boundary condition at an inner radius.

This is done for cases (1b) and (2b), setting $\phi = 520$ for the nodes at $r = 1$. Agreement of the two FEM results is now good and agreement with the expected (logarithmic) decay results is reasonable with such coarse meshes and such a rapid decay rate.

Finally, note that from Eqn (23) it follows that $\partial\phi/\partial r = -\phi_0/2\pi r)$ and this can be set as a boundary condition in Fig. 5 (at $r = 4$) but this gives little change in the results of Table 3 (for the cubic element).

Appendix C: A Facet Element for 3-D Analysis

Extracts from paper on a new facet shell element (the best yet?).

Such elements are what FEM was originally aimed at, i.e. stress analysis of aircraft shells etc. Here Mohr's *method of nested interpolations,* a *basis transformation* technique, is used to formulate an accurate 9 *freedom* thin plate element (historically a difficult problem) and a unique 9 freedom plane stress element including the in-plane *drilling freedom* (very rarely attempted and never before as successfully). The two component elements are then combined to obtain an accurate *facet* element for stress analysis of 'shell' structures. An important feature is that the two 9 df component elements have the same *kernel stiffness matrix*, that of the classical *linear strain triangle LST)* element, similar to that of Sec. FM9 but with translational df *u,v* at each node.

FORMULATION OF THE ELEMENT

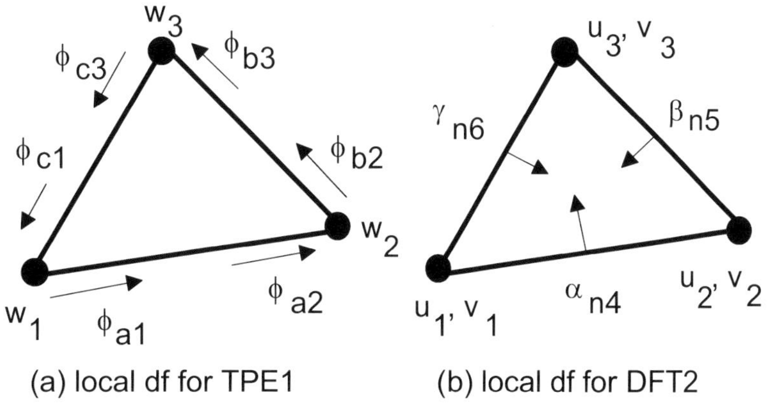

Fig. 1. Local freedoms for the component elements

In the present work the accurate 9 d.f. thin plate element (TPE1)[3,6] and the new 'drilling freedom triangle' (DFT2) of Mohr are combined and 14 d.p. computation used. The plate element is derived by transforming the global slopes $\phi_x = \partial w/\partial x$, $\phi_y = \partial w/\partial y$ to the natural slopes parallel to the sides shown in Fig. 1(a). Then using cubic interpolation on each side and assuming linear variation of the normal slopes the basis transformation

$$\{\phi_x, \phi_y\}_{i+3} = T_f\{w, \phi_x, \phi_y\}_i \qquad i = 1, 2, 3 \tag{1}$$

yields the slopes at the midsides.

Now a kernel stiffness matrix k^* can be obtained for the freedoms ϕ_x, ϕ_y at the vertices *(i = 1,2,3)* and midsides *(i = 4,5,6)* and this is exactly that for the classical linear strain triangle (LST),[4] the final stiffness matrix for flexure being given by the congruent transformation

$$(2) \qquad k_f = T_f^t\, k^*\, T_f$$

The new DFT2 element is derived by assuming that, on each side, the natural derivatives of the transverse natural displacements at its ends are equal to the vertex drilling freedom, that is

$$(3) \qquad (\partial a_n/\partial s_a)_1 = \phi_1, \ (\partial a_n/\partial s_a)_2 = \phi_2$$

on side 12. Then applying quadratic interpolation to the transverse natural displacement the value at the middle of this side (a fictitious node designated 'local' node 4) is expressed in terms of the vertex

freedoms. Repeating on the other two sides and assuming a linear variation of the parallel displacements (α, β, γ) the basis transformation

$$(4) \quad \{u, v\}_{i+3} = T_e\{u, v, \phi\}_i \qquad i = 1, 2, 3$$

yields the displacements at the midside nodes.

Again the kernel stiffness matrix is that for the LST (obtained here using three point numerical integration) so that the final extensional stiffness matrix is given by

$$(5) \qquad k_e = T_e^t\, k^*\, T_e$$

The final 18 x 18 element stiffness matrix is given by

$$k = T_s^t \begin{bmatrix} k_e & O_9 \\ O_9 & k_f \end{bmatrix} T_s \tag{6}$$

where O_9 is a 9 x 9 null matrix and

$$T_s = \begin{bmatrix} T_n & O_6 & O_6 \\ O_6 & T_n & O_6 \\ O_6 & O_6 & T_n \end{bmatrix}, \quad T_n = \begin{bmatrix} T_c & O_3 \\ O_3 & T_c^* \end{bmatrix}. \tag{7}$$

in which T_c is the 3-D coordinate transformation matrix of Mohr,[4,9] that is

$$\begin{Bmatrix} x^* \\ y^* \\ z^* \end{Bmatrix} = \begin{bmatrix} c_x & -s_x t_y & s_x \\ -s_y t_x & c_y & s_y \\ -c_y s_x & -c_x s_y & c_x c_y \end{bmatrix} \begin{Bmatrix} x \\ y \\ z \end{Bmatrix} = T_c\{x\} \quad (8)$$

in which

$$t_x = -(y_{32}z_1 + y_{13}z_2 + y_{21}z_3)/2\Delta, \; t_y = (x_{32}z_1 + x_{13}z_2 + x_{21}z_3)/2\Delta$$

$$s_x = \sin(\tan^{-1}(t_x)) \; etc., \; x_{21} = x_2 - x_1 \; etc., \; 2\Delta = |x_{21}y_{32} - x_{32}y_{21}|$$

and

$$T_c^* = \begin{bmatrix} 0 & 1 & 0 \\ -1 & 0 & 0 \\ 0 & 0 & 1 \end{bmatrix} T_c \quad (9)$$

is a Boolean transformation required because globally the rotational freedoms are the right handed system

$$\phi_x = -\partial w/\partial y, \; \phi_y = \partial w/\partial x, \; \phi_z = \partial u/\partial y - \partial v/\partial x \quad (10a)$$

whereas matrix k_f is derived using local freedoms

$$\phi_x^* = \partial w/\partial wx \text{ and } \phi_y^* = \partial w/\partial y \quad (10b)$$

SPHERICAL SHELLS

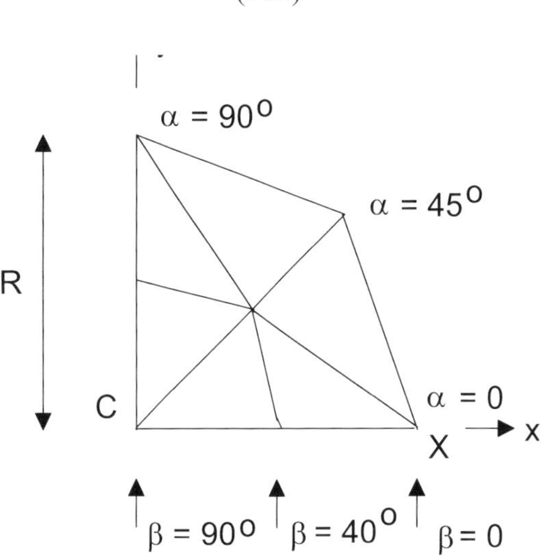

Fig. 3.
Spherical coordinates for coarse mesh for octant of a sphere

Fig. 3 is a plan view of the seven node mesh used for an octant of a spherical shell. The nodal coordinate data is spherical in α and β from which the Cartesian coordinates are easily calculated as

$$(11) \quad z = R\sin\beta, \; R_p = R\cos\beta, \; x = R_p\cos\alpha, \; y = R_p\sin\alpha$$

The meshes used had 10, 13, 16, 25 and 34 nodes, $\delta\alpha = 22.5$ deg. (after the first $\delta\beta$), the increments in β, beginning from the crown C, being

10 nodes: $\delta\beta = 2 \times 22.5 + 45$; 13 nodes: $\delta\beta = 3 \times 18 + 36$; 16 nodes: $\delta\beta = 4 \times 15 + 30$

25 nodes: $\delta\beta = 6 \times 10 + 2 \times 15$; 34 nodes: $\delta\beta = 10 \times 7.5 + 15$

here using large elements near the 'waist' of the sphere to reduce the tendency for comparatively steep elements which tend to reduce solution accuracy.

The problem of a pinched sphere is considered with data and boundary conditions

$$E = 1,\ \nu = 0,\ R = 4,\ t = 0.5 \text{ and } 0.05,\ P = 1 \text{ at C}$$
$$u,\ v,\ \phi_x,\ \phi_y,\ \phi_z = 0 \text{ at } C,\ \ v,\ \phi_x = 0 \text{ along CX (curved)}$$
$$u,\ \phi_y = 0 \text{ along CY (curved)},\ \ w,\ \phi_z = 0 \text{ along XY (curved)}$$

combining these 'line' boundary conditions at points X and Y.

The results are given in Table 3 compared to the exact solutions which are given by[11]

$$(12) \quad w = \sqrt{3}\,(1 - \nu^2)PR/4Et^2$$

and note that P = 4 (or unity in the FEM analysis for an octant of the sphere).

The numerical results are excellent with no more than 34 nodes and variations of the normal displacements close to the crown (for $\beta = 65 - 90$ deg.) is also close to the analytical solution.[11]

The stress solutions are generally reasonable but a much finer mesh is needed near the crown where the problem may be treated as that of a shallow spherical cap to obtain solutions of greater accuracy (and in line with the manner in which the classical analytical solution is obtained.[11]

Table 3. Deflections under load on a pinched sphere

Nodes (mesh)	t = 0.5		t = 0.05	
	DFT1	DFT2	DFT1	DFT2
10 (2 x 3)	20.392	28.512	1166.3	1101.8
13 (2 x 4)	23.827	28.160	1632.9	1475.7
16 (2 x 5)	25.782	28.098	1945.6	1827.2
25 (2 x 8)	27.006	27.517	2549.7	2554.7
34 (2 x 11)	27.663	27.703	2766.3	2770.3
Theory		27.713		2771.3

As does the DFT1 formulation, the new DFT2 formulation (+ TPE1) also gives satisfactory solutions to the problem of a pressurized sphere,[6] but here the main accuracy problem is that of calculation of nodal loads. Overall, however, both elements perform satisfactorily over a range of shell problems but the DFT1 element does poorly on constant stress patch tests.[1] The new DFT2 element, however, passes these exactly,[1] also performing slightly better on shell problems than the original element. As derivation of both the TPE1 and DFT2 elements is remarkably simple, it is expected that their combined used as a facet shell element will be popular.

Appendix D: The Large Curvature Correction FEM Analysis

Introduction

The LCC for Finite Element Method analysis (FEM) was first developed in Cartesian form by Mohr in 1979 (Mohr & Milner, 1981), and Milner added a curvilinear form for this correction (Milner, 1981). The original Cartesian correction had a slight error which did not affect results noticeably, whilst the original curvilinear correction claimed impossibly good results with only 1 or 2 elements and only one load step, thanks to an erroneous, if not ridiculous, cosine term associated with moment loadings (Mohr & Argyris, 2001).

The work was corrected in a paper faxed to the late John Argyris in Stuttgart. On the phone he applauded the work and suggested he lend his name to the work so I wrote a part II of the paper and posted this to Stuttgart. In the end part I was lost, whilst part II was typeset and queued for production in *Computer Methods & Applied Mechanics,* for which Argyris was the chief editor.

As a result of my complaining to a US editor about slowness reviewing a paper combining the part I and part II papers the typeset part II stayed in the publication queue for a few years at Elsevier Science and then disappeared leaving no trace, despite many enquiries about it.

Circa 2006 I used many more elements to obtain very accurate results that did, at last, prove the Large Curvature Correction (LCC) beyond all doubt, putting these results in a final combined paper.

The key equations and results from that work are given in this Appendix.

The Cartesian LCC

Normally direct strains S_x in the x direction in a material are calculated as $S_X = du/dx$, where u, v are the Cartesian displacements in the x and y directions, and du/dx here denotes the partial derivative of u with respect to variation in the x direction only. If, for example, the *interpolation function* for u is the bilinear function $u = a + bx + cy$, then $du/dx = b$, and $du/dy = c$.

In a beam subject to bending the Cartesian curvature for small displacements is calculated as simply: $C = d^2v/dx^2$

When the beam undergoes large displacements the axial direct strain must be calculated as:

$S_X = du/dx + (dv/dx)^2/2$

Large displacements alter the geometry of the system and render the problem nonlinear so that a stepwise solution method must be used. For this a 'virtual' variation in the extensional strain is calculated as:

$V(S_X)=V(du/dx)+V[(dv/dx)^2/2] = V(du/dx)+(dv/dx)V(dv/dx)$

and this term is used to calculate *residual loads* which are recalculated at each step of the nonlinear solution procedure, and which gradually diminish as the accuracy of the solution improves.

For consistency, I decided to introduce the Large Curvature Correction which in Cartesian form calculates the beam's curvature from the well-known formula:

$C = d^2v/dx^2/F^3$ where $F = [1 + (dv/dx)^2]^{1/2}$

Then a virtual curvature increment is calculated as:

$$
\begin{aligned}
V(C) &= V(d^2v/dx^2)F^{-3} + (d^2v/dx^2)\ V(F^{-3}) \\
&= V(d^2v/dx^2)F^{-3} - 3(d^2v/dx^2)(dv/dx)F^{-5}\ V(dv/dx) \\
&= V(d^2v/dx^2)[1 - 3(dv/dx)^2/F^2]/F^3
\end{aligned}
$$

here using reciprocity to exchange incrementation in dv/dx with incrementation in d^2v/dx^2 in the second term, and this LCC is included in the residual load calculation.

The curvilinear curvature correction

Alternatively, the beam's curvature can be calculated with respect to its curvilinear coordinate s, which follows the curved shape of the beam:

$C = (d^2v/ds^2)/F$ where $F = [1 - (dv/ds)^2]^{1/2}$

Then a virtual increment in this is given by:

$$
\begin{aligned}
V(C) &= V(d^2v/ds^2)F^{-1} + (d^2v/ds^2)\ V(F^{-1}) \\
&= V(d^2v/ds^2)F^{-1} + (d^2v/ds^2)(dv/ds)F^{-3}\ V(dv/ds) \\
&= [V(d^2v/ds^2)/F][1 + (dv/ds)^2/F^2]
\end{aligned}
$$

and again reciprocity is used to obtain the final result.

Numerical results

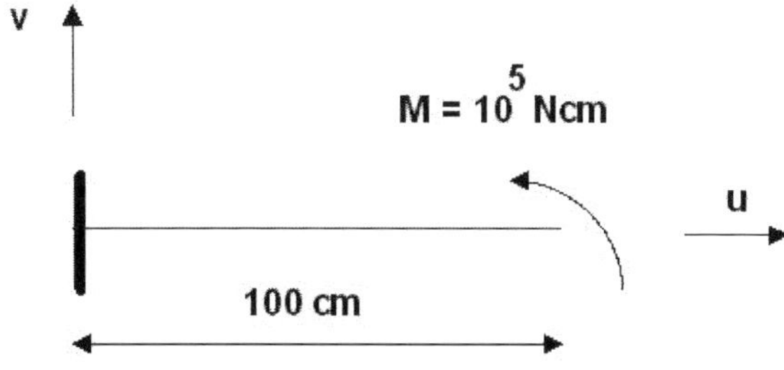

Figure. D.1. Large displacement of a beam,

$A = 10\ cm^2$, $I = 5\ cm^4$, $E = 2 \times 10^6\ cm^2$With the usual 3 degrees of freedom per node, namely u, v and dv/dx, the results obtained for the simple beam problem shown in Figure D.1 are shown in Table D.1.

Table D.1. Results using 3 d.f./node.

e	s	i	u	v	dv/dx
With Cartesian curvature correction					
4	10	3	-9.3152	36.6826	0.7441
10	10	3	-13.7880	43.3140	0.9261
10	10	5	-13.7831	43.3070	0.9259
10	20	3	-15.2040	45.2057	0.9780
10	40	3	-15.6558	45.7853	0.9942
With curvilinear curvature correction					
4	10	3	-9.2879	36.6699	0.7401
10	10	3	-13.5845	43.1156	0.9125
10	10	5	-13.5724	43.0090	0.9121
10	20	3	-15.1177	45.1203	0.9730
10	40	3	-15.6305	45.7586	0.9928
Exact			-15.8529	45.9698	1.0000
Small displacement solution			0.0	50.0	1.0

Here A = cross sectional area, I = moment of inertia of the beam cross section, and E = Young's modulus (of elasticity). For the FEM analysis 'e' = 4 or 10 elements are used with the total moment loading (M) at the end of the beam applied in 's' steps with 'i' iterations of the residual load solution technique used at each load step.

Here both the Cartesian and curvilinear LCCs require 40 load steps to give a reasonably accurate solution for the lateral displacement 'v' at the end of the beam.

As shown in Table D.2, better results are obtained using four freedoms/node, the added freedom being dv/dx. Stress calculations for the problem are satisfactory (Mohr & Argyris, 2001) and to prove the LCC beyond all doubt results were obtained using up to 100 elements and 100 load steps, as shown in Table D.3.

Table D.2. Results with 4 df/node.

e	s	i	u	v	dv/dx
With Cartesian LCC (4 df/node):					
20	10	3	-16.1959	46.3145	1.0173
20	20	3	-15.9300	46.0581	1.0043
20	40	3	-15.8656	45.9953	1.0010
With curvilinear LCC (4 df/node):					
20	10	3	-15.7576	45.8890	0.9934
20	20	3	-15.8224	45.9528	0.9983
20	40	3	-15.8388	45.9690	0.9996
Exact:			-15.8529	45.9698	1.0000

Previous curvature correction results were obtained using single precision MegaBasic computation (8 figures). To provide the greater memory needed for larger problems Visual Basic was used to obtain the results of Table D.3. Single precision (7 figures) gave slight errors for e = 50 and serious errors for e = 100 so that double precision (15 figures) was used for all the results of Table D.3. The results for increasing numbers of load steps are extrapolated by assuming that the solution error decreases according to the inverse square of the number of load steps so that the ordinal intercept of the regression line for the plot of v against $1/s^2$ is the extrapolation result.

For all three columns of data a coefficient of correlation = 1 to 5 decimal places was obtained. Accurate regression lines for increasing e can be obtained in the same way.

Table D.3. Tip deflection v using 3 iterations per load step

Load steps, s	e = 25	e = 50	e = 100
10	45.88721	45.88530	45.88483
20	45.95118	45.94906	45.94853
40	45.96736	45.96514	45.96436
50	45.96931	45.96708	45.96652
100	45.97193	45.96967	45.96910
Extrapolated	45.97270	45.97046	45.96984
Exact		45.96977	

It has been suggested to me that the foregoing Large Curvature Correction might have application in the theory of relativity, but I doubt it. More obviously, small curvatures in light deflected by stars could be calculated using the small curvature approximation of structural mechanics, i.e. curvature = d^2v/dx^2.

The LCC does illustrate, however, that physical systems involving large curvatures can be studied with reference to an orthogonal frame of reference and there is no need to consider a curved coordinate system as is used in the General Theory of Relativity.

FM References

Southwell RV, Relaxation Methods in Theoretical Physics, OUP Oxford, 1946.

Prezmieniecki, JS. Theory of Matrix Structural Analysis, McGraw-Hill, New York, 1967.

Zienkiewicz OC, The Finite Element Method, McGraw-Hill, London, 1977.

Brebbia CA, The Boundary Element for Engineers, Pentech Press, Plymouth, 1980.

Budnick, FS, Mojena, R, Vollmann TE, Principles of Operations Research for Management, RD Irwin, Homewood Il. 1977,

Chung TJ, Finite Element Analysis in Fluid Dynamics, McGraw-Hill, NY, 1978.

Crandall, SH, Engineering Analysis: A Survey of Numerical Procedures, McGraw-Hill, New York. 1956.

Irons BM, Ahmad S, Techniques of Finite Elements, Ellis Horwood, Chichester, 1980.

Jennings, A., Matrix Computation for Engineers and Scientists, Wiley, Chichester, 1977.

Mohr GA, A triangular finite element for thick slabs, *Computers & Structures,* Vol. 9, pp 595-598, 1978.

Mohr GA, Power AS, Elastic boundary conditions for finite elements of infinite and semi-infinite media, Proc. Instn Civ. Engrs (UK), part 2, vol. 68, p 675-684, 1978.

Mohr GA, Elastic and plastic prediction of slab reinforcement requirements, *Proc. Instn Civ. Engrs,* Part 2, Vol. 67, pp 851-852, 1979.

Mohr GA, Design of shell shape using finite element, *Computers & Structures,* Vol. 10, pp 745-749, 1979.

Mohr GA, Elastic and plastic predictions of slab reinforcement requirements, *Instn Engnrs Australia Civil Engineering Transactions,* pp 16-29, 1979.

Mohr GA, On triangular displacement elements for the bending of thin plates, *Proc. 3rd Int.. Conf. in Australia on Finite Element Methods,* Univ. of NSW, pp 159-175, 1979.

Mohr GA, Numerically integrated triangular element for doubly curved thin shells, *Computers & Structures,* Vol. 11, pp 565-571, 1980.

Mohr GA, A contact stiffness matrix for finite element problems involving external elastic restraint, *Computers & Structures,* Vol. 12, pp 189-191, 1980.

Mohr GA, A simple rectangular membrane element including the drilling freedom, *Computers & Structures,* Vol. 13, pp 483-487, 1981.

Mohr GA, Milner HR, Finite element analysis of large displacements in flexural systems, *Computers & Structures,* Vol. 13, pp 533-536, 1981.

Mohr GA, A doubly curved isoparametric shell element, *Computers & Structures,* Vol. 14, No.1-2, pp 9-13, 1981.

Mohr GA, Application of penalty factors to a doubly curved quadratic shell element, *Computers & Structures,* Vol. 14, No. 1-2, pp 15-19, 1981.

Mohr GA, Quadratic finite elements for shells, *Mathematics and Models in Engineering Science,* DSIR, pp 23- 33, Wellington, New Zealand, 1982/

Mohr GA, Finite element formulation by nested interpolations: application to the drilling freedom problem, *Computers & Structures,* Vol. 15, No. 2, pp185-190, 1982.

Mohr GA, Application of penalty functions to a curved isoparametric axisymmetric thick shell element, *Computers & Structures,* Vol. 15, No. 6, pp 685-690, 1982.

Mohr GA, Broom ND, A Finite Element Lubrication Model, *Fourth Int. Conf. in Australia on Finite Element Methods,* pp 90-93, Melbourne, 1982.

Mohr GA, Medland IC, On convergence of displacement finite elements, with an application to singularity problems, *Engineering Fracture Mechanics,* Vol. 17, No. 2, pp 481-491, 1983.

Mohr GA, Reduced integration and penalty factors in an arch element, *International Journal of Structures,* Vol. 3, No. 1, pp 9-15, 1983.

Mohr GA, Paterson NB, A natural differential geometry scheme for a doubly curved shell element, *Computers & Structures,* Vol. 18, No. 3, pp 433-439, 1984.

Mohr GA, Finite Element Analysis of Viscous Fluid Flow, *Computers & Fluids,* Vol. 12, No. 3, pp217-233, 1984.

Mohr GA, Development of a new thin plate element using a small computer, *Int. Conf. on Education, Practice and Promotion of Computational Methods in Engineering Using Small Computers,* (EPMES), Macau, 1984.

Mohr GA, Cook PL, On near equivlance of assumed stress and reduced integration formulations of the bilinear plane stress finite element, *Computers & Structures,* Vol. 21, No. 3, pp 475-478, 1985.

Mohr GA, Caffin DA, Penalty Factors, Lagrange Multipliers and Basis Transformation in the Finite Element Method, *Civ. Engng Trans IEAust.* Vol. CE27, No. 2, May 1985, pp 174-180.

Mohr GA, Mohr RS, A new thin plate finite element by basis transformation, *Computers & Structures,* Vol. 22, No. 3, pp 239-243, 1986.

Mohr GA, Milner HR, A Microcomputer Introduction to the Finite Element Method, Pitman, Melbourne, 1986; Heinemann, London, 1987.

Mohr GA, Finite Elements for Solids, Fluids, and Optimization, OUP Oxford, 1992.

Mohr GA, Finite element optimization of structures - I (solids applications), Computers & Structures, vol. 53, p 1217, 1994.

Mohr GA, Finite element optimization of structures - II (fluids applications), Computers & Structures, vol. 53, p 1221, 1994.

Mohr, GA, Optimization of critical path models using finite elements, Australian Civil Engineering Transactions, IEAust, vol. CE36, p 123, 1994.

Narus JA, Anderson JC, Rethinking distribution: adaptive channels, Harvard Business Review, July-August, 1996.

Zhao C, Steven GP, Xie YM, Effect of initial non design domain on optimal topologies of structures during natural frequency optimization, Computers & Structures, vol. 62, no. 1, p 119, 1996.

Mohr GA, Improving an accurate thin plate element, *Computer Methods in applied mechanics and engineering,* Vol. 166, pp 341-348, 1998.

Mohr GA, On two equivalent thin plate bending elements, *Communication in Numerical Methods in Engineering,* Vol. 14, pp 271-275, 1998.

Mohr GA, Finite element solutions for optimal triangular plates, *Int. J. Mechanical Sciences,* Vol. 41, pp 1289-1300, 1999.

Mohr GA, Finite element solutions for optimal square plates, *Int. J. Mechanical Sciences,* Vol. 42, pp 2337-2345, 2000.

Mohr GA, Polynomial solutions for thin plates, *Int. J. Mech. Sci.,* Vol. 42, pp1197-1204, 2000.

Mohr GA, An improved facet shell element, *Int. J. Arts & Sciences,* Vol. 1, No. 1, pp 19-26, 2001.

Mohr GA, Argyris JH, The large curvature correction in finite element analysis - I, Int. J. Arts & Sciences, Vol. 1, No. 1, p1. 2001.

Mohr GA, Argyris JH, The large curvature correction in finite element analysis – II, *Int. J. Arts & Sciences,* Vol. 1, No. 2, pp 27-35, 2001. [this and part I to appear in Computer Methods in Applied Mechanics and Engineering].

Mohr GA, A New Facet Shell Element, *Int. J. Arts & Sciences,* Vol. 1, No. 2, pp 36-49, 2001.

Mohr GA, The Finite Patch Method: a nodal equation method based on FEM, *Advances in Engineering Software,* Vol. 32, pp 327-335, 2001.

Mohr GA, *Finite Elements and Optimization for Modern Management,* Independent Publishers Ltd, Melbourne, 2002.

Mohr GA, Mohr PE, An accurate facet shell element, *Int. J. Arts & Sciences,* Vol. 2, No. 1, pp 1-13, 2002.

Mohr GA, *Natural Finite Elements Using Basis Transformation,* Independent Publishers Ltd, Melbourne, 2003.

Mohr GA, Power AS. Natural cubic element formulation and infinite boundary modeling for potential type problems, *Australian and New Zealand Institute of Applied Mathematics Journal,* Vol. 44, pp133-143, 2003.

Mohr GA, Finite element modeling and optimization of traffic flow networks, *Transportmetrica*, Vol. 1, No. 2, pp 151 – 160, 2005.

Mohr GA, *Elementary Thinking for the 21st Century,* Xlibris (2014).

Mohr GA, Richard Sinclair, Edwin Fear, *The Evolving Universe: Relativity, Redshift and Life From Space,* Xlibris (2014).

Award

THE SCIENTIFIC MBA

This book is the final edition of the handout lecture notes for this course, the DBS/MBS, now printed rather than photocopied for the first time. The course was written in pencil in 1994 and first presented in part the following year. A typed edition appeared in 1996, followed by a word-processed edition in 2001, both of these undergoing occasional corrections, revisions and extensions over the years. The course has always had the following 14 subjects:

1. **BP** **Business Policy**
2. **BL** **Business Law**
3. **MS** **Mathematics and Statistics**
4. **BF** **Business Finance**
5. **MP** **Management Psychology**
6. **MR** **Marketing Research**
7. **IT** **Information Technology and Computing**
8. **NM** **Numerical Methods**
9. **IE** **International Economics (Macroeconomics)**
10. **ME** **Managerial Economics (Microeconomics)**
11. **OT** **Optimization Techniques**
12. **OR** **Operations Research**
13. **PP** **Project Planning and Control**
14. **FM** **Finite Methods**

THE AUTHOR

Dr Geoff Mohr did his PhD working on optimization of structures using the Finite Element Method (FEM) at Cambridge University, where his father helped split the atom. He did pioneering work on FEM in England, Australia and New Zealand. He wrote circa 60 papers for 20 scientific journals and published more than 20 books, including *Finite Elements for Solids, Fluids, and Optimization* (OUP); *A Microcomputer Introduction to the Finite Element Method* (Pitman & Heinemann); *Finite Elements & Optimization for Modern Management;* and *Natural Finite Elements using Basis* Transformation (Independent Publishers Ltd); The *Pretentious Persuaders: Heart Disease, Cancer & Aging;* and *The History & Psychology of Human Conflict* (Horizon); *Curing Cancer & Heart Disease; The Variant Virus; The Doomsday Calculation; The War of the Sexes; 2045, A Remote Town Survives Global Holocaust; and Elementary Thinking for the 21st Century* (Xlibris); *The 8-Week+ Program to Reverse Cardiovascular Disease* (Book Venture), and the present book.

He also co-authored 5 other books with *Richard Sinclair* and *Edwin* Fear: *The Evolving Universe: Relativity, Redshift and Life from Space*; and *World Religions: The History, Issues, and Truth* (Xlibris); and *World War 3: When & How Will It End?*; *The Brainwashed: From Consumer Zombies to Islamism and Jihad;* and *Human Intelligence, Learning and Behaviour* (Inspiring Publishers).

COMMENTS ON GEOFF MOHR'S WORK HAVE INCLUDED:

Some provocative and timely issues such as econobabble.

I wish I had never heard of the Finite Element Method **– Cambridge student finishing PhD.**

This book is sure to become one of the most influential of modern times.

The legendary and prolific pioneer of Matrix Structural Analysis and the Finite Element Method, civil and aeronautical engineer John Argyris, said to G. A. Mohr:

- ***You have done much more work than I.***
- ***You are much more intelligent than me.***
- ***The greatest scientist in Australia***
- ***You are the hope of the future.***
- ***Of course!*** **– in reply to the question: "Is the problem of the human race anthropology?"**

Printed in the United States
By Bookmasters